MACHIAVELLI'S ETHICS

MACHIAVELLI'S ETHICS

ERICA BENNER

PRINCETON UNIVERSITY PRESS   *Princeton and Oxford*

Published by Princeton University Press, 41 William Street, Princeton, New Jersey 08540

In the United Kingdom: Princeton University Press, 6 Oxford Street, Woodstock, Oxfordshire OX20 1TW

Library of Congress Cataloging-in-Publication Data

Benner, Erica.

    Machiavelli's ethics / Erica Benner.

        p. cm.

    Includes bibliographical references and index.

    ISBN 978-0-691-14176-3 (hardcover : alk. paper) — ISBN 978-0-691-14177-0 (pbk. : alk. paper)

1. Machiavelli, Niccolò, 1469–1527.   2. Ethics.   I. Title.

    B785.M24B46 2009

    170.92—dc22   2009002603

British Library Cataloging-in-Publication Data is available

This book has been composed in Minion Pro with Trajan Pro

Printed on acid-free paper. ∞

press.princeton.edu

Printed in the United States of America

10 9 8 7 6 5 4 3 2 1

For Patrick

"Ἀνάγκης θυγατρὸς κόρης Λαχέσεως λόγος. Ψυχαὶ ἐφήμεροι, ἀρχὴ ἄλλης περιόδου θνητοῦ γένους θανατηφόρου . . . ἀρετὴ δὲ ἀδέσποτον, ἣν τιμῶν καὶ ἀτιμάζων πλέον καὶ ἔλαττον αὐτῆς ἕκαστος ἕξει. αἰτία ἑλομένου· θεὸς ἀναίτιος." . . .

ἔνθα δή, ὡς ἔοικεν, ὦ φίλε Γλαύκων, ὁ πᾶς κίνδυνος ἀνθρώπῳ, καὶ διὰ ταῦτα μάλιστα ἐπιμελητέον ὅπως ἕκαστος ἡμῶν τῶν ἄλλων μαθημάτων ἀμελήσας τούτου τοῦ μαθήματος καὶ ζητητὴς καὶ μαθητὴς ἔσται, ἐάν ποθεν οἷός τ᾽ ᾖ μαθεῖν καὶ ἐξευρεῖν τίς αὐτὸν ποιήσει δυνατὸν καὶ ἐπιστήμονα, βίον καὶ χρηστὸν καὶ πονηρὸν διαγιγνώσκοντα, τὸν βελτίω ἐκ τῶν δυνατῶν ἀεὶ πανταχοῦ αἱρεῖσθαι· . . . ἀδαμαντίνως δὴ δεῖ ταύτην τὴν δόξαν ἔχοντα εἰς Ἅιδου ἰέναι, ὅπως ἂν ᾖ καὶ ἐκεῖ ἀνέκπληκτος ὑπὸ πλούτων τε καὶ τῶν τοιούτων κακῶν, καὶ μὴ ἐμπεσὼν εἰς τυραννίδας καὶ ἄλλας τοιαύτας πράξεις πολλὰ μὲν ἐργάσηται καὶ ἀνήκεστα κακά, ἔτι δὲ αὐτὸς μείζω πάθῃ . . .

Εἰπόντος δὲ ταῦτα τὸν πρῶτον λαχόντα ἔφη εὐθὺς ἐπιόντα τὴν μεγίστην τυραννίδα ἑλέσθαι, καὶ ὑπὸ ἀφροσύνης τε καὶ λαιμαργίας οὐ πάντα ἱκανῶς ἀνασκεψάμενον ἑλέσθαι, ἀλλ᾽ αὐτὸν λαθεῖν ἐνοῦσαν εἱμαρμένην παίδων αὐτοῦ βρώσεις καὶ ἄλλα κακά· ἐπειδὴ δὲ κατὰ σχολὴν σκέψασθαι, κόπτεσθαί τε καὶ ὀδύρεσθαι τὴν αἵρεσιν, οὐκ ἐμμένοντα τοῖς προρρηθεῖσιν ὑπὸ τοῦ προφήτου· οὐ γὰρ ἑαυτὸν αἰτιᾶσθαι τῶν κακῶν, ἀλλὰ τύχην τε καὶ δαίμονας καὶ πάντα μᾶλλον ἀνθ᾽ ἑαυτοῦ.

"Here is the message of Lachesis, the maiden daughter of Necessity: 'Ephemeral souls, this is the beginning of another cycle that will end in death. . . . Virtue has no master. Each will have more or less, depending on whether he values or disdains it. The choice is your own responsibility. God has none.'" . . .

Now it seems that it is here, Glaucon, that a human being faces the greatest danger of all. And because of this, each of us must be most concerned to seek out and learn those subjects that enable him, by his own powers and knowledge, to distinguish the good and useful life from the worthless, and always to make the best choice possible in every situation. . . . We must go down to Hades holding adamantly to this belief, lest we be dazzled there by wealth and other evils, rush into tyranny or some other similar course of action, do irreparable evils and suffer even worse ones. . . .

He said that when the Speaker had told them this, the one who came up first chose the greatest tyranny. In thoughtlessness and greed he chose it without adequate examination and didn't notice that, among other evils, he was fated to eat his own children as a part of it. When he examined at leisure the life he had chosen, however, he beat his breast and bemoaned his choice. And having ignored the prophet's warning, he did not take responsibility for these evils. Instead he blamed fortune, daemons, and everything but himself.

—Plato, *Republic* 617d–619e

CONTENTS

ACKNOWLEDGMENTS

This book was conceived and written in Berlin. Long periods of work were interrupted by breaks spent with friends on Hufelandstrasse, in the Volkspark Friedrichshain, and at the now non-existent British Council in Hackescher Markt. I am deeply grateful to them, and above all to Herr Drux for looking after things *zuhause* during my frequent absences.

Many of my academic debts predate the conception and writing of this book. Nevertheless, I thank friends, colleagues, and former students at Oxford University, the London School of Economics, and the Central European University for supporting me in various ways. The Alexander von Humboldt Foundation, Tulane University, and Yale University provided fellowships that supported different stages of research and writing. I am especially grateful to Dominic Byatt, Margaret Canovan, Alison Carter, Giovanni Giacoppini, Andrew Hurrell, Meg Keenan, Mária M. Kovács, David Miller, Mark Philp, Kleon Satraptos, Hagen Schulze, Avi Shlaim, Anthony D. Smith, Steven B. Smith, the late Geoffrey Stern, Rick Teichgraeber, and Peter Wilson. I also thank my editor at Princeton University Press, Rob Tempio, for a remarkably swift review process and for his good advice and humor in addressing other matters; my production editor, Natalie Baan, for her support in dealing with many last-minute details; and Richard Isomaki for his excellent copyediting.

My mother, Gretchen Benner, has remained as interested in and supportive of my work as ever. I thank her for everything, again. Thanks too to my friends for their solidarity over many years. And special thanks to Rosamund Bartlett, who always asked after my Machiavelli, and cheered me on even when I seemed to need no cheering.

My husband Patrick has lived with this book from the start. He listened, counseled, encouraged, made sure I was fed, and graciously befriended this Other Man who demanded so much of my time. I am quite sure that no scholar living or dead has ever had a better spouse, *compagno*, or friend. Had fortune not blessed me with his company, I would have had far less pleasure in writing this book. It is dedicated to him in deepest love and gratitude.

ABBREVIATIONS

Citations from Machiavelli's writings give the work, book (where relevant), and chapter first, followed by page number from English translation, then by page number from the original as in the *Opere*.

AW	Machiavelli, *Art of War* (*Dell' arte della guerra*). Original in *Opere*, vol. 1.
BH	Leonardo Bruni, *History of the Florentine People*
D	Machiavelli, *Discourses on Livy* (*Discorsi sopra la prima deca di Tito Livio*). Original in *Opere*, vol. 1.
Discursus	Machiavelli, "Discourse on Remodeling the Government of Florence" (*Discursus florentinarum rerum*). Original in *Opere*, vol. 1.
FH	Machiavelli, *Florentine Histories* (*Istorie fiorentine*). Original in *Opere*, vol. 3.
GD	Guicciardini, *Dialogue on the Government of Florence*
HH	Herodotus, *Histories*
LH	Livy, *Histories* (*Ab urbe condita*)
MF	*Machiavelli and His Friends: Their Personal Correspondence*. Trans. and ed. James B. Atkinson and David Sices. Original in *Opere*, vol. 2.
P	Machiavelli, *Prince* (*Il principe*). Original in *Opere*, vol. 1.
PolH	Polybius, *Histories*
PL	Plutarch, *Parallel Lives of Greeks and Romans*
PM	Plutarch, *Moralia*
SBC	Sallust, *Bellum Catilinae*
TPW	Thucydides, *Peloponnesian War*
XC	Xenophon, *Cyropaedia*
XH	Xenophon, *Hiero*

It is necessary that we add to the knowledge of history that branch of philosophy which deals with morals and politics. . . . Nor in this connection do I hesitate to speak of the most distinguished of his class, and to set up as a model for imitation Machiavelli and his precious *Observations on Livy*. . . . I do not defend his impiety or his lack of integrity, if he actually had such faults. And yet . . . if I give a just estimate of his purpose in writing, and if I choose to reinforce his words by a sounder interpretation, I do not see why I cannot free from such charges the reputation of this man who has now passed away. . . . If our plan is to interpret authors favorably, we shall palliate many faults in this man also, or we shall at least tolerate in him those that we tolerate in Plato, Aristotle, and others who have committed offenses not unlike his. (Alberico Gentili, *de Legationibus* [1594], III.ix)

Since his death in 1527, Machiavelli's thought has been subject to widely differing interpretations. On the one hand, he is credited with the "Machiavellian" doctrine that prudent rulers should shed moral scruples, adopting whatever means are necessary to preserve their state. This doctrine has been evaluated both critically and positively. Machiavelli's early critics claimed that he defended the evil methods of tyrants. Since the nineteenth century, many sympathetic readers have argued that "Machiavellian realism," as they see it, sets out the necessary foundations of stable government or national independence.[1] On the other hand, many early readers argued that Machiavelli's main purpose was to offer advice on how to preserve popular freedoms in republics.[2] More recently, scholars who identify Machiavelli with a wider "civic humanist" tradition have done much to explain these early republican readings. These scholars have not systematically explored Rousseau's assertion that the *Prince* is a "book of republicans." Yet they have made it much harder to read any of Machiavelli's works as straightforward defenses of a politics indifferent to all ends except self-preservation.[3]

Disagreements between "realist" and republican or "civic humanist" readings have dominated Machiavelli scholarship for decades. But remarks made by some

[1] For examples of the critical view see Anglo 2005. For early examples of the sympathetic view see Hegel 1999 (1800–1802), 553–58; and Fichte 1971 (1807), 400–453. Strauss (1958) regards Machiavelli as a teacher of evil, yet offers a nuanced analysis of the reasons that brought him to these teachings.

[2] Gentili 1924 (1594), III.ix; Spinoza 1958 (1677), V.7; Rousseau 1964 (1762), III.6.409.

[3] Rousseau, 1964 (1762), III.6.409. "Realist" and republican interpretations are not, of course, mutually exclusive. According to Fichte, Machiavelli sought to combine the two ideas: while his ultimate goals were strongly republican, he believed that it was sometimes necessary to use any available methods to preserve republics and national freedoms from monarchist enemies and foreign threats. See Fichte 1971 (1807); and Meinecke's (1998 [1925]) influential exegesis.

of Machiavelli's early readers raise even more fundamental problems of interpretation. These have, however, received surprisingly little scholarly attention. The remarks in question are not idiosyncratic or off the cuff. They are made by a number of authors who give ample evidence of having read Machiavelli's works with great care, and who all attribute similar purposes to his writings. The remarks do not occur in the context of polemical diatribes, unlike interpretations offered by some of Machiavelli's fiercest critics. Many are found in works authored by some of the most perceptive readers and thinkers of the sixteenth through eighteenth centuries, including Francis Bacon, Benedict Spinoza, and Jean-Jacques Rousseau. In addition to stressing Machiavelli's sympathies with republics and "peoples," these and other authors make three striking claims that deserve a fuller examination than they have so far received.

One claim is that Machiavelli should be regarded as a moral and political philosopher. According to Alberico Gentili, an Italian Protestant exile who became professor of jurisprudence at Oxford, Machiavelli "assumes the role of philosopher" when discussing historical examples, excelling in "that branch of philosophy which deals with morals and politics [*moribus et civitate*]." Gentili compares Machiavelli's aims with those of ancient philosophers such as Socrates, Plato, and Cicero, who believed that moral philosophy was a necessary foundation of both statesmanship and citizenship.[4] In 1605 Francis Bacon seconded Gentili's view of Machiavelli as an exemplary philosophical "politician" and moral thinker. More than any other recent writer, Bacon suggests, Machiavelli showed that policy was "a great part of philosophy" and vice versa.[5] Toward the end of the seventeenth century, the English republican Henry Neville hailed Machiavelli as the most profound moral thinker of modern times. In a dialogue entitled "Plato Redivivus" (1681) Neville describes "the divine Machiavel" as "the best and most honest" of political thinkers, who, like the "divine Plato" before him, wrote as a philosophical "physician" seeking to treat mankind's recurrent moral and political disorders.[6]

The claim that Machiavelli wrote as a moral philosopher is usually linked to two more specific views that help to explain the claim. One is that unlike writers whose aims are more polemical and partisan than philosophical, Machiavelli does not take sides with any sectional interest, or pit "peoples" in an all-out conflict against "princes" or nobles. In the role of civil physician, he hoped that his writings would make him "tolerated as an educator and teacher by those who held the tiller of government" in a *principato* or a republic, so that his advice might help to steer either government away from ruin.[7] The other view is that Machiavelli wanted to teach people how to *see through* deceptively good appearances in politics, not how to *generate* them. According to Bacon, Machiavelli's main ethical problem was one familiar to ancient philosophers. It often happens that people unwittingly embrace

---

[4] Gentili 1924 (1594), III.ix–xi, xxi; II.iv–vi.

[5] Bacon 2001 (1605), 67.

[6] Neville attributes aims of moral and religious "renovation" to Machiavelli that suggest that his references to "the divine Machiavel" are not ironic, though they are undoubtedly provocative.

[7] Gentili 1924 (1594), III.ix; Bacon 2001 (1605), 169; Spinoza 1958 (1677), V.7.

unwise or evil courses of action because these appear wise or good. How then can "philosophical" reflections help them to recognize all the "forms and natures of evil" that assume benign colors? Machiavelli's great service, Bacon claims, was not to show that moral standards should be lowered in the light of "what men do." It was to show how to recognize corrupting conduct that goes under decent appearances, so that higher standards may be preserved. The attentive study of how corruption operates behind apparent virtues is, Bacon observes, "one of the best fortifications for honesty and virtue that can be planted." For "as the fable goeth of the basilisk, that if he see you first, you die for it; but if you see him first, he dieth: so it is with deceits and evil arts."[8]

A second striking claim is that Machiavelli purports to uphold the "rule of law" against the "rule of men" as the principal antidote to civil disorders, whether in principalities or republics. James Harrington offers an emphatic version of this claim on the opening pages of his *Oceana* (1656). He expounds an ideal of government according to "ancient prudence," that is, "government de jure . . . an art whereby a civil society of men is instituted and preserved upon the foundation of common right or interest; or, to follow Aristotle and Livy . . . the empire of laws, and not of men." This kind of government, Harrington asserts, "is that which Machiavel (whose books are neglected) is the only politician that has gone about to retrieve." Harrington does not pause to ask why the Florentine's name was widely identified with the unscrupulous wiles of "extraordinary" individual rulers instead of with the rule of law. He simply states what he regards as the correct understanding of Machiavelli's purposes, claiming that among modern writers Machiavelli should be seen as the leading reviver of "ancient" rule-of-law thinking, which held that "the liberty of a commonwealth consists in the empire of her laws, the absence whereof would betray her to the lust of tyrants."[9] Harrington's good friend Neville echoes this claim. He repeatedly invokes the "incomparable Machiavel" to support arguments for upholding the strict rule of law, even when one's aim is to reform or "purge" corrupt forms of government.[10] Building on arguments from the *Discourses* and *Prince*, Spinoza's *Tractatus Politicus* defends extensive freedoms of speech and religion, and the equal freedom of all citizens to stand for office. Spinoza describes Machiavelli as a consistent defender of the rule of law who, while canvassing the common opinion that virtuous one-man rulers are needed to cure corruption, ultimately exposes fatal flaws in it.[11]

---

[8] Bacon 2001 (1605), 169. In an apocryphal letter, Neville has "Nicolas Machiavel" insist that by laying bare the corrupt maxims "most in vogue" in his times, he did not mean to recommend them, or to reconcile readers to the harsh reality that "de facto the infamy of the breach of Word would quickly be forgotten and pardoned by the World." His "only scope and design is to promote the Interest and welfare of mankind, and the peace and quiet of the world" by exposing the grim realities of moral corruption behind appearances of "greatness," virtue, or religion (Neville 1691, 5–8).

[9] Harrington 1901 (1656), 183–84, 193.

[10] "Plato Redivivus" claims to follow Machiavelli in seeking to "make the law and the judges the only disposers of the liberties of our persons" and to establish distinct "powers and jurisdictions of . . . several councils (wherein the protection of liberty, as Machiavel calls it, it now to be placed)" (Neville 1681, III.20–21).

[11] Spinoza 1958 (1677), VI.4–5, VII.1, X.1, 10; see chap. 11.

A third claim is that in seeking to "renovate" ancient wisdom, Machiavelli drew as much on Greek as on Roman sources, and on Greek philosophy as well as history. Indeed, early readers denied that sharp distinctions can be made between historical and philosophical aspects of Machiavelli's writing, since like many of his favorite ancients he "assumes the role of philosopher" when discussing historical examples. Neville's "Machiavel" acknowledges Greek philosophers among his chief inspirations, while modestly disavowing the capacity to imitate their methods. According to "Plato Redivivus" Machiavelli sought to revive "a wise custom amongst the ancient Greeks" who, "when they found any craziness or indisposition in their several governments, before it broke out into a disease, did repair to the physicians of state . . . and obtained from them some good recipes, to prevent those seeds of distemper from taking root." In its manner of enquiry Neville's text imitates Machiavelli as well as Plato, "the greatest Philosopher, the greatest politician (I had almost said the greatest divine too) that ever lived": his dialogue does not seek "to dispute . . . for victory" but "to discover and find out the truth" by means of familiar, unstudied discourse. Neville treats Machiavelli as the main modern exponent of arguments that he attributes to Plato, Aristotle, and Cicero, as well as to the historians "Thucydides, Polybius, Livy or Plutarch."[12] A recent scholar has noted that Bacon selected much of the same canon of ancient historians as Machiavelli, including Livy and Tacitus but also Xenophon, Polybius, and Thucydides, whom Machiavelli "uses and cites . . . as Bacon does."[13] The same scholar omits, however, to point out that Bacon frequently identifies his predecessor's moral teachings with those of Greek philosophers such as Socrates, Plato, or Aristotle. Gentili offers one of the most direct, and tantalizingly unexplained, identifications of this kind. "If our plan," he writes, "is to interpret authors favorably, we shall palliate many faults" in Machiavelli too; "or we shall at least tolerate in him those that we tolerate in Plato, Aristotle, and others who have committed offenses not unlike his."[14]

All these claims characterize Machiavelli's thought in ways that challenge widespread assumptions found in both realist and civic humanist interpretations. While some scholars refer to "Machiavelli's philosophy," few refer to his ethics or moral philosophy.[15] Although recent scholars have emphasized Machiavelli's preference for the rule of laws over the "rule of men," so far none have tried to reconstruct the philosophical reasons for this preference, instead presenting it in conventional or "rhetorical" terms. Moreover, even the most vigorous defenders of the rule-of-law reading remain ambivalent on one point: Machiavelli, they suggest, believed that exceptional individuals must play a key role in founding, ordering, or purging

---

[12] Neville 1681, Pref.3, II.3, I.2–3. Neville criticized writers who misinterpreted Plato and Aristotle as defenders of monarchy or tyranny.

[13] Wormald 1993, 223–24, 199.

[14] Gentili 1924 (1594), III.ix. Gentili stresses the value of Greek language and learning throughout the *Legationibus*, paying special attention to Greek practices and judgments about the ethics of war and peace; see Gentili 1924 (1594), I.xviii, III.vii.

[15] For example, see Strauss 1958, 294–98; Skinner 1981, 48–77; Viroli 1998, 11–41, 176–88; de Alvarez 1999, esp. 68–71; and Fischer 2000. Other recent scholars deny that Machiavelli can be called a philosopher; see chap. 1.

polities, if necessary using extralegal means.[16] As for ancient sources, scholars influenced by the work of Leo Strauss frequently compare Machiavelli with Greek writers. Yet they tend to argue that he broke with their main ethical positions, as well as with those of other ancient, theological, and humanist thinkers.[17] Civic humanist readings generally stress Roman sources more than Greek.[18] An exception is J.G.A. Pocock's argument that together with other Renaissance republicans, Machiavelli drew heavily on Aristotle's conception of civic life and the responsibilities of active citizenship. But Pocock's main concern is to identify a few general ideas that were developed by later British and American writers, not to offer a fine-grained interpretation of either Aristotle or Machiavelli. His readings of both authors are therefore too broad-brushed to support claims about the Aristotelian ancestry of Machiavelli's thought.[19]

This book presents an interpretation of Machiavelli's writings that helps to account more fully for all three of the claims just outlined. It explains how early philosophical readers could reasonably see Machiavelli as a fellow moral philosopher who identified the strict rule of laws as the key to avoiding and correcting civil disorders, and who drew extensively on Greek as well as Roman arguments. Once the textual basis for their claims has been clarified, it also becomes clearer why early readers could characterize the *Prince* as an ethical and republican text. None of these readers left detailed commentaries on Machiavelli's writings, though some of them imitated aspects of his manner of writing and endorsed many of his arguments. While the interpretation offered in the present study was originally inspired by some of the readings just set out, in the end I had to work out my own answers to questions posed by early readers. Nonetheless, this is not intended as an interpretation sui generis, but as a renewal of a very old tradition of Machiavelli readership: one that sees him as a moral philosopher whose political theory is based on the rule of law, and whose "manner" and "matter" of writing are heavily indebted to ancient Greek ethics.

Arguments: Philosophical ethics and the rule of law

This book suggests that Machiavelli's positions are closer to those of other humanist republicans than to amoral political realism. But he used ancient sources in

---

[16] While defending the view that Machiavelli preferred the rule of laws over that of men, Viroli (1998, 146–47) nonetheless concludes that "The restoration of liberty in a corrupt city" is for Machiavelli "the work of one man alone, not of the laws. . . . Rule of law and rule of men are both essential components of Machiavelli's republican theory."

[17] Some of Machiavelli's Greek sources are explored thoughtfully in Strauss 1958 and de Alvarez 1999.

[18] Skinner (2002, 184) describes Machiavelli as a "neo-Roman theorist" while saying very little about his Greek sources. In a valuable recent study, Eric Nelson (2004) discusses some of the neglected Greek sources of Renaissance and modern republican thinking. Yet his treatment of Machiavelli is brief, and deals specifically with his idea of the republic.

[19] Pocock 1975; see Sullivan's (1992) apposite criticisms. I see no evidence that Machiavelli drew on Aristotle more than other Greek writers. If we let ourselves be guided by Machiavelli's own explicit statements and allusions, it seems likely that his most important ancient—as distinct from Hellenistic— Greek sources predate Aristotle, who himself built on their legacies.

highly individual ways, and urged readers to think critically about humanist and republican conventions that, in his view, had been reduced to vague generalities by the political rhetoric of his own times.[20] All four of his main political works (the *Prince, Art of War, Florentine Histories,* and *Discourses*) contain a strong Socratic element. They do not offer judgments that can be attributed to Machiavelli himself without careful interpretation. Instead they present various opinions commonly expressed by political leaders, religious authorities, or men in the piazza, then proceed to examine them in the light of examples and reflective "reasoning" (*ragionare*). Machiavelli seldom draws unequivocal conclusions at the terminus of his reasonings; he invites readers to make their own judgments. Nevertheless, I argue that Machiavelli himself has very clear and distinctive ethical commitments. These can be identified through a comparative reading of all his main works, not one that starts from a casual reading of the *Prince* and imposes preconceptions about that work on the longer texts.

Machiavelli's ethics may be described as an ethics of self-legislation. A basic premise of all his political works is that human beings have no choice but to establish their own laws and orders, *leggi* and *ordini*, through their own corruptible powers of reasoning. They should expect little help from nature, God, or the natural sciences, but must exercise their free will—always under severe constraints—to impose and uphold fully human orders. The ethical value of free agency is fundamental for Machiavelli's arguments. He treats it as an innate capacity that explains the possibility of human *virtú*, and thus deserves respect (*respetto, rispetto*) regardless of the specific ways in which agents exercise it. At the same time, he argues that ordered civil life is impossible unless free agents impose constraints on their own movements, consistent with respect for the freedom of others. Political orders acquire stability when citizens see their own self-imposed constraints as having the quality of *necessità*, a word that has the sense of an ethical imperative or *obligo* for Machiavelli as well as that of physical compulsion. *Leggi,* the laws, are the appropriate form of any ethical or political "necessity" for human beings. In the absence of any other reliable source of authority, the laws must be based on free public *ragionare* and freely authorized by whoever is expected to uphold them.

Starting from these premises, Machiavelli develops a consistent set of arguments about what any political "orderer" (*ordinatore*) must do to acquire and maintain authority among free human agents who have the power to make or unmake their own laws. Against the widespread view that he neglects considerations of justice or subordinates them to self-interest, I argue that justice (*giustizia, iustizia*)—often expressed through paraphrases such as *leggi* or *respetto*—is a fundamental concept in all Machiavelli's writings. This becomes apparent once preconceptions about his views have been set aside in favor of a careful, independent reading. He frequently invokes justice even in the *Prince,* though that work assumes that most readers are too corrupt to be moved by appeals to justice unless these are concealed within arguments from self-interest. Arguing, for example, that princes are strongest when they form transparent, uncoerced contractual ties (*contratto*) with subjects and

---

[20] *Discursus,* 106/737.

foreign allies, Machiavelli explains why brute force is seldom enough to under-write political power. "Victories are never so clear," he points out, "that the win-ner does not have to have some respect, especially for justice [*le vittorie non sono mai sí stiette che el vincitore non abbia ad avere qualche respetto, e massime alla iustizia*]."[21] Such views, I argue, form part of the main line of ethical reasoning that runs through all Machiavelli's writings, though often beneath skillfully crafted, surface appearances of amoralism. He makes readers work hard to identify and keep hold of the ethical line in the midst of numerous corrupt opinions also found in his texts, which mimic the unreflective and corrupt opinions found in civil life.

I try to retrieve these arguments by paying close attention to Machiavelli's noto-riously puzzling modes of writing, discussed in Part I ("Contexts"). The arguments are similar, and expressed in nearly identical language, across the four major po-litical works. Part II ("Foundations") starts by reconstructing Machiavelli's critical theory of knowledge, which he develops through the concepts of historical *imi-tazione* and *cognizione* (chap. 3). Chapter 4 offers a close analysis of two of his most important concepts, *necessità* and *virtú*. I argue that previous studies have not fully grasped the demanding normative sense that Machiavelli gave to both concepts. Chapter 5 reappraises his conception of human nature in the light of this read-ing. Part III ("Principles") reconstructs the implicit, ethical reasoning behind his overtly prudential arguments for respecting popular "desires for freedom" and the "limits" of justice (chaps. 6–8). Part III concludes by questioning the standard view that Machiavelli held that "ends justify means" (chap. 9). I try to show that when his statements to this effect are reread in their textual context, it becomes clear that they cannot be taken as straightforward expressions of Machiavelli's own views. On the contrary, he usually presents them as among the widespread, self-serving "opinions" that stand in need of critical examination. Finally, against the backdrop of my interpretation of his ethics, Part IV ("Politics") reexamines Machiavelli's arguments on how to "order" and maintain political authority, both within and among polities (chaps. 10–12).

Although most chapters offer detailed discussions of Machiavelli's historical examples, I understand his main purposes to have been philosophical, and con-cerned primarily with the foundations of *normative* judgments about actions. I ac-knowledge that rhetorical arguments on the one hand, and the attempt to develop empirically well-founded analyses of human conduct on the other, have an impor-tant place in his thought. Both, however, are subservient to a more basic interest in identifying standards and principles of "reasonable" or right action. Machiavelli's criteria of reasonableness or rightness are not exhaustively grounded in empirical analyses or instrumental considerations, that is, judgments about what it takes to achieve particular aims in specific conditions. A philosophically sensitive reading suggests that an adequate understanding of his central normative concepts such as *virtú*, free will, and order depends on imputing capacities to human beings beyond what can be seen or measured, and which furnish standards that may be used critically to evaluate particular ends and actions. This understanding is reflected

---

[21] *P*, XXI.90/181.

in how I set out my reading of the texts. Since reflectiveness about the adequate use of concepts is fundamental for Machiavelli's ethical "reasonings," each chapter is organized around key concepts used throughout his works.

The reading presented here seeks to avoid what I see as two equally serious methodological pitfalls. One is to subordinate the interpretation of Machiavelli's texts to the study of wider literary and political contexts while playing down puzzling arguments and idiosyncratic uses of key words that cry out for closer analysis. The other pitfall is to treat textual interpretation as a free-ranging activity, whereby readers express their personal response to a text while offering little in the way of a reasoned account. My argument starts by locating Machiavelli's thought in what I consider to be the most important political and intellectual contexts that influenced his views. But the bulk of the book is concerned with textual exegesis and the analysis of arguments. While my concern is to recover the meaning of Machiavelli's texts, I try to give clear reasons for considering one interpretation as stronger or weaker than another, and to explain my use of textual evidence within or across different works. I have no illusions that this will forestall serious disagreements with my reading. Yet I hope it may provoke more rigorously reasoned debates about how to interpret Machiavelli's writings.

Sources: Greek ethics

The book's main contributions are interpretative and philosophical. But it also seeks to contribute to the history of ideas. My main argument here is that Machiavelli's Greek antecedents have been badly underexamined. Readers can gain a better understanding of his often enigmatic arguments and use of examples if they go back to the ancient Greek and Hellenistic texts he frequently invokes, as well as to Roman and humanist sources. An important part of the work presented in these pages has been to look closely at Machiavelli's use of authors such as Thucydides, Xenophon, and Plutarch, whose works he often cites in his main works on politics, as well as in letters and shorter pieces.[22] Part I identifies some of the most important affinities between his implicit ethical arguments and those found in Greek writings. The affinities relate both to substantive judgments and to formal features

---

[22] My interpretation does not oppose Machiavelli's Greek sources to Roman ones. The ancient Greek writers I see as his main models were also models for his Romans. Both Livy and Sallust, for example, took Thucydides as a model in matters of style and often of substance. See Walsh 1963, 21–23, 40–44, 83–85, 105, 206–12; Fornara 1983, 106–7, 175; Bringmann 2007, 118–22. Livy often drew on Polybius, a Greek who lived under the Roman Empire. Cicero was a great admirer of Greek philosophy, writing dialogues on the *Republic* and *Laws* that sought to renovate Plato. While Machiavelli drew broadly on Roman and Greek texts, his main selection can be narrowed down to authors who wrote in one of two main, arguably related traditions: critical philosophical history, tracing its main lineage to Thucydides; and Socratic writing in various genres, best represented by Xenophon, Plato, and Plutarch. It seems unlikely that he or his humanist contemporaries would have accepted sharp distinctions between Greek and Roman approaches, or the oppositions sometimes posited today between, say, Thucydides and Plato or Cicero and Tacitus.

of his arguments, including many of his key evaluative concepts and oppositions. More cautiously, I suggest similarities with arguments found in Plato's dialogues.

This lacuna in the Machiavelli scholarship is so large and persistent that one might expect to discover good reasons for it. One possible reason is simply a lack of clear evidence that Machiavelli read Greek. But by the same token, there is no firm evidence that he did not.[23] Even if his Greek was poor or non-existent, the writings of Thucydides, Xenophon, Plato, Aristotle, and Plutarch—though possibly not of Polybius—were all available to him in Latin translation, and in some cases in Tuscan vernacular. I consider it unlikely, however, that a writer of Machiavelli's outstanding literary and linguistic talents would not have consulted the original Greek of works he mentions and "imitates," even if he first encountered them through translations.

Another rationale might be that Machiavelli did not express anything like the same admiration for Greek political models, whether Athenian or Spartan, as he did for ancient Rome.[24] This view assumes that Machiavelli's most important judgments relate to concrete political practices rather than general standards, and focus on what ancient practices got right, not on what they got wrong. But Machiavelli's appraisals of ancient works do not deal only, or even mainly, with examples of excellence. They are just as concerned with the causes of disorders, and with the corruption of sound standards of judgment as well as of institutions. The same can be said of his favorite Roman authors. Livy, Sallust, and Tacitus were not primarily eulogists of Rome, but critical analysts of the causes that corrupted the Roman republic's once virtuous orders. These Romans drew heavily on the concepts, judgments, and literary genres developed by Greek writers. Machiavelli's grim analysis of contemporary conditions in his native city, Florence, has many similarities with Thucydides', Xenophon's, or Plato's critical analyses of Athens' self-destructive democracy. His analysis of fratricidal conflicts between different Italian cities draws heavily on Athenian authors and on Plutarch, a Greek who, living under the Roman empire, looked back on his country's former glories and self-inflicted disasters.

Yet another possible explanation for the neglect of Machiavelli's Greek sources turns on the problematic distinction between philosophy and history. The view that Machiavelli "attacks" or is hostile to Greek philosophy is frequently asserted in the scholarly literature, although in my view no persuasive case has yet been offered to support it.[25] As I argue in chapter 1, the assertion often rests on a questionable account of the main intellectual contexts that helped to shape Machiavelli's thinking.

[23] Mansfield conjectures that Machiavelli deliberately concealed his knowledge of Greek, "playfully extinguishing the preceding philosophical sect and perverting the memory of antiquity *a suo modo*" and thus liberating the Romans and their imitators from their "tutelage to Greek political philosophy" (1979, 206). I find the deliberate-concealing thesis plausible, although my reading challenges the argument that Machiavelli broke with the Socratic tradition.

[24] See Gilbert 1965, 203–8, and the remarks on Roman and Greek sources of the republican tradition in Pettit 1997, 285–86.

[25] Strauss (1958) outlines a fascinating case, but does not flesh it out with detailed comparisons of Machiavelli and Greek philosophers.

The most serious error is to presume that Florentine and Italian humanism *tout court* was concerned to promote the *vita activa* above the *vita contemplativa*, where the former is identified with politics or rhetoric, and the latter with philosophy. This picture of humanist thinking about the relation between politics and philosophy stands in urgent need of reappraisal. I further question the assumption that since Machiavelli does not call himself a philosopher, and did not write scholastic treatises that explicitly distinguish philosophical subject-matter from historical and political themes, he must have had little interest in anything that would have been recognized in his times as philosophy—especially Greek philosophy.[26] The Greeks he admired philosophized about ethics and politics through historical and biographical writing (Thucydides, Xenophon, Polybius, Plutarch's *Lives*), characterless "discourses" in the form of essays (Xenophon, Plutarch's essays), dialogues on political matters (parts of Thucydides' histories, Xenophon's *Hiero*, Plato's *Gorgias*, *Republic*, *Statesman*, and *Laws*), and other genres that clearly differed from scholastic treatises or commentaries. The content of these ancient writings was recognized as philosophical by readers such as Gentili, Bacon, Neville, Hobbes, Spinoza, and Rousseau,[27] who apprehended similar philosophical purposes in Machiavelli's partly imitative works—which include a philosophical history modeled on Thucydides as well as Livy (the *Florentine Histories*), a collection of numerous short essay-like *discorsi* (the *Discourses*), and a long dialogue (the *Art of War*).

The problem of Machiavelli's relations with Plato and various branches of Platonism has been almost entirely neglected in the scholarly literature, notwithstanding the parallels alluded to by Machiavelli's early philosophical readers. The subject is at once potentially rich and a hazardous minefield for any scholar who remains unconvinced—as I do—by textbook oppositions between Machiavelli's alleged realism and empiricism and a strongly transcendentalist interpretation of Plato's idealism. Textbook oppositions often sound plausible to people who lack the time or interest to read difficult works with the care they demand.[28] They add interesting dramatic tension to what might otherwise be much duller surveys of the history of ideas, and thus come to be valued as expository or teaching tools. But even plausible or interesting accounts of the relations between authors need to be evaluated by close, reasoned readings of their texts, and by independent judgments about their content. This book is about Machiavelli, and it is quite long enough without any further examination of how my interpretation might challenge preconceptions

[26] Felix Gilbert (1965, 193) states that "Machiavelli was not a philosopher. He intended neither to outline a philosophical system nor to introduce new philosophical terms." Gilbert's definition of philosophy here is unduly narrow. If these were its definitive features, the entire tradition of Socratic philosophy discussed in chap. 1 must be considered as non-philosophy.

[27] See Hobbes' (1989 [1629], 570–86) remarks on Thucydides' philosophical education under Anaxagoras, who was also Socrates' mentor, and the historian's commitment to non-partisan truth in "Of the Life and History of Thucydides." Unlike the others in this list, Hobbes does not explicitly acknowledge Machiavelli as an inspiration for his own arguments. But an examination of their use of ancient—and especially Greek—sources might suggest the need for further comparative studies of Machiavelli and Hobbes; see Conclusions.

[28] The present author has often been such a person, not least when pressures to write quickly or to teach fast-paced courses on the history of ideas left precious little time to read.

about his affinities with Plato's philosophy. I do, however, consider this an extremely fruitful area for future research. To avoid introducing such a controversial set of side issues into the main text, I have consigned many of my direct comparisons between Machiavelli and Plato to footnotes, where I hope they might nonetheless stimulate further thought and argument.

The proposal that Greek sources provide an indispensable key to reading Machiavelli is by no means an elegant solution to all the puzzling features of his writing. Some of the original Greek texts discussed here are as ambiguous as Machiavelli's own renovations. In saying that highly problematic works such as Thucydides' histories, Xenophon's *Cyropaedia* and *Hiero*, or Plato's *Statesman* or *Laws* provide a key to Machiavelli's enigmas, I certainly do not mean that they supply clear-cut answers that can resolve interpretive debates once and for all. Fortunately for future generations of readers, it is most unlikely that any interpretation of Machiavelli's endlessly intriguing texts will ever be regarded as definitive. Debates will rage on, but perhaps they will take on new dimensions if we examine Machiavelli's ancient sources more closely, along with his humanist contexts. Until we have a fuller appraisal of these sources, we will fail to appreciate the extent to which later thinkers who built on his ideas, such as Harrington, Spinoza, and Rousseau, saw a revival of ancient ethical traditions as necessary for "modern" enlightenment. Instead of regarding Machiavelli as a late humanist whose ideas represent the waning of Renaissance enthusiasm for ancient teachings, they saw him as what might be called a critical humanist: one who pointed out many corrupt features of humanist thought in his own time, including corrupt and self-serving uses of ancient models, and who offered a fresh reconstruction of very ancient teachings about political order and virtue. This is the view defended in this work.

CONTEXTS

I

Civil Reasonings: Machiavelli's Practical *Filosofia*

It is widely assumed that Machiavelli either had little interest in philosophy, or thought that its role in human enquiry should be subordinated to practical political concerns. In its simplest form, the assumption rests on a sharp distinction between philosophy as a "contemplative" activity and politics as a realm of "practical" action. Thus one scholar has written recently that Machiavelli cannot be called a philosopher at all, but a "practitioner of politics" who engaged himself "heart and soul" in political, administrative, military activity.[1] A more nuanced view is that there are philosophical elements and implications in Machiavelli's writings, but that the kind of philosophy found there is radically empirical. By treating "what is" in human conduct as the sole standard for what "ought" to be done, Machiavelli is supposed to have subordinated ethical judgments to a new "science of politics" that broke with both ancient and Christian conceptions of philosophical ethics.[2] Another view is that Machiavelli redefined the idea of philosophy in ways that reject any ethical limits, including those derived from what empiricists regard as objective or natural data, unless the limits are determined by a more fundamental criterion of political necessity. Thus Leo Strauss sees it as an error to deny "the presence of philosophy in Machiavelli's thought." But whereas for ancients "philosophy transcends the city, and the worth of the city depends ultimately on its openness, or deference, to philosophy," Machiavelli's "new notion of philosophy" remains "on the whole within the limits set by the city *qua* closed to philosophy" and despises the ancients' "concern with imagined republics and imagined principalities." Philosophy on this view must not set its sights on standards beyond what the prince or the *demos* sets, but accept them as "beyond appeal" and simply look for the "best means conducive to those ends."[3]

A few recent scholars have suggested that Machiavelli reevaluated the role of philosophy in several later writings and identified his own purposes with those of ancient philosophers. But no systematic case is made for this alternative view, nor is it treated as the basis for a philosophical reinterpretation of Machiavelli's major works.[4] This chapter questions the first three views, and outlines a more systematic set of arguments against the presumption that Machiavelli subordinated philosophy to politics. This prepares the ground for two further arguments that are

---

[1] Bec 1996, Pref.iii; also see Gilbert 1965, 193, and Morfino 2002, 17.
[2] Berlin 1981 (1958), 73; Meinecke 1998 (1925), 39–43; Cassirer 1946, 129–43.
[3] Strauss 1958, 294–97.
[4] See de Grazia 1989, 142, 249, 375–76, 384–85; Viroli 1998, 48–54.

developed throughout this book. One is that although Machiavelli did not openly proclaim or disavow philosophical intentions, all his main writings refer to and build on a particular ancient tradition of philosophically informed politics. This tradition did not conceive of philosophy as an "otherworldly," purely contemplative, or elite activity, but as an indispensable element of a well-ordered civil life in which all citizens should participate. The second argument is that while Machiavelli does argue from observations and common opinions concerning what is or has been, he does not treat empirical data as an exhaustive or sufficient basis for reasoning about human conduct.

I start by locating Machiavelli's main ethical and political concerns in the context of his own times, in relation to what he saw as the most pressing problems that his writings sought to address. Many studies of Machiavelli contextualize his views by examining how other Florentine humanists viewed the problems of maintaining or expanding republics. Yet few take his own mature writings on Florence as a starting point. There are good reasons to begin, then, with Machiavelli's unjustly neglected *Florentine Histories*. His general diagnosis of how political corruption sets in and spreads is developed most clearly here, as are his views on the rise of "entrepreneurial" princes in unstable republics.[5] Moreover, just because the *Histories* is less widely read than the *Prince* or *Discourses*, it offers a way to approach Machiavelli's ideas afresh.

1.1.
Florentine Histories: Decent words, indecent deeds

The *Histories*, completed around 1525, was Machiavelli's last major work.[6] Whereas his previous political writings had been entirely independent, the *Histories* was commissioned by government bodies under the auspices of Giovanni de' Medici, then Pope Leo X, and Giulio de' Medici, who became Pope Clement VIII. Since the return of the Medicis to power in 1512, Machiavelli had been out of favor with the city's authorities and proscribed from employment as a civil servant, having served for many years as a loyal diplomat under the republican Soderini government.[7] By 1520 several prominent Medici scions, particularly Giovanni, sought to strengthen their regime's position by inviting known critics such as Machiavelli to express their views more openly. As Machiavelli's correspondence with close friends shows, he was well aware of the need to remain guarded when responding to such apparently liberal-spirited invitations.[8] His dedicatory letter is cautious and

---

[5] Some scholars believe that Machiavelli changed his mind on these matters after he wrote the *Prince* in 1513–14. The evidence presented throughout this work suggests that his main positions are consistent across his political works.

[6] Unlike the *Prince* and *Discourses*, which were published posthumously, the *Histories*—like Machiavelli's dialogue the *Art of War*—was published during his lifetime.

[7] Machiavelli was imprisoned and tortured by returning pro-Medici authorities before his proscription from public life.

[8] See sec. 1.5. For further background on the commissioning of the *Histories* see Ridolfi 1963, 176–85, 195–206; Gilbert 1972, 75–99; Skinner 1981, 78–88; Garin 1993, 29–61. Gilbert notes that while

respectful. But it states up front that the *Histories* will neither celebrate Florence's greatness nor pretend that generations of Medici dominance had brought unmitigated boons to the city. Machiavelli notes that he "was particularly charged and commanded by Your Holy Blessedness that I write about the things done by your ancestors" in a manner that would show "that I was far from all flattery (for just as you like to hear true praise of men, so does feigned praise presented for the sake of favor displease you)." True to his word, his account of Florentine domestic and external politics under various Medici princes is unflattering. Yet Machiavelli insists that his sponsors should not take this critical portrayal as a slight to their own or their family's honor. According to his analysis, the principal causes of present-day Florentine "disorders" (*disordine*) long predate the Medicis' emergence as effective *principi* in the republic.[9] The *Florentine Histories* puts these causes under a searingly harsh spotlight.

According to Machiavelli, throughout its history Florence's most noteworthy characteristic was not the outstanding reputation of its high culture, its free republican institutions, or the greatness of its dominions in Tuscany and beyond. Above all else, Florence had long been distinguished by the variety and intensity of its internal dissensions. "If in any other republic there were ever notable divisions," Machiavelli observes, "those of Florence are most notable." Other republics have typically had one principal division, such as that between plebs and the patrician Senate in Rome, which often proved a source of strength and a contributing cause of freedom.[10] But in Florence divisions were multiple, and endlessly multiplying. There "the nobles were, first, divided among themselves; then the nobles and the people; and in the end the people and the plebs: and it happened many times that the winning party [*parte*] was divided in two." The result was continual civil strife; for "from such divisions came as many dead, as many exiles, and as many families destroyed as ever occurred in any city in memory."[11] According to Machiavelli, the root cause of Florence's divisions was the "unreasonable" desire of each party to dominate all the others. Not only the nobles but various popular parties too refused to share power on terms acceptable to their rivals. "The prize they desire to gain" through unrestrained political rivalry was not "the glory of having liberated the state," thereby serving the common good. Each *parte* was motivated by private

---

Machiavelli "had to disguise his anti-Medicean feelings" in the work, nevertheless "an attentive reader can discover these feelings behind the praising and glorifying words." My analysis agrees with this assessment, and with Gilbert's judgment that the *Histories* "contained the same political message as his other works." As I hope this and later chapters will show, Chabod's (1960, 29) view that the *Histories* shows a decline in Machiavelli's "creative vigor" rests on a superficial reading of this marvellously rich text, written in the Thucydidean tradition of critical philosophical histories.

[9] The Medicis were not officially princes until 1531, four years after Machiavelli's death, when Charles V forced Florence to accept hereditary Medici rule. Cosimo is reported to have said, "I am not a prince" to Pope Pius II, preferring (like Julius Caesar in Rome) to describe himself as "first citizen" of the republic (Findlen 2002, 14, 33). Charles' decree turned what Machiavelli regarded as the Medicis' de facto princely regime or *principato*, which had hitherto retained the name of republic, into a regime that was also non-republican de jure.

[10] See chaps. 4, 7.

[11] *FH*, Pref.6–7.

ends, seeking only "the satisfaction of having overcome others and having usurped the principality of the city." One of the main lessons of the *Histories* is that when competing parties regard unilateral dominance as a reasonable aim, partisans lose respect for the juridical and ethical limits that are necessary for political order. As Machiavelli has a prudent speaker note, rivals in this kind of struggle for dominance reach a point at which "there is nothing so unjust, so cruel, or mean that they dare not do it."[12]

This point was repeatedly reached in Florence long before the Medicis came to power. Indeed, such conflicts paved the way for one *parte* dominated by a single family to assert control over the divided republic. In Florence, Machiavelli writes,

> orders and laws are made not for the public but for personal utility; hence wars, pacts, and friendships are decided not for the common glory but for the satisfaction of few. And if other cities are filled with these disorders, ours is stained with them more than any other; for the laws, the statutes, and the civil orders have always been and still are ordered not in accordance with free life but by the ambition of that party which has come out on top.[13]

If Florentine divisions had undermined civil orders for so long, how then did the city manage to remain intact under nominally republican institutions, let alone increase its territorial dominions and reputation for *grandezza*? Machiavelli's answer is that until his own time, generations of Florentines had deployed a specific set of civic skills to conceal the most crippling deficiencies in their institutions. The ambivalent effects of these skills on Florentine politics are examined throughout the *Histories*. Although "the things done by our princes outside and at home may not be read, as are those of the ancients, with admiration for their virtue and greatness," Machiavelli observes wrily that they may "be considered for other qualities with no less admiration when it is seen how so very many noble peoples were held in check" by badly ordered armies and badly enforced laws. The admirable "other qualities" are not "the strength of the soldiers, or the virtue of the captain, or the love of the citizen for his fatherland"; of these the honest historian of Florence "does not tell," for his subject presents scant evidence of them. The qualities that maintained Florence's reputation and dominion are skills of making men or deeds appear better than they are. In each successive period described in Machiavelli's *Histories* "it will be seen with what deceits, with what guile and arts [*con quali inganno, astuzie, arti*] the princes, soldiers, and heads of republics conducted themselves so as to maintain the reputation they have not deserved." The city might be corrupt, divided, and compromised by dependence on foreign powers. But so long as its republican and "princely" leaders were adept at creating appearances of civic virtue, concord, and independence, the Florentines' idea of themselves—and their image in Italy and the world—remained that of a serious regional power governed by impeccably free institutions.[14]

---

[12] *FH*, III.5.110/429–30.
[13] Ibid.
[14] *FH*, V.1.186/520–21.

If the *Florentine Histories* has a single leitmotif, it is the disparity between good words, appearances, or reputations and the less praiseworthy deeds that these may gloss. In the dedication Machiavelli declares that "in all my narrations I have never wished to conceal an indecent deed with a decent cause [*una disonesta opera con una onesta cagione ricoprire*], or to obscure a praiseworthy deed as if it were done for a contrary end."[15] Throughout the work he urges readers, particularly citizens of republics such as Florence, to consider how genuinely *onesto* actions aimed at serving the public good can be distinguished from *disonesto* deeds that pursue private or partisan aims in the name of the republic. The great difficulties of seeing through *onesto* appearances are underscored in Book III. Here Machiavelli has a group of citizens, "moved by love of their fatherland," put forward a scathingly critical diagnosis of Florentine disorders. They note that in Florence and the rest of Italy notions of duty, religion, legality, and justice had become so corrupted by sectarian divisions that they were treated as mere weapons in struggles for dominion. "Because religion and fear of God have been eliminated in all," the main speaker notes,

> an oath and faith given last only as long as they are useful; so men make use of them not to observe them but to serve as a means of being able to deceive more easily. And the more easily and surely the deception succeeds, the more glory and praise is acquired from it; by this, harmful men are praised as industrious and good men are blamed as fools. . . . From this grows the avarice that is seen in citizens and the appetite, not for true glory [*vera gloria*], but for the contemptible honors on which hatreds, enmities, differences, and sects [*sètte*] depend; and from these arise deaths, exiles, persecution of the good, exaltation of the wicked. . . . And what is most pernicious is to see how the promoters and princes of parties give decent appearance to their intention and their end with a pious word [*la intenzione e fine loro con un piatoso vocabolo adonestono*]; for always, although they are all enemies of freedom, they oppress it under color [*sotto colore*] of defending the state either of the optimates [*ottimati*] or of the people.[16]

Though it reverberates throughout the *Histories*, the distinction between *onesto* words, names, or appearances and *disonesto* deeds sharpens up in later books where Machiavelli discusses the Medicis' rise to power. With Cosimo and Lorenzo, the creation of decent appearances to "color" dubious deeds reaches an apogee. Machiavelli acknowledges that these popular princes were largely responsible for giving Florence a name for greatness and glory throughout Italy and beyond. But he also implies that their actions greatly diminished the city's already brittle internal freedoms, and undermined its external security. Instead of stating his critical judgments directly, Machiavelli employs various indirect techniques to imply them. One technique is to praise Cosimo and Lorenzo's ancestors for more consistently placing the public good above private ambitions than their descendants.

---

[15] *FH*, Ded.4/306–7.
[16] *FH*, III.5.109–10/428–32; translation slightly modified. Compare Thucydides, *TPW*, III.82–83, discussed in chap. 2.

Of one Medici ancestor, Machiavelli writes that many Florentines "agree that if Messer Veri had been more ambitious than good, he could without hindrance have made himself prince of the city." But when relatives tried "to persuade him to seize dominion over the republic," Veri de' Medici refused to seize power through any "extraordinary" or illegitimate means; instead he urged the people to "put down their arms and obey the Signori."[17]

Like his more cautious forebears, Machiavelli's Cosimo is highly skilled at avoiding any appearance of illegality in the deeds that bring him to power. Whereas other leaders slandered their opponents with trumped-up or false charges, Cosimo appeared to stand above the fray. He governed himself "with greater spirit in public things and with greater studiousness [*studio*] and more liberality [*liberalità*] toward his friends than his father had done." Cosimo was, Machiavelli writes, "a very prudent man, of grave and pleasing appearance, quite liberal, quite humane [*umano*]; he never attempted anything against either the Party or the state but took care to benefit everyone and with his liberality to make many citizens into his partisans [*partigiani*]." These "arts" of appearing good made it hard to oppose him openly. As his most prudent opponent, the elder statesman Niccolò da Uzzano, observes, the deeds that made critics suspect that Cosimo harbored illegitimate intentions appeared to most citizens as irreproachably "decent": he helped people with his money, handing out or writing off loans to prospective "partisans," and secured public positions of honor for his friends. "Thus," Uzzano remarks, "one would have to allege as the causes for driving him out" of public life "that he is merciful [*piatoso*], helpful, liberal, and loved by everyone." But what law "blames and condemns in men mercy, liberality, and love?" While Uzzano himself "perfectly understood" that these "modes" of gaining popular support corrupt republican liberties and "send men flying to a princedom," a majority of his compatriots were taken in by Cosimo's *onesto* appearances. And since Florentines had long lived with corruption and party divisions, most people simply failed to see what was wrong with Cosimo's methods of "making partisans."[18]

Machiavelli draws further contrasts between Cosimo and prominent citizens who opposed his partisan and "private" ambitions. One was Uzzano, who saw clearly that behind decent appearances the Medici party's "extraordinary modes of proceeding" tended to destroy the rule of law.[19] Machiavelli's Cosimo is prepared to use questionably legal modes to secure his preeminence, though always under the

---

[17] *FH*, III.25.139–40/464–66. Machiavelli's portrait of Cosimo's father, Giovanni de Bicci, is more ambivalent. He appeared as a defender of popular rights, but was "deservedly suspect to the wiser" because the latter saw that Giovanni tended to stir up old dissensions between people and nobles. Machiavelli attributes to Giovanni some of the most prudent maxims in the *Histories*, such as the advice to his sons, "In regard to the state, if you wish to live secure, accept from it [only] as much as is given to you by laws and by men." But Giovanni also says that with his "arts" of appearing upright "in all his speech" he had "not only maintained but increased my reputation in this city"—raising doubts as to whether these arts aimed to serve the common good, or simply to gain a reputation that served private ends. *FH*, IV.3.147–48/475–76; IV.11.156/484–85.

[18] *FH*, IV.26–27.172–75/505–9.

[19] See chap. 10 on the distinction between "extraordinary" and "ordinary" modes.

banner of urgent "necessity." Uzzano, by contrast, "was first among those to whom extraordinary ways were distasteful."[20] Another opponent whose qualities stand in silent contrast to Cosimo's apparent virtues is Neri di Gino Capponi. Machiavelli reports that Cosimo "feared his reputation more than any other's" because, "having been at the head of the Florentine armies many times," Neri had earned "great credit" with soldiers as well as civilians "with his virtue and his merits." Cosimo's reputation derived as much from the wealth and reputation of his forebears as from his own merits. Moreover, Neri gained his authority from public, transparent procedures: he "was one of those who had acquired his reputation by public ways, so that he had many friends and few partisans." Cosimo, on the other hand, "had the private and public ways open to his power," and "had many friends and partisans." Since in Machiavelli's lexicon, private and partisan ways of gaining authority have questionable legitimacy, his description of Cosimo's methods raises serious doubts about their contribution to political order:

> It is to be known [da sapere] that citizens in cities acquire reputation in two modes: either by public ways or by private modes. One acquires it publicly by winning a battle, acquiring a town, carrying out a mission with care and prudence, advising a republic wisely and prosperously. One acquires it in private modes by benefiting this or that other citizen, defending him from the magistrates, helping him with money, getting him unmerited honors, and ingratiating himself with the plebs with games and public gifts. From this latter mode of proceeding, sects and partisans arise, and the reputation thus earned offends as much as reputation helps when it is not mixed with sects, because that reputation is founded on a common good, not on a private good.[21]

After Neri's death the "enemy party" was greatly weakened, and Cosimo's friends set to work destabilizing the Florentine republic. Cosimo "pretended" to stand above these partisan conflicts, posing as disinterested champion of popular wishes; thus "when some deliberation arose that might please the people, he was the first to favor it." Nevertheless, Machiavelli states that the "quality of government" dominated by Cosimo's party became "unbearable and violent" (*insupportabile e violento*), Cosimo himself too "old and weary" to control disturbances.[22] Read in the light of the distinction between *onesto* words and *disonesto* deeds, Machiavelli's epitaph on Cosimo implies that the celebrated man's own conduct contributed to the malaise left at his death. While again we read that Cosimo was "the most reputed and renowned citizen" who above all other men was "liberal and magnificent," the main evidence of his "liberality" is that he lent large sums of money to citizens "who had any quality," and helped any "noble man" under "necessity."[23]

[20] *FH*, IV.27.174–75/506–8.

[21] *FH*, VI.6.236/580–81; VII.1–2.276–77/628–31.

[22] *FH*, VII.2–4.278–80/630–33.

[23] See the early description of Cosimo as taking care "with his liberality to make many citizens into his partisans" (*FH*, IV.26.172–73/505); also later "Cosimo, in order to gain partisans in Florence and friends outside, had been very liberal in sharing his property with everyone" (VII.10.288/642–43).

These private loans were presumably given for partisan ends, and went to well-to-do citizens, not to public works aimed at alleviating poverty in the city. Wanting to "be known" for his magnificence beyond Italy, Cosimo built a hospital for "poor and sick pilgrims" in Jerusalem. But Machiavelli mentions no comparable public services that he funded at home. His magnificence "appeared" in "the abundance of buildings built by him," but these were for "adornment" or private use rather than the public good. He spared no expense to fill churches with raiments "necessary to the adornment of divine service" and built many "private houses" that Machiavelli describes as resembling "palaces not of private citizens but of kings." Cosimo "knew how extraordinary things that are seen and appear every hour make men much more envied than those that are done with the deed and are covered with decency." He therefore took care to generate decent appearances, especially when his deeds were likely to attract envy or indignation. He managed it so that "civil discords always increased his state in Florence, and wars outside increased his power and reputation."[24] Nonetheless, the great man's anxieties increased late in life as he surveyed his own dubious legacy. "It distressed the greatness of his spirit," Machiavelli writes, "that it did not appear to him" that "he had increased the Florentine empire by an admirable acquisition" or improved Florence's security. Indeed, Cosimo realized that his policies had helped rival neighbors to become more threatening to Florence.[25]

Numerous conspiracies against Medici rule follow Cosimo's death. Machiavelli has a nameless conspirator "calling to his aid the people and liberty." In earlier chapters of the *Histories*, these words could still elicit bursts of republican zeal, even in periods of oppression or corruption. Now the noble words *popolo* and *libertà* ring hollow in the piazza. For "the one had been made deaf by the fortune and liberality of the Medici and the other was not known in Florence." Toward the end of the *Histories* words such as "pomp," "magnificence," and "splendor" appear more and more, alongside "terror" and "God."[26] Spectacles, ornaments, and dramas, balls, and banquets proclaim "the greatness of the house of Medici and *its state*" now that the republic had become in effect the private property of a single family.[27] Machiavelli has Cosimo's son Piero suffer pangs of "conscience" when he sees how badly Florence is afflicted by conspiracies. He berates his friends for treating the city as their own private trough:

> it is not enough for you to be princes in such a city and for you few to have these honors, dignities, and advantages with which previously many citizens were wont to be honored . . . it is not enough for you to be able to afflict

---

[24] *FH*, VII.5.281–82/634–36; compare *P*, XVI on liberality as a merely apparent virtue, discussed in chap. 9.

[25] *FH*, VII.6.284/636–38.

[26] Compare Thucydides' remarks about the "most costly and splendid [*polutelestatē . . . kai euprepestatē*]" preparations made in Athens for their ill-advised assault on Sicily, including the comment that to some Athenians "the whole thing seemed more like a display of riches and power" than a well-calibrated "preparation against enemies." The hollowness of the enterprise is underlined by descriptions of the Athenians' expensive and ostentatious public prayers; TPW, VI.31–32.

[27] *FH*, VIII.8.325/688, emphasis added; VII.21.300/657–58.

all others with public burdens and for yourselves, free from those, to have all the public profits. . . . You despoil your neighbor of his goods, you sell justice, you escape civil judgments, you oppress peaceful men and exalt the insolent.

Unfortunately, Piero dies before he can restore the exiles banished by his father's partisans, a move that might have "checked the rapacity" of those who remained in Florence.[28]

The *Histories* ends with the death of Piero's son Lorenzo, widely celebrated in his own time and after as a skilled practitioner of what would come to be called political "realism" or realpolitik. Machiavelli portrays Lorenzo as a chip off Cosimo's block whose consummate self-presentational skills outstripped those of his hugely popular grandfather. Already in his youth Lorenzo speaks with a "gravity and modesty" that inspired trust far beyond what was due to one so young.[29] Machiavelli's Cosimo is an unpolished merchant-prince whose persuasive abilities had less to do with his use of words than with skillful avoidance of overtly illegal actions. His Lorenzo, who enjoyed the best humanistic education, is a master of rhetorical spin as well as a shrewd political operator. The decent words "liberty," "common good," and "fatherland" never sounded better than in Lorenzo's public addresses. The good citizens of Florence lap it all up. While declaring that they will gladly fight for Lorenzo's reputation and state, however, they show little concern to defend the principles implied by the good name of republic, in particular the principle that laws should rule over men.[30] Lorenzo's partisans frequently invoke God's support for all their enterprises, and God's wrath against their critics. Having crushed a conspiracy in which he was a target, Lorenzo declares that "God, who has never in the past abandoned our house, has again saved us and taken up the defense of our just cause." To lend further dignity to his family name, he made his son a cardinal, thus erecting "a ladder enabling his house to rise to heaven."[31] Yet behind Lorenzo's populist spin, "the princes of state" restricted the government so that fewer citizens were permitted to deliberate important matters, thus putting "a check on the spirit of those who were seeking new things."[32] Outside Florence, Lorenzo's aggressive methods of expanding Florentine "dominions" eroded trust among Italian cities that should, in Machiavelli's view, have been forming more effective alliances against foreign intruders. Having wearied citizens with increasingly violent wars against fellow Italians, Lorenzo and his friends sought new "friends" outside Italy, seeking to defend themselves with foreign arms instead of strengthening defenses closer to home.[33]

---

[28] *FH*, VII.23.302/659–60.

[29] *FH*, VII.24.303/661. Compare Livy (*LH*, XXVI.xviii.70–73) on Cornelius Scipio (Africanus), who like Lorenzo sought to salvage his family name while increasing his personal reputation; see chaps. 9, 12.

[30] *FH*, VIII.10.330/693–94; compare IV.33.184/517–18.

[31] *FH*, VIII.10.328/691–92; VIII.36.361/730–32.

[32] *FH*, VIII.19.340/705–7.

[33] See, e.g., *FH*, VIII.14.334/698–99; VII.32.311–12/672; VIII.17.337–38/702–3. For Machiavelli's views on Florentine expansion see esp. chaps. 6, 12.

These policies were conducted behind a persuasive façade of Florentine military and commercial power and cultural prestige. If Florence's republican freedoms had become a fading memory under Lorenzo's watch, he had at least made his city "more beautiful and greater than ever" with private houses fit for kings instead of citizens. Like Cosimo, he maintained his friends in stipends and pensions, and "kept his fatherland always in festivities." All these things, Machiavelli remarks with unmistakable irony, were "like solid ramparts to the city."[34] Cracks in the façade appear in Machiavelli's closing words about Lorenzo in the last pages of the *Histories*. On his deathbed in 1492, Lorenzo is a man "full of distress," "marvelously afflicted," and "oppressed by intolerable stomach pain." Moreover, "that very great disasters must arise from his death, heaven showed many evident signs." Even without heavenly forebodings, serious disorders can be foreseen in Machiavelli's earlier accounts of Lorenzo's harmful policies and methods. The *Histories'* pathetic final sentence implies that at least some of the "bad seeds" that flourished after Lorenzo's death, and that "ruined and are still ruining Italy," were planted by him and his forebears.[35]

If Machiavelli took such a critical view of the Medicis in the *Histories*, it might seem puzzling that his dedicatory letter apologizes to Giulio for failing to abstain from flattery when writing about his ancestors. "I very much fear," he writes there, "that in describing the goodness of Giovanni, the wisdom of Cosimo, the humanity of Piero, and the magnificence and prudence of Lorenzo, it may appear to Your Holiness that I have transgressed your commands" to avoid undue praise. His excuse, Machiavelli says, is that he had to rely on records left by writers who were themselves shameless flatterers. So "when I found that the records of those who described" earlier Medicis "were full of praise for them, I was obliged either to describe them as I found them, or out of envy to be silent about them." Even if he is not at complete liberty to criticize the Medici *principi*, he remains free to omit remarking on errors he does not altogether "know." For "if under those remarkable deeds [*egregie opere*] of theirs was hidden an ambition contrary to the common utility, as some say," Machiavelli observes wryly, "I who do not know it am not bound to write about it."[36] If he suspects that there is a darker side to the deeds he recounts than what the usual encomiums say, yet cannot claim to know it, he will let readers examine for themselves whether the deeds he describes fit the flattering words usually ascribed to them. If the Medicis' deeds show an ambition contrary to the common utility, Machiavelli will not say so in so many words; he simply makes the deeds speak louder than words, names, and reputations. The truth of the *onesto* words he uses to describe the Medici princes must be measured against his indirectly critical, sotto voce account of their deeds and legacies.[37] Readers themselves must judge which comes closer to the truth, the good words or the deeds.

---

[34] *FH*, VIII.36.361/730.

[35] *FH*, VIII.36.361–63/730–32.

[36] *FH*, Ded.4/306.

[37] Many elements in his account of the Medicis resemble traditional topoi in Greek "rise-to-tyranny" literature; see Gray 1997. In Herodotus and earlier writers, (1) new tyrants generally emerge from conditions of civil strife or *stasis*, promising to restore order; (2) they gain supporters by cultivating ap-

1.2.
Flawed remedies: Rhetoric and power politics

While the *Histories* deals with particular events in a particular city, Machiavelli's diagnosis of Florentine disorders highlights a general problem facing any republic, however well ordered. On the one hand, citizens committed to defend the republic against partisan or princely usurpers must rely on their powers of persuasion to secure popular support. On the other hand, there are many different modes of persuasion; and since those who want to acquire princely powers in a republic are often skilled rhetoricians and spin-mongers, their opponents must choose their own counter-persuasions with great care. Drawing mainly on the *Prince*, scholars have offered diverse arguments about how Machiavelli proposed to address endemic problems of persuasion in republics. Before considering some of these arguments, let us reconstruct Machiavelli's diagnosis as it is presented in the *Histories*.

Numerous episodes there suggest that when fighting to defend republican orders against internal threats, persuasion and public laws are the only weapons that are wholly compatible with republican principles. Those who resort to unlawful force or violent conspiracies undermine commitments to the public standards of legitimacy appropriate for republics. Machiavelli vividly illustrates this point when he describes the confrontation between Cosimo de' Medici's partisans and their leading opponents, led by Rinaldo degli Albizzi. Rinaldo is presented as a sincere and passionate patriot, though also personally ambitious, who tried hard to block the Medici *parte* from seizing princely power in the republic. Machiavelli's account acknowledges that Rinaldo had formidable opponents, and does not hold him wholly responsible for failing to preserve the republic. It does suggest, however, that Rinaldo's efforts were weakened by his excessive reliance on the use of force to combat the Medici party's much subtler maneuvers. Whereas the Medicis were masters of sophisticated persuasive arts, Rinaldo tried to fight by means of force, even when force was unauthorized by the laws of the republic. This openly offensive approach played straight into his opponents' hands. They could plausibly claim to be more respectful of public laws and deferential to the popular will than Rinaldo, and thereby garner undeserved credit from their enemy's mistakes.[38] Similarly, after the Pazzi conspiracy against his family has been crushed, Lorenzo de' Medici is able to present himself as a champion of popular legitimacy as against a handful of conspirators who acted without popular authorization. He reminds citizens that the "extraordinary" authority his family has in the city was not seized

---

pearances of justice, liberality, and honest dealing, so that their ascent to tyranny occurs by popular will, not undue violence; (3) when they finally seize power, some deception is used to create an aura of legitimacy for their actions; (4) once in power, tyrants typically rely more and more on mercenaries for defense. They often engage in expensive building projects to keep up their reputation, including houses "fit for kings"; and their often rustic origins are contrasted with the magnificence and pomp of their later way of life. For example, see HH, I.59–96, 114. Most such tyrants leave behind material evidence of greatness (*megalos*), but in other respects leave their cities worse off than before. Machiavelli's *Life of Castruccio Castracani* also includes all these themes.

[38] See chap. 9, sec. 9.5.

by violence. It was willingly "given" by the Florentine people themselves, who "exalted" the Medicis because they had been seen to strive "with humanity, liberality, and with benefits, to surpass everyone." If the conspirators acted "out of the hatred and envy they have of our authority, they offend you," the people, "not us, since it was you who gave it to us." For "truly, those authorities deserve to be hated that men usurp, not those that men earn by their liberality, humanity, and munificence." And "my house could not have ruled and would not be able to rule this republic if you together with it had not ruled and did not rule now."[39]

This speech epitomizes the *Histories*' theme that the most *onesto* words and legal forms often "color" *disonesto* deeds that undermine the rule of law. At the same time, it underscores the point that extralegal violence is a high-risk, self-defeating response to those who gain power by such means. A more effective range of responses can be made through counter-persuasions. The problem of how to distinguish persuasions that tend to support stable republican orders from those that corrupt them is at the heart of Machiavelli's *Histories*. Both the Medicis and the men who tried to contain that family's ambitions used persuasive speech to seek popular support. But there are distinct differences between the forms of speech that Machiavelli gives to men who sought to "seize" the republic for their own private or partisan ambitions, and to those he presents as the republic's most prudent defenders. Both sides invoke the good words republic, freedom, fatherland, and justice. Yet the Medicis and other tyranny-prone individuals who appear earlier in the work use them much more liberally to arouse popular passions, adding heavy doses of God and religion to their rhetoric.[40] By contrast, speakers who Machiavelli portrays as reliable defenders of the republic steer clear of emotive rhetoric, aware that *onesto* words are easily abused. If they do use hot-button words, they take care to give clear, transparent accounts of the deeds needed to match them. When the men who place themselves "in the middle" between warring "sects" try to persuade both sides to negotiate their differences, they avoid inflammatory language, simply explaining to each side why it is in their own interest to put down arms. When the *Histories*' exemplar of prudent statesmanship, Niccolò da Uzzano, seeks to dissuade his compatriots from following Rinaldo's urgings to an ill-advised war, he says that he will deliberately refrain from speaking about the justice of the war, and only discuss its utility in non-partisan terms.[41]

In the *Histories*, then, Machiavelli treats emotionally loaded, imprecise, or partisan forms of rhetoric as destabilizing for republics. Persuasions that give straightforward, transparent reasons for and against a policy or a candidate for office, without resorting to manipulation, deception, or intimidation, are most *compatible* with the ideal of a *res publica*.[42] It does not necessarily follow, however, that they are also most suitable for *defending* republican orders against partisan or princely usurpations. The outcome of the *Histories* must disappoint readers who

---

[39] *FH*, VIII.10.329/642–43.
[40] *FH*, VII–VIII.
[41] *FH*, IV.19.165–66/495–97; see chap. 9, sec. 9.3.
[42] Compare Plato, *Gorg.* 517a, 527c.

believe that genuinely *onesto* persuasions always succeed in countering *disonesto* ones. On the contrary, Machiavelli's narrative shows how seldom the former win out over the latter. The work's "sad and lamentable" end brings home how hard it is for straight-talking, *onesto* men devoted to the public good to compete for popular favor against skilled manipulators of words and reputations.[43] This suggests two possible conclusions about the value of transparently reasoned persuasions as a means of public defense.

One is that they are ultimately useless. Over and over, well-meaning patriotic men employ them in the *Histories*, with ephemerally effective results. If it is assumed that Machiavelli judged persuasions and policies by their results rather than by their intrinsic value, it might seem reasonable to interpret the frequent failures of *onesto* persuasions as evidence of their disutility. The only rational response to this inescapable fact, it might be supposed, is to embrace a knowing skepticism about the value of honesty and transparency in politics. The message of the *Histories* is perhaps the same as that often attributed to the *Prince*: namely, that in politics the most important means of self-defense is knowledge of how to manipulate words and appearances. Instead of clinging to lofty standards of truthfulness, transparency, and public reasoning, people should wake up and see these for what they are in reality: attractive but empty words used in the rough game of political appearance-mongering, for bad as well as for good ends. Those wise enough to recognize this can learn to improve their game and win; those who persist in moralistic denial are doomed to failure. So far the corrupt, overambitious Medicis have been winning. Their opponents should therefore try a different tack: accept the rules of their *disonesto* game, and learn to play it better than they.[44] If political disorders often stem from people's failure to see through specious appearances of virtue, then those who wish to restore order must simply become better than everyone else at generating such appearances. This logic would make the *Histories* consistent with the view that Machiavelli defended the need for "entrepreneurial" princes to seize power in corrupt republics. Only charismatic individuals, on this view, are able to purge partisan corruption, clamp down on popular "licentiousness," discard moral inhibitions, and do whatever is needed to save Florence and Italy.[45]

But a close reading of the *Histories* suggests reasons to doubt whether Machiavelli consistently favored such an approach. Far from implying a relativist or cynical view of standards of transparency, honesty, or public reasoning, the work offers a trenchant critique of various modes of persuasion that flout those standards. The standards themselves are not discredited by recurrent abuses of *onesto* words in the narrative and their failure to defeat *disonesto* dealers. Nor are they treated as valid only in non-corrupt contexts. When Lorenzo defends his family's apparently legitimate modes of gaining authority near the end of the *Histories*, his good

---

[43] *FH*, VII.34.316/677.

[44] Cassirer 1946, 140–43; Berlin 1981 (1958), 73; Strauss 1958, 294, 232–35.

[45] Skinner, Viroli, and other proponents of "civic humanist" readings argue that while Machiavelli was committed to republican principles, he also thought "princely" one-man orderers were needed to eradicate political corruption; Skinner 1978, 114, 138; Viroli 1998, 145–47.

words ring hollow to anyone who has noticed the gulf between his party's good words and corrupt deeds in the preceding pages. These subtly critical features of Machiavelli's *Histories* cast doubt on the view that in the politics of persuasion, the sole criterion for success is how effectively people are persuaded to embrace a policy, party, or person at the time of sale. The *Histories* judges success from a longer and more reflective standpoint. The basic criterion is not whether acts of persuasion secure a name or reputation for greatness, a vast groundswell of popular support, or even a semblance of civil order for a time. It is how much stable order is achieved as a result of persuasions; or to put it negatively, whether certain persuasions tended to intensify partisan conflicts, undermine standards of public transparency, and create a legacy of disorder.

The same persuasive act may be judged differently depending on which criterion one applies. As Machiavelli shows, Cosimo and Lorenzo may be judged as highly successful, indeed "admirable," on the first criterion: they were good at seizing power and converting the republic into their family's "private" *principato* while persuading people that they acted only under popular authority. The more fundamental criterion, however, is whether or not the works in question strengthened the city's orders and defenses or weakened them. On this criterion, the Medicis failed dismally. Under *colore* of good words and appearances, their policies led to the loss through exile of many good and wealthy citizens, undercut the rule of law, deepened partisan divisions, and strained or wrecked Florence's valuable alliances with neighboring cities. All these disorders rendered both Florence and Italy vulnerable to foreign interlopers. The end of the *Histories* is "sad and lamentable"—and the entire work "tragic"—not because another great Medici has died, but because Lorenzo has exacerbated the sad legacy of corruption set in train by his ancestors.[46] The notion that extraordinary entrepreneurial princes are needed to save the corrupt republic is exposed as an empty shell, bringing more wars and internal strife in its train. It may have sold easily to the Florentine people, but an effective sale is not an effective solution. The *Histories* shows what happens when politics is reduced to a competitive game in which success is measured by transient appearances rather than stable legacies. It seems unlikely that having identified the abuse of *onesto* appearances as a contributing cause of his city's disorders, Machiavelli would urge more of the same, advising readers to join the fray on what he saw as deeply corrupting terms.

The other possible conclusion to draw from the failure of transparent persuasions is that they are a necessary yet insufficient component of republican defenses. The question is then, what is needed to supplement them in order to make those defenses more effective? One solution proposed by recent scholars also treats the skillful use of rhetoric as the key component of more adequate defenses. On this reading of Machiavelli, transparency, truthfulness, and reasoning are well-meaning but weak weapons in corrupt times. Machiavelli therefore sought to fight

---

[46] In a letter to Guicciardini of October 21, 1525, Machiavelli signs himself as "Historian, Comic Author, and Tragic Author [*Historico, comico, tragico*]," this last epithet evidently referring to his recent *Histories* (MF, 371/411).

rhetoric used for bad aims with rhetoric used for the common good. He treated political theory as "a rhetorical practice based upon historical knowledge which aims at verisimilitude rather than truth, and endeavors to impel passion and commitment, in addition to conquering reason's consent."[47] Machiavelli is said to have added two essential supplements to bolster republican defenses. One is an infusion of "passions" to compensate for motivational shortcomings of *ragionare*. The other is the replacement of "verisimilitude" for truth as standard of knowledge needed for political action. More efficacious "rhetoric" is the main instrument for arousing passions and creating verisimilitudes. On this reading Machiavelli "practiced political theory, not as the work of a philosopher, nor as the work of a scientist, but as the work of an orator." He "wrote on politics to offer counsel and advice on the most useful way to found, govern, and redeem a principality or a republic, not to identify political or moral truths, and even less to frame universal laws of politics based upon observation of facts."[48]

There are two problems with this account of Machiavelli's solutions. First, few ideas are further from the general tenor of his writing than that arousing "passions," even passions for liberty or the republican *patria*, should play a leading role in resolving civil disorders. The language of passions is extremely muted in all of Machiavelli's works. In the *Histories*, the word "passions" is usually coupled with the words "partisan" or "private."[49] In his correspondence Machiavelli remarks that although he knows his own feelings, he always endeavors to keep them out of his analyses and evaluations of politics. If this cannot be done completely, he says clearly, it should nonetheless be attempted when reasoning in and about republics, as author or as citizen.[50] For the most part he is true to his word. When he does speak of the strong feelings aroused by the name of *libertà* or republic, he uses the words "love" (*amore*) or "desire," not *passione*. To be sure, he writes with great feeling about the desires peoples have for a free way of life in both the *Histories* and the *Discourses*, while his famous appeal for a redeemer of Italy in the *Prince* is a clear example of impassioned rhetoric. But the presence of these elements in his writings does not mean that passionate rhetoric constitutes the main part of his renewed defense of republics. If his writing is designed to stir strong feelings as well as to gain "reason's consent," the moving of passions is subordinate to the dispassionate analysis of the underlying causes of Italian disorders or threats to freedom. He consistently stresses that the results of actions motivated by the love of *libertà* or *patria* depend on how well they are "ordered." By themselves, even passions for good things lack the qualities of order or *virtù* that are needed to compensate for deficiencies in transparent public reasoning.[51]

[47] Viroli 1998, 112–13.

[48] Viroli 2001, 10, 186; 1990, 156–57; 1998, 148–74, 73–113. Also see Sullivan 2004, 33, 78–79.

[49] For example, *FH*, III.16.126; V.13.201; V.21.210–11; V.31.222–23.

[50] See letters between Vettori and Machiavelli in 1513–14 (*MF*, 253, 305).

[51] As later chapters argue, Machiavelli did seek to take passions, appetites, and humors into account when reasoning about political ordering. His aim, however, was not to transform corrupting passions into good ones, but to find more effective orders to *regulate* natural dispositions, personal feelings, and conflicting humors.

Second, in the *Histories* and elsewhere, "verisimilitudes" constructed without any concern "to identify political or moral truths" are treated as an unstable basis for better political ordering. Rhetorical verisimilitudes may inspire people to support men and policies, often with great passion. But even if they are meant to serve good ends, they can only have lasting success if they are based on sound analyses of the causes of disorders, and sound practical judgments about how to address them. In fact, as the next section suggests, well-meaning republican rhetoric is often part of the problem as Machiavelli describes it, not the spearhead of a well-considered solution. Machiavelli argues that chronically quarrelsome peoples like the Florentines would be better equipped to construct stable orders if they examined themselves honestly and faced up to at least one unalloyed "truth." This is that they are not a uniquely freedom-loving, tyranny-hating people, as their inspirational rhetoric says they are, but a population that has the same ambitious, envious, and suspicious "humors" as every other, and that often brings tyranny on itself by failing to reflect prudently on how to regulate these humors. Inspiring rhetoric may cover up these uninspiring "political and moral truths" for a time; but this can hardly help citizens to reflect on what might constitute more solid defenses. Simply arming citizens with better rhetoric for a better cause does not help them to become better *judges* of what is needed to establish good orders.

It is thus highly questionable that Machiavelli believed it was possible to discover "the most useful way to found, govern, and redeem a principality or a republic" without first trying "to identify political or moral truths" and distinguish them from errors and illusions. The claim that he did not regard standards of truth and error as essential to practical deliberations about "usefulness" and order will be further assessed later.[52] I will suggest that for Machiavelli the demand for moral and political *verità*, or for the "true knowledge" (*vera cognizione*) of histories, does not involve a quest for absolute judgments that admit of no further examination. To search for what is true is to look for the best possible account, based on reasons that are not arbitrary, partisan, or private, but general and open to continuous critical scrutiny. Rhetorical appeals are not likely to be useful for founding or redeeming polities if the conditions for a truly well-ordered republic, a *vera repubblica*, are not reasoned about in this way, and defended against unreflective or merely self-serving interpretations.[53]

1.3.
Flawed analyses: Self-celebratory versus self-critical histories

This suggests a more adequate response to the frequent failure of transparently reasoned persuasions. The response just considered is right to see such persuasions as a necessary but insufficient part of republican defenses. Yet its notion of how to supplement those defenses is flawed. To identify what more fundamental defenses are needed to supplement them, Machiavelli calls for a better grasp of

---

[52] See chap. 3, sec. 3.5.
[53] See sec. 1.7.

the reasons why republican orders are valuable, and a better understanding of the conditions needed to sustain them. The *Histories'* opening remarks about the responsibilities of historians state clearly that a frank, historically probing analysis of current civil disorders is an essential background for seeking well-judged remedies. Machiavelli argues that historians who want to defend their city's republican institutions have a special responsibility to set out the weaknesses of republican government as well as its strengths; and not merely to praise their ancestors, but also to examine their errors. The most useful republican histories do not conceal mistakes, divisions, and other blemishes on the record of the civic body. They depict all these quite distinctly, so that future generations can learn from past difficulties and take prudent measures to rectify them. The Roman historian Livy took this responsibility very seriously; so did Livy's Greek model, Thucydides.[54] Before Machiavelli, humanist writers such as Leonardo Bruni (1370–1444) adapted formal features of their own histories of Florence from these ancient historians, particularly the use of invented speeches. Machiavelli introduces his *Histories*, however, by asserting that Bruni and other previous historians of Florence shirked their civil responsibilities in their writings.

In his preface Bruni declares that "if I am not mistaken, the special duty of scholars has ever been to celebrate the deeds of their own time and so to rescue them from oblivion and the power of fate—indeed, to render them hallowed and immortal."[55] Machiavelli takes issue with this conception of scholarly duties. While Bruni and his successor as "official" historian of Florence, Poggio Bracciolini (1380–1459), wrote extensively about struggles to establish the city's republican orders, Machiavelli claims that they said too little about the difficulties involved in defending these orders from internal threats. These "very excellent historians," Machiavelli writes, wrote in detail about the city's history up to 1434.

> But when I had read their writings diligently so as to see with what orders and modes they proceeded in writing, so that by imitating them our history might be better approved by readers, I found that in the descriptions of the wars waged by the Florentines with foreign princes and peoples they had been very diligent, but as regards civil discords and internal enmities, and the effects arising from them, they were altogether silent about the one and so brief about the other as to be of no use to readers or pleasure to anyone.

Machiavelli considers two possible reasons why his predecessors might have omitted such important matters. One is that "these actions seemed to them so feeble that they judged them unworthy of being committed to memory by written word." The other is that "they feared that they might offend the descendants of those they might have to slander in their narrations." Whatever their motives, their failure to examine internal disorders more self-critically led them to take "appearances" of greatness in "the actions of governments and states" at face value, "however they are treated or whatever end they may have." Had they scrutinized

---

[54] See chap. 2, sec. 2.5, on Thucydides' views, and chap. 3, sec. 3.1. on Livy's.
[55] BH, Pref.4–5.

internal enmities in more "detail," the underlying weakness of Florence's republican orders would have become clear, and the appearances of cohesion and greatness exposed as skin-deep. This is one kind of unpleasant but necessary truth that is needed, at minimum, as the basis for more effective political ordering. Machiavelli announces that he will offer a more critical account of Florence's histories than Bruni or Poggio. He promises to describe internal conflicts "in detail," without hiding any shameful blemish on Florence's good name. His histories will show how "divisions in the city" formed and caused disorders in the past so that citizens who read his account may learn from these "dangers" how to "maintain themselves united."[56]

A small puzzle emerges if we turn from these remarks to Bruni's histories: in fact, Bruni does mention numerous internal enmities and disorders throughout his work. Above all, persistent enmities between nobles and popular classes or plebs, and the struggles of the latter to win their rightful place in the republic, are central to Bruni's narrative.[57] Read alongside Machiavelli's *Histories*, however, Bruni's work reveals several features that Machiavelli might have found problematic. In the first place, Bruni frequently invokes the idea of a free and powerful republic in a self-congratulatory way, as an element of what might be called a unifying ideology of the Florentine citizenry.[58] He starts by describing the often violent internal and external conflicts that made it difficult to establish stable republican orders. In the course of the narrative, however, he depicts the progressive emergence of a common popular consciousness making for an increasingly cohesive, powerful, freedom-loving "Florentine People" (*florentinus populus*), all the more united and free because of their earlier struggles.[59] Bruni was a prominent statesman as well as a scholar, and his history soon acquired the status of a civic and patriotic text for educated Florentines. It might well be regarded as an example of an inspirational "verisimilitude" whose primary purpose was to arouse civic pride and forge a sense of common purpose, both for the sake of healing Florence's internal divisions and for pursuing an ambitious program of external expansion.[60]

Machiavelli undoubtedly shares Bruni's desire that an entity that deserved the good name of the Florentine "people" should take shape and maintain itself as a stable, effective political agency. But Machiavelli's Florentine people has no identity or existence independent of specific actions taken by its diverse parts. Nor is it a category defined by birth, social background, or even common historical travails and achievements. Machiavelli's *popolo* is an agency that takes shape or disintegrates through the actions of its constituents. The *Histories* speaks of the "people" when different "parties" or mutually suspicious sections of the population put their differences aside to cooperate in a common enterprise. To constitute a people

---

[56] *FH*, Pref.6–8.

[57] BH, IV.420–23 and discussion below.

[58] See Hankins 2000.

[59] For example, BH, II.108–9. Bruni's histories were written in Latin and translated into Tuscan vernacular soon after.

[60] On Bruni's support for an assertive Florentine expansionism and his relation to the Medicis, see Hankins 2000; Brown 2000b; and Mansfield 2000.

in any reflective sense of the word, Machiavelli implies, diverse parties and social groups must demonstrate the will to share power, and "the desire to live according to the laws" instead of by partisan interests. Only demonstrative acts of this kind can turn what Machiavelli calls a mere "multitude not tempered by any check" into a stably ordered people. Conversely, a people once formed may dissolve again into a multitude or into various divisions based on class or status or party.[61] This usage implies that it is up to each generation of citizens to earn the good name of *popolo*. They cannot rest on the laurels and hard work of their ancestors, since complacency may corrupt even the greatest historical achievements.[62]

Bruni's unabashedly partisan bias is a second feature that differentiates his histories from Machiavelli's. Bruni's idealized "Florentine people" is essentially Guelf, non-noble, and not very poor. When internal discords occur in his narrative, some group that does not form part of the popular core is usually behind them. The pro-imperial Ghibellines, traditional nobility, or some other marginal party often incites the indigent rabble—naturally envious of their superiors and always itching for a street fight—against the sound core of the *populus* proper.[63] When discussing recent times, Bruni uses the Latin words *diversis* (partisanship) and *factiones* in ways that clearly indicate his own party preferences. Whereas the Albizzi and Ricci families who opposed Medici aspirations "generate partisanship among the citizenry" and are called leaders of *factiones*, their rivals are not described as partisan. Bruni considers it justified that "a law was passed prohibiting the leaders of these families from taking part in the governance of the state," thus silencing factions.[64] More generally, Bruni is indeed "silent or very brief" about the disorders that helped to pave the way for the Medici family's rise to effective princely power. His account gives almost no weight to their opponents' reasons for seeking to block them, but simply presumes that readers will recognize the necessity to grant extraordinary authority to Cosimo and his offspring in order to rescue the ailing republic.

Machiavelli may well have had these features in mind when he wrote that his predecessors' histories are "of no use to readers" concerned to understand the causes of Florence's recurring ailments. His own descriptions of various "discords" in the city reflect the view that responsibly written histories should not seek mainly to inspire civic pride, or to foster positive self-conceptions by painting others in a negative light. By comparison with Bruni's, Machiavelli's histories are remarkable in their attempt to give an evenhanded account of the claims made by rival parties,

---

[61] *FH*, II.12, 64/375–76; II.32.87/401–3; III.22.135/460–61.

[62] The distinction has Greek origins in *ochlos* (mob) or *plēthos* (many) vs. a *dēmos* ordered under laws. Compare the distinction between disordered "multitudes" and well-ordered "peoples" in Hobbes 1998 (1642), VI.1–2.75–77.

[63] For example, BH, I.100–103; II.164–65, 176–77; IV.358–61; VII.298–99; VIII.381–87, 410–17; IX.1–9. Hankins suggests that for Bruni "a republic is better off when governed by the middling sort of citizen, frugal, hardworking, and peaceloving," while "the lowest classes should be kept out of power at all costs" (introduction, BH, xix).

[64] BH, VIII.479–81.

social groups, or powerful families.[65] Through speeches given to different characters or in his own commentary, Machiavelli consistently presents opposing sides of each case. In a few cases where one side advocates what Machiavelli sees as a reckless or transparently self-serving policy, he gives the advocate weak arguments and his opponent strong ones. But even in such cases, he refrains from dismissing imprudent arguments as nothing but partisan troublemaking. He acknowledges that a case was made, and that reasons were given that persuaded some hearers, sometimes many. When discussing long-standing conflicts between Guelfs and Ghibellines, nobles and non-nobles, or different sections of the people, Machiavelli deliberately strives for a balanced treatment. In his *Histories* every Florentine citizen bears some share of responsibility for the city's seemingly endless troubles, and therefore for trying to establish better orders; no section of the population or party is exempted.[66]

Machiavelli's emphasis on critical self-examination and self-responsibility differentiates his histories from Bruni's in a third respect. As Machiavelli remarks, Bruni does spend a good deal of time describing "wars waged by the Florentines with foreign princes and peoples." The implicit criticism is not simply that Bruni should have paid more attention to internal affairs. Bruni's account of Florence's early struggles and disorders, Machiavelli implies, ascribes too much responsibility to foreign powers while failing to examine the errors of Florentines themselves. The concern to evoke appearances of collective unity against external aggressors is palpable in Bruni's narrative. Foreigners are often singled out as the source of disorders, both individually and collectively. Ferocious anti-German sentiments are expressed in his earlier books, later giving way to anti-French remarks. This strain of anti-foreign rhetoric appears as part and parcel of an anti-imperial, Guelf ideology.[67] At one point, apparently without irony, Bruni expressly states that external enemies may serve a valuable purpose in providing a focus for internal unity. "If there had been a fight with some entirely foreign, external enemy and not with fellow-citizens," he remarks, "the common danger to both the ordinary folk and to the optimates and a resolute devotion to country would have united them in the common defense."[68]

Machiavelli shares Bruni's desire for a strong, independent Florence, and clearly wants to minimize foreign interference in the city's affairs. But the *Histories* never uses anti-foreign rhetoric as a substitute for self-critical examination of the causes of internal conflicts, or indeed of external ones. Indeed, the very first paragraph of Book I provocatively inverts Bruni's tendency to blame internal troubles on outsiders. Here Machiavelli describes the peoples who overran Italy after the fall of the Roman Empire not as lawless barbarians preying on a superior civilization, but as rational agents who left their homelands in a highly "ordered" fashion, following

---

[65] See esp. chap. 8, secs. 8.2.–8.3..

[66] For example, Machiavelli notes that Guelfs as well as Ghibellines were responsible for ushering in foreign kings and emperors against their internal enemies; see *FH*, II.6–7.58–59/368–70.

[67] BH, II.126–27, 200–201.

[68] BH, II.170–71.

their countries' established "modes and orders" for dealing with the genuine necessity imposed by overpopulation. The *Histories* continues in this vein, refusing
to shirk the responsibility of self-evaluation by scapegoating foreigners. Whenever
external "necessity" impends, some internal party always shares responsibility.[69]
This rigorous demand for self-responsibility is as fundamental to the *Prince* as it
is to the *Histories*. When calling for a prince who will effectively resist Italy's foreign invaders, Machiavelli's "rhetoric" does not blame the latter for Italians' present
troubles. It seeks to motivate action informed by the reflections offered earlier in
the work, summed up near the end with the discussion of free will and Italians' own
responsibility to put themselves under better "orders." If Italy has been "reduced"
to such a condition that it is "more enslaved than the Hebrews, more servile than
the Persians, more dispersed than the Athenians," lacking a head, "without order,
beaten, despoiled, torn, pillaged, and having endured ruin of every sort," passionate
patriotism alone is unlikely to save it. "New laws and new orders" are, Machiavelli
argues, the "true foundation of every undertaking." If Italians fail to reflect on what
is needed to stabilize and "maintain" these new orders, they will not escape their
plight.[70] A first step is to study their own histories carefully, asking whether there
were causes closer to home that allowed foreign peoples to overrun Italy and Rome
in the past, and foreign powers to dominate Italian cities in the present.

A fourth, more general contrast between Bruni's and Machiavelli's histories is
suggested by their statements of what each takes to be any historian's chief "duty"
to his readers. Whereas Bruni thinks that scholars should "celebrate the deeds of
their own time" and render them "hallowed" for posterity, Machiavelli insists that
histories should seek to be "useful." And the best way to be useful is to strive to
identify the most fundamental and recurrent causes of disorders.[71] The search for
"truer" causes than those depicted by partisan and anti-foreign rhetoric forms the
analytical backbone of Machiavelli's *Histories*. He suggests that responsible historians should think of themselves as civic "physicians" who diagnose and try impartially to address a city's disorders, not as civic mythmakers who play down its
diseases or give a superficial, self-serving account of its causes.[72] Bruni frequently
explains various conflicts as the result of hatreds and envy, implying that these
passions are unreasonable. Machiavelli wants to diagnose the "causes of hatreds"
in the city, and assumes that at least some of these hatreds had reasonable cause.
A precondition for eliminating civic hatreds is to distinguish such causes from

[69] See chap. 4, secs. 4.1.–4.3.
[70] *P*, XXV–XXVI.98–105/186–92.
[71] Compare Hobbes' (1989 [1629], 579–85) remarks on Thucydides' purposes: the Athenian believed that to be "profitable" for future generations, history should not conceal the "calamities" suffered by his countrymen, least of all those that were self-inflicted. Instead it should present them "truly . . . for that men profit more by looking on adverse events, than on prosperity"; and miseries "better instruct, than . . . good success." Thucydides wrote "without affection to either side, and not as a lover of his country but of truth." Hobbes follows Plutarch in blaming Herodotus, by contrast, for recording only the glorious actions of his own country; he was merely "a rhetorician" pleading a special case, not, like Thucydides, a great historian who meets the highest rhetorical *and* philosophical standards.
[72] See chap. 2 on Socratic writers' comparisons of philosophers with physicians.

their less reasonable effects, and address the legitimate grievances expressed by different parties and social groups. Both the *Histories* and *Discourses* identify two general, conflicting human dispositions or humors (*umori, omori*) as the most basic source of conflicts within and between cities: dispositions to dominate or command on the one hand, and to resist being dominated or commanded on the other. This simple anthropological thesis allows Machiavelli to question several ideological and partisan accounts of conflicts in Florence, or indeed in "any city whatever."[73] He notes, for example, that by 1282 "the wars outside and the peace within had almost eliminated the Ghibelline and Guelf parties in Florence." On a Bruni-like pro-Guelf analysis, Florence's main conflicts should have been put to rest. But deeper, more persistent causes of conflict remained that were only contingently related to this particular division, or indeed to any other. These were the "humors" that are "naturally wont to exist in all cities between the powerful and the people." Since in every city "the people want to live according to the laws and the powerful want to command by them, it is not possible for them to understand [*cappino*] together."[74]

Note that "the powerful" (*potente*) and people are abstract concepts with no necessary connection to specific social groups or parties. The powerful are defined *qua* those who command, the people as those who want to live according to laws. Similarly, when Machiavelli says later that the "cause of all evils that arise in cities" is "the grave and natural enmities that exist between the men of the people and the nobles, caused by the wish of the latter to command and the former not to obey," he does not mean that the groups who go under the names of nobles and people have innate differences that explain their antipathies.[75] The categories "nobles" and "people" are man-made concepts, expressing standards and relationships that human beings impose on themselves and on others. Conflict between the two groups is natural only in the sense that it follows from the dispositions ascribed to whoever is born into the group that goes under the name of nobility or the people. The deeper roots of conflict are found in all human "orders": in universal human tendencies to set up ranks of commanders and followers, and in the presence of some "humors" that seek to dominate or "command" others. Even if particular expressions of these tendencies are eliminated—Guelfs versus Ghibellines, or nobles versus people—others will soon crop up in their place. Machiavelli has a concerned citizen observe that whenever "one party is driven out and one division eliminated, another emerges. For in the city that prefers to maintain itself with sects rather than with laws," he continues, "as soon as one sect is left there without opposition, it must of necessity divide from within itself." Thus when the Ghibellines were destroyed, people thought that the Guelfs "would live for a long time happy and respected"; instead they soon divided into Whites and Blacks. When the popular "party" overcame the power of the nobility, few believed that "any cause of scandal or party would ever arise again in Florence, since a check had

[73] *D*, I.1.4–7/208–20, I.16/240–43; *P*, IX.39/143–44.
[74] *FH*, II.12, 64/376.
[75] *FH*, III.1.105/423.

been put on those who by their pride and unbearable ambition appeared to have been the cause." But "now it is seen through experience how mistaken the opinion of men is and how false their judgment," since "the pride and ambition of the great was not eliminated but taken from them by our men of the people" who now, in exactly the same manner as the nobles, "seek to obtain first rank in the republic" while refusing to share political authority with anyone born into the nobility.[76]

If divisions in any city stem from inevitable, chronic mistrust among more ambitious humors and the rest, it might seem impossible to escape the "necessity" that makes "a city divide within itself." But Machiavelli does not say that the necessity leaves citizens no choice but to play hardheaded power politics. He says only that their present "modes" of defense are inadequate "because the city cannot defend itself by those private modes that it had ordered in the first place for its own safety."[77] If the root cause of conflict is clashing humors, the solution is to regulate these by means of more effective "laws and orders" based on public rather than private and partisan modes. It is most certainly not to persist in the exhausting cycles of conflict described ad nauseam in the *Histories*, whereby one party then another persuades a majority, often with *onesto* words and great rhetorical skill, violently to confront their rivals. Nor is it the solution canvassed and discredited in many episodes of the *Histories*: a leader who claims to have such extraordinary political acumen and popular support that he, and few others, can be expected to restore order.

Bruni's histories do not provide this more general, critical diagnosis. His idealizing treatment of the Florentine people reflects fundamental differences between his and Machiavelli's civic humanist aims and ethical standards. Bruni's account is structured around a central conflict between the essentially good Florentine people, treated as the personification of republican ideals, and various enemies they must fight off. Machiavelli's *Histories* is structured around a tension between such simplifying rhetoric and the far more complex realities it glosses. He goes beyond Bruni and many other humanists in demanding a more precise, non-rhetorical account of sound republican institutions and values. Machiavelli's vocabulary may resemble Bruni's, and they seem to have the same political values at the level of names: republic, people, liberty, rule of law. But he often uses the same words to criticize policies praised by Bruni under the names of republic or *libertà*. Whereas Bruni's histories "celebrate" the Medici-led republic, Machiavelli's writings underline Florence's failures to deserve the name of true republic, in Bruni's times or his own.

1.4.
Philosophy and the *vita activa* in Florentine humanism

In the *Florentine Histories*, at least, Machiavelli sees technical proficiency at the "game" of politics as a deeply flawed remedy for civil corruption. If speeches, common opinions, and rhetoric are important elements of Machiavelli's own writings, he does not treat them as the key to solving problems of civil self-defense. He

---

[76] *FH*, III.5.110–11/428–32.
[77] Ibid.

presents them, rather, as a starting point for examining the conventional wisdom, unreflective assumptions, and errors of judgment that lead people to accept persuasions that harm the public good. By studying examples of detrimental forms of persuasion, people can sharpen their abilities to identify manipulative strategies and build up resistance to them. Learning to discriminate between more and less reflective uses of rhetoric, and to *recognize* corrupt or ill-judged uses of good words, is indeed a key part of Machiavelli's proposed remedy for political disorders. Learning to *exercise* rhetorical skills is a secondary element, and one that he treats as only conditionally valuable for defending republics from corruption.

To know how to wield a rhetoric that is persuasive yet non-corrupting, speakers must first reflect carefully on several issues that relate to sound ordering. These include how to distinguish adequate senses of words such as "freedom" and "republic" from uses that fall short of the true or best possible account of standards upheld by those words. They also include reflections on the "natural and ordinary" humors found in all human cities; on the limits set on human action by necessity, fortune, or other human beings' motions and desires; and on the possibilities for self-directive human action afforded by free will. Genuinely efficacious rhetoric—rhetoric that contributes to stable orders—presupposes some previous engagement with these ethical and philosophical questions. I will argue that this is among the "covert" teachings of the *Prince*, as it is the overt starting-point of the *Discourses* and a message brought home over and over in the *Florentine Histories*.

The suggestion that Machiavelli wants civic founders, orderers, and legislators to adopt a more philosophical approach to politics, let alone to treat a philosophically reflective ethics as the bedrock of political judgment, runs against the grain of most previous interpretations. It is often supposed that Machiavelli regarded all philosophy as of little use to men engaged in politics, whether as leaders or as ordinary citizens. A few passages in the *Histories* intimate that Machiavelli saw some kinds of philosophy as elements of the Medicis' machinery of self-promotion. He observes that Cosimo sponsored a new Platonic Academy in Florence, and sought to "use conveniently" (*sua commodità usare*) Marsilio Ficino (1433–1499), known as "second father of Platonic philosophy," to demonstrate the Medicis' commitment to humanist high culture. This, Machiavelli remarks wrily, made Cosimo "feared and loved in Florence by citizens and marvelously esteemed by princes not only in Italy but in all Europe."[78] Whether or not they believe that Machiavelli took a cynical view of philosophy, many scholars assume that he did see philosophical reflection as inherently competitive with, and inferior to, political activity. On this view, he considered his own writings as practical treatises aimed at getting better results for practical-minded readers. Moreover, he presumably saw this aim as incompatible with the systematic reflections on metaphysics, epistemology, or ethics that tend to occupy philosophers—particularly those grounded in "a certain Athenian tradition," that is, Socratic and Platonic philosophy.[79] Proponents of this

---

[78] *FH*, VII.6.283/636–38. The Florentine Academy was founded in 1462 or 1463. Under the auspices of the academy, Ficino completed the first Latin translation of Plato's complete works.

[79] Lynch 2003, 221; Skinner 2002, 139–42.

claim see Machiavelli as heir to a tradition of Italian humanism that "stems from the confrontation with philosophy, whose values were contemplative, and rhetoric, whose values were civic and active." For humanists *tout court*, on this account, philosophy and politics are activities that must take place in very different spheres of life. Philosophy was "non-political," while rhetoric was "political by its nature."[80]

Both in Bruni's time and in Machiavelli's, however, numerous examples can be found of Italian humanist writers who were deeply involved in politics, yet upheld a very different conception of the relation between civil life and philosophy than the competitive one just sketched. This treated the two activities as complementary, even as mutually necessary. Instead of regarding philosophy as "contemplative" or otherworldly, it insisted that philosophy properly understood is centered on human beings, humanly possible knowledge, and rigorous reflections on whatever is necessary to order human life. Philosophy in this sense has all-important practical aims and uses, and philosophical men should also be practical men who are actively committed to ordering a human life in their own cities and, if needed, beyond them.[81] A good example of this view can be found in the biographical writings of Gianozzo Manetti (1396–1459), a student of Bruni. Having criticized Cosimo de' Medici's foreign policy and under suspicion of espionage, Manetti was forced into exile late in life and spent his last years serving in administrative posts outside Florence.[82] His "Life of Socrates," dedicated to King Alfonso of Aragon, begins by urging the monarch to "join the study of moral philosophy to that of rhetoric and history." The biographical sketch presents the ideal of a civil philosopher as anyone who helped statesmen and fellow citizens examine the beliefs, opinions, or appearances that influence their actions. "Although he was a great philosopher," Manetti writes, Socrates by no means saw the life of a mystical hermit as his vocation. On the contrary, "he still led a civic life like any other Athenian citizen, conversing with his fellow citizens, marrying, and holding civic magistracies." In short, he omitted "nothing he considered pertinent to citizenship." Citing Cicero, Manetti declares that Socrates was "the first to call philosophy down from the heavens and set her in the cities of men . . . compelling her to ask questions about life and morality and things good and evil."[83]

This integrated ideal had not died out among Italian or Florentine humanists by Machiavelli's time. It can be found, for example, on a close reading of the *Dialogues* written by Francesco Guicciardini (1483–1540), a participant in Machiavelli's discussion circle at the Orti Oricellari and one of his most interesting correspondents.[84] His dialogues start by alluding to the artificial, excessively scholastic character of what is called philosophy today, so that the leading interlocutor declares that he will

---

[80] Siegel 1968, cited and mostly seconded by Pocock (1975), 55–64. Bruni is often cited as a spokesman for this view. In his *Isogogican moralis philosophiae*, for example, we read that "both kinds of life have their proper esteem and merit. The contemplative life is, to be sure, the more divine and rare, but the active is more excellent with respect to the common good" (cited in Baron 1988, 149–50).

[81] See Cassirer 2000 (1926) for a fine account of this sense of humanist philosophy.

[82] See the introduction to Manetti 2003, vii–x.

[83] Manetti 2003, 170–71, 200–201, 180–81.

[84] See next section.

"leave aside" philosophy in the ensuing discussion. It later becomes clear, however, that philosophy as such has not been dismissed, only certain kinds of argument that go under the name of philosophy. The dialogue itself is philosophical in a more adequate sense of the word: it starts with opinions that appear sound to "natural reason," examines them from different angles, and gradually leads speakers toward a more reflective account of various political questions.[85] The discussion considers certain ancient philosophers as particularly valuable sources of contemporary political wisdom. Guicciardini's key speakers hint at an integrated conception of civil "philosophizing" and attribute it chiefly to "your philosophers, or as you called them just now political writers" such as Plato, Aristotle, and Xenophon. All three are described as "philosophers . . . who have written about political life" and who sought through writing to address civil disorders.[86]

According to this type of humanist account, what makes philosophy philosophical is not its abstract or contemplative character, but the demanding standards it imposes on reasoning about anything. Continuous, deeply reflective reasoning about what is needed to guide practical activity is no less "philosophical" than scholastic studies in logic or metaphysics. Manetti stresses that the "true philosophy" introduced by Socrates concerned ethical questions whose answers require no expert knowledge; indeed, Socrates was famous for his ironic denial that he himself knew anything. His main aim was not to demonstrate ultimate truths or refute false beliefs, but to "purge the corruption of vice" in himself and anyone who wished to converse with him. By debating constantly with "friends and learned men," he induced them to recognize weaknesses in their conventional or unreflective views and to seek better accounts of the matter at hand. These accounts could be considered as "probable truths" to which further reasoning must always be applied.[87] Socrates' methods showed that philosophy should not be practiced only by leading statesman or administrators, but also by citizens on whose good judgment civil orders depend in a republic. Similarly, Guicciardini's dialogue implies that true philosophical discussion should take its lead not from quotes by famous thinkers, but with "what the man on the street can understand." His main speaker gives an example: since it seems evident to any man on the street that the rule of one good man is better than any other form of government, the present discussion will start with this common opinion, and examine it from various angles. By the end of the dialogue, the opinion has not been explicitly refuted. But many reasons have been given for doubting whether government by one can be stable; although "natural reason" suggests that one man is best, "philosophical" reasoning of this dialectical kind enables participants to understand why the ideal invariably fails.[88] Though neither Guicciardini nor his speaker names his source, the one-man ruler example comes from one of Plato's non-Socratic dialogues, the *Statesman*, which proceeds in much the same way: having considered flaws in the "first-best" one-

---

[85] GD, I.12.14–15.
[86] GD, I.17, 33, 4.
[87] Manetti 2003, 178–81, 188–89, 194–211.
[88] GD, I.12–13; II.94–95.

man ruler ideal, it outlines a "second-best" solution more suitable for corruptible human beings.[89] Guicciardini's dialogue ends with a reflective position that differs from both the prereflective "first-best" and the cynical rejection of any standards of better or worse. The aim of philosophy should not be to construct imaginary republics remote from ordinary people's natural reason; it should acquaint people with their own human limitations, giving them a clearer view of what is "reasonably possible" within those limits and what is not. On this criterion it is quite reasonable to "seek a government that can be totally good, or at least good in the most important matters, not one that will necessarily be evil." Understood in this way philosophy has much to say "about our duty to our country and our duty to others."[90] Without it, the foundations of civil order will remain vulnerable to men who use good words and appearances to seduce others for their own one-man or partisan purposes.

These examples sit uneasily beside claims that by Machiavelli's time, Italian humanists generally accepted a sharp distinction between practical political rhetoric and an abstract, contemplative philosophy. They also raise doubts about claims that Platonic philosophy had, through Cosimo's support for Ficino, become so strongly associated with anti-republican interests that defenders of the republic such as Machiavelli and Guicciardini must have been hostile to it. Quentin Skinner writes that Platonism provided resources that enabled some Florentine humanists "to repudiate their republican heritage" and express their preference for monarchy. "Plato's authority" enabled Lorenzo's humanist supporters "to mount a more direct attack on the participative ideals of Florentine republicanism" by arguing that the best form of government is that of a wise guardian or philosopher-king, not government in the hands of committed citizens.[91] It is easy to see how Machiavelli and his politically oriented friends might have seen this kind of philosophy as an impediment to civil involvement on behalf of republican orders. But it is important to note, first, that not all specialist scholars of Ficino's Academy agree with this account of its philosophical positions or political legacy. According to Arthur Field, the thesis that Medici patronage took humanists outside the city into villas where closed, elite circles engaged in intellectual life, eschewing civic participation, is extremely misleading. For many who defended the *vita contemplativa*, this had "nothing to do with the renunciation of worldly life in any literal sense. Indeed, it implied the opposite," since individuals who examine themselves inwardly are better able to exercise virtue in the political world. Thus one Academy member, Cristoforo Landino (1425–1498), wrote that "true wise men ought not to dedicate themselves to the speculative life that they might forsake the active" but follow Aeneas in applying what one learns about oneself and others through continuous speculation to active, moral, and political life.[92]

---

[89] See chap. 11, sec. 11.4.

[90] GD, II.95, 5.

[91] Skinner 2002, 139–42.

[92] Field 1988, 3–51, 260, 273–74. On Florentine Platonism and Ficino also see Garin 1965, 81–104; 1994, 93–118. On Aeneas, see chap. 11, sec. 11.2.

Second, both Field's study and a wider reading of writers connected with the Academy supply reasons to question the suggestion—usually implied rather than systematically defended—that Platonism or "Plato's authority" was interpreted in an anti-republican or anti-political way by most Academic humanists. As Field points out, Landino and others stressed that Plato himself did not advocate the avoidance of public life in favor of pure contemplation. On the contrary, he taught that a philosophical man sees as the "first of his duties that he dwell in cities, look out for the republic, safeguard his fellow citizens, protect friends . . . and look out for the common good."[93] In first half of the fifteenth century, Italian humanist writers repeatedly called attention to the fact that Aristotle was the teacher of Alexander the Great, while Plato had tried to educate the kings of Sicily in hopes that they would give up their tyrannical ways. These writers did not praise ancient philosophers' political activities over their contemplative ones. They simply stressed the complementarity of philosophy and civil commitment.[94]

Third, even if the names of philosophy and Platonism in Florence came to be associated with apolitical discussions among a pro-Medici elite, it does not follow that critics of the Medici regime must have accepted this understanding of philosophy, let alone that they sought to confront it with a ruthlessly practical orientation. To eschew *any* philosophy was not the only possible reaction against the specific, apolitical kind of philosophy ascribed to Ficino academicians. Another option was to recall the classical ideal of an integrated civil philosophy whose roots were traced by many Italian humanists to Socrates, Plato, Xenophon, and Aristotle.

The thesis that Machiavelli's interests were unphilosophical rests, then, on a questionable picture of the humanist context that influenced him.[95] The classical and humanist repertoires available to Machiavelli included various conceptions of the proper relationship between philosophy and practical life. This does not prove that Machiavelli held a more philosophical conception than is usually supposed. It does show that contextualist arguments cannot rule out the influence of a very

[93] Cited in Field 1988, 261.

[94] Martines 2002, 196–99, 331. Machiavelli's early admirers endorsed these views of Platonic and Socratic traditions. Plato, writes Bacon, could not agree with the corrupt manners of his country and refused to hold office; yet he still sought to serve his country as a philosophical doctor "with humble persuasions, and not with contestations." Bacon also commends "Xenophon the philosopher, who went from Socrates' school into Persia" as a model who combined military virtue and learning (2001 [1605], 20, 55–56). Gentili (1924 [1594], III.ix–x) upholds the ideal of "a legal, ethical, and . . . political philosopher [*legalem, ethicum, politicum . . . philosophum*]" who is also "educated in practical politics and in the administration of his offices . . . for even Plato regards those philosophers who have done otherwise as very incompetent [*ineptissimos*]." Compare Neville's (1691, 2) robust objections to those who misread "Aristotle, and even Plato himself" as defenders of monarchy.

[95] In his essay "The Florentine Revival of the Philosophy of the Active Political Life" Baron (1988, 1:134–57) argues that Florentine humanists sought to upgrade the importance of politics in relation to philosophy. But he does not claim that this entailed the downgrading of philosophy, particularly philosophy in the "activist" Socratic or Platonic tradition. Moreover, while some humanists discussed by Baron opposed the practical life to "the philosophical conceits of Plato," many others he mentions, such as Landino, disputed this apolitical view of Plato's philosophy.

different kind of civil-philosophical thinking on Machiavelli, and suggests prima facie reasons to further explore his relationship to it.[96]

1.5.
What is, has been, and reasonably can be: Machiavelli's correspondence

Let us now move from broad-brushed accounts of the humanist contexts presumed to have shaped Machiavelli's thinking, and ask what can be learned about his philosophical purposes by examining a narrower kind of context: that formed by his first readers, trusted friends, and political fellow-travelers. Insofar as this can be reconstructed from their personal correspondence, it can help us to assess the widespread assumption that Machiavelli and his friends must have been skeptical about the value of philosophy, especially Platonic philosophy, for civil life. Support for this assumption is sometimes found in the contrast between the philosophical discussions that formed the core of discussions in Ficino's Academy, on the one hand, and what is presumed to have been the more practical political content of Academic discussions later on. The Academy's activities were severely curtailed after the Pazzi conspiracy (1478) against the Medici regime. Its meetings resumed after the Medicis' return from exile in 1512. They were now held in the Rucellai Gardens (Orti Oricellari) and hosted by the young Cosimo Rucellai, to whom, with Zanobi Buondelmonti, Machiavelli dedicated the *Discourses*. Now excluded from Florentine politics, Machiavelli became a senior participant in the Orti Oricellari circle from around 1515. Despite the paucity of evidence about their discussions, it has usually been assumed that Machiavelli and his friends in the Orti distanced themselves from philosophy, steering the rump Academy in a much more practical direction.[97] This assumption is based partly on the circle's apparent connection with anti-Medici conspiracies. It is also based on prevailing interpretations of Machiavelli's own writings and interests, which played an important role in shaping the Orti discussions. It may be, however, that these interpretations rest on a sharper distinction between practical politics and philosophy than Machiavelli and his friends endorsed.

The correspondence between Machiavelli and his friends contains one explicit reference to Machiavelli's philosophy. In 1509 Filippo Casavecchia wrote to congratulate his friend on his role in securing a peace settlement between Florence and Pisa. Guicciardini would later mention the settlement in his own histories,

---

[96] Machiavelli's early philosophical emulators insist on the need to integrate politics and philosophy, if anything placing greater stress on the latter. Bacon (2001 [1605], 178, 45) argues that men are not "fit auditors of policy, till they have been thoroughly seasoned in religion and morality; lest their judgements be corrupted, and made apt to think that there are no true differences of things, but according to utility and fortune." He agrees with Plato that people and states were happy "when either kings were philosophers, or philosophers kings." Compare Spinoza's (1958 [1677], 1–2) ironic remarks in the *Tractatus Politicus* on the common opinion that only practical "statesmen" (*politici*) are qualified to write about politics, whereas philosophers are regarded as unfit to govern or advise.

[97] See Gilbert's fascinating essay "Bernardo Rucellai and the Orti Oricellari: A Study on the Origin of Modern Political Thought" (1977). As I suggested earlier, however, Gilbert (237) exaggerates the division between the "historico-political method" adopted by Machiavelli's group and philosophical pursuits.

writing that Machiavelli's negotiations were a rare example of fair treatment from the Florentine side, which had so often bullied Pisa and other smaller cities or broken faith with them. Whereas in previous and subsequent settlements the Florentines "preferred to be certain of their victory under iniquitous treaty conditions," Machiavelli's diplomacy gave the Pisans firm promises in an "easy and clement" spirit, and helped to ensure that the Florentines observed them faithfully.[98] In a somewhat cryptic passage that appears to praise Machiavelli's practical ideas for unifying neighboring cities under Florentine leadership, perhaps with a view to achieving wider Italian unity, Casavecchia writes:

> Niccolò, this is a time when if ever one was wise it should be now. I do not believe your ideas [*vostra filosofia*] will ever be accessible to fools, and there are not enough wise men to go around: you understand me, even if I am not putting it very well. Every day I discover you to be a greater prophet than the Hebrews or any other nation [*altra generazione*] ever had.[99]

This reference to Machiavelli's *filosofia* can be interpreted in ways that justify the translation as "ideas" instead of "philosophy," thus attenuating any connection with philosophy as an activity that is not subservient to practical aims. Casavecchia is congratulating Machiavelli on a practical achievement, not writing to discuss his profounder ruminations on the ethics of military conquest or political unification. Machiavelli had not yet written the *Prince* or other works in which he discusses free will, the difference between unreflective opinions and well-founded knowledge, or the relationship between *necessità* and *virtú*. Finally, like other letters from Casavecchia, the tone is often camp and teasing. Perhaps by hailing Machiavelli's prophetic *filosofia* his friend wanted jokingly to exaggerate the visionary thinking behind his friend's practical peacemaking achievement, or even to flirt with him through flattery.[100] But other letters suggest that Machiavelli's closest friends, who were the first readers of his political and historical writings, considered his "ideas"—particularly those he wrote down after he was prohibited from public service—as having more philosophical content than any of these explanations suggest. The correspondence indicates that Machiavelli's friends considered his *filosofia* as coherent, rigorous, and remarkably consistent over time. Most importantly, they regarded his ideas as remote from both the reductive empiricism and unprincipled realism that are often ascribed to Machiavelli.

Shortly after his imprisonment and proscription from politics, Machiavelli replied to a gloomy letter from his friend Francesco Vettori, who was allowed to continue work as a public servant under the Medici regime. It is true, Machiavelli

---

[98] Guicciardini 1969, VIII.203–7. See Viroli 2001, 103–6, on the context and content of Machiavelli's negotiations. Following Guicciardini, Viroli stresses that while under the settlement Pisa acknowledged the superiority of Florentine jurisdiction, Machiavelli showed an exceptional willingness to compromise, and especially to persuade the country-dwellers around Pisa to end their frequent revolts against Florentine *dominio*.

[99] Casavecchia to Machiavelli, 17 June 1509, *MF*, 181–82/189–90.

[100] Compare *MF*, 133, 157, 164, 185.

writes, that practical affairs often "turn out differently from the opinions and ideas [*discorsi et concetti*] we have." Nevertheless, the current gap between practice and *concetti* cannot induce Machiavelli to embrace political facts-on-the-ground or compromise his own *discorsi et concetti* in a pragmatic fashion. Indeed, he tells Vettori, "if I could talk to you" directly instead of through letters, where he cannot risk expressing himself in complete frankness, "I could not help but fill your head with castles in the air [*castellucci*], because Fortune has seen to it that since I do not know how to talk about either the silk or the wool trade, or profits or losses, I have to talk about politics [*ragionare dello stato*]."[101] This is often taken simply as a statement of Machiavelli's frustration at being excluded from political life. But he also alludes to a broader theme found in other letters and writings: namely, that reasoning about civil matters can and should be conducted in speech and imagination even when it cannot be done in practice. Writing later in the same year, Vettori uses similar language to consider how men used to reasoning about politics should behave when they are out of power and prevented from expressing themselves freely. Although, Vettori writes,

> it often appears to me that things do not proceed reasonably [*non procedino con ragione*], and because of this I judge it to be superfluous to speak of them, to discuss them, and to argue about them, nonetheless someone who has grown accustomed to one way until the age of forty finds it hard to give up and to get used to other habits, to other ways of talking and thinking [*altri ragionamente e pensieri*]. Therefore for every reason, and especially for this one, I wish I could be with you and see whether we could organize [*rassettare*] this world, and if not the world, at least this part here, which seems to me very hard to organize in fancy [*nella fantasia*], so that if it came to having to do it in fact [*al fatto*] I should think it was impossible.[102]

Here Vettori intimates that Machiavelli's impatience to reenter practical politics may not have been motivated only by personal vocation or ambition. It was also motivated by the desire, shared with friends like Vettori, to organize a more reasonable kind of politics: at least "in fancy," through "castles in the air," since in practice the political standards they uphold seem impossible to implement.

The language used in other letters hints more strongly at a philosophical dimension in Machiavelli's political and historical writings. Responding to his friend's concerns about writing a history of Florence under Medici auspices, Guicciardini urged Machiavelli to go ahead with the project. It would of course be necessary, Guicciardini acknowledged, for his friend to disguise his own critical judgments in order to avoid offending the ruling party. In the turbulent history of their city, Guicciardini writes, "we do not see any incident that has not been seen in other times." But "changing the names and forms [*nomi e figure*] of things means that only the prudent recognize them; therefore history is good and useful, because it sets before you and makes you recognize and see again what you have

---

[101] Machiavelli to Vettori, 9 April 1513, *MF*, 225–26/240–41.
[102] Vettori to Machiavelli, 12 July 1513, *MF*, 241–44/267–70.

never known or seen."[103] The paradox that history can make people "see again" what many have never "seen" finds echoes in Machiavelli's *Discourses*. Taken in by the variable appearances of events—what Guicciardini here calls "extrinsic colors" (*colori estrinseci*)—most people think that the problems faced in each time and place are unique, arising from particular features of each context. They therefore fail to recognize the recurring patterns of conduct that bring the same benefits or disorders to every city. Machiavelli's histories, Guicciardini suggests, will no doubt be informed by a penetrating analysis of the recurrent, general causes at work beneath the particular "names and forms" found in Florentine history. These will be recognized by "the prudent" alone, who will understand the critical undertones of Machiavelli's outwardly inoffensive narrative. Whoever follows the general reasonings in the text will be able to "see again" recurrent truths—for example, about the root causes of corruption in republics—that "prudent" observers "saw" clearly in previous eras, but which are obscured by "names and forms" that make old things look new and bad things look better than they are.

Guicciardini further implies that he expects Machiavelli's histories not just to examine general *causes* of particular events, but also to evaluate them according to general *standards*. He makes a teasing, oblique reference to Machiavelli's own standards, remarking on how his friend is constantly observing different modes of life, in this instance a community of monks with whom he was staying. You will, Guicciardini writes, no doubt "make use of that model [*modello*] for some purpose" in his histories, "comparing it or measuring it against some of those forms of yours [*vostre forme*]." Guicciardini's mock-Platonic language is playful, but not obviously ironic. His letter concludes: "you have always been considered exceedingly extravagant in your opinions by most people, and the inventor of new and outlandish things [ut plurimum *estravagante di opinione . . . et inventore di cose nuove et insolite*]."[104] Read in isolation from other passages, of course, this last could be read as consistent with the view that Machiavelli's "new modes and orders" did not respect any particular, predefined standards at all, but urged princely "entrepreneurs" to impose their will by sheer virtuosity. But this reading ignores the many references in the correspondence that suggest that his evaluative standards were stable and rigorous. A year before Machiavelli's death, for example, an exchange of letters between Guicciardini and Florence's ambassador to France, Roberto Acciaiuoli, refer to some of Machiavelli's "outlandish" inventions or "castles in the air." "Machiavelli is here," Guicciardini reports from Lombardy, where Machiavelli had been invited to put into practice his ideas about military organization set out in the *Art of War*. "He came to reorganize the militia; but, seeing how rotten it is, he has no hope of having any respect from it. Since he is unable to remedy the faults of mankind, he will do nothing but laugh at them." Acciaiuoli wrote back:

I am glad that Machiavelli gave the orders to discipline the infantry. Would to God that he might put into action what he has in mind, but I doubt whether

---

[103] Guicciardini to Machiavelli, 18 May 1521, *MF*, 338–39/377–78.
[104] Ibid., 339/377–78.

it is like Plato's *Republic*. Hence it would seem to me better if he were to return to Florence and carry out his duty of fortifying the walls because the time when we will need them is rapidly approaching.[105]

This letter, of course, does not constitute evidence that Machiavelli or anyone else saw his dialogue on the *Art of War* as having any connection with Plato's political philosophy.[106] It might just be a joke among friends about his unrealistically high expectations from a "rotten" army. But this too is noteworthy, since it goes against the grain of accounts that see Machiavelli as an arch-pragmatist prepared to lower his standards regarding "the faults of mankind." Like other letters, it affirms his friends' view of Machiavelli as a man of high standards who demanded more of human beings and institutions than most; and who when disappointed by others' conduct found ways to laugh while holding on to his standards, instead of lowering them to fit facts on the ground that did not fit his *forme* or *concetti*.

There is no evidence in either Machiavelli's letters or those of his friends that he departed from his core "ideas" even when he was proscribed from public service and sought to return. Many letters suggest instead that he sought to serve his city in writing when he was prevented from doing so through direct action. In 1521 he wrote to Guicciardini that he never disappointed his republic "whenever I was able to help her out—if not with deeds, then with words; if not with words, then with signs [*cenni*]." He added: "I have no intention of disappointing her now" although "I know that I am at variance with the ideas [*oppinione*] of her citizens, as I am in many other matters." He might have to rely heavily on signs, coded language, and oblique modes of writing because in these corrupt times his compatriots tended to oscillate between credulity and cynicism: they were quick to embrace appearances of goodness while mistrusting genuine decency and truthfulness. Since "I am aware," Machiavelli writes, "of how much belief there is in an evil man who hides under the cloak of religion, I can readily conjure up how much belief there would be in a good man who walks in truth, not in pretense [*in verità e non in simulazione*]."[107] Far from arguing that politics and ethics should embrace the corrupt standards found in most actual histories and cities, Machiavelli found ways to defend higher standards without preaching or haranguing, methods sure to backfire in times such as his.

Several letters also confound the common view that Machiavelli treats what is "seen," what "has been," or "what is" as an exhaustive basis for the standards he uses to judge present and future orders. Writing to Vettori, Machiavelli acknowledges that it is "natural" for human beings to doubt that "what has not been" and is not "seen" can ever come to be. "I am aware," he writes, "that natural human shortcomings [*naturale difetto degl'uomini*] are at variance with my idea [*opinione*]" about

---

[105] *MF*, 376. By this time Machiavelli's rights to serve in public posts had been partially restored, so that he was permitted to engage in select military and diplomatic activities.

[106] Despite first appearances, the *AW* does not only discuss military organization in a narrow sense. The dialogue contains subtle reflections on the conditions for stable political order, as well as on the true meaning of virtue, justice, and sources of ethical knowledge. See chaps. 3, 8.

[107] Machiavelli to Guicciardini, 17 May 1521, *MF*, 336–37/372–74.

necessary reforms to Florentine foreign policy. These shortcomings include "first, wanting to live from day to day; second, not believing that what has not been can be [*che possa essere quel che non è stato*]; third, always sizing people up in the same way." Against these defective views, Machiavelli consistently maintains that some dangers that have not yet been seen by people who focus on particular, transient appearances may loom large on closer examination; and remedies that have not been tried or "seen" to work may later be tried, and succeed.[108] For example, Vettori cites Aristotle as saying that since "confederated republics" (*republiche divulse*) have never performed well in the past, they probably never will.[109] Machiavelli's reply questions this judgment by doubting whether observed experience is ever a sufficient basis for judging what might succeed. "I do not know, he writes, "what Aristotle says about confederated republics, but I certainly can say what might reasonably exist [*che ragionevolmente potrebbe essere*], what exists [*che è*], and what has existed [*che è stato*]." Observations about what is or has been should undoubtedly be given weight in assessing future possibilities; but one should also consider what "might reasonably exist," a phrase that Guicciardini would echo in his *Dialogue*. Machiavelli insists that he will not derive his own standards for judging whether voluntary confederations can ever succeed from any particular classical authority. Instead he will canvass a wide range of historical examples, including many not often "seen" in extant historical records. And as a final appeal, he will exercise his own judgment about what might "reasonably exist," although no examples can be found.[110]

Machiavelli's rejection of Aristotle as ultimate arbiter on this issue does not entail a rejection of *all* philosophical approaches to this practical question. It rather implies that insofar as Aristotle or any other philosopher takes (or is thought by some readers to take) known experience as a sufficient template for future possible orders, while neglecting what "might reasonably exist," his reasoning is perhaps not philosophical enough. A concrete, relatively uncontroversial example of Machiavelli's own lifelong commitment to what he saw as a "reasonable" idea, regardless of past or present examples of success, is his conception of a civilian militia. He was invited to put it into practice under the Soderini republic and much later in Lombardy, where the rottenness of the troops made him laugh. Although both attempts proved disastrous, he continued to defend his conception, pointing out in writing that its success depended on political and juridical reforms, not just on military ones.[111] The next section suggests that he applied a similar standard of what "might reasonably exist" to defend the idea of a "true republic." He argued that this idea was needed to guide reforms in Florence, although it was not derived from any particular example of really existing republics, past or present.

---

[108] Machiavelli to Vettori, 10 August 1513, *MF*, 247–50/274–79.

[109] Vettori to Machiavelli, 20 August 1513, *MF*, 251–56/279–85.

[110] Machiavelli to Vettori, 26 August 1513, *MF*, 257–60/287–90. In this instance he gives the example of the ancient Etruscan confederation as a successful model seldom mentioned by ancient or modern writers; see chaps. 3, 12.

[111] See chap. 8, sec. 8.1.

The passages just set out are undeniably ambiguous, and my suggestion that they have philosophical content still needs to be demonstrated more fully in later chapters. At this early stage, I simply want to assemble prima facie contextual evidence that Machiavelli's thought is less narrowly practical or empirical than is often presumed; and that recurrent references in his letters and works allude to a kind of philosophical thinking that has affinities with Socratic and Platonic traditions, without deferring completely to any particular ancient authority.[112]

1.6.
The Socratic tradition of philosophical politics

This brings us to another type of context that influenced Machiavelli's writings, and that may shed more light on his thought than somewhat random comparisons with other humanists.[113] All of Machiavelli's main political works refer to ancient writers whose ideas and methods of writing inspired him. In the next chapters I suggest that he drew on his ancients in a highly individual way. He wrote not as a worshipful disciple of any particular ancients, Roman or Greek, but as an independent thinker who made his own judgments about which ancient genres, literary techniques, and arguments to renovate. In particular, his conception of the relationship between his writings and public service has affinities with that implicit in Roman writers such as Livy, Cicero, and Sallust. The most striking affinities in this respect, however, are with two of the Greek writers most frequently mentioned or alluded to in Machiavelli's works: Xenophon (c. 430–360 BC) and Plutarch (c. AD 45–120). A student of Socrates, Xenophon seeks to convey his teacher's ethical teachings, especially his ideas about the role philosophy should play in public life.[114] The next chapter will consider how these ideas and Xenophon's modes of literary "dissimulating" might have inspired Machiavelli. Plutarch was a Greek who held Roman citizenship under the empire. Through numerous essays and many of his *Parallel Lives* of famous Greeks and Romans, he sought to pass on what he took to be Socrates' and Plato's teachings about the need for philosophers to involve themselves in politics; and,

---

[112] There are four references to "philosophers" in Machiavelli's most philosophical work, the *Discourses*. All four can be traced, *inter alia*, to Plato's *Timaeus* or *Critias*, two of the most widely read dialogues in Machiavelli's time; until Ficino made his complete Latin translation, parts of the *Timaeus* were the only pieces of Plato's writing accessible to readers without knowledge of Greek. Compare (1) the *Discourses'* passage about the limited knowledge of things natural and supernatural (*D*, I.56.114) to *Tim.* 29c, *Crit.* 107b; (2) on mountain men and lost memories after floods (*D*, II.4.138) to *Tim.* 22–26; (3) on the universe not being eternal (*D*, II.5.138) to *Tim.* 28; (4) on necessity perfecting the hands and tongue of men (*D*, III.12.246) to *Tim.* 47–48, 68–69, 75–76.

[113] If common elements are sought, it is important to choose carefully which humanists are picked out as having affinities with Machiavelli. His positions should not be assimilated to those of writers like Bruni, whom he openly criticizes, on the basis of superficial similarities, but rather with contemporaries such as Guicciardini whose views were closer to his own.

[114] Strauss (1958, 161–62, 291) sees Xenophon as Machiavelli's main political philosopher; also see Nadon 2001, 13–24, on Xenophon and Machiavelli.

conversely, the need for statesmen and captains to seek guidance through philosophical reflection.[115]

In an essay on "The Education of Children," Plutarch argues that the best men are those "who are able to combine and mingle political capacity with philosophy." The contemplative life alone, he writes, "is not useful, while the practical life which has no portion in philosophy" is based on inadequate knowledge (*epistēmē*) of its subject matter.[116] How then should the two activities be integrated? Addressing this question from the perspective of practical men of state, Plutarch points out that any adequate conception of statesmanship consists

> not only in holding office, being ambassador, vociferating in the assembly, and ranting round the speakers' platform proposing laws and making motions. Most people think all this is part of statesmanship, just as they think of course that those are philosophers who sit in a chair and converse and prepare their lectures over their books; but the continuous practice of statesmanship [*politeia*] and philosophy, which is every day alike seen in acts and deeds [*en ergois kai praxesin*], they fail to perceive.[117]

Statesmen who live up to the standards implied by that name, Plutarch continues, do not "court the mob, deliver harangues, arouse factions," or perform public services only when compelled to do so. The truly statesmanlike man, "although he never put on a uniform" or held public office, "is always acting as a statesman by urging those on who have power, guiding those who need guidance, assisting those who are deliberating, reforming those who act wrongly," and "encouraging those who are right-minded."[118] If true statesmen can be identified through these actions and not just by official titles, the same holds for men who deserve the name of philosopher. For

> being a statesman is like being a philosopher. Socrates at any rate was a philosopher, although he did not set out benches or seat himself in an armchair or observe a fixed hour for conversing or promenading with his pupils, but jested with them . . . and drank with them, served in the army . . . and finally was imprisoned and drank the poison. He was the first to show that life at all times and in all parts, in all experiences and activities [*pathesi kai pragmasin*], universally admits philosophy.[119]

This conception of philosophy calls not for a life of contemplation divorced from politics, but for a high degree of ethical reflectiveness about political activity. This, according to Plutarch, Socrates, Xenophon, and Plato, is a condition for any worthwhile *vita activa*. Those who practice this kind of philosophy do sometimes have to step back from the political fray and learn how to give reasoned accounts

[115] Most *Lives* discuss the philosophical education of each famous man.
[116] Plutarch, "The Education of Children," PM, I.36–37.
[117] Compare Plato, *Gorg.* 500c–501c, 521d–522a.
[118] Plutarch, "Whether an Old Man Should Engage in Public Affairs," PM, X.144–47.
[119] Ibid.

(*logoi*) of the causes of political problems, and reasoned judgments about how to address them. But these philosophical modes of reasoning do not compete with practical political deliberations. On the contrary, they play an indispensable part in sound political reasoning. Both citizens and rulers need practical philosophy if they wish to avoid serious errors of political judgment. Philosophers are thus like doctors who treat political disorders "as if they were diseases," making for them "a secret political medicine" kept "within the state, so that it may have as little need as possible of physicians and medicine drawn from the outside." Plutarch regards true philosophers as "men of public spirit" who are always "eager to converse with the prominent and powerful" not because they are personally ambitious, but because they seek to benefit their cities and mankind. This was why Plato "sailed to Sicily in the hope that his teachings would produce laws and actions in the government of Dionysius." Although he found the future tyrant already too corrupt to be guided toward justice, Plato's efforts were still worthwhile. They remain an example of reasonable aims pursued against empirical odds, yet which were not shown to be unreasonable by this particular failure.[120] Statesmanlike philosophers should never stop exerting themselves on behalf of the public good even when they must act under severe constraints. At the very least they must use "frankness of speech" (*parrēsian*) to address dangerous problems, even if this involves great risks for themselves.[121] In a short essay entitled "That a Philosopher Ought to Converse [*dialegesthai*] Especially with Men in Power [*hēgemosi*]" Plutarch treats Socrates as the original inspiration for these ideas, and Plato as a role model in both his efforts to reform unjust rulers and in his views on public education as a foundation of stable republics.[122]

When affinities are recognized between these positions and Machiavelli's view of his own civil responsibilities, many difficulties relating to his methods of writing and the content of his arguments become easier to resolve. Although Machiavelli does not announce his philosophical aims in so many words, I will argue that he practiced philosophy in the sense defined by Plutarch and other ancient writers, both Greek and Roman.[123] Ancient philosophers who held this view by no means restricted themselves to general and abstract studies, leaving "particulars" to biographers and historians.[124] Most obviously, Xenophon and Plutarch wrote about particular men and deeds in order to demonstrate what they saw as general ethical and political truths.[125] Socrates' (468–399 BC) contemporary Thucydides (b. 471 BC) is treated by Plutarch as a writer whose histories have philosophical content

---

[120] Plutarch, "Precepts of Statecraft," PM, X.158–61, 246–47; "That a Philosopher Ought to Converse," PM, X.28–27; "To an Uneducated Ruler," PM, X.52–53.

[121] Plutarch, "Precepts," 246–47. Plutarchian frankness includes a range of subtle dialogical techniques; see chap. 2.

[122] See Plato, *Seventh Letter*; *Laws*, esp. 653a–674c, 764c–773e, 857e–862e, *et passim*.

[123] Here again, I take issue with scholarship that contrasts "Roman" ideals of public participation and the *vita activa* with more contemplative "Greek" philosophy. As will become clearer in chap. 2, this distinction is a misleading caricature of arguments found in both Greek and Roman writing.

[124] See Pocock's (1975, 55–57) overly sharp distinction.

[125] See Plutarch, "Fortune of Alexander," PM, IV.420–21.

in the sense just described. I have suggested that Machiavelli's *Florentine Histories* should be read in a similar way: as philosophical history that seeks to address civil disorders by encouraging citizens to understand their causes, recognize their symptoms beneath misleading appearances, and respond in more effective ways than they could discover without such an account. Significantly, the most prudent characters in his *Histories* are presented as reflective men of letters, not as dynamic men of action who have no time to read ancient works or engage in longwinded *ragionare*.[126] Although his unnamed "men in the middle" who reason frankly with warring parties are not called philosophers in name, their diplomatic deeds reveal them as civil physicians who try to address disorders through a non-partisan understanding of their deepest causes.

If Machiavelli had a *filosofia*, why did he not say so? Plutarch's remarks on who or what goes under the name of philosophy may help to illuminate this matter. When young men first embark on philosophical studies, he observes, they often seek out the branch of study that brings greatest repute. Some beginners are led to what they imagine are "the resplendent heights of the Natural Sciences"; others go in for endless "disputations, knotty problems, and quibbles," while still others "enter a course in Logic and Argumentation, where they straightaway stock themselves up for the practice of sophistry." Others count up their "literary stock" based on derivative "apothegms and anecdotes." But those who make real progress "do not arrogate to themselves, as before, the name of philosophy and the repute of studying it, or even give themselves the title of philosopher," which would now strike them as presumptuous. There is a saying, Plutarch reports, that many who came to Athens to study "were, at the outset, wise; later they became lovers of wisdom, later still orators. As time went on, however, they at last became "just ordinary persons [*idiōtas*], and the more they laid hold on reason the more they laid aside their self-opinion and conceit."[127] This recalls Guicciardini's *Dialogue*, which begins with young men trying to do what they take to be philosophy by citing famous names, until the leading interlocutor says he will put philosophy aside and start by discussing what seems natural and obvious to most people. This turns out to be a more effective way to distinguish errors from truer opinions, and is thus more philosophical, even without the name of philosophy.[128]

The idea that most people use that name in self-serving and corrupt ways is a leitmotif of Plato's and Xenophon's Socratic writings as well as Plutarch's. Socrates gave the ironic label *sophistēs*, "the wise ones," to men who wanted to be called philosophers although their practices gave true philosophy a bad name.[129] He accused the sophists of subordinating the pursuit of knowledge to practical ends that were not themselves

---

[126] Chiefly Uzzano, Palla Strozzi, and Neri di Gino Capponi; see chaps. 7–9.

[127] Plutarch, "Progress in Virtue," PM, I.418–19, 432–35. In their correspondence Machiavelli and his friends called themselves collectively "dotards" (*barbogeria*) (MF, 407, 453). Vettori, Casavecchia, and others mocked the superior attitudes of men who want to be esteemed for their ranks and titles instead of valued for their deeds and demonstrated qualities.

[128] Compare Hobbes' (1998 [1642], 7–8) opening remarks in *De Cive* on Socrates and the corruption of philosophy.

[129] For example, see Plato, *Gorg.* 527a, *Rep.* 598d.

subjected to philosophical examination. Their teachings provided the sons of the wealthy with tools to campaign effectively for power, especially teaching them how to make speeches and public appearances likely to attract popular support. What they called philosophy was merely the technical knowledge (*technē*) needed to make students appear knowledgeable, not the reflective knowledge (*epistēmē*) that is the proper aim of philosophy. The sophists filled their own pockets by giving their students an undeserved reputation for knowledge.[130] An appreciation for this tradition may help to explain why, his friend Casavecchia notwithstanding, Machiavelli did not describe himself as a philosopher as well as a "historian, comic writer and tragic writer." If he and other members of his circle had read their Plutarch and Xenophon as well as Plato's *Gorgias*, *Republic*, and other well-known dialogues, they would have been familiar with the tradition. And given Machiavelli's concerns about how good names are used to color indecent deeds, and specifically about how Cosimo de' Medici "used conveniently" philosophy as part of his appearance-making apparatus, it is unsurprising that he did not claim the name of philosopher.

What then should be made of the following passage from the *Florentine Histories*:

> It has been observed by the prudent that letters come after arms and that, in provinces and cities, captains arise before philosophers. For, as good and ordered armies give birth to victories and victories to quiet, the strength of well-armed spirits cannot be corrupted by a more honorable leisure than that of letters, nor can leisure enter into well-instituted cities with a greater and more dangerous deceit than this one. This was best understood by Cato when the philosophers Diogenes and Carneades, sent by Athens as spokesmen to the Senate, came to Rome. When he saw how the Roman youth was beginning to follow them about with admiration, and since he recognized the evil that could result to his fatherland from this honorable leisure, he saw to it that no philosopher could be accepted in Rome.[131]

If Machiavelli means simply that all letters corrupt young men in republics, taking them away from the *vita activa*, then his own writings are as guilty of doing this as the rest. A more likely meaning is that philosophers and men of letters are always under suspicion of corrupting young men in corrupt times. Machiavelli perhaps thought he was so regarded at the time of writing. Plutarch, his probable source for this episode, presents Cato's sweeping ban on all philosophers as a symptom of dangerous ignorance and defensiveness in the late Roman republic, reminiscent of Socrates' death sentence on the charge of corrupting Athenian youth.[132] By banishing all philosophers from Rome, Cato failed to differentiate among different kinds

---

[130] See Plato, *Phaed.* 274e–275c, *Prot.* 312c–319a, *Soph.* 222a–223b, *Rep.* 493a–495e, Xenophon, "On Hunting" in *Scripta Minora*, 448–57.

[131] *FH*, V.1.185/519.

[132] The Greek philosophers' mission was to persuade the Romans to leave Greeks their autonomy. Carneades gave public talks that caused a scandal by implying that Romans used the word "justice" in different ways to suit their own imperial purposes, thus challenging those who believed that Romans only fought just wars. See Bringmann 2007, 121.

of "philosophy," excluding more adequate kinds that might have purged Rome of corrupting influences that were already rife.[133] It seems unlikely that Machiavelli's closest friends would have read the passage as a non-ironic condemnation of philosophy and letters *tout court*. The correspondence suggests that they would have seen Machiavelli's *Histories* as an attempt to inject a much-needed dose of philosophical medicine into a disordered political and military scene.[134]

1.7.
Forming republics in writing and in practice: The *Discursus*

Among Machiavelli's writings, one unambiguous example can be found of an attempt to do what Plutarch and other Socratic writers suggest: to address questionably legitimate rulers through frank yet diplomatic discourses, trying to persuade them to convert their tyranny or principality into a republic. This is exactly what Machiavelli does in his "Discourse on Remodeling the Government of Florence" (*Discursus florentinarum rerum post mortem iunioris Laurentii Medices*, henceforth *Discursus*). The piece was written around 1520 at the request of Giovanni de' Medici, then Pope Leo X. As a gesture of goodwill, Giovanni had invited several well-known critics of his family's princely position in the nominal republic to state their case. Machiavelli seized the opportunity to write in a more directly critical manner than he did elsewhere. His persuasions contain several elements characteristic of a Socratic *dialogos* with men in power. The *Discursus* starts with frank yet scrupulously diplomatic attempts to show its addressee the basic causes of current problems. It then examines common opinions about the topic at hand, and only after that offers a modest presentation of what the speaker considers more reasonable views.

Machiavelli begins by offering a frank diagnosis of present Florentine disorders. While he refuses to pretend that these are not very serious, he does not hold the Medicis or any other single party responsible for them. As he would argue in the *Florentine Histories*, the first step toward finding a remedy must be to acknowledge

---

[133] PL, *Cato Major* 368–73. Having criticized the claims of self-styled "practical" men that letters and philosophy harm the public good, Bacon (2001 [1605], 10–16) writes that Cato "was well punished for his blasphemy against learning" by being seized afterward with the desire "to go to school again, and to learn the Greek tongue" in order to "peruse the Greek authors; which doth well demonstrate that his former censure of the Grecian learning was rather an affected gravity, than according to the inward sense of his own opinion." Similarly, Socrates' accusers were later blamed while the philosopher accumulated "honors divine and human; and those discourses of his which were then termed corrupting of manners, were after acknowledged for sovereign medicines of the mind and manners, and so have been received ever since till this day." These points, Bacon concludes, should answer those unlearned "political men" who have "presumed to throw imputations upon learning."

[134] In a letter to Guicciardini written in 1526, Machiavelli writes that when "Count Pietro," a Spanish military engineer commissioned to fortify Florence, arrives to confer with him, "we shall do our best to pick his brain as much as possible; I have held off in order to hear what he has to say, so that what happened to the Greek with Hannibal does not happen to me"; Machiavelli to Guicciardini, 4 April 1526, *MF*, 385–86. The Greek with whom Machiavelli identifies himself was the philosopher Phormio, who expatiated to Hannibal on "the duties of a military commander" and on military matters in general. When the lecture was over, Hannibal promptly rejected Phormio's ideas as those of a madman—and lost the war against Rome. See note in *MF*, 553.

that the disease is serious, and that the constitution introduced by the Medicis—an unstable hybrid of princely and republican modes—cannot be part of the cure. The deeper cause of Florence's disorders, however, is the general disease of partisanship: not the existence of different parties as such, but the conviction found in all parties that one of them must permanently dominate the others. All previous governments in Florence, Machiavelli points out, have been afflicted by partisanship, so that "the alterations in them have been made not for the fulfilment of the common good, but for the strengthening and security of the party." The belief that the dominance of some party or family is the only possible basis for stable order had caused endless strife in Florence long before the Medicis came to power; Machiavelli sees their rise to princely status as a symptom of this deeper disease, not as its cause. He hopes that with the recent death of Lorenzo II, to whom he had dedicated the *Prince*, powerful Medicis such as Giovanni will recognize the urgent need for change. Matters have, he writes, now reached a point where it is necessary "to reason about new modes of government [*ragionare di nuovi modi di governi*]."

Again speaking frankly, Machiavelli acknowledges current obstacles to reform. These include Giovanni's concerns to maintain princely powers for his family and safety for his friends. In good Plutarchian and Socratic form, Machiavelli does not second-guess or criticize these concerns. Instead he takes them as a starting point for considering reforms that might accommodate them, at least for a time. He knows, Machiavelli declares, that his princely addressee is "much inclined" toward a republic, and believes that

> you defer establishing it because you hope to find some arrangement by which your power in Florence will continue great and your friends may live in security. Since I believe I have discovered one, I hope Your Highness will give attention to my discovery, so that if there is anything good in it, you can make use of it and also learn from it how great is my wish to serve you. And you will see that in this republic of mine your power is not only preserved but is increased, your friends continue to be honored and safe, and the whole body of citizens has evident reasons for being satisfied. With the utmost respect, I beg Your Holiness not to condemn and not to praise this discourse of mine without first reading it through.[135]

True to his assurances, Machiavelli's proposals take account of the current facts of Medici dominance and partisanship. He does not insist that these corrupt elements must be thoroughly purged before republican orders can be established. Yet it would be wrong to see this transitional position as a pragmatic acceptance of certain distasteful political facts, nor does it indicate a willingness to compromise his fundamental aims. Machiavelli's pragmatism is merely provisional. It involves no lowering of his republican standards, but serves as a more effective means to promote those standards.[136] In current conditions, the best hope of promoting

---

[135] *Discursus*, 107/738.
[136] Note that Machiavelli relies on frank truth-telling, not manipulative forms of rhetoric, in attempting to persuade Giovanni to give up his principality.

them without creating further disorders is to persuade Giovanni himself to implement Machiavelli's republican proposals "from above." This would allow a non-
revolutionary transition from princely to stable republican government.

To dispel any lingering illusions that the status quo can be sustained, Machiavelli
examines the "opinions of others" that are at variance with his own judgments. He
respectfully acknowledges the widespread opinion that "no government can be
established firmer than that existing in the times of Cosimo and Lorenzo." People
who harked back to a golden age when Florence seemed great and stable, and
who believe that things really were as they appeared, upheld the early-Medici form
of popular-princely government as their model. Machiavelli rejects this opinion,
while diplomatically avoiding any direct criticism of the idealization it involves.
Instead of arguing that Cosimo and Lorenzo used corrupt means to generate appearances of *grandezza*, thereby undermining the rule of law and external defenses,
he simply points out that the causes that induced people to support their government at the time no longer exist. In Cosimo's time the hybrid "princely republic"
appeared strong because it had popular approval. But since then, Florentines have
"experienced" a different, more fully republican form of government "that they
think more just [*civile*] and that pleases them better." Although Machiavelli refrains from specifying what this was, he evidently means the republic in which
he himself served under Piero Soderini's leadership until the Medici restoration
of 1512. Moreover, the first Medici princes gained popular approval because they
came from the *popolani* and appeared to be like them, behaving in a friendly way
to ordinary citizens. Now, however, their family has become so great that "there
cannot be such intimacy and consequently such favor." It once seemed "natural"
for the people to back Medici rule. But as the *Florentine Histories* suggests and the
Discursus subtly hints, this appearance was based more on Cosimo's and Lorenzo's
skills in fostering it than on natural sympathies between their family and the Florentine *popolani*. Machiavelli concludes that since "we cannot call a government
modeled on Cosimo's either safe or firm [*né sicuro né stabile*]," it "should not be
acceptable to Your Holiness and your friends."[137]

Machiavelli deals more briefly with a second opinion given by "those who
prefer a government more inclusive [*piu largo*] than Cosimo's." This, Machiavelli
remarks, might sound appealing to citizens who see themselves as defenders of
republican ideals. Unfortunately, too many of these people argue in vague "generalities" (*e' generali*) and have defective notions about what stable republican orders
require. Although inclusiveness (*larghezza*) may be one criterion for republican
government, it is insufficient. There are more and less well-ordered ways to make
republics inclusive, and standards of good order should be more fundamental than
"general" ideals of inclusiveness. Unless a republic "is inclusive in such a way that it
will become a well-ordered [*ben ordinata*] republic," Machiavelli contends, "its inclusiveness is likely to make it fall more rapidly." This is true, for example, of inclusive orders that fail to address the more basic problem of partisan strife, whereby

---

[137] *Discursus*, 106/737.

different parties refuse to share authority and see any increase in their opponents' power as a reason to break public laws.[138]

Despite his wistful allusion to the republic of his own earlier years, Machiavelli neither idealizes nor proposes a return to its often unstable orders. A truthful diagnosis indicates that a new constitution is needed to address Florence's disorders. Having considered defects in other proposed solutions, Machiavelli now gives his "own opinion." He starts by arguing that no government is stable (*stabile*) unless it is a true principality or a true republic (*vero principato, vera repubblica*). All hybrid forms of government tend either to "rise" toward *principato* or descend to *repubblica*. The only way to stabilize government, then, is to settle firmly on the one or the other, and order it for a long life. Machiavelli does not presume to tell Giovanni that he should opt for a republic because principalities are "pestiferous."[139] Refraining from direct criticisms of principality, he simply proceeds to offer a criterion for a true republic, and to prescribe specific institutions that meet it. The definitive criterion for a *vera repubblica* is, Machiavelli proposes, government that has "its distinctive parts" (*le parti sue*). He then presents reasons for judging that this general criterion must be the basis for any solution. All cities contain diverse and conflicting humors and parts. Stable order depends on establishing terms of coexistence among these parts. Instead of seeking to eliminate any of them through exile, repression, or other modes of exclusion, Florence's leaders should opt for a government that obliges each part to share authority with the rest, on terms that seem just to everyone.[140] "Without satisfying the generality of the citizens [*all' universale*]," Machiavelli declares, "to set up a stable government is always impossible." General satisfaction depends not on ephemerally effective rhetoric, but on orders that give "the whole body of citizens . . . evident reasons for being satisfied [*l'altra universalità di cittadini . . . cagione evidentissima di contentarsi*]." A government ordered according to the standards of a "true republic" is, Machiavelli argues, one "which everybody will see and realize needs to be just as it is." "There is," he declares, no other way to escape Florence's ills

> than to give the city institutions [*ordini*] that can by themselves stand firm. And they will always stand firm when everybody has a hand in them, and when everybody knows what he needs to do and in whom he can trust, and no class of citizen, either through fear for itself or through ambition, will need to desire revolution [*innovazione*].

[138] *Discursus*, 107/737–38.
[139] *D*, I.2 says that there is only one "true" mode, republic, which can stabilize different forms of government. Machiavelli avoids saying this here, presumably because he is addressing a "prince" who remains attached to the mode of *principato* and who is suspicious of republican opposition. The *Discursus*' arguments also imply that *principato* cannot be stable, since government by princes always tends toward tyranny; but Machiavelli leaves it to Giovanni to work this out for himself.
[140] This is different from many conceptions of "mixed" governments or constitutions that have been attributed to Machiavelli; his remarks here and in *D*, I.2 show that he saw hybrid forms as inherently unstable.

He then outlines concrete suggestions for reforms likely to satisfy these general standards, based, yet improving on, institutions that already exist or have existed in Florence.[141]

Machiavelli nowhere suggests that this cure depends on finding examples of actual republics that instantiate the standards of a *vera repubblica*. As I argue in later chapters, his basic criterion for identifying those standards is not what is or has been "seen" in ancient or recent times, but what is reasonably possible and indeed "has to be" if civil disorders are to find a durable cure. There may be no known examples of republics in which the chief normative criterion for a true republic—sharing authority among distinct parts under the common rule of law—was fully met, let alone respected by all parties. Even Rome experienced frequent, dangerous bouts of corruption because the nobles constantly sought to dominate the plebs, while the plebs were constantly suspicious of the nobles.[142] Nonetheless, so long as the reasonable *principle* of shared authority was upheld against the actions that incessantly challenged it, Rome remained great and free. It was this principle and the laws and orders that enforced it, not the absence of destabilizing humors, that kept corruption in check in Rome. And the general principle of shared power under strict public laws, not particular Roman institutions, is what Machiavelli wants Giovanni to adopt. The principle itself is not exclusively Roman; it also has Greek antecedents.[143] So has the idea of a true republic as a set of normative standards that are not themselves derived from particular examples, although they may be illustrated by examples that approximate them.[144] The standards are set partly by reflecting on what is or has been, but also by considering what orders are reasonably possible for human beings.[145]

---

[141] *Discursus*, 106–15/737–45.

[142] *D*, I.1.4–7/199–202.

[143] See TPW, VIII.89-97 on the idea that sharing (*metechtō*) authority and shared rule (*sunkrasis*) underpin stable order in cities. Thucydides remarks that for the first time in his own lifetime, Athens finally achieved a good constitution when both the few and the many were given their share. Also see XC, I.126.

[144] In addition to several distinct types of constitution seen in experience, Aristotle (*Politics*, IV.iv.7) also presents a general normative conception of *politeia*—variously translated as "constitution" or "republic"—which can be used to judge whether or not any actual constitution deserves that good name. His chief criterion: "where the laws do not govern there is no *politeia*." Plato (*Statesman*, 297d–303c) gives a similar criterion for the only conception of *politeia* that is "correct in the strict sense [*orthēn akribōs monon politeian*]." More specifically, the same dialogue suggests (308a–311c) that true statesmanship involves knowing how to order all the "parts" of a city through "sharing of opinions, through honors, dishonor, esteem, and a giving of pledges to one another," and "always entrusts offices in cities to these [parts] in common" so that none try to dominate the rest. In *Laws* 715b–c the main interlocutor doubts that a constitution can be regarded as a genuine *politeia* with genuine (*orthos*) laws unless its laws are established for the good of everyone in the city. If the authors of laws are not citizens but party men, they have no claim to be obeyed, or indeed to be called "laws" (*nomoi*). A more specific, procedural criterion is introduced later: a genuine *politeia*, as distinct from "party rule," should be based on the consent of the governed (*Laws* 832c–d). In the *Republic* 590c–d we read that the aim of the law, "which is the ally [*summachos*] of everyone in the city," is as far as possible to make all equal and friends (*omoioi . . . kai philoi*). This is a condition for any city that "deserves to be called a city [*polin*]" not only in reputation but in truth (*hōs alēthōs*) (*Rep.* 422e–423a).

[145] See chap. 5, sec. 5.7.

Machiavelli's concrete proposals for institutional reform try to show how the standards of *vera repubblica* may be applied even in corrupt conditions. This, he assures Giovanni, need not involve dangerous upheavals or undermine his own safety and authority. If Giovanni is persuaded by Machiavelli's arguments, he himself may initiate reforms "from above," thus effecting a non-revolutionary transition to a constitution that meets true republican standards. So as long as Giovanni lives, Machiavelli concedes, he should retain certain powers that reflect his princely status. After his death, however, those powers should be transferred to the republic. The penultimate paragraph appeals to Giovanni's private interests again, declaring that if he does undertake the proposed reforms, he will find himself free from many "vexations" that must weigh on a man in his position. The final paragraph offers an ominous prediction: if the republican principle of shared authority remains unheeded, many new dangers will necessarily come to Florence, not least to Giovanni's friends. The city's present unstable government must either rise to tyranny or descend into licentious violence, as such governments always do. In "riot and haste a head will be set up who with arms and violence will defend the government," or "one party will run to open the Hall of the Council and plunder the other party." In either case, Machiavelli concludes, "Your Holiness can imagine how many deaths, how many exiles, how many acts of extortion will result, enough to make the cruelest man—much more than Your Holiness, who is most merciful—die of sorrow."[146] Here is a good example of Machiavelli's use of rhetoric to drive home his point. But as with the end of the *Prince*, the rhetoric comes only at the end of a rigorously reasoned, diplomatic discourse that urged readers to step back from common opinions about how to achieve stable rule, and to seek a truer account of what standards the idea of a true republic requires.

Shortly before the rhetorical end, Machiavelli identifies his attempt to persuade Giovanni to apply republican principles with the similar aspirations of ancient philosophers. He begins by acclaiming public service, especially civil reforms, as the most praiseworthy of human activities:

> I believe that the greatest honor possible for men to have is that willingly [*voluntariamente*] given to them by their native cities; I believe the greatest good to be done and the most pleasing to God [*Dio*] is that which one does to one's native city. Besides this, no man is so much exalted by any act of his as are those men who have with laws and with institutions remodeled [*con leggi e con istituti reformato*] republics and kingdoms; these are, after those who have been gods [*iddi*], the first to be praised.

However, this does not imply that practical politicians deserve more praise than philosophers who discharge their civil duties through writing or *discorsi*. Many men are constrained to reform cities on paper because they lack the power to reform them in practice.

---

[146] *Discursus*, 115/745.

And because they have been few who have had opportunity to do it, and very few those who have understood how to do it [*saputo fare*], small is the number who have done it. And so much has this glory been esteemed by men seeking for nothing other than glory that when unable to form a republic in reality [*in atto*], they have done it in writing [*in iscritto*], as Aristotle, Plato, and many others, who have wished to show the world that if they have not founded a free government [*fondare un vivere civile*], as did Solon and Lycurgus, they have failed not through ignorance but through their impotence for putting it into practice [*dalla impotenza di metterlo in atto*].[147]

Perhaps Machiavelli is being ironic about philosophers here, suggesting that their only reason for writing about republics was the desire for personal glory and to prove that they were not ignorant of politics, though they were ineffectual participants in it. If so, he is as guilty of these vanities as they, for he too is writing when he cannot act otherwise than to write. As he wrote to Guicciardini, in corrupt times no one believes that a man who claims to have good intentions really "walks in truth." Such men are more readily trusted when they profess to be vain or ambitious, since people do not understand other motives for writing things that bring them no wealth or glory. From the perspective of corrupt men, philosophers who wrote about republics when they could not form them must have been motivated by vanity; surely Machiavelli is no different. It seems doubtful, however, that Machiavelli believed this of himself, or of ancient philosophers like Aristotle and Plato. After all, both he and they could have gone in for teaching young men how to generate appearances of wisdom under the name of philosophy. Instead they wrote about the principles of a true republic, defending reasoned standards of conduct in times when standards of honesty and reasonableness were ridiculed or abused. While recognizing that incivility often reigned in practice, they still tried to teach citizens and rulers to reflect on the conditions for a *vivere civile*. Machiavelli does not assign highest honors to the founders of actual civic orders such as Solon and Lycurgus; he gives at least equal praise to Aristotle, Plato, and others who were able only to write about republican principles. Moreover, the passage slyly raises the question whether all those who try to found civil orders in practice have always "understood how to do it."[148] It may be that they could benefit from the advice of others who lack the power to do it *in atto*, but whose writings show that they have thought a great deal about the foundations of a *vivere civile*.

The *Discursus* and correspondence cast doubt on the notion that Machiavelli regarded demanding philosophical standards, especially those that do not conform to corrupt realities, as imaginary castles in the air of little interest for practical men. Despite their wide currency, I hope to show that there is no convincing basis for the assertions that Machiavelli "despises the concern with imagined

---

[147] *Discursus*, 113–14/744. Compare Gentili's remark cited in the introduction.

[148] As Plato wrote in his own name, many people think they know (*epistasthai*) the tones or languages of various constitutions, but most fall short of understanding them, and therefore produce mere imitations that soon go to ruin. See his further explanation in the *Fifth Letter*, 321d–322b, of why he preferred to advise others on politics without speaking in his own city's assembly.

republics and imagined principalities"; that his writings judge human conduct by a "sub-human" standard; or that "he is good at bringing fantasies down to earth, but he assumes . . . that this is enough," while allowing "too little to the ideal impulses of men."[149] The position that emerges from both the *Florentine Histories* and *Discursus* is that what exists and is seen through much of human history is disordered. But standards for human conduct do not have to be derived from examples of disordered conduct. They can and must be sought in some way other than by accepting whatever is said in corrupt times to be true or false, praiseworthy or bad.

The rest of this book enquires how Machiavelli proposed to identify and defend properly human ethical standards. In the same letter to Guicciardini where he says that no one trusts men who "walk in truth," Machiavelli further observes that many of his fellow citizens, unsure how to take responsibility for their own troubles or unwilling to do so, sit back and pray for God or some holy man to save them.[150] "They would like a preacher who would teach them the way to paradise," he writes, while "I would like to find one who would teach them the way to go to the Devil." The usual reading is that Machiavelli wants to pry his contemporaries away from Christian morality so that, by going to the devil, they will discover more efficacious if less moral means to defend themselves. But Machiavelli does not say here or anywhere else that he wants someone to teach men how to be less good, let alone how to become pragmatically amoral. He says that people should learn the way to the devil not in order to follow it, but in order to *avoid* it. "I believe," he writes, "that the following would be the true road to paradise: learn the way to Hell in order to steer clear of it."[151] Most people use the word "paradise" to express an ideal of the highest possible bliss for human beings. Machiavelli doubts that human beings can ever find the kind of perfect happiness that some of his contemporaries desire. If there is a road to some human condition that might approach the idea of paradise, that best possible condition must consist in avoiding evils made by human beings themselves, not in maximizing bliss. And the best way to teach human beings how to avoid evils is to show how they themselves produce them, sometimes unwittingly, and often under self-deceptions about their own virtue or prudence.[152]

The *Histories* shows Florentine citizens, and anyone else who recognizes the general arguments and principles set out in the work, their own share of responsibility

---

[149] Strauss 1958, 296–97; Berlin 1981 (1953), 73.

[150] In part a reference to Friar Girolamo Savonarola; see chaps. 10–11.

[151] Machiavelli to Guicciardini, 17 May 1521, *MF*, 336–37.

[152] Neville's (1691, 5) "Machiavel" affirms these aims in his "Vindication," declaring that he hopes to show both tyrants and "the poor people who are forced to live under them" the danger each faces. His writings do this "by laying before the former, the hellish and precipitous courses they must use to maintain their power," and by showing peoples "what they must suffer" if they allow ambitious leaders to act outside limits established by public laws. "If any man will read over my Book of the Prince with impartiality and ordinary Charity," Neville has Machiavelli say, "he will easily perceive, that it is not my intention therein to recommend that Government, or those men there described"; it is only to analyze their manipulative methods so that others can avoid falling prey to them.

for the political hell they long to escape.[153] By describing these deeds in detail, Machiavelli makes it hard for his compatriots to blame foreigners, fortune, or rival parties for their collective troubles. "God does not," Machiavelli declares at the end of the *Prince*, "want to do everything" toward the redemption of corrupt and downtrodden cities; most of the work "you must do yourself."[154] His ethics is an ethics of human self-responsibility. It treats humans as corruptible animals capable of great evil, but also as self-ordering animals capable of setting demanding yet reasonable standards for themselves. They seldom live up to their highest standards, to be sure. But they constantly employ them anyway—to judge others' conduct if not their own. The clarification and reasoned defense of what he saw as the most important standards form the philosophical underpinning of all Machiavelli's main writings. Both his choice of basic standards and his methods of reasoning about them owe much to ancient Greek writers, as the next chapter argues.

[153] Compare Plato's (*Rep.* 565c–569c) Socrates on how peoples are often responsible for allowing tyrants to emerge, by "setting up one man as their special champion, nurturing him and making him great," only to realize their mistake when civil order has been destroyed. Similarly, Machiavelli's analysis in the *Histories* traces the origins of various tyrannical regimes—most dramatically that of Walter, Duke of Athens, and more subtly that of the Medicis—to popular habits of mistaking "license" for appropriately measured freedom. For Machiavelli as for Plato (in *Rep.* 571a–590d) this freedom depends on setting the rule of laws above that of men; see chaps. 6–7.

[154] *P*, XXVI.103/189–92.

CHAPTER 2

Ancient Sources: Dissimulation in Greek Ethics

In the first few centuries after Machiavelli's death, many independent-minded readers considered not only the *Florentine Histories* and *Discourses* but also the *Prince* as republican texts.[1] In the *Social Contract,* Rousseau called the *Prince* a "book of republicans"; he, Gentili, Bacon, Spinoza, Herder, and other philosophers had no doubt that its fundamental teachings were consistent with the more open defenses of human and political freedom that appear elsewhere in Machiavelli's corpus. But these philosophers also noted an apparent contradiction in Machiavelli's writings. On the one hand, they describe him as an "honest man" and praise his unwavering commitment to the truth. On the other, the same authors refer to Machiavelli's "secret" methods of writing, saying that he was "forced to hide" his commitment to freedom. Gentili remarks, paradoxically, that Machiavelli "makes all his secrets clear" to readers who recognize the subtle signs he gives pointing to his true intentions. Rousseau notes that Machiavelli's "choice of his execrable Hero," the corrupt, self-promoting Prince, "is in itself enough to make manifest his hidden intention." If the *Prince* has usually been taken at face value, Rousseau continues, this proves merely that "this profound political thinker has had only superficial or corrupt readers until now."[2] By crafting appearances that are not what they seem, Machiavelli was able to convey truths that he could not have expressed openly at the time, or that would not have been believed sincere if he had done so. Under color of seeking to advise princes to act in unprincipled ways, the *Prince* uses indirect methods of writing to teach "lessons" that can help peoples better to defend themselves against corruption.

One reason why these philosophers were unmystified by Machiavelli's truthful-yet-opaque modes of writing is that they were familiar with, and sometimes imitated, ancient literary techniques and genres that inspired Machiavelli's. Most of these styles have roots in ancient Greek writings, particularly those of Socratic writers such as Xenophon, Plato, and Plutarch, or in Thucydides. Until we have a fuller account of Machiavelli's ancient sources, Machiavelli's affinities with other humanist writers such as Bruni may be overestimated, while his affinities with earlier philosophers whose ideas he tries to renovate go unrecognized. Each of the following

---

[1] By this I mean men who wrote independently of any princely or monarchical court or papal authority. On Machiavelli's collisions with "the court of Rome" see Neville 1691 and Rousseau 1964 (1762), III.5–6 n. 1.

[2] Rousseau 1964 (1762), III.5–6 n. 1.

sections examines an ancient text, genre, or method of writing that Machiavelli alludes to in his works, and that provides clues to how these should be read.

2.1.
Constructive dissimulation: Writing as civil "medicine"

A central aim of all Machiavelli's writings is to instruct readers how to see through misleading political appearances—not, as is sometimes thought, how to construct them. He observes in the *Discourses* that "many times, deceived by a false image of good, the people desires its own ruin; and if it is not made aware that that is bad and what the good is . . . infinite dangers and harms are brought into republics." Easily impressed by *onesto* words and promises of quick results, people will often support a policy that "appears spirited, even though there is the ruin of the republic concealed underneath."[3] Machiavelli does not distinguish sharply between ordinary people who are incapable of recognizing these dangers and wise elites who know better. In the *Prince* we read that "the vulgar are taken in by the appearance and outcome of a thing, and in the world there is no one but the vulgar." The statement mimics the opinion of self-styled wise men who regard "the many" with contempt, seeing them as gullible consumers of false appearances. If, however, there is no one in the world but the vulgar, those men who consider themselves wise are no more immune to deceptions than the coarse multitude.[4] Everyone, Machiavelli implies, should be wary of being taken in by good political appearances, and arm themselves against their seductions. However shrewd they may be in their other fields of activity, most citizens have to evaluate "great" actions from a distance, without the detailed information they would need to judge well. This often leads them to judge badly, since opinions often "from a distance appear true" that on closer scrutiny prove "altogether alien from the truth." And "the generality of men feed on what appears as much as on what is; indeed, many times men are moved more by things that appear than by things that are [*le cose che paioni che per quelle che sono*]."[5]

Clearly there is no way to put a stop to *disonesto* speech, short of silencing everyone who is not godlike and incorruptible. All cities are made by and for human beings; human beings must use speech to constitute and run their cities; and no human being or mode of speech is immune to corruption. The *Florentine Histories* present a first-best remedy: to find prudent citizens and leaders who use transparent reasoning to point out the hidden dangers behind good words and appearances, helping others to judge policies more carefully. But some times are so corrupt that direct modes of reasoning go unheeded, with anyone who appears honest held in particular mistrust. This leaves honest men two choices: either to opt out of civil life altogether, or to find unusual ways to reason with fellow citizens and leaders.

---

[3] *D*, I.53.105/305–6; see also II.22.179–81/385–87.
[4] *P*, XVIII.71/167.
[5] *D*, II.22.180/385–86; I.25.60/257.

In works where he chooses the second, Machiavelli was able to draw on a rich repertoire of ancient models. Many of these used what Roman writers called dissimulation (*dissimulatio*) and Greeks irony (*eirōneia*), understood as a form of concealment that differs from both deception and secrecy. Secrecy involves hiding without providing any access to one's intentions or qualities. Deception involves the attempt to persuade others that one's intentions or qualities are altogether different from what they truly are. By contrast, dissimulation conceals some intentions and qualities while revealing others in indirect ways. As Francis Bacon put it, deception or "simulation" occurs "when a man industriously and expressly feigns and pretends" to be other than he is; dissimulation occurs "when a man lets fall signs and arguments, that he is not that [which] he is" or appears. Used judiciously, Bacon argues, dissimulation can be a valuable means of helping people to see through falsehoods and deceptions.[6] Prodded by subtle "signs and arguments" to notice the true qualities or judgments that a dissimulation conceals from full view, the attentive can pick up the clues and try to interpret the dissimulator's true purposes for themselves. This kind of interpretation gives them training in critical observation, since they must work hard to spot the scattered "signs" and piece them together in a coherent account of the person or argument that remains concealed beneath very different appearances. Ancient writers such as Xenophon, Plato, Aristotle, and Plutarch used dissimulation as an important tool of moral and political education. Its main purpose was to develop capacities for independent, reasoned judgment, especially by teaching boys and practical men how to distinguish appearances of virtue or wisdom from qualities that deserve those names. By reading works that "imitate" the misleading appearances seen in the public realm, attentive readers learn how these phenomena are generated, and thus become better equipped to avoid traps set for them by demagogues.[7]

Of course, dissimulation may have other aims than to teach people to be sharper judges of appearances. It may be used for comedic purposes, to make people laugh when they recognize the gap between what is said or shown and the real qualities obliquely exposed. It may be used to mock one's subject, or to provoke an antagonist.[8] These uses of dissimulation presuppose that an audience already has a fairly clear notion of the truth beneath the appearance, so that, say, a portrayal of a man reputed to be corrupt as a law-abiding citizen is readily recognized as ironic. More opaque forms of dissimulation assume that an audience has either a false or deeply flawed idea about a subject, or no clear preconceptions about it at all, so that they must form their views with the help of the dissimulating account. In such cases dissimulation may have two main purposes. One involves a large element of secrecy: to disguise a speaker's or writer's intentions from most of his audience, while communicating it indirectly through "signs and arguments" to a few. The other is non-esoteric and philosophical. It aims to provoke anyone attentive enough to

---

[6] Bacon 1985 (1597–1625), 76–78. Compare Bacon 2001 (1605), 193–94, where dissimulation and counterdissimulation are described as means to "tell a lie and find a truth."

[7] See chap. 5, sec. 5.6. on foxes and snares.

[8] See Vlastos 1991, 21–44.

pick up the clues to exercise his capacities for judgment, especially moral and political judgment. Many examples of the first can be found among writers critical of the Roman Empire, and in other periods when writers could be persecuted for expressing political or religious dissent.[9] The second, more philosophical forms of dissimulation were developed in Athens, especially after the Peloponnesian War, in conditions that their authors regarded as extremely corrupt but not so oppressive that they were forced into secrecy. The sentencing of Socrates to death alerted his students Xenophon and Plato to the risks of free speech even in their democracy. But it did not prevent them from writing down their own accounts of this grave injustice; and their highly creative uses of ironic dissimulation are designed not to disguise the truth from all but a select few, but to encourage any receptive reader to reflect philosophically on first appearances or his own opinions.[10]

Two of Machiavelli's favorite ancient writers, Polybius and Plutarch, were Greeks who wrote under constraints of censorship in the Roman Empire but whom authorities regarded as loyal. Both combine an element of esoteric dissimulation with the aim of stimulating critical reflections among a wide audience. Aware of official constraints, they take care to conceal direct criticisms of the empire and to avoid provoking offense. Readers will more readily recognize elements of double-writing in some of Plutarch's *Lives* and essays if they are familiar with "signs and arguments," key words and topoi, that are characteristic of earlier Greek forms of dissimulation. Plutarch was not, however, secretly addressing only the most educated Greeks or critical Romans and provincials who read Greek. While such readers were most likely to recognize subtly critical elements in his writings, Plutarch's aim is neither to identify an elite of like-minded men nor to stir up dissent behind innocuous appearances. He sometimes dissimulates in order to avoid offending the authorities, but his more important purpose is to urge as many readers as possible, particularly among the young, to arm themselves with the most basic skills needed for civil life. These were not skills in producing good appearances through rhetoric, as the so-called *sophistēs* taught, but skills in seeing through spurious appearances and resisting their appeal.[11] Such aims transcended the specific context of Plutarch's writings. They served the general purpose of urging people to adopt a more reflective approach to civil life, whatever form of government they happened to live under and whatever prospects they might have of engaging directly in politics. The interpretation proposed in this study holds that all Machiavelli's political writings, including the *Prince*, dissimulate in similar ways for similar purposes. On the one

---

[9] Roman examples include Sallust and Tacitus: see chap. 3. Also see Strauss 1952 on diverse traditions of "esoteric" writing.

[10] The Socratic and Platonic solution to the problem of people being taken in by appearances is not, though it is often taken to be, rule of knowledgeable philosophical elites. In the *Republic*, *Statesman*, and *Laws* the ideal of elite rule of experts is advanced early on only to be greatly complicated later in the dialogues; see chap. 11, sec. 11.4.

[11] Plutarch ("Precepts," PM, X.172–75) warns men in power not to rely too much on appearances, since "the people see through the characters, counsels, acts, and lives of public men, even those that seem to be very thickly cloaked." When addressing ordinary citizens, however, he does not take their immunity from deception for granted, but urges them to seek continuous exercise in seeing through it.

hand, Machiavelli was "forced," as Rousseau says, "to disguise his love of freedom" and his view that the Medici party had long been thoroughly corrupt. On the other hand, he also sought to teach "great lessons to peoples," not just to a select group of wise readers or to Italian contemporaries.[12] His purposes in dissimulating seem less arcane or idiosyncratic when they are examined against the backdrop of Greek antecedents, whether composed under the Roman Empire or before.

Paradoxically, Plutarch treats dissimulation as one means of practicing "frankness" (*parrēsian*) toward people one regards in a friendly way. In his essay "How to Tell a Flatterer from a Friend" he argues that since only good things are sought for one's friends, they should be addressed in ways that aim to help and not to harm them. But what gives pleasure is not always helpful, whereas unpleasant truths often are. Friends do not recommend whatever gives pleasure, but only the best things. This raises a problem about the most efficacious means to good ends: how can salutary but unpleasant truths be conveyed to a friend without injuring his pride, shattering beliefs he finds comfortable and familiar, or turning him against the speaker, thereby defeating the latter's persuasive intentions? Plutarch's answer is that since people may not want to hear harsh truths, friendly interlocutors must find oblique, diplomatic ways to convey them while showing respect for their independent judgment. Forms of address that fail to do this, such as haranguing, threatening, or talking-down, are less respectful and less effective ways of revealing what the speaker takes to be true. If a speaker or writer wants a friend "who tells the truth as I do," he should also want one who "decides for himself as I do" instead of depending wholly on his friend's judgment. Plutarchian "frankness" allows for different degrees of what might be called constructive dissimulation, which are particularly valuable for addressing men in power.[13] The essay itself exemplifies the diplomatic frankness it advocates. It seems to be an apolitical piece about private friendship, but drops hints that it is also concerned with questions about political engagement where freedom of speech is constrained.

Plutarch acknowledges that dissimulative writing is often taken at face value or misinterpreted. When this happens, unphilosophical readers may blame the writers for the corrupt or dangerous views that they describe. They should rather, Plutarch argues, ask themselves whether they have tried hard enough to understand his meaning. But since it can be very difficult indeed to identify a writer's own views among the half-truths, unreflective opinions, and outright lies in his writings, how can readers trust their own abilities to differentiate the one from the other? While there is no simple formula for getting it right, Plutarch does offer some helpful pointers on how to read texts that give signs of dissimulating. His essay "How a Young Man Should Study Poetry" recommends using poetry as "an introductory exercise in philosophy." To begin with, readers should give a writer

---

[12] I agree with Strauss (1958, 297) that disguising intentions for safety was part of Machiavelli's purpose, but not that he sought to select a knowledgeable ruling elite through his "subtle rhetoric." The second aim outlined here, as recognized by earlier philosophical readers, better captures his fundamental purposes.

[13] Plutarch, "Flatterer," PM, I.276–87.

the benefit of the doubt. They should presume that his judgments are generally consistent and reasonable, instead of leaping to criticize every apparent inconsistency, or assuming that distasteful or violently expressed opinions must represent the author's own views. Careful distinctions should be made between the judgments portrayed in a text and the judgments of the poet, whose own views are not necessarily those he describes. Poetry, Plutarch observes, "often gives an imitative recital of base deeds, or of wicked experiences and characters" without openly describing them as bad. Listeners should "not accept as true what is admired and successful" in the literary account. Instead they should simply recognize that it is fitting for the "base" characters portrayed to see bad deeds as good, because their values and evaluative language are debased. It is unreasonable to blame writers who portray such unpleasant subjects, or to assume that they wish to promote base values. Readers should "commend the faculty and art which imitates these things," often with the aim of helping readers to judge them more prudently for themselves. They should "repudiate and condemn" not the writer but "the disposition and the actions" imitated in his work. If readers are not altogether corrupted, the very vileness of certain actions or words should arouse suspicion that discredits them, and alert the audience to the writer's critical intentions.[14]

Moreover, as soon as readers notice signs that a text contains dissimulation, they should sharpen up their senses and pay close attention to what they read, since judgments are "given silently" in such writings rather than spelled out. Plutarch offers a variety of suggestions on how to read between the lines. If a text seems to put forward an opinion that readers find shocking, they should consider whether the author writes something "to the opposite effect" elsewhere that "nullifies the effect" of the first statement. Sometimes authors pose particularly hard puzzles by asserting an "unjustifiable saying" (tōn atopōs eipēmenōn) that they never explicitly contradict elsewhere. If they encounter such sayings, readers should look for hints that the author is silently opposing this assertion to a better argument by some other writer, whether named or unnamed; and then readers should presume that the present author prefers the more reasonable argument. The "means for rectifying a statement" that sounds preposterous or unjust can often be found "in words that lie near, or by the context." If a word or phrase placed alongside another "blunts the point which the passage, in its worse interpretation, would have," readers should "seize upon it" and ask if the writer really believes the bad words he writes. Plays on ambivalent meanings of words are one of the principal methods of dissimulation used by poets and philosophers. Ambivalence "works through the normal usage of words," so that readers must constantly ask themselves whether a writer is using a given word in one sense or another. Sometimes the difference is between literal and metaphorical meanings, as when "hunting" refers literally to the pursuit of wild game but metaphorically to chasing away tyrants or pursuing philosophical truths.[15] In these cases both sets of meanings may point equally to truths, albeit different kinds. Alternatively, the same word may be used to express meanings that

[14] Plutarch, "How a Young Man Should Study Poetry," PM, I.74–113.
[15] See chap. 3, sec. 3.4.

are more or less true or adequate. "Virtue" may be understood as "repute and influence" or as whatever qualities render men just and good; "happiness" as influence,
wealth, and repute, or as "complete possession or attainment of good." When a text
that contains signs of dissimulating seems to define a word in the less adequate
sense, readers should "transfer from the worse to the better sense" in a "suspicious
passage" and presume that this substitution conveys the writer's own views.[16]

Plutarch's advice to readers applies as much to biographical and historical writing as to Homer and Pindar. It calls into question one-dimensional readings of
well-known texts by Greek writers who were masters of constructive dissimulation. One glaring example, as the next section shows, is Xenophon's portrait of
Cyrus, a work whose reputation has long suffered from commentators who read
it as a straightforward defense of monarchy or a portrait of the "ideal prince."[17]
Plutarch's remarks explain why and how a writer who wishes to expose the faults
in his subject might appear to do nothing but praise it. A biography of a famous
man may be dominated by overt praise for his virtues, yet also describe deeds
whose harmful effects emerge in the narrative. Though the deeds are not openly
criticized, careful readers will detect the difference between good words used to
express sound judgments and the same words used to color base conduct.[18]

Their familiarity with Plutarch, Xenophon, and other masters of philosophical
dissimulation may help to explain why readers such as Gentili, Bacon, Neville,
Spinoza, and Rousseau rejected the view of Machiavelli's *Prince* as an amoral treatise for princes. Machiavelli himself frankly admitted that he practiced dissimulation. "For a long time," he wrote to Guicciardini, "I have not said what I believed,
nor do I ever believe what I say, and if indeed I do happen to tell the truth, I hide it
among so many lies that it is hard to find." He describes himself here as "a doctor
of this art" of lying while telling the truth.[19] One reason for perfecting the art of
dissimulation is suggested in a letter written while he was completing the *Florentine Histories*: the need to avoid offending suspicious authorities in conditions of
limited freedom. "Here in the country I have been applying myself . . . to writing
the history," Machiavelli writes, again to Guicciardini,

> and I would pay ten *soldi*—but no more—to have you by my side so that I
> might show you where I am, because, since I am about to come to certain
> details, I would need to learn from you whether or not I am being too offen-
> sive in my exaggerating or understating of the facts [*le cose*]. Nevertheless,

[16] On the meanings of virtue and happiness, see Plutarch, "Poetry," PM, I.126–33; on virtue opposed
to fortune, "On the Fortune or the Virtue of Alexander," PM, IV.476–77.

[17] For a useful discussion of the debates, see Nadon 2001, 1–13.

[18] Plutarch ("Poetry," PM, I.96–105) distinguishes between what one learns from (*a*) a text or oral
poetry and (*b*) actions and "declarations or opinions." Several of Plutarch's own works may be read as
exercises designed to equip readers to recognize signs of corruption behind deceptively good appearances. His essay "Fortune of Alexander" (PM, IV.398–485) seems to praise the great conqueror unreser-
vedly, but overt praise is subtly interwoven with critical analysis. Plutarch sometimes does the contrary:
he seems to criticize a subject while praising deeds "between the lines," notably in his *Life* of Nicias, the
Athenian general who tried to oppose Athens' assault on Sicily during the Peloponnesian War.

[19] Machiavelli to Guicciardini, 17 May 1521, MF, 336–37/372–73.

I shall continue to seek advice from myself, and I shall try to do my best to arrange it so that—still telling the truth—no one will have anything to complain about.[20]

Although Machiavelli nowhere describes this mode of writing as *dissimulazione*, his correspondence often mentions his own use of signs (*cenni*), codes (*cifra*), ambivalence, and other techniques of dissimulative writing in his political works and plays.[21] While he sometimes states that political oppression forced him to write in this way, his letters also point to a different, more constructive reason to dissimulate: to teach people "the way to hell" so that they may learn to avoid it. His writing often mimics the unreflective or corrupt opinions or maxims that lead people to embrace self-destructive policies, thus creating their own political hell by their own unforced choices. By seeming to endorse these opinions while "letting drop" arguments that hint at their shortcomings, Machiavelli tries to provoke readers into recognizing the errors for themselves, ensuring that they work harder to avoid them in future.

In these respects Machiavelli's methods and aims have clear precursors in the Greek writings he cites in various works. He frequently echoes a Socratic metaphor that identifies philosophical discourse with medicine for corrupt souls and cities, and calls for a "physician" who can introduce it.[22] As later chapters argue, while the medicine he has in mind includes stronger "arms," Machiavelli's *armi* are never only military; and not just any strongman prince can satisfy his standards of a good physician.[23] One of the indispensable foundations (*fondamenti*) of good republican or princely arms is the ability to "recognize snares" and resist the appeal of misleading appearances.[24] Writings that dissimulate about politics can serve as a valuable medicine for those who need to build up better defenses. If readers recognize the dissimulation, and if their judgment has not been so corrupted by the times that they misinterpret the writer's intentions, such writing can help to purge readers of flawed opinions while pointing the way toward sounder judgments. It is also a more effective means of inoculating them against further errors. This is because the purgative is not thrust on readers by a writer who claims to be wiser than they. It is introduced through modes of writing that imitate "discourses" between friends, and must ultimately be accepted and self-administered by individual readers.

---

[20] Machiavelli to Guicciardini, 30 August 1524, *MF*, 351/389.

[21] For direct references to Machiavelli's and his friends' use of codes in their personal correspondence, see *MF*, 51–53, 365, 393–95, 398. Also see *AW*, VII.123–33.

[22] Plutarch ("On Listening," *PM*, I.204–9, 229, 211) describes philosophical speech acts as "pungent discourse" that purges harmful emotions and opinions. Philosophical purging is not forced on patients, but offered to them to administer by themselves in their own time and according to their own reasonings.

[23] The language of physicians and purging recurs throughout Machiavelli's works. For example, see *D*, I.Pref., I.14, I.39, II.5, III.1, III.49, noting how the theme frames the beginning and end of Book III; *P*, III.8, 12, VII.30, XIII.57; *AW*, I.94. Compare *TPW*, VI.14; Plato, *Gorg.* 500e–501c, 517d–522e. On Thucydides' and Plato's application of medical analogies to moral and political disorders see Moes 2007, esp. 62–68.

[24] See chap. 5, sec. 5.6.

Machiavelli's dissimulations are well suited to the delicate task of setting out harsh truths to agents who are both corruptible and free. Readers who simply take a writer's own judgments as authoritative, while lacking an independently reasoned account of why they should be, will remain susceptible to any writer and speaker who appears to know more than they do. A city full of such passive readers will lack one of the fundamental components of good "arms." Untrained in independent, critical judgment, its citizens become easy prey to bad persuasions, partisan discords, and tyrants. Athenian writers such as Thucydides, Xenophon, and Plato understood this danger well. Their works generally avoid stating their own reflective judgments, instead presenting different opinions for readers to examine for themselves.[25] Machiavelli, as I will try to show, adopts these ancient models of writing for similar reasons.

2.2.
Inoculation for citizens: Words and deeds in Xenophon's *Cyropaedia*

The contrast between decent words and less decent deeds is a recurrent theme in Greek writing. Thucydides evokes it throughout his history of the Peloponnesian Wars to explain how his Athenian contemporaries' political and military judgments were corrupted by excessive ambition, arrogance, and self-congratulatory rhetoric.[26] Plutarch cites Thucydides in the essay "How to Tell a Flatterer from a Friend," suggesting that the great historian offers important philosophical and ethical lessons for posterity. Thucydides casts a harsh light on one of the main symptoms of civil disorder: the tendency to invest vice with the names that belong to virtue. Amid factions and wars, Thucydides says, "they changed the commonly accepted meaning of words when applied to deeds [*tēn eiōthuian axiōsin tōn onomaton es ta erga*] as they thought proper. Reckless daring [*tolma . . . alogistos*] came to be regarded as devoted courage [*andreia philetairos*], watchful waiting as specious cowardice, moderation [*sōphron*] as the craven's pretext [*tou anandrou prochēma*], a keen understanding [*pros apan suneton*] . . . as want of energy to undertake anything [*epi pān argon*]."[27]

The lesson to be drawn from this, Plutarch concludes, is that "we should be observant and on our guard against prodigality being called 'liberality' [*asōtian—eleutheriotēta*], cowardice 'self-preservation' [*deilian—asphaleian*] . . . frivolous talk 'wise moderation' [*mikrologian—sōphrosunēn*] . . . the irascible and arrogant 'spirited' [*orgilon kai huperēphanon—andreion*] the insignificant and weak 'humane' [*eutelē kai tapeinon—philanthrōpon*]." Such misuses of good words "accustom a man to treat vices as virtues, so that he feels not disgusted with them but delighted, which also takes away all shame for his errors." The corruption of ethical language starts as a symptom of corrupt practices, but may also become a contributing cause

---

[25] Following Plato, Plutarch ("Precepts," PM, X.180–83) argues that dialogical methods are the appropriate means of persuasion for free people as opposed to a mob.

[26] See sec. 2.5.

[27] Compare e.g. Plato, *Rep.* 560e–561a.

of civil disasters. It brought disaster to the people of Sicily, Plutarch argues, because they misidentified the savage cruelty of its tyrants as a laudable "hatred for wicked-ness." It ruined Egypt because people were unable to distinguish genuine "piety" and "devotion to the gods" from Ptolemy's religious mania. Finally, it "subverted and destroyed the character [*ēthē*] of the Romans" because, by growing accustomed to call Antony's luxuriousness and excesses *philanthrōpia* (humanity), the proper sense of that word was forgotten. Those whose actions conformed to its corrupt uses were praised, while anyone who attempted to show proper respect for human-ity was mocked or mistrusted.[28]

Close readers of Plutarch and Thucydides encounter numerous examples where deeds that cause grave civil disorders are colored with good words—sometimes by a particular character in a speech, sometimes by a narrative voice that seems to be the author's own. As Plutarch explains, the tension between words that praise and deeds that condemn one and the same act is supposed to provoke readers to reexamine their own judgments about what constitutes praiseworthy conduct. His aim and, he suggests, that of Thucydides, Plato, and other philosophical writers is to forearm citizens against all-too-common misuses of language that corrupt practical judgment. By learning to spot tensions between writer's words of praise for a character and the deeds he ascribes to him, readers may develop their pow-ers of independent judgment, and train themselves to avoid traps similar to those encountered in much political speech.

One of the most finely crafted examples of a text that dissimulates in order to educate citizens is Xenophon's *Cyropaedia*. After Livy's histories, Machiavelli di-rectly cites the *Cyropaedia* more than any other ancient work.[29] On a casual read-ing, Xenophon's portrait of the Persian prince appears as an unqualified ideal. He seems to present Cyrus as a model monarch who displays all the qualities that kings in all times and places should imitate.[30] According to the *Cyropaedia*, Cyrus' supreme achievements were, first, to gain the obedience of subjects throughout his vast empire by means of persuasion rather than violence; second, to order an effective army out of men taken from diverse countries; and finally, to acquire extremely loyal associates in his court and wider empire. His subjects "were so devoted to him that those of every nation [*ethnos*] believed that they did them-selves an injury if they did not send to Cyrus the most valuable productions of their country"; and "every private individual thought he should become a rich man if he should do something to please Cyrus."[31] On closer scrutiny, however,

[28] Plutarch, "Flatterer," PM, I.300–305. In the *Prince* Machiavelli refers to many of the same "vir-tues," telling princes to avoid those that are widely praised—such as liberality and mercy—and boldly adopt "modes" that are called vices in corrupt times. See esp. chaps. 5, 9, 11.

[29] The *Prince* mentions Cyrus in four chapters, the *Discourses* in five. It is usually stated or appar-ent that Machiavelli's source is Xenophon's *Cyropaedia*. On the *Prince*'s relation to the *Cyropaedia* see Strauss 1958, 59, 161–63, 291–92; and de Alvarez 1999, 69–70.

[30] For example, see the "Introduction" to the text in XC and debates discussed in Nadon 2001 and Due 1989.

[31] XC, I.106–7; II.318–19; VIII.420–21.

Xenophon's account of the means Cyrus used to gain such popularity raises doubts about whether he deserves unqualified praise.

Xenophon tells us, for example, that Cyrus "held the opinion [*dokoumen*] that a ruler ought to excel his subjects not only in point of being actually better than they, but that he ought also to cast a sort of spell on them." Outward appearances, particularly the use of clothing in the extravagantly regal style of the neighboring Medes, were among his chief means of entrancing subjects. For Cyrus "thought that if anyone had any personal defect, that dress would help to conceal it." He also encouraged "the fashion of pencilling the eyes, that they might seem more lustrous than they are, and of using cosmetics to make the complexion look better than nature made it," so that he and his closest associates appeared to their subjects as superior beings. Even as a youth Cyrus perceived that "nothing is more effectual toward keeping one's men obedient than to seem wiser than they," and thus sought to acquire a "reputation" (*doxan*) for wisdom by whatever means best succeeded in doing so.[32]

Some readers might be tempted to play down the potential for corruption inherent in these methods because to his own close associates, at least, Cyrus is disarmingly frank about his own human weaknesses. He does not insist that he must be superior to everyone else in the ways that gods are superior to men; his superiority remains that of one man in relation to others.[33] Readers might well ask, however, whether Cyrus is not prone to err in the other direction: instead of demanding more of himself than is proper for a human being, he sometimes demands too little. His specific admissions of human frailty betray self-indulgence, one of the greatest failings in Socratic ethics. Blaming the gods for giving him passions that often stand in need of self-discipline, he admits that he does not trouble to set limits on them. For example, when discussing "the passion for wealth which the gods have put into the human soul" Cyrus admits that he is "as insatiate as other people" and, following the lead of the gods, "always grasping for more." He tries to extenuate this admitted shortcoming by pointing out that he uses his wealth to enrich others, winning their friendship and loyalty and reaping as his reward "security and good fame" (*asphaleian kai eukleian*). Cyrus therefore speaks truly enough when, approaching death, he thanks the gods that "in my successes [*epi tais eutuchais*, lit. "good fortune"]" he never "entertained proud thoughts transcending human bounds [*oudepōpote . . . huper anthrōpon ephronēsa*]."[34] The question silently posed to readers is whether he allowed his god-given weaknesses more free rein than is proper for men who deserve to be called virtuous, thus lowering kingly and human standards in corrupting ways.

The same question arises with respect to Cyrus' methods of courting goodwill. Since the obedience of his soldiers and loyalty of political associates is unforced, it might appear more stable than obedience shown to tyrants who use more violent methods. But Xenophon's descriptions of Cyrus' alternative methods raise doubts about whether they could form the basis for durable order. One method

---

[32] XC, VIII.324–25; I.108–9.
[33] Unlike Plutarch's Alexander in "Fortune."
[34] XC, VIII.342–43, 422–33.

is to make sure that powerful men were "better friends to himself than to one another."[35] Another is to show at all times great *philanthrōpia*, translated here as "kindness of heart" but better rendered as "humanity."[36] The main expression of Cyrus' *philanthrōpia* is to do favors for whomever he wanted as a supporter, often "through gifts of money," honoring supporters with presents in the belief that "this would implant in them a certain amount of good will, just as it does in dogs." Xenophon "praises" Cyrus for far surpassing all others in every "way of courting favor"; indeed he says that it was Cyrus "who began the practice of lavish giving [*poludōria*]" among seekers after political power, which "among the kings . . . continues even to this day." This conduct explains why no one before Cyrus "ever gained an empire [*archē*] by conquest," and why even to his death he "was called 'father' by the people he had subdued." Still more questionably, Cyrus "acquired the so-called 'king's eyes' and 'king's ears' in no other way than by bestowing presents and honors" on partisans. By "rewarding liberally those who reported to him whatever it was to his interest to hear," he encouraged the growth of informal surveillance networks, prompting "many men to make it their business to use their eyes and ears to spy out what they could report to the king to his advantage." As a result, Xenophon observes, "the people are afraid everywhere to say anything to the discredit of the king, just as if he were listening."[37] The initial distinction between force and persuasion turns out to be too sharp to make appropriately nuanced judgments about these methods of government. Persuasion, it seems, may appeal to the judgment of free men; conversely, it may involve intimidation, or manipulative actions that reduce men to the status of domestic animals. Xenophon does not spell out these distinctions, but leaves it to his readers to pick up the "signs and arguments" that reveal less attractive aspects of Cyrus' rule.

   These undertones indirectly call into question the appearances of virtue behind the model prince. Cyrus' methods of rule magnify his own fame and temporarily increase Persia's empire. But they also erode the rule of law, produce an atmosphere of fear, and corrupt the moral virtues that Xenophon ascribes to Persia before Cyrus' reign.[38] In the course of the narrative he introduces characters who appear to have benefited from Cyrus' generous "humanity." Some express a longing, however, to live again as free men unburdened by the wealth they have gained in exchange for doglike obedience.[39] Near the end of the work one of Cyrus' close friends remarks that he used to think that the king surpassed all other men in military matters; but now he swears by the gods that he seems to excel even more in *philanthrōpia* than in generalship.[40] Since by now the good word *philanthrōpia*

---

[35] XC, VIII.328–29.

[36] Latin *humanitas*.

[37] XC, VIII.330–39.

[38] Before Cyrus, Persia is portrayed as a disciplined, warlike, law-abiding polity and contrasted with Media as corrupt, effeminate, and depending on the personal rule of kings instead of the rule of law.

[39] For example, see XC, VIII.362–75.

[40] XC, VIII.378–79. The critical point is underlined by accounts of Cyrus' military dealings; in contrast to earlier accounts of his brilliant battlefield strategies and diplomacy, these now consist mainly in distributing spoils of war among soldiers and partisans.

has quietly been shown to be corrupt in Cyrus' new Persia, a near-synonym for buying obedience with gifts and bribes, the friend's words are poor praise indeed. Close to death, Cyrus declares that "as far as I know, there is nothing that I ever attempted or desired and yet failed to secure [*out' epicheirēsas out' epithumēsas oida hotou ētuchēsa*]."[41] The word translated here as "to secure" is derived from the verb *tugchanō*, to chance or hit upon; it connotes an achievement or acquisition based on fortune (*tuchē*) rather than on careful planning or hard effort. Events after Cyrus' death show that he while he may have "secured" friends and empire for himself, he failed to secure good order or empire that would last beyond his own life. His realm was governed by the "single will" of Cyrus, who treated his subjects "as if they were his own children" or domestic animals, and foreign countries as game to be "hunted."[42] As soon as he died "his children at once fell into dissension, cities and peoples began to revolt, and everything began to deteriorate [*poleis kai ethnē aphistanto, panta d' epi to cheirōn etrepeto*]."[43]

Xenophon hints that this unhappy outcome can be explained by Cyrus' deviations from the sound religious teachings (*didaskōn ek tōn theiōn*) he received as a youth, in accordance with Persian custom. The ethics taught in Xenophon's ostensibly Persian system of education are quintessentially Socratic. Transparency and trust are presented as fundamental tenets of Persian morals, and as necessary foundations of stable government. Near the end of the *Cyropaedia* Xenophon tells us that in "early times" Persian kings and their officers, "in their dealings with even the worst offenders, would abide by any oath [*horkos*] that they might have given, and be true to any pledge that they might have made." Had they not done this, "not a man would have trusted them, just as not a single person any longer trusts them, now that their lack of character is notorious." The *Cyropaedia*'s chief spokesman for these good precepts is Cyrus' father, Cambyses, portrayed here as the last truly upright Persian king. After his son has made great conquests, Cambyses warns him not to become "puffed up by your present successes and attempt to govern the Persians as you do those other nations" such as the Medes, with the informal methods of control described earlier. He urges Cyrus to rely on covenants and oaths to keep good order, as his ancestors did to good effect.[44] While Xenophon does not say that Cyrus actually violated oaths himself, he does imply that by placing personal loyalty based on financial inducements ahead of principled commitments, his methods undermined the "attitudes" needed to maintain respect for oaths and formal agreements.[45] Cyrus' conduct paved the way for his successors to show open contempt for oaths, especially in foreign relations. Xenophon recalls the hapless Greeks who, "trusting in the previous reputation of the Persian kings" and sharing Cambyses' old-fashioned confidence in oaths,

[41] XC, VIII.424–25.
[42] See chap. 3, sec. 3.4.
[43] XC, VIII.438–41;V.106–9.
[44] XC, VIII.440–41, 406–9. Machiavelli has Cosimo de' Medici's father Giovanni give similar prudent advice in the *FH*.
[45] This, I will argue, is one of Machiavelli's central arguments; see chaps. 8–9.

went in good faith to negotiate with Cyrus the younger "and had their heads cut off," contrary to all the customary norms of Persia and other civilized countries. While Cyrus' own conduct stopped far short of such excesses, it is partly responsible for the erosion of ancient religion.[46] "For whatever the character of the rulers is," Xenophon writes, "such also that of the people under them for the most part becomes"; and "in this respect they are now even more unprincipled than before" Cyrus' time.

Without directly criticizing his princely subject, Xenophon does let drop suggestions that Cyrus' undoubted virtues were mixed with disturbing tendencies. As a child he is described as "most generous of heart [*philanthrōpotatos*], most devoted to learning [*philomathestatos*], and most ambitious [*philotimotatos*], so that he endured all sorts of labor and faced all sorts of danger for the sake of praise." He also shows an early tendency to claim more than his share (*pleonexia*) in praise and in power. Xenophon illustrates this disposition by describing the young Cyrus' attitude to hunting, an activity central to "Persian" education and strictly regulated by "Persian" laws. Ignoring all the careful teaching he receives about what animals should or should not be approached, Cyrus is unable to stop himself from wanting to hunt all kinds of game without distinction. Once in the heat of the chase, he loses all self-restraint and becomes "reckless," soon exhausting the supply of animals in his father's park. Although Cyrus learns to discipline himself in other respects as he grows older, he never ceases to indulge his vast appetite for hunting. He soon turns to a different sort of game: foreign lands, kings, and peoples that he seeks to domesticate for no purpose except to gratify his desire for praise and power.[47] Xenophon connects *pleonexia* and *philotimia* (ambition) to another corrupting disposition shown by Cyrus as a boy: a tendency to subordinate standards of justice to instrumental judgments about what actions are most likely to bring success. Cambyses frequently urges his son to give principled respect to the gods and the laws, not wavering when he thinks that he will gain less by acting according to duty. Cyrus' replies seem to agree with this traditional Persian teaching. Yet his reason for agreeing is not that the gods, laws, and other people deserve respect, or that such respect is a necessary condition for well-ordered civil life. It is that by conforming to his father's principles—or seeming to—he might be able to increase his own influence over gods and men. When Cambyses urges his son to understand and obey the counsels of the gods, Cyrus replies that he will do so in order that the gods may help him and that he might be more likely to "have power with the gods, even as with men." Cambyses expresses awe before the counsels of the gods; Cyrus expresses a familiarity with them, and a belief that he can use their commands for his own advantage, that borders on *hubris*.[48]

The *Cyropaedia* begins by reflecting on how most men who are disposed to tyranny (*turannidos*) have "been deposed once and for all and that right quickly." The few who remain in power even for a short time become "objects of wonder

---

[46] Compare the critical remarks on Cyrus' legacy in Plato, *Laws* 694a–695a.

[47] XC, I.10–11, 48–59.

[48] XC, I.89–91.

as having proved to be wise and fortunate [*sofoi . . . kai eutucheis*] men."[49] Since Cyrus' qualities made him happy, fortunate, and more loved than hated throughout his life, it might be thought that his flaws were remote from the dispositions that lead to tyranny. But a closer examination suggests otherwise. Xenophon hints that *pleonexia*, the demand for more than one's share, and the related tendency to place one's own advantage above respect for laws are precisely the dispositions that lead to tyranny.[50] If tyranny is "the government of unwilling subjects and not controlled by laws but imposed by the will of the ruler," then Cyrus himself did not become a full-blown tyrant insofar as his subjects willingly embraced his rule.[51] But the lines between his methods of princely rule and those of tyrants are very fine indeed, and his conduct lowered standards so that his successors crossed the lines more brazenly.[52] When painted in subtle and attractive colors, most of a prince's subjects—and most readers of the *Cyropaedia*—may not notice the hidden dangers. Whoever does recognize the warning signs scattered throughout the narrative will not fall into the error of reading Xenophon's work as a naïve "romance" of the "ideal prince," let alone as praise for monarchy. Perceptive readers in Machiavelli's time and after recognized the work's skillful dissimulations, and understood its educational purpose: to train readers to scrutinize men and actions that appear impeccably decent, so that they may better defend their own and their cities' freedom.[53]

Plutarch criticizes those who admire "Plato and Xenophon for their language . . . but have no desire for their sedative and purgative virtues, nor the power to discern them." Readers who make philosophical progress, however, "are always able to derive benefit, not only from what is said, but also from what is seen and done, and to gather what is appropriate and useful therefrom."[54] Given Machiavelli's own fascination with various techniques of dissimulation, it is unlikely that he would have failed to recognize their uses in Xenophon's *Cyropaedia*.[55] His comments on the work are as studiously ambivalent as the original. Xenophon "toils very much,"

[49] However, in Xenophon's "dialogue on tyrants," as Machiavelli calls it, the tyrant Hiero's wisdom and fortune did not make him happy; see sec. 2.4 below. Machiavelli frequently uses "wise" and "fortunate" or "happy" in similar ways to suggest inadequate judgments.

[50] Compare HH, I.114–15.

[51] Xenophon, *Memorabilia*, IV.vi.12. Compare Rousseau, who, expressly following Greek authors, argues that the basis for the distinction is not whether rule is good or bad but whether it is acquired by the will of the ruled or usurped (1964 [1762], III.10.441–43). Also see the approving remark on Xenophon's "Persian" notion of justice in Rousseau 1964 (1762), I:266 n. 1.

[52] I suggest in chap. 11 that the distinction between princes and tyrants has the same fluidity for Machiavelli; see Mattingly 1958 for a similar view.

[53] See Guicciardini on Xenophon, GD, Pref. 4. Also compare Kant's interpretation of the *Cyropaedia*, which he saw as demonstrating that a host of particular attributes of good princely conduct still may not add up to a good prince; Kant, "Lectures on the Philosophical Doctrine of Religion" (1996 [1783–84], 342).

[54] Plutarch, "Progress," PM, I.422–23.

[55] Indeed, he imitates it in his epitaphs on Cosimo and Lorenzo de' Medici, and in his "history" of the tyrant Castruccio Castracani. Like the *Cyropaedia*, this short work is often misread as portrait of an ideal—in this case "entrepreneurial"—prince, with an almost identical sorry end.

Machiavelli remarks in the *Discourses*, "to demonstrate how many honors, how many victories, how much good fame being humane [*umana*] and affable brought to Cyrus." The writer imitates his subject in this respect, since Cyrus himself took great care not to give "any example" that would show him "either as proud, or as cruel, or as lustful, or as having any other vice that stains the life of men."[56] A few chapters later, however, he makes it clear that he does not see Xenophon's prince as a model of corruption-free rulership. He distinguishes two methods of seeking glory, those necessary in republics and those necessary for princes, citing Xenophon's Cyrus as an example of the latter. In republics, glory comes to leaders who show themselves "always harsh to everyone" alike and who, "loving only the common good," are unable to "acquire partisans" to serve their "private ambition." Since leading men in republics must "live under the laws and obey the magistrates" in the same way as everyone else, they must be as strict in enforcing public laws against their friends and partisans as against their enemies. But princes who aspire to have more power than the laws must seek obedience by different means. Thus Xenophon's Cyrus, "being a prince particularly well wished for and having the army as his partisan," courted people's "love" for his person instead of seeking authority through public laws.[57]

These comments are sometimes taken at face value twice over: Xenophon as recommending Cyrus' methods of going slyly behind the laws instead of over them, and Machiavelli as seconding this "realistic" advice. Contrary to these appearances, the *Cyropaedia* is a masterwork of Socratic ethics and a fine example of constructive dissimulation. It remains to be seen whether Machiavelli's *Prince* and *Discourses* use similar methods toward the same aims. At this point, it is worth noting that Machiavelli says Cyrus did more or less what, in the *Florentine Histories*, he says the Medicis did: they courted "love" by scrupulously avoiding appearances of injustice or illegality, buying "partisans" with private means to promote private ambitions. If Machiavelli thought Cyrus should be commended for these actions, he must have thought the Medicis were almost as praiseworthy. For reasons set out earlier, this seems most unlikely.

2.3.
Conversations with rulers: Plutarch and Xenophon on purging tyranny

Another genre of dissimulative writing addresses men in power, as Machiavelli's *Discursus* addresses Giovanni de' Medici, with a view to checking or purging their tendencies to injustice. Plutarch's short piece "To an Uneducated Ruler" (*Pros hēgemona apaidegton*; Lat. *Ad principem ineruditem*) explains why dissimulation

---

[56] *D*, III.20.262.

[57] *D*, III.22.267–68. Cyrus is ambivalent in the *Prince*: he is sometimes classed with virtuous orderers of armies and peoples, such as "Moses, Cyrus, Romulus, Theseus" (*P*, VI., XXVI), but elsewhere with men whose methods left a legacy of corruption and disorder. Thus Machiavelli (*P*, XVI.64–65/157–59) classifies as very liberal "givers" Cyrus, Caesar, and Alexander, who maintained a "name" for liberality because their imperial conquests allowed them to give away what did not belong to themselves or their own subjects.

is often needed in such discourses. It is difficult to give advice to rulers because many "are afraid to accept reason as a ruler over them, lest it curtail the advantage of their power by making them slaves to duty." Nonetheless, public-spirited "philosophers" should use diplomatic "frankness" to try to cure rulers of *pleonexia* and the unbounded "desire to be first and greatest [*tēn toû prōton einai kai megiston epithumian*]."[58] Although philosophical education for statesmen ought to begin in childhood, Plutarch, Xenophon, and Plato suggest that it can be effective even for old men.[59] Diplomatic conversations can help them to revise some of their traditional shibboleths, prejudices, and authoritarian attitudes toward the young. But what if a grown man in a position of power shows dangerously corrupt or tyrannical inclinations? The public-spirited citizen, Plutarch insists, should not "be afraid of being called a courtier and a toady" if he seeks to serve his city by engaging such rulers in *dialogos*. Nor, however, should he rebuke or bombard them with "sophistical disquisitions" on good government. He should simply let rulers know that "when they wish it, he will be glad to converse and spend his leisure with them." Whoever "removes evil from the character of a ruler, or directs his mind toward what is right, philosophizes, as it were, in the public interest and corrects the general power by which all are governed." If his teachings are philosophical in the Socratic sense, they will derive from principles that, "if they are firmly engraved in the souls of rulers and statesmen" and regulate them, "acquire the force of laws."[60]

If a ruler has become an outright tyrant, it may seem that well-meaning conversation can do no good, and that conspiracy or revolution are the only means to purge tyranny. But since these methods risk creating new sources of discord and injustice, philosophers are reluctant to encourage them. A different option is try to persuade men in power to restore the rule of law of their own accord, before opponents are driven to use violence against them. This strategy, which Machiavelli uses in the *Discursus*, has roots in a variety of ancient writings in which tyrants effectively eliminate themselves *qua* tyrants as the direct result of philosophical dialogue.[61] As we saw in chapter 1, with those who have or seek absolute power it is especially important to enter discussion by addressing their own avowed concerns, without openly questioning their entitlement to that power. Hence the emphasis in such writings is on how tyranny endangers the personal well-being of powerful

---

[58] Plutarch, "To an Uneducated Ruler," PM, X.52–57; "Old Man," PM, X.78–79, 106–7. Plutarch (Precepts," PM, X.218–19, 234–35) cites Xenophon to support this recommendation. The idea of tyranny-preventing dialogue is described in detail in the *Cyropaedia,* where "Persian" education based on Socratic ethical teaching is upheld as the foundation of political order. Only youths who "complete the course required by law" are allowed "to join the class of mature men and to fill offices and places of distinction." The dialectical giving and demanding of reasoned accounts is central to this education.

[59] For example, see Plutarch, "Old Men," and Plato, *Laws.*

[60] Plutarch, "Old Man," PM, X.138–39; "Philosopher Ought to Converse," PM, X.30–37. Compare Plato, *Rep.* 571a–592b, *Laws* 960c–961a. The last books of both dialogues stress the need to establish the rule of law and reason both in the souls of every individual, so that they can regulate themselves without external force, and in the constitutions of cities.

[61] On the theme of "disappearing" rulers and philosopher kings, see Schofield 1999.

men.[62] In the self-reforming tyrants literature, the writer or a fictional speaker starts by discussing what matters most to the tyrant, his own private happiness and safety, as if these constitute the main touchstone for appraising his methods of rule. That the tyrant's ends should be personal power, glory, and safety is never directly questioned. The speaker appears to accept that these ends are legitimate, or at least off-limits in the discussion, and that he is concerned only to help the tyrant discover better means to achieving them.

Xenophon's *Hiero* is a well-known example of a dialogue through which a tyrant recognizes the need to convert himself into a law-abiding prince. The titular character, Hiero I of Syracuse (478–467 BC) is drawn into conversation by the poet Simonides. Simonides starts by seeming to praise the life of a tyrant, remarking on the great personal advantages that he imagines must come with unchecked power. Prodded into candid self-examination by the poet's apparently naïve, deferential questioning, Hiero admits that the tyrant's life makes him miserable. Before he became a tyrant he longed for absolute power and the advantages that he, like most people, imagined it must bring. But now that he has such power, he sees that the advantages it brings are nothing as compared with the vexations. The power that comes from being above the laws might be expected to bring boundless pleasures and complete security. In fact it has the opposite effects. Since a tyrant's lawless conduct creates many enemies and conspiracies, he cannot trust anyone, cannot sleep well at night, or freely enjoy even the simplest bodily pleasures without anxiety.

Simonides feigns astonishment at all this. Surely the experience of tyranny from the inside, so to speak, cannot be so remote from common beliefs about its boons for the tyrant himself? Hiero says he is not surprised "that the multitude [*plēthos*] should be deceived" by tyrannical power, since "the mob [*ochlos*] seems to guess wholly by appearances that one man is happy, another miserable." Tyranny, he observes, "flaunts its seeming treasures outspread before the gaze of the world," while keeping its woes "concealed in the heart" of the tyrant. Hiero expresses surprise that his interlocutor, whose poetic-philosophical "intelligence [*gnōmēs*] is supposed to give you a clearer view of most things than your eyes," remains "blind" to the truth about tyranny.[63] But Simonides, of course, is practicing constructive dissimulation. By gently drawing Hiero to confront the stark contrast between outward appearances and his own miserable experience, the philosopher-poet encourages the tyrant to purge himself of any remnant of his previous desires for absolute power. Having recognized his old errors, Hiero is now able to see what corrective measures are needed. So far the dialogue has focused only on the adverse effects of tyranny on the tyrant's own life: nothing has been said about justice toward subjects, legitimate and illegitimate authority, or the common good. Having lured Hiero into an admission of grave error based on concern only for his own well-being, however, Simonides takes a more active role at the end of the dia-

---

[62] It does not indicate a greater concern in Greek ethics for individual souls than for the relations between human beings who stand in unequal positions of power; see White 2002 for many apposite criticisms of this characterization of Greek ethics in general.

[63] XH, 16–19.

logue, cautiously introducing these wider considerations. Once Hiero himself has reaffirmed his longing to give up tyranny, the poet seizes the opportunity to give him more positive advice about how to leave tyranny behind while still advancing his previous goals: personal safety, glory, and happiness.

According to Hiero himself, the most crippling disability faced by tyrants is that they find themselves at war with their own countrymen and fatherland. This forces them to depend on foreign mercenaries as their bodyguard and external allies to keep them in power, thus making "foreigners more formidable than the citizens." And this in turn makes the tyrant all the more unpopular and insecure among his own people.[64] Hiero asks Simonides' advice on how to escape his vexations. How can mercenaries be employed without making him unpopular? Or does Simonides think that "a ruler, once he becomes popular, will have no need of a bodyguard?" The philosophical poet replies that of course any ruler needs defending, for some human beings are like horses—when allowed to drive completely out of their proper bounds (*ekplea ta deonta exōsi*), they are prone to run riot (*hubristoterois*). The verb *hubrizō* is sometimes used to describe unruly plants or animals, but also refers to wanton or licentious conduct in human beings who fail to respect proper bounds (*deon*), especially in relation to others. In this regard, to commit *hubris* may mean to outrage, assault, or wantonly violate, usually because of poorly restrained passions, ambitions, or desires for more than one's share (*pleonexia*). Simonides' statement furnishes a good example of double-writing: it seems to warn rulers against unruly individuals who threaten them, but simultaneously hints that the most *hubris*-prone individuals are rulers themselves, especially when they do not respect legal restraints. The implication is that if Hiero wants to become more popular and more secure, he might have to take radical measures.

First of all, if he must keep mercenaries, he should he cease to treat them as his private defense force and enjoin them "to act as the bodyguard of the whole community [*hos pantōn . . . doruphorous tōn politōn*] and render help to all." For if they "were under orders to guard the citizens as well as the despot, the citizens would know that this is one service rendered to them by the mercenaries," who would also "be able to give fearlessness and security" to laborers in the countryside. A subtle shift in language begins to occur in what follows. So far, Hiero and Simonides have spoken of the tyrant's "subjects" (*archomenoi*). Now, when advising the tyrant to share his defenses with others in the "community," Simonides begins to refer to these others as citizens (*politois*) or allies (*summachoi*), words more appropriate for people who are treated in the ways he now says Hiero should treat them. For example, shared defenses should afford citizens more leisure to look after their private affairs, now free from the suspicious scrutiny of the tyrant's rule. Hiero should not hesitate to draw on his private property for "the common good" (*ton koinon agathon*). By sharing his defenses and property with subjects, or rather citizens now unburdened by tyrannical control, Hiero will reduce his own

---

[64] XH, 30–53. Compare Plutarch's ("Uneducated Ruler," PM, X.65) "kings fear for their subjects, but tyrants fear their subjects." Also see Plato, *Rep.* 619c–d on the foreseeable miseries of those who choose a tyrant's life.

absolute powers but greatly strengthen his glory and ensure that he has true victory (*nikē*). Indeed, Simonides declares, "you are the victor [*nikōn*] in the noblest and grandest competition in the world." He will have "secured" the conversion of hostile subjects into civil friends, so that "all the world will tell of your virtue"; he will be admired abroad and at home, "in public among all men" as well as in private. At the end of the dialogue Simonides assures Hiero that if he undertakes the necessary reforms,

> you will have the willing obedience of your subjects . . . and should any danger arise, you will find in them not merely allies [*summachous*], but champions and zealots. Accounted worthy of many gifts, and at no loss for some man of goodwill with whom to share them, you will find all rejoicing in your good fortune, all fighting for your interests, as though they were their own. . . . Take heart then, Hiero; enrich your friends, for so you will enrich yourself. Exalt the city [*auxe de tēn polin*], for so you will deck yourself with power [*dunamin periapseis*].[65]

Chapter 11 will consider whether the *Prince* might have dialogical aims similar to those of the *Hiero*, that is, to show one-man rulers why it is their interest to found or refound government on a wider, non-arbitrary basis. For now, note simply that Machiavelli's remarks about a later Syracusan Hiero (Hiero II, 306–215 BC) echo the language and themes of Xenophon's dialogue on the self-reforming tyrant.[66] In chapter 6 of the *Prince*, entitled "Of New Principalities That Are Acquired through One's Own Arms and Virtue," Hiero is named as an example of a prince who

> eliminated the old military and organized a new one; he left his old friendships and made new ones; and when he had friendships and soldiers that were his own, he could build any building on top of such a foundation; so he went through a great deal of trouble to acquire, and little to maintain.[67]

In chapter 13 Machiavelli draws lessons for his contemporaries from the military aspects of Hiero's reforms. The Syracusan general saw that his country's "mercenary military was not useful because they were *condottieri* set up like our Italians." After leading them to destruction in battle, he "then made war with his arms and not with alien arms."[68] In the *Prince* as in Xenophon's *Hiero* these reforms involve a significant reduction in the ruler's personal power, and the transfer of certain powers to the people. Machiavelli appeals to princely readers to undertake reforms that strengthen their "own arms" by befriending their own people, making them

---

[65] XH, 50–57.
[66] The *Prince* mentions Hiero of Syracuse twice, the *Discourses* four times. Many themes in the *Hiero* are echoed in Machiavelli's writings, notably the dangers of excessive desires for honor and praise (XH, 36–43), and the *Prince*'s theme of relying on one's own arms and people instead of on mercenaries (XH, 30–35, 44–53).
[67] P, VI.25/131–32.
[68] P, XIII.55–56/154–56. Compare PolH, I.8.16; VII.8.357.

responsible for their own country's defenses, and thus ending the prince's dependence on mercenaries and foreign monarchs.

Other themes touched on in Xenophon's dialogue indicate that the *Hiero* is much more than "a naïve little work" advising tyrants to be more like kings. Nor is it concerned only with the tyrant's personal happiness.[69] Hiero's criticisms of his own tyranny reveal elements of a substantive political theory that reappear in Machiavelli's writings.[70] In addition to making enemies of one's own people, another self-disabling feature of tyrannical rule is that it cannot employ ordinary citizens' virtues to improve defenses and government. Hiero tells Simonides that tyrants recognize a stout-hearted, a wise or a just (*dikaious*) man "as easily as private citizens do. But instead of admiring such men" and putting them to good use in the city, "they fear them—the brave lest they strike a bold stroke for freedom [*eleutheria*], the wise lest they hatch a plot," and the just "lest the people desire them for leaders." Once tyrants "get rid of such men through fear," however, no one is left for their use but the unjust, the vicious, and the servile (*hoi adikoi kai akrateis kai andrapodōdeis*). The unjust are trusted because, like the tyrant, "they fear that the cities may some day shake off the yoke and prove their masters"; the vicious "on account of the license they enjoy as things are"; and the servile "because even they themselves have no desire for freedom." It is a "heavy trouble" indeed, Hiero admits, "to see the good in some men, and yet perforce to employ others."[71] Simonides briefly addresses this complaint at the end of the dialogue, saying that Hiero should "contrive to bring the capital of all the citizens into employment." The capital in question is not just their wealth; more importantly, it includes whatever virtues they may be able to contribute to common defenses and the common good: courage, wisdom, justice, and the like.

These arguments are echoed in the *Discourses* and more subtly, but unmistakably, in the *Prince*. A chapter entitled "What a Prince Should Do to Be Held in Esteem" starts by seeming to recommend "great" gestures that give a prince "fame," then moves on to propose shrewd maneuvers that can help him maintain power. The chapter ends by declaring,

> A prince should also show himself a lover of the virtues, giving recognition to virtuous men [*dando ricapito alli uomini virtuosi*], and he should honor those who are excellent in an art. Next, he should inspire his citizens [*cittadini*] to follow their pursuits quietly, in trade and in agriculture and in every other pursuit of men, so that one person does not fear to adorn his possessions for fear that they may be taken away from him, and another to open up a trade for fear of taxes. But he should prepare rewards for whoever

---

[69] The editor's remarks in the Loeb edition (introduction, xvi) are quaintly obtuse: "The *Hiero* is a naïve little work, not unattractive. . . . The gist of Xenophon's counsel" is that tyrants should try to rule like good kings.

[70] Though it should be stressed that the theory is not Xenophon's alone; its main elements can also be found in Herodotus, Thucydides, Plato, and Aristotle. This makes it difficult to pin Machiavelli's main Greek sources to any single author.

[71] XH, 28–31.

wants to do these things, and for anyone who thinks up any way of expanding [*ampliare*] his city or his state.

Behind skillfully crafted appearances of caring only for a prince's reputation, passages such as these imply that genuine strength in any form of government, princely
or republican, depends on recognizing and rewarding merit and virtue among all
citizens. The quiet shift from the *Prince*'s usual talk of "subjects" (*sudditi*) to *cittadini* might signal to some readers that a prince who seeks strong foundations for
his rule should consider adopting modes of government that treat peoples more
like citizens, free and active participants in a *vivere civile*, than subjects of another's
dominant will.[72]

More than this: the call to recognize virtue, honor excellence, reward anything
that amplifies the public good, respect individuals' private property and choice of
activities, and avoid arbitrary actions that intimidate citizens sounds suspiciously
like an old-fashioned concern for justice. If some readers reject this suspicion on
grounds that Machiavelli does not speak of justice in the *Prince*, they have not
read the chapter carefully. Two paragraphs before the one just cited, we read that
"victories are never so clear that the winner does not have to have some respect,
especially for justice [*le vittorie non sono mai sí stiette che il vincitore non abbia ad
avere qualche respetto, e massime all' iustizia*]."[73] The sentence's immediate context
is advice to princes to take clear sides in conflicts and deal honestly with those
they support, respecting contractual agreements with allies through defeats as well
as victories. In the broader context of a chapter on what princes should do to
gain esteem, it foreshadows the unstated message that emerges more clearly in the
last paragraph: whether dealing with foreign countries or with his own people,
not even the most powerful ruler can afford to act entirely without "respect" for
justice. Later sections consider other ancient writings that appear only to discuss
expediency but, often without using the word, also discuss justice.

2.4.
Dissimulating about deception: Xenophon's Cambyses

A fine illustration of the difference between constructive dissimulation and falsify-
ing deception occurs in the *Cyropaedia*, in the form of a dialogue between young
Cyrus and his father Cambyses. The discussion begins when the precociously cynical prince, having realized that "nothing is more effectual toward keeping one's
men obedient than to seem wiser than they," asks his father how one can acquire
a reputation (*doxan*) for wisdom. Cambyses, the exemplar of traditional, non-
corrupt Persian ethics, realizes that his son's question fails to distinguish between
reputations and true qualities. Even as a boy Cyrus assumes that appearances are

---

[72] The theme of self-reforming tyrant also occurs in Books IV and V of Aristotle's *Politics*. Similarities between Xenophon's *Hiero* and Plato's *Rep.* IX are often noted; it seems likely that Aristotle was
inspired by one or both of these earlier treatments.

[73] P, XXI.90–91/180–81. Also see XXIII on whether princes should allow advisers to speak freely,
discussed in chap. 9, sec. 9.1. and chap. 11, sec. 11.5.

all that matter, so long as they serve one's own purposes. His father takes this defective opinion as the starting point for a nuanced enquiry into the question of when deception is acceptable and when it is wrong. The enquiry proceeds through three main steps.

First of all, Cambyses replies that there is no quicker way to gain a reputation for wisdom than "really to be wise in those things in which you wish to seem to be wise." He then points out some of the disadvantages of seeking to gain any reputation through deceptive appearances. If you wish to seem a good farmer, doctor, or flute-player when you are not, he tells his son, "just think how many schemes you must invent to keep up your pretensions [*dokein*]." Moreover, even if you do persuade some people to praise you "in order to give yourself a reputation," you would eventually "be found to have practiced deception [*doloseis*]" and be "convicted as an impostor."[74]

A few pages later, however, Cambyses complicates this old-fashioned account. At this second stage of the enquiry, he now tells his son that the use of cunning and deception is sometimes acceptable when dealing with enemies in war. Cyrus is taken aback by what he takes to be a hypocritical position. If deception in general is wrong and disadvantageous, yet acceptable and advantageous in some circumstances, this seems to imply a general rule that calculations of advantage trump judgments of right and wrong. Cyrus infers that, according to the "Persian" ethics his father espouses, justice should be subordinated to utility since "it is useful to know [*epistasthai*] both how to do good and how to do evil to men." One must apply completely different standards to friends and enemies, and be ready to compromise standards of justice whenever they are inconvenient for oneself.

Cambyses concedes that this is how his advice looks at first glance. But he then tells a story that corrects Cyrus' cynical understanding of the permission to use deception in some matters of war. There was, Cambyses says, a teacher "in the time of our forebears" who used to teach justice in the way Cyrus proposes. He taught his young pupils "to lie and not to lie, to cheat and not to cheat, to slander and not to slander, to take and not to take unfair advantage [*pleonektein*]." This teacher also "drew the line between what one should do to one's friends and what to one's enemies." Once standards of justice were subordinated to utility and personal relationships, they lost any power to constrain utterly self-serving actions. At this point, on Cambyses' account, moral and social anarchy broke out. It soon appeared right to deceive (*exapatan*) friends as well as enemies "provided it were for a good end," and permissible "to steal the possessions of a friend for a good purpose." When as a result of this teaching some people had become experts in deception and taking more than their share (*pleonexia*) from friends as well as foes, others realized that they needed to rethink how the young learn about justice. They decided that it was best to proceed as Cambyses is doing in the present dialogue: first teach clear, simple principles of justice to the young, and only afterward discuss the particular conditions that determine how they are applied. Cambyses ties up this part of the discussion by returning to his initial defense of a general

---

[74] XC, I.108–9.

prohibition on deception. His story about the corrupting teacher has set out some additional reasons for the prohibition, which now looks even better founded than before. To underline this provisional conclusion, Cambyses tells Cyrus that as a result of the hard moral lessons he has just described, "an ordinance was passed which obtains even unto this day, simply to teach our boys . . . to tell the truth and not to deceive and not to take unfair advantage." If anyone "should act contrary to this law, the law [ethei] requires their punishment" so that they may become better-disciplined citizens.[75]

This brings us to the third step of Cambyses' discourse, which deals with the apparent contradiction between the permission to deceive enemies in war and the newly affirmed, traditional view that justice is the same for everyone and not subordinate to utility. The ancient Persians, Cambyses says, began as he did by outlining general principles of justice because the young, being inexperienced, find it hard to grasp the important distinction between general principles and particular applications. As the preceding dialogue demonstrated, if teachers try to draw this distinction before pupils have recognized clear reasons for the general principles, some may wrongly assume—as Cyrus just did—that the principles are dispensable, or less compelling than some other criterion. This misunderstanding corrupts judgment in the ways that Cambyses' story describes. First, enemies are not considered as subjects of justice, even if one has made commitments to them under treaty or oath. Soon commitments made to friends are regarded as dispensable too, if one's own purposes conflict with them.

But now that Cyrus has been duly warned about these corruptions, Cambyses will explain how one can affirm a general prohibition against deception yet admit it in certain dealings with enemies at war. When boys "came to be as old as you are now," Cambyses tells his son, "then it seemed to be safe to teach them that also which is lawful toward enemies [pros tous polemious nomima]." It seems safe at this stage of education because it seems less likely that "you would break away and degenerate into savages after you had been brought up together in mutual respect." Note that the more mature view does not simply depend on a clearer understanding of the justice due to friends, but also on the understanding that enemies too should be treated according to what is "lawful."[76] Cyrus should now be ready to understand that in war some matters are regulated by treaties, customs, and informal standards of justice: for example, cease-fires, the treatment of prisoners, the protection of enemy ambassadors, and the like. It is no more acceptable to deceive enemy combatants over such matters than to deceive friends with whom one has tacit or explicit commitments. According to Persian-Socratic ethics, treaties and oaths undertaken are sacrosanct, whether the parties are friends or enemies. However, there are some areas of warfare that are not generally regulated by mutual undertakings, and where it is generally agreed that the use of deception is acceptable. Good military strategy often relies on ruses that mislead an enemy about the size, condition, or layout of one's troops, or which lure enemy forces into a vulnerable

[75] XC, I.112–19.
[76] XC, I.116–19.

position.[77] The mature, nuanced position is therefore that as a general principle of justice it is wrong to deceive. But it is acceptable to practice forms of strategic deception on enemies in war, so long as this is done in ways that do not violate sworn oaths and treaties that regulate what is "lawful towards enemies."

Cambyses' discourse both explains and illustrates the distinction between deception and constructive dissimulation. Deception aims at hiding the truth or breaking commitments, whereas Cambyses' "Persian" teachings include an element of constructive dissimulation: they seek to reveal the full truth about deception by withholding part of it until their audience is ready to grasp it correctly. If Machiavelli too uses dissimulation as a general means of revealing truths, might his remarks on deception also resemble Xenophon's and Cambyses' dissimulations? When he discusses deception in the *Discourses*, he does indeed cite the *Cyropaedia* as a key source. In Book II he notes that Xenophon shows the "necessity to deceive" in various ways. First he considers "that the first expedition that he has Cyrus make against the king of Armenia is full of fraud, and that he makes him seize his kingdom through deception and not through force." Later Xenophon has Cyrus "deceive Cyaxares, king of the Medes, his maternal uncle, in several modes; without which fraud he shows that Cyrus could not have attained that greatness he came to." Machiavelli appears to accept the view that a reputation for "greatness" in the sense alluded to here is the proper aim of anyone who seeks to become a prince and "attain great empire."[78] But as in Cambyses' discourse, Machiavelli's opening remarks are only the provocative starting point for much more nuanced reflections on acceptable uses of deception.

These are set out near the end of the *Discourses* in a chapter whose title announces "That to Use Fraud [*fraude*] in Managing War Is a Glorious Thing." It is almost universally accepted that Machiavelli endorses instrumental deception in many areas of political and military action, not just in aspects of warfare that are unregulated by treaties or informal agreements. But when preconceptions are set aside, his treatment of deception in the *Discourses* appears to recommend a nuanced view similar to Cambyses' Persian-Socratic position in the *Cyropaedia*. The first sentence proposes a teasing paradox: "Although the use of fraud in every action is detestable, nonetheless in managing war it is a praiseworthy and glorious thing." Here Machiavelli draws Cambyses' distinction between the general principle that deception is wrong, and the recognition that some forms of deception are an accepted part of military strategy and tactics, to which standards of justice need not apply. Machiavelli insists that the exception does not apply to every aspect of warfare; indeed, he directly echoes Cambyses' mature judgment. "I shall only say this," he writes: "that I do not understand that fraud to be glorious which makes you break faith given and pacts made." For while "this may at some time acquire state and kingdom for you . . . it will never acquire glory for you." Nor does Machiavelli accept the view that deception practiced against enemies is generally less

---

[77] XC, I.122–25. This is followed by a discussion of another form of deception: deception in hunting, and by analogy in trying to ensnare one's enemy.

[78] D, II.13.155–56/358–59.

culpable that that used against friends. When remarking that fraud is praiseworthy, he refers to a specific kind of fraud employed under specific battlefield conditions, where since no agreements based on mutual trust have been made, there are
none to be violated. "I speak," he writes, only "of the fraud that is used with the
enemy who does not trust you [*nimico che non si fida di te*] and that properly consists in managing war [*che consiste proprio nel maneggiare la guerra*]." Examples
include "that of Hannibal when at the lake of Perugia he simulated [*simulò*] flight"
to enclose the Roman army, and when as a defensive stratagem "he lit up the horns
of his herd to escape the hands of Fabius Maximus."[79] These forms of fraud have a
very specific provenance, and do not involve violations of good faith, which are as
necessary for the orderly and humane conduct of war as they are for civil order.

2.5.
Dissimulating about justice: Thucydides' Diodotus

Thucydides' history of the Peloponnesian War provides another rich source of
examples of dissimulation, both through speeches attributed to historical figures
and in the historian's own narrative. Born three years after Socrates and himself
a general who fought for Athens, Thucydides' analysis of how ethical values become corrupted under pressure of war and civil war was often cited by later Greek
and Roman writers.[80] As with Machiavelli's *Florentine Histories*, a central theme
of Thucydides' work was the difficulty citizens face in making political judgments
where ethical standards are corrupt. The Greeks' collapse into political and moral
disorder involves a fall from a better, though non-ideal, condition: what had been
accepted or customary (*eiōthōs*; n. *ethos*, *ēthos*; v. *ethō*) among Greeks in cities
that had often been rivals, but were now mortal enemies. Even in the best of
times, Thucydides says, people in cities thought about how to seize power or how
to take revenge instead of seeking justice. Under pressure of civil conflict, accepted ideas about taking power became even more cunning, while ideas about
revenge became crueler. People even changed the accepted values of words (*tēn
eiōthuian axiōsin tōn onomatōn*) in order to misrepresent their deeds as just. The
cause of all this, Thucydides suggests, was the quest for dominion (*archē*) pursued
through excessive self-seeking (*pleonexia*) and ambition (*philotimia*), which in
turn led to zealous partisanship (*philonikein*). Each party operated not according
to established laws in the interests of the society as a whole, but against existing
customs to claim more than their share (*para tous kathestōtas pleonexia*). Oaths
were taken only under duress and broken as soon as possible. In their battle to
the death for supremacy over others, each party committed terrible crimes that
"escalated to ever greater revenges [*timōrias*], never to promote justice and the
best interests of the city," but setting whatever limits (*horizontes*) happened to
please each party. Neither side "observed the rules of piety," gaining more respect

---

[79] *D*, III.40.299–300/514.
[80] Such as Plutarch, cited in sec. 2.2. above.

for "the high words [*euprepeia logou*] with which they got away with performing their base actions."[81]

Thucydides points out that the basic dispositions that produce partisanship, debase values, and drive people to reject any limit on their actions are found in all cities. Even under the constraints ordinarily imposed by customs and laws, human nature is prone to violate the laws (*para tous nomous adikein*). But it does not always strive to be above all constraints of justice, or become an enemy to any authority (*kreissōn de tou dikaiou, polemia de tou prouchontos*). This diagnosis implies that it is not human nature as such that should be blamed for the corruptions described, but those who allow human nature to predominate over and rule (*kratēsasa*) the laws. Human beings always have a choice, although in extremely turbulent conditions they may not realize it: to let themselves be ruled more by reflective prudence (*sōphrosunē*) or by violent self-assertion (*hubris*), by respect for sacred laws or by revenge, by justice (*dikaiois, dikē*) or by self-seeking.[82] Thus Thucydides' deeply pessimistic account of unregulated human nature also identifies correctives. Ambition and *pleonexia* do not always produce the disorders he describes in Book III; they are ordinarily contained by respect for customs, justice, and fear of the laws. These set clear limits on each person's or party's or city's share of power, so that none are permitted to exercise unwanted dominion over others. Similar ideas can be found in Xenophon, Plato, and Plutarch's writings, as well as in Machiavelli's.[83]

The ethical standards implicit in Thucydides' digression on words and deeds provide a touchstone for evaluating the counsels offered in various speeches he attributes to political and military leaders.[84] Even before the war, the Athenians are portrayed as prone to arrogance and *pleonexia*, thinking themselves deserving of more power than others and caring little whether others voluntarily accept their dominion.[85] A high estimation of their own greatness leads them dangerously to underrate their opponents' capacities. In their deliberations about how to deal with other cities they are complacent, quick to apply double standards, and overeager to find excuses for their own errors and unfair dealings. These deficiencies are subtly woven into speeches Thucydides attributes to the Athenian

[81] TPW, III.82–84; compare the *FH* passage quoted in sec. 1.1, at note 16 in chap. 1.

[82] TPW, III.82–84. The translation is mine, based loosely on Blanco 1998, 131–32.

[83] Many of the basic ethical concepts and judgments implied in Thucydides' history have clear affinities with Socratic ethics. As Hobbes (1989 [1629], 570–71) notes in his biographical essay on Thucydides, Socrates and Thucydides were contemporaries; both fought in the Peloponnesian War, and both were students of Anaxagoras, a philosopher who like Socrates was put to death for his "irreligious" teachings. Socrates' students Plato and Xenophon allude admiringly to the historian; I see no evidence at all of significant tensions between Plato's philosophy or ethics and Thucydides' thought, nor did later students of both such as Plutarch. See Strauss 1964, 236–40, and Hornblower 1987, 112, 120–25, for perceptive comparisons of Thucydides with Socrates and Plato.

[84] As his translator Hobbes (1989 [1629], 577) remarks, Thucydides does not lay down "open conveyances or precepts" or openly condemn those responsible for making poor choices. Instead he "so clearly set before men's eyes the ways and events of good and evil counsels, that the narration itself doth secretly instruct the reader, and more effectually than can possibly be done by precept."

[85] The Spartans symbolize greater respect for customary ways, but are also prone to excessive narrowness and formalism.

general Pericles. In his first oration delivered before the war, Pericles imprudently declares that since the Spartans and their allies are weaker, poorer, and politically less efficient than the Athenians, the latter need not worry about fighting them. In his second speech, the famous Funeral Oration, he praises some of the ideas that Thucydides associates with non-corrupt Greek customs, notably fear of breaking the laws; but he identifies this and other admirable qualities exclusively with Athens, treating them as marks of superiority that justify that city's imperial policies. His third speech abandons all his earlier restraint and declares that Athenian sea power can enable Athenians to spread their power even further than they already have. Like Machiavelli's praise for Cosimo and Lorenzo in the *Florentine Histories*, Thucydides' apparent praise for Pericles is undermined by the sharp tensions he sets up between good words and self-serving deeds. It gives way in the last speech to an open admission that Athens' empire (*archē*) was acquired unjustly and is run like a tyranny (*hōs turannida*), but should nonetheless be preserved by any available means: go then, he declares, and fight your enemies "not just with spirit, but with a spirit of contempt [*kataphronēmati*]."[86] Neither Thucydides' comments nor speeches by prudent characters suggest that it was *necessary* for Athens to hold its empire like a tyranny. There were other, more legitimate ways to exercise political and military authority that are more consistent with customary ethics, respect for the rule of law, and indeed with the Athenians' own interests. Pericles and his compatriots simply did not choose to recognize this alternative before they got deep into the war; and now, knowing that they risked losing their reputation as well as power, they became more assertive than ever.

One of the signs Thucydides uses to signal whether or not a speaker's advice is prudent appears in what he says about the relation between fortune or chance (*tuchē, eutuchē*) and the actions he proposes. In Thucydides' lexicon—as in Livy's, Plutarch's, and Machiavelli's—those who rely on fortune often expect success to come easily (*rhadiōs*), then blame everyone but themselves if they fail. Pericles' first speech promised the Athenians an easy victory; when this proves elusive, his third blames bad fortune (*kakotuchē, atuchē*) instead of Athenian misjudgments.[87] A better basis for success is set out in an early speech by Athens' Corinthian opponents. Those who overreach themselves because of good fortune in war (*ho te en polemō eutuchia pleonazōn*), they warn, are unaware that a "treacherous audacity" makes them bold. Prudent men depend on their own courage (*eupsuchia*) and good nature (*phusei agathon*). In contrast to the Athenians' presumption that they could easily win, their enemies do the opposite, understanding that prosperity comes through hard work (*ek tōn ponōn*).[88] Though the Corinthians' good words are no less motivated by self-interest than Pericles' advice to the Athenians, their sense is closer to the traditional customs that regulated relations among Greek cities before the war.[89]

---

[86] TPW, I.140–44; II.35–46; II.60–65.

[87] TPW, I.140, II.44 (x4), II.60, 62. See Machiavelli on Athens' attitude to fortune, *D*, I.1.

[88] TPW, I.120–24.

[89] See the very critical views of Pericles' leadership in Plato, *Gorg.* 515d–519e.

These elements of Thucydides' ethics are further developed through debates during the war.[90] Numerous speeches illustrate the basic problem of corrupt judgment described in Book III: that in conditions of extreme rivalry and mistrust, it becomes difficult for citizens in democracies to make sound judgments about the policies set before them. Speakers who advocate policies based on narrow or emotionally distorted notions of self-interest find it easier to win a following, while citizens who urge self-restraint are suspected of being cowards or traitors. In such conditions, prudent counselors may have to present their advice in ways that shield them from suspicion. When no one trusts a man who argues in favor of justice, speakers are more likely to persuade others to act justly if they avoid the language of justice, concealing their principles behind a mask of hardheaded instrumentalism.

An example of such constructive dissimulating occurs in the Mytilenean debate in Book III. Here Thucydides narrates how Athens' ally, the city of Mytilene, decided to withdraw from the league and join the Spartan-led enemy alliance. Explaining their decision to the Spartans, the Mytileneans point out that Athens had long since ceased to treat its allies as equals, instead "contriving to enslave" those who supported them. The Mytileneans now realized that they had become "free and independent [*autonomoi . . . kai eleutheroi*] in name only" and could no longer trust the Athenians. Although Athens' present subjects (*archomenoi*) had originally accepted the city's leadership as free allies (*summachoi*), the city they had willingly accepted as leader (*hēgemonas*) had begun unilaterally to exercise dominion through empire (*archē*). The result, as even Pericles admitted, was that Athens now ruled as a tyranny. "It seemed unlikely," the Mytileneans tell the Spartans, that the Athenians "would enslave some of those they had made allies with our help, and then refrain from doing the same thing to the rest of us if they could."[91]

The Mytilenean revolt failed. Having crushed and blockaded their former allies, Thucydides reports that the Athenians had a debate about the Mytileneans and, enraged by the betrayal of allies they had treated better than others, decided to inflict an extremely violent punishment: they would kill not just all the men in the city but all males above the age of puberty, not differentiating between those who had supported the revolt and those who had not. The next day, however, the decision "to annihilate the Mytileneans" seemed unreasonably cruel (*analogismos ōmon*) to many Athenians who had at first agreed with it, so another assembly was called to reconsider their decision. The first speaker is Cleon, by far the most aggressive of the leading citizens and "the most trusted by people in those days." He had won the first debate that decided to annihilate Mytilene, and now tries to dissuade his compatriots from changing their minds. Like Pericles, Cleon openly admits that Athens holds its empire like a tyranny, but does not admit that tyranny is unjust. The only wrong he acknowledges is that of Athens' unwilling subjects. Since these are all treacherous plotters, he argues, only overwhelming force can put them in their place. Having demonstrated the apparently flagrant injustice of

[90] For valuable discussions see Hornblower 1987; Cawkwell 1997; Rood 1998; de Romilly 1956 and 1997.
[91] TPW, III.9–14; see chap. 12.

the Mytileneans' actions, Cleon presents the Athenians with a choice. Either they must admit that their empire is unjust and that the Mytileneans were justified in rebelling, or they must punish the rebels with the utmost violence, reasserting their claims to dominion and making it clear to all their other subjects that no apostasy will be tolerated. Cleon strongly advises them to choose the second of these options, arguing that it is both just (*dikaia*) and expedient (*sumphora*) to follow through with the punishment already decided. If the Athenians do not inflict violent revenge they will do wrong to themselves, because if the rebels "were justified in rebelling, you must be wrong to exercise dominion over them."[92]

The persuasive force of Cleon's rhetoric depends on hearers not noticing, or not caring about, a basic tension in his position. On the one hand, Cleon claims that his proposed policy is just as well as expedient. On the other, he defends Athens' tyrannical methods of rule and exonerates unfair punishments if they help to preserve its empire. There are two ways to resolve the tension. One is to argue that the justice of a policy depends solely on the justice of the ends it seeks to promote. But Cleon has not tried to demonstrate that the ends of Athenian empire are just, any more than its methods. All he has done is to assume that his audience want to preserve the empire, and that to do so is expedient. He does not ask his compatriots to ask themselves whether or not their desires for absolute empire, *archē*, are reasonable. In effect, those desires themselves become the sole criterion of what is expedient. So long as the ends of Athenian *archē* are immune from scrutiny, and are taken as the ultimate touchstone of expediency, the justice of means used on their behalf is also spared closer examination. On this conception it is easy to claim that justice is wholly congruent with one's own advantage, since justice is by definition whatever appears to serve one's own advantage, and one's advantage is simply whatever one currently desires. On this account, it appears logical to brand efforts made by opponents to defend their legitimate interests as unjust or ambitious.[93]

The other way to resolve the tension between Cleon's assertions is to understand justice as nothing more than revenge for perceived wrongs. Cleon's rhetoric presumes that his audience's newly reignited rage will drive them to accept this primitive, one-sided notion of justice.[94] When he declares that the massacre of the Mytileneans is at once just and expedient, justice here is synonymous with vengeance, and involves a refusal to consider whether wrongs might have been committed by both sides. If justice is unilateral vengeance, and expediency is doing whatever one wants without considering the wishes of those affected by one's actions, then the annihilation of the Mytileneans does seem a just and expedient response to their revolt. If hearers uncritically accept the sense Cleon gives to these words, his reasoning seems logical. Since it also accords with their desire to rule

[92] TPW, III.36–40.

[93] Compare Pericles' (TPW, 60–65) third speech, where he admits that Athens now "holds its empire like a tyranny" and declares that whether or not others willingly accept Athenian dominion is immaterial; for if "taking it is thought to have been unjust [*adikon*], letting it go would be extremely dangerous."

[94] Conceptions of justice as revenge are implicitly criticized in TPW, III.82–84.

other Greeks without consulting their will, whoever opposes Cleon's arguments will need to use very effective persuasions indeed.

Thucydides tells us that the next speaker, Diodotus, had opposed the killing of the Mytileneans in the first assembly. Diodotus has an unenviable task. Cleon has preemptively accused anyone who opposes the massacre of taking bribes; whipped up popular rage against the upstarts who dared to reject Athenian dominance; and made an apparently logical argument that both justice and expediency demand the annihilation of the Mytileneans. Diodotus starts by pointing out that "two things most opposed to good counsel [*euboulia*] are anger and haste." Reminding citizens that reasoned discussion (*logos*) is the only means people have to educate themselves in practical affairs and plan for an uncertain future, he asks hearers not to "dismiss the practical utility [*chresimon*] of my argument in favor of the attractive appearance [*euprepei*]" of Cleon's.[95] Yet Diodotus is wary of presenting his own case in a straightforward way. If there is one thing no one trusts in Athens—like Machiavelli's Florence, a city full of talkers—it is transparent efforts to speak truthfully for the sake of what is right. "It has come to a point," Diodotus observes, "that things customarily set down as good [*kathestēke tagatha*] are no less suspect than what simply is bad [*einai tōn kakon*]." Using deceit (*apatē*), people convince others to do the most terrible things, while anyone who defends a good cause has to lie if he wants to be believed. Indeed, "it is impossible to do good openly and without lying all the time. And the man who openly does good," Diodotus continues, "is rewarded with the suspicion that he will secretly be getting a payoff from somewhere."[96] Since corrupt practices make it difficult for Athenians to distinguish good from bad counsels, Diodotus must tailor his own rhetoric to his audience. He cannot speak with complete openness, nor can he claim to be concerned with doing what is right or good. His solution is to dissimulate. He appears to argue only from one set of premises that he knows his audience accepts, but lets drop "signs and arguments" that reveal more fundamental commitments that he seeks to defend by indirect means. Both his general methods of argument and specific positions would be imitated by many later writers, including Livy and Machiavelli.[97]

Diodotus proposes a much simpler criterion than Cleon's: he will, he says, judge the matter only from the standpoint of expediency, setting aside all considerations of justice. "In view of your present anger against the Mytileneans," he tells his hearers, "the greater justice of Cleon's argument might well appeal to you. But there is no need for us to deliberate about what is just," he argues, "since we are not putting them before a law-court. We are trying to decide only what to do with them, and how they can be most useful [*hopōs chrēsimōs*] to us." By feigning indifference to justice and injustice, Diodotus evades the trap Cleon tried to set when he identified justice with whatever measures Athenians imagined might preserve their empire. Had Diodotus questioned this equation, he would have come under suspicion as a traitor who dared to doubt whether that empire should be preserved,

[95] TPW, III.42.
[96] TPW, III.43–44.
[97] See chaps. 8, 9, 12.

and who evaluated it by independent standards of legitimacy. Instead he carefully avoids any criticism of imperial ends, claiming only to evaluate the best means to advance them. Even if it could be shown that the Mytileneans were thoroughly in the wrong, he says, "I would not for that reason call on you to execute them unless it was expedient to do so." By the same token, "if there were some reason to pardon them, why then, let them be, unless that did not seem good for the city."[98]

Diodotus then sets out a more reflective conception of expediency than the one proposed by Cleon. Cleon's main argument is that it is better for Athens to kill all the Mytileneans because this will deter future rebellions. Diodotus argues that the opposite result is more likely. A policy of annihilation risks "driving the rebels past the point of no return," making it "impossible for them to change their thinking [*metagnōnai*] and make up for their error." What the Athenians now have on their hands is a rebel city that, "realizing that it will not survive, can come to terms while it still has the resources to pay reparations and can then go on to pay its taxes in the future." If Athens goes the other way, however, "do you think there is any city at all that wouldn't make even better preparations than it does now and drag the siege out to the bitter end," if it made no difference whether it capitulated quickly or slowly? Moreover, Diodotus asks, "how can it not hurt our interests if we spend our money during a siege, and then if we do conquer the place, take control of a wasteland that can give us no revenues?" Prudent reflection suggests, then, that the Athenians would harm themselves more than the "criminal" Mytileneans if they take the course of annihilation.[99]

These arguments are grounded in an account of human beings as naturally prone to fight to the death against those who seek to deprive them of freedom. Diodotus emphasizes how difficult it is to "subdue a free man who is dominated by force [*bia archomenon*], and who has revolted in favor of self-government [*pros autonomian*], as of course he should be expected to do."[100] Judged by Cleon's standards of justice, such men might seem to deserve violent punishments. But, Diodotus argues, the most expedient course is not "excessively to punish free men who have rebelled," but rather to "keep a careful watch to prevent rebellion and to prevent the notion of it even entering their heads; and then when we do use force, to prosecute as few of them as possible." Otherwise, as the Mytileneans' earlier speech made clear, the ruler will cease to be trusted even by his less downtrodden allies, who may all turn against him as the Mytileneans turned against Athens. By "executing moderate [*metriōs*] punishments" against disgruntled subjects, Athens might continue to rule strong cities whose taxes and troops help its cause. In the name of expediency alone, Athens should stop relying on the terrors inflicted by excessively punitive "laws" or "justice" and rely instead on responsible actions (*apo tōn ergōn tēs epimeleias*) to preserve power.[101] The most expedient way to hold an

---

[98] TPW, III.44.

[99] See chap. 12 on similar arguments in Livy and Machiavelli about the necessity to choose between extremes.

[100] Compare Machiavelli, chaps. 6–7.

[101] TPW, III.45–46.

empire, Diodotus concludes, is "to willingly let yourselves be wronged before you justly annihilate" others—where the paradoxical idea of "just annihilation" is understood according to Cleon's corrupt, one-sided notion of justice as revenge.

Like Cleon, then, Diodotus presents his fellow citizens with a stark choice. They may come to terms with the rebel city, thereby keeping a taxpaying ally that at present still contains many loyal citizens. Or they may conduct an indiscriminate massacre and create an enemy to the death, thus weakening Athens' hold on its empire and undermining the city's own security. Diodotus concludes by declaring that "as to Cleon's equation of justice with expediency in his call for revenge, we have found that it is not possible to have both."[102] *If* justice is taken to mean vengeance, *then* justice is incompatible with the reflective conception of expediency just set out, since wanton vengeance invariably destroys the most basic conditions for human coexistence: trust and respect for other people's freedom. If the word "justice" is understood in a more adequate sense, however, it clearly is compatible with Diodotus' reflective conception of expediency. Some elements of an adequate conception of justice are set out in his speech. Justice properly understood aims to restore order, not eliminate offenders. It appeals to people's sense of responsibility instead of terrifying them with immoderate penalties. It takes different sides' legitimate claims into account, instead of treating one's own desires as the touchstone of right and wrong. Prudent observers of human nature conceive of justice in these ways because they recognize that human beings consider themselves as naturally free, and should thus be expected to fight back to the death when others show contempt for their freedom.

Not only does Diodotus say a great deal about justice "between the lines"; he demonstrates the opposite of his overt, dissimulating claim that judgments about expediency should be treated as prior to claims of justice. On close scrutiny, his arguments suggest that reflective expediency requires respect for justice in the more adequate sense just outlined. Actions that are judged to be unjust on those criteria always, Diodotus implies, provoke reactions that are harmful to the unjust agent. The reactions are not always immediate or strong enough to seem threatening. But human nature being what it is, jealous of freedom and resentful of offenses, agents can be reasonably certain that people they unjustly offend or oppress will fight back. If they eliminate one group of such people, others will be angered by this arrogant violence or *hubris*, and fight back even harder. Whereas Cleon defined justice in terms of an unreflective notion of expediency, Diodotus demonstrates that a reflective conception of expediency must include respect for justice. He avoids making this argument directly because he is addressing an audience who, for the most part, have long ceased to value the standards customarily upheld by the good word "justice."[103] Carried away by arrogant self-regard, the desire for more than

---

[102] TPW, III.47.

[103] Compare Plato, *Laws* 906b–c: "What ruins us is injustice and senseless aggression [*adikia kai hubris*]; what protects us is justice and prudent moderation [*sōphrosunē*]." The greatest threat to the benefits of these virtues is *pleonexia*, the desire for more than one's share. It is represented metaphorically as "disease" when it appears in flesh and blood, and "plague" when brought by the seasons or at intervals of years; while if it occurs in the city and constitution, the same vice emerges under yet another name:

their share of power, and the corrupt moral language of popular orators, Diodotus' compatriots can be brought to respect justice in their deeds only under color of words that feign indifference to justice. His arguments win the debate by a very narrow margin, and Mytilene avoids massacre.

Although Machiavelli does not directly acknowledge Thucydides as a source in the *Florentine Histories*, the most prudent character in that work, Niccolò da Uzzano, opposes an ill-advised war with arguments remarkably similar to Diodotus'. Realizing that his overambitious fellow citizens are only moved by self-interest, Uzzano says he will set aside questions of justice and speak only of utility, and makes other specific arguments that echo those presented by Thucydides.[104] A different kind of dissimulation about justice occurs in the debate about whether Athens should attack Sicily. Athens' senior general Nicias strongly opposes the expedition with arguments similar to Diodotus'. "It is senseless," he argues, "to assault people whom you can't hold on to [*mē kataschēsei*] after you conquer them, while failure would leave you worse off than before you attacked."[105] In Thucydides' account, Nicias' reasons for opposing the expedition betray a deep reflective prudence that ought to be valued in responsible citizens, but which is ridiculed in such times as excessive caution or timorousness. In the end, he warns, it is not good or bad fortune that decides a contest, but planning and hard work, through which the Spartans might yet prevail. Echoing earlier maxims that warn against *hubris* and *pleonexia*, Nicias argues that Athenians should not endanger their city by "reaching for another empire before we have secured the one we have." Nicias' appeal for restraint is ridiculed by the young Alcibiades, who insists that "if we don't rule over others, they will rule over us." Nicias opposes this assertion by echoing Diodotus' analysis: when dealing with large, independent cities or with free men, it is "unlikely that they would accept our rule in exchange for their freedom [*eleutherias*]." This time the assembled citizens of Athens opt for preemptive unilateralism, rejecting Diodotus' and Nicias' maxim that unwanted rule is seldom lasting. Nicias is obliged to sail into Sicily against his better judgment, and after a long siege Athens suffers massive defeat.[106]

Almost identical arguments are evaluated throughout all Machiavelli's main works. Among the many formal and substantive similarities that can be found between Machiavelli's and Thucydides' writings, one of the clearest is a theme stressed in Nicias' speech against assaulting Sicily: that it is the height of imprudence to try to take what you cannot hold.[107] Commenting on Nicias' arguments

"injustice." Thucydides and Livy frequently describe diseases and plagues in language that echoes their descriptions of unjust conduct.

[104] *FH*, IV.19.165–66/495–97; see chap. 9, sec. 9.3.
[105] TPW, VI.9–14.
[106] TPW, VI.9–23.
[107] Compare Plato, *Seventh Letter* 331e–332c, and Xenophon's (XC, I.126–29) remark that men who appear wise have often "persuaded states to take up arms against others"; then "the states thus persuaded to attack have been destroyed" because they did not recognize bad advice. Many "who might have treated people as friends" but did not "have received their just deserts from these very people, because they preferred to treat them like slaves rather than as friends." Still others, "not satisfied to live

in the *Discourses*, Machiavelli suggests that they lost the debate not because they were weaker than Alcibiades', but because at this stage in the war, Athenians' judgment was so deeply corrupted that even prudent appeals to self-interest had poor chances of prevailing. "In Greece, in the city of Athens," Machiavelli writes, "Nicias, a very grave and prudent man, was never able to persuade that people that it might not be good to go to assault Sicily." Thus "when that decision was taken against the wish of the wise, the entire ruin of Athens followed from it." The *Histories* presents comparable examples of prudent statesmen advising restraint but failing to carry the majority against more incendiary persuasions. In each case, the failure to take prudent advice resulted in serious harm to Florence's interests. And in each case the prudent statesman's failure to dissuade others is not due to his own shortcomings as leader or orator; Machiavelli makes it clear that ultimate responsibility for ill-advised policies lies with the people who adopt them, not with those who tried their best to prevent their adoption.[108] The next three chapters examine the main elements of the philosophical medicine he offers as a prophylactic against such misjudgments.

---

contentedly, in enjoyment of their own proper share [*autois to meros*], have lost even that which they had, because they have desired to be lords of everything."

[108] *D*, I.53.107/305–7; compare III.16.255/465–67. See chaps. 8–12.

FOUNDATIONS

II

CHAPTER 3

Imitation and Knowledge

The *Discourses* begin by observing that in modern times antiquity is never "imitated" in the field of politics. On the whole "the most virtuous works the histories show us, which have been done by ancient kingdoms and republics, by kings, captains, citizens, legislators, and others who have labored for their fatherland" are, Machiavelli notes, more often admired than imitated. Indeed these works "are so much shunned by everyone in every least thing that no sign of that ancient virtue remains with us." This, Machiavelli declares, makes him "marvel and grieve."[1] Yet his own admiration for the ancients is not naïve or undiscriminating. He is well aware that modern princes and republics frequently mimic the names, maxims, and other appearances of antiquity in the hope of lending an aura of greatness to imprudent or *disonesto* deeds. It is unlikely that Machiavelli wants his contemporaries to imitate ancient political works in this shallow way. Yet he raises two sets of questions that underscore very serious difficulties involved in any more substantial kind of imitation. One concerns the epistemic grounds for judging what works it is reasonably *possible* to imitate, especially if imitators hope to achieve the same results as their ancient models. In Machiavelli's view, precious few historical records show as much concern for the truth as for partisan or private purposes. How then can contemporaries be sure that the ancient works they want to imitate came about in the ways described by the records? Indeed, given the frequent attribution of supernatural aid or powers to the most reputed kings, captain, and legislators, can imitators have any well-founded confidence that their actions are humanly imitable at all? A second set of questions is normative. Regardless of what seems possible, what standards *should* be used to decide which ancient political works are worth imitating? Many ancient works reported in the histories had undoubted *grandezza*. But do all political actions that embody greatness deserve equal praise, or are some praised more reasonably than others?

3.1.
The ancient tradition of imitating ancients

The theme of imitating ancients was a well-established topos in Greek, Roman, and Hellenistic writings.[2] Machiavelli's use of the theme echoes a long tradition in

---

[1] *D*, I.Pref.5–6/197–98.

[2] Mansfield (2000, 234) makes the puzzling assertion that "the ancients had no ancients." They certainly thought they had.

which historical and philosophical writers criticized the present in an indirect way by discussing comparable events in the past.[3] Critical uses of the topos took present times as corrupt, and evoked antiquity or the deeds of "our ancestors" as sources of excellent laws and customs that were in danger of being forgotten. An example familiar to Roman and Hellenistic writers as well as Machiavelli's contemporaries appears in Plato's dialogues *Timaeus* and *Critias*, which Plato presents as companions to the *Republic*. The *Republic*'s overt subject is how to build a well-ordered city based on justice. It shows very young men trying, within the limits of their nascent abilities, to legislate according to what they take to be philosophical principles. The *Timaeus* underscores the need to supplement these reasonings with historical knowledge of how different cities have been built and destroyed in the past. What, it asks, can builders of new cities learn by studying the causes that strengthened and weakened ancient polities? Are new systems of laws likely to last longer if their founders imitate older models of long-lasting constitutions? The ensuing discussion suggests that there are no simple, unphilosophical answers to these questions such as many young or narrowly practical men seek. New legislators should certainly study past examples. But their studies will prove useless if they are not guided by highly reflective judgments about two things: the scope and limits of their own legislative powers, and what ancient deeds deserve to be imitated.

The *Timaeus* uses the idea of imitating ancients to argue that city-building should be informed by mature reflections on how different kinds of necessity (*anangkē*) impinge on human works. Since necessity ensures that no such works are eternal or incorruptible, human legislators should not aspire to imitate the quality of immortality ascribed to the divine, let alone see themselves as godlike authors of all the matter for which they legislate. Only God creates matter *and* imposes order on it; human builders must impose order within constraints set by divine and material necessity.[4] The practical implications of these arguments are vividly illustrated in the *Critias*, where the eponymous character recounts the rise and swift collapse of a very great power, Atlantis. The Atlantis myth conveys a timeless message: that even the greatest human works may be swept overnight into oblivion when the people responsible for upholding them fail to respect constraints placed on their actions by necessity, not least the ethical necessity to avoid acting as a tyrant over others. The circumstances of Atlantis' rise and fall have obvious parallels with the Peloponnesian War, in which an overconfident Athens' attempt to dominate the Hellenic world had destroyed all that had once been good in Athenian orders, while exposing all of Greece to the expansionist thrusts of better-ordered foreign powers. Affirming the *Timaeus*' point that human builders must develop a clear sense of their own limited legislative powers, Critias' narra-

---

[3] Fornara (1983, 106–9) identifies Xenophon, Livy, Tacitus, and Sallust as authors of "critical histories." The last three were influenced by Thucydides. My brief discussion here includes Plato as a philosopher who made frequent use of "mythical" histories for similar critical purposes. Also see Brisson 1999, esp. 128–33.

[4] Plato, *Tim.* The dialogue stresses the positive role of necessity in eliciting the best human works, both corporeal and moral; see 46e–48a, 53d, 56c, 68e–70b. Also compare 75e–76e and D, III.12.246/456 on how necessity improves the "hands and tongue of men."

tive implies that they also need mature capacities of evaluative judgment in order to learn from past experience. At the very least, anyone who wants to imitate ancient works should be able to distinguish true greatness or virtue from mere appearances. Judged by its size, wealth, and military power, Atlantis appeared to be the greatest of known cities. Its total collapse under pressure of war showed how brittle its powers were, calling into question the adequacy of any idea of greatness derived from such ephemeral attributes.[5] The parable suggests that when legislators encounter historical examples that seem eminently worthy of imitation (*mimēsis*), they should pause before rushing to imitate them, and first examine the standards they use to make such judgments. Otherwise, philosophically inexperienced legislators may imitate mere appearances of greatness or justice in ancient works, unaware that the original works were less well made than they seemed, and ultimately led to great disorders.[6]

The twin dangers of overestimating one's own powers and failing to distinguish imitation-worthy qualities from appearances came again to the fore in writings composed under the late Roman republic and empire. When critical Romans debated whether and how to imitate their ancient ancestors or the more ancient Greeks, their chief concern was not to identify ways to enhance military or imperial greatness, but to warn contemporaries against *hubris* and encourage a more reflective approach to judging what is imitation-worthy. "What chiefly makes the study of history profitable," Livy writes in the preface to his *opus magnum*, is

> that you behold the lessons of every kind of experience set forth as on a conspicuous monument; from these you may choose for yourself and for your own state what to imitate, from these mark for avoidance what is shameful in the conception and shameful in the result.[7]

Livy acknowledges from the outset that the main subject of his histories, the Roman republic, will meet an unhappy end in "these modern times" (*ad haec nova*), when "the might of a people which has long been very powerful is working its own undoing [*quibus iam pridem praevalentis populi vires se ipsae conficiunt*]."[8] His histories do not describe an idealized antiquity that serves as an escapist diversion from, or reproach to, the corrupt present.[9] On the contrary, his accounts of the "brave days of old" show that from its earliest beginnings Rome was wracked by internal struggles and external wars, which often came close to destroying the

---

[5] Plato, *Crit.* 108d–121b.

[6] As argued in *Rep.* 598a–c. A story told in *Tim.* 21a–26d intimates that the Greeks—Athenians above all—were susceptible to this kind of error. When Athens' ancient lawgiver Solon travels to Egypt in search of archaic wisdom about how to legislate, he is told by a very old Egyptian priest that the Greeks are mere children as compared with peoples who have firmer beliefs about antiquity (*palaian doxan*) that regulate their conduct.

[7] *LH*, Pref.6–7.

[8] Compare *FH* on the self-inflicted undoing of the Florentine republic.

[9] Despite his admission that he takes pleasure in dwelling on the past so that he "may avert my gaze from the troubles which our age has been witnessing for so many years" and become "absorbed in the recollection of the brave days of old, free from every care which, even if it could not divert the historian's mind from the truth, might nevertheless cause it anxiety." *LH*, Pref.4–5.

city altogether. The causes of such near-fatal crises were, on Livy's accounts, largely self-inflicted. In the most serious cases they involved overstepping restraints on conduct set down by ancient customs and religion, whose articles included the sanctity of oaths among compatriots, allies, and enemies. Rome recovered its strength only when the city publicly acknowledged its errors, made amends to the parties it had wronged, and abandoned aggressive or unjust methods in favor of more moderate policies.[10] The purging of corrupt moral standards—reflected in the corrupt use of words used to praise or blame men and deeds—is an essential part of this remedy for Livy as for Thucydides, Socrates, and Xenophon. Such purging took Romans back, as it were, to the sound ordering standards embodied in their ancient customs. The deeds that followed or restored these customs and standards emerge as most worthy of imitation. If his contemporaries applied these standards to their own times, Livy implies, they should be appalled by the extent of their decline.

In Rome under the emperors, some of Machiavelli's favorite writers used the ancient Greek topos of imitating ancients to criticize imperial censorship and political oppression while appearing to discuss more innocuous pedagogical matters. In his "Dialogue of Oratory," a fictional debate about the comparative merits of ancient and modern rhetoric, Cornelius Tacitus (c. AD 56–117) obliquely examines how the empire's institutions tried to impose conformity to a rigid set of behavioral and cognitive norms, with the aim of eliminating any dissent—and indeed any genuine freedom—among citizens. The ostensible target of the dialogue's criticisms are Tacitus' self-satisfied contemporaries, who see the most recent styles of oratory as superior to older methods. Expressing this view, a first speaker challenges the very distinction between ancients and moderns. Many orators who his opponents praise as practitioners of good "ancient" rhetoric are not, he points out, very ancient at all; people who dislike present practices use the word "ancient" for anything they admire, while taking an unjustly dim view of modern innovations. In reply, Tacitus has the dialogue's main speaker give a robust defense of critical uses of the ancients versus moderns distinction. He gladly admits that he himself employs the concept of "ancients" in an evaluative way, evoking specific ancient practices in order to criticize defective modern ones. The examples he holds up for imitation are not idealized; they also have deficiencies. But these are minor indeed as compared with the defects of present corrupt practices. For example, defenders of modern practices charge that ancient rhetoric was undisciplined and idiosyncratic, reflecting the individual styles of orators instead of following conventional rules. Though this may be true, readers should ask themselves which is worse: individualism in modes of speaking or the heavy-handed, uniform rules imposed in modern times by state-controlled schools. Imperial authorities criticize ancient and more recent pre-imperial orators for fomenting "license" and destabilizing the republic by appealing to popular passions. The speaker again concedes that this is true. But he asks readers to consider whether the conduct called licentious by its

---

[10] Most notably during the wars with Gaul and Rome's Italian neighbors, and later with Carthage; see chaps. 5–8, 12.

authoritarian critics, however harmful, was worse than the so-called order that is destroying freedom in the present-day Roman empire.[11]

Outside the city of Rome itself, Tacitus' Greek contemporary and fellow Roman citizen Plutarch developed a wide range of subtly critical uses for the theme of imitating ancients. His *Parallel Lives* and essays show that Plutarch was deeply interested in examining the causes, especially internal causes, that had destroyed the independence of Greek cities and that of the "province" as a whole. Like Thucydides and Plato, he sees the corruption of "ancient" morals in the leading city of Athens as one major cause, overconfidence in the city's power to dominate others as another. In earlier times the Athenians were praised for building the "far-shining foundation of freedom" as a beacon to Greeks and other peoples; after their disastrous failure in Sicily their "fame" came to rest on the glories of their theater. Where at one time their actions merited high praise, now one saw only images of past glory painted by writers and mimicked on stage. Since the Peloponnesian War Athenians had become famous for their skills in creating appearances. But, Plutarch implies, they were deplorably bad at seeing through them.[12] Far from blaming Athenians for the Greeks' current subjection to Rome, however, his *Lives* show that poorly regulated ambitions could be found in all Greek cities in every period of Hellenic history, as they can in Rome. Plutarch employs the topos of imitating ancients to stimulate critical self-examination among his compatriots. His *Lives* remind readers living under the Roman yoke—Romans as well as Greeks, and by extension any other subject peoples—of the deeds that made their ancestors free and deserving of praise. At the same time, they cast a glaring spotlight on homegrown negligence, errors, and injustices that led them to sell out their own hard-won freedom. In most cases these causes did not involve outright viciousness, but ordinary human weaknesses. Nonetheless, by studying ancient examples, later generations can reflect on how similar weaknesses may be anticipated and corrected.

Plutarch's writings encourage readers to exercise their capacities for ethical discrimination so that they might become better at seeing through virtuous appearances, and therefore better judges of what ancient deeds are worth imitating. Like other Socratic writers, he held that these capacities could not be taught by sermons or treatises. Individuals had to develop them for themselves through reading and free discussion.[13] Ancient examples should inspire readers to desire a life of honorable acts, and perhaps to imitate what they see as best in ancient deeds. But far from involving hero-worship or uncritical mimicry, imitation understood in an adequate sense is a highly individual matter. As a recent scholar puts it, for Plutarch good imitation rests on reasoned moral choice, and therefore individual choice.[14] He wants his readers, especially the young, to recognize the

---

[11] Tacitus, "A Dialogue on Oratory" (1979, 270–347).

[12] For example, Plutarch, "Were the Athenians More Famous in War or in Wisdom?" PM, IV.492–527.

[13] Plutarch, "Listening," PM, I.204–59.

[14] See Duff 1999, 38–41; Plutarch, "Progress," PM, I.448–53.

harm that may be done through actions that appear great, liberal, or humane, so that they will become more vigilant defenders of their countries and of justice. This requires a kind of critical judgment that is incompatible with excessive deference to authority, even toward writers such as Plutarch or great teachers like Socrates. While Plutarch often offers evaluations of his own, he does so only after presenting evidence and weighing good reasons for different views. By proposing a tentative case for his judgments and avoiding polemic, he invites readers to develop their own balanced, reasoned appraisals of each *Life*. With few exceptions, the men and deeds he presents are not thoroughly praiseworthy or vicious. Idealized accounts of ancient deeds discourage independent, critical reasoning about what deserves to be imitated and how. It is better, Plutarch argues, for readers of histories or poetry not to regard everything with awe, but to "acquire the habit of exclaiming with confidence 'wrong' and 'improper' no less than 'right' and 'proper.'" If a young man rushes to embrace exalted "opinions" about "good and great names . . . he will be greatly injured if he approves everything, and is in a state of wonderment over it, but resents nothing" in his heroes. For the man who admires everything and "whose judgement, because of his preconceived opinion, is enthralled by the heroic names" will often "be inclined to conform to much that is base" while imagining that he imitates what is best.[15] Young men must first learn how to judge different accounts of deeds that inspire desires for emulation; then to distinguish good from bad actions; and only later try to imitate what they judge to be good. For this purpose, those accounts are best that show "both virtue and vice commingled" in the acts and characters held up as models for study.[16] To bolster their defenses against those who seek to enslave them, readers should train themselves not only to see through misleading appearances but also to rely on senses other than sight and hearing, which often deceive the young or unwary.[17]

Plutarch's deceptively subtle modes of writing reflect both his Socratic inspiration and the constraints on freedom of expression placed on writers under the empire. In "provinces" such as Greece, talk of revolt against the imperial administration rumbled on beneath quiet appearances. Plutarch occasionally criticizes such anti-imperial rumblings. He observes, for example, that local officials and demagogues often "foolishly urge the people to imitate the deeds, ideals, and actions of their ancestors, however unsuitable they may be to the present times and conditions." Plutarch does not try to hide his own regret for his country's lost freedoms. His essay titled "Precepts of Statesmanship" notes sadly that peoples living under Rome's imperium have no need for many of the statesman's skills. Under the nominal peace imposed by the one universal power, now "of liberty the peoples have as great a share as our rulers grant them" and not a whit more. His remark that "perhaps more would not be better for them" is clearly ironic. But as the

---

[15] Plutarch, "Poetry," PM, I.132–37.

[16] Ibid., PM, I.124–31.

[17] Plutarch, "Fame of Athenians," PM, IV.508–9; "Listening," PM, I.207; "On Chance [*Peri tuchēs*]," PM, II.78–79. See next section on similar themes in Machiavelli.

last chapter suggested, Plutarch prefers persuasion over violent revolution as an agency of political change. Moreover, given the "weak condition of Greek affairs," those who poisoned their air with "bad words, malice, and threats" only invited further repression. Some ancient deeds of Greeks should be imitated, especially those apt for repelling tyranny and corruption close to home. But the great battles, uprisings, and conspiracies of the past that led some Greeks "vainly to swell with pride" are, Plutarch argues, best "left to the schools of the sophists." Greece now needs statesmen who remain blameless in the eyes of their Roman rulers and work quietly, for example through the "medicine" of writings such as Plutarch's, to keep up the spirit of freedom.[18]

3.2.
Inadequate imitation: The "unreasonable praise of antiquity"

Xenophon's *Lacedaemonians* starts by describing some of the excellent laws given by the Spartan lawgiver Lycurgus, who "laid on the people the duty of practicing the whole virtue of a citizen as a necessity irresistible [*anangkēn askein apasan politikēn aretēn*]." Then Xenophon remarks:

> Now that these laws [*nomoi*] are of high antiquity [*palaiotatoi*] there can be no doubt. . . . Nevertheless, in spite of their antiquity, they are wholly strange to others even at this day. Indeed, it is most astonishing that all men praise such institutions, but no state chooses to imitate them [*mimeisthai de auta oudemia polis ethelei*].[19]

Xenophon's main explanation for this astonishing fact is that the ethical and political judgment of his contemporaries has been corrupted by the excessive ambition on the part of men who "strive far more earnestly to exercise rule than to be worthy of it." Spartan kings are no longer regarded in honor "as mere men" but as "demigods."[20] This makes it seem impossible to emulate the high standards set for them by Lycurgan laws.

Machiavelli adopts a similar tone of astonishment when he remarks at the beginning of the *Discourses* that while his contemporaries praise the political works of the ancients, none go so far as to imitate them.[21] Like Xenophon, he attributes this reticence to tendencies found in corrupt times to idealize the less corrupt past. By depicting ancient "kings, captains, citizens, legislators" as almost godlike figures who bear scant resemblance to their living counterparts, some writers make their deeds seem so remote that no one thinks of imitating them, "judging that imitation is not only difficult but impossible—as if heaven, sun, elements, men had varied in

---

[18] Plutarch, "Precepts," PM, X:238–41, 290–99, 244–45.

[19] Xenophon, "Lacedaemonians" in *Scripta Minora*, 168–71.

[20] Ibid., 184–89. Xenophon hints at another explanation: that the laws themselves set standards that were too high for mere mortals to achieve; see chap. 11, sec. 11.1.

[21] D, I.Pref .5/197–98. He makes a similar remark on the Roman mode of expansion in D, II.4, discussed in chap. 12.

motion, order, and power from what they were in antiquity."[22] Machiavelli counters these judgments by arguing that the world has always been "in the same mode" and the virtue praised in the past has not completely forsaken even the most dejected provinces; indeed, "the virtue that is desired and is praised with true praise" could be found in many places even after "the Romans were ruined."[23]

In the preface of Book II, however, Machiavelli complicates his apparently straightforward call to imitate antiquities. He now declares, "Men always praise ancient times—but not always reasonably [*ragionevolmente*]—and accuse the present." We have just noted one sense in which such praise may be unreasonable: when "partisans of the past" exaggerate ancient glories by contrast with present ills. Another form of unreasonable praise is even more common: when people admire ancient deeds that have a name for greatness, without examining their true quality.[24] Machiavelli alludes to this error in the *Histories*, suggesting in the preface that readers should avoid the temptation to admire or imitate all those deeds that have "greatness [*grandezza*] in themselves." Such deeds "always appear to bring men more honor than blame" but turn out on closer scrutiny to have produced grave disorders.[25] Instead of rushing to imitate whatever deeds are "seen" to have *grandezza*, *reputazione*, or *onore*, readers should strive to imitate only the "most virtuous works the histories show us," which may not be those that attract the most praise.[26]

How then does Machiavelli propose to distinguish genuinely praiseworthy works from those that are praised unreasonably? He hints in the first preface that since the capacity to make evaluative judgments cannot be learned in the same way as technical skills, political imitation is much more demanding than purely aesthetic and technical kinds.[27] Indeed, the need to make such judgments helps to explain why people are so reluctant to imitate ancients in matters such as "ordering republics, maintaining states, governing kingdoms, ordering the military and administering war, judging subjects, and increasing empire." Judgments about what deserves praise or blame are arguable even in the best of times. In corrupt times when *onesto* words such as "freedom," "justice," and "greatness" are routinely used

---

[22] *D*, I.Pref.6/198. Compare Livy, who points to the opposite source of error found in complacent, *hubris*-prone cities: poor judgment in choosing what to imitate is caused by a lack of interest in what people consider the remote past, often under the conceit that what is thought and done in their own times must represent a clear improvement on the past.

[23] *D*, II.Pref.124/325–26.

[24] For example, the modern Venetians "disposed themselves to have a spirit of monarchy made like the Roman," a mode of imitation that would soon weaken the city's internal freedoms and force its rulers to rely on external support. Elsewhere Machiavelli says that the "sayings and deeds" of the modern French imitate the maxims of ancient patriotism "so as to defend the majesty of their king and the power of their kingdom." *D*, III.31.282–83/494–97; III.41.301/515. These examples suggest that Machiavelli must not mean it literally when he says that moderns never imitate the ancients in political matters; he must mean either that modern imitators have not tried to imitate the right ancients, or that they have not imitated the right ancients in the right way.

[25] *FH*, Pref.7–8/308–11.

[26] *D*, I.Pref .5/197–98.

[27] Compare Plutarch ("Old Man," *PM*, X.114–17): "Treatises on navigation do not make ship-captains" of men who lack experience and study; it is even harder to teach political expertise through treatises, since it requires knowledge of virtue.

to color *disonesto* deeds, even good men may be crippled with doubt about their own capacities to judge well. This helps to explain the surprising fact that while Machiavelli's contemporaries are wary of imitating ancient political *opere*, they are happy to follow ancient models in the fields of plastic art, civil law, and medicine. Imitation in these fields requires technical knowledge and technical judgment. Modern statue-makers, lawyers, and doctors are "taught" by studying the ancient works directly, and faithfully following the authority of their authors. Ancient works of art have "intrinsic glory" that is not much disputed; ancient statutes and medical prescriptions also lay out clear codes, cures, and cases that are taken by all as authoritative. The works being imitated are "nothing other than verdicts given by ancient jurists, which, reduced to order, teach our present jurists to judge" and "experiments performed by ancient physicians, on which present physicians found their judgements." By contrast, there are no works available to political imitators that have such clear or undisputed authority. Whereas the arts have "clarity in themselves," this cannot be said about "the lives and customs of men, of which such clear testimonies are not seen."[28] Before political actors can think of imitating the ancients, they must use their own judgment to decide which of the many ancient works recounted in histories deserve to be imitated.

While Machiavelli is encouraged by the fact that contemporaries imitate ancients in some fields, then, he does not want readers to imagine that imitating the deeds of "kings, captains, citizens, legislators" and the like is as straightforward a matter as imitating ancient art or medicine. If they approach political imitation as if it involves mainly technical kinds of expertise but fail to develop capacities for evaluative judgment, they risk imitating unworthy deeds, or worthy ones in the wrong way. Broadly speaking, imitation in the arts, civil law, and medicine aims to *reproduce* an existing object or a condition. Legal statutes and ancient medical prescriptions are reproductive in the sense that they aim to regulate existing conditions, rather than seeking to establish new ones. When moderns imitate ancient political deeds, however, they cannot simply copy the originals. For one thing, there are no original deeds at hand, but only records that are often fragmentary or untrustworthy. For another, the circumstances that condition political actions are never identical. Political imitators therefore cannot avoid innovating much more extensively than imitators of ancient statutes or medicine. They must use their own judgment to generate a coherent, attractive account of the deeds they want to imitate, aware that historical records may be unreliable, incomplete, or open to vastly different interpretations.

In the plastic arts a reproduction may serve wider aesthetic or private purposes: it may produce aesthetic pleasure in observers, or confer an aura of honor on the owners.[29] These effects, the pleasure or the aura, are what make people value the copy; and the quality of the original may have no bearing at all on the valued present effects. Political actors often seek to imitate ancient works merely to confer an air of ancient greatness on their own. But since the effects they seek to produce are

[28] *D*, I.Pref.5–6/197–98.
[29] *AW*, I.10–11/533–35; VII:163–64/688–89.

public and far-reaching, the value of the original must be assessed by some more than private, subjective, or wholly conventional criterion. Otherwise political imitation is reduced to mere appearance-making uninformed by any "reasonable" standards of prudence and imprudence, goodness or badness, order or disorder. While masters of this mode of imitation are often considered wise, in the *Florentine Histories* and elsewhere Machiavelli shows that their technical skills lack any stable compass capable of building or sustaining political orders. Imitators who have the kind of virtue that is "praised with true praise" examine ancient works in order to identify publicly defensible standards for stable building, not simply to persuade people to support their badly ordered modes of government.

Machiavelli frequently uses the language of the senses to contrast more and less discriminating forms of imitation. His contemporaries do not imitate the "most virtuous" ancient works, he writes, because they lack "a true knowledge of histories [*vera cognizione delle storie*] through not getting from reading them that sense nor tasting that flavor that they have in themselves [*quel senso né gustare di loro quel sapore che le hanno in sé*]." If people "got from reading" histories the full "sense" they have, they might stop "judging that imitation is not only difficult but impossible." Senses such as taste are needed to gain a "true knowledge" of histories because the main sense used in reading, sight, is an extremely unreliable guide for making evaluative judgments.[30] Machiavelli alludes to this problem when he observes that when considering what political acts deserve praise or blame, we are "not reasoning about the arts, which have so much clarity in themselves" that the times cannot alter their intrinsic glory." It is necessary to reason in a much more critical way about "the lives and customs of men, of which such clear testimonies are not *seen*."[31] Original works of ancient art can be observed directly, but ancient political works can only be "seen" through the imitative and selective medium of records or testimonies, that is, through others' eyes, which should never be taken as an adequate authority. Like Xenophon and Plutarch, Machiavelli urges readers to activate senses other than sight when reading ancient histories or his own, so that they may develop more effective defenses against attempts to seduce them with virtuous appearances. Many puzzling parts of his texts can be read as exercises in "seeing through" an overt message to a very different, covert one, not so much by sharpening one's sense of sight as by considering what "taste" is left in one's mouth by an account of apparently virtuous deeds, or how an account "smells." If readers do not get from histories the sense they contain or taste their flavor, this may be due to their own unwillingness to engage thoughtfully with what they read. Passive reading that takes words or the images they convey at face value will either fail to inspire imitation, or furnish a very poor basis for it.[32]

---

[30] Compare TPW, I.10, III.103–4, VI.16, VI.30–31 on misleading appearances of greatness or wisdom.

[31] *D*, I.Pref .6/198; II.Pref.123/324; emphasis added.

[32] For example, in the *Histories'* accounts of the "works" of the Medicis the most striking words—"pomp," "magnificence," "reputation," "greatness," "extraordinary"—evoke splendid appearances. Yet the accounts of deeds, and subtler choices of words, leave behind a bad taste. The *Prince* too calls for sensitivity to what is not seen, through the sense of touch: "Men judge by their eyes more than their

3.3.
Historical judgment: Criticism of sources and self-examination

In the *Discourses* and elsewhere, Machiavelli offers several more specific suggestions about how prospective imitators should and should not approach the study
of "histories." A first condition for attaining a "true knowledge" of ancient works
has already been mentioned: avoid taking judgments about what deserves to be
imitated on anyone else's authority. Machiavelli frequently distinguishes between
judgments based on what is "known" according to common opinion or reputed authorities, on the one hand, and judgments based on reasons (*ragioni*) independent
of examples, convention, tradition, or the views of the powerful.[33] Independent
reasoning (*ragionare*) enables readers to scrutinize various ideals of ancient virtue,
subject them to critical analysis, and emerge with a more discriminating account
of the elements that deserve to be praised or imitated and others that do not. The
Art of War dramatizes this approach by describing the interlocutors' uncertainty
about what parts of ancient life they should imitate and, more importantly, how
much independent judgment is needed to evaluate the ancient models they discuss. At the end of the dialogue the main speaker, Fabrizio Colonna, recalls that
at the outset his younger friends had been perplexed by an apparent tension in his
views on imitating ancient things:

> If you remember well, Cosimo, you said to me that you were unable to find
> out the cause for this: that, on the one hand, I am the exalter of antiquity
> and blamer of those who in grave things do not imitate it, and, on the other,
> I have not imitated it in the things of war, where I have exerted myself. To
> this I responded that men who want to do something, must first prepare
> themselves to know how to do it, so as then to be better able to do it when
> the opportunity permits. Whether I would know how [*sapere*] to return the
> military to ancient modes or not, I want for judges you who have heard me
> dispute at length on this matter.[34]

At the start of the dialogue Fabrizio's position seemed incoherent to young men
unused to dialectical reasoning. They assumed that any practical man who "exalts"
ancient works should be eager to imitate them without discussion or delay. By the
end of the dialogue, the young speakers can more easily understand why Fabrizio
can praise antiquities yet insist on the need for careful preparation in order to know
how to imitate them well. And a first step toward this know-how (*sapere*)—which
may or may not lead toward knowledge (*cognizione*)—is for each participant in the
dialogue to shed any youthful inclination to accept judgments about "grave things"

---

hands, because seeing is given to everyone, touching to few"; "Everyone sees [*vede*] how you appear,
few touch [*sentono*] how you are" (*P*, XIV.71/157–58). As the next section shows, Machiavelli's notion
of how to read "between the lines" involves more than intuition or subjective hunches. It is based on
a context-sensitive understanding of why an author wrote the way he did, and on a reasoned account
of his methods of writing.

[33] On the relation between reasons and examples, see below and *AW*, III.73/600–601.

[34] *AW*, VII.160–61/685.

on others' authority.[35] Although Fabrizio is much more experienced in war and politics, he urges his interlocutors not to accept uncritically anything he says. They must question him from many angles, and judge for themselves whether Fabrizio would know how to return to the ancient modes he praises. It is essential that they trust their own judgment more than his or anyone else's because they, in the end, must take responsibility for military and civil orders in their city. Fabrizio declares that despite his wide experience, he is too old and lacks the ability (*facultà*) to "show the world how much ancient orders are worth." He hopes, however, that his friends will continue to evaluate the ancient orders they have discussed so that in the future they may "help and counsel your princes to their benefit."[36]

A second condition for working toward a more adequate "knowledge of histories" is closely related to the first: never take written historical accounts at face value, but learn to read between the lines. In the *Discourses* Machiavelli observes that if "the truth of ancient things is not altogether understood [*non s'intenda al tutto la verità*]," this is in part because in the writings of ancients who recorded the deeds of their own times, "most often the things that would bring infamy to those times are concealed and others that could bring forth glory are rendered magnificent and very expansive."[37] Historians may have very different motives for concealing blemishes in their subjects while exaggerating their merits. Discriminating readers may reasonably conclude that the accounts of some ancient writers, like those of many modern ones, show little concern to meet standards of truth (*verità*) or knowledge. Their main purpose was not to be useful to readers who seek a reflective understanding of how good orders are built and undermined. Instead of treating history as an aid to a more philosophical approach to politics, they make history serve private or partisan purposes. Such histories seek not to stimulate discriminating evaluations but to forestall independent judgment. Ancient writers had the same motives as modern historians for this kind of "concealing." One was ambition: some writers were eager to flatter the powerful in hopes of gaining honors or material advantages. Bearing this in mind, no reader should "deceive himself because of the glory of Caesar, hearing him especially celebrated by the writers." In most cases "those who praise him are corrupted by his fortune and awed by the duration of the empire" that ruled "under that name" after Caesar. Another motive for concealing or glorifying ancient deeds is fear: repression under the de facto empire founded by Caesar "did not permit writers to speak freely of him."[38] Clearly, anyone who seeks to imitate the deeds of Caesar as they appear in such accounts must be wary of trying to accomplish what Caesar himself may never have done. In particular, they should not imagine that the deeds praised by fearful or ambitious writers could have been accomplished without unlawful, excessive, or violent means. Although these writers omit these acts or play them

---

[35] See the next section on this distinction. The end of the *AW* (158/683, 161/685, 164/689) has a rare use of *conoscere-conoscitore*.

[36] *AW*, VII.164–65/683–85.

[37] *D*, II.Pref.123/324–25.

[38] *D*, I.10.31–32/226–28.

down in their histories, imitators of Caesar's deeds will surely find that they must take blame along with praise.[39]

Among ancient writers who were constrained to conceal or magnify, however, a few can be found whose works defend freedom while appearing to praise Caesar and blame his enemies.[40] These writers were neither ambitious enough to subordinate standards of truth to partisan ends, nor frightened enough to stop looking for ways to tell the truth as they saw it. We have seen that many of Machiavelli's favorite ancient writers developed a range of literary techniques that overtly praise powerful men, but indirectly question the virtue of their characters, deeds, and legacy. What readers at first see in texts such as Xenophon's *Cyropaedia* or Sallust's *Bellum Catilinae* does not necessarily embody the authors' most considered judgments. Careful readers can identify these less superficial meanings if they learn to rely on senses other than sight. Although Sallust seems to present Caesar as a virtuous defender of the republic against Catiline's conspiracy, Machiavelli reads the historian's apparent praise as dissimulating. The words Sallust gives to Caesar appear liberal and humane; but readers who know about Caesar's personal ambitions might smell bad faith and hypocrisy in them, and suspect that Sallust's narrative is covertly critical.[41] Unable "to blame Caesar because of his power," Machiavelli's preferred writers intimate criticism by lavishing praise on his enemies, or by attributing his defects to other men. Thus "whoever wishes to know what the writers would say of [Caesar] if they were free," Machiavelli advises, "should see what they say of Catiline," the conspirator who tried and failed to make himself effective tyrant in the Roman republic not long before Caesar tried and succeeded. Sallust draws subtle parallels between Caesar's later, successful coup and Catiline's failed one, hinting that the former deserves the same condemnation as the latter. Indeed, "Caesar is so much more detestable," Machiavelli adds, "as he who has done an evil" and pulled it off "is more to blame than he who has wished to do one" but failed.[42] Readers who become adept at spotting these clues in ancient writings will find it easier to work out Machiavelli's similarly dissimulated judgments.

The *Discourses* mention a third condition for acquiring the "knowledge of histories" needed to judge what to imitate: do not take surviving historical records as an adequate or exhaustive source for such judgments. As Plato's wise Egyptian points out in the *Timaeus*, vast quantities of human experience have been consigned to oblivion by floods or fires, natural and man-made causes. He presents the story of Atlantis as a case in point: an extraordinary human achievement that met an extraordinary and violent end, so that its lessons for posterity had been forgotten until now. Machiavelli echoes these themes, declaring that "it would be reasonable that there be memory of more than five thousand years" of human civilizations

[39] See chaps. 10, 11.

[40] Hence the common misapprehensions that Sallust was a partisan of Caesar, Tacitus a supporter of Roman empire, or Xenophon's *Cyropaedia* a monarchist tract.

[41] SBC, 51–52.

[42] *D*, I.10.31–32/226.

"if it were not seen how the memories of times are eliminated by diverse causes, of which part come from men, part from heaven." Plagues, famines, and floods may be counted as causes from heaven. Floods are the "most important" because the only survivors "are all mountain men and coarse, who, since they do not have knowledge [*notizia*] of antiquity, cannot leave it to posterity."[43] If the heavens do leave any remnant of human memories intact, someone's private ambitions will soon corrupt them. For even coarse mountain men are prone to ambition; and "if among them someone is saved who has knowledge [*notizia*]" of antiquity, "to make a reputation and a name for himself he conceals it and perverts it in his mode so that what he has wished to write alone, and nothing else, remains for his successors." The causes of forgetfulness that "come from men" are exemplified by the early Christian sect, which sought to "extinguish the old" religions "to give itself reputation." The church's leaders sought to eliminate knowledge of "ancient theology" by persecuting "all the ancient memories" and "burning the works of the poets and the historians."[44] These acts of cultural and spiritual vandalism greatly impoverished the stock of ancient wisdom available in present times.

Prospective imitators-of-ancients may well ask, then, whether there might be ancient works that have been undervalued or nearly forgotten, but whose slight traces are worth investigating as possible candidates for imitation. To spot such traces, let alone appreciate their value, students of histories must rely on their own judgment, not accept common opinions or defer to received authorities; and know how to read between the lines. For example, though extant histories say very little about the ancient Tuscans, it is still possible to find "some little memory" of their orders "and some sign of their greatness." Before the Roman Empire the Tuscans "were very powerful by sea and by land," maintaining a league of equal confederated cities for many centuries. This, Machiavelli writes, "was secure for a great time, with the highest glory of empire and of arms, and special praise for customs and religion [*con somma gloria d'imperio e d'arme, e massime laude di costumi e di religione*]." It should not "seem difficult" for present-day Tuscans or others to imitate these ancient modes. For if the paucity of historical records makes it hard to glean a "true knowledge" of Tuscan orders, at least the merits of what is reported are clear in themselves, although few writers praise them to the skies. By contrast, there is no shortage of ancient or modern writings that lavish praise on Roman modes of *imperio*, just as they praise the greatness of Caesar or Alexander. Yet detailed accounts of these modes, such as Livy's or Polybius', describe many specific deeds that prudent contemporaries are reluctant to imitate.[45] If the ancient works that are most lavishly praised are also the hardest to imitate, this may not be due to their intrinsic greatness but to the fact that their reputation rests on one-sided or inflated appraisals. Men and empires who try to imitate this superhuman kind of *grandezza* seldom succeed, whereas those who imitate the more modest "works"

[43] See Plato, *Tim.* 22b–e and *Laws* 677a–e.
[44] *D*, II.5.139–40/343–45. See chap. 10, secs. 10.5.–10.6. on the distinction between religious "sects" and non-sectarian forms of religion.
[45] *D*, II.4.135–38/337–41.

of peoples like the Tuscans have better chances of recapturing what was good in their "empire and arms, customs and religion." Such unsung works, Machiavelli suggests, should be taken seriously as candidates for imitation along with selected *opere* of Romans, Greeks, and others. Indeed, the very first ancient example that the *Discourses* say "should be imitated" is the "kingdom of the Egyptians"; the first modern examples are "the kingdom of the sultan, and the order of the Mamelukes and of their military before they were eliminated by Selim the Grand Turk." If the "names" of the former "had not been eliminated by antiquity," Machiavelli asserts, "they would be seen to merit more praise than Alexander the Great and many others whose memory is still fresh."[46]

A fourth condition for moving toward more adequate "knowledge of histories" is rigorous self-examination. When considering which ancients to imitate, readers are naturally affected by the same motives that influence historians: ambition, fear of power, partisan sympathies, or hatred. Machiavelli urges readers to examine their own responses to histories before leaping to imitate whatever deeds arouse their passions. People often praise the past "unreasonably," he observes, because "men hate things either from fear or from envy," and these feelings are aroused much more strongly toward what is close at hand. Since the "entire knowledge" (*la intera cognizione*) of present things "is not in any part concealed from you, and, together with the good, you know [*conoscendo*] many other things in them that displease you," the present is judged "much inferior to ancient things, even though [it] may in truth deserve much more glory and fame" than deeds praised in the past.[47] Hatred of the present is usually strongest in ambitious men whose own times prevent them from acquiring the power and rank they think they deserve. This makes them idealize the past as a time when, as they imagine, men who possessed virtues comparable to their own had free rein to seek the glory that was due to them.[48] Machiavelli is consistently critical of laws and policies that frustrate the desires of ambitious men to seek public offices and honors. Such men err, however, when their hatred of the present prevents them from critically examining the deeds of reputedly great ancients. Since ancient things no longer "offend you or give you cause to envy them," their flaws are readily excused or overlooked; but if the same deeds were before your eyes, you might be more wary of trying to imitate them. In corrupt times many ambitious men are tempted to imitate famous examples of extraordinary ancient energy, self-assertion, or military prowess. But prudent imitators should resist these urges, lest they act on opinions about the past that have "certain reasons that at a distance appear true but are altogether alien from the truth."[49] Ambitious men and cities should check their own impulses to imitate images of ancient greatness without considering whether the originals really were so great, let alone whether they themselves know enough to produce good imitations.

[46] *D*, I.1.16–18/199–202.
[47] The idea that things most admired that are farthest away occurs in TPW, VI.11, VI.49.
[48] *D*, II.Pref.123–25/324–27.
[49] *D*, II.22.180/385–87.

While enjoining readers to hold their passions in check when judging ancient deeds, Machiavelli admits that he himself is not immune to such lapses in reasonableness. He too cannot help blaming his own times and wanting to see the past as a source of higher standards that can be used to criticize the present, but also to inspire modern men to correct present ills. Readers are warned that Machiavelli's own reasonings may be distorted by his desire for reforms that fortune prevents him from implementing.[50] Like ancient philosophers who could only write down their political ideas because they lacked the power to realize them, Machiavelli is aware that he may overestimate human capacities for achieving good orders because he unwittingly idealizes those found in the past. "I do not know," he concedes, "if I deserve to be numbered among those who deceive themselves, if in these discourses of mine I praise too much the times of the ancient Romans and blame ours. And truly," he goes on, "if the virtue that then used to reign and the vice that now reigns were not clearer than the sun, I would go on speaking with more restraint" for fear of "falling into this deception [inganno] of which I accuse some."[51] If readers can trust his "discourses" more than those of some other writers, it is not because Machiavelli is less affected by natural passions and appetites than they. It is only because he admits that his judgments may be thus affected, and urges readers to take nothing he says on absolute authority. He will say "manifestly that which I may understand [intenderò]" of ancient and recent times, "so that the spirits of youths who may read these writings of mine can flee the latter and prepare themselves to imitate the former at whatever time fortune may give them opportunity for it." For "it is the duty of a good man to teach others the good" they could not do "because of the malignity of the times and of fortune, so that when many are capable of it, someone of them more loved by heaven may be able to work it."[52] But given all the passages that urge readers to take a critical view of everything they read, including the Discourses itself, it seems unlikely that the youths Machiavelli hopes will be among his readers would be hero-worshippers looking for a leader whose teachings serve as a beacon. His modes of writing are not those of a writer seeking deference from admirers who hope to imbibe vera cognizione secondhand, but of one who wants to provoke readers to think for themselves.

3.4.
The Socratic metaphor of hunting

Further clues as to how a vera cognizione of histories may be approached are found in Machiavelli's discussions of "hunting" in the Prince and the Discourses. Chapters in both works recommend hunting (le cacce) as a means of exercising for war; the title of the Prince's chapter 14, which deals with hunting, is "What a Prince Should Do Regarding the Military" (Quod Principem Deceat Circa Militiam). Both

---

[50] Compare Thucydides' remark that it is usual for men to claim what they want to be true "even on an unfounded hope, and what they wish not, to reject" with authoritative arguments; TPW, IV.108.

[51] D, II.Pref.125/326–27.

[52] Ibid.

chapters stress the importance of "mental" exercises, knowledge of military art or "science," and the "knowledge of sites" as elements of military expertise that may be developed through hunting.[53] Both, moreover, refer to Xenophon's *Cyropaedia* as a source. The *Prince* explicitly advises readers to consult for themselves "the life of Cyrus written by Xenophon" if they wish to grasp more fully the reasons for Machiavelli's remarks. Let us take Machiavelli at his word and examine some possible connections.

In the *Cyropaedia* hunting is said to afford "the best training for war [*pros ton polemon malista paideusi*]" in all its aspects.[54] There is much more to hunting, however, than this military language suggests. Xenophon and other Socratic writers used hunting as a complex metaphor which, as we will see, includes training in philosophical discussion and ethical judgment. On close reading, these skills turn out to be as important for the effective defense of cities as military arms. Xenophon presents hunting as part of the Persians' excellent moral and political education, saying that Persian kings used it as a regular exercise for war. "It is not easy," Xenophon remarks, "to find any quality required in war that is not required also in the chase [*tē thēra*]."[55] Cyrus' attitudes to hunting soon prove to be symptomatic of his main personal flaws: unrestrained competitiveness and *pleonexia*, which eventually impel him to use corrupt means to sustain his over-extended empire. As a youth his love of the chase grew so great that "before long he had exhausted the supply of animals in the park by hunting and shooting and killing them," so that there were no more animals left for him or others to hunt. Cyrus then asks to be taken out hunting in the wilds with the adult men, declaring that there he shall "consider that all the animals I see were bred for me." His Persian education taught him that certain beasts and sites were dangerous, and should be avoided. Nevertheless "when he saw a deer spring out from under cover, he forgot everything and gave chase, seeing nothing but the direction it was making." This excessive single-mindedness, amounting to obsession, is soon displayed in his approach to hunting men in war. Ignoring the cautionary urgings of his elders—and his early philosophical education—Cyrus advises a bold charge on enemies in Mede territory. "As a well-bred but untrained hound rushes recklessly upon a boar, so Cyrus rushed on," Xenophon writes, "with regard for nothing but to strike down every one he overtook and reckless of anything else." Though his assault produced an outstanding victory, it also shows Cyrus' total disregard for considerations of prudence or justice when in the heat of chase; his sole concern is to hunt beasts or men, and to capture them.[56] Once he catches his prey, to be sure, he proves skilled at handling them so that they do not try to escape, and in many cases do not wish to. But Xenophon's description of Cyrus' unrestrained assaults on his prey and his insatiable appetite for more leave a bad

---

[53] *P*, XIV.58–60/157–59, *D*, III.39.297–99/512–13.

[54] Xenophon, "On Hunting" in *Scripta Minora*, 442–43. The word for hunting in this piece is *kunēgetikos*.

[55] *XC*, I.16–19.

[56] *XC*, I.48–71.

taste, alerting readers to look out for later examples of questionably virtuous conduct that appear praiseworthy.[57]

Xenophon has Cyrus himself use the language of hunting to speak of human conquests when he tells his troops that the king of Armenia "is the game we have come to catch."[58] This points to one of Cyrus' key shortcomings as a ruler, as judged by standards set out early in the *Cyropaedia*: his failure to recognize the difference between methods needed to rule a collection of human beings and those needed to govern a herd of non-human animals. Herds of animals, Xenophon observes at the start of Book I, obey their herdsmen "more readily than men obey their rulers." Herds follow their keeper uncritically, never questioning his authority or asking for reasoned accounts of his decisions. They allow him to profit from them without demanding any share; and "we have never known of a herd conspiring against its keeper, either to refuse obedience to him" or to deny him profits from their use. None of these things hold for men, who "conspire against none sooner than those who they see attempting to rule over them." Xenophon concludes that "for man, as he is constituted, it is easier to rule over any and all other creatures than to rule over men." He then hails Cyrus as a remarkable example of a man who both succeeded in acquiring vast conquests, and secured rule over men who obeyed him willingly. This shows that despite the difficulties just outlined, human animals can be ruled "if one should only go about it in an intelligent [*epistamenōs*] manner."[59] Cyrus avoided violence once he conquered new enemies, and made friends among them through gifts and favors. By these means he managed—in his own lifetime, at least—to hold the conquests he made. But if these means of courting goodwill were more humane than brute force, Xenophon suggests that they were still unworthy of self-respecting men who value their freedom.[60] Cyrus honored his supporters with gifts in the belief that "this would implant in them a certain amount of good will," Xenophon notes, "just as it does in dogs."[61] Cyrus treats human beings and countries as wild game that he can domesticate, reducing them to uncritically loyal dependents. Ultimately, his ill-disciplined appetite for hunting far and wide leads him to neglect matters close to home.[62] After his death, the collapse of his empire and any semblance of domestic order shows that Cyrus' many particular virtues do not add up to the complete virtue needed for rulership. That virtue requires a philosophical understanding of conditions for stable rule over

---

[57] Xenophon's judgments about Cyrus' military record, like those regarding his methods of rule, are ambivalent. At first Cyrus establishes a broadly based military based on "equal shares," but these good orders are gradually eroded throughout the narrative; see XC, II.140–45, 166–67. By the end, Xenophon says that as a result of Cyrus' later actions no one in Persia ever goes to war any more without the help of Greek mercenaries, even when at war with Greeks (XC, VIII.452–53).

[58] XC, II.208–11; see Machiavelli on this episode, *D*, III.39.298/512.

[59] XC, I.4–5.

[60] See the captive king of Armenia's remarks on the love of freedom, XC, III.222–25.

[61] XC, VIII.330–31.

[62] Near the end of Cyrus' life he used to take his associates out hunting "whenever there was no need of his staying at home, but even when there was some need of his staying at home, he would himself hunt the animals that were kept in the parks" (XC, VIII.322–23).

human beings, as distinct from herding wild beasts; and in Xenophon's account, the rule of law based on principles of justice, backed by "customary" religion, is fundamental to such understanding.[63]

The *Cyropaedia* uses hunting as a metaphor for the methods used by corrupt rulers to capture and rule subjects. In Xenophon's deceptively unphilosophical essay "On Hunting," by contrast, corrupt or tyrannical rulers are the wild, lawless beasts who must be hunted down and disciplined by any man or woman who wishes to defend justice.[64] Xenophon's well-educated huntsmen (*kunēgetai*) are not just good at fighting external enemies. They attack any wild beasts (*thēria*) that assert "powers hostile to the whole community" from inside or out. Their aims are not those of politicians "whose objects are selfish practices for victory over friends," but to prevail over "common foes."[65] Readers who become skilled at this kind of hunting learn not to be conquerors of human game or tyrants, but vigilant defenders of their cities against wild human animals who refuse to stay within bounds of law and justice. The essay begins by stressing the connection between hunting and virtue (*aretē*), and ends by contrasting the virtue proper to "huntsmen" with the errors of those "who recklessly seek their own advantage [*pleonexias*] whether in private or public life." They "offer their lives and their property in sound condition for the service of the citizens [*to koinon tois politais*]" and attack only "wild beasts," whereas "those others"—the wild human animals among them—attack their fellow citizens and friends." As part of an education in virtue, hunting includes learning to reason well about "how to capture game" and thus avoid the evils of tyranny. Hunters should learn to detect signs of tyrannical conduct early on, behind seductively decent appearances. Hunting teaches virtuous practitioners to act with prudent moderation (*sōphrosunē*) instead of rashness, and in accordance with religion (*ta theia*), a concept that Xenophon associates with both civil justice and the keeping of oaths in the absence of civil laws. Above all, a good education gained through hunting "teaches a man to observe laws [*chrēsthai nomois*], to talk of righteousness [*tōn dikaiōn*] and hear of it." Those "who have given themselves up to the continual toil and learning [*mochthein te kai didaskesthai*] hold for their own portion laborious lessons and exercises" but "hold safety for their own cities [*sōterian de tais heautōn polesin*]."[66]

In Xenophon's essay, virtuous hunting is associated with a specifically Socratic philosophical ethics and opposed to the appearance-making activities of sophists. In a passage cited in Machiavelli's *Prince*, Xenophon writes that virtue was learned

<hr />

[63] XC, I.40–43. Xenophon suggests that an education in Socratic philosophy may help to check tendencies to *pleonexia* and *hubris* in hunting and ruling. When as a youth Cyrus used to go hunting with Tigranes, son of the king of Armenia, Tigranes would take along "a certain philosopher" who was put to death by his father on grounds that the philosopher was corrupting his son. In a clear reference to Socrates, Xenophon has the unnamed philosopher urge the son not to be angry with his father, since he acted out of ignorance (XC, II.229–45).

[64] The last sentence of the essay stresses that "huntsmen" should include huntswomen; Xenophon, "On Hunting" in *Scripta Minora*, 456–57.

[65] Ibid., 366–457.

[66] Ibid., 336–73, 452–57, 446–47. Compare Xenophon's "Agesilaus" in *Scripta Minora*, 98–10.

by "the companions of Cheiron" in ancient times, beginning with hunting, which teaches in the first instance that virtue does not come easily; great toil and discipline (*paideuseis*) are needed to capture it.[67] Hunters learn that many fail to hold on to virtue because it cannot be seen, and because poorly disciplined people dislike the hard work needed to secure it. Philosophical hunting, practiced through dialectical reasonings with others, teaches the young not to rely on appearances when judging whether virtue is present or not. The sophists, on the other hand, "profess to lead the young to virtue" but in fact "lead them to the very opposite." Masters of "the art of deception [*tōn exapatan technēn*]," they "hunt the rich and the young" for their own profit and vanity. They teach the young how to make a good impression with words, but are unable to make them better judges of what is or is not virtuous: and "words [*onomata*] will not educate," though teachings (*gnōmai*) based on wisdom may. Sophistic rhetoric, Xenophon claims, "consists of words and not of thoughts [*noēmasi(n)*]." These spurious teachings are among the enemies of virtue and good civil defenses that philosophical hunters must track down and confront. Properly philosophical hunting includes learning to recognize the difference between words that express reflective thinking and words that "seem" (*dokein*) useful or virtuous but may not "be" (*einai*) either. Constant exercise in making such discriminating judgments is a condition for doing virtuous deeds, as well as for recognizing virtue and its absence in the actions of others.[68] Hunting helps to form reflectively prudent (*sōphronas*) and just (*dikaious*) men "educated in truth" (*to en tē aletheia paideuesthai*). These are the people to whom cities "owed their success in war, as in other matters." Of such philosophically disciplined citizens, Xenophon concludes,

> are good soldiers and good generals made. For they whose toils root out whatever is base [*aischra*] and froward [*hubristica*] from mind and body and make desire for virtue to flourish in their place—they are the best, since they will not brook injustice [*adikoumenē(n)*] to their own city nor injury [*kakōs*] to its soil.[69]

Hunting is used as a similar complex metaphor in several of Plato's dialogues. The *Sophist* contrasts two opposed forms of hunting (*thēreutikon*): one favored by sophists who hunt rich, prominent young men for their own gain, the other by true philosophers who "hunt" for knowledge for its own sake and in order to defend virtue. The discussion illustrates the dialectical methods used in philosophical hunting, described as a particular "method of hunting and way of talking" that is opposed to the methods of the sophists. Having found that the name *sophistēs* is commonly used for different things, the interlocutors try to identify the true sophist by characteristics they can agree on and to agree on "a clear account of

[67] See *P*, XVIII and discussion in chap. 5. In Xenophon's essay ("On Hunting," 366–67, 372–73, 448–49) Cheiron, half-brother of Zeus, is mentioned at the beginning and near the end as a source of teaching that includes the military, political, and ethical dimensions of "hunting."
[68] Ibid., 446–53.
[69] Ibid., 444–45.

what he is."[70] In a subtler use of the metaphor, Plato's *Laws* links hunting to military defenses, philosophical self-examination, and the public good. The main interlocutor proposes that "everyone who means to play his part in keeping his country safe must throw himself heart and soul" into a regimen that includes "hunting [*thērous*] with dogs and other types of chase." They should "investigate the entire country, summer and winter, in arms, to protect and get to know every district in succession." Each "hunter" should take turns serving as master and servant, never employing farmers and villagers "for their own private needs, but only for public tasks." The discussion stresses that "everyone should be closely familiar with his own country [*akribeias epistasthai pantas tēn autōn*, lit. 'everything of his own']; probably no study is more valuable."[71]

These ancient uses of the hunting metaphor furnish an essential backdrop for understanding how Machiavelli uses it.[72] Chapter 14 of the *Prince* begins by asserting that any prince "should have no other object, nor take anything else as his art but that of war and its orders and discipline [*ordini e disciplina*]; for that is the only art [*arte*] which is of concern to one who commands." A prince who "does not understand [*non si intenda*] the military" will not trust his soldiers or win their esteem. To acquire the requisite understanding, a prince should "never lift his thoughts from the exercise of war, and in peace he should exercise it more than in war." He can do this either with deeds (*opere*) or with the mind (*con la mente*). Under the heading of deeds he says that "the prince should always be out hunting [*debbe stare sempre in su le cacce*]." Hunting accustoms the body to hardships, and enables hunters to "learn [*imparare*] the nature of sites." This knowledge (*cognizione*) is useful, first, because by "learning to know" (*impara a conoscere*) one's own country one can better understand how to defend it. Second, "through the knowledge of and experience [*cognizione e practica*] with those sites, one can comprehend [*comprendere*] with ease every other site that it may be necessary to explore as new." By acquiring particular knowledge of one's own terrain, one learns to draw effective conjectures about any other site.[73] "For the hills, the valleys, the plains, the rivers, and the marshes that are in Tuscany, for example, have a certain similarity to those of other provinces."[74]

If these passages seem to highlight merely military and logistical benefits of hunting, the next paragraph gives the meaning of the word a distinctly Socratic twist. It describes the valuable practice of the Achaean "prince" Philopoemen who "when he was on campaign with friends . . . often stopped and reasoned with them [*ragionava*]" about questions of military strategy.[75] He would set out different "chances that can occur to an army," and then "listened to their opinions, gave his

---

[70] Plato, *Soph.* 218d–226. On hunting for knowledge, also see *Statesman* 264a–c.

[71] Plato, *Laws* 763a–c.

[72] That Machiavelli gives "hunting" a philosophical sense is recognized by Mansfield (1979, 421–25) and de Alvarez (1999, 57, 67–68, 137–40).

[73] On conjectures see sec. 3.5 and chap. 5, sec. 5.7.

[74] *P*, XIV.58–59/157–58.

[75] Philopoemen (mentioned by Machiavelli in *D*, II.4) was head of the Achaean League. Also see *LH*, XXXV.28 and PL, *Philopoemen*.

own, supported it with reasons [*corroboravala con le ragioni*]." In this way "because of these continued cogitations there could never arise . . . any accident for which he did not have the remedy." Princes are advised to keep up such modes even in peaceful times so that if their fortune changes for the worse, they will be prepared to meet adversity with virtue. These remarks erode the initial distinction between exercising for war with deeds or with the mind, and imply that discursive reasoning is an essential part of a prudent prince's defensive activities. The understanding needed to secure authority and military power in fact depends on exercises that involve the mind in reflecting on past and future actions. This kind of "hunting" reminds generals and princes that the knowledge they need for defense must be acquired through respectful discussion with friends or subjects, based on the free and transparent exchange of reasons.

A subtler indication that there may be more to Machiavelli's remarks than meets the eye is his unusual emphasis on cognitive aspects of hunting. In the *Prince*'s chapter 16, we read four times in the same paragraph that knowledge (*cognizione*) is among the main conditions and goals of hunting, while the verb *conoscere* appears twice. In the discussion of hunting near the end of the *Discourses*, the word *cognizione* occurs eight times in one short chapter and *conoscere* three times. This is a remarkably insistent repetition of a word that Machiavelli uses in a selective way throughout his writings.[76] *Cognizione* and *conoscere* invariably refer to reflective forms of cognition, involving more demanding standards or more stable objects of knowledge than *intendere* (usually translated as "to understand"), *sapere* (usually "know how to" in a technical sense), or *notizia* (like *cognizione*, usually translated as "knowledge") for ways of cognizing (or objects of cognition).[77] The word *cognizione* occurs only one other time in the *Prince*: in the dedication, where Machiavelli says that he values none of his own possessions more than his "knowledge of the actions of great men, learned by me from long experience of modern things and a continuous reading of ancient ones." He would not offer this *cognizione* as worthy of a prince's attention were it not based on long and deep reflec-

---

[76] Whereas the *Prince* connects *cognizione* gained through hunting with an "art" of establishing *ordini* and *disciplina*, the *Discourses* links it to "science" (*scienza*). See also Xenophon on how cavalry commanders should, if they lack personal experience, consult the men in their force who have the best knowledge (*tous epistēmonestatous*) of various sites ("The Cavalry Commander," *Scripta Minora*, 228–29).

[77] In the *Art of War*, for example, the most common word for "knowing" is *sapere* in military matters, with its connotations of technical know-how. If we look at every instance in the *Discourses* of the two main nouns translated as "knowledge," *cognizione* and *notizia*, we see three main differences in how Machiavelli uses them. (1) One relates to differences in the epistemic quality of knowledge: he uses *notizia* when the type of knowledge in question is slight, poorly grounded, or corrupted by those who have it, *cognizione* when it is "true" or otherwise more adequate (*D*, I.56; II.Pref., II.5., II.24; III.27; *P*, I–II). The choice of *cognizione* or *notizia* may also depend on (2) whether the objects of knowledge are general or particular (*D*, I.47; II.4–5, 12, 33; III.34, 39); or (3) whether the objects are variable or unchanging (*D*, I:39; *P*, II). These passages suggest that it is not just an insufficiency of particulars that falls short of *cognizione*; the quality of *notizia* itself may be deficient. The significance of these uses and the connections they make from one part of the text to another are lost in translations that render *vera cognizione* "proper appreciation" (*The Discourses*, ed. Crick) or "true understanding" (Bonadella 1973).

tions; it presumably deserves to be called *cognizione* only because Machiavelli has "thought out and examined these things with great diligence for a long time [*con gran diligenzia lungamente escogitate ed esaminate*]."[78]

By insisting on the connection between hunting and reflective forms of knowledge, Machiavelli hints that there is more to the sport than stalking wild game and appraising military sites. The *Discourses'* remarks about the kinds of knowledge hunting yields recall Plato's view that everyone should achieve a precise knowledge (*akribeias epistasthai*) of his own country, and all that is "his own," through "hunting with dogs and other types of chase." The "knowledge of countries" (*cognizione de' paesi*) in general, Machiavelli writes, may be acquired through the close study of one, since "every country and every member of the latter have some conformity together, so that one easily passes from the knowledge of one to the knowledge of the other [*dalla cognizione d'uno facilmente si passa cognizione dell'altro*]." It would be odd indeed if Machiavelli meant that the topography of any one country is much the same as that of another, since this is clearly false. The statement seems most reasonable when it is read metaphorically, to mean that a close examination of everything that is "one's own"—one's own desires and humors, unreflective opinions, and civil orders and disorders close to home—must be the foundation of more general knowledge of histories, other countries, and other individuals. Machiavelli notes that this kind of "practice [*pratica*], or truly this particular knowledge [*particulare cognizione*]," was shown by Xenophon to be "acquired more through hunts than by any other training."[79]

Chapter 14 of the *Prince* also touches on the question of how hunting can generate the kinds of ethical *cognizione* needed to imitate ancient works. Machiavelli advises princes to exercise their minds on warfare by reading histories, where they may find some "excellent man" in the past to imitate, enabling them to be as "praised and glorified" as their models. He then names several such great men who themselves imitated an earlier model of excellence: Alexander the Great imitated Achilles; Julius Caesar, Alexander; Scipio Africanus, Cyrus. While Machiavelli here seems to see their reputation for greatness as thoroughly deserved, his remarks elsewhere are critical of these "extraordinarily" ambitious men. All were famously flawed, and failed to leave a lasting legacy of good internal orders or external defenses for their countries. This raises the question of whether historical accounts that describe the virtues of such men might have been read too uncritically by their imitators. Alternatively, it may be that some writers did show the flaws behind the great men's reputations, yet the imitators overlooked them because they were dazzled by appearances or seduced by ambition. While this uncritical type of imitator may take the following sentence at face value, more discriminating readers will smell the irony:

whoever reads the life of Cyrus written by Xenophon will then recognize [*riconosce*] in the life of Scipio how much glory that imitation brought him,

---

[78] *P*, Ded.3–4/117–18.
[79] *D*, III.39.298–99/512–13.

how much in chastity, affability, humanity, and liberality Scipio conformed to what had been written of Cyrus by Xenophon.[80]

If Scipio took Cyrus to be the "ideal prince" portrayed at the overt level of Xenophon's work, chances are that he imitated a deeply flawed model: one that appears praiseworthy in all outward respects, yet whose corrupt deeds led to ruinous disorders. A few chapters later in the *Prince*, Machiavelli suggests that this was indeed the case. Like Xenophon's Cyrus, the celebrated Roman conqueror of Carthage was skilled at projecting appearances of virtue even when his deeds showed excessive ambition. Scipio gained popular favor through his chastity, affability, humanity, and liberality, all extremely ambivalent words of praise that Machiavelli, like his ancient writers, often uses for conduct that corrupts good political *ordini e disciplina*.[81]

Machiavelli's discussions of hunting provide important, seldom-noticed evidence of his affinities with Socratic ethics and political philosophy. His hunting teaches princes and citizens how to improve their defenses not just by acquainting them with physical terrains, but by urging them to reflect in a philosophical way on the civil conditions for maintaining a strong state.[82] He concurs with Socratic writers who held that an adequate military or political *scienza* must rest on a bedrock of practical philosophy. Discriminating ethical judgments, as the next section further argues, are the core of these philosophical foundations.

3.5.
Ethical judgment: The "true knowledge of histories"

Two views sometimes attributed to Machiavelli are clearly incompatible with the reading proposed here. One is an extreme form of skepticism that makes it difficult, if not impossible, to distinguish what deeds have genuine value from what falsely appears valuable or praiseworthy. The other is a reductive form of empiricism that subordinates ethical considerations to undeluded observations about what is or has been in the past. This section outlines some prima facie objections to both views. Later chapters more fully demonstrate my alternative positions.

Machiavelli has often been portrayed as a defender of the view that appearances constitute the only knowable reality, so that learning to manipulate appearances must be considered the height of practical knowledge. Previous sections examined Machiavelli's remarks about the unreliability of extant sources, the self-deceptions of readers, and above all the ability of those skilled in generating appearances to gain a name for greatness that often survives the disastrous results of their deeds.

[80] P, XIV.58–60/157–59.

[81] In Machiavelli's works as in the *Cyropaedia*, *umanità* and *liberalità*—Xenophon's *philanthropia* and *gennaion*—are names given by the corrupt to generous or merciful conduct that aims to secure loyal political friends. Machiavelli's judgments of Scipio echo those of Livy and Plutarch. The latter ("Precepts," PM, X:192–93, 228–29) writes that the Roman people, impressed by his youthful victories in Spain, appointed him consul "suddenly and contrary to law." For Livy's critical views on Scipio see, for example, LH, XXVI.19, and chap. 12, sec. 12.5.

[82] Compare Hobbes 1994 (1650), 32 and 1996 (1652), 21–22, on "hunting" for *sagacitas* or wisdom.

If the purgative and constructive purposes of these remarks are played down, they may appear as elements of a searingly critical exposé of naïve aspirations to discover any secure historical or ethical knowledge in histories or through any other human science. This extreme skepticism, one might suppose, forces both Machiavelli and his most *virtuoso* readers to break from the past once they have recognized the impossibility of any safe modes of *imitazione*. Instead of imitating ancient deeds they must take a wholly new path of their own, knowing that they cannot rely on reports of past deeds or standards of value found in ancient works to guide their own founding, ordering, and commanding. This uncharted new path is both dangerous and liberating. If Machiavelli's great insight is that there are no defensible standards of truth or knowledge that should guide historical studies aimed at practical imitation, then it is up to orderers, captains, and legislators to create their own standards and persuade others to accept them. Instead of searching in vain for standards vindicated by past experience or dialectical reasoning, let alone those advanced in theological or natural law doctrines, political actors should not hesitate to generate their own standards and virtuous appearances. The only limits they must acknowledge are the power political pressures generated by rival *virtuoso* actors. Otherwise their *virtú* is a mainly creative, self-assertive force that enables them, first of all, to establish whatever political "facts" they choose; and having done this, to persuade others to acknowledge their facticity through methods such as those described in the *Prince* and *Discourses*.

To assess these views, let us start by distinguishing two kinds of standard that Machiavelli is supposed to have questioned or dismissed: the *epistemic* standards involved in assessing the truth or knowledge claims in various historical accounts, and the *evaluative* standards invoked in judgments about what historical works deserve praise or blame. Taking epistemic standards first, it is unclear how proponents of the skeptical reading just outlined can explain Machiavelli's non-ironic uses of the concepts of *cognizione* and *verità* to assess the adequacy of different opinions, accounts, or standards of judgment. The *Discourses* start and end by affirming the need to search for *cognizione*. The first preface notes that Machiavelli's contemporaries lack a "true knowledge of histories," and concludes by expressing the hope that readers will draw from his ensuing commentaries "that utility for which one should seek knowledge of histories."[83] These opening remarks are echoed, now with added philosophical and ethical dimensions, in the discussion of *cognizione*-seeking "hunting" near the end of the *Discourses*. In the second preface and elsewhere, Machiavelli acknowledges that "the judgment of men" is inescapably fallible, corruptible, and easily taken in by whatever is "seen." Nevertheless, "it is necessary that [men] sometimes judge the truth [*è necessario che giudichino la verità*]" about the remote past as well as in matters close at hand.[84] All of Machiavelli's main works use *verità* and *cognizione* in ways that show a keen awareness of the pitfalls of dogmatism and naïveté, yet conclude that it is necessary to defend some standards of

---

[83] *D*, I.Pref.6/197–98. The word *cognizione* is used three times in a pointed repetition here, as compared with eight times in III.39.

[84] *D*, II.Pref.123–25/325–27.

truth and knowledge when reasoning (*ragionare*) about different accounts of any phenomenon. It would be implausible to read into these passages the ironic, arch-skeptical claims that true knowledge consists only in the realization that there is no truth, and that knowledge is an illusion.

Machiavelli's conceptions of truth and knowledge are non-dogmatic and critical, but entail the rejection of extreme skepticism. What Machiavelli counts as true, or an object of knowledge, is the best possible account of a thing; and one can only judge whether a particular account is best if it is compared with others. His methods of writing demonstrate his commitment to this dialectical position. The merits of different accounts must be taken seriously, while whatever account one prefers must be subjected to the same harsh scrutiny as all the others. Moreover, if what one is after is the best *possible* account, then whatever is judged the best account at the end of a particular discussion remains only provisionally best, since further discussions might well improve on it.[85] When discussing histories Machiavelli does not use the words *cognizione* and *verità* to demand a single, final account of how things were or of what causes produced which effects. Like the Greek authors whose modes of writing he sometimes imitates, Machiavelli recognizes the permanent possibility of reasoned disagreement about what really happened in the past, the relationship between different events, and responsibility for what are taken as outcomes. His remarks about hunting and the dangers of uncritical *imitazione* treat the recognition of this possibility as a condition for any discussion aimed at seeking *cognizione* in good faith. Anyone, that is to say, who joins in *discorsi* aimed at a "true knowledge of histories" should realize that both their own and other human beings' grasp of the truth is always partial and possibly corrupted by ambition, fear, hatred, or partisan sentiments. This is as true of Machiavelli, Livy, and other historians as of young or inexperienced readers. But even if participants in a *discorso* start with very different accounts of the past, they can still try to identify common standards that allow them to distinguish more and less well-founded accounts. In relation to historical epistemology, Machiavelli's concepts of *cognizione* and *verità* are best understood as regulative standards that should apply to the reasoned discussion of the past. They include the conditions set out in previous sections: the need to check for extreme partiality when appraising sources, to take account of what may not be known because of past accidents or deliberate distortions, and to acknowledge the possibility that one's own reasonings might be unduly influenced by various humors and passions.[86]

Conceived in this way, historical standards of knowledge and truth are essentially regulative and critical, serving as checks that allow participants to identify extremely naïve, one-sided, or partial accounts. They do not yield accounts of the past that can be considered as final, complete, or immune to further critical scrutiny; the search for such accounts is indeed illusory. Standards of *cognizione* and

---

[85] This conception of what "truth" means and how to seek it stands in contrast to polemical approaches to discovering truth, and dogmatic and skeptical conceptions of what truth is.

[86] The Tuscan word *cognizione* carries connotations of reasoned judgment, especially in legal and ethical matters.

verità are themselves as susceptible to unreflective uses and self-serving abuses as other human standards such as greatness, virtue, and justice. They are none-theless necessary conditions for any discussion among free persons who seek, by means of transparent reasoning, to narrow the gap between their understanding of the past and that of others. There are of course other ways to narrow the gap: through empathy, for example, or the use of less transparently critical means of persuasion. But these methods are less likely to bridge sharp disagreements, let alone to support judgments that are widely thought to transcend partisan or private views. When Machiavelli says that "Good historians, as is ours," strive to "put certain cases particularly and distinctly so that posterity may learn how they have to defend themselves in such accidents," he does not mean that they should use history as a platform to make a polemical case for whatever cause they might choose.[87] Those who discuss the past responsibly do not shy away from making judgments, or omit matters that might offend contemporaries. In the manner of Livy's or Thucydides' writings and his own *Florentine Histories*, they highlight and examine the recurring dangers against which, in the historian's judgment, readers might need to "defend themselves." The demand that accounts given by historians and political actors meet standards of truthfulness in these respects—giving their own reasoned judgment in good faith on the one hand, not concealing potentially dangerous features of human nature and conduct on the other—is often expressed by Machiavelli as a necessity for self-defense in cities. Like the *cognizione* discovered through hunting, *verità* is an indispensable component of the good military and political "arms" discussed at length in the *Prince* and *Discourses*.

As for *evaluative* standards invoked when judging what deserves praise or blame, it is true that the incurable corruptibility of moral standards is a central theme not just of the *Prince* but of all Machiavelli's main works. Book I of the *Histories* sets the stage for the rest of his tragicomic narrative by describing how, in various times and places, *onesto* names are assigned to things or people of little value that then gain a *reputazione* for greatness. When an insignificant man called Osporco trades in this absurd name for the name of pope, suddenly he is considered to *be* God's own representative-in-chief. When any random collection of predatory invaders, gang of robber-warriors, or rich men assume the "name of nobility," they are miraculously transformed into heroes and demigods who demand deference for themselves and their descendants, regardless of whether it is merited by their deeds. If such satirical observations exhausted Machiavelli's analysis of how names seem to produce new kinds of value, it might appear to support a skeptical form of nominalism, whereby names constitute the only cognizable normative reality. But Machiavelli's position is remote from this kind of skepticism. His comments parody and reject the belief that by renaming people or things one can alter their essential attributes, let alone their true value. New names merely assign new proprietorship to things, or appear to elevate and humble men who do not change their underlying nature. An Osporco is still a country bumpkin beneath the robes and names of a pope; a man is still an ordinary mortal, not a demigod, whether he

---

[87] *D*, III.30.280/493.

is named Giovanni or Caesar; without arms—which for Machiavelli require much more than troops, swords, and guns—the name of nobility is an empty shell.[88] Machiavelli never says that priests "became" cardinals or Giovannis and Pieros princes, or that some members of the Florentine people rose to "become" nobles while others sunk to become lesser plebs. He says only that people took the names of cardinal or prince, nobleman, or lesser plebs. While he clearly regards some such names as normatively empty or symptomatic of corrupt times, others have more adequate uses. By clarifying and defending these labels, it becomes possible to make reasoned judgments about the true value of deeds, people, or cities that go under the names.

Machiavelli underscores the importance of distinguishing between nominal and true values on the first page of the *Discourses*. In the dedication to his young friends from the Orti Oricellari, Zanobi Buondelmonti and Cosimo Rucellai, Machiavelli suggests that while most writers praise whoever holds power or a recognized title, he prefers to recognize the intrinsic quality of persons and their actions. This is why, he says, "I have gone outside the common usage of those who write, who are accustomed always to address their works to some prince." These people, "blinded by ambition and avarice, praise him for all virtuous qualities when they should blame him for every part worthy of reproach." For his own dedicatees, by contrast, "I have chosen not those who are princes but those who for their infinite good parts deserve to be." The chief quality that makes these men deserve to be princes is that they are among "those who know [*sanno*], not those who can govern a kingdom without knowing [*sanza sapere*]."[89] The distinction between princes in name and princes by desert signals Machiavelli's concern to reason about the true value of the qualities and actions that are praised, blamed, or concealed under various decent-sounding names. For readers about to embark with Machiavelli on the "dangerous" search for new modes and orders in ancient histories, it is a matter of the utmost importance to avoid the error of assuming that what are commonly praised as the "virtuous qualities" proper to princes deserve to be so praised. The same goes for virtues commonly ascribed to republics: Florence went under this *onesto* name during all the upheavals recounted in the *Florentine Histories*, and kept it long after it had become, in effect, a Medici princedom.[90] Machiavelli does not conclude from this that any polity may reasonably be called a republic, or anyone deserves to be called prince, if enough people can be persuaded to accept these designations. On the contrary, he urges readers to step back from uses of these words that reflect unreflective or corrupt standards, and to consider for themselves what ought to constitute adequate standards for a deserving prince or a "true republic."[91]

[88] *FH*, I.5.14–15/318–19, 7.17/321–22, 11.22–23/327–28.
[89] *D*, Ded.3–4/195–96. While the choice of *sapere* (know-how) instead of *cognizione* here seems to suggest that the *Discourses* will focus on practical and technical questions of government, the work soon turns out to involve much more.
[90] As Rome remained a republic in name under the emperors.
[91] The idea has Socratic antecedents in the idea of a true "statesman" (Lat. usually *principe*). See PM, X.179, 145; PL, *Cleomenes*, 974.

The need to reexamine old names extends, as we will see, to core concepts used to reason about personal and political values: virtue, necessity, and order as well as *grandezza* or *giustizia*, *libertà* or *umanità*. The aim of good imitators of ancients should not be to reproduce mere appearances of these things, or to persuade naïve or corrupt contemporaries that their works possess them. They must try to elucidate what they judge to be non-corrupt, reflectively adequate standards expressed by any of these concepts, and give as clear an account as they can of the reasons why others should respect these standards. Machiavelli's own attempts to do this for specific evaluative concepts are discussed in the remaining chapters.

This brings us to a second position often imputed to Machiavelli: a reductive empiricism that examines questions concerning human actions, including evaluative questions about proper ends and acceptable means, only in relation to observed "facts" identified through history or anthropological study. Ernst Cassirer argues that in Machiavelli's "new science" of politics "the facts of political life are the only valid arguments," adding that Machiavelli "never argues about political doctrines or maxims." Isaiah Berlin asserts that Machiavelli's "method and tone" are wholly empirical. Friedrich Meinecke proposes that Machiavelli offered a radically modern perspective that subordinated "supra-empirical" moral necessity to the empirical necessities of brute power, producing a new opposition "between absolute and relative standards of value."[92] These readings offer fascinating diagnoses of the ruthless, amoral forms of so-called realpolitik that affected important strands of political thinking in the first half of the twentieth century. They are not, however, grounded in thorough readings of Machiavelli's writings, or in analyses of the forms of corruption he sought to address in his own times. Later chapters develop more detailed arguments against reductive empiricist readings. Here I outline a few points arising from Machiavelli's discussions of knowledge that suggest prima facie reasons to question these readings.

First, two key passages mentioned earlier allude to the insufficiency of empirical methods as a basis for practical *cognizione*. The idea that experience may be a misleading or corrupt source of knowledge is strongly underlined in Book II, chapter 5 of the *Discourses*. Machiavelli here affirms the critical point made in Plato's *Timaeus* that much of "known" experience is the product of self-serving and destructive human actions which incurred the loss of many "memories" that might have had practical value. The philosophical implication is that it is wise to doubt whether we know all that human beings are capable of, for better or worse, since records of their greatest or basest deeds may have been wiped out or "perverted" by some ambitious survivor. If it is possible that whatever slice of experience we take as our source of knowledge is misleading in one of these ways, then experience must be an insufficient source. Prudent seekers of knowledge must frequently turn to conjecture (*coniettura*) and other modes of reasoning that do not rely wholly on what can be directly observed, in records or in present actions.[93]

---

[92] Cassirer 1946, 136; Berlin 1981 (1958), 37; Meinecke 1998 (1925), 39.

[93] *D*, II.5; compare the crpytic remark in III.18 that Epaminondas says that knowledge (*cognizione*) of enemies' decisions and policies is difficult and must be found by conjectures, not only experience.

The other passage comes from the *Discourses'* discussion of hunting. Here we read that hunters gain political and military knowledge not by studying and comparing different examples, but by closely examining only one site—their own country— very closely. This methodology, Machiavelli says, provides a sufficient basis for acquiring a profound knowledge of other sites and countries.[94] It is difficult to see how the methods of knowledge acquisition recommended here can be squared with those used in empirical political sciences. According to Machiavelli, knowledge of generals and invariables cannot always be gleaned from the accumulation and comparison of particulars and variables. Nor, presumably, would a wider sample of examples improve the quality of the kind of philosophical *cognizione* that "hunters" should be seeking.[95]

Second, it is doubtful whether Machiavelli thinks that evaluative standards applicable to human works can be derived from a more rigorously scientific knowledge of history or of nature, including those aspects of human nature that can be identified through observation and analyzed by empirical methods. We have already discussed the problems that arise when people take what is seen in extant historical records as a sufficient basis for evaluative judgments. Machiavelli also hints at reasons to doubt the sufficiency of any humanly possible knowledge of nature as a foundation for ethical judgments. Although some men may claim to have "knowledge [*notizia*] of things natural and supernatural," he concedes that "we"—he and like-minded, unpresumptuous reasoners—"do not have" it.[96] Instead of drawing skeptical conclusions from this admission of ignorance, however, Machiavelli alludes to a different kind of truth suggested by "some philosophers [*alcuno filosofo*]." These hold that the results of human actions may be foreseen "by their natural virtues [*per naturali virtú*]" and reasonably attributed to divine or supernatural "intelligences." Although the supernatural sources of these forebodings can never be proven empirically, one "sees it . . . to be the truth" that whenever some grave wrong has been committed, natural events such as floods, thunderbolts, and the like are widely imputed to supernatural causes and interpreted as warnings from on high.[97] The truth in these "philosophical" judgments, found in the critical histories of Livy and Thucydides as well in Plato's dialogues, is ethical rather than theoretical. The judgments do not primarily seek to identify the "natural or supernatural" causes of disasters that follow on human misconduct. Rather, they evaluate the ethical quality of actions that are seen to bring on grave disorders.[98] Chapter 5 will argue that while Machiavelli does think that a better empirical knowledge of human nature should inform ethical and political judgments, he does not reduce such judgments to empirical investigations of human or any other kind of nature.[99]

---

[94] *D*, III.39.298–99/512–13.

[95] Machiavelli frequently distinguishes empirical arguments and "reasons," usually offering both as complementary but sometimes pitting one against the other—in which case arguments from "reasons" prevail over arguments based on experience or examples alone.

[96] Compare HH, II.3; Plato, *Euth.* 2c–15e, *Apol.* 29a–b, *Crat.* 400d–401a.

[97] *D*, I.56.114/314; see chap. 5, secs. 5.3 and 5.4, for further discussion.

[98] Compare Plato, *Tim.* 29c; *Crit.* 120d–121c.

[99] Compare Hobbes 1994 (1650), 33–34.

Third, reductive empiricist readings overlook an unannounced yet crucial component of Machiavelli's writings: his implicit, constant demand for the closer examination of more and less adequate uses of key concepts or names as a means of identifying reasonable normative standards. We saw earlier that even when imitators examine their *sources* critically, they may still make unreasonable judgments about the past because they are insufficiently reflective about the *concepts* they use to analyze and evaluate histories. Machiavelli's new path toward more adequate *cognizione* includes this indispensable conceptual element. It calls for the critical examination of concepts employed in the empirical study of histories, both to examine causes and to evaluate actions.[100] The concept of necessity, for example, is often used in ways that presuppose a set of observable, brute facts that self-evidently constrain action, often forcing supra-empirical moral necessities to take second place. This uncritically empiricist view of necessity is often imputed to Machiavelli. The next chapter tries to show, however, that the critical examination of various unreflective and un-*virtuoso* uses of *necessità* is fundamental for Machiavelli's ethics and political theories; and that his concept of necessity has important ethical dimensions that have not been adequately studied. It is harder to see how more and less adequate uses of words such as "prince" or "republic," "virtue" or "order," "freedom" or "justice" might be distinguished on empirical criteria alone. These words do not refer, in Machiavelli's view, to qualities or templates that may be discovered through more accurate empirical studies of nature, or of what most people in fact do. They express normative standards that human beings set for themselves, thereby placing demands on themselves that are not found in nature per se. If analogous standards are found in all times and places where cities have existed, this is not because all human beings instinctively follow the same natural patterns. It is because beings who have the specific mix of dispositions and capacities found in humans realize that unless they uphold adequate standards expressed through concepts of order, virtue, or justice, they will be unable to sustain any forms of life that they regard as worthy of beings with the order-making and deliberative capacities they ascribe to themselves.

If these standards cannot be derived from *nature*, the empirical study of *history* should also be considered as only a secondary source for identifying them. Historical examples of what are called princes or republics, or of deeds that are called virtuous, furnish material on which readers may exercise their judgment about the standards adequate to these names. But Machiavelli does not suggest that full or secure *cognizione* of standards of princeliness, virtue, or order can be *derived* from examples. Nor does he say that standards are only defensible if they can be shown to have been realized in past or contemporary instantiations. On the contrary, he says that some eminently defensible standards, such as those expressed in the phrase

---

[100] Here is another intriguing point of comparison with Hobbes, who treats reasoning about the "proper use of names" as the foundation of "science." For example, see Hobbes 1994 (1650), 169–72 and 1996 (1652), 24–31. Further research into the ancient Greek sources of both Hobbes' and Machiavelli's arguments may illuminate seldom-noticed similarities and differences between the two authors, in this and other respects.

"true republic," may never have been adequately exemplified at all. Yet this does not discourage Machiavelli from identifying those standards and applying them to remedy contemporary disorders. Analogously, even if no examples of princes who meet Machiavelli's standards could be found in historical records, the idea of a prince-by-merit would still stand as a defensible regulative norm for political judgment, and as a reasonable aspiration. Machiavelli could still, that is, demand that anyone who goes under the name of *principe* should have the infinite good parts and knowledge possessed by his friends Rucellai and Buondelmonti. If no examples can be found of men with their "parts" being given the name of prince, this does not make it pointless to insist that they *should* exercise princely forms of authority. The relevant standards do not derive from actual princes, but from the reasonable demands human beings place on those in positions of public authority.

The question of what demands human beings may reasonably impose on themselves and others is, as I argue in the next chapter, much more fundamental for Machiavelli's ethics than observations about what demands they do in fact impose. He treats the clarification of normative standards as a condition for adequately reasoned reflection on experience. Empirical examples form the overt subject-matter of his writings, but the critical examination of names and concepts used in these examples forms the philosophical backbone of every major work. As the rest of this study tries to show, Machiavelli does not underestimate the difficulties involved in identifying adequate uses of the concepts he examines. Nor does he imagine that it is easy to persuade readers to accept the standards he proposes. Once the name of prince has become associated with claims by one man to stand above public laws, forms of princely authority that should be held by those who deserve it also become suspect. Once the decent words "republic" and "freedom" have been identified with weak authority and license, people invoke them to defend badly ordered polities or to reject authority in any form. Once "justice" is associated with partisan revenge for past injuries, people use it only to fight their enemies, not knowing how to use it to settle disputes according to principles that everyone considers reasonable. Machiavelli's remedy is neither skeptical relativism nor a blunt, dogmatic empiricism. In both form and substance, it has much more in common with ancient dialectical remedies than is usually recognized.

3.6.
Machiavelli's dangerous new reasonings

This brings us back to Machiavelli's claims to take a wholly new path at the beginning of the *Discourses*. In the first preface he observes that "it has always been as dangerous to "find new modes and orders" as to set off in search of unknown (*incognite*) seas and lands. Despite these dangers, Machiavelli resolves "to enter a path as yet untrodden by anyone." How can this be reconciled with his claims that those who wish to build anew should start by imitating ancient "modes and orders"? I propose the following solution. For Machiavelli, reasonable imitation involves, first, identifying reasonable action-guiding standards met by ancient works; second, giving a reasoned account of why those standards should be defended; and third, trying to work out and establish new political orders that meet those standards. The first of these elements looks backward, as it were, stressing recurrently valuable lessons that Machiavelli thinks may be derived from ancient authors. The second and third look forward: they require new reflections on old problems and standards, and possibly new kinds of action that may be or appear dangerous.

In relation to the first element, the next chapters will argue that Machiavelli derives normative standards from reasonings about dispositions, capacities, and desires that he sees as unchanging in the human species. In contrast to most previous interpreters, I argue that Machiavelli does not consider all of the normatively relevant, unchanging features of human nature as empirically observable. Nor does he claim to be the first to discover these features and infer correct precepts from them. His favorite ancient writers identified similar precepts and applied them to their own times. Machiavelli's methods of writing and judgments about ethical standards should, I suggest, be seen as highly creative *renovations* of what he saw as the most "reasonable" positions in ancient ethics and political thought. His writings offer a new interpretation and robust defense of ideas found in a number of different ancient authors, Greek and Roman, most of whom acknowledged a common core of influences. Machiavelli does not present his new beginning as a radical break with the past but, on the contrary, as a contribution to the renewal of a perennially rich source of non-dogmatic ethical, political, and indeed religious wisdom. Some of the reasonings he offers for his ethical standards have a distinctive form, so that their content appears to differ, or even dissent, from that of the standards upheld by his ancients. But the basic content of Machiavelli's ethical standards is not radically new, nor did he aspire to make this kind of innovation. Nothing in his writings suggests that there can be progress in these practical kinds of *cognizione* as there can be in the natural sciences. What one needs to know about human dispositions and capacities in order to work out reasoned action-guiding standards was very well known to many ancient writers. Machiavelli's remarks about human nature and the conditions for stable order build on anthropological and ethical premises set out by Thucydides, Xenophon, Plato, and Plutarch, and renovated by Roman writers such as Livy and Sallust. In these fundamental respects Machiavelli did not aspire to improve on ancient knowledge, let alone transcend it. He sought to remind readers of practical truths demonstrated in ancient works that had, in his view, too often been misunderstood or ignored.

It is unnecessary to posit a radical break between Machiavelli's ethics and everything that came before it to see why this approach might lead his writings, and some of his readers, down a dangerously new path. What Machiavelli proposes is a careful, independent re-reading of ancient authors who themselves called for boldly critical, independent thinking about ethics, politics, and history. Like Plutarch and Plato, Machiavelli insists that well-considered imitation depends on this kind of thinking; it cannot suffice to copy the actions described in ancient texts, or appeal to known authorities. Whenever someone embarks again on such investigations, they must look for new reasons and examples that will resonate with contemporaries. They might defend the same standards as the ancient writers, but their reasonings will be their own. And while the renewed orders they propose may be inspired by standards exemplified by ancient cases, they may find it impossible or unreasonable to follow ancient models wholesale. Reflective imitation in practical matters always involves renovation. Good imitators identify the most reasonable standards they can find in ancient examples, and apply these to criticize the present, to propose remedies for disorders, or to build new orders. Machiavelli suggests that this kind of renewal should happen very frequently. From the perspective of rulers or institutions whose authority rests on dogmas, corrupt opinions, or fear, this calls for a critical stance in citizens and subjects that might well be perceived as dangerous. From the imitator's perspective, the dangers might appear even greater. Reflective imitation requires confidence in one's own powers of judgment, a willingness to question popular opinions and received authorities, and the courage to defend one's reflective judgments against those who attack them as dangerous innovations. If these critical, non-dogmatic urgings foreshadowed the arguments of certain Enlightenment thinkers, they can also be found in the writings of ancient authors whose ideas Machiavelli renovates.

CHAPTER 4

Necessity and Virtue

Necessità and *virtú* are two of the most widely discussed concepts in Machiavelli's writings. The two concepts often appear together, paired or contrasted, to explain, justify, or critically evaluate actions. In classical history and philosophy, the word *necessity* (Greek *anangkē*, Latin *necessitas*) identifies very strong causalities that constrain human actions. Virtue (*aretē, virtus*) has many specific senses, but broadly speaking refers to specifically human capacities to respond in appropriate ways to natural, supernatural, or man-made constraints. While it is generally acknowledged that Machiavelli's *necessità* and *virtú* retain these broad meanings, the precise content he gives each word is disputed. There is surprisingly little disagreement on one point, however. Both among scholars who see Machiavelli primarily as continuing a civic humanist tradition and those who see him as a realist who broke with that tradition, the overwhelming majority assume that he uses the concept of *necessità* in a fairly straightforward way. When Machiavelli says that agents act under necessity, it is generally assumed that he wants to underscore the hard realities of conflict and power that limit human choices, rendering ideally moral actions impossible. On this view, Machiavelli uses the concept of *necessità* to mark out objective limits on moral choice. Where necessity is not pressing, people may indulge their pious desires to be or appear good; but when necessity bears upon them, such conduct is irresponsible. Wherever *necessità* comes into play, conventional ethical constraints must be subordinated to the objective needs of self-preservation.

This understanding of Machiavellian *necessità* informs several common interpretations of his related concept of *virtú*. One sees *virtú* primarily as a capacity to dominate or master constraints of all kinds, including necessity and fortune. If necessity consists of overwhelming constraints that limit human freedom, the argument goes, then *virtú* must be the power that enables some extraordinary men to overcome any such constraints. Thus Leo Strauss argues that for Machiavelli "the domination of necessity remains the indispensable condition of every great achievement," while Quentin Skinner describes Machiavelli's *virtú* as "a creative force able to master the world's disorder and 'remake' it."[1] Some versions of this self-assertive conception strip ancient and humanist virtue of its moral content, reducing *virtú* to a purely instrumental capacity: for Machiavelli, we are told, "there is no other way to look at virtue than politically, that is, for what it gets you."[2]

---

[1] Strauss 1958, 298; Skinner 1978, 92–98, 152.

[2] Mansfield 1998, 22–38; compare Meinecke 1998 (1925), 36–37; Skinner 1988, 434.

This chapter argues that Machiavelli's concepts of *necessità* and *virtù* have a far richer ethical content than these accounts appreciate. The first three sections consider Machiavelli's subtly critical analyses of necessitarian rhetoric. Later sections examine important yet seldom-noticed nuances in his arguments about more and less responsible—that is, *virtuoso*—responses to *necessità*.

4.1.
The rhetoric of necessity

The language of necessity has two main uses in political rhetoric. One is explanatory: it explains why agents must act in certain ways, or why they could not act in others. The other use is justificatory: to say that an agent acted under necessity is to suggest that the range of responses open to him were severely limited. Agents who invoke necessity as a justification often imply that since they had little or no choice in their responses, these should be exempt from moral evaluation. If an agent had very little room for choice, the argument goes, he cannot be held fully responsible for the consequences of his actions, even if these appear weak or excessive.

In ancient histories and philosophy, discussions about the role of necessity in human affairs are often a medium for examining questions of ethical or political responsibility. How far should agents be praised or blamed for whatever they do under the extreme constraints they call *anangkē* or *necessitas*? If they have little room for choice, in what sense can they be held responsible for whatever decisions they make within very narrow margins? Ancient writers often discuss these questions through speeches they give to historical figures, who offer opposing judgments about whether to go to war, launch a battle, or punish rebels with extreme measures. One character typically presents the case for swift, assertive action by invoking necessity; his arguments are then countered by a more circumspect speaker, who questions whether the necessity at hand rules out all courses of action except the one proposed by the previous speaker. Perhaps in his haste for action the latter has failed to examine other possible responses, including some that might prove more advantageous than the one he urges. Perhaps he has failed to weigh the foreseeable dangers of rushing to meet a situation of civil or external emergency with force unmodulated by prudent judgment. Readers of the debates recounted by Thucydides, Livy, or Sallust, or conversations between impetuously assertive and circumspect characters in Xenophon or Plato, are seldom told which side was more reasonable. The writers leave such judgments to readers themselves, merely hinting at their own positions through the intrinsic merits of certain arguments and by their accounts of the results of actions taken.[3]

Machiavelli's writings, especially the *Florentine Histories*, contain many similar examples of rhetoric invoking necessity. The dialectical aspects of his treatment of *necessità* are less obvious in other writings. Many passages in the *Prince* and *Discourses* seem to cut straight through all the nuanced philosophical and ethical considerations weighed by ancient authors, brushing these away in favor of blunt

---

[3] See chap. 2.

assertions about what *necessità* self-evidently requires. Thus in the *Discourses* we read of men who faced the "necessity" to kill "infinite others" who opposed their plans, of celebrated founders of cities who committed fratricide under a necessity to "be alone" when ordering a republic, of others whose actions show a necessity to deceive, and many similar statements.[4] Much of the most striking rhetoric of *necessità* occurs in Machiavelli's discussions of relations between polities: sometimes to explain weakness, sometimes to justify extreme violence, deception, or taking what many people would regard as unfair advantage. These statements are usually taken as straightforward expressions of Machiavelli's own views. So long as amoralism is presumed to be the bedrock of Machiavelli's judgments, the context and dialectical functions of statements that seem to confirm that presumption remain under-examined. Even scholars who dispute amoralist readings of Machiavelli ask fewer and less interesting questions about passages where he invokes *necessità*, especially in relation to external self-defense. When the *Discourses* declare that "the fatherland is well defended in whatever mode one defends it, whether with ignominy or with glory," few have thought it necessary to ask whether or not Machiavelli's surrounding remarks suggest his agreement with this statement, let alone to analyze ambiguities in its meaning and practical implications.[5] When we read in the *Histories* that "things done out of necessity neither should nor can merit praise or blame [*cose fatte per necessità non se ne debbe ne puote loda o biasimo meritare*],"[6] there seems little reason to doubt that this is just vintage Machiavellianism—unless we look more closely at the rhetorical context, the reliability of the speaker, and contrasting arguments made by other speakers in comparable situations.

The usual readings err in assuming that Machiavelli uses the concept of *necessità* in only one way: to identify serious constraints on action that deserve to be treated as a bedrock of political and ethical reasoning. Machiavelli does use the concept of *necessità* to pick out very strong constraints on action, and admits that these constraints should be taken into account when evaluating responsibility. But his statements about *necessità* also function in a more philosophical way: to put rhetorical claims under dialectical scrutiny, in order to assess responsibility for actions taken under the "banner" of *necessità*. He invokes *necessità* not to foreclose critical discussions about the most responsible or ethical response to extreme pressures but, like his ancient models, to stimulate such discussion. This becomes clearer when statements such as those just cited are read in context. Those found in the *Florentine Histories* occur in speeches by characters whose judgment is marred by narrow self-interest or extreme insecurity. Many speakers use the language of necessity in a self-serving way to color ineffectual, counterproductive, or uncompromising reactions to internal and external pressures. In the *Discourses*, statements about the "ultimate necessity" to save the fatherland are often sayings or "maxims" attributed to particular individuals, some of whose judgments are sounder than others. Machiavelli suggests that they may be

---

[4] *D*, III.30.280/492–93; I.9.28–30/223–24; II.13.155/358–59.
[5] *D*, III.41.300–301/515.
[6] *FH*, V.11.197–99/534–35.

understood in more and less reasonable ways, depending on how well one has understood what measures are needed to "save one's fatherland" in a more than temporary or partisan sense.[7] In both longer works and in the *Prince*, arguments frequently heard in political life are "quoted" in speeches or *discorsi* mimicking the mixture of sound, corrupt, and unreflective views found in "any city whatever," inviting readers to examine them critically in the light of Machiavelli's examples and reasonings.

Machiavelli's manner of writing implies that readers should respect whatever is reasonable in the opinions presented, taking care not to reject grains of truth along with the dross. Yet they should accept no excuse or pretext without rigorous, independent examination. People who are used to taking the lead from others but "do not know how to reason [*non sappiendo ragionare*] about either public defense or public offense" easily fall prey to corruption and tyranny.[8] Machiavelli was well aware that one of the most ancient, widespread, and effective ways to short-circuit public reasoning is to invoke urgent necessity.[9] It would be astonishing if a writer so attuned to the uses of *onesto* words to color *disonesto* deeds always presented *necessità* as an objective datum, somehow immune to partisan abuses. The *Florentine Histories* has speakers of all parties use inflammatory or scaremongering rhetoric invoking *necessità*. Some use it to defend republican institutions, others to subvert them. When used in speeches, the rhetoric of necessity always has an urgent tone. Speakers generally want to push policies through against the resistance of those who demand more time to evaluate the situation, consider different courses of action, and weigh foreseeable consequences. Machiavelli uses necessitarian rhetoric in his writings in order to put it under a spotlight, training readers to see through its abuses and to demand more carefully reasoned arguments for policies it is used to defend. Some constraints on action do deserve the name of *necessità*; the use of necessitarian language is by no means always a ruse to justify weakness or self-indulgent amorality. But many appeals to necessity do fall short of Machiavelli's demanding standards of explanatory and normative adequacy. His *Histories* describes numerous situations where people deny that they can be held responsible for failures or their gross injustices, since necessity left them no choice but to do as they did. Machiavelli questions such irresponsible uses of the word *necessità*. The most profound reasoning in all his main works suggests that even people who act under very severe constraints—Moses in Egypt, Aeneas cast adrift from the ashes of Troy, prospective redeemers of his downtrodden Italy—may

---

[7] See chap. 9, especially sec. 9.7.

[8] *D*, I.58.116/316; I.16.44/240.

[9] The institutions of Medici control were often justified with reference to the needs of external defense; the phrase "Necessitas imminet" (necessity is impeding) was famously used by Medici counsellors in June 1458 to argue that the government would have to be retaken by force from its opponents. Sympathetic humanist writers including Tignosi and Poggio Bracciolini echoed this rhetoric, defending power-political theories that favored Medician "necessity." Field sees these as "proto-Machiavellian" theories that see law as a function of power; on my reading, it is more likely that Machiavelli presents such maxims not to affirm them but to examine their shortcomings. See Field 1988, 28, 42, 145–46, 158, 176–77.

choose among different courses of action for which they must be held responsible. Machiavelli's discussions suggest that irresponsible agents use the rhetoric of *necessità* in ways that reflect one or more of the following defects.

First, they have a *self-excusing* account of the causes that generate situations of extreme *necessità*. Irresponsible agents treat whatever constraints they call *necessità* as alien and hostile pressures that have no genetic connection to their own conduct, seldom scrutinizing their own actions or omissions to ask whether these might contribute to a future situation of urgent necessity. Responsible agents, by contrast, constantly ask themselves what they can do to avoid being placed under extreme pressures, even in quiet times when no great pressures seem to loom. Recognizing that in cities "accidents [*accidenti*] arise every day that have need of a physician" they seek to address "strange and unhoped for" pressures before they develop into situations of dangerous *necessità*.[10]

Second, irresponsible agents view necessity from a narrowly *unilateral* perspective. They show little interest in how the people or cities with whom they interact might be expected to respond to their own movements, tending to overrate their own powers and merits while badly underrating those of others.[11] This one-sided perspective often leads them to undertake unilateral actions that provoke foreseeably violent or counterproductive reactions. By contrast, reflective agents avoid taking a narrow view of the situations that involve *necessità*. When considering how to deal with imminent or future pressures, they try to examine them from the standpoint of other agents as well as from their own. By "beginning to know and manage [*conoscere e maneggiare*]" the motivations of opponents inside one's own city or in external relations, prudent agents cease to regard the latter with "the terror that fame and reputation" give them, instead coming to see them as men driven by the same desires and humors as themselves.[12]

Finally, irresponsible agents often undertake *badly ordered* measures in response to whatever pressures they describe as *necessità*. Machiavelli's word "orders" (*ordine*) and cognate terms such as *ordinario* express the appropriate mode for responsible responses to necessity. "There is," on the other hand, "no more dangerous nor more useless defense than that which is done tumultuously and without order."[13] Blaming others when extreme necessities constrain them, such agents tend to flee, lash out violently or recklessly, or collapse in abject defeat. In most instances, disordered modes of action intensify necessitarian pressures instead of relieving them. Reflective and responsible agents waste little time blaming others for their difficulties. They examine their own past actions and omissions, asking whether they might have done more to avoid the present situation; and in the light of these reflections, assume full responsibility for whatever actions they take in response to necessities, including new measures aimed at correcting previous shortcomings.

---

[10] *D*, III.16.255/465–66; III.49.308–9/524.
[11] See Thucydides on Athens, chap. 2.
[12] *D*, III.37.294/508.
[13] *D*, III.30.280/491–93. See chap. 10, sec. 10.1.

4.2.
Necessità as an excuse

The tendency to blame one's difficulties on outside forces beyond one's control—fortune, foreigners, fate, or the heavens—is a recurrent theme in all Machiavelli's writings. The *Histories* begin by announcing the author's intention to avoid this kind of irresponsible analysis of his city's travails. As we saw in chapter 1, Machiavelli regrets that historians such as Bruni and Poggio Bracciolini had not shown their compatriots how to examine their own and their ancestors' errors prudently, but frequently blamed civil discords on rival parties or foreigners.[14] The *Histories'* opening chapter confronts these self-excusing tendencies through gently satirical remarks about the *necessità* involved in what others called the barbarian invasions of Rome. Machiavelli's remarks look especially provocative when compared with Bruni's account of the same events.[15] Bruni describes Rome's Gothic invaders as "a formidable race" who inflicted "devastation" wherever they went. Their princes were "fierce by nature" and when inspired by a "lust for revolt" attacked Romans, massacred them, and inflicted "great slaughter" among provincial peoples. Later hordes of Goths "rampaged through Etruria with barbaric fury," making Rome tremble at the "fearful approach." At last victorious, they came "sweeping through Italy with frightful force" and "wrought devastation wherever they marched with fire and sword." If the Germanic invaders appear in Bruni's account as an uncontrollable natural force impervious to reasoned negotiation, the Huns were even worse: Attila was "cruel and fearsome by nature" and "seemed born to be the terror of the world."[16]

Machiavelli slyly challenges this conventional description of the "barbarian" invaders. First, he uses the language of necessity not to describe pressures inflicted on Romans by "barbarians," but to identify the causes that drove these peoples out of their own homelands toward Rome. If there was a pressing necessity involved in this great confrontation, he implies, it was faced not by the Romans but by their invaders. Inhabiting regions so bountiful that their populations grew too large to support on their land, it became "necessary for a part of them abandon their fathers' lands and to "seek new countries to inhabit." By contrast, the supposed necessity these "northern peoples" brought upon Rome was largely self-inflicted by Roman authorities themselves. Outsiders were able to wreak such destruction because of the Romans' own negligence and corruption. Goths and Huns merely seized the opportunity "given to them by the emperors" when the latter abandoned Rome, exposing the western empire to pillage. Some imperial ministers directly incited the invaders; motivated by private ambi-

---

[14] *FH*, I.5.14/318–19.

[15] Bruni's (BH, I.52–53) account, like Machiavelli's, reflects a strongly republican interpretation of history, since both suggest that the emperors' neglect of the western empire was largely to blame. Unlike Machiavelli, Bruni also blames the rarity of external wars, which led the emperors and the Roman nobility to wage wars against their fellow citizens instead of concentrating on external defenses.

[16] *FH*, I.1–9.9–20/312–26.

tion, they secretly invited Vandals and later Huns into Italy to overthrow their internal rivals.[17]

Second, Machiavelli's description of the invaders' response to the pressures that drove them toward Rome overturns the caricature of the invasions as a raging, disordered flood that inundated the civilized world with no rationally explicable cause. Most historians treated the invasions or Rome as outbursts of feral greed or envy, showing no interest in the political deliberations that might have guided invaders' actions. By contrast, Machiavelli focuses on the prudent orders (*ordine*) followed by these peoples when they decided to leave their own countries. His language in the opening passages of the *Histories* could hardly stand in starker contrast to the descriptions of chaotic savagery conventionally applied to Rome's invaders. "The order they follow," he writes,

> when one of these provinces wants to unburden itself of inhabitants, is to divide into three parts [*parti*] and assign each person a place so that each part may be equally supplied with nobles and base, with rich and poor; then the part to which the lot falls goes to seek its fortune, and the two parts, un-burdened of the third, remain to enjoy their fathers' goods.[18]

Once again, this laconic account contrasts more and less responsible ways of dealing with urgent *necessità*. It alludes to the advantages of responding to pressures preventively before they take on more critical dimensions. The general form of the response is also a model of responsible action on other criteria set out earlier. Machiavelli describes people responding to necessities by imposing judicious "orders" on themselves, instead of lashing out or fleeing in a disorderly way. His northern invaders regard necessity not as a hostile force to be overcome by any means; instead they see it as an opportunity to establish good orders among themselves.[19] Machiavelli notes that even when Roman governors tried to play one rival group of invaders off another, those that found themselves at a disadvantage treated necessity as an opportunity to put themselves "in better order to seek revenge for their injury."[20] Moreover, at least some barbarian rulers imposed far better orders than Roman emperors had provided their peoples for a long time.[21] Faced with these well-ordered conquerors, the Romans simply crumbled under their old self-inflicted disorders. "And truly," Machiavelli observes with some exasperation, "for the ruin of such an empire founded on the blood of so many virtuous men, there could not have been less indolence in princes nor less infidelity in ministers," and no "less force nor less

---

[17] *FH*, I.1–8.12–18/312–24. This foreshadows his analysis of Florentine and Italian travails in the next millennium, when native rulers and party leaders frequently gave foreign powers the "opportunity" to meddle in their cities' affairs.

[18] *FH*, I.1.9/312.

[19] Compare HH, I.94.

[20] *FH*, I.1.9–10/324–27.

[21] *FH*, I.3.12–13/315–17.

obstinacy in those who attacked it; for not one but many populations conspired in its ruin."[22]

Machiavelli's account of the *ordine* imposed by Italy's northern invaders suggests a further point which, as we will soon see, he also uses to set out his ethical theory in the *Discourses*. The point is that responsible agents do not just respond to necessity with raw force or energy. They seek to impose new, well-ordered necessities on themselves and their environment, thereby making themselves less vulnerable to future pressures. The first individual who wins Machiavelli's praise in the *Florentine Histories* is the Ostrogoth emperor Theodoric. In war, Machiavelli writes, Theodoric was always victorious, while in peace he greatly benefited his cities and peoples. He restored Rome to civil order, allowed Romans every honor except military training, and contained all the barbarian kings in the empire "without the tumult of war, but by his authority alone." He built new towns and fortresses to impede further movements of populations seeking to attack Italy. If "so many virtues had not been sullied" by suspicions of cruelties committed under his watch, Theodoric would deserve honor "from every side, because through his virtue and goodness not only Rome and Italy but all the other parts of the western Empire, free of the continual battering they had suffered" from outside inundations "recovered and settled down into good order [*buono ordine*] and a very prosperous state [*assai felice stato*]."[23]

4.3.
Necessità as a pretext

In the *Discourses* Machiavelli describes the extreme violence of wars fought by "entire peoples" who, "necessitated by either famine or war," are forced to leave their homes and "seek a new seat and a new province" by possessing land occupied by other peoples and expelling or killing "the ancient inhabitants of it." Such peoples are "very frightful, since they have been expelled by an ultimate necessity; and if they do not encounter good arms, they will never be contained."[24] The phrase "ultimate necessity" (*ultima necessità*) recurs in the *Florentine Histories*, where a speaker exhorts his compatriots to war with the words: "There is an ultimate necessity that ought to make us obstinate in defense." The same speaker, one of the "older and wiser" citizens of Florence's neighboring city Lucca, further

---

[22] *FH*, I.1.9/321–23. Specific features of these northern *ordine* exemplify principles that Machiavelli later argues ought to govern the distribution of benefits and burdens in any political order: procedural fairness in deciding who should leave by means of lot; equal opportunity in dividing the population in a way that gives people an equal chance to stay or go regardless of wealth or social status; and the idea that polities should be mixed bodies, in which rich and poor, noble and ignoble share burdens and benefits even under extreme necessity.

[23] *FH*, I.4.13–14/329–31.

[24] *D*, II.8.143–45/346–49, discussed in chap. 11. His main examples in the *Discourses* are the Hebrews and Maurusians; in the *Histories* (*FH*, I.3.117/315–16) the Britons exemplify peoples who, "dispossessed of their fatherland" by violent expulsions, "became ferocious through necessity and thought that although they had not been able to defend their own country they might seize one belonging to others."

declares that "things done out of necessity neither should nor can merit praise or blame."[25] If readers assume that these passages express Machiavelli's own considered judgments, then it would seem that he acknowledges at least some situations of extreme danger that are not avoidable or self-inflicted, but imposed on agents by hostile forces beyond their control. Such situations might seem to justify any "things done" as reasonable or unavoidable responses to extreme *necessità*. In the *Discourses* Machiavelli reports a Roman legate as saying "that it did not appear to him that any policy whatever for saving the fatherland was to be avoided" and that it "appeared to him . . . that the fatherland is well defended in whatever mode one defends it, whether with ignominy or with glory." Elsewhere he quotes a passage from Livy which has a captain of the Samnites, neighbors and often enemies of Rome, declare, "War is just to whom it is necessary, and arms are pious to those for whom there is no hope save in arms [*iustum est bellum quibus necessarium, et pia arma quibus nisi in armis spes est*]."[26] Before concluding that these passages express Machiavelli's views, however, they should be read in the context of the speeches or *discorsi* where they appear. In most cases, it becomes clear that passages that invoke *necessità* as a pretext for uncompromising action cannot simply be identified with Machiavelli's own judgments. Rather, they quote familiar opinions or maxims that stand in need of critical scrutiny. Let us consider several examples that illustrate diverse ways in which the word *necessità* is used in political speech, ranging from crudely self-serving to more reasonable uses.

Machiavelli attributes some of his most glaring examples of self-serving, irresponsible rhetoric to early popes and emperors in the fractured Roman Empire. Early in the *Histories* he describes the wars launched by these rulers against the Saracens as a case in point. Echoing his opening discussion of the "northern" invasions of Rome, Machiavelli presents the first Saracen incursions into Italy as a self-inflicted blight. First, he writes, the emperor Romanus, outraged by the Italian provinces' rebellion against his rule, let the Saracens in to attack Puglia and Calabria; later emperors hired Saracens to counter papal authority. The emperors, in other words, were responsible for giving these new "barbarians" a stronghold in Italy. Having opened the door to this external threat, a long string of popes and emperors proceeded to invoke *necessità* as a pretext for unnecessarily long, violent, and fruitless wars against the Saracens. Machiavelli describes these wars with dry irony, insinuating that they were caused as much by papal ambition as by genuine threats. The pontiffs, he writes, found ingenious ways to use the Saracen menace to their own advantage. Hated by the Roman people and realizing that "because of the disunities in Italy he could not be secure," Pope Urban II

> turned to a generous enterprise [*una generosa impresa*], went away to France with all the clergy, and in Auvergne gathered up many peoples to whom he made a speech against the infidels. This speech so inflamed their spirits that they decided to make a campaign in Asia against the Saracens.

---

[25] *FH*, V.11.197–99/534–35.
[26] *D*, III.41.300–301/515; III.12.248/458–59, discussed in chap. 9.

This campaign along with all the others like it were called the Crusades [*Crociate*] because all those who went on them had their arms and clothing marked with a red cross.[27]

The "generous enterprise" soon fizzled out to an ungenerous and inglorious end. It was "glorious in the beginning," Machiavelli writes, "because all Asia Minor, Syria, and a part of Egypt came under the power of the Christians," and because several "celebrated new orders of knights were born." Among these were "the Order of the Templars," which, despite the good word *ordine* in its name, "shortly after disappeared on account of their bad customs [*cattivi costumi*]." Famous emperors such as Frederick Barbarossa, having been deprived by the pope of authority over Rome, joined "the enterprise in Asia" so as "to vent [*sfugare*] against Mohammed the ambition that he had not been able to vent against the vicars of Christ."[28] This was followed "at various times various unforeseen events [*accidenti*] in which many nations and particular men were celebrated" or "acquired great reputation [*reputazione grandissima*]." *Onore* and *reputazione* notwithstanding, the crusaders fought with only "varying fortune" until they were trounced by the Saracen leader Saladin. Machiavelli says that this defeat was due to Saladin's "virtue and the discords of the Christians," which "in the end took from them all the glory they had acquired in the beginning." After only ninety years, he observes ironically, "the Christians were driven out of the place they had successfully recovered with such honor."[29]

Machiavelli treats the wars against the Saracens as a textbook case of an irresponsible appeal to *necessità*. The wars involved using badly ordered means to fight against a largely self-inflicted threat. Moreover, the popes and emperors he mentions were uninterested in weighing the responses their actions were likely to provoke from agents at the receiving end. Absorbed with their own ambitions or seeking to deflect hatred from themselves at home, it soon became apparent that their "generous enterprises" in Asia had been predicated on overconfidence in their own fortune and a gross underestimation of their opponents' *virtú*. Machiavelli regards actions framed with such navel-gazing disregard for other people's responses as badly ordered, and almost always self-defeating. He does, however, recognize important differences between crudely self-serving appeals to *necessità* and appeals based on the sincere belief that an unbearable price must be paid if urgent, uncompromising action is not taken. His appraisals of how such appeals are made under different kinds of constraint can be seen in several examples from the *Histories* and the *Discourses*.

A first example involves an appeal to *necessità* that has some reasonable cause, and which is motivated by a sincere love of fatherland as well as by personal am-

---

[27] *FH*, I.12.23/328–29; I.21.33/339–40; I.17.27–28/334.

[28] Like the Crusades themselves, on Machiavelli's (*FH*, I.19.30–31/336–37) account Frederick's venting came to an inglorious end. For "having arrived at the river [Cidnus] he was lured by the clarity of its waters into washing himself in them, from which disorder"—presumably the attempt to cleanse his rotten self—"he died."

[29] *FH*, I.17.27–28/334. In a similar vein, he plays down the Ottoman threat later; see VI.33.268–69/620.

bition. Machiavelli puts it in the mouth of the exiled Rinaldo degli Albizzi, one of the *Histories*' most complex characters. The "use of arms," Rinaldo declares, should never be condemned in situations of *necessità*; for "many times infirmities arise that cannot be healed without fire and iron" so that "the good citizen, even if iron should be necessary, would sin much more by letting them go uncured than by curing them." And "I do not know," Rinaldo continues, "what necessity is greater than ours or what piety can exceed that which takes our fatherland out of slavery." Read out of context, these words might seem to exemplify Machiavelli's own patriotic values, and his conviction that any external threat should be met by assertive force. Placed back in context, matters look more complicated. Rinaldo's passionate patriotic rhetoric is not addressed to his Florentine compatriots but to a foreign prince. He is not exhorting compatriots to defend their own city, but inciting a foreigner to attack Florence in order to topple his own enemies, hoping to place own party in power by means of "others' arms" instead of by popular will. The ends he pursues through necessitarian rhetoric are both partisan and imprudent, since in effect if not intent Rinaldo offers an ambitious foreign ruler power to determine who holds authority in Florence. Machiavelli casts further doubts on the prudence of Rinaldo's appeal to *necessità* by making him insist that an attack on Florence would be easy.[30] He underestimates the defensive reactions of citizens whose city is invaded by a foreign power, especially one whose intentions they have reason to distrust.

In this case, Machiavelli implies that Rinaldo exaggerated the *necessità* faced by his city in order to justify self-serving and excessive actions. A few chapters later he presents a more difficult case: a confrontation between Florence and the neighboring city of Lucca. The words "There is an ultimate necessity that ought to make us obstinate in defense" are uttered by a "wise" citizen of Lucca, a city with a long history of fighting for independence against Florentine dominance. Inciting his people to defend themselves once again, the same speaker declares: "You must always have understood that things done out of necessity neither should nor can merit praise or blame." Describing the Florentines as "perpetual enemies" (*perpetui nimici*) of the Lucchese people, the speaker tells his countrymen to disregard all restraints in the ensuing all-out struggle.[31] Machiavelli leaves little doubt that the necessity faced by the Lucchese was severe, and that they had reason to be indignant at the constant threats posed to their freedom by Florentine ambitions. When the episode ends in failure for Florence and Machiavelli reports that an accord was pressed on the Florentines to leave the Lucchese their liberty, he can scarcely contain his disdain for his compatriots' sullen reaction. "Rarely does it happen," he writes, "that anyone is so displeased at having lost his own things as were the Florentines for not having acquired those of others."[32]

Nevertheless, Machiavelli does not suggest that the Lucchese should have considered themselves exempt from restraints when responding to *necessità*. While

---

[30] *FH*, V.8.193–95/529–31.
[31] *FH*, V.11.197–99/533–36.
[32] *FH*, V.14.203/540.

weaker or less culpable parties may have cause for forcible resistance, Machiavelli still holds them responsible for choosing prudent modes of resisting.[33] A close reading suggests several flaws in the Lucchese citizen's argument that "things done out of necessity neither should nor can merit praise or blame." First, the speech shows an inadequately responsible approach to *necessità* in its tendency to blame others or brute bad luck for the present dire situation, without asking whether past omissions or actions on the part of one's own city might have contributed to it. Thus "the ancient hostility of the Florentine people" against Lucca is said to be due not to Lucchese actions, but only to their weakness or bad luck and the Florentines' "ambitious nature." Second, Machiavelli hints at partisan motives behind the "wise" speaker's rhetoric. Lucca's leading citizens, he notes, welcomed war with Florence as a means of deflecting internal hatreds from themselves, since they feared the "inconstant spirits" of their own plebs almost as much as foreign conquest. The speaker, Machiavelli implies, exaggerates Florence's ill-treatment of Lucca in order to whip up fear and rage among the lower classes. A third dubious feature of the speech is revealed in its portrayal of war with Florence as an all-out war between "perpetual enemies." The speaker describes a clash that must inevitably result in either "salvation" or enslavement for the Lucchese people, and which could in neither case alter their view that the Florentines are their "perpetual enemies" with whom no terms of partnership (*compagni*) can be worked out. Earlier in the *Histories*, Machiavelli has a group of mediators explain why this attitude is unreasonable: they "recalled that it was not prudent always to want the ultimate victory."[34] Later chapters show that this maxim applies in the same way to relations between cities seeking to live on decently ordered terms of coexistence.[35]

More generally, the assertion that "things done out of necessity neither should nor can merit praise or blame" sits uneasily beside one of Machiavelli's recurrent arguments: namely, that even under extreme constraints agents must choose between different ways to respond; and they can, indeed must, be held responsible for their choices. At the very least they can choose to flee or to stay and fight. And then they must choose *how* to flee or fight: by lashing out in a ferocious, unreflective way, or by "ordering" themselves for their future security. Since these choices are always available even under an "ultimate necessity," there is always room for praise or blame. Even responses to overwhelming pressures may still be judged more or less prudent or *virtuoso*. Some responses seize the occasion to establish new and better orders. Others strike back violently, but do nothing to rectify the shortcomings that allowed *necessità* to wreak havoc in the first place. Machiavelli regards even much weaker and oppressed agents as nonetheless free agents who must share responsibility for seeking solutions to conflicts. The Lucchese too had a choice: either to fight a war of mutual extermination between "perpetual enemies,"

---

[33] This speech calling for ruthless self-defense by a weaker city is analogous to an incendiary speech by a downtrodden woolworker in Book III: the latter focuses attention on the responses of the weakest groups inside a city to deprivation, the former on those of the weakest cities in a region (or dominion) to attacks on its freedom. See chap. 8, sec. 8.2.

[34] *FH*, V.11.197–99/533–36; II.14.67/378–79.

[35] Compare Thucydides' Diodotus, discussed in chap. 2, sec. 2.5.

or to be prepared to make an accord (*accordo*) with the Florentines that would enhance the security and freedom of both.[36]

4.4.
Imposing and removing *necessità*

While Machiavelli shows understanding for the desperation of people under extreme pressures, he consistently holds that responses to *necessità* must be prudently ordered. He identifies two broad ways to order responses: necessities may be "imposed" by various means, or they may be "removed" by prudent agents. This section considers what he says about "removing necessities" and how he relates removing to imposing. The remaining sections discuss different ways of imposing necessities, relating them to Machiavelli's concept of *virtú*.

Machiavelli mentions this mode of responding to necessity in Book III of the *Discourses*, where he quotes from a speech in Livy's histories: "War is just to whom it is necessary [*Iustum est bellum quibus necessarium*], and arms are pious to those for whom there is no hope save in arms."[37] Livy gives these words to a captain of the Samnites, an Italian people who recurrently resisted Roman attempts to make them subjects (*subietti, sudditi*) instead of partners (*compagni*). The context of the speech is analogous to that of the Lucchese speech in the *Florentine Histories*. In both cases, appeals to necessity are made on behalf of peoples who judge that they have been treated unjustly by powerful neighboring cities that seek to dominate them, and whose methods of exercising *dominium* have caused them to mistrust the stronger city's proposals for peace. Livy's Samnite speech illustrates the same tendency to relativize standards of justice under extreme pressure that Machiavelli depicts in the Lucchese oration. But once again, Machiavelli's own commitment to the maxims he presents is called into question by several features of the context.

The chapter begins by recalling to readers the many points in which previous *Discourses* have "discoursed of how useful [*utile*] is necessity to human actions and to what glory they have been led by it." The next sentence connects Machiavelli's own investigations of this theme with that of "certain moral philosophers [*alcuni morali filosofi*]" who consider that "the hands and tongue of men—two very noble instruments for ennobling him—would not have worked perfectly nor led human works to the height they are seen to be led to had they not been driven by necessity."[38] The philosophical question of how necessity can be "useful" is the main subject of the chapter. The nuances in Machiavelli's appraisal of the Samnite claim that "war is just to whom it is necessary" are best understood when this claim, made in the heat of war, is set alongside more reflective judgments about the utility

---

[36] *FH*, V.11.197–99/533–36. The idea that accords allowing cities to support each other's freedom should be preferred to the illusory quest for "ultimate victory" is expressed clearly in *FH*, II.38.99–100/416–17.

[37] *D*, III.12.248/458. The same quote appears at the end of *P*, XXVI, and nearly the same in *FH*, V.8.

[38] As noted previously, in my view one likely source for this is Plato's *Tim.*, esp. 47d and 75a–76e. The note in the Mansfield translation (*D*, III.12.246 n. 2) cites Plato's *Laws* 628c–d as presenting an opposed view, without explaining the interpretation. I see no basis for any opposition.

of *necessità*. By considering what kinds of action taken with respect to necessity are most "useful," the chapter will also point toward a more adequate, non-relativist account of what is "just" in relation to necessity.

The key element in Machiavelli's dialectical examination is set out clearly: necessity is most useful and leads to glory, he says, when agents view it as their own necessity. He alludes to two main ways in which agents may come to see necessities as their own self-imposed constraints rather than as alien and hostile impositions. One is by deciding to accept *pre-existing* constraints they have not chosen as conditions for their future actions. The other is by making *new* orders to serve agents' own freely elected purposes. This second way of ordering one's own necessity was, Machiavelli writes, "known by the ancient captains of armies." They used it in two distinct but complementary ways: by imposing new necessities on their own men to make them more obstinate; and by removing necessity from their enemies, to make them less so. Thus ancient captains strove to "do every work so that their soldiers were constrained by necessity" to fight in a disciplined, highly motivated way. At the same time "they used all industry so that enemies would be freed from" necessity.

Here then is an important distinction between the modes of ordering necessity that are appropriate for oneself and one's own friends, partners, or willing subjects, on the one hand, and those appropriate for dealing with other people, especially with enemies, on the other. The rationale for this distinction has already been set out. Necessity is useful when agents see it as self-imposed and freely accepted. But it is very dangerous when they see it as imposed from without, since people grow more obstinate in their resistance when necessity is forced on them by others. "Such obstinacy," Machiavelli observes, "also arises from the natural hatreds that neighboring princes and neighboring republics have for one another, which proceeds from the ambition to dominate and from jealousy for their state." Here as in the *Histories*, Machiavelli stresses the near impossibility of achieving "ultimate victory" in conflicts where one or both sides consider themselves under pressure of necessity inflicted by the other. "Such rivalry and contention," he points out, "have made and always will make the capture [*espugnazione*] of one by another difficult."[39] This is why it is imprudent to leave opponents no choice but to order themselves better and fight back more effectively. Prudent orderers ought rather "to contrive with all diligence to lift [*levare*] such necessity . . . and in consequence such obstinacy" from their enemies.

The distinction between removing and imposing necessities relates in the following way to the differences between more and less responsible actions. Irresponsible agents may think that the only way to deal with enemies is to eliminate them with violence. Responsible agents know that unilateral and immoderate measures might eliminate some enemies, while creating many more. Irresponsible agents endorse ruthlessness toward enemies because they view conflicts only from their own perspective. They spend little time considering how their

[39] *D*, III.12.246–47/456–57.

opponents are likely to react, or if they do consider this, grossly underestimate their capacities for *virtuoso* resistance. Responsible agents recognize that their opponents are human beings like themselves who tend to respond in similar ways to necessities they regard as inflicted by others. Reflecting that they themselves would fight obstinately against perceived aggression or humiliation, they work hard to avoid creating a cause for such fights against themselves, and try to remove such causes as already exist.

These arguments suggest that the Samnite captain's assertion "war is just to whom it is necessary" is not a straightforward expression of Machiavelli's own views, but a statement he presents in order to stimulate reflections on how necessity is perceived from the standpoint of agents other than oneself. Considered as a description of how people often judge things under extreme conditions of conflict, the statement serves as a warning to those who fail to take sufficient account of opponents' responses to their actions. If they attack too aggressively or refuse to make compromises, their enemies will have reason to consider themselves under harsh necessity; and this is likely to make them more dangerous, since it stimulates indignation and efforts to impose better orders on themselves. Machiavelli reinforces this point with another quote from Livy: "alike in virtue, you are superior in necessity, which is the last and greatest weapon [*virtute pares, quae ultimum ac maximum telum est, necessitate superiores estis*]." It is more prudent to lift the pressure of urgent necessity from enemies by offering them alternatives to all-out, perpetual war. So long as "necessity constrained" the enemies of Rome to combat, "they combated very ferociously; but when they saw the way open" to a reasonably favorable settlement, "they thought more of fleeing than of engaging in combat."

Machiavelli offers several examples of policies that relieved the necessity pressing on enemies, thereby depriving them of cause for obstinacy in their resistance. "If they have fear of punishment," he suggests, a prudent agent lifts their sense of urgent necessity by promising pardon. If his enemies "had fear for their freedom," he shows "that he does not go against the common good but against the ambitious few in the city."[40] He describes the means used by Camillus, "the most prudent of Roman captains," to "take away from the enemy the ultimate necessity [*ultima necessità*] of defending themselves." Camillus achieved this by commanding "that no one should hurt those who were unarmed, so that when the arms were thrown to earth" the enemy city "was taken almost without blood. Such a mode," Machiavelli notes approvingly, "was later observed by many captains."[41] Knowing when and how to "remove" necessity from one's enemies in order to attain one's ends turns out to be an important element of Machiavellian *virtú*. *Virtuoso* orderers not only judge well how to impose necessities on themselves and their environments, in ways discussed shortly; they also judge well when and how to "lift" those that they had a part in imposing on others.

---

[40] Compare TPW, IV.19–20: prudent men and cities can always "vanquish" their enemy by acting not with violence (*biasamenois*) but with generosity (*charisamenois*), offering moderate terms of reconciliation.

[41] D, III.12.249/459.

4.5.

Virtú as reflective prudence: Taking stock of ordinary constraints

This brings us to another important and neglected feature of Machiavelli's distinctions between more and less responsible conceptions of *necessità*. I noted above that responsible agents attend as much to "ordinary and natural inconveniences" posed by human drives, desires, and accidents as they do to crises that seem to call for extraordinary responses.[42] How does Machiavelli relate these ordinary constraints on action to the harsher constraints that are usually called *necessità*? A clearer understanding of the relationship between *ordinario* constraints and Machiavelli's reflective conception of necessity, I suggest, sheds valuable light on his concept of *virtú*.

Machiavelli uses the word *necessità* to designate constraints that have various sources. Natural constraints include the physical attributes of the sites at one's disposal and, in some cases, natural disasters such as floods that force people to change their location and build new cities from scratch. Constraints attributed entirely or in part to supernatural agencies include those said to be imposed by fortune, fate, or the will of gods. Human *necessità* encompasses historical, economic, or political pressures that motivate people to build new cities, including external wars that drive people from their homelands. Machiavelli also implies that certain desires, humors, and drives exhibited by human beings in all times and places have a distinctive quality of *necessità*. Early in the *Prince* we read that it is a "natural and ordinary [*naturale e ordinario*] necessity" that "one must always offend those over whom he becomes a new prince." The *Discourses* make the related point that tyranny brings "natural and ordinary dangers" to tyrants, as well as their enemies. It is also "a very natural and ordinary thing to desire to acquire," and "very ordinary and reasonable [*ordinario e ragionevole*]" that a prince will lose what he acquires if he fails to observe "any of the conditions observed by others who have taken provinces and wished to hold them."[43]

While the words "ordinary," "natural," and "reasonable" might at first seem to have little connection to the sense of urgency and emergency conveyed by the rhetoric of *necessità*, Machiavelli's reflections suggest that adequate conceptions of *necessità* do not focus only on extraordinary constraints. On the contrary, prudent agents should take the ordinary and natural or reasonable constraints that confront them every day as seriously as necessities that arise *in extremis*. Such ordinary necessities include all the humors and desires that explain why new princes always "offend" their new subjects. As later chapters argue, desires "not to be dominated" and desires to live free and secure are among the most pressing *ordinario* constraints on princes'—and any other agents'—actions.[44] Since these human desires are extremely strong and can emerge at any time in "any city whatever," princes and republics underestimate them at their peril. Some of the most basic necessities that princes should attend to are ordinary and quotidian, such as accidents that

---

[42] *D*, III.37.294/508.

[43] *P*, III.8/120; *D*, III.6.234/442; *P*, III.14–16/124–26.

[44] *D*, I.5, I.16, II.2.

arise every day. Other ordinary necessities are shown in the obstinacy that "arises from the natural hatreds that neighboring princes and neighboring republics have for one another, which proceeds from the ambition to dominate and from jealousy for their state." The mix of good and evil in human works is another "ordinary and natural inconvenience" that agents must learn to "know and manage" if they want to take part in shaping their own fortune instead of being subject to another's.[45] If the word *necessità* identifies constraints that should be treated as very serious limits on action, then Machiavelli implies that all these desires, humors, and inconveniences are as "necessitating" as constraints posed by emergencies. Indeed they are more fundamental, ubiquitous necessities that must be taken into account by anyone who orders civil life, fights wars, or seeks to regulate relations with other polities. "Ordinary and natural" desires and humors can never be completely eliminated; they are simply part of everyday human social life, inside cities and among different peoples.[46] They ensure that even the most powerful agents are subject to infinite constraints posed by other people's desires, movements, and repulsions, which prevent them from doing whatever they choose. While Machiavelli presupposes that human beings have free will, he also stresses that they exercise it under numerous, ineliminable constraints, most of which are simply "natural and ordinary" inconveniences or "ordinary and reasonable" difficulties that arise from having to share the world with other people.[47]

This analysis has important implications for understanding Machiavelli's concept of *virtù*. He uses *necessità* to designate strongly constraining causality, and *virtù* for an enabling causality that makes some choices and actions possible even under constraints imposed by *necessità*. Irresponsible necessitarian rhetoric treats *virtù* and *necessità* as rival forms of causality. It considers the constraints imposed by necessity as extreme and hostile pressures that must be dominated, and *virtù* as the power that enables individuals or cities to dominate them. Machiavelli's emphasis on ordinary constraints calls this view into question. His arguments imply, first, that *necessità* does not always involve extreme pressures or situations of crisis; and second, that agents show deficient *virtù* who focus their energies on dealing with critical situations but fail to "know and manage" more "ordinary" pressures. While Machiavelli does hold that *virtù* only shows itself under necessity, *necessità* includes serious constraints of an everyday character. His most *virtuoso* agents are not those who seize the occasion given by *necessità* to justify "extraordinary"

---

[45] *D*, III.49.308/524–25; III.12.246–47/456–57; III.37.294/508.

[46] *D*, I.3.15/207–8.

[47] A similar idea is expressed in Thucydides by the Spartan king Archidamus, who urges his compatriots "to consider that the thoughts of our neighbors are very much like our own. . . . We must not think there is much difference between men, but only that the best have been educated among the severest necessities [*en tois anangkaiotatois paideutai*]"; TPW, I.84. Archidamus further stresses the need not only to measure opponents' present power and military knowledge, but also to realize that both they and you have the capacity to become stronger and wiser through hard work and self-imposed discipline. He points out that the temptation to underestimate enemies on the basis of their present condition is the greatest danger for cities and armies—a truth borne out by Thucydides' subsequent narrative.

actions, but those who labor even in "quiet times" to found and maintain quite ordinary, regulative orders.[48] He frequently suggests that *virtú* calls less for grandiose exertions than for continuous hard work or *industria*.[49] An important element of *virtú* in this sense is a specific kind of prudence. This involves taking a broad view of the small and large, immediate and future constraints on one's actions, including those imposed by other agents' "ordinary and natural" reactions to pressure: their ambitions, aversions to being dominated, and obstinacy when fighting under extreme *necessità*. Machiavelli argues that whoever fails to take stock of these constraints must either fail in his enterprises, or achieve ephemeral success without forging stable orders. A basic condition for calling agents *virtuoso*, then, is that they should exhibit a high degree of reflective prudence, habitually considering ordinary humors, desires, and reactions of others as "necessary" constraints on their own field of action. Actions that show boldness, energetic exertion, or stubborn determination may show *virtú* if and only if they are based on a prudent assessment of the ordinary constraints on one's own actions.

Machiavelli frequently alludes to a common error that indicates a shortfall in *virtú*: the failure to differentiate between "ordinary" constraints on action that need continuous regulating, on the one hand, and more urgent pressures that require more assertive responses. In particular, ordinary and ineliminable divisions in cities encourage people to exaggerate dangers posed by opponents. Motivated by ambition to dominate or fear of being dominated, these people use the rhetoric of necessity to (mis)represent quite ordinary and reasonable constraints on their own actions as threats to public order. The entire *Florentine Histories* can be read as a cautionary lesson about what happens to cities that succumb to these kinds of imprudence. Both nobles and people in Florence showed a chronic deficit of reflective prudence, and hence of *virtú*, in viewing necessity from a unilateral perspective. Perceiving their rivals' ordinary desires to share authority as threats to order, both sides constantly rang the alarm bells of *necessità* at the slightest provocation.[50] In contrast, Machiavelli argues, sound republican orders in Rome were based on the recognition that most "tumults" (*tumulti*) were the "ordinary and natural" by-products of the two main, opposing humors (*umori*) found in any city, some wishing to dominate and others not to be dominated. Roman orderers showed their *virtú* by preserving and regulating these humors instead of trying vainly to repress them.[51] Roman orders showed *virtú* by accepting different humors as a "natural and ordinary" necessity in any free city and giving them room to "vent" (*sfugare*).

No other act of ordering, founding, or fighting, however grandiose, receives higher praise from Machiavelli than the ordinary yet supremely virtuous recognition that conflicting humors and tumults are an ineliminable feature of any civil

---

[48] Examples include Camillus and Fabius Maximus in Rome and Uzzano in the *FH*, described as a man "hostile to every extraordinary mode" and obstinate in defending established orders when they were good. See chap. 1, sec. 1.1., and chap 10.

[49] For example, *P*, II.6–7/120; *D*, I.1.7–10/199–202; III.12.246–49/456–59; *FH*, II.1.52–53/361–62.

[50] *FH*, II.14.67/378–79.

[51] *D*, I.4–5.16–19/208–12.

life.[52] Unlike the Romans, Florentines never learned to live with their "ordinary and natural" tensions, or to regulate them in ways that strengthened common freedoms. Where Rome's republican orders resolved conflicts by disputing (*disputando*), Florentines sought to end them by fighting (*combattendo*). Rome ended conflicts with a law (*con una legge*), Florence "with the exile and death of many citizens." The Florentine people fought "to be alone in the government without the participation of the nobles," not seeing that civil order would only be preserved if they agreed to pass a law preventing any part from dominating another, thus removing the necessity for partisan warfare. Popular desires to govern alone were, Machiavelli states, "injurious and unjust [*ingiurioso e ingiusto*]."[53] The Roman people nurtured the "more reasonable" desire to share access to the highest honors in the city with the nobles.[54] By agreeing to do so, the plebs took away the necessity that would have constrained the nobles to fight against them had they been deprived of their share.

These contrasts highlight the distinctive forms of prudence that Machiavelli treats as conditions for *virtú*. Orderers show a very high degree of *virtú* who realize the futility of trying to repress different humors or to dominate those hostile to them. *Virtú* is shown most powerfully in actions that involve self-restraint as well as self-assertion, and which accept limits on one's own powers so that civil power is shared with other parts on terms that order tumults without eliminating them. In these examples Machiavelli clearly values the capacity for reflective self-restraint much more highly than capacities for unilateral self-assertion, and identifies the former but not the latter with *virtú*. All his works examine the grave disorders that flow from unilateral or aggressive attempts to dominate any natural or social environment, whether clement and friendly or hostile. For Machiavelli the "domination" of *necessità*, especially of "ordinary and natural" necessities, is not a reasonable aim of *virtuoso* action. *Virtuoso* orderers recognize that the most persistent, ubiquitous constraints on their ordering are simply indomitable, and that they must accept other people's conflicting desires and wills as an ineliminable part of political life. They treat collisions with these *ordinario* necessities as opportunities to exercise their self-ordering capacities in ways that are constrained by, but need not be subjected to, other people's desires and motions. For this reason, Machiavelli's *virtú* can be seen more in men and works that regulate (*regolare*) necessity than in those that aspire to dominate (*dominare*) them.

4.6.
Under- and overassertive responses to necessity

This interpretation rejects the widespread assumption that Machiavelli's *virtú* is a quality manifested most strongly by *estraordinario* men in extraordinary times,

---

[52] Compare the discussion of venting humors (*chumoi*) in individual and civil bodies in Plato, *Tim.* 86e–87c.

[53] When dealing with Rome Machiavelli treats overambitious *nobili* as more deficient in *virtú* than the plebs. His analysis of Florentine disorders lays more blame on the people.

[54] *FH*, III.1.105–6/423–24; also III.2–6.106–12/423–33 and episodes discussed in chaps. 7–8.

and the related view that his concept of *virtú* has more to do with energetic self-assertion than with prudent self-restraint. To regulate the effects of natural, ordinary, and extreme pressures, self-imposed necessities must be well *ordered*; and effective orders necessitate by *regulating* actions. Ill-directed bursts of energy or unilateral assertions of an agent's will lack *virtú*, and are unlikely to constrain anything or anyone effectively. Moreover, individuals or cities who seek *only* to author new necessities of their own, but who refuse to recognize any pre-existing necessities as limits on their actions, are clearly deficient in *virtú*.

It has seldom been recognized that for Machiavelli, responses to necessity may be overassertive as well as underassertive. Underassertive agents respond to ordinary or urgent necessities by fleeing from situations of intense pressure and seeking out easier ways to live, instead of staying put and working harder to impose their own "ordered" necessity. Overassertive agents respond to any *necessità* with resolute opposition and confrontation, believing that *virtú* is shown by "overcoming" or "mastering" necessity. Machiavelli sees both responses as deficient. If some choices show too little *virtú* because they do not try hard enough in the face of necessity, other choices fail to show adequate *virtú* because agents do not take constraints on their choices seriously enough.[55]

Machiavelli underlines the defects of over- and underassertive modes of action by examining different choices of site in Book I of the *Discourses*. The metaphorical aspects of Machiavelli's writing in this key chapter are usually overlooked: when he speaks of sites (*siti*) he mentions not only natural environments but also the human and social matter that any builder (*edificatore*) of cities must handle. Underassertive agents are right to prefer sites for building new cities that are fertile and thus able to support large populations for defense and other public goods. They go wrong in relying too much on natural advantages for their security and flourishing. Overassertive agents seem to show more *virtú* because they recognize that stable orders depend on imposing new necessities that "the site does not provide." They go astray when they view the imperative to impose new necessities as a mandate to repress whatever old ones—natural, historical, or anthropological—they might find on site. Responsible ordering should not try to make things easy for orderers of cities and future generations of citizens. But neither should it involve the self-deception that any orderer can completely dominate necessity, least of all "natural and ordinary" necessities posed by diverse humors, tumults, and human desires for freedom. *Virtuoso* "orderers" recognize that their ordering capacities are always exercised under constraint; and further, that when insufficient constraints are imposed from without, they should impose more on themselves. Indeed, the first chapter of the *Discourses* insists that human beings *only* show *virtú* under pressure of necessity. Builders show their *virtú*, Machiavelli argues, by imposing their own necessities on sites that are too agreeable, since sites that do not severely constrain their inhabitants cause the latter to become idle. When agents are not constrained by either externally inflicted or self-imposed necessity,

---

[55] Or as Machiavelli sometimes says, they may show an "excessive" *virtú* which, by exceeding bounds of prudence, disqualifies them from deserving that good name; see chap. 6, sec. 6.1.

or do not regard themselves as so constrained, they invariably fail to maintain *virtú* in their own actions and their cities.[56]

One of Machiavelli's most vivid illustrations of the difference between virtuous and *virtú*-deficient responses to necessities imposed by site occurs in the *Histories*, with reference to the Venetians. In contrast to his more critical account in the *Discourses*, Machiavelli here presents the first Venetians as *virtuoso* orderers who turned harsh *necessità* into an opportunity for self-improvement, not an excuse for living disordered or oppressed.[57] Venice was established when, "constrained by necessity," several populations fled from the invasions by Attila and the Huns to inhabit the swamps around Rivo Alto. Machiavelli notes that the migrants "left very pleasant and fertile places to live in places that were sterile, deformed, and devoid of every comfort." They might have responded to these constraints with fatalistic passivity, blaming ill fortune; or by succumbing to a bestial life dictated by their natural environment. Instead they ordered themselves for a life better than the one they left. Venice was located in "a swampy and diseased place," yet its inhabitants "at a stroke rendered it healthy" through their own industry. Since "many peoples were brought together at a stroke," there was all the more need to cooperate in building institutions to regulate their common life. So "in a very short time they made those places not only habitable but delightful; they established laws and orders among themselves, and amidst so much ruin in Italy, they enjoyed security." Venetian commerce provided what their denizens and "other men had need of," not primarily luxury goods. Moreover, Venetians did not yet exert their commercial strength to seek to dominate other cities or peoples; they did not aspire to "any other dominion than of what might make the traffic of their merchandise easier." As long as they "lived in this form their name became terrible on the seas and venerated within Italy," and in Italian squabbles "they were most often the arbiters" whose judgment was respected, making it into "a republic that for order and for power [*per ordine e per potenza*] ought to be celebrated above every other principality in Italy."[58]

Machiavelli uses this example not just to illustrate adequately virtuous responses to extreme necessity, but also to demonstrate that even the most successful achievements of *virtuoso* building are vulnerable to corruption. The greatest danger faced by descendants of such exemplary builders is to rest on ancient laurels, forgetting that necessity is never wholly dominated but must always be present for *virtú* to remain robust. The first Venetians knew that "as necessity had led them to live in the waters, so it forced them to think of how they could live decently [*onestamente*] when they had no use of the land." So they sailed forth "in ships throughout the world," filling their city with merchandise, which attracted numerous traders to the

---

[56] D.I.1. This point is developed further in the next sections.

[57] D.I.1. The difference can be explained by Machiavelli's allegorical aims: he is less interested in giving the single most accurate account of Venetian history than in making ethical points about more and less virtuous responses to necessity.

[58] *FH*, II.1.52–53/361–62; I.28–29.40–41/347–50. The deliberate equivocation between designating Venice as republic or principality reflects Machiavelli's critical view of its particular mixed form of government, which leaned heavily toward aristocracy while maintaining the name of republic.

city. Later generations took these achievements for granted. Forgetting that well-ordered restraints must be part of any successful strategy for dealing with necessity, they were carried away by their city's commercial success and began to seize surrounding cities. The motives for these seizures had little to do with genuine *necessità*. Their cause, Machiavelli writes, was the Venetians' "lust for domination [*cupidità del dominare*]," which gave them "so great an opinion of their power" that both Italian princes and kings beyond the Alps "were in terror [*terrore*] of them." The Venetians paid a high price for demanding excessive power. By trading in the role of judicious arbiter of Italian affairs for the part of would-be empire-builder, they so antagonized various princes and kings that these "together conspired against them and in one day took from them that state which they had won for themselves in so many years with infinite expense." And now although they have "reacquired something," they "have reacquired neither their reputation nor their forces" and so live like all the other Italian princes "at the discretion of others."[59]

This example shows again that Machiavelli's conception of *virtuoso* self-imposition has at least as much to do with ordered self-*restraint* as with self-*assertion*. The most virtuous agents do not seek simply to beat down obstacles; they meet them head-on, yet deal with necessities that cannot be permanently eliminated by making them accomplices in further "building." Even optimally free human actions are constrained and overdetermined in innumerable ways. No choices are made in a vacuum; every human choice involves a response to some pre-existing natural or historical conditions, and to choices made by others that now confront agents as necessities. Agents who realize that their choices are always constrained are more likely to make prudent use of the narrow margin for choice that they do have. Knowing that choice and free will are not boundless powers, but capacities that always operate within the narrow margins left by nature, fortune, and the past and present actions of other men, they develop an economy of choice that they use prudently. Men or cities that imagine they can "master" all such constraints, seeking to impose their will on others and calling this *virtù*, suffer from one of the deepest delusions human beings can have. Those who refuse to accept "ordinary and natural" constraints are bound to overextend their own capacities, bringing disorder on their cities and hardships on themselves.

4.7.
Virtù as self-responsibility: Authorizing constraints on one's own forces

I have suggested that Machiavelli's *virtuoso* agents show reflective prudence, first, in their ability to distinguish among different kinds of necessity; and second, in working out appropriate ways of ordering their responses to them. Since *virtuoso* agents know that they must always act under the ordinary constraints posed by

---

[59] *FH*, I.29.41–42. Machiavelli compares Venice to Athens in these respects in D.I.1.7/199. Compare Plato's (*Crit.* 108e–121c) discussion of Atlantis as a great power disordered by its own good fortune, mythically foreshadowing the rise and decline of Athenian power.

other people's desires and humors, they see themselves under some kind of necessity all the time, not just in times of "extraordinary" crisis. Agents show *virtú* who regard extreme constraints as opportunities to examine what "orders" they may have lacked before, or to ask what was deficient in the orders they already had. The *virtú*-deficient consider the same necessities merely as negative, external threats to their free agency, treating constraints as an excuse for their own weakness or a pretext for extreme reactions. We have mentioned two distinct *virtuoso* ways of addressing necessities: by "imposing" necessities of one's own in response to those inflicted on one, and by "removing" necessities that one's own previous actions have inflicted on others. Let us now look more closely at what Machiavelli says about what is involved in "imposing" one's own necessities and how this relates to *virtú*.

By arguing that orderers or captains may impose ordered *necessità* on "their own" subjects, troops, or actions, Machiavelli implies that necessity need not be perceived as an external or hostile force; on the contrary, necessities may be ordered or imposed by agents on themselves and on those under their authority. So long as the latter continue to accept the orderer's authority, both they and the orderer can reasonably regard necessities imposed in this way as their own self-imposed necessities. These become conditions they willingly accept as limits on their actions, as necessary conditions for personal or civil *virtú*. By accepting certain necessities in this way, both orderers and followers manifest their *virtú* in a more profound way than those discussed earlier: they assume *responsibility* for their actions and orders by voluntarily setting constraints on themselves.

The idea that *virtú* involves the capacity—and the willingness—to assume responsibility by imposing constraints of "one's own" can be found though a philosophically sensitive reading of Book I, chapter I of the *Discourses*. Here phrases translated as "imposing [*posto, costringhino*] necessities" or "necessity ordered by the laws" occur many times in short succession. In the following, dense passage Machiavelli gives his first indications as to what *virtú* is and how it should be exerted in relation to *necessità*:

> Because men work either by necessity or by choice [*o per necessità o per elezione*], and because *there is greater virtue to be seen where choice has less authority*, it should be considered whether it is better to choose sterile places for the building of cities so that men, constrained to be industrious [*constretti a industriarsi*] and less seized by idleness [*odio*], live more united, having less cause for discord, because of the poverty of the site. This choice would without doubt be wiser and more useful if men were content to live off their own and did not wish to seek to command others. . . . Therefore, since men cannot secure themselves except with power [*potenza*], it is necessary to avoid this sterility in a country and to settle in the most fertile places where, since [the city] can expand [*ampliare*] because of the abundance of the site, it can both defend itself from whoever might assault it and crush anyone who might oppose its greatness. As to the idleness that the site might bring, *the laws should be ordered to constrain* [*costringhino*] it

by imposing [*ordinare*] such necessities as the site does not provide [*quelle necessità le leggi . . . che il sito non la costrignesse*].[60]

As noted earlier, Machiavelli presents necessitating constraints as a valuable counterweight to natural human tendencies that tend to corrode virtue, here summed up metaphorically as "idleness." Necessitating constraints are so useful, in fact, that they should be imposed and multiplied wherever too few are found in pre-existing "sites." The passage also suggests that necessity is not always an unchosen force imposed from without. On the contrary, when Machiavelli first mentions necessity in the *Discourses*, he speaks of *necessità* freely chosen and "ordered" by agents themselves.

A further important idea is implied in the last sentence: namely, that "ordering laws" is among the principal "modes" used by *virtuoso* builders to impose well-ordered necessities. Machiavelli directly links the ideas of "choosing necessities" and ordering them by laws to the normatively adequate concept of *virtù* that informs his judgments throughout the *Discourses*. "[A builder's] virtue," he declares, "can be recognized [*conosce*] in two modes: the first is in the choice of site [*nelle elezione del sito*], the other in the ordering of laws [*nella ordinazione delle leggi*]." Choosing sites and ordering laws are, I suggest, two distinct but complementary ways in which *virtuoso* agents impose their own necessities on whatever conditions—harsh or clement, fortunate or unhappy—may confront them. On the one hand, agents may recognize that some pre-existing constraints set inescapable or valuable limits on their actions. They therefore choose to **authorize** these necessities as constraints they willingly accept, although they did not originally choose or intentionally impose them. Indeed, reflectively prudent *virtuoso* agents realize that they *must* authorize some such constraints as conditions of their own action, since not even the most powerful individuals or cities are free from all such limits. On the other hand, agents may impose their own necessities not only to address pre-existing pressures, but also to **author** new constraints that serve their own purposes.[61] Even very weak agents may take responsibility for their actions under pressure by imposing their own orders on themselves and on their natural and social sites. The rest of this section looks more closely at the idea that initially unchosen necessities may be authorized, converting them into objects chosen by agents. The next section examines Machiavelli's remarks on self-authored necessities.

No matter how severe the constraints they work under, Machiavelli presupposes that human beings are able to exercise choice in limited yet important ways. If the constraints leave only two options—stay or go, live or die—agents can, indeed must, choose to do or not to do one or the other. Further, if there are more than two options, agents can and must choose among them. Both kinds of choice show responsible agency, even when agents are heavily constrained. Both involve a capacity that is extremely important in Machiavelli's ethics and political theory:

---

[60] *D*, I.1.14–16/200–201; emphasis added.

[61] Machiavelli sometimes speaks of the "author" (*autore*) of laws, as in the chapter title: "Nonobservance of a law that has been made, and especially by its *author*, is a thing that sets a bad example" (*D*, I.45.93/291). The ideas of authoring and authorization are implicit in his concept of *autorità*.

the capacity to give or withhold authority (*autorità*) to or from any person, power, or state of affairs. Agents show their *virtú* in how they use this capacity to authorize constraints they have not made or chosen, as much as in their more assertive *virtuoso* acts of ordering and imposing. Authorizing constraints is for Machiavelli one of the most important means people use to "impose necessities" on themselves. As later chapters will argue, authority willingly given by the people who are expected to obey it is the principal means for any prince, republic, or order to secure power and greatness. Machiavelli implies that the capacity to choose or authorize pre-existing necessities, however constrained it may be, is necessary and sufficient for agents to be held responsible for actions they take in response to necessity. It is also a necessary and sufficient reason to regard agents as having free will, as chapter 6 will argue further.

In Book I, chapter 1 of the *Discourses* Machiavelli's examples of two "free builders," Moses and Aeneas, illustrate the point that harsh necessities can be chosen by as well as inflicted on agents. Paradoxically, these builders were "free" because they were "constrained" by the most adverse conditions to leave their previous homes and to seek "a new seat" elsewhere. Under identical constraints, *virtú*-deficient agents might have acted differently. Instead of choosing to authorize the necessities inflicted on them as an opportunity to seek new lands and build anew, less *virtuoso* men would have viewed the extreme pressures that faced Moses and Aeneas only as obstacles to their freedom. More fatalistic agents might have stayed in devastated Troy and languished in its ruins instead of following Aeneas to new shores where he built Rome; or remained in slavery under Egyptian despotism instead of moving with Moses to reunite the scattered Hebrews. Badly ordered, aggressive agents might have tried to take revenge against those who destroyed or enslaved them, while doing little to improve their own defective orders. Both fatalistic and reckless agents reject pre-existing necessities as inescapable conditions for their own redemptive actions: the one passively succumbing to external constraints, the other lashing out against them in a disordered way. Moses and Aeneas showed their virtue by exercising the extremely narrow margin of freedom left to them, and accepting the constraints of defeat or past slavery as conditions for their own *virtuoso* choices. In moving with their followers to a new seat, they acknowledged the force of necessity and the limits of their own powers, and built on this prudent understanding of their own limitations when they set up new laws and orders. Instead of bemoaning their inauspicious beginnings, they willingly embraced harsh necessity as a spur to their own acts of self-renovation.

Machiavelli's subtly philosophical reasonings at the beginning of the *Discourses* recognize the *virtú* of these builders not insofar as they opposed or tried to dominate necessity, but because and insofar as they chose to "second" it. Their examples show that when a given necessity is willingly accepted as among the conditions for future action, it influences new building but does not completely determine its course. Indeed, the act of authorizing pre-existing constraints makes agents free from complete external determination, since their act of choosing or "willing" makes them a contributing cause of new actions. Agents who must build on "sites" constrained by war, floods, or famine can nonetheless authorize such conditions to act as "necessities" that they will take into account in their new cities, and perhaps—like well-ordered tumults in Rome—turn them into advantages. Elsewhere Machiavelli implies that when agents willingly accept certain pre-existing constraints, thereby recognizing them as a *legitimate* influence on subsequent actions, this improves their prospects of pursuing well-ordered courses of action in future. When measures to put one's affairs in order are taken under the pressure of necessity but not "willingly," he says, "the remedies are not useful."[62] Prudent agents do what they can to avoid having to work under such unwanted pressures by taking preventive measures. But if pressures come anyway, the *virtuoso* apply remedies willingly, authorizing at least some unchosen necessities as conditions for their own subsequent actions.

This creates possibilities to authorize necessities in the second, more expansive sense: to choose among more than two options. Once builders have chosen to second necessity by moving to a new seat instead of staying put, they now face a further, often highly constrained choice: the choice of site. All possible sites for new building impose some natural or human constraints. Either they have physical inconveniences relating to location, landscape, or resources; or they have human and social inconveniences posed by pre-existing settlements, which may be more or less extensive and ordered. Machiavelli mentions two kinds of choice faced by Aeneas and Moses regarding human necessities. One is the choice between building an entirely new city among previous inhabitants of a land, or establishing one's migrant people in cities already established and belonging to others. The other choice concerns "modes" of dealing with the populations found in lands where builders seek a new seat. When the refugees are few, they are more constrained to seek the goodwill of locals and make them partners in city-building. When they are many and desperate, they face strong pressures to force out locals by violence. Even under such extreme constraints, Machiavelli suggests that *virtuoso* agents can always find more than one way to respond, discrediting unvirtuous claims that necessity left *no* choice. As we will see when discussing Aeneas and Moses in chapter 11, Machiavelli identifies degrees of *virtù* by examining how agents choose even under harsh constraints. He is particularly interested in whether builders choose to authorize some constraints posed by pre-existing human settlements as necessary restraints on their own action, or whether to reject all such constraints as obstacles they need not respect.

In the long passage cited above, Machiavelli underlines an essential point about how to judge the quality of such choices. The most *virtuoso* builders understand that in the end it matters little whether a site is clement or harsh, since either way it will carry inconveniences that necessitate *virtuoso* industry. If a site is harsh and unwelcoming, laws and orders will be needed to supply whatever amenities the site does not provide. If a site is fertile, abundant, and appears secure, *virtuoso* builders realize that these qualities "might bring" idleness, and therefore that "the laws should be ordered to constrain it by imposing such necessities as the site does not provide." Whether you start out with harsh or with easy conditions, in

---

[62] *FH*, II.8.60; compare *D*, I.38.81–82.

other words, you will need to "order laws" to counteract the disadvantages found in each: harsh external necessities in the one case, excessive amenities in the other. In short, Machiavelli conceives necessity in terms of equal opportunities and disadvantages, since these tend to balance out over time. What makes the difference in any individual's or city's success or failure is not site or fortune but *virtú*.[63]

4.8.
Virtú as autonomy: Imposing one's own orders and laws

If agents have little or no choice of site, the capacity to impose new necessities—here in the form of laws "ordered to constrain" whatever site one finds—allows them to show *virtú* even under conditions they did not choose. The capacity to author new constraining necessities is identified at the start of the *Discourses* as essential for *virtú*. The study of history shows "how many necessities the laws made by Romulus, Numa, and the others imposed," so that "the fertility of the site, the advantages of the sea, the frequent victories, and the greatness of its empire could not corrupt it for many centuries" and "maintained it full of as much virtue as has ever adorned any other city or republic."[64] The most *virtuoso* builders are those who do not wait for a crisis to impose their own necessities, but impose them preventively. Thus "those who have had the wisdom to prevent the harms that the agreeableness of the country would have caused through idleness" acted virtuously "by imposing a necessity [*hanno posto una necessità*] to exercise on those who had to be soldiers, so that through such an order [*ordine*] they became better soldiers than in countries that have naturally been harsh and sterile." Machiavelli adds that in Egypt the necessity imposed by the laws (*necessità, ordinata dalle leggi*) did much to bring forth excellent men in that country, compensating for disadvantages—including an excess of natural amenities—in site.[65]

The *virtuoso* capacity to author one's own necessities presupposes reflective prudence, self-responsibility, and the capacity to authorize pre-existing necessities as conditions for further building. Yet it also involves a more substantive causality. Self-imposed laws and orders bring something new to sites that are not given by nature or previous history.[66] These man-made forms of *necessità* compensate for any dearth of constraining necessities furnished by nature, fortune, or previous human orders. They enable agents to establish a more symmetrical relationship

---

[63] Compare the lesson of the Myth of Er at the end of Plato's *Rep.* 616c–619d. Here an apparently deterministic treatment of the necessity (*anankē*) governing all human things opens up into a discussion of the scope left for choice (*hairesthō*), suggesting the necessity for self-responsible choice even when one's fate seems to have been determined in advance by lot. Necessity turns out to be a condition for well-examined, responsible choice, not an excuse for poor choices or fatalism; each individual's fate depends on virtue (*aretē*), which "knows no master [*adespoton*]; each will possess it to a greater or lesser degree, depending on whether he values or disdains it. The responsibility [*aitia*] lies with the one who makes the choice; God has none [*theos anaitios*]." Compare *Tim.* 42d–e and *Laws* 904a–905a.

[64] *D*, I.1.8–9/200–202.

[65] See HH, I.142, II.4–11.

[66] *FH*, II.1.52–53/361–62.

between their own, always severely limited causality and other causalities that constrain them. When constrained to leave home and build anew, agents who exercise their virtue to impose *new* necessities on their site and themselves thereby increase the balance of their own power as against necessities imposed from outside by the given conditions in a site. Their own newly authored necessities limit and manage the impact of external causalities on their actions, and exert causalities that they recognize as their own works.[67] Good laws and orders can make a bad site into the seat of an excellent, virtuous polity. If a site is barren, inclement, or hard to defend, good laws can still compensate for these disadvantages. If a site is rich in resources and easy to defend, on the other hand, good laws will be no less necessary to compensate for excessive advantages. Bad laws and man-made disorders can destroy the benefits afforded by an excellent site, turning its advantages into causes of idleness, luxury, or excessive ambition. Choices about how to regulate human actions by self-authored laws and orders are thus more important than pre-existing geographical or natural features of a site, and have a greater influence on a city's defenses or economic flourishing. Human agents' powers to author necessities to regulate their environments and themselves are, on Machiavelli's account, undoubtedly small. Nevertheless, this small power can produce highly effective works if it is exercised responsibly by agents who gauge its inherent limits as well as its potential.

Machiavelli's concept of *virtú* has often been related to human powers of resisting fatalism or founding new cities, but it is seldom associated with human capacities to make their own laws. Yet the passages just cited suggest that human lawmaking capacities are essential to Machiavelli's conception of *virtú*. I propose that the connection between *virtú*, human laws, and self-imposed necessity is fundamental to Machiavelli's ethics.[68] The connection is made clearly in first chapter of the *Discourses* and developed systematically throughout that work. In the first chapter the main necessities imposed by *virtuoso* agents are described as "orders" or as "laws": what *virtuoso* agents should order include, very importantly, necessities that take the form of laws. The necessities imposed on new sites by free foreign builders such as Romulus and Aeneas are specifically "imposed by laws," not by brute force or the unilateral will of these builders. Again, in ancient Egypt "the necessity ordered by the laws was able to do so much that most excellent men arose there, notwithstanding that the country is very agreeable"; and "the kingdom of the sultan, and the order of the Mamelukes and their military" prevented idleness from growing out of the "kindness of the country" by imposing "very strong laws." Over and over in this key opening chapter, Machiavelli stresses the connection between forms of *virtuoso* ordering needed to meet necessity and self-imposed laws. Laws are human beings' chief means of exerting and securing *virtú*. Thus Machiavelli notes "how many necessities *the laws* made by Romulus, Numa, and

---

[67] See Plato, *Gorg.* 503e–504a on the relation between regularity and order (*taxis, kosmos*) and imposing one's own necessities; and similar relations in TPW, VI.72 between good order (*eukosmos, kosmos, taxis, eutaxias*) and imposing *anangkē* on one's own forces.

[68] As it is to Socrates' and Plato's, and arguably Thucydides' (see chap. 2, sec. 2.5).

the others imposed" to keep that city full of virtue notwithstanding the fertility of its land, advantages afforded by its seas, and its "frequent victories" in war. Self-imposed laws establish virtue both by constraining pre-existing necessities within human orders, and by imposing new necessities that "the site does not provide." Similar connections between optimal expressions of *virtú* and human lawmaking are made in Machiavelli's other works. In the *Histories* we read that the founders of Venice "established laws and orders among themselves" so that "amidst so much ruin in Italy, they enjoyed security" and other advantages of civil life.[69]

It may reasonably be inferred from such passages that self-imposed laws and orders, *leggi e ordini*, are the most adequate expression of human and civil *virtú* for Machiavelli. *Virtú* allows human beings to establish a measure of independence from fortune, natural pressures, and other human beings. When the products of *virtú* are orders framed as laws, however, this allows human beings—whether considered as individuals, cities, or species—to exercise a degree of *autonomy* in relation to the constraints that always bear on them. Through the responsible exercise of *virtú*, individuals and cities can avoid being dominated by forces that they perceive as external to their own. Indeed, Machiavelli implies that the exercise of self-legislating and self-ordering *virtú* offers the *only* means human beings have to escape such domination. It must be exercised constantly or, whenever an agent fails to reflect prudently before acting or to take full responsibility for his own actions, external pressures will enter the vacuum and begin to govern agents more than they govern them.

Although Machiavelli does not use the Greek word *autonomia*, a compound of *autos* (one's own) and *nomos* (laws), later chapters will argue that his concept of political *libertà* assigns fundamental value to the capacity of agents to author and authorize their own laws. On this view true *libertà* consists not in the absence of constraints, but in conditions where agents regard the most commanding constraints on their action as self-imposed by laws they willingly authorize. For Machiavelli the crucial difference between the constraints on free and unfree agents lies in the source of authority that agents themselves give to them. While many natural and man-made constraints undoubtedly have objective power to *influence* an agent, it is up to agents to decide whether and how much *authority* they will allow a constraint to have on their choices and actions. Because *virtuoso* agents make extensive, reflectively prudent use of their powers of authorization, they are able to achieve a high degree of autonomy in relation to other causalities. *Virtú*-deficient agents, on the other hand, depend too much on other causalities—fortune, fate, the heavens, or the arms of others—to achieve autonomy or secure political *libertà*. Since they fail to impose necessitating constraints—laws and orders—on themselves, and only recognize constraints forced on them from without, they remain at the mercy of causalities that are more violent or better-ordered than themselves.[70]

---

[69] *FH*, I.29.41–42/349–50; compare *P*, XXIII–XXVI.

[70] Thus it is better "to do now, with the benignity of laws, that which, after deferring, men may be required by necessity to do with the support of arms" (*FH*, III.5.112/428–32).

Self-imposed laws are thus the paradigm of freedom-conducive necessity for Machiavelli. As with other key concepts, he implicitly distinguishes normatively adequate from inadequate conceptions of *leggi*. Most generally, specific positive laws are judged as adequate to the normative concept of law only if they meet two standards also required of orders that deserve the name. A first standard is *voluntary authorization*: laws are not adequately lawlike, or orders adequately order-producing, if they are imposed unilaterally and remain unauthorized. Machiavelli uses the word *leggi* for man-made constraints that acquire authority through the assent of those who live under them. The "necessitating" force of laws is backed by physical force, but that force itself is strictly regulated by the public authority given to enforcers through self-imposed laws. So-called laws enforced in the absence of such authority depend on the brute power or ephemeral fortune of individual rulers, and cannot produce stably virtuous orders. Second, Machiavelli's *leggi* always connotes *regularity*. Laws are human beings' chief means of regulating their social landscape or site. Where the quality of lawfulness is found in abundance, one also finds order, respect for authorities, and reliance on transparent criteria for distributing public goods. Where good *leggi* are lacking, one sees disorder, licentious disdain for other people's claims, and arbitrary private criteria corrupting the distribution of public offices and judicial processes.

Laws for Machiavelli are always the product of human ordering activity; not even the most "natural and ordinary" or "ordinary and reasonable" regularities in human conduct are grounded in natural laws. Nor does Machiavelli think that such regularities should be taken as naturalistic evidence from which prescriptive natural laws can be derived. For reasons explained further in the next chapter, Machiavelli argues that self-imposed laws are the only valid prescriptive laws known to men. *Virtú* therefore cannot involve obedience to laws presumed to issue from nature or God. On an adequate understanding of the word, it must refer to the capacities exerted by human beings to work out laws and orders of their own making, and which are the only means they have to establish stable relations of authority and obedience among themselves. *Leggi e ordini* are human beings' distinctive, *virtuoso* means of imposing their own compelling necessity on events, making them independent of fortune and "the arms of others." The capacities associated with *virtú* enable human beings to establish ways of life for themselves that are distinctively human: ways that are not found ready-made in nature, determined by natural instincts, or given by presumed supernatural authority.[71]

If I am right that the most adequate expression of Machiavelli's *virtú* occurs through legislative acts that make autonomy possible and sustainable, then his notion of self-imposed *necessità* takes on a rich ethical significance that has seldom been recognized. As just observed, the "necessity" imposed by laws involves ethical compulsion as well as physical compulsion or force. The optimal forms of

---

[71] Compare the relationship between virtue and laws in Plato, *Tim.* 24b–d; *Laws* 829a–846c; and *Rep.* 590c–d: "it is better for everyone to be ruled by divine reason, preferably from within himself and his own [*oikeon echontos*], otherwise imposed from without, so that as far as possible all will be the same and friends. That is the aim of the law, which is the ally of everyone in the city."

self-imposed necessity, laws and orders, combine force with ethical compulsion or obligation (*obligo*): they recognize ethical reasons for constraints on action, then give these reasons a compulsory authority backed by public force. To become a stably ordered causal force, Machiavelli suggests, human "orders" should be given the form of laws, which combine humanly authorized force with moral authority. Self-imposed necessities are the best guarantee of human orders and the optimal expression of *virtú*; and self-imposed necessities in the form of *leggi e ordini* involve ethical constraints or obligations, not the arbitrary or lawless use of force.

The ethical dimensions of Machiavelli's *necessità* will be further examined in other chapters. One of his most striking illustrations, to which we will recur, can be found in an episode adapted from Livy. During the wars with Gaul Rome's ambassadors, members of the Fabii tribe, violated a sacred duty under the "law of nations" to refrain from fighting the enemy while on a diplomatic mission. When the Roman Senate declined to punish the ambassadors, the Gauls launched a massive assault, nearly destroying Rome's defenses and so terrifying its inhabitants that most wanted permanently to abandon the city. At this critical juncture, the general Furius Camillus stopped his *virtú*-deficient compatriots from fleeing and ordered them for renewed self-defense. Under these new orders, the Romans beat back the Gauls and laid the foundation for improved military *ordini* in Rome. On Machiavelli's account, however, Camillus' *virtuoso* response sought not only to restore Roman power, though this was one desired effect. Its first aim was to pull Rome back to the "limits" that had been overstepped when the Senate refused to punish the Fabii ambassadors for transgressing the *ius gentium*. Camillus' virtuous "orders" included acts of public repentance for Rome's egregious arrogance. Military reforms were also adopted, but they were founded on acts of justice that involved acknowledging past errors and restoring juridical and moral "discipline" in Rome. Camillus took the *occasione* inflicted by dire necessity to improve Roman orders in this fundamental sense, purging his countrymen of the *hubris* and moral corruption that provoked their enemies to inflict such violent retribution.[72]

Camillus' response exemplifies Machiavellian *virtú* in the ethically rich sense I am proposing. Faced with pressures of genuine urgency, often largely of the Romans' own making, Camillus and other *virtuoso* citizens met necessity not only by asserting strong counterpressures but also by "drawing back to the limits" and reaffirming their "religious" commitment to respect the "law of nations."[73] By these

---

[72] *D*, II.28–29; III.1.

[73] In Thucydides, the Spartan king Archidamus best exemplifies all these aspects of a good or virtuous statesman. He refuses to invoke necessity as a pretext or excuse for precipitate action, advising his countrymen not to be ashamed of what the hotheaded call slowness and procrastination (*bradu kai mellon*). This trait may be a symptom of good order (*eukosmon*) and be considered as "in the truest sense intelligent self-control [*sōphrosunē*] which alone prevents us from becoming insolent [*exubrizomen*] in prosperity and from succumbing to adversity as much as others." He recommends ruthlessly critical self-examination when deciding whether or not to go to war, noting that since we ourselves must be thought the causers (*aitias exomen*) of all events, good and bad, we must bear responsibility to appraise likely consequences of our own actions. Above all, Spartans should not be ashamed that they are educated too simply to despise the laws and with too much strict discipline to disobey them. TPW, I.83–84.

means they restored—and ultimately increased—Roman strength on foundations that respected ordinary and necessary limits on any city's power. In this case, these limits include the need to coexist with other people and cities that also have legitimate desires for freedom or security, and that can be expected to react ferociously when insulted as the Romans insulted the Gauls. Camillus treated extreme necessity as an opportunity to make Romans "examine themselves" critically, make amends for their past offenses, and recognize the limits they must impose on themselves even while they sought to recuperate strength. These moderate aims did not preclude the "natural and ordinary" desire to acquire further glory and strength for Rome. They simply recognized the need to respect restraints on the means used to pursue these aims. Insofar as less prudent Romans aimed to *dominate* necessity instead of making prudent, Camillus-like judgments about how to work with it, they exceeded the limits needed for adequate *virtú*. Insofar as the prudent acknowledged those limits and made them the basis for their own self-imposed laws and orders, they displayed the highest *virtú* possible for human beings.

4.9.
Necessità and *fortuna*

Let us briefly summarize differences between the concept of *virtú* I am imputing to Machiavelli and conceptions more usually attributed to him. First of all, Machiavelli's *virtú* does not involve pragmatic adaptation to whatever standards are found in various environments, regardless of whether agents judge the standards as reasonable. The capacity to use one's own judgment to set standards for action and adhere to them through variations in fortune is a core value embodied in Machiavelli's *virtú*. Second, *virtú* is not just any form of hard work, or any robust force imposed in the name of order. The sheer energetic force of an agent's will may temporarily impose restraints that appear to control natural or social sites. But unless those restraints are given a form that enables them to *regulate* sites over time, they are unlikely to maintain stable orders or civil *virtú*. Third, Machiavelli's *virtú* does not involve the unconstrained exercise of free will; self-limitation and self-restraint are at its core. *Virtú* depends on an agent's exercise of free choice, but the exercise of choice per se is not what shows an agent's *virtú*. Only the quality of his choices does so. *Virtuoso* agents gauge the limitations and possibilities presented by nature, history, or fortune and work within them to produce something stable of their own. Finally, *virtú* is not a capacity unilaterally to impose constraints of one's own without regard for responses at the receiving end. Virtuous imposing involves taking pre-existing necessities seriously, and authorizing some as conditions for further building.

As for *necessità*, it should be clear by now that Machiavelli uses the concept in more discriminating ways than most readings have assumed. It is not the case that agents have no significant range of options about how to respond to pressures they call *necessità*. Machiavelli does not claim that necessity exempts agents from the responsibility to work out careful responses, or gives them license to subordinate ethical restraints to supposed needs of self-preservation. On the contrary, he usually invokes *necessità* to provoke reflections on the range of choices agents have even under harsh constraints. Agents always have at least one choice when under extreme necessity: they may choose to rely on their own *virtuoso* resources to respond, or to rely on fortune and hence on "the arms of others." Agents who rely on *virtú* do not "vary" in good or bad fortune but "keep their spirit firm and joined with their mode of life so that one easily knows . . . that fortune does not have power over them."[74] Being self-reliant, they assume responsibility for whatever actions they take under pressure of *necessità*. Agents who choose to rely on fortune shirk this responsibility to some degree.

Despite superficial affinities, the relationship between *necessità* and *virtú* is very different from that between *virtú* and *fortuna*. Machiavelli consistently treats *necessità* and *virtú* as interdependent types of causation, not antithetical ones. Whenever he says that an action displays *virtú*, some necessity can always be found behind it. There can be no *virtú* without *necessità* in some form, external or self-imposed or both. Responsible agents see *necessità* not as a threat to their *virtú* but as a stimulus to it; the narrower their range of choices, the more they must exercise *virtú* in choosing to act as they do, and the more praiseworthy will be their good choices. Since extreme *necessità* tends to elicit greater *virtú*, virtuous "works" must always be attributed to both. Moreover, necessities can be imposed by acts of will and even chosen. All these features erode the sharp distinction between externally imposed *necessità* and an agent's own *virtú*, since the production of *virtuoso* effects requires a prudently judged use of both. Those who recognize the constant pressures exerted by necessity need not consider themselves to be in a permanent state of war with these pressures. They deal in much the same way with extreme pressures as with everyday tumults: by examining themselves and existing orders critically, seeking to influence external necessities in various ways and to improve themselves in an orderly manner.[75]

Fortune and *virtú*, on the other hand, are always antithetical forms of causation for Machiavelli. Agents who rely on *virtú* rely primarily on their own resources. Machiavelli associates *virtú* with self-reliance, independence, and self-responsibility, and *fortuna* with causal resources that are not an agent's own. Whenever he describes an individual or city as "fortunate," Machiavelli implies that it relies too much on something other than its own virtue.[76] Agents who rely on *fortuna* are dependent on external forces that may happen to support their enterprises at one moment but frustrate them at the next, often leading to their "ultimate ruin." Machiavelli repeatedly insists that agents must choose which kind of causation they want to rely on most. They cannot rely equally on *fortuna* and

---

[74] *D*, III.31.281–82/494–97. Compare II:30.202/407: "For where men have little virtue, fortune shows its power very much."

[75] Fabius Maximus is another Roman example of properly assertive virtue; see chaps. 5, 12.

[76] See, for example, *P*, VI–VII. In *P*, XXVI–XVI, Machiavelli does suggest that steady good "fortune" can be won by effective exercise of virtue. But when this happens, credit properly goes to *virtuoso* men or orders, not to fortune at all; the word "fortune" becomes redundant in describing it.

virtú, for the more *fortuna* is said to cause events, the less they can be attributed to *virtú*.[77] Fortune may temporarily produce similar effects to those of *virtú*: security for a prince in his state, the goodwill of those he rules, stable orders in and around his city. But what fortune gives, it also easily takes away. This is why agents who rely more on fortune easily lose their acquisitions, while those who rely more on *virtú* maintain them more securely. Although reliance on fortune may produce temporary appearances of successful acquisition, only one's own *virtú* can convert resources given by or taken from others into one's own. The next chapter examines the implications of these arguments for Machiavelli's account of human nature.

[77] In the *Prince* (VI.22/131–32) we read that "the result of becoming prince from private individual presupposes either virtue or fortune," and both of these causes "appear" to relieve some of his difficulties in maintaining power. Beyond appearances, however, it is always true that "he who has relied less on fortune has maintained himself more."

CHAPTER 5

Human Nature and Human Orders

Some scholars have claimed that Machiavelli rejected traditional ethics, both Christian and classical, in favor of a "a new naturalistic ethic" that represented a decisive break from "premodern" thinking. This "ethic" dismissed all man-made standards and restraints as arbitrary, subjective, and ultimately toothless. In their place it set the unalloyed "dictates of nature," demanding that men follow them "impartially and resolutely." Although according to Friedrich Meinecke ethics for Machiavelli "is always a question of following the natural forces of life," it is also one "of regulating them by means of reason." Machiavelli's regulative reason, however, is said to be narrowly instrumental: it helps agents to work out the most efficient means to their ends, but is indifferent both to their choice of ends and to considerations of justice and injustice. Indeed, its distinctive contribution to modern, demystified ethics consists in stressing how to use "the bestial element in Man" even if this sometimes required agents to descend into "the filth of bestiality."[1] Similarly, Ernst Cassirer describes Machiavelli as the founder of a "new science" of politics that ignored all religious and ethical considerations, constructing a theory of practical action from empirical observations alone. Machiavelli did not give laws for this new political science; he "discovered" them through close observation of human behavior. Empirical findings about what human beings actually do were his sole source of action-guiding norms. The only rules and restraints that Machiavelli takes seriously in politics, Cassirer asserts, are those he saw operating throughout history. While he "studied the rules of the game very thoroughly," he "had not the slightest intention of changing or criticizing the rules"; he sought only "to find the best move—the move that wins the game."[2] If these influential readings are right, Machiavelli's "new" political science would leave very little room indeed for self-imposed ethical constraints and standards that I have associated with his concepts of *leggi e ordini*.

The last chapter acknowledged that one of Machiavelli's criteria for *virtuoso* agency is the capacity to recognize what is "natural and ordinary" for human beings, and accordingly to recognize the limits set by anthropological "necessities" on any agent's actions. But our discussion also suggests that the interpretations just outlined stand in need of reappraisal. It is far from clear that natural drives,

---

[1] Meinecke 1998 (1925), 31–42.

[2] Cassirer 1946, 129–43. Compare Strauss 1958, 296–97; Skinner 1988, 434; Parel 1993, 270–71; Mansfield 1998, 36–39.

appetites, and dispositions exhaust Machiavelli's conception of human nature. He also alludes to human capacities for exercising free will and self-legislative *virtú* as among the *naturale e ordinario* considerations that prudent agents should take into account. This raises the question whether Machiavelli thought that adequate action-guiding rules could be derived *only* from empirical study of the political games human beings play in all times and places. He may have argued that this kind of study was a necessary yet insufficient condition for working out better rules: that one must analyze the games people play not just in order to win on their terms, but also in order to identify flaws in the rules as they stand. This chapter argues that Machiavelli's "renovated" ethics is based partly on an empirical account of "natural and ordinary" human drives and dispositions, but also on an account of the ethical demands that human beings place on themselves when they use words such as "necessity" or "fortune," "order" and "virtue," "law" and "justice." Far from breaking with all classical as well as Christian ethics, Machiavelli's arguments have much in common with a critical tradition of philosophical anthropology that can be traced to Thucydides, Xenophon, Plato, and Plutarch.

5.1.
Fortune and free will

Machiavelli's views on fortune and free will often appear contradictory because he does in fact set out opposing prescriptions on how people should deal with changing fortunes. As we will see below, sometimes he praises pragmatic adaptability, seeming to identify the ability to "vary one's mode with the times" with *virtú*. At other times he does the exact opposite, praising those who realize that *fortuna* is a woman, that is, an inferior power that wants to be dominated by assertive *virtuoso* men.[3] The most plausible solution to this paradox is that Machiavelli treats both views as incompletely reflective opinions that stand in need of further examination. He uses the word *fortuna* to echo everyday common usage: to characterize a causality that human beings experience as independent of their own best or worst efforts, and which produces results that appear indifferent to those efforts. When people are uncertain whether specific human actions can be held responsible for a state of affairs, and unwilling to attribute responsibility to God or some other agency, they often attribute it to *fortuna*. When they impute Roman successes or Florentine disorders to fortune, they imply that these conditions cannot be fully explained in terms of deliberate actions. That element of arbitrariness is what everyday language refers to as *fortuna*.

Machiavelli's own references to *fortuna* mimic such views in order to examine them more closely. It has widely been assumed that Machiavelli's remarks on fortune reflect an interest in cosmological or theoretical questions about fortune's influence over human affairs, and that his answers to these questions determine his ethical positions. I suggest, however, that Machiavelli's fundamental concerns are ethical. His primary question is not, How much room do fortune, necessity, or

[3] See sec. 5.2.

the heavens leave for human *virtù* and free will? It is rather, If we presuppose that there can be no decently "ordered" life unless human beings are regarded as having free will, then how should we discriminate between more and less responsible—or virtuous—ways of exercising that will? Machiavelli's aim in assessing the power of fortune is to evaluate claims about the limits of human beings' *responsibility* for their own actions. Such claims may reflect the underassertive view that fortune constrains human actions in such serious, unforeseeable ways that much of what agents do must be imputed to brute luck; or the overassertive view that fortune can be mastered once and for all by the right kind of man. Machiavelli highlights the shortcomings of both, and suggests more adequate ways of appraising responsibility in relation to causalities that seem indifferent to self-directed action. Sometimes he echoes opinions that stress fortune's powers, and that use the word *fortuna* as a synonym for good or bad luck; at other times, the converse opinion that fortune can ultimately be mastered. He defends neither view, but examines the ethical implications of each.

Consider, for example, the passage in the penultimate chapter of the *Prince* where Machiavelli sets out his most general views about *fortuna*. The passage starts by noting a widespread, fatalistic opinion based on traditional cosmological beliefs: namely, that various natural and supernatural causalities always dominate feeble human powers, leaving very little room for responsible human actions:

> It is not unknown to me [*non mi è incognito*] that many have held and hold the opinion that worldly things are so governed by fortune and by God, that men cannot correct them with their prudence, indeed that they have no remedy at all; and on account of this they might judge that one need not sweat much over things but let oneself be governed by chance [*sorte*]. This opinion has been believed more in our times because of the great variability [*variazione*] of things which have been seen and are seen every day, beyond every human conjecture [*umana coniettura*].

Far from dismissing this deterministic opinion, Machiavelli starts by expressing sympathy with it. "When I have thought about this sometimes," he ruminates, "I have been in some part inclined to their opinion." Indeed, if what is seen now and through past experience were all there is to go by, then the view that one need not sweat (*insudare*) much over things would seem eminently reasonable. But Machiavelli clearly does not regard what has "been seen and is seen every day [*viste e veggonsi*]" as a sufficient basis for deciding the issue. For, he goes on to reason,

> Nevertheless, so that our free will not be eliminated [*il nostro libero arbitrio non sia spento*], I judge that it might be true that fortune is arbiter of half our actions, but also that she leaves the other half, or close to it, for us to govern.[4]

Free will is not a datum that can be seen, yet Machiavelli suggests that it can be presupposed despite overwhelming evidence that appears to rule it out. He does

---

[4] *P*, XXV.98/186–87.

not explain here why he "judges" that free will should not be "eliminated" (*spento*) in spite of the compelling evidence "seen every day." However, other examples and reasonings scattered throughout the *Prince* and other writings may help to explain this judgment.

First, what might be called negative epistemic grounds are suggested in the passage just cited: free will cannot be ruled out because neither Machiavelli nor any trustworthy authority can possibly *know* exactly how much power fortune has over human actions. In the absence of such knowledge, some margin may be assumed for the exercise of free will. Epistemic modesty, not arrogance, suggests that fortune cannot control all. Epistemic modesty also suggests that reasonable people must acknowledge limits set by chance, accidents, and other unforeseeable factors on their own choices. If we do not know how far fortune can govern us, we also cannot know how far we are able to govern it. Because human agents cannot completely predict or control fortune, "They should indeed never give up [*non si abbandonare*] for, since they do not know its end and it proceeds by oblique and unknown ways [*per vie traverse ed incognite*], they have always to hope and, since they hope, not to give up in whatever fortune and in whatever travail they may find themselves."[5] These non-fatalistic judgments are already implicit in ordinary, reflective uses of the language of *fortuna*. If human beings cannot completely "know the ends" of fortune as "it proceeds by oblique and unknown ways," this is partly because responsible uses of the word *fortuna* do not refer to causes that have rationally explicable operations. On the contrary, responsible agents try to explain their conditions in terms of identifiable actions and reactions, especially their own, reserving "fortune" for whatever small remainder they consider to have been extremely difficult to foresee or to influence. Although they cannot predict or control all the incalculable factors that they call *fortuna*, they do know that these cannot be completely known or controlled; and this allows agents to focus attention on regulating better what can be known and regulated, not least their own reactions and *virtuoso* choices.

Second and more importantly, Machiavelli refuses to rule out free will on practical grounds. In the *Prince* he appeals to readers' self-interest in presupposing that human beings have free will. If free will were eliminated as a causal force, this would not only spare human beings their share of responsibility for hardships and evils. It would also render them unworthy of praise or glory. If they could not hold themselves responsible for their troubles, they could not take credit for their successes. This would deprive them of incentives to work for the good. His closing arguments in the *Prince* also allude to distinct ethical reasons for presupposing free will as a severely constrained yet effective causality. Free will is among the most basic qualities ascribed to beings who define themselves as human. The idea that responsible agency and free will are inseparable from any adequate concept of a human being is expressed in Machiavelli's claim that "God does not want us to do everything, so as not to take [*non ci tòrre*] free will from us and that part of the glory that falls to us."[6] Fatalistic men hold God or fortune

[5] *D*, II.29.199/406–7.
[6] *P*, XXVI.103/190.

responsible for their human condition. But Machiavelli argues that adequate conceptions of God and fortune do not subsume all human affairs under these powerful causalities. Rather, they distinguish these causalities from a human causality, called free will in its most basic form and virtue when exercised responsibly, and presume that God and fortune gladly leave to human beings a "remainder you must do yourself."

These ethical arguments for self-responsibility are expressed obliquely in the *Prince*, usually in the outward form of pragmatic political or military advice. The argument that God wants to leave us some "part of the glory that falls to us" echoes a similar passage from a few pages earlier, where Machiavelli writes:

> For one should never fall in the belief that you can find someone to pick you up. Whether it does not happen or it happens, it is not security for you, because that defense was base and did not depend on you. And those defenses alone are good, are certain, are lasting, that depend on you yourself and on your virtue.

The same point is developed when Machiavelli illustrates the respective powers of fortune and free will by comparing fortune to "violent rivers" which, once "enraged," force all to flee before their impetus "without being able to hinder them in any regard." Free will can do little to stop such floods once they break out. But human agents can still be held responsible for the destructive effects ascribed to *fortuna*, since violent outbreaks of bad "fortune" can usually be traced to previous failures to exercise virtue. Thus even if the slings and arrows of fortune governed more than "half our actions," a further reflection would still be pertinent:

> it is not as if men, when times are quiet, could not provide for [floods] with dikes and dams so that when they rise later, either they go by a canal or their impetus is neither so wanton nor so damaging. It happens similarly with fortune, which demonstrates her power where virtue has not been put in order [*ordinata*] to resist her and therefore turns her impetus where she knows that dams and dikes have not been made to contain her.[7]

Free will, in short, is a condition for human self-responsibility, individual or collective. The notion of practical *judgment* would make little sense if human actions and choices were considered as completely determined by other causalities: fortune, God, fate, or "the arms of others." The concept of *virtù* too would be

---

[7] *P*, XXIV–V.97–99/186–87. A similar idea occurs in a speech by the Spartan general Hermocrates in Thucydides. "I do not blame," he declares, "those who wish to rule [*archein*], but those who are too willing to be subjects; for it is the nature of man everywhere to rule those who give in, but to guard against those who attack. If we know how things stand and yet fail to take the right precautions, ordering ourselves against the common fear, we are in error." TPW, IV.61. Thucydides has many speakers underscore the perils of relying on fortune; see chap. 2, sec. 2.5. and TPW, VI. 9–14, 17–19, 23, 65; VII.63. Also compare Plato, *Laws* 874e–845d: "It is vital that men should lay down laws for themselves and live in obedience to them; otherwise they will be indistinguishable from wild animals of the utmost savagery," since without "laws and regulation" each man's "human nature will always drive him to look for his own advantage."

redundant. Judgments ascribing *virtù* to actions or works refer to the quality of choices shown in those works, and choice depends on agents who possess free will, however severely constrained.

If Machiavelli refuses to rule out free will on non-empirical, purely practical grounds, it might seem puzzling that he sometimes discusses the relation between fortune and free will in what sounds like a language of empirical measurement. But when Machiavelli writes that "it might be true that fortune is arbiter of half our actions, but also that she leaves the other half, or close to it, for us to govern," he is not interested in establishing a science for measuring the precise provenance of fortune or free will.[8] That would be an idle exercise, since neither concept has empirical or mathematical referents; the causalities they refer to cannot be directly seen or calculated. They are causalities that human beings attribute to themselves and their fields of action in order to assess practical responsibility. The proposition that fortune and free will each govern half of human actions must therefore be seen as metaphorical and ethical, not theoretical. If the exact margin could somehow be measured, this would make no difference for Machiavelli's basic ethical point that agents should "never give up" their practical presupposition of free will even under the worst constraints. If in a given situation or in general one could ascertain that fortune had 99 percent influence and free will only 1, that 1 percent would still leave room for the exercise of self-ordering *virtù*. The failure to do whatever one could within that margin would still be an avoidable, human failure.

For Machiavelli, then, *fortuna* refers to the incalculable, apparently arbitrary factors that always influence human actions, no matter how much theoretical knowledge may be gleaned about their natural operations. Free will and *virtù* are self-moving causalities that enable human beings to make and evaluate their own actions, no matter how much fortune or necessity constrain them.[9] Both kinds of causality are equally essential to our notions of responsible human agency. A world conceived as entirely subject to the accidents and irregularities commonly called "fortune" would be equally inhospitable to any responsible agency, that is, *virtù*. But by the same token, *virtuoso* agents need to conceive of their world as governed partly by *fortuna*. If all the factors that constrain action could be foreseen in advance, this would presuppose a world where all the outcomes were also predetermined, and where free will had nothing to say about the proper ends of actions. The inhabitants of such a world would have no need to make deliberative judgments, and hence no need for a concept of *virtù*. Although Machiavelli sees ample evidence of its weakness in his own times and cannot demonstrate it with evidence, he will not eliminate free will because this would eliminate responsibility, virtue, and deliberative judgment. Even if empirical science could prove that these were illusory, Machiavelli's arguments imply that they would still be necessary for an acceptably human life.

[8] *P*, XXV.98/186–7.
[9] On the relations between free will and *virtù*, see chap. 6.

5.2.
How to manage *fortuna*: Impetuosity and *respetto*

Let us now consider some plausible objections to this reading. Undeniably, Machiavelli's writings do set out practical precepts that seem to suggest that genuinely
virtuoso action requires the weakening of ethical constraints. One set of precepts
asserts that agents are invariably ruined who do not know how to vary their modes
and nature with changing times. In the *Prince* we read that if a prince "would
change his nature with the times and with affairs (*se si mutassi natura con e' tempi
e con le cose*)," his fortune would not change; the *Discourses* contain a chapter entitled "How One Must Vary with the Times If One Wishes Always to Have Good
Fortune."[10] These precepts are easily assimilated to an ethic stressing the virtues of
pragmatic adaptation to shifts in fortune over commitment to unchanging principles. A second set of practical precepts seems to confirm a less deferential view
of fortune's powers and a corresponding view of *virtú* as a highly self-assertive capacity. The *Prince* memorably declares that when confronted with fortune's slings
and arrows

> it is better to be impetuous [*impetuoso*] than cautious [*respettivo*], because
> fortune is a woman; and it is necessary, if one wants to hold her down, to beat
> her and strike her down. And one sees that she lets herself be won more by
> the impetuous than by those who proceed coldly [*freddamente procedono*].
> And so always, like a woman, she is the friend of the young, because they are
> less cautious, more ferocious, and command her with more audacity.

These precepts undoubtedly seem hard to square with the ethically demanding
conception of *virtuoso* self-ordering I have imputed to Machiavelli. But the texts
offer reasons to doubt whether either set of precepts is based on Machiavelli's own
reflective judgments.

The first view that agents should "vary their modes with the times" sits un-
comfortably beside an argument that is repeated with great vigor in surrounding
chapters in the *Discourses* and *Prince*: namely, that virtuous agents should not wait
for fortune to change their modes, but should impose clear orders of their own
to check the effect of "variations" imposed from without. It is wrong, Machiavelli argues, to think that men "cannot correct" worldly things "with their prudence" but should let themselves be governed by chance. Instead they should work
continuously to impose their own orders on themselves and their environments.
Variations in fate or fortune are symptoms of grave disorders; whereas "if diked
by suitable virtue," such variations would be regulated. Over and over Machiavelli
identifies variation and variability with fortune. Order and virtue are opposed to
variation, as causalities that aim to produce works capable of regulating changes.
Prudence and virtue consist not in varying but in ordering. The message of these
reflective arguments is precisely *not* to vary with the times or wait for conditions
to change before imposing one's own orders. *Virtuoso* men impose "new laws and

[10] *P*, XXV.100/188; *D*, III.9.239–40/449–50.

new orders" of their own before external events can inflict troubles on them.[11] It is hard to see how agents can show optimal virtue both by varying their nature and modes with fortune, *and* by avoiding dependence on fortune by building stable "dikes and dams" to contain it. One kind of action or the other, adaptive or self-ordering, must be a more adequate manifestation of *virtú*.

The self-ordering view is more consistent with positions Machiavelli develops throughout the *Discourses*. In a chapter entitled "Strong Republics and Excellent Men Retain the Same Spirit and Their Same Dignity [*Dignità*] in Every Fortune," Machiavelli quotes words ascribed by Livy to the Roman general Camillus, frequently presented by both writers as a model of *virtú*. "Among the other magnificent things that our historian makes Camillus say and do," Machiavelli begins,

> so as to show how an excellent man ought to be made, he puts these words in his mouth: "Neither did the dictatorship ever raise my spirits nor did exile take them away." Through them one sees that great men are always the same in every fortune; and if it varies—now by exalting them, now by crushing them—*they do not vary* but always keep their spirit firm and joined with their mode of life so that one easily knows [*facilmente si cognosce*] for each that fortune does not have power over them.[12]

According to this passage and the rest of the chapter, varying one's mode with fortune is assuredly not the way to avoid dependence on it and thus show *virtú*. Indeed, Machiavelli says the exact opposite. The most *virtuoso* attitude to *fortuna* is to regulate or order whatever powers are ascribed to it. Agents can and should try to regulate fortune before it shows great variations instead of simply adapting to its changes. Thus "where men have little virtue, fortune shows its power very much; and because it is variable, republics and states often vary and will always vary until someone emerges who is so much a lover of antiquity that he regulates it [*la regoli*] in such a mode that it does not have cause to show at every turning of the sun how much it can do."[13] Machiavelli gives no reason, as he does in the *Prince*, for readers to suspect that he sees this opinion as inadequate; on the contrary, he affirms it with many "reasons and examples" throughout the *Discourses*. Here excellence, prudence, and *virtú* in individuals and orders are repeatedly identified with steadfast adherence to the same modes, at least when those modes are based on reflective prudence and a commitment to promises undertaken. In fact Machiavelli argues that "the sudden variation of fate [*sorte*]" occurs when agents fail to impose steady orders of their own on their conduct.[14]

If variations of fate or fortune may be caused by a failure to establish firm orders, then men who try to deal with variations of fortune by varying their own modes of action fall far short of *virtú* in two ways: by failing to regulate both the variations themselves and their underlying causes. Since *fortuna* is variable, the *virtuoso* way

---

[11] P, XXV–VI.101–4/189–92.
[12] D, III.31.281/494; emphasis added.
[13] D, II.30.202/409–10.
[14] D, III.33.286/499, 34.289–90/501–2, 49.309–10/524–25; III.31.281/494.

to escape dependence on it is always to be the same—to impose orders that are steady and unvarying so that they can regulate *fortuna*'s variations, irregularities, and caprices.[15] The most judicious reasonings in the *Prince* also treat steadying, self-imposed orders as the most *virtuoso* way to meet vicissitudes of fortune. Machiavelli makes it quite clear that agents who dismiss cautious prudential reasoning as a waste of time show defective virtue, and that *virtuoso* agents "order" effective precautions to avert or deal with crises, steadily regulating fortune in "quiet times."[16] The final chapter calls for a redeemer (*redentore*) of Italy who is not a master of variability but "someone prudent and virtuous" enough "to introduce a form [*forma*] that would bring honor to him and good to the community [*università*] of men there," based on firm new "laws and orders" that fortune cannot overturn because they "have been founded well [*bene fondate*]" without depending in any way on fortune.[17] In both works, moreover, Machiavelli suggests that the kind of prudence required to change one's nature in conformity with the times cannot be found in mortal men. He contrasts merely "human prudence" (*umana prudenza*) with the illusion that some men have superhuman powers to come out on top in every fortune, even if they do not take the trouble to order it.[18]

This brings us to the second set of precepts outlined at the beginning of this section, which assert that it is better to deal impetuously with fortune than to proceed with caution. The implicit contrast between modest powers of "human prudence" and a superhuman prudence that allows for infinite flexibility is made in relation to the example of Pope Julius II, who always "proceeded impetuously in all his affairs." The pope himself, Machiavelli writes, was happy (*felice*) in meeting success in all his enterprises beyond what anyone acting with "all human prudence" could have achieved. But his happiness depended entirely on fortune, and not at all on virtue. Despite the superhuman appearance of his feats, the pope was no different from all other men in that "he would never have deviated from those modes to which nature inclined him." Thus, "If times had come when he had needed to proceed with caution [*con respetti*]," Machiavelli argues, "his ruin would have followed."[19] Prudent readers should not, then, imitate the pope's impetuous modes of action in the hope of becoming as happy as he. Instead they should recognize the ordinary inconvenience that their nature inclines them more toward impetuosity or "caution" (*respetto*) and, instead of trying in vain to vary their nature to suit fortune's moods, try to order themselves to a stable virtue that avoids the extremes of both. Machiavelli elaborates on this theme at many points in the *Discourses*, writing, for example, that "one sees that some men proceed in their works with impetuosity, some with hesitation

---

[15] *D*, III.31.281–84/494–97; compare *P*, XXIV.97/186.

[16] Compare Archidamus' speech in TPW, I.80–86, where the values of modesty, careful deliberation, and temperance are defended against impatient men who want to act more assertively. The latter, Archidamus warns, usually harm themselves through their arrogance (*hubris*), while those who are guided by more cautious virtues thereby show their good orders (*eukosmon*). Also see Nicias' unsuccessful warnings against Athens' Sicilian expedition, TPW, VI.9–14.

[17] *P*, VII.25–26/133–34, XXV.98–99/186–87; XXVI.101–4/189–92.

[18] *P*, XXV.100/188.

[19] *P*, XXV.101/188–89.

and caution [*con rispetto e con cauzione*]." But since in both modes "suitable limits are passed [*passano e' termini convenienti*]" which make actions deviate from the "true way" (*la vera via*), prudent men should not try to change their nature—as later sections suggest, a pointless aim—but rather order their actions to stay within due "limits."[20] This kind of ordering calls for a steadiness in character and commitment, an integrity, that does not permit either pragmatic adaptation to fortune or impetuosity as it is commonly understood. Since we are dealing with merely human prudence, the right question is not which is absolutely better, impetuosity or caution, but rather which has better chances of not straying from the *vera via*.

Machiavelli considers this question by discussing notable examples of caution and impetuosity during one of Rome's gravest military crises, the second Punic War. The Roman general Fabius Maximus, he notes, wore down Carthaginian forces in Italy by proceeding "hesitantly and cautiously [*rispettivamente e cautamente*] with his army, far from all impetuosity and from all Roman audacity." The times, Machiavelli says, were suitable to Fabius' modes, which brought him glory. He then suggests that when the times changed, it was good that Fabius was not king of Rome but, living in a republic, had to concede supreme military command to other men, such as the younger Scipio, who were prepared to act impetuously against Hannibal's armies. First the Roman republic was rescued by Fabius, "who was best in times proper for sustaining [*sostenere*] war"; later "it had Scipio in times apt for winning it."[21] Machiavelli's general point here is political: since different humors are needed in men who exercise authority in different circumstances, good political orders allow for well-regulated variations in military and civil leadership so that the men best qualified to deal with particular matters can take office. But this does not alter his judgment that it is neither possible nor desirable for individuals to vary their natural dispositions with the times. Fabius' caution proved a great boon to Rome when the city's armies had been decimated in battles launched by more impetuous—on Livy's account, reckless—men.[22] Machiavelli does not argue that Fabius should later have changed his nature to be more like Scipio; when the times called for more risk-taking action, good Roman orders made it possible for naturally less cautious leaders to take over. On balance, however, Machiavelli suggests that since men cannot change their mainly *respettivo* or impetuous nature, it is better to have men in high political or military office who err on the side of *rispetto e cauzione* than men who err on the side of impetuosity. This preference becomes clear on a close examination of his various remarks about Fabius and Scipio. Machiavelli's apparent praise of the impetuous younger man, a paragon of "Roman audacity," is interwoven with sharp criticisms of various corrupting modes used in his campaigns and his bids for political authority.[23] Toward

---

[20] *D*, III.36.292–93/506–7.

[21] *D*, III.9.239–40/449.

[22] See *LH*, XXII.12, 39–40, XXVII.16, and esp. XXX.26: "Fabius has been accounted a man of caution rather than of action. And while one may question whether he was the 'Delayer' by nature, or because that was especially suited to the war then in progress, still nothing is more certain than that one man by delaying restored our state [*rem*]." Compare Machiavelli's views discussed in chap. 12.

[23] See chap. 12, sec. 12.5.

the end of the *Discourses,* moreover, impetuosity in armies is explicitly contrasted to good order, and therefore to *virtú.* Armies whose operations are not "regulated" are not, Machiavelli declares, "true armies"; they act with "fury and impetuosity, and not by virtue." Although neither caution and impetuosity is good when taken to extremes, the thrust of Machiavelli's reasonings is that impetuosity endangers order more than *rispetto,* and ought therefore to be held in firmer check.[24]

In view of these judgments, it seems unlikely that passages that seem to defend impetuosity as the height of *virtú* express Machiavelli's own views. This is rather a naïve opinion commonly found among young, less experienced men such as Scipio and his admirers. Machiavelli's prime examples of Roman virtue are mature men who err on the side of *respetto,* not the "young men" who fortune is commonly thought to favor.[25] If excessive caution or respect does not always vanquish enemies once and for all, it at least sustains good orders of combat; whereas impetuous self-assertion without respect invariably causes disorders.

Reflections on the importance of *respetto* form one of the main subjects of the *Prince*'s penultimate chapter. The word and cognate terms occur eight times in its four paragraphs. *Respetto* is connected with "art" and "patience," while impetuosity is linked to "violence" and impatience. The usual translation as "caution" or "hesitation" suggests that Machiavelli regards *respetto* mainly as an instrumentally valuable quality, not an ethical one.[26] But a few chapters earlier he implies that its instrumental meaning is closely linked to an ethical notion of "respect" for limits imposed by other people's dispositions and motions—that is, with consideration for the "ordinary and natural" constraints stressed at the beginning of the *Prince*: "victories are never so clear that the winner does not have to have some respect, especially for justice."[27] This sentence is seldom noticed because it seems foreign to the usual interpretation of the *Prince* as a treatise advising indifference to justice. Against the backdrop of other arguments examined here and in the last chapter, however, it seems reasonable to see it as a summation of one of Machiavelli's core ethical positions. It prefigures several more direct arguments given to prudent speakers in his later works, the *Histories* and *Discourses*: notably the arguments that is it never wise to seek ultimate victory, and that victors who fail to respect the limits set by their enemies' natural dispositions make them more obstinate in defense. *Respetto* is thus a condition for giving *virtuoso* orders to *fortuna,* and therefore for *virtú* properly understood.[28]

---

[24] *D,* III.36.292–93/506–7.

[25] *P,* XXV.101/189.

[26] In the Mansfield-Tarcov translation of *D,* III.9.239 *rispetto* is given as "hesitation" and *cauzione* as "caution." In the *Prince* Mansfield renders *respetto* and its cognates as "caution," with the exception noted in n. 27 below.

[27] *P,* XXI.90/181. Here, unusually, the Mansfield translation renders *respetto* as "respect" instead of "caution."

[28] Compare *D,* III.36.292–93/506–7 and Plato, *Seventh Letter, Laws* 337a–d. Plato writes here that conflicts among factions or cities can only be brought to a stable resolution if the victor "controls itself and enacts laws for the common good" so that "the defeated party will be doubly constrained, by respect and by fear [*aidoi kai phobō*], to follow the laws—by fear because the other party has demonstrated its superior force, and by respect because it has shown that it is able and willing to conquer its

5.3.
Practical theology: Heavenly judgments and human reasons

Machiavelli's remarks about the heavens (*il cieli*) and God further reflect the priority he gives to ethical concerns about human responsibility over both traditional
cosmology and theoretical science. He shows little interest in evaluating the epistemic quality of beliefs about God. He neither affirms beliefs in divine intervention,
miracles, prophecies, or the revelation of God's will, nor criticizes them for lacking
natural foundations. In fact, Machiavelli's references to the heavens acknowledge a
sense in which such "superstitious" beliefs can be considered as natural and, when
understood in that way, as reasonable.

When people impute events in the natural and human worlds to supernatural
causalities, Machiavelli suggests, they are not always failing to explain things rationally. Many writers who usually explain human events in terms of natural human
causes, including "our Livy" and Thucydides, also consider the same events from a
different standpoint that has little to do with natural sciences.[29] The usual explanation for the coexistence of these different standpoints in the same texts is that "premodern" authors, however rigorous their naturalism in other respects, allowed a
residue of superstition to creep into their incompletely scientific accounts.[30] This
explanation, I suggest, misunderstands the relation between historical explanation
and ethical judgment in many ancient writings, and therefore in Machiavelli's renewals of ancient ethical arguments. At one level, histories in the tradition founded
by Thucydides, developed by Livy, and renewed by Machiavelli were concerned to
identify the most natural causes of events. All these authors focus on causes that
are traceable to widespread, easily intelligible human motives. When they report
that a speaker or popular opinion imputed some event to supernatural causes, they
seldom see it as their business to affirm or dismiss these opinions as theoretical
claims about causation. As Machiavelli says, claims about divine causes of events
should "be discoursed of and interpreted by a man who has knowledge [*notizia*]
of things natural and supernatural, which we do not have."[31] Yet the same opinions
can be evaluated from an ethical standpoint, where the kinds of truth embodied
in statements about heavenly causation are quite distinct from, do not depend on,
the truths of natural science. This and the following section argue that Machiavelli
is happy to acknowledge the reasonableness of certain judgments that attribute
events to the heavens so long as these judgments are understood as ethical, not
explanatory, judgments.

---

desires and serve the law instead. . . . If the victors show themselves more eager than the vanquished
to obey the laws, then everything will be safe, happiness will abound, and these evils [of party strife]
will take their flight."

[29] See Machiavelli's (*D*, II.29.197/404–5) approving remark that Livy demonstrates "the power of
heaven over human affairs."

[30] For example, Parel 1993.

[31] *D*, I.56.114/314. Compare Plato, *Rep.* 427b–c: since we have no knowledge of things relating to the
gods and other supernatural beings, Socrates says, we should not presume to over-legislate on such
matters.

Machiavelli often treats fortune and the heavens as cooperative causalities, and at times seems to treat *fortuna* and *il cieli* as near synonyms.[32] However, his remarks about the heavens ascribe one important power to them that is entirely missing in his descriptions of *fortuna*, and indeed stands in direct contrast with it. *Fortuna* is willful, capricious, and lacks any moral compass. It is a morally vacuous causality that only acquires ethical order when the latter is given by human *virtú*. When Machiavelli refers to the heavens, on the other hand, he always imputes to them the power of moral judgment. Whenever the heavens are said to wish, will, or cause natural and human events, they do not wish or cause randomly; nor are they motivated by sentiments of sympathy or antipathy to particular human beings. What the heavens "wish" is to punish and correct gross deviations from standards of correct or just human conduct. When Machiavelli seconds Livy's judgment that "heaven for some end wished the Romans to know its power [*volendo il cielo a qualche fine che i romani conoscessono la potenza sua*]," both writers mean something very different than that the Romans were subject to random variations of *fortuna*.[33] The most reasonable interpretation of Livy's account is ethical; it transcends mere superstition.

Machiavelli's comments on the reasonable use of statements about heavenly causation appear in Book II, chapter 5 of the *Discourses*. He begins by noting that among the "diverse causes" that may erase memories of past times, "a part comes from men and a part from heaven." The causes that Machiavelli says "come from heaven" include plagues, famine, or "an inundation of waters."[34] He notes that the most venerated authors of antiquity often invoke such causes, and does not second-guess them. On the contrary, he says that these things should not "be doubted." One reason to take them seriously is empirical: "all the histories are full of them," and "this effect of the oblivion of things is seen." It also "seems reasonable" to attribute apparently natural disasters to the heavens on ethical grounds. Machiavelli's next remarks invoke standards of reasonableness that are ethical rather than theoretical. He makes his key point through a naturalistic analogy. Just as people find it "reasonable" that "simple" natural bodies sometimes need to be purged of corrupting elements, so do they judge it reasonable that "purging" is needed to restore health to "mixed" bodies such as "the mixed body of the human race."[35] When events happen that produce such ethically necessary purging, no matter what their natural causes, it is not unreasonable to suppose that some supremely wise being wished them to occur. The necessity for renovative purges here is recognized by applying standards of good order. It is not simply a matter of

---

[32] For example, *D*, II.29.197/404–5.

[33] Ibid. Compare HH, I.87, I.91.

[34] By contrast, the causes that come from men include the creation of new religious "sects" whose leaders wish to extinguish older religions "to give themselves reputation." Machiavelli (*D*, II.5.139/342) gives the "Christian sect" as his chief example, writing that it "persecuted all the ancient memories, burning the works of the poets and the historians . . . and spoiling every other thing that might convey some sign of antiquity."

[35] *D*, II.5.138–40/341–43.

physical survival.[36] It may of course also become that, since for Machiavelli cities that fail to maintain standards of order and virtue are also vulnerable to severe internal and external pressures. But if ethical and physical necessity are interdependent here, the priority for human cities must be to clarify and defend standards for self-imposed orders. When people impute natural disasters to supernatural intentions, then, this is reasonable insofar as they consider events from an ethical standpoint, not a theoretical one. They express a moral judgment that bad conduct merits punishment and corrupt cities need to be purged before they can be restored to ethical and political health.

The distinction between theoretical and ethical judgments explains Machiavelli's apparently credulous reports of natural catastrophes in the *Florentine Histories*.[37] These reports do not signify a residue of pre-scientific superstition in Machiavelli's writings any more than similar reports in Livy or Thucydides show shortfalls in ancient rationality. When any of these writers mention events that were widely seen at the time as punishments sent by God, they imply that people were able to recognize when serious wrongs had been committed even though, confused by the corrupt standards of their corrupt times, they were unable to articulate "ordinary and natural" reasons for their judgments. Indeed, those who ascribe moral judgments to the heavens may doubt that any merely human standards can be trusted to assess responsibility and issue judicious punishments.[38] When people find no reliable standards upheld in their own cities, recourse to explanations invoking the judgment of the heavens indicates that their own powers of ethical judgment have not been entirely extinguished by corrupt times. By imputing the "power of heaven" to devastating events, they exhibit uncertain, but still intact, powers to judge human actions.

In Book II of the *Discourses* Machiavelli gives a good example of how people may "reasonably" attribute heavenly causation to events that they interpret as punishments and warnings. He recalls Livy's account of the near-destruction of Rome by the Gauls, including "our historian's" report that many Romans at that time saw this event as a divine reproach for the arrogant "modes" used by Rome in its foreign relations. This example, Machiavelli remarks, "is very notable for demonstrating the power of heaven over human affairs." Livy "demonstrates" this power "extensively and in very efficacious words," saying that since heaven for some end wished the Romans to know its power," it set off a chain of events to punish the Romans for their multiple transgressions. Rome's ambassadors, members of the Fabii family, violated the "law of nations" by taking up arms against their Gaulish hosts, who quite reasonably demanded redress. When the Roman Senate derided these demands, the Gauls launched a ferocious assault on Rome that almost wiped the city off the map. Knowing who was at fault, the heavens at first "ordered that nothing worthy of the Roman people should be done in Rome to put down that

[36] This appeals to a Greek tradition that metaphorically associates natural necessity with ethical necessity, without implying any causal connection between the two. See White 2002, esp. 120–23; Plato, *Tim.* 46e–48b, 87a–d.

[37] See *FH*, VII.28.307; V.21.210–11/548–49.

[38] See chap. 8, sec. 8.4.

war." Machiavelli follows Livy in seeming to endorse the common opinion that Roman errors were caused by heavenly intentions. But what both historians accept is not a theoretical or speculative claim about supernatural causation, but the ethical judgment that the Romans deserved a harsh punishment. Far from arguing that judgments about human responsibility should be reduced to theoretical judgments about causation, Machiavelli follows his ancients in implying that when *judging* the quality of human actions, standards of reasonableness are distinct from those used to *explain* the same actions. Machiavelli admits that since he himself lacks "knowledge" of "things supernatural," he cannot judge with certainty whether specific events have heavenly or natural causes or both. But any human being can judge whether human agents acted in ways that undermine good orders or respect constraints posed by other people's "ordinary" humors. It is not unreasonable to ascribe powers of moral judgment to the heavens when these appear to concur with ordinary human judgments about responsibility.

Further, people who judge the matter reasonably do not impute events to the heavens in order to avoid responsibility, but to underscore the ethical necessity for human agents to assume responsibility for their errors. Machiavelli scarcely mentions the heavens in his detailed account of Roman errors following the assault. The Romans themselves, without any divine prodding, failed to display the virtue that might have averted disaster.[39] When Romans claimed that these errors were willed or "caused by" the heavens or by fortune, this judgment was reasonable insofar as it pointed to culpable failures arising from their own shortage of self-ordering *virtú*.[40] Understood in this way, statements about heavenly causation may play an important regulative role in practical reasoning, checking presumptuous conduct and *hubris*. Claims that attribute human errors to the heavens may reflect the eminently reasonable judgment that there are limits any individual's, party's, or city's power; that these limits should be respected even by agents who rate their own powers highly; and that violating limits incurs disorders that may reasonably be represented as divinely sanctioned chastisements.[41]

Machiavelli never seeks to expose the non-rational theoretical basis of supernatural concepts or to belittle the childish superstitions of the "many." On the contrary, he consistently criticizes the view that there is nothing but superstitious illusion in popular or religious notions of divine or supernatural power.[42] This attitude may be as damaging for human orders as the unreasoning belief that God is always on your side, no matter how bad your orders:

> To believe that without effort on your part God fights for you while you are idle and on your knees, has ruined many kingdoms and many states. . . . But

---

[39] *D*, II.29.197–98/405.

[40] Thus "after speaking of all the disorders spoken of above, Titus Livy concludes by saying, "So much does Fortune blind spirits where it does not wish its gathering strength checked" (ibid.).

[41] Compare TWP VI.27 on Athenians' fears of divine retribution, reflecting uneasiness about their audacious decision to invade Sicily.

[42] Except when these notions involve beliefs about godlike powers in men. See chaps. 10 and 11.

there should be no one with so small a brain that he will believe, if his house is falling, that God will save it without any other prop, because he will die beneath the ruin.[43]

From an ethical standpoint, popular judgments that cite supernatural causes are often more reasonable than arguments that reduce practical judgments to natural causation. They are certainly more reasonable than the view that human actors are under no necessity to show *respetto* toward constraints imposed by other people's ordinary and reasonable humors. Further, even people who have a thoroughly secular, naturalistic view of causation in human life should acknowledge that they cannot "eliminate" the existence of gods on the basis of experience.[44] Secular rationalists should recognize that concepts of the divine or supernatural are frequently used to express reasonable ethical judgments about human self-responsibility. Unlike reductive naturalists, Machiavelli seems happy to leave to the "heavens" a non-necessary but valuable supplementary role in helping people to recognize the disorders they bring on themselves when they fail to impose ordering restraints on their actions. At the same time, he warns men who lean too much on expectations of divine favor that this presumptuous faith threatens their own *virtú*. Men "who live ordinarily in great adversity or prosperity," Machiavelli observes, "have been brought to ruin or to greatness through a great advantage [*commodità*] that the heavens have provided them, giving or taking away from them an opportunity to be able to work virtuously."[45] The "advantage" conferred by heaven only provides the opportunity to do one's own work. Whether the end result is *grandezza* or ruin depends entirely on the quality of that work.[46]

5.4.
Practical prophecies: Foreseeing the future by "natural virtues"

On the reading just presented, a reasonable meaning of the statement that "heaven caused" the Romans to err would be that there were strong practical reasons for the Romans to see the Gauls' devastating attack as a wake-up call to "purge" themselves of tendencies to disrespect the "laws of nations." The notion of a cause (*cagione*) here has the ethical sense of "good" reason or just cause.[47] Machiavelli connects natural and ethical causes when discussing how it is possible to foresee

---

[43] Machiavelli, "Asino," lines 115–27/67–68 (*Opere*, vol. 3).

[44] Machiavelli's relative silence on cosmological questions does not obviously signify a considered rejection of any propositions about supernatural influences on human affairs. His position in these passages is remote from atheism or a thoroughgoing scientific skepticism. It is a position defined only in relation to practical judgments; its theological and theoretical content is insubstantial.

[45] *D*, II.29.198/406. Compare *P*, XXVI: since "God does not want to do everything; the rest you must do yourself"; and Plato, *Rep.* 617e.

[46] Compare Plato, *Crit.* 120d–121c on the fate of Atlantis.

[47] Machiavelli's (and Latin) *causa* has this sense as well as the explanatory sense; one does not depend on the other. Two Greek words often translated as "cause," *aitia* and *prophasis* (as in Thucydides' much-discussed phrase "the truest cause" of war) also relate mainly to ethical responsibility, not to natural or mechanical causation.

the effects of actions. One kind of foresight became notorious in Florence during Machiavelli's lifetime through the ominous prophecies of Friar Girolamo Savonarola, a charismatic opponent of Medici power who gained a mass following in the late 1490s. When Machiavelli evaluates opinions that ascribe prophetic powers of foresight to individuals, he implies that a distinction should be made between more and less reasonable senses of prophecy. Less reasonable senses include those invoked by men who claim to have privileged access to God, who conveys knowledge of his purposes, and commands them to act on this knowledge. Some of Machiavelli's most sharply ironic remarks concern this kind of claim to prophetic knowledge.[48] Whether or not he approves of the political ends at issue, he objects to the manipulative methods used by self-proclaimed prophets such as Savonarola. But Machiavelli discusses more reasonable forms of foresight that are sometimes called prophetic. "Whoever considers present and ancient things," he writes in the *Discourses*,

> easily knows [*conosce facilmente*] that in all cities and in all peoples there are the same desires and the same humors, and there always have been. So it is an easy thing for whoever examines past things diligently to foresee [*prevedere*] future things in every republic and to take the remedies that were used by the ancients, or if they do not find any that were used, to think up new ones through the similarity of accidents. But because these considerations are neglected or not understood [*non intese*] by whoever reads, or, if they are understood, they are not known [*conosciute*] to whoever governs, it follows that there are always the same scandals in every time.[49]

One kind of reasoning needed to "foresee" future developments is to reflect on past experience to identify recurrent patterns of conduct caused by "desires and humors" found in all times. Another kind draws partly on knowledge gained through experience, but goes beyond it. Machiavelli presents this in Book I of the *Art of War* by a distinction made between experience and "conjecture" as a basis for judging goodness in men. Outlining procedures for selecting good soldiers, the protagonist Fabrizio says that "the goodness of one whom you have to select as a soldier is known [*si conosce*] either by experience through some outstanding deed of his or by conjecture [*o per esperienza, mediante qualche sua egregia opera, o per coniettura*]." He explains that when one is choosing among inexperienced men, "proof of virtue cannot be found"[50] since they have not yet had the training needed to develop the qualities necessary for a good soldier. Thus "lacking this experience, it is necessary to recur to conjecture," which is made from a man's "years, his art, and his bearing [*presenza*]." These last include physical attributes but also much more: "One should above all look to his customs [*costumi*], and what in them is honest and shame-filled [*onestà e vergogna*], otherwise one selects an instrument

---

[48] See chaps. 10, 11.

[49] D, I.39.83–84/282.

[50] Gilbert (1989, II:588) translates this as "evidence of fitness," sacrificing Machiavelli's ethical strand of reasoning in favor of colloquial and pragmatic rendering.

of scandal and a beginning of corruption."[51] Similar conjectural precepts apply when trying to judge future events such as successes or failures in war, or the likelihood of future stability or upheavals in a polity. Just as one cannot know the fitness of men to serve as soldiers until they have experience that provides "evidence," one can only know the likelihood of success in battles or longevity of polities after the fact. But one can still make reasoned conjectures about an army or a polity's prospects by examining their orders, asking how well or badly they are regulated. These judgments, Machiavelli suggests, can allow one to "foresee" the future career of armies, governments, and polities with a high degree of accuracy.

He notes elsewhere that conjecture is often needed to show people the intrinsic goodness or badness of things, especially when bad habits and experience have corrupted their judgment. When people are "used to living in one mode," he notes in the *Discourses*, they often do not see its potentially fatal weaknesses and "do not wish to vary it." Since men living in corrupt conditions "do not look evil [*male*] in its face," they "have to have it shown to them by conjecture."[52] Just as military orderers may make sound conjectures about the future performance of soldiers if they know what qualities to look for, anyone may make sound conjectures about the likely response of other agents to a particular action if they prudently examine "ordinary and natural" human desires, drives, and humors. Agents who let themselves be constrained by such considerations are able to avoid the kinds of errors committed by the Romans, who faced ruin "only through the inobservance of justice [*solo per la inosservanza della giustizia*]" when their ambassadors "sinned 'against the law of nations' [*peccato i loro ambasciatori* <contra ius gentium>]."

As we saw in chapter 4, men who are not guided by an adequate account of these features of human "nature" often under- or overestimate their own powers in relation to those of others. They then act in ways that *predictably* provoke responses that tend to defeat their own purposes. Machiavelli does not suggest that such errors can be completely avoided by agents who have *cognizione* of "ordinary" drives and desires. He does imply that at least some important effects of actions can usually be "foreseen" by conjecture from this reflectively prudent basis. Such conjectures supplement Machiavelli's account of reasonable ethical causes. The relationship between the two can be analyzed more clearly if we distinguish between two ways of considering human "nature" that emerge from Machiavelli's arguments.

> (N1) identifies dispositions, drives, and desires that should be taken as *naturale e ordinario* constraints on limits on any action. These are "natural" to human beings in that they can never be eliminated from the species of beings designated by the concept of *umanità*. They are known through prudent observation based on experience, or on seeing these aspects of

---

[51] *AW*, I.26–27/553.

[52] *D*, I.18.51/247. For similar uses of *coniettura* as necessary when experience is unavailable as a basis for judgment or when it corrupts judgment see *D*, I.28, 31 *et passim*.

human nature at work through the study of histories. For this reason (N1) can be described as the *empirical* strand of Machiavelli's philosophical anthropology.

(N2) includes capacities for self-ordering acts of *virtú* that are made possible only on a prior presupposition of free will. Free will and *virtú* can be considered as natural in a different sense from (N1). Without using the word "innate," Machiavelli's arguments suggest that they are innate capacities that may be activated or not by an agent's choice. Here is one key difference between the two concepts of naturalness: the "motions" described under (N1) are always present and observable even when agents regulate them, while capacities for free will and *virtú* must be presupposed whether or not they are exercised. Since they cannot always be observed in action, and for long periods appear to have abandoned whole provinces or the human species, it is easy to doubt whether they should be regarded as part of human nature, or indeed that they exist at all. Nonetheless, they must be presupposed if human beings want to consider themselves responsible for their actions, orders, and laws, and deserving of praise and blame; or if they want to hold other human agents so responsible.[53] This is the *ethical* side of Machiavelli's philosophical anthropology.

Both (N1) and (N2) are equally important components of Machiavelli's practical anthropology, or his account of the features of human "nature" that should guide and constrain actions. Judgments based on (N1) take a mainly prudential form. They consider actions from the standpoint of an agent's own avowed purposes, and evaluate the prudence of his action by asking whether it took stock of the features of (N1) that were likely to affect its results. From this standpoint, the Roman Senate's violations of the *ius gentium* in the Fabii episode could easily have been judged imprudent before the Gauls took revenge, since a ferociously indignant response could be predicted on the basis of (N1). Unlike prudential judgments, which proceed from the standpoint of a particular agent's avowed aims, Machiavelli's implicit ethical judgments consider actions from the standpoint of what is appropriate for any beings that have the capacities described under (N2) as well as (N1): that is, for human beings generally. Judgments about reasonable or unreasonable causes for actions based on (N2) evaluate actions not by considering their effects on agents, but by asking whether they respect the capacities for ordered *virtú* and independence that must be presupposed in people affected by an action. From an ethical standpoint, the Senate's violations of the *ius gentium* should have been judged as injurious whether or not they provoked a violent response in this case, with disastrous consequences for Rome. Their actions were imprudent from the standpoint of (N1), and wrong when considered under (N2). Had the Gauls been too divided, weak, or weary to punish the Romans as they did, so that the immediate results of Roman violations did not appear disastrous, anyone with

[53] See *D*, I.3.15/207–8; I.16–18.44–52/240–48.

knowledge of (N2) would still judge their actions as ethically wrong. They freely chose to violate their legal and informal commitments several times, even after the Gauls appealed to them for justice; and in so behaving they treated the Gauls with contempt, instead of as agents who deserved respect and were capable of responding effectively to Roman offenses.[54]

Machiavelli implies that people who claim to foresee future disasters often do this by what might be called an ethical process of conjecture. Prophecies that interpret natural disasters as forebodings of future disasters are widely believed when people are aware that some grave wrong has been done or that their conditions of life are corrupt and in need of purging. Thus he writes in a mock naïve voice: "Whence it arises I do not know [io non so], but one sees by ancient and modern examples that no grave accident in a city or a province ever comes unless it has been foretold either by diviners or by revelations or by prodigies or by other heavenly signs."[55] His first example comes from Florentine history, when "before the death of Lorenzo de' Medici the Elder, a cathedral was struck in its highest part by a heavenly dart, with very great destruction for that building." People made their own connection between this extraordinary natural event and the politically significant event of Lorenzo's death because, perhaps without articulating the view, they were conscious at some level that his legacy had increased corruption in Florence and weakened its security. By reflecting on the unjust methods used under Medici rule, prudent judges could foresee that disorders would follow, even before the consequences were fully exposed after Lorenzo's death.

The paragraph goes on to juxtapose this Florentine example with analogous prophecies that preceded the Gauls' attack on Rome. Machiavelli reiterates Livy's account of how before the attack a plebeian "reported to the Senate that . . . he had heard a voice greater than human that admonished him that he should report to the magistrates that the French were coming to Rome." Machiavelli's main interest in such reports is what they tell us about human beings' sense of responsibility for their own errors in the past, and their will to correct or make amends for them. In both his modern and ancient examples, people project onto natural events ethical judgments that they did not perhaps make openly at the time, and perhaps still have been unable to articulate. The reasonableness of "prophecies" is not susceptible to empirical evaluation; as Machiavelli admits, the cause of such events themselves "I believe is to be discoursed of and interpreted by a man who has knowledge of things natural and supernatural, which we do not have. Yet it could be," he continues,

> as some philosophers would have it, that since this air is full of intelligences [intelligenze] that foresee future things by their natural virtues [per naturali virtú preveggendo le cose future], and they have compassion for men,

---

[54] In Thucydides those who view and treat their opponents with contempt (kataphronēsis) invariably inflict harm upon themselves over time.

[55] Emphasis added.

they warn them with like signs so that they can prepare themselves for defense.[56]

One reading of the claim that future things can be foreseen by their "natural virtues" might be that "intelligences" beyond the grasp of ordinary human cognition convey foreknowledge to a few human beings, whose natural virtues enable them to receive this knowledge. A different reading, however, is more consistent with Machiavelli's arguments in this chapter and elsewhere: namely, that human *intelligenze* are able to "foresee future things" by their own *naturali virtú*, without supernatural aid. Reflective human prudence, which is one part of *virtú*, can foresee future human responses to actions by taking stock of the natural dispositions described in (N1). Agents who seek to impose their own *leggi e ordini*, which constitute the most adequate expression of *virtú*, must also take into account the basic ethical constraints set by other agents' free will (N2) in order to find the right "limits" for their self-ordering works. If they do not currently see evidence of free will or *virtú* in the people affected by their actions, they should use conjecture to infer that these capacities are still present, and accord them the respect they deserve.

Machiavelli defends this "ordinary" kind of "foreseeing" against those who argue that some actions are neither good nor bad in themselves, but can only be judged by their effects. Early in the *Prince* he observes that "King Louis lost Lombardy for not having observed any of the conditions (*termini*, translated elsewhere as "limits") observed by others who have taken provinces and wished to hold them. Nor," he goes on, "is this any miracle" that could not have been foreseen from an examination of his numerous "errors." On the contrary, the result was "very ordinary and reasonable [*molto ordinario e ragionevole*]," and therefore foreseeable.[57] Other examples involve the predictably bad effects of breaking faith and violating treaties.[58] From this human standpoint, a reasonable sense of "prophecy" would simply involve foreseeing the effects of actions by considering what would be ordinary (judged by N1) and reasonable (judged by N2) reactions to them.[59] Men who foresee in this way are sometimes ascribed prophetic powers by the less prudent, and thought to have supernatural vision. In fact, Machiavelli implies, they foresaw future consequences from their quite *ordinario* knowledge of human nature (N1), which preserved them from self-serving delusions about the weakness of human desires to acquire, to live secure, or to live free. But they were also helped by knowledge of (N2), which made them recognize other people's free will and *virtú* as a necessary "limit" on actions.

[56] *D*, I.56.113–14/313–14.

[57] *P*, III.15–16/126.

[58] See chaps. 8 and 9. This is one of the main themes in Greek historical writing, discussed throughout Herodotus' and Thucydides' works.

[59] Compare the distinctions between more and less reasonable uses of prophecy in Spinoza 2007 (1669–70), 13–42 and Hobbes 1996 (1652), 287–300. When discussing prophecies and religion in Part III of the *Leviathan*, Hobbes makes very liberal use of Machiavelli-like language of "ordinary" and "extraordinary" events, causes, or knowledge.

5.5.

Moral psychology: The *malignità* of human nature and the discipline of *virtú*

One of the most widespread assumptions about Machiavelli's anthropology is that he had a "pessimistic" view of human nature. On this view, human nature itself is the greatest constraint on human attempts to legislate good orders. Whereas philosophers such as Plato and many humanists urged men to develop what was more "godlike" in their being, it is commonly argued that Machiavelli wanted to strip away illusions about human beings' quasi-divine essence, exposing human nature as scarcely different from that of other beasts. Indeed, Machiavelli states bluntly that the human is the most bestial of animal species.[60] By rejecting the notion that man partakes of divine qualities, Machiavelli is said to have produced a new "naturalistic ethic" that recognized the necessity for man to sink into "the filth of bestiality" in order to survive.[61] When he advises "orderers" of cities to make laws for man as he is, instead of trying to legislate for an idealized species of virtuous beings, many readers have assumed that this advice is based on the view that human nature is essentially bad. The following well-known passage, among others, seems to support this reading:

> As all those demonstrate who reason on a civil way of life, and as every history is full of examples, it is necessary to whoever disposes a republic and orders laws in it to presuppose that all men are bad [*rei*], and that they always have to use the malignity of their spirit [*la malignità dello animo loro*] whenever they have a free opportunity [*libera occasione*] for it.

A few chapters later we read that "men are more prone to evil than to good [*piú proni al male che al bene*]," and that prudent orderers should take this into account.[62] Some readers have argued that in practical terms, this pessimistic view of human nature lowers the standards that lawmakers and other political actors should use when deciding how to order civil life.[63] Once prudent orderers face up to the truth that human beings are naturally bad, they will shed their own moral scruples and begin to do whatever is necessary to preserve their own rule and the glory of their own city.

The arguments developed previously suggest, however, that a more nuanced account is needed of Machiavelli's views on this issue. To start with a point that has been underemphasized by most scholars, although Machiavelli does say that men are "more prone" to evil than to good, he never says that human nature is thoroughly or mainly bad. His scattered remarks on what he takes to be unvarying human dispositions pass no such sweeping verdicts. Rather, they amount to a view of human "nature" as prone to both bad and good *actions*. Machiavelli notes in the *Discourses* that men "do not know how to be altogether wicked or altogether good"

---

[60] See Machiavelli, "Asino," *Opere*, vol. 3.
[61] Meinecke 1998 (1925), 41–42.
[62] *D*, I.3.15/207–8; I.9.29/224.
[63] Strauss 1958, 296–97.

and, not knowing how to be "honorably wicked" or "perfectly good" (*onorevolmente cattivi, o perfettamente buoni*), often take harmful "middle ways."[64] Later he writes, "I judge the world always to have been in the same mode and there to have been *as much good as wicked* in it."[65] Restored to its original context, the statement that those who order laws in republics should "presuppose" human badness supports this mixed—or rather, action-dependent—view of man's moral character. The first sentence of the chapter says that whoever orders laws in republics should "presuppose that all men are bad." Near the end, however, we read: "it is said" that "the laws make them good." In the chain of reasoning that connects the first to the second statement, Machiavelli makes it clear that his concern is not simply to underline the badness in human nature. More importantly, it is to reinforce a key point made in the first chapter of the *Discourses* and developed throughout the work: that however bad the natural conditions of a site or the natural humors found in men, human capacities to "order laws" can always be used to turn these more toward good than bad.

Machiavelli does, to be sure, hold that all human beings are corruptible. They can never be "made good" if this is taken to mean permanently transformed from one wholly bad nature into another purged of dispositions to act badly. If the common opinion that "the laws make men good" is taken to mean that human laws somehow eliminate natural dispositions that produce bad conduct, the opinion clearly reflects wishful thinking. But Machiavelli uses the words "good" (*buono*) and "bad" (*rei, male, cattiva*) not for qualities found in human nature, but to describe how people ordinarily evaluate the quality of actions or works. Goodness or badness are almost always qualities of human actions in his lexicon, not of individual men or the human species. If "making good" means correcting men's actions rather than changing their nature, the old saw that "laws make men good" accords with the reflective judgments already set out in the *Discourses'* first chapter. Laws make men good by setting limits on license and placing them under "necessity"—in both the ethical sense of obligation and the physical sense of force—to direct their own actions toward good and away from the bad.[66]

Understood in this way, the presupposition that all men are bad and "prone to evil" need not imply a pessimistic account of human nature. Far from discouraging *virtuoso* self-ordering, it provides a strong stimulus to exercise *virtú* continuously and reflectively. The *naturale e ordinario* dispositions identified above under heading (N1) are ineliminable, and prone to corrupt uses. But Machiavelli argues that these dispositions need not be seen as obstacles to those who wish to improve the quality of their own actions, or that of the people for whom they order laws. The first chapter of the *Discourses* argues that adverse natural conditions in a site should stimulate agents to improve it by imposing good laws and orders; the third chapter makes an analogous argument about the human moral character and the corrective properties of self-imposed laws. If the *virtú*-deficient see badness in human nature,

---

[64] *D*, I.26–27.62–63/258–59.
[65] *D*, II.Pref.124/325; emphasis added.
[66] *D*, I.3.15/207–8.

like poverty in sites, as cause for pessimism, this is because they have not reflected prudently enough on how they might order laws to improve given conditions. *Virtuoso* agents regard the same badness and poverty as necessities that constrain them to impose better orders, knowing that this is entirely their own responsibility. They would of course be wrong to harbor optimism about their chances of transforming human nature, let alone of eliminating tendencies to corruption; such beliefs are symptoms of overassertive *hubris*. It is misleading, however, to describe as pessimism the self-critical prudence that Machiavelli sees as appropriate for virtuous legislators. If human nature consisted only of malignant drives and passions, *and* human beings are entirely responsible for making their own laws, it is hard to see how any human being could be trusted to make laws designed to stem corruption. Those who order laws in republics are themselves only human beings. When presupposing that all men are bad, they must do so of themselves as much as of all the others. Despite this self-critical stance, *virtuoso* orderers are not discouraged from trying to make laws that improve the quality of their own actions and those of others. They start by presupposing their own badness as much as anyone else's, yet also presuppose that they and everyone else has free will. And since the prudent know that free will may be used for bad or for good, with or without *virtú*, they work all the harder to design laws and orders that improve the quality of actions, if not of natural humors.

The usual pessimistic reading of Machiavelli's account of man's moral nature needs to be corrected, then, through closer attention to his remarks on free will and self-ordering *virtú*. The two aspects of his anthropology should not be identified with a simple dualism between bad, non-rational natural dispositions (N1) and good, rational capacities for virtue (N2). Machiavelli does not trouble to challenge this kind of dualism. He simply ignores it, and harks back to an ancient picture of man as having both ineliminable natural drives *and* innate capacities to regulate those drives.[67] It would be misleading to characterize the practical judgments that follow from reflecting on both aspects of human nature as pessimistic or optimistic. Pessimism and optimism are attitudes toward expected future conditions or results. Machiavelli's philosophical anthropology implies that the results of actions depend only on agents' own efforts, not on the intrinsic quality of their empirical nature. While his naturalistic account of human desires and drives identifies serious constraints on ordering, it does not form the normative *foundations* of his ethics or political theory. The recurrent drives, desires, and passions (N1) are simply the raw material that any human orderer must work with. They lack any intrinsic normative force. And since all men have innate capacities for ordering laws (N2) as well as for acting badly, it does not matter what proportion of good or bad might be in their nature. What matters is what they do to order themselves and their common life.

---

[67] See chap. 2, 2.5. on Thucydides; Plato, *Rep.* 571b–c, 572b, 609a–612a, and *Laws* 874e–875d: "It is vital that men should lay down laws for themselves and live in obedience to them; otherwise they will be indistinguishable from wild animals of the utmost savagery." Such arguments and others discussed in chap. 2 show how mistaken is Wolin's (1960, 237–38) claim that Machiavelli's sense of evil sets him apart from the Greeks, who "never considered that men would always act malignantly if given free rein."

I suggest that Machiavelli's statements about human badness are best under-stood as cautionary and regulative judgments that apply to agents seeking to exer-cise their *virtù*, not as part of his empirical anthropology. They identify tendencies to corruption that should be presupposed by prudent orderers if they want to use their free will for *virtuoso* works and not for bad.[68] The statements function pri-marily as a warning against complacency in well-ordered or powerful cities. Their main message is that it is better to err on the side of caution than to depend on man's natural or God-given goodness when regulating human actions. The warn-ing is needed because, as Machiavelli frequently observes, men become compla-cent in periods when civil life appears to be well ordered, imagining that they are immune from the badness found in other cities. Such people want simply to be happy in their good fortune, not wanting to dwell on their own corruptible dispo-sitions.[69] When "any malignity remains hidden for a time," it may go unregulated because it is "concealed" under good appearances of order to which "no contrary experience has been seen." But it will, Machiavelli says, be exposed over time, "which they say is the father of every truth."[70] Instead of expecting good actions to spring spontaneously from human nature, or indeed from insufficiently examined orders, one should always assume that "men never work any good unless through necessity." Laws and orders impose both a physical necessity (force, *forza*) and an ethical necessity (obligation, *obligo*) for those who live under them to make their actions work for good not bad.

The statements about human badness regulate legislating and ordering in a second, complementary way. While mainly cautionary, they also offer a construc-tive spur to *virtuoso* ordering. If human nature were any better than it is, human capacities for virtuous self-regulation would not be activated. In corrupt times it seems to many people that the virtue seen in ancient histories has abandoned the human species altogether, or at least fled from some provinces. When those who order laws in cities share this view, one sees the converse error of that shown by those who are complacent about their city's unvarying goodness: excessive fatalism about prospects for making their bad orders better.[71] Read from this perspective, Machiavelli's remarks about human badness serve as incitements to necessary self-improvement. Prudent agents, they suggest, should not despair of doing any good in their cities. They should rather presuppose that their own free will and *virtù* give them some room for maneuver, however narrow, and treat the appearance of incurable corruption as a challenge to use their capacities more effectively.

In contrast to these regulative judgments, Machiavelli's empirical anthropol-ogy (N1) treats "ordinary and natural" dispositions as neither good nor evil in

---

[68] Machiavelli (*D*, I.18.49–52/245–48) makes this clear when he says that he will "presuppose a very corrupt city" in order to underscore the great difficulties of maintaining freedom in corrupt conditions, then goes on to outline laws and orders that the Romans used to attempt to maintain it.

[69] People who live in corrupt modes do not want to change and "do not look evil in the face," so they "have to have it shown to them by conjecture" (*D*, I.18.51/247).

[70] *D*, I.3.15/208; I.37.

[71] *D*, I.16–18.44–52.

themselves. Most dispositions may be directed for better or for worse according to how virtuously agents choose to exercise their free will.[72] The moral quality of human nature depends on human beings' own self-imposed orders. It may be natural that "all err equally when all can err without respect [*tutti equalmente errano, quando tutti sanza rispetto possono errare*]," which happens in cities that lack good laws. But human laws regulate actions for better or worse; and if well-ordered peoples are better than princes who do not subject their own actions to laws, the goodness of one and the badness of the other "arises not from a diverse nature [*natura diversa*]—because it is in one mode in all . . . but from having more or less respect for the laws [*rispetto alle leggi*] within which both live." The nature of princes and peoples is the same; the difference between them is their attitude to the laws, which makes one deserve to be called good and the other less so. A people that "commands" and is well-ordered will be "stable, prudent, and grateful no otherwise than a prince" not because the people are inherently good but because under these conditions they tend to exhibit more "respect for the laws."[73]

The same holds for the "common opinion" about the varying, mutable, and ungrateful nature of multitudes (*moltitudine*). One can consider it their nature, Machiavelli argues, to create disorders only if it is part of the definition of a multitude to be a mass of people unregulated by public laws, whereas a "people" in a normatively adequate sense of the word is regulated by laws. Once again, it is the presence or absence of orders and laws that causes the characteristics identified by many as their nature. "Everyone who is not regulated by laws [*non sia regolato dalle leggi*]," Machiavelli points out, "would make the same error" as those attributed by many writers to the "unshackled [*sciolta*] multitude." A "multitude regulated by laws" will always have "the same goodness [*bontà*] that we see" in well-ordered kingdoms or principalities. Indeed it will be even better, since unlike kings and princes "it will be seen neither to dominate proudly nor to serve humbly [*né superbamendiamo dominare né umilmente servire*]." Good and bad "dispositions" (*disposizioni*) in peoples are also caused by the quality of their orders, not by nature. "No great account," Machiavelli insists, "should be taken of what a people says about its good or bad disposition if you are ordered so as to be able to maintain it if it is well disposed, and to provide that it should not hurt you if it is badly disposed." In provinces such as France and Spain, where one sees relatively few disorders, this "derives not so much from the goodness of the peoples, which is in good part lacking" as "through the order of those kingdoms, which is not yet spoiled." Goodness in people can be found in other provinces such as Germany, where orders are maintained not by kings, but by the people's own self-ordering

---

[72] Free will may be exercised to regulate (N1) for virtuous order, but it may also be used for disorder; see chaps. 6–7.

[73] *D*, I.58.116–17/316–17. "Natural" here does not mean these hatreds must be taken as givens; they issue from "the ambition to dominate and from jealousy for their state." Although these rivalries can never be entirely eliminated, in relations between polities as in internal relations, they can be mitigated through prudent orders (*D*, III.12.247/456–59).

virtue. This "makes many republics there live free, and they observe their laws so that no one from outside or inside dares to seize them."[74]

These passages imply that when assessing man's moral character, it makes no sense to consider only the natural dispositions and drives described by (N1). Men are capable of *malignità*, but also of ordering themselves to check badness. Machiavelli's *Tercets on Ambition* relate natural human "instincts" to the self-imposed necessity of laws in the same way:

> Oh human spirit insatiable, arrogant, crafty, and shifting [*varia*], and above
>   all else, malignant, iniquitous, impetuous, and feral [*maligna, iniqua,*
>   *impetuosa e fera*], because through your longing so ambitious, the first
>   violent death was seen in the world. . . .
> From this it results that one goes down and another goes up; on this
>   depends, without law or agreement [*sanza leggi o patto*], the shifting of
>   every mortal condition. . . .
> Every man hopes to climb higher by crushing now one, now another,
>   rather than through his own wisdom and goodness [*sua propria*
>   *virtue*]. . . .
> To this our natural instinct draws us, by our own motion and our own
>   feeling, if laws and greater forces do not restrain us [*se legge o maggior*
>   *forza non ci affrena*].

The poem stresses the devastating effects on Italy of the failure to establish strong laws setting limits on ambition:

> I say that if with Ambition are joined a valiant heart, a well-armed vigor
>   [*una virtute armata*], then for himself a man seldom fears evil. . . .
> And when someone blames Nature if in Italy, so much afflicted and worn,
>   men are not born so ferocious and hardy [*feroce e dura*],
> I say that this does not excuse and justify our lack of worth, for discipline
>   [*l'educazion*] can make up where Nature is lacking.

Machiavelli wants virtue and the laws to *regulate* ambition and other human drives, appetites, and passions, not to eliminate them. His concepts of *educazione*, *disciplina*, and *virtú* do not involve repression or denial of what is corruptible in the human character. Orderers can hardly be expected judiciously to regulate *naturale e ordinario* dispositions if they do not recognize the deeply ambivalent effects these may have on human life. What Machiavelli says about ambition applies to other similarly basic drives and desires:

> Since no man has power to drive her out of himself [*cacciarla*], needful it is
>   that Judgement and Sound Intellect, with Order and Ferocity [*l'iudizio e*
>   *l'intelletto sano con ordine e ferocia*], be her companions.[75]

[74] *D*, I.58.115–16/315–16; I.55.110/310.
[75] "Tercets on Ambition," 735–39/44–46; translation slightly modified.

It is seldom noticed that Machiavelli defines goodness and wickedness in terms of self-imposed "limits" (usually *termini*) or lack thereof.[76] What he calls "evil" results from serious and avoidable failures of human self-regulation: a failure of human responsibility to set necessary limits on one's actions when one has the capacity to do so.[77] This stands at odds with the view that according to Machiavelli, ethical judgments based on (N2) should be subordinated to empirical claims about allegedly natural human drives (N1). This kind of empirical reductionism has been read into Machiavelli's remarks about human nature by scholars who hail him as having pioneered a salutary break from both ancient and Christian ethics, placing practical judgments on a more scientific basis. I see no convincing evidence, however, that Machiavelli wanted to subordinate ethics and politics to the new methods of natural science. Although he analyzes human conduct in a ruthlessly rational manner, he nowhere suggests that ethical judgments and precepts can be *derived* from empirical observations. Nor does he imply that empirical observations about human nature are a sufficient *foundation* for practical judgments.[78] He does hold that observations about human nature should *inform* ethics, not least by underscoring the folly of trying to make human beings better than they can ever be. But the limits on human ordering powers are not hard-and-fast constraints that leave no room for choice. Orderers must still decide what to take as natural or supernatural limits on their own choices, and this itself is a choice for which they can be held responsible, praised, or blamed.

Thus Machiavelli's remarks about human desires, appetites, and passions do not function only to give a realistic description of the human animal, stripped of illusions and reduced to low standards of conduct. They also underline the capacity human beings have to regulate, redirect, or discipline their own nature in accordance with standards not found in biological nature or unregulated humors. Pessimistic accounts of Machiavelli's anthropology tell only half the story. The missing half is that he sets self-legislative virtue alongside natural impulses, not in the vain hope of making man a better quality of animal, but at least a more self-regulating animal. Machiavelli calls for both a more naturalistic view of man *and* a greater appreciation of human powers of self-ordering. This does not mean that

[76] The Greek roots of this idea can be recognized in the ethical concepts and contrasts discussed earlier. All the Greek writers discussed here associate order (*taxis, cosmos*) with the basic values of temperate self-restraint (*sōphrosunē*), respect (*aidō*), and reverent shame (*aischunē*). These values are necessary foundations of security (*sōtēria, asphaleia*) as well as of justice (*dikē*), and are realized only by means of laws (*nomoi*). Insecurity and injustice result from lawlessness (*paranomia*), since there are insufficient limits on vices antithetical to the virtues needed for order: chiefly excessive self-seeking and unrestrained desires (*pleonexia, philotimia, epithumia*), arrogance (*hubris*), and contempt for others (*kataphronēsis*). Nearly identical language and standards of judgment occur in Herodotus, Thucydides, Xenophon, and Plato. For concise summaries of these ideas and their relation to *philosophia*, see "Fragments from an Anonymous Work" in Iamblichus 1996, chap. 20; and implicitly, TPW, III.82–84.

[77] See *D*, I.29.65/261–63: "the nature of men is ambitious and suspicious and does not know how to set a limit to any fortune it may have"; also see I.46.95/293–94.

[78] In these respects Machiavelli anticipates Rousseau and Kant, who develop this position more explicitly. All three, in my view, owe more than is usually acknowledged to ancient Greek arguments about the limited relevance for moral judgment of judgments about empirical nature.

human beings should hope for progressive improvement in the moral quality of human nature, even under the best possible orders. The best human agents can do is to order laws that encourage better conduct and punish worse, in this modest way seeking to "make men good." This requires constant hard work that may, if done prudently, lead to reasonably stable—though always reversible—progress in the quality of human orders and actions. Because it is reversible, people need constant reminders of how things that seemed on a straight path up in the past then went downhill, often very quickly.[79]

5.6.
Human zoology: The ways of men and beasts

What then should be made of well-known passages such as the one in the *Prince* where Machiavelli seems to advise readers *not* to follow only the law-governed "way of men," but also the force-governed "way of beasts"? The passage begins:

> (I) You must know [*sapere*] that there are two kinds of combat: one with laws [*con le leggi*], the other with force [*con la forza*]. The first is proper [*proprio*] to man, the second to beasts; but because the first is often not enough, one must have recourse to the second. Therefore it is necessary for a prince to know well how to use [*usare*] the beast and the man.

This is almost always read as advice to any prudent political actor to rely less on law and more on force than conventional morality dictates. Prudent princes, Machiavelli seems to say, know when to thrust law aside and use force like lions or cunning like foxes.[80] But on a closer reading, it is unclear that Machiavelli's distinction between men and beasts has the practical implications usually ascribed to it. Consider what he says that princes should learn from beasts:

> (II) Thus, (1) since a prince is compelled of necessity to know [*sapere*] well how to use the beast [*bene usare la bestia*], he should pick the fox and the lion; (2) because the lion does not defend itself from snares and the fox does not defend itself from wolves. (3) So one needs to be a fox to recognize [*conoscere*] snares and a lion to frighten [*sbigottire*] the wolves. (4) Those who stay simply with the lion do not understand this [*non se ne intendano*].[81]

If the first part of clause (1) says that princes are forced to learn to "use" bestial qualities, the second adopts a discriminating tone. Not just any beasts will do; rather, very specific qualities of lions and foxes are put forward for imitation. Clause (2) says what these are. Significantly, it points not to the strengths of foxes and lions that princes should imitate, but to their weaknesses: lions do not defend themselves against snares, while foxes are vulnerable to wolves. Human beings often display the same weaknesses. The first thing to learn from these beasts, then,

---

[79] See *D*, III.31.283/494–46; III.29.277/490.
[80] See Skinner 2002, 125, *inter alia*.
[81] *P*, XVIII.69/165.

is their means of *self-defense*, including defensive modes of *combattere*. Sentence (3) clarifies this: one must be a fox to "recognize snares" and a lion to "frighten off" wolves. Both are defensive, not aggressive, aims.

Note that the skills needed to recognize snares and frighten off wolves are not what they have sometimes been taken to be. Most importantly, the fox's distinctive skills are not cunning and fraud. Machiavelli's foxes are quite unlike Cicero's. Whereas the Roman treats foxes as creatures of deception (*fraude*), Machiavelli presents deception as a quintessentially human skill; nowhere does he suggest that other animals practice it.[82] His imitation-worthy foxes are not cunning fraudsters; they are simply good at "recognizing snares [*conoscere e' lacci*]." If readers assume that Machiavelli identifies foxes with cunning, they may overlook the extremely important difference—one of the *Prince*'s key themes—between the skills needed to *generate* appearances and those needed to *see through* them. Foxes can do the second but not the first. By contrast, human beings do know many ingenious ways to create traps by covering *disonesto* deeds with *onesto* words and appearances. Men do not need to learn arts of appearance-making from foxes or other beasts, since those arts are altogether human. But they are deplorably bad at recognizing snares created by their fellow human beings. Men fail to see through techniques of creating *onesto* appearances because they rely too much on one frequently misleading sense, sight; and spin-adept princes know how to color their deeds in appealing shades. To recognize these traps, citizens need like foxes to use all their senses, not rely on sight alone. Whereas foxes know how to do this by instinct, humans have to work hard to develop an ability to "recognize snares," whether in military tactics or in political stratagems and rhetoric. In corrupt times men fail to do this work, and thus become bad at defending themselves.

Machiavelli's deceptively conventional use of Ciceronian topoi therefore has provocative undertones. A central aim of all Machiavelli's writings is to teach readers how to see through dangerously misleading rhetoric and other all-too-human modes of generating deceptive appearances in politics. His advice to use more of the fox aims to make readers better at seeing through these ubiquitous, man-made snares; not a word is said about learning to deceive or ensnare others. Machiavelli certainly never attributes these skills to foxes, just as he never applauds princes who use fraud. When he discusses deception and fraud in princes later in the same chapter, he does not say that princes *should* use deception, only that many *do*. Moreover, Machiavelli's philosophical zoology is rather generous to foxes, and critical of the human beings who project their own self-destructive traits onto other, ostensibly wilder animals. To this extent, the view that Machiavelli wants to bring human standards closer to the ways of beasts is right. But his discussion of foxes teasingly questions the Christian and Ciceronian assumption that human beings who use the beast thereby *lower* standards of human conduct. A close reading suggests that he abandons the negative descriptions of behavior said to be typical of certain beasts, instead ascribing traits to them that have a positive value. The unstated implication is that the lowest standards of conduct found in the animal king-

---

[82] In Cicero, *De Officiis* I.xiii.44–47, widely viewed as a reference for Machiavelli's chapter.

dom are not subhuman at all. They are set by human beings, not by other beasts. Humans may also set the highest standards, but they should not delude themselves into thinking that their nature always aims for better rather than for worse, let alone that they can learn nothing from other animals of value for civil orders.[83]

So far, the message of the *Prince*'s discussion of men and beasts can be characterized thus: princes (and other readers) should imitate beasts in a *discriminating* way, especially in their methods of *self-defense,* and most particularly the fox's ability to *recognize snares*.[84] What then about lions? Princes also need to use something of the lion's ability to "frighten wolves," since men too must combat predators. At first glance, sentence (3) seems to say that the natures of foxes and lions are complementary and equally valuable as models for human princes. But sentence (4) suggests an unequal estimation of their strengths and weaknesses. It stresses the disadvantages of acting *only* like lions: ferociously but without the *conoscere* of foxes. Since there is no parallel assessment of those who imitate foxes but neglect to act like lions, this introduces a jarring asymmetry into an otherwise symmetrical treatment of foxes and lions. It implies that prudent users of the beast should give priority to imitating those bestial behaviors that have a large cognitive element, not to those rooted in simple instincts of self-preservation. A discriminating "use of the beast" does not mean acting more on instinct and less on prudential reasoning or reasoned self-restraint. Even when using lionlike ferocity, human princes should guide this use with a keen sense of the snares involved, using powers of *conoscere* that foxes have by instinct and humans must develop by their own efforts. Princes remain weak who use lionlike ferocity to attack, but lack the ability to defend themselves preemptively by knowing how to "recognize snares." Such imprudently aggressive princes come off worse in Machiavelli's discussion than those who defend themselves well but do not know how to attack. Machiavelli neither recommends offensive ferocity to his readers nor advises them to relax discriminating restraints when using animal instincts. Instead he urges them to develop an ability to temper ferocity with knowledge of how to defend themselves against snares—not least those that entrap men who use their ferocity to attack, but who do not use prudent foresight to avoid getting trapped by others' snares and, all too often, by their own. This reading is supported by other nuances in chapter 18 of the *Prince*. We read here, for example, that the proper use of the beast "was taught covertly [*copertamente*] to princes by ancient writers, who wrote that Achilles, and many other ancient princes, were given to Cheiron the centaur to be raised, so that he would look after them with his discipline [*disciplina*]."[85] Note that Cheiron does not teach princes to be more ruthless or forceful. He teaches them *disciplina*, a word closely related to *virtú* in Machiavelli's vocabulary.[86]

[83] For a similar argument see Plutarch's satire "On the Use of Reason by 'Irrational' Beasts," PM, XII.
[84] Recall the remarks of Bacon, Neville, et al. about Machiavelli's purposes; see introduction.
[85] See chap. 3, sec. 3.4. on Xenophon's Cheiron and "hunting."
[86] The idea that the *disciplina* of self-imposed orders can make any "nature" good recurs in a complex irony in the *Discourses*. Machiavelli (*D*, III.36.292–93/506–7) notes that "many believe" that it is the "nature" of the French to fight like men at the beginning of a fight but come out "less than women." While adding that he "believes" this to be true, his message is not as crudely Gallophobic as it first appears. It

Despite first appearances, then, nothing in Machiavelli's advice to "use the beast" suggests the need to relax human powers of self-regulation, let alone to release the beast in man from the fetters of ethical restraint. Recall that passage (I) says that "a prince must understand how to make a good use of the beast *and* the man," not *only* how to use the beast. A good use of the beast is only half of the work princes should do. Simply unleashing the lionlike beast in man is bad strategy; what is needed, paradoxically, is to make men more "ferocious" by giving them good disciplinary orders and self-restraint. What then would constitute a good "use" of the ways of men? A reflective answer emerges when we reconnect the discussion of lions and foxes in passage (II) to the distinction made in (I) between force and laws as two modes of *combattere*.

When Machiavelli says that *forza* is proper to beasts and *leggi* to men, he has usually been taken as suggesting that force and laws are antithetical modes, so that when a prince uses more of one he must use less of the other. It is far from clear, however, that Machiavelli does treat *forza* and *leggi* as mutually restrictive modes of action. Passage (I) does not say that *forza* is for fighting, *leggi* for taming, ordering, and pacifying, let alone that the use of force necessarily threatens the rule of law. The laws are also described as a mode (or rather one of *dua generazioni*) of *combattere*; and Machiavelli implies that the two modes of *combattere* are complementary and equally necessary. He never says that princes can or should dispense with the "human" use of *leggi* or subordinate it to the prudent use of force. He says only that since fighting by law is not always *sufficient* without force, princes must learn how to make good use of "the beast and the man," force as well as law. He does not explicitly give primacy to *forza* or to law, but says that the use of one without the other *non è durabile*. Laws need to be backed by force; for Machiavelli as for his ancient writers, force is a necessary element of law.[87] But no less does force need to be regulated by law. The first is a matter of *prudential* necessity, dictated by human dispositions that make men break laws or manipulate them for private ends. The second is a matter of *ethical* necessity, an imperative dictated by standards of human life set by men themselves.[88] Although *forza* may be the means proper for beasts, then, it need not be exercised in brutal or unrestrained ways. If beasts such as lions—and many human beings—lack the understanding needed to do otherwise, those with better cognitive capacities know how to use force with restraint. And though *leggi* are the means proper to men, human laws must be backed by force. If human beings were naturally so good that they did not sometimes need to use force to compel obedience to laws, then laws would not be necessary, any more than force.[89]

---

is that even if the French or any other human beings are naturally weak—which Machiavelli believes we all are—they can still order themselves to make their *actions* more effective.

[87] The idea that both law and force, and modes of men and beasts, are needed to sustain human orders appears in Plato, *Rep.* 589b–590b. Here Socrates says that those who want to preserve justice in cities should make the lion's nature their ally (*summachon*); so long as they do not subordinate human reason to it, this alliance involves no debasement of human character.

[88] Though this ethical necessity for law and justice can be argued from a standpoint of expediency, as seen in chap. 2, sec. 2.5.

[89] *D*, I.3.15/207–8.

By seeming to oppose force and law, Machiavelli challenges readers to exercise the foxlike skills needed to see through rhetorical "snares." His chapter 18 purports to teach princes how to manufacture appearances of virtue while breaking faith behind the scenes. One of the commonest rhetorical sleights-of-hand used by actual princes is to appeal to an antithesis between the ways of men, equated with the laws, and the ways of beasts, equated with force. If these crude oppositions are accepted, the following specious arguments might seem convincing: "In an ideal world human beings would only use laws. But since in the real world laws are not enough, it is often necessary to use force. It is therefore necessary that I, the prince, often use force without recourse to laws, in effect acting above the law." It is easy enough to agree with the proposition that laws without force are not enough, and that it is often necessary to use force. But the opposition between force and laws is classic sophistry: the necessity to use force in no way reduces the necessity to use laws to regulate it. Readers who fall into the sophistical trap and unreflectively identify force with bestial ways fail to see that force can and should be regulated by human laws. If they accept the further false conclusion that inhumane ways are often necessary because force is often necessary, they allow themselves to be ensnared by one of the oldest tricks in the princely-tyrannical book, and fail to defend civil orders. Far from urging readers to abandon ethical or juridical scruples about using force, then, the *Prince* covertly urges princes and citizens of republics to use more of the properly human means of *leggi* to defend themselves and their cities.

5.7.
Human cities, where modes are neither delicate nor too harsh

For Machiavelli *leggi* and *ordini* can only be human products, the work of human *virtú*. The concept of a natural law, whether attributed to divine authorship or not, makes little sense in Machiavelli's vocabulary. Human beings may discover and analyze orderly processes in nature, but these cannot be normative for human orders. Machiavelli's position might be expressed as follows: when making laws and orders, human beings must start by recognizing the overwhelming constraints placed on their actions by accidents, natural processes, their own inextinguishable passions, and perhaps by God. Some of these constraints are so pervasive and clear that it is tempting to call them laws and thus make them normative for human action. But this temptation should be resisted. In the same way, natural science may identify regularities that have an overpowering *influence* on human conduct. But science offers no conclusive reasons why human beings should take these regularities as normative for their own choices and actions.

A close reading of the first chapter of the *Discourses* helps to clarify Machiavelli's thinking about how human ordering can acquire normative bearings. When men find themselves cast adrift from pre-existing orders and decide to build new ones, two sets of conditions always influence their building. One are external constraints, which include conditions such as "disease, hunger, or war" that first drove them to seek "new beginnings" and the hard material obstacles they must confront wherever they seek to "build anew": the challenges of reconfiguring an uninhabited site to suit their needs, or those posed by the presence on their chosen territory of other peoples living under their own laws.[90] The other conditions are anthropological. They include both the "natural" constraints I identified with (N1) and builders' *innate* capacities to "impose" their own laws and orders in spite of these constraints (N2). Machiavelli argues that builders of cities suitable for human beings must take both conditions into account. External constraints should not be taken as absolute limits on their actions, or be granted the status of natural laws that dictate the aims and character of civil life independently of human choices. Builders may take their initial physical bearings from the site and other external constraints. But the normative standards that guide judgments about the kind of life they want to promote in their cities, and their choice of laws supporting such a life, cannot be derived from a purely empirical study of natural or social sites. They must be defined through reasoning about the necessary conditions for coexistence among beings that have *both* natural dispositions (N1) and innate capacities (N2). And as I have argued, Machiavelli treats self-legislative and self-ordering capacities (N2) as the key—indeed, the only—source of norms that distinguish human forms of life from those of beasts.

What kinds of city are appropriate for the corruptible self-legislating animals that human beings are? Drawing on previous arguments, we can infer that cities built for men rather than for gods or beasts must meet several broad criteria. Their builders should accept natural dispositions (N1) as constraints on building, and give them a place to vent. Yet they should not treat them as sufficient foundations of civil order or *civiltà*. Such *fondamenti*, to be stable, must be based on self-imposed necessities that take the "human form" of orders and laws (N2). The relation between (N1) and (N2) should not involve the overassertive domination or control of either one by the other. Rather, (N2) should regulate and order (N1) in non-repressive ways, respecting the ordinary and natural limits set by the latter.

These features of a properly human city are illustrated by an example that appears near the end of the *Florentine Histories*. In the Genoese commune of San Giorgio, Machiavelli writes, laws are regarded as the foundation of arms, money, and government, not vice versa; arms and government there are the defenders of laws. When someone "has taken over the state," the "company" (*Comune*) of San Giorgio makes him

> swear to observe its laws, which have not been altered up to these times, because San Giorgio has arms, money, and government, and one cannot alter the laws without danger of a certain and dangerous rebellion. An example truly rare, never found by the philosophers in all the republics they have imagined and seen; to see within the same circle, among the same citizens, liberty and tyranny, civil life and corrupt life, justice and license, because that order alone keeps the city full of its ancient and venerable customs

[90] *D*, II.8.

[*la libertà e la tirranide, la vita civile e la corrotta, la giustizia e la licenza: perché quello ordine solo mantiene quella città piena di costumi antichi e venerabili*].[91]

Machiavelli's quasi-mythical San Giorgio captures the inescapably mixed character of any well-ordered human city. What he presents here is a regulative ideal of a city that is both optimal and possible for human beings. The ideal rejects idealistic aspirations to build a city that transcends corruption, license, and the dangers of tyranny. It recognizes that human beings will never produce cities where freedom, *civilità*, and justice reign completely secure and unchallenged. No city built by and for men can expunge the conflicting humors that make them prone to disorders. Yet the citizens of San Giorgio refuse to let these omnipresent human conditions dominate political life or undermine their own demanding, self-imposed standards of *civilità*. They neither give free rein to corruption-producing conditions nor try forcibly to repress them. Instead they regulate them by means of laws that citizens recurrently "swear to observe." San Giorgio's solution to chronic human corruptibility is to acknowledge it fully, then to give it rigorous orders to prevent corrupting dispositions from taking over civil life. By accepting their own tendencies to *malignità* as an ineliminable part of civil life, citizens do not draw the "realistic" conclusion that they must sometimes use force unregulated by laws or use fraud against compatriots or foreigners in order to survive. On the contrary, they see that the only way to maintain stable orders is to authorize the strict rule of law in their city. Only self-authorized laws enable them to preserve their own "ancient and venerable" standards of conduct amid constant—and often self-inflicted—dangers of corruption. The mythical-philosophical example of San Giorgio illustrates the point that while builders of cities should not idealize human nature, or imagine that its corrupting dispositions can be overcome, nor should they conclude that the only alternatives are to repress natural drives or to leave them unregulated. The venting of human ambitions and other humors is needed for freedom and stable orders, but it can and should be ordered by laws that set clear limits on everyone's freedom. According to Machiavelli, such laws are every bit as human as the humors that need venting. And the laws and orders, not the humors, are what make civil life possible.

Machiavelli uses the example of San Giorgio to suggest that all human beings, not least his fellow Florentines, would do themselves a great service if they would realize that the kind of *vita civile* appropriate for them must always have the mixed character he ascribes to his non-idealized yet properly human city. Unfortunately, the idea of corruptible yet self-ordering *umanità* is seldom taken as a standard for building cities. Instead people oscillate between trying to build cities suitable for incorruptible beings, that is, gods, and when this fails—as it always does—building to subhuman standards. This debases the good name of *umanità*. Machiavelli often uses the word in ways that imitate its frequent abuses. What people call *umanità* in

[91] *FH*, VIII.29.352/720.

corrupt times, he suggests, is really excessive indulgence of others for the sake of one's own private or partisan interests.[92]

The fact that standards of *umanità* are easily corrupted does not mean that the good word lacks more adequate meanings. In the *Discourses* Machiavelli distinguishes between the genuine "humanity and integrity" of Romans like Camillus, and the mere "reputation" for being humane and affable gained by more self-indulgent men whose misnamed *umanità* introduced fatal elements of corruption into the republic.[93] Machiavelli discusses the basis for this distinction in the first book of his dialogue *Art of War*. Here he identifies "modes" as "more humane" (*modi più umani*) that are neither too delicate (*delicate*) nor too harsh (*aspre*). These distinctions are set out in a dialectical progression at the start of the dialogue. First, the chief interlocutor Fabrizio Colonna expresses the wish that eminent contemporaries had sought

> to be like the ancients in the strong and harsh things, not in the delicate and soft ones [*cose forti e aspre, non nelle delicate e molli*], and in those that they did under the sun, not in the shade [*l'ombra*], and to take up the modes of the true and perfect antiquity, not the false and corrupt one. For after these studies pleased my Romans, my fatherland went to ruin.

Fabrizio's young host Cosimo Rucellai responds by agreeing that men like his grandfather Bernardo, in whose famous gardens the dialogue is set, should have imitated what was "harsh" rather than "delicate" in ancient things.[94] He excuses him by noting that in the very corrupt times when Bernardo lived, men were judged "crazy" (*pazzo*) who adopted harsh modes of life that the ancients used to "harden them to be able to withstand evil and . . . make them love life less and fear death less." Frightened (*sbigottito*) by the common opinion that self-privation and self-exposure to the elements were unworthy of praise, Bernardo had abandoned these harsher ancients and imitated only those who had the approval of his own society: those who preferred a "soft life" (*il vivere molle*).[95]

Fabrizio replies by questioning common opinions about what is worth imitating in *both* delicate and harsh modes of life. When he praised what was "strong and harsh" in ancient ways, he explains, he did not have in mind those extremely "hard modes of living [*modi di vivere duri*]" mentioned by Cosimo. If delicate ancient modes are rejected, this does not mean that one must go to the other extreme and imitate the excessively harsh. The more adequate sense of Fabrizio's initial statement that people should be more like the ancients "in the strong and harsh

---

[92] *P*, XVII.67–68/162–64. In seeming to praise humanity while criticizing corrupt uses, Machiavelli follows Xenophon's *Cyropaedia*; see chap. 2. The *Discourses* frequently note that princes and generals gained a "reputation" for *umanità* when they refrained from punishing their own "partisans," allowing private ambitions to override the rule of law.

[93] *D*, III.20.262/472–73.

[94] See Gilbert 1977, 215–46, on Bernardo's complex relations with the Medicis and his writings on antiquities.

[95] A veiled reference to Bernardo's half-hearted acquiescence in Medici rule, in contrast to his grandson's preference for hazarding the "harsh" conditions of resistance.

things" is, he explains, that they should imitate "other more humane modes [*modi piú umani*] and those that have more conformity with life today, which I do not believe would have been difficult to introduce for one who is numbered among the princes of a city." The standards adequate to the word *umana* are neither very harsh nor delicate. They are represented by the "modes of the true and perfect antiquity [*modi di antichità vera e perfetta*]," as distinct from the corrupt one where people did things "in the shade." Transparency and commitment to public well-being are among the standards found in Fabrizio's notion of true antiquity. When they were flouted by "shady" private and partisan dealings, good Roman orders were quickly ruined. But the main characteristic Fabrizio ascribes to standards of humane antiquity is good ordering based on a prudent appraisal of human weaknesses and strengths. He foreshadows some of these humane orders here, saying that he would like to introduce the following ancient modes:

> To honor and reward the virtues [*le virtú*], not to despise poverty, to esteem the modes and orders of military discipline [*disciplina*], to constrain [*constringere*] the citizens to love one another, to live without sects [*sètte*], to esteem the private less than the public, and other similar things that could easily accompany our times. These modes are not difficult to persuade [men of] when one thinks about them much and they are entered into by due degrees. For in them truth appears so much that every common talent [*ogni comunale ingegno*] can be capable of it.[96]

Here Fabrizio rejoins *umanità* to integrity, virtue, discipline, concern for the public good, and love of truth. Like the non-idealized ideal of San Giorgio, this account of humane ancient modes holds up as ideals practices that accept human corruptibility as their premise. Fabrizio does not want to make all men or orders thoroughly virtuous, since this would be impossible, but simply to order things so that virtues are honored and rewarded. He does not dream of eliminating poverty, but seeks orders where it is not despised. Unlike some imitators of very harsh ancient modes, he does not wish to esteem martial things indiscriminately, but only those "modes and orders of military discipline." Nor does Fabrizio want to subordinate private to public interests, but only to "persuade" citizens to "esteem" the private less than the public. His desire to live without sects might sound unrealistic until we recall that Machiavelli uses *sètte* for any groups, political or religious, that seek complete dominance or "ultimate victory" over rivals; whereas rivalry per se, producing "tumults" among different humors, he considers as an *ordinario e naturale* inconvenience that may be ordered for freedom and civil life.

Remarks scattered throughout the *Discourses* confirm this adequate sense of *umanità* as a standard based on both a non-idealized, naturalistic conception of human dispositions (N1) *and* knowledge of human capacities for self-ordering (N2). Excessively harsh modes, Machiavelli observes, are rightly called brutal, cruel, or barbaric, not human. Although human beings are in a sense naturally prone to all these modes when they live under bad orders or no orders, they fall short of the

---

[96] *AW*, I.10–12/534–36.

standards of humanity that become clear when one recognizes innate human capacities to constrain their own actions. Machiavelli describes a prince as "barbarian"
who is "a destroyer of countries and waster of all the civilizations [*dissipatore di tutte
le civiltà*] of men." Since such men show no respect for limits or human orders, they
fall short of *umanità*. By contrast, "if he has within himself human and ordinary orders" a prince will refrain from such excessive violence and leave to his subjects "all
their arts and almost all their ancient orders."[97] As seen with foxes and lions, brute
force unregulated by any laws or prudent reasoning is stupid. It involves only "using"
the way of beasts instead of a judicious use of the man *and* the beast, force *and* law.

In corrupt cities, the need to check "delicate" self-indulgence and leniency toward partisans is greater than the need to check excessive harshness. Machiavelli's
frequent remarks recommending harsh measures as a matter of *necessità* should
be read with this in mind. A "citizen who lives under the laws of a republic" should
not, he writes in the *Discourses*, seek to found his authority on his reputation for
umanità, since this often rests on corrupt modes that benefit his supporters at
the expense of transparency, good orders, and the rule of law. When Machiavelli
argues that the mode of "harsh commands" is a "more praiseworthy and less dangerous" source of authority in republics, "harsh" has the same sense as it did for
Fabrizio Colonna: he means harshness defined in terms of humane orders and
discipline, not the harshness of "hard living" or "barbarian" cruelty. The mode he
recommends is good because it "is wholly in favor of the public and does not in
any part have regard to private ambition."[98]

The "harshness" Machiavelli frequently recommends as a condition for republican orders is not the cruel, inhumane harshness involved in violent repression. It
is analogous to the sense of "force" invoked in the phrase "force of law": a force or
harshness necessitated by a clear recognition of natural tendencies to corruption,
and seeking to regulate these tendencies by general, non-arbitrary, and publicly
known standards. In this sense "it is a very true rule [*una regola verissima*] that
when one commands harsh things, one must make them observed with harshness
[*asprezza*]."[99]

5.8.
Who is responsible for the laws? Human reasoning and *civiltà*

This and the previous chapter questioned the view that Machiavelli's anthropology
paves the way for a wholly new natural science of humanity, and the related view

---

[97] *D*, II.2.133/335.
[98] *D*, III.22.265–67/476–80. Similar dialectical reasoning occurs in a well-known passage on the
difference between ancient and modern forms of religion in *D*, II.2.131/334–35. Here Machiavelli seems
to hold up ancient forms of undisciplined "harshness" as a valuable corrective to the "delicate" modes
encouraged by Christianity. But if the Christian conception is too delicate and otherworldly, the "Gentile" conception described here focuses too one-sidedly on physical strength, while saying little about
the ordering needed to maintain oneself "strong."
[99] On the need for harsh but necessary remedies in corrupt cities, see Plato, *Gorg.* 518c–519b,
521a–522a.

that he subordinates ethical judgments to empirical analyses of human nature. His anthropology seeks rather to renovate ancient ethical traditions that identify free will and virtue as distinctive human causalities, which allow human beings to establish some degree of autonomy from both divine and natural determination. On the reading proposed here, Machiavelli does not reject divine or superhuman standards in favor of subhuman ones. He calls on human beings to order their own lives and actions without depending too much on God or nature, while respecting both. His renovated, highly individual version of ancient self-legislative ethics stresses human self-responsibility for making and maintaining human moral and political orders. Human order and dignity are not seen as gifts from nature or God, but fragile, easily reversible achievements that must be won through human beings' own continuous efforts. This makes it all the more marvelous when well-ordered human cities and human laws are founded and sustained for more than a few generations.

What means should then be used to establish and uphold the humane orders needed for civil life, if not sheer force, natural law, or appeals to the heavens? Machiavelli's consistent answer is ordinary human reasoning, *ragionare*.[100] The give-and-take of reasons and their critical appraisal is the main tool human beings must use for their self-legislative ordering. The reasons presented in Machiavelli's writings are, earlier sections argued, primarily practical rather than theoretical or theological. They assess the implications and intrinsic merits of *actions*, and seldom try to evaluate various theological doctrines or naturalistic theories. His concept of self-legislative *ragionare* should be distinguished from several other conceptions of practical reasoning that have been attributed to him. First, for Machiavelli *ragionare* is not mainly adaptive, aimed at the bare survival of individuals or of the species. Agents who conceive of practical reasoning in this way show a serious lack of *virtú*, allowing natural instincts or what they see as external nature to control their actions. Second, the self-ordering tools supplied by *ragionare* are not only instrumental: reasoning is not used only to choose the most efficient means to attain whatever ends agents happen to have, but also to identify ends adequate to self-imposed human standards. Third and finally, Machiavelli does not treat *ragionare* as a higher set of intellectual faculties that deserve to command man's baser drives, passions, and appetites, or which render human beings superior to other animals. Machiavelli never identifies *ragionare* with specifically intellectual or scientific cognitions available only to those who have the leisure to immerse themselves in specialized studies. Nor does he describe reasoning as a commanding faculty whose use guarantees the choice of prudent or virtuous ends. *Ragionare* is a necessary condition for *virtú*, but hardly a sufficient one. Machiavelli denies that the possession of complex rational faculties makes humans better animals than other beasts. On the contrary, they may use their rational faculties for evil ends as well as good; indeed, they more often use them to deceive and mislead by a variety of sophisticated ruses than to defend stable orders. Reasoning directs agents to *virtú* when agents themselves choose to direct it to *virtú*.

[100] Also see chap. 10.

The importance of reasoning both in private and in public is stressed throughout the *Discourses*, where Machiavelli suggests that "knowing how to reason" is a condition for upholding up even minimal standards of *umanità* and *civilità*. Peoples who lack this knowledge become easy prey for homegrown tyrants and external predators who treat them more like beasts than fellow men. "That people," Machiavelli writes,

> is nothing other than a feral animal [*animale bruto*] that, although of a ferocious and feral nature, has always been nourished in prison and in servitude. Then, if it is left free in a field to its fate [*lasciato a sorte in una campagna libero*], it becomes the prey of the first one who seeks to rechain it, not being used to feed itself and not knowing [*né sappiendo*] places where it may have to take refuge. The same happens to a people: since it is used to living under the government of others, not knowing how to reason about either public defense or public offense [*non sappiendo ragionare né delle difese o offese publiche*], neither knowing princes nor known by them [*non conoscendo i principi né essendo conosciuto da loro*], it quickly returns beneath a yoke that is most often heavier than the one it had removed from its neck a little before.[101]

Just as the ferocity of princes, armies, and lions is useless if undirected by orders grounded in reflective *ragionare*, the unreasoning ferocity of peoples does not help them to defend themselves from internal and external oppressors; it only makes them more vulnerable. But whereas princes who rely one-sidedly on the ways of beasts do so because of ambition or obtuseness, Machiavelli suggests, unreasonable ferocity in peoples is most often caused by lack of political freedom. One of the chief ways in which unfreedom keeps peoples at the level of feral animals is by denying them opportunities to reason "about either public defense or public offense." Reflective peoples "become wise from their afflictions"; unreflective ones stay caught in cycles of decline and ruin, blame fate or other people for their downfall, and fail to take advantage of opportunities for personal or civil redemption.[102] Maintaining freedom, or indeed any human *civilità*, depends on "knowing how to reason" about public actions. Machiavelli's laws are only *effective* if they are backed by force, but they only have legitimate *authority* if they can be explained by clear justificatory reasons. While recognizing that there are circumstances where it is necessary to grant the one or a few men authority to reason without public consultation, Machiavelli denies that public scrutiny of these men's work should ever be curtailed, or that any authorities are exempt from giving reasoned accounts of their actions. Similarly, while acknowledging the value of some non-rational modes of persuasion such as religious rituals or customs, Machiavelli does not exempt these from standards of civil reasoning. On the contrary, as chapter 10 argues, he treats the latter as a standard for regulating uses of the former, and as the only legitimate source of political authority.

---

[101] *D*, I.16.44/240.
[102] *FH*, V.1.185/520–21; *P*, XVIII and XXVI; *D*, III.2, 34, 40, *inter alia*.

Machiavelli's own writings demonstrate the value of critical *ragionare*. He urges readers to take nothing on unexamined authority, including any conclusions they might attribute to him. When he announces that he will oppose a view held by virtually "all the writers" ancient and modern, he defends his apparent audacity by saying, "however it may be, I do not judge nor shall I ever judge it to be a defect to defend any opinion with reasons, without wishing to use either authority or force for it [*io non guidico né giudicherò mai essere difetto difendere alcuna opinione con le ragioni, sanza volervi usare o l'autorità o la forza*]."[103] In short, "it is good to reason about everything [*essendo bene ragionare d'ogni cosa*]" even when people are "used to living in one mode" and are reluctant to "look evil [*male*] in its face."[104] For Machiavelli, reasoning is in the first instance an individual activity that proceeds from the cognition and reflections of individual minds. Reasoning about the conditions for civil coexistence, however, requires both generalizations beyond one's own case and the exchange of reasons among persons and groups of people. If public *ragionare* is to produce virtuous order rather than an anarchy of self-assertive demands and dogmas, it needs to be ordered through procedural restraints authorized by everyone. As the next chapters suggest, one of the most distinctive aspects of Machiavelli's defense of republican orders is his insistence on the need for procedures of transparent public reasoning as their indispensable foundation.

If ordinary reasoning is the chief instrument of self-legislation, it is also the most reliable means human beings have of checking the excesses or abuses of reasoning. This does not mean that Machiavelli regards any form of human *ragionare*, whether instrumental, theoretical, juridical, or discursive, as inherently trustworthy; on the contrary, he is a most penetrating analyst of its limitations and abuses. All forms of reasoning are vulnerable to ordinary, all-too-familiar human weaknesses. Two are particularly dangerous for moral and political self-legislation. One weakness is overconfidence or ambition that leads to precipitate judgments, or assertions about truth in matters on which mere human reason cannot have certain knowledge. The other is excessive caution or fear that causes people to distrust their own ordinary capacities for reasoned judgment. When such doubts result in a refusal to exercise one's reflective and deliberative capacities, people may fall into a passive, indifferentist relativism, take refuge in unreasoning dogmatism, or simply hand over their own powers of reasoning to authorities. Machiavelli is highly alert to these dangers. After weighing the alternatives, however, he repeatedly returns to the same conclusion: namely, that ordinary reasoning is the best means we have for making practical judgments about justice and the laws. It may be untrustworthy. But other methods of grounding legislative and political authority can be trusted even less.

[103] *D*, I.58.116/315–16. The opinion is that "multitudes" cause disorders in republics.
[104] *D*, I.18.49–51/245–48.

PRINCIPLES

III

CHAPTER 6

Free Agency and Desires for Freedom

Although Machiavelli's concept of freedom has been widely discussed, scholarly interest has focused on his thinking about political freedom. One influential interpretation asserts that "the only freedom Machiavelli recognizes is political freedom, freedom from arbitrary despotic rule, i.e. republicanism," and "the freedom of one state from control by other states." On this view, Machiavelli does not consider human desires for freedom as strong or ethically compelling. He ostensibly holds that human beings "care little for liberty—the name means more to them than the reality—and they place it well below security, property or desire for revenge." As a motive for action, freedom is "automatically" outweighed by "the motive of self-preservation," which Machiavelli, like Hobbes, is said to rank above all others.[1] Other scholars acknowledge that desires for freedom have a central role in Machiavelli's moral psychology and political ethics. Many argue, however, that he ascribes value to those desires only insofar as they contribute to the collective good of the polity or *patria*, while giving little weight to more individualistic desires to be respected as free agents irrespective of the wider good one pursues.[2] A few recent scholars have tried to show that Machiavelli's concept of *libertà* involves the protection of individual rights to security, free speech, and appraisal according to personal merit when competing for public honors.[3] I second this view in the next few chapters. I doubt, however, whether it is possible to appreciate what is most distinctive about Machiavelli's conception of freedom when it is examined only from a political or sociological standpoint.[4] A closer study of its ethical and philosophical premises is needed to complete and support readings that see Machiavelli's *libertà* as requiring respect for certain individual claims, identified in advance of specific notions of the public good.

Against the widespread views that he reduces ethics to political prudence, or seeks to separate ethics from politics, this chapter argues that independent ethical principles guide Machiavelli's judgments about what constitutes political *libertà* in an adequate sense of the word. Principles restrict the ends that may be pursued

[1] Berlin 1981 (1958), 38–41.

[2] For example, Pocock 1975, 194–218; Skinner 2002, 177–85; Sullivan 2004, 31–78.

[3] Notably Viroli 1998, 118–31; Tarcov 2007.

[4] Pocock (1975, 211) identifies an emerging "sociology of liberty" in Machiavelli's writings, "founded very largely upon a concept of the role of arms in society and in a *vivere civile*." Viroli (1998) also discusses the relation between political freedom and the civil or political life in Machiavelli's writings. Neither offers a detailed analysis of the ethical foundations of political freedom.

under the name of freedom, and regulate the choice of means used to found or renovate free orders. In order to make a clearer case for the priority of ethical principles as the touchstone of political freedom, I have divided my discussion of Machiavelli's *libertà* into two chapters, one focusing on ethical premises and the other on free political orders. Machiavelli's own discussions do not, of course, distinguish sharply between principles and prudence, or between ethical principles and the political *ordini* that they recommend. His principled lines of reasoning have to be identified through close reading, attentive to the unstated implications of his arguments and examples as well as to the positions he spells out.

6.1.
The *Discourses* on desires for freedom in and among cities

Books II and III of the *Discourses* give numerous examples of peoples conquered or fought by the Romans whose desires for freedom made it impossible to defeat them by military power alone. These views are summed up in one of the *Discourses*' most eloquent chapters, entitled "What Peoples the Romans Had to Combat, and That They Obstinately Defended Their Freedom." "Nothing," Machiavelli declares here,

> made it more laborious for the Romans to overcome [*superare*] the peoples nearby and parts of the distant provinces than the love [*amore*] that many peoples in those times had for freedom; they defended it so obstinately that they would never have been subjugated if not by an excessive virtue [*una eccessiva virtú*] . . . in every least part of the world the Romans found a conspiracy of republics very armed and very obstinate in defense of their freedom.[5]

Such passages do not simply describe Rome's historical experience. They make a judgment about the quality of the *virtú* that enabled Rome to "overcome" other peoples. The most usual reading assumes that Machiavelli's views on Rome's republican *modi e ordini* are entirely positive, and remain so until he reaches the time of Caesar's coup d'état. Book I of the *Discourses* holds up many internal modes as worthy of imitation. And despite its preface's opening remark, "Men always praise ancient times—but not always reasonably,"[6] Book II seems to extend praise for Rome's internal orders to the modes the republic used to dominate Italy and other provinces. If this uncritical stance is assumed, the main purpose of passages describing other people's obstinate struggles to defend their *libertà* is to underscore Rome's vastly superior capacities for *virtuoso* self-ordering. Various chapters throughout the *Discourses* provide examples of this superiority not just in the republic's military *ordini*, but also in the political orders that helped to give it such strong arms and in its judicious use of religion.[7] Since Machiavelli's judgments on many of these Roman *modi* are unequivocally positive, casual readers

---

[5] *D*, II.2.131–33/330–34.
[6] *D*, II.Pref.123/324.
[7] See chaps. 10, 11.

might well interpret his remarks about other people's love of freedom simply as further evidence in his case for imitating republican Rome in every respect. The comments are not, it might seem, meant to direct readers' attention to the long-forgotten merits or legitimate claims of the losers, but only to highlight the rare *virtù* of the victors.

The words Machiavelli uses to evaluate Rome's modes of "overcoming" other peoples, however, raise doubts about whether his judgment is altogether positive. In the statement that Rome could never have "subjugated" (*soggiogati*) these freedom-loving peoples without *una eccessiva virtù*, the italicized phrases offer highly problematic praise when considered in the light of the concept of *virtù* attributed to Machiavelli in preceding chapters. If the arguments offered there are correct, "excessive virtue" is a Machiavellian paradox that, under closer scrutiny, dissolves into an oxymoron. For Machiavelli, I have argued, modes of action that deserve to be called *virtuoso* are by definition modes that recognize the necessity to respect constraints or limits (*termini*). Among the strongest constraints are those posed by various "natural and ordinary" necessities. These include desires found in "any city whatever" to acquire and command; they also include desires to live secure and to live free. Even in the *Prince* Machiavelli observes that "victories are never so clear that the winner does not have to have some respect, especially for justice," and earlier that "one cannot call it virtue to kill one's citizens, betray one's friends, to be without faith, without mercy, without religion; these modes can enable one to acquire empire [*imperio*], but not glory."[8]

If *virtù* rightly understood is a capacity whose exercise is always limited by the agent's respect for such constraints, then *eccessiva virtù* is at best a questionable kind of *virtù*, at worst a form of self-assertion that oversteps prudent bounds and thus ceases to deserve the good name of *virtù* at all. Even if it is possible that in this particular instance Machiavelli *might* have meant to praise the Romans rather than to question their methods, his highly unusual use of the adjective "excessive" with *virtù* should provoke readers to follow his next *discorsi* on Roman modes of "expansion" very carefully before jumping to firm conclusions. Recalling the opening sentence of Book II, "men always praise ancient times, but not always reasonably," they should ask whether the specific *modi* described in subsequent chapters meet the criteria for adequately *virtuoso* "orders" set out in Book I. A close reading of Machiavelli's often enigmatic reasonings suggests that many of the Roman methods he describes in Books II and III exceed the limits of prudent action. They involve perceived betrayals of other cities that had considered themselves friends of Rome, violations of good faith toward friends as well as enemies, merciless cruelty toward peoples defeated in war, and disastrous neglect of the soundest injunctions of Rome's ancient religion. So long as Roman methods of subjugating others did not overstep these limits, Machiavelli suggests, they deserve to be praised. As we saw in the case of the Fabii episode, where the Romans "pulled back to the mark" after violating the "law of nations," Machiavelli follows Livy in distinguishing overassertive Roman policies from virtuous ones, presenting exemplary *prudentissimo* men

---

[8] *P*, XXI.90/181; VIII.35/140.

such as Camillus as models worthy of imitation. But when overassertive methods were responsible for the republic's subjugation of neighboring peoples, as they often were, he questions contemporary opinions that ascribe *virtú* to these modes. If there are now fewer republics than there were in antiquity, and far less "love of freedoms seen in peoples as . . . then," Machiavelli believes

> the cause of this to be rather that the Roman Empire, with its arms and its greatness, eliminated all republics and all civil ways of life. And although that empire was dissolved, the cities still have not been able to put themselves back together or reorder themselves for civil life except in very few places in that empire. However that may be, in every least part of the world the Romans found a conspiracy of republics very armed and very obstinate in defense of their freedom. This shows that without a rare and extreme [*rara ed estrema*] virtue the Roman people would never have been able to overcome them.[9]

Here and elsewhere, Machiavelli does not make critical observations about the Roman *imperio* only to distinguish its freedom-destroying methods from those of the earlier republic. Neither he nor Livy draws a sharp temporal line between the good early republic and later, corrupt empire. Both show the republic struggling to assert and maintain *virtuoso* orders from its birth, facing numerous nearly fatal setbacks throughout its history. Like Livy, Thucydides, and Xenophon, Machiavelli uses history to reexamine the seeds of corruption that were often scarcely noticed at the time, and which posterity tends to ignore because it focuses on dramatic consequences instead of subtler causes. He invites readers to scrutinize the actions of the expanding young republic, asking whether some of the methods used by specific leaders or some of the ambitions of the Roman people complied with the standards of *virtuoso* self-restraint outlined in the last chapter. Were there some modes of action employed by the republic even in its better days that overstepped virtuous limits, thereby introducing elements of corruption that would eventually destroy Rome's internal freedom and produce long-lasting disorders in many parts of the empire?

Machiavelli's passages about the love of freedom exhibited by subjugated peoples do not only function, then, to underline the exceptional quality of Roman *virtú*. They also serve as warnings to agents who imagine that their own city's virtue or power is sufficient to overcome other peoples, but who fail to take stock of feelings at the receiving end of their power.[10] Among the various *naturale e ordinario* "inconveniences" he discusses, I suggest that Machiavelli treats the love of freedom as by far the most powerful obstacle to unilateral, assertive actions. In the *Discourses*, other people's "desires for" or "love" of freedom are invoked as a warning against overassertive agents who think that their material power or superior *virtú* entitles them to impose their will on others.[11]

---

[9] *D*, II.2.132/334.

[10] Recall Archidamus', Diodotus', and the Melians' advice in TPW, I.84, III.45–49, and V.100–102.

[11] Compare Thucydides' (TPW, III.45) remark that it is natural for a free man to revolt against rule by force; and Xenophon, XC, II.223.

The *amore* that peoples have for freedom is not simply love of external independence, although independence is often a precondition for enjoying other forms of freedom. In Book I, chapter 2 of the *Discourses* Machiavelli says that he will take as his main subject cities "that had a beginning [*principio*] far from all external servitude and were at once governed by their own will [*governate per loro arbitrio*]."[12] Both kinds of freedom, independence and self-government, are presented as equally desirable. Later sections will consider whether Machiavelli sees them as sufficient to satisfy the ethical demands of *libertà* as he conceives it. In Book II, chapter 2 he implies that the chief objects of *amore* found in peoples who love *libertà* are free forms of internal order, which he also calls a "free way of life" or *vivere libero*. He uses *libertà* in these two distinct senses throughout the chapter, while suggesting that both have roots in the same basic desires and capacities. On the one hand he distinguishes "the servitude into which the cities come as serving a foreigner" from "that to a citizen of their own."[13] On the other hand, he clearly implies that people who desire the one kind of freedom should, if they reflect prudently, desire the other with equal intensity. The *vivere libero* inside cities cannot be established or maintained securely if a city is too dependent on others, let alone if it is a "subject" city. Conversely, Machiavelli argues that cities with free republican orders are better at using their "own arms" to defend themselves than cities with less free forms of government.[14] Since cities whose citizens cherish their *vivere libero* are less likely to experience the kinds of internal disorders that are often a pretext for foreign intervention, and less dependent on foreign arms for their defense, internally free cities are better at maintaining their independence over time. Machiavelli alludes to the profound interdependence of internal and external *libertà* when he writes that in Italy during the earliest period of Roman expansion

> from the mountains that now divide Tuscany from Lombardy to the point of Italy, all were free peoples [*popoli liberi*]. . . . One sees quite well that in those times . . . Tuscany was free [*libera*] and enjoyed its freedom so much and hated the name of prince so much that when the Veientes, having made a king in Veii for their defense, and asked for aid from the Tuscans against the Romans, they decided after many consultations not to give aid to the Veientes so long as they lived under the king. For they judged it not to be good to defend the fatherland of those who had already submitted [*sottomessa*] to another.[15]

Machiavelli presents the Tuscan decision not to help the Veientes as based on sound prudential reasoning. They judge that cities living under free forms of government—here understood in the classical republican sense of government without kings or princes—are responsibly organized to depend on their own best efforts

[12] *D*, I.2.10/202.
[13] *D*, II.2.133/335.
[14] On the idea that free men are most warlike and the best defenders of "their own," see Hippocrates I, "Airs, Waters, Places," pars. 16 and 23.
[15] *D*, II.2.129/331.

for their self-defense. If they should need external support from other republics, the latter can go to their aid confident that the city they support will not idly depend on others to do their defensive work for them, but that their own citizens will fight hard for their own freedom. If, however, a republic has "made a king for their defense," this action shows its poor judgment about what kind of orders are needed for good defenses, and makes it doubtful that citizens will fight as well as they would on behalf of free orders.

In this crucial chapter and elsewhere, warnings against underestimating others' desires for freedom apply in nearly identical ways whether the *libertà* in question refers to internal forms of government or to independence from unwanted foreign control.[16] When Machiavelli remarks that it is "not good to defend the fatherland of those who had already submitted to another," the one to whom the Veientes had submitted was a king established among themselves, not a foreign power. He implies that acts of submission, whether to a homegrown or a foreign power, show the same unvirtuous lack of self-responsibility in their willingness to depend on "others' arms." Conversely, the willingness to fight for one's own *libertà* is praiseworthy whether the main threats to freedom come from inside or outside a city. For Machiavelli these are simply two distinct contexts where people assert the same, generically human desires. This is especially clear in the narrative structure of Book II, chapter 2 of the *Discourses*, which moves seamlessly from discussing one sense of *libertà* to the other, while treating basic desires for freedom as having the same motives and practical implications in both. The chapter starts by discussing Rome's early difficulties in trying to dominate other peoples and provinces. Yet it goes on to explain these difficulties not through examples of conflicts between peoples, but primarily with examples of popular resistance to tyranny *inside* cities. This suggests motivational affinities between the opponents of internal tyranny and the opponents of external dominion.

Machiavelli's first examples are drawn from ancient Greek writings, not from Roman authors. Readers who want a good account of why uncorrupt peoples value freedom should start, he proposes, with Xenophon's *Hiero*. He begins by noting that one of the chief hallmarks of an internally *un*free city is that a prince or a tyrant "alone, and not his fatherland, profits from his acquisitions. Whoever wishes to confirm this opinion with infinite other reasons," he continues,

> should read the treatise Xenophon makes *Of Tyranny*. It is thus not marvelous that the ancient peoples persecuted tyrants with so much hatred and loved the free way of life, and that the name of freedom was so much es-

---

[16] I follow Machiavelli's usage when distinguishing between "foreign" or "external" and native or internal. His concepts of foreigner (usually *forestiere)* and extrinsic (*estrinseca)* have an important perceptual dimension, especially in relation to neighboring Italian cities and regions. As numerous examples from the *FH* suggest, Florence's neighbors clearly perceive it as a foreign city when it treats them as subjects (*sudditi, subietti)* of its unauthorized dominion. The distinction becomes less sharp when other cities are treated as partners or friends (*compagni, amici)*. Common causes may turn erstwhile foreign enemies into partners who see a region (such as Tuscany) or a province (such as Italy) as their common *patria*.

teemed by them. Thus it happened that when Hieronymus, grandson of Hiero the Syracusan, was killed in Syracuse and the news of his death came to his army . . . it began first to raise a tumult and take up arms against his slayers; but when it heard that freedom was being cried out in Syracuse, being attracted by that name, it became entirely quiet, put down its anger against the tyrannicides, and took thought of how a free way of life could be ordered in that city.

This is followed by a discussion of an episode from Thucydides to demonstrate Machiavelli's next argument: namely, that "it is also not marvelous that peoples take extraordinary revenges against those who have seized their freedom." The example involves the "nobles" inside the city of Corcyra who "took away freedom from the people" during the Peloponnesian War. In response, the popular party regained its strength with Athenian help and imprisoned or killed many nobles. When the rest tried to flee, "the people made a crowd," uncovered the upper part of the prison, and suffocated the nobility with its ruins. "Many other similarly horrible and notable cases," Machiavelli concludes, "also occurred in the said province [of Greece]." This dramatic illustration underlines his point, made again and again from different angles in the chapter: "one sees it to be true that freedom that is taken away from you is avenged with greater vehemence than that which is wished to be taken away [*che quella che ti è voluta tôrre*]."[17] This "extraordinary revenge" by the freedom-loving populace was "not marvelous" but, on the contrary, easily foreseeable by anyone armed with a prudent assessment of *ordinario* and reasonable desires for freedom.

Having begun with these cautionary examples of what peoples may do if deprived of freedom inside their cities, the chapter goes on to draw parallels between Greek and Roman experiences. The Roman examples concern struggles for freedom in relations between Rome and other peoples. In the Greek cities of Syracuse and Corcyra, such struggles took place against native tyrants. In the Roman context as Machiavelli treats it here, the main struggles for freedom were fought by cities and peoples who feared that Rome showed tyrannical tendencies in relation to themselves. He does not mention Rome's internal orders here; the qualities that made them free before the republic was corrupted have already been examined in detail in Book I. In fact, in this extremely important chapter on freedom, the Roman republic is scarcely mentioned at all, except in the passing comment that Rome arrived at "greatness" after it was "freed from its kings."[18] Otherwise only the Roman Empire is discussed, in the unflattering description of its freedom-destroying legacy cited earlier. The Italian analogues to the freedom-loving Syracusans and Corcyrans in Greece are not Romans but the Samnites, one of the nearby peoples who resisted Roman *dominium* most ferociously, first in the Italian Wars described by Livy in the fourth and third centuries BC, and later in revolts

---

[17] *D*, II.2.130–31/332–33. Compare Thucydides, TPW, III.70–85; IV.46–48.
[18] *D*, II.2.129/331.

against Rome in the first century BC.[19] "It seems a wonderful thing," Machiavelli writes, that the Samnites "were so powerful and their arms so sound that they could resist the Romans" for forty-six years "after so many defeats, ruinings of towns, and so many slaughters received in their country. . . . So much order and so much force were there then," he continues in language that echoes the opening lines of the chapter, "that it was impossible to overcome [insuperabile] were it not assaulted [assaltato] by a Roman virtue."[20]

This is the third time in a few pages that Machiavelli has made this kind of paradoxical remark. The first sentence of the chapter says that only an "excessive virtue" could have "subjugated" peoples such as the Samnites who desired freedom so obstinately. In the next paragraph we read that without a "rare and extreme" virtue the Romans could not have "overcome" (superare) the armed and obstinate "conspiracy of republics that opposed them. Now, a few lines later, the desire of non-Romans for freedom is said to have been insuperabile if it had not been "assaulted" by "Roman virtue." I have already questioned whether Machiavelli thinks that virtú can be eccessive without losing the right to the name. In the same way, the phrase estrema virtú strikes a false chord if, as I argued in chapter 4, an adequate conception of virtú involves responsible self-restraint—what Machiavelli described as self-imposed necessità. The third phrase in the series, "a Roman virtue" (una virtú romana), sounds less problematic in terms of Machiavelli's normative vocabulary. But the notion that Roman virtue should "assault" other peoples seeking to defend their own freedom is as disturbingly paradoxical as the concept of an excessive virtue. If virtú depends on ordering and not brute self-assertion, readers might ask, surely it cannot be asserted by means of assaltato, a word that normally connotes unjust violation. Moreover, if another condition for virtú is reflective prudence about the nature of the human material affected by one's actions, then Machiavelli's unequivocal message is that agents who underestimate other people's desires for freedom are both imprudent and deficient in virtú. If it is ever prudent and virtuous to "assault" others, it is least likely to be so when they are seeking to defend their libertà.

The chapter ends by distinguishing more sharply than before between "the servitude [servitú] into which the cities come as serving a foreigner [servendo a un forestiero]" and servitude "to a citizen of their own." By this time it should be clear that the two kinds of servitude do not involve fundamentally different kinds of affront to people who love freedom. On the contrary, Machiavelli pointedly underlines their basic affinity. The love of freedom that induces people to resist both kinds of servitú has, he implies, the same sources in the same human drives. In terms of practical anthropology, other people's desires for freedom should be considered as posing quite ordinary and reasonable—and very strong—constraints on actions, whether the main object of their current desires is external independence or internal political freedom.[21]

---

[19] Livy, LH, VI–X. For a detailed analysis of Rome's recurrent difficulties with its Italian neighbors see Keveaney 1987.

[20] D, II.2.132/334.

[21] See P, II–III.6–16/119–27.

6.2.
The *Florentine Histories* on freedom and the need for self-restraint

Book II of the *Florentine Histories* contains one of Machiavelli's most emphatic accounts of why others' desires for freedom should be taken as a serious limit on any agent's actions. Here he has a group of leading magistrates approach the Duke of Athens, who gained popular support to become prince within the Florentine republic, then set himself up as tyrant. The speakers implore the duke to end his tyranny of his own accord.[22] First they point out that despite his initial popularity, the duke lost popular faith by using "extraordinary" methods to achieve "that which we [citizens] have not granted to you in the ordinary way [*per lo ordinario*]." They then tell the tyrant to beware of the harm he will bring on himself if he persists in flouting popular desires for *libertà*. He should think twice when "seeking to enslave a city which has always lived free," as the risks of doing this are always extremely high. "Have you considered," they ask the tyrant, "how important this is in a city like this, and how vigorous is the name of freedom [*quanto sia gagliardo il nome della libertà*], which no force can subdue, no time consume, and no merit counterbalance?" The speakers appeal to the duke's own self-interest, describing the ever-deepening plight of the tyrannical life in terms that recall the complaints voiced by Xenophon's Hiero. Foreign forces are not enough to hold power; even the most powerful rulers need to trust their own people. The citizens urge the duke to consider "how much force will be necessary to keep such a city enslaved," reminding him:

> That there is not enough time to consume the desires for freedom is most certain, for freedom, one knows, is often restored in a city by those who have never tasted it but who loved it only through the memories of it left to them by their fathers; and thus, once recovered, they preserve it with all obstinacy and at any peril. And even if their fathers had not recalled it to them, the public palaces, the places of the magistrates, the ensigns of the free orders [*liberi ordini*] recall it. These things must be recognized [*cognosciute*] with the greatest desire by citizens.

The speakers then ask whether any policy short of restoring freedom might make it easier for the tyrant to overcome resistance. Can any "merit counterbalance" loss of freedom, they ask rhetorically, or any "deeds" serve as a "counterweight to the sweetness of free life [*contrappesino alla dolcezza del vivere libero*]"? The speakers' answer is clear: "even if your habits were saintly, your modes benign, your judgments upright [*giudizi retti*], they would not be enough to make you loved." If the tyrant believes that any aspects of his personal conduct make a difference when people regard themselves as oppressed, they assure him, "you would be deceiving yourself." Another common stratagem used by tyrants to deflect internal hatreds is to seek external glory for their city as compensation for the loss of internal freedoms. Again, the speakers pour cold water on any thought the duke might have

---

[22] Compare Hiero's voluntary shedding of tyranny, discussed in chap. 2, sec. 2.3.

of trying to secure his tyranny in this way. "Not if you were to add all Tuscany to this empire" would people stop caring about their own freedom, even "if every day you were to return to the city in triumph over our enemies." The speakers explicitly identify the tyrant's foreign conquests with his acts of internal oppression. The more he oppresses other peoples abroad, they argue, the more obvious it will become to his own subjects that they suffer the same oppression. For "all the glory" derived from foreign conquest would not accrue to the people of the city but only to the tyrant; "and the citizens would not acquire subjects [*sudditi*] but fellow slaves [*conservi*] in whom they would see their own slavery aggravated." This would create sympathies across city borders that were bound to work against the tyrant, instead of helping him to divide native from foreign subjects with a view to oppressing both. In short, no matter what precautions he takes, a tyrant will inevitably confront serious threats that stem from popular desires for freedom. He should understand that freedom cannot be traded off against other political goods, or "colored" in ways that prevent people from noticing their oppression. The speakers conclude by laying down a basic maxim of prudent action: "that dominion is alone lasting which is voluntary [*quello dominio è solo durabile che è voluntario*]."[23]

These prudent words, Machiavelli says, "did not move the obdurate spirit of the duke in any part." He insisted that he had no intention to deprive the city of its freedom but only to restore it, arguing that "only disunited cities were enslaved and united ones free." At first, this false conflation of freedom with unity proved rhetorically effective, and a population weary of partisan violence rallied to the duke's side. No sooner had he persuaded the people to grant him power for life, however, than the duke set about destroying popular liberties. In matters of law his sentences were unjust (*ingiusti*), and "the severity and humanity [*severità e umanità*] that he had feigned were converted into arrogance and cruelty [*superbia e crudeltà*]." He gave the most important offices to foreigners, disregarded all civil life, and did violence "without any respect" to women, until the citizens were "full of indignation as they saw the majesty of their state ruined, the orders laid waste, the laws annulled, every decent being corrupted [*ogni onesto vivere corrotto*], all civil modesty eliminated." Just as the Signori had foreseen, the usually fractious population soon put aside sectarian differences, and "the whole people" took up arms, "armed with a cry for liberty." Confronting his now formidable enemies, the duke tried one last time to win the people over with "some humane act." But by now it was too late to hide his true colors under *colore* of feigned *umanità*. And since "indignation appears greater and wounds are graver when liberty is being recovered than when it is being defended," anyone who tried to negotiate with the duke came to a violent end. The duke was sent into exile. The multitude "purged itself" of its rage against the tyrant by mutilating and feasting on the flesh of two

<hr />

[23] *FH*, II.34.92–93/407–8. On the idea of willing as a condition for stable rule, compare TPW, IV.19: "It is natural for men cheerfully to accept defeat at the hands of those who make willing [*hekousiōs*] concessions, but to fight to the bitter end, even against their better judgement, against an overbearing [*huperauchounta*] foe." Later we read that neither force nor betrayal, but only mutual consent (*homologia*), brings stable peace (V.17). Also see TPW, III.46–47, VI.76, IV.107–8.

other men, one an innocent youth. Machiavelli's deadpan, graphic description of this grisly purging outdoes the vivid account in the *Discourses* of the Corcyrans' "horrible" revenge. In both cases, the descriptions of extreme violence aroused by the theft of freedom have both a cautionary and a purgative function. They warn readers to take stock of the predictably violent reactions of people who consider themselves oppressed; and they offer readers a strong, repellent medicine aimed at purging any overambitious humors that they themselves may have.[24]

Machiavelli does not disguise his own judgment in this case. The Duke of Athens deserved harsh retribution, he writes, because "he wanted the slavery [*servitú*] and not the good will [*benivolenza*] of men."[25] He refused to recognize the simple, unmarvelous truth of basic maxims derived from the prudent reflection that people tend to resist attempts to remove their freedom. One is the maxim that stable orders depend on the express or tacit consent of those who live under them: princes and cities "have to be content with the authority [*autorità*]" given them by those they seek to rule, for "that dominion is alone lasting which is voluntary." Variations on this maxim are repeated in various contexts in the *Histories*, with reference to both internal freedom and external independence. Machiavelli has Giovanni de' Medici give his son Cosimo similar advice, which the latter took as a maxim regulating appearances rather than actions. "In regard to the state, if you wish to live secure, accept from it as much as is given to you by laws and by men." This way of seeking public *autorità* brings "neither envy nor danger, since it is what a man takes himself" from others, "not what is given to a man, that makes us hate him."[26]

Throughout the *Histories*, nearly identical maxims apply to the conduct of cities in their external relations. In the Duke of Athens episode, Machiavelli moves back and forth from the civil aspects of the conflict to external ones, using the same language to describe attempts in both contexts to gain power without respecting the will of subjects. His remark that *imperio* is more easily acquired and securely held when one avoids using "all force and obstinacy" echoes the maxims expressed in relation to civil authority. Just as those who wish to rule inside cities are more secure if the people willingly "give" them authority, those who want to build a strong *imperio* should prefer to do so through the support of free cities that help them as "friends" rather than as weak, dependent, and potentially unreliable "subjects."[27] "Being free" themselves, the other towns that Florence had sought to dominate by force were now more willing and better equipped with internal virtue to "help maintain the Florentines' own freedom." From a standpoint of reflective prudence, and without any reference to justice, these remarks suggest that there is greater profit in methods that strengthen one's "own arms" through voluntary friendships and agreements than in attempts to gain power through making subjects.[28] The principle that informs these positions is the same, whether it appears in the context of civil or external relations:

---

[24] *FH*, II.36.94–95/409–10; II.37, 98–99/414–15.

[25] *FH*, II.37.99/416.

[26] *FH*, IV.16.161/491.

[27] The Greek antithesis, found throughout Herodotus, Thucydides, and Xenophon, opposes *philoi* (friends) and *summachoi* (allies) to subjects (*hupēkooi*) or slaves (*douloi*). See chap. 12.

[28] *FH*, II.38.99–100/416–17.

namely, that respect for the free will of subjects is a condition for stable orders. Machiavelli presents the principle through examples suggesting that overassertive agents recognize its force only when it is framed as a prudential maxim, consistent with their own utility. But if appeals to utility are needed for pragmatic reasons to persuade corrupt agents to adopt better methods, the underlying principle holds in the same way whether or not the appeal succeeds in a given case, and whether or not the subjects who assert their free will are compatriots.

One interpretation of these passages about the advantages that flow from respecting the freedom of one's foreign "subjects" is that Machiavelli treats the view they express as hopelessly naïve.[29] This reading is unsupported by any convincing evidence from the text of the *Florentine Histories*, and ignores ample evidence here and in other works that Machiavelli approves of policies that respect other peoples' desires for freedom, even when they have been subjects of one's *imperio*. Indeed, he repeatedly suggests that the naïve ones are those who think it is always naïve to "placate" (*placare*) one's "subjects with peace" rather than "make enemies of them with war."[30] The truly imprudent are those who so underestimate their freedom-loving opponents that they think they are being wise in taking advantage of them. In the Duke of Athens episode Machiavelli draws a direct connection between the internal and external contexts in which desires for freedom may be asserted, underscoring the similar constraints these desires place on prudent action. He directly links the Florentine people's internal struggle to overthrow tyranny with the outbreak of demands for freedom among its subject cities. By throwing out their internal tyrant, the Florentines

> inspired all the towns subject to the Florentines [*terre sottoposte a' fiorentini*] to get back their own freedom. Arezzo, Castiglione, Pistoia, Volterra, Colle, and San Gimignano rebelled, so that with one stroke Florence was left deprived of its tyranny and its dominion [*dominio*]. In recovering its freedom, it taught its subjects how to recover theirs [*nel recuperare la sua libertà insegnò a subietti suoi come potessero recuperare la loro*].[31]

Machiavelli not only describes the *civil* war against tyranny as the direct inspiration for subject cities to regain their external freedom; he also says that the rebellion of the cities left Florence "deprived of its *tyranny*" over them, not of legitimate claims to leadership. The clear implication is that Florence had to change its modes of exercising *autorità* over neighboring cities, or risk facing disorders comparable to those that brought down the tyrant within their city.[32] Internal and external

---

[29] Most recently, Hörnqvist 2004.

[30] See chap. 12, secs. 12.3.–12.7.

[31] *FH*, II.38.99/416.

[32] Compare Thucydides, as discussed in chap. 2. To be clear, Machiavelli's point here is not that Florence behaved as a "tyrant" to other cities only when it was ruled by a tyrant, and necessarily behaved in a friendlier manner when it was freed from tyranny. Not all cities that deprive others of freedom have unfree internal orders, and Florence was a case in point. It had extensive "dominions" that many in the subject cities regarded as depriving them of freedom. Yet this "empire," like Rome's, had largely been established when Florence lived under republican orders.

demands for *libertà* are described as arising from the same generic human desires; the reasons why people fight for civil *libertà* inside cities are fundamentally the same as their reasons for seeking external freedom. This is why Machiavelli can say that "in recovering its freedom" from internal tyranny, Florence "taught its subjects how to recover theirs" against their externally imposed *tiranno e dominio*.

These maxims stress the utility of self-restraint for ambitious men and cities. They say that if they want their *autorità* to be secure rather than fleeting, they have to restrict the means they use when seeking authority to modes that respect the choices of free men. But if appeals to utility are not enough to discourage men or cities from overstepping these limits, sterner warnings must come into play. Machiavelli's maxims of negative prudence stress the great disutility to overassertive agents of seizing or using power without regard for the will of their subjects. Once again, his arguments and language echo Thucydides and Xenophon. Those "lords can keep their lordship safe," he has the Signori warn the duke, "who have few enemies, whom either by death or by exile it is easy to eliminate." But he whose methods create "universal hatred . . . never finds any security, because you never know from whence evil may spring, and he who fears every man cannot secure himself against anyone." Tyrants deceive themselves who imagine that they can ever have complete security while maintaining tyranny. If you try to do this "you aggravate the dangers, because those who remain," and there are always a few, "burn more with hatred and are readier for revenge."[33] In case the reasons Machiavelli presents in support of these maxims still fail to persuade ambitious agents to set limits on their quest for greater authority, his cautionary descriptions of the violent revenge inflicted on tyrants might give them pause where *ragionare* carries no weight. And although it is harder to persuade ambitious cities or peoples to regulate their methods of acquiring power, his vivid descriptions of the disasters brought on Florence whenever the city tried to win "ultimate victory" over neighboring cities have purgative functions similar to his accounts of the revenge taken against tyrannical individuals. The most direct analogue to this technique in the *Discourses* is Livy's episode of the Fabii and the Roman Senate inviting the near-destruction of Rome as a result of having violated the "law of nations." A more oblique warning can be detected in the passage on the legacy of Roman *imperio* cited earlier in this section: the much-vaunted arms and *grandezza* of that empire were used to "eliminate" all republics and all *viveri civili*, which over a thousand years later were still unable "to put themselves back together or reorder themselves for civil life except in very few places."[34]

These and other parts of the *Florentine Histories* carry the same message as Book II, chapter 2 of the *Discourses*: the failure to take seriously people's desires for freedom is one of the most dangerous errors that political actors can make. In both these works and the *Prince* we find the important argument that there are no "middle ways" between "placating" desires for freedom or crushing them ruthlessly.[35] The

---

[33] *FH*, II.34.92/407.

[34] *D*, II.2.132/334.

[35] Machiavelli's notion of a middle way (*via del mezzo*) is easily misconstrued. A middle way is not a happily balanced "mean" between extreme modes of action. Policies that follow middle ways try to

main point of this antithesis is not to say that rulers should be prepared to eliminate all opposition arising from desires for freedom. As Machiavelli observes elsewhere, it is never prudent to seek ultimate victory, and in any case victories made without respect for justice never last.[36] The point is, rather, that if you fail to address desires for freedom, you will face such serious opposition that you will almost certainly be unable to be able to eliminate it. The more realistic of the two options is clearly to respect desires for freedom, since attempts to eliminate opponents driven by those desires are almost always doomed to fail—or at best, lead to victories that carry unbearably high costs for oneself. As the members of the Signori put it when addressing the duke: "you have to believe either that you have to hold this city with the greatest violence (for such a thing the citadels, the guards, and friends from outside many times are not enough)," or "you have to be content with the authority that we have given you." The realistic choice here is the second, freedom-respecting one, since "that dominion is alone lasting which is voluntary."[37]

6.3.
Are desires for freedom universal?

In view of Machiavelli's remarks about the dangers of neglecting others' desires for freedom, it seems reasonable to conclude that these desires should be treated as among the basic anthropological data that must be "presupposed" by civil builders and orderers. In the first book of the *Discourses* he sets down the general maxim that "if a prince wishes to win over a people that has been an enemy to him" in his own fatherland, "I say that he should examine first what the people desires; and he will always find that it desires two things: one, to be avenged against those who are the cause that it is servile; the other, to recover its freedom."[38] Once agents recognize that peoples "always" hate servility and seek freedom, prudent orderers should make it a high priority to "examine what causes are that make [them] desire to be free." If they fail to understand this popular desire, they will fail to establish stable orders as surely as if they underestimate natural human tendencies to *malignità*. Orderers who presuppose *malignità* but do not carefully examine desires for freedom in their subjects, allies, or enemies have only part of the anthropological *cognizione* needed to make sound laws and orders.

Consider, however, two possible objections to this reading. One is that Machiavelli's remarks on desires for freedom do not imply that these desires are universal; they are not obviously found in all times and all cities, but only in some. The other is that he does not regard desires for freedom as equally spread throughout any given population, even in those times and places where they are asserted. If one or both

combine elements of under- and overassertive modes. Since both are *virtú*-deficient, the results are unstable mixtures of modes that sometimes "placate" and sometimes use extreme violence. More prudent modes of action avoid both the extremes and the unstable mixtures. See chap. 1 on "true republics" and chap. 12 on "true" modes of external expansion.

[36] *FH*, II.14.67/378–79; *P* XXI.90/180–81.
[37] *FH*, II.34.92–93/407–8.
[38] *D*, I.16.45/242.

of these objections is fair, this would cast doubt on my argument that Machiavelli treats desires for freedom as a fundamental constraint on any prudent agent's actions. If unlike ambition, envy, or *malignità* desires for freedom are non-universal or held with unequal intensity by different groups of people, this leaves room to argue about how serious a constraint it is in particular cases. It may be that some individuals, sects, cities, or peoples desire freedom less ardently than others, so that the desire cannot be seen as a serious obstacle to assertive action in the way that other *naturale e ordinario* constraints can. Let us look at each objection in turn.

Machiavelli frequently remarks that whereas some peoples display strong desires to enjoy and defend their freedom, others conspicuously lack such desires. He alludes to two causes that might explain their absence. One is that some peoples have never known freedom in the first place, so do not miss it: "that people is nothing other than a brute animal that, although of a ferocious and feral nature, has always been nourished in prison and in servitude." When such a chronically oppressed people is "left free in a field to its fate, it becomes the prey of the first one who seeks to rechain it, not being used to feed itself and not knowing places where it may have to take refuge." The other cause that explains the non-existence of desires for freedom is that people once had then lost it, so that after a time they forget its value. Growing "used to" living without freedom, they do not exercise their capacities for self-legislative reasoning that are constantly at work in the *vivere libero*. They may cease to believe that they have these capacities or, if some seek to use them, find that they do not know how. Whichever the cause, the effects on desires and capacities for freedom are similar. A people "used to living under the government of others" is critically disadvantaged by "not knowing how to reason about either public defense or public offense, neither knowing princes nor known by them." Such a people "quickly returns beneath a yoke that is most often heavier than the one it had removed from its neck a little before." Again, Machiavelli makes clear that the phrase "the government of others" here covers both externally imposed government and government by homegrown tyrants or princes.[39] In these passages desires for freedom are not tied to inextinguishable *natural* drives, but are presented as desires that develop only through the experience of *political* freedom. Moreover, despite the Signori's argument in the *Histories* that people in cities whose freedom has been lost keep recalling its value through the memories of their ancestors, Machiavelli seems to concede that such memories may be enfeebled or extinguished. As we have seen, he argues that after the Roman Empire destroyed civil ways of life in so many provinces, especially Italy and Greece, desires as well as capacities for reconstituting free republics seem to have been fatally weakened. Machiavelli notes with regret that in his own times "there is only one province," presumably Germany, "that can be said to have free cities in it."[40] Since any recent experience of political freedom was so rare, desires for freedom were seldom manifested.

---

[39] The discussion begins: "Infinite examples read in the remembrances of ancient histories demonstrate how much difficulty there is for a people used to living under a prince to preserve its freedom afterward, if by some accident it acquires it" (*D*, I.16.44/240).

[40] *D*, II.2.129/331.

It might seem, then, that desires for freedom are not as universal or timeless as desires to acquire, desires to command, or desires not to be commanded—all of which are different, as we will soon see, from *libertà*. On this view desires for freedom are not part of all human beings' most primitive motivational makeup, but must be nourished through life under free political orders. If we consider empirical evidence, such as the number of free polities, effective popular rebellions, or other overt expressions of desires for freedom among people who currently lack it, we would probably conclude that evidence of the desire for freedom is always uneven across the human species. If so, perhaps we should also conclude that it is a less important constraint on action than generic human *malignità* or other widespread desires. The thrust of Machiavelli's arguments might seem to be that desires for freedom should be taken very seriously *when* someone asserts them strongly, but not that they should presupposed of all individuals or peoples at all times, regardless of their own avowals.

But if the last chapter was right to argue that Machiavelli's anthropology is not based solely on these kinds of empirical evidence, then judgments about the universality of desires for freedom must also be made on other grounds. The chief ground is implied in the distinction between the "natural" condition of being "left free" to one's unregulated fate and the ordered condition of a "free way of life." This corresponds to the distinction drawn in the last chapter between two senses of human nature found in Machiavelli's thought. One refers to *naturale e ordinario* dispositions, appetites, and desires (N1) that do not arise from human acts or self-ordering; the other to human beings' innate capacities (N2) to order, regulate, and discipline their own dispositions, appetites, and desires. I have argued that Machiavelli treats these ordering capacities (N2) as universal, although the extent to which they are manifested in human works varies.[41] If works of *virtù* appear in some places or among some peoples more than others, this does not mean that there are any good grounds for judging that the *capacities* those peoples or places have for *virtù* are innately superior to anyone else's.

The same holds for desires for freedom. Machiavelli is the first to admit that few examples can be found of peoples who asserted desires for a *vivere libero* after a long time without freedom. There are far more examples of peoples who successfully toppled foreign and indigenous kings, princes, or tyrants yet failed to order themselves afterward for a free way of life, and soon fell under an even heavier yoke than the one recently "removed from its neck." Machiavelli often contrasts the ancients' love of freedom with most of his contemporaries' apparent indifference to it.[42] He does not brush any of this depressing evidence under the carpet. Nor, however, does he take it as sufficient reason to abandon efforts to awaken desires for freedom by pointing to notable examples. The discouraging evidence is, after all, based solely on empirical observations. Innate capacities for exercising free will, and hence for *virtuoso* deeds, cannot be known or measured by this kind of evidence. If human desires for freedom are rooted in these innate capacities,

---

[41] *D*, III.43.302/517. See chap. 5.
[42] *D*, II.2.131/333.

and not *only* formed through the experience of political freedom, then the universality of those desires may be presupposed even among people—if there are any such people—who appear never to have asserted them.

Machiavelli never actually says that desires for freedom are rooted in innate, universally human capacities for free will, while he does say that they are formed by the non-universal experience of living under free orders. Why should we conclude that he holds the former view, as well as the latter? The most compelling reason is that at the core of all of his main works is the assumption that strong desires for freedom may be awakened among people who have never yet lived under free orders. Florence is his main case. On the one hand, both the *Discourses* and the *Florentine Histories* present that city as a sorry example of all the attributes that should discourage anyone who wants to awaken desires for *libertà* in people who have never experienced it. On Machiavelli's various accounts, Florence began life as a dependent and unfree city built by an already corrupt Roman Empire. Any observer who did not presuppose the free will of its people might well conclude that they would never develop desires for freedom, since they had no previous experience of self-government. Nevertheless, by Book II of the *Histories* and after over a thousand years of dependence, disorder, and oppression, the Florentines exercise their narrow margin of free will to create an independent republic. Machiavelli does not expressly say that this evidence supports his presupposition, stated in the *Prince*, of innate capacities for free will. But if peoples such as the Florentines can assert desires for independence or self-government before experiencing these forms of *libertà*, it seems reasonable to suppose that those desires have anthropological roots that run deeper than experience.

True, having won their freedom, the Florentines found it excruciatingly difficult to maintain. Yet despite the bitter end of Machiavelli's chronicle, the tone of the work as a whole is instructive and constructive rather than disheartening. No one who reads the speech he gives to the Signori in Book II and notices its plaintive, dying echoes in later chapters can doubt that Machiavelli wants his work to demonstrate the fundamental value of freedom for any decent human life, as well as its fragility. He clearly does not want compatriots to conclude from his narrative of Florence's painful struggles for freedom that because their ancestors had so far failed to secure a stable *vivere libero*, they themselves should abandon hopes of ever succeeding. The moral of his tragic story is exactly the same as that of his depressing account of the state of Italy at the end of the *Prince*. Italy was at the time of writing "more enslaved than the Hebrews, more servile than the Persians, more dispersed than the Athenians." She was "without a head, without order, beaten, despoiled, torn, pillaged, and having endured ruin of every sort." Having said all that, Machiavelli concludes that one must "never give up" hope, not because God or fortune might come to Italy's aid but because even the most downtrodden people still have free will and the capacity to give themselves "new orders."[43] For the same reasons that he refrains from eliminating free will despite weighty evidence against the view that it governs human actions, he insists that desires to "live free"

---

[43] *P*, XXVI.102–5/189–92; XXIV.96–95/185–86.

may be awakened even among people who have long seemed resigned to the un-free conditions in which they live. Some currently downtrodden peoples may not express desires for freedom; some may even seem attached to their slavery. But if desires for freedom may emerge even in conditions of abject slavery, simply because people exert their innate free will in the face of necessity, it follows that it is always imprudent to rule out or underestimate the possibility that *anyone* might assert such desires under pressure.

This brings us to the second objection mentioned above: namely, that it is unclear whether Machiavelli regards desires for freedom as *equally* strong or widely spread across different social classes, occupational groups, peoples, and provinces. In Book I of the *Discourses* he notes that those who command are often able to "so blind the multitude" that the latter fails to "recognize the yoke that it was putting on its own neck." Taken out of context, such remarks might seem to imply that the "multitude" do not desire freedom enough, or in the right way. If they did, they would not be so easily led to abandon freedom, displaying "such corruption and slight aptitude for free life." But Machiavelli offers numerous examples showing that desires for freedom are not found only in men or peoples of superior mettle, education, or leadership capacities. They are connected to concerns about security among the many as well as to desires of the few to command, and can be observed in members of all social groups and occupations. An orderer who examines well "what causes . . . make [peoples] desire to be free," Machiavelli declares, "will find that a small part of them desires to be free so as to command." But "all the others, who are infinite, desire freedom so as to live secure." Desires for freedom, then, are at least as intense among the many in any city or province as among the few. In cities that have been deprived of freedom, princes "will *always* find" that the people has two desires: "one, to be avenged against those who are the cause that it is servile; the other, to recover its freedom."[44]

If Machiavelli implies that desires for freedom are found in equal force among the "many," he also suggests that those desires have more appropriate objects and modes of expression among the many than among those who regard themselves as their superiors. The majority of people can "easily be brought to live free and ordered" so long as they have not been corrupted, and corruption springs from the "heads," not from the "trunk."[45] For this reason Machiavelli advises orderers who seek "to constitute a guard for freedom" to imitate the Romans, who put this guard in the hands of "popular men" rather than those of the "great." "One should," as he says, "put on guard over a thing those who have less appetite for usurping it."

> Without doubt, if one considers the end of the nobles and of the ignobles, one will see great desire to dominate in the former, and in the latter only the desire not to be dominated; and, in consequence, a greater will to live free, being less able to hope to usurp it than are the great. So when those who are popular are posted as the guard of freedom, it is reasonable that they have

---

[44] *D*, I.17.48–49/244–45; I.16.46/242, emphasis added.
[45] *D*, I.16.46/242; I.17.47/243–44.

more care of it, and since they are not able to seize it, they do not permit others to seize it.[46]

Here Machiavelli touches on a point that is essential for identifying what is most distinctive in his conception of political freedom, or *vivere libero*. Desires for freedom may be deficient, excessive, or ordered to avoid both deficiency and excess. They are most obviously deficient when they do not motivate people to resist internal or external oppression. They can be judged excessive when they lead to actions that overstep the limits set by others' actual or potential desires for freedom. Excessive desires can only be satisfied by dominating others and usurping freedom that is rightly theirs. When desires for freedom are excessive in this sense, they cease to deserve the name of *libertà* at all: they are more accurately called *ambizione* or *dominio*.[47] Desires for an appropriately limited kind of *libertà*, Machiavelli suggests, are therefore more often found in the popular and the many than in the few. If there is an unequal distribution of desires and aptitude for ordered, law-governed freedom across social and economic groups, the deficit is on the side of the powerful few, not the "blind multitude."

These arguments suggest that it is prudent to consider the potential for such desires as universal and spread equally among different parts of any given population, since they are rooted in innate capacities for free will. Orderers should consider desires for freedom as a limit on their legislation in two respects. From an empirical standpoint (N1), they should recognize the connection between those desires and other natural drives, such as self-preservation. From an ethical standpoint (N2), they should recognize that desires for freedom are strong and universal because they are rooted in innate human capacities for self-legislative virtue. When considered from the first standpoint, desires for freedom must be respected for reasons of prudence; if a legislator ignores them, he will almost certainly provoke resentment and resistance to his laws' authority. When considered from the second standpoint, a people's current disinclination to resist subjection should not be written off as unthreatening to their oppressors. Even without visible *evidence* that a subject people or classes of people inside a polity desire equal freedom, there are good *reasons* for presupposing their equality in this respect.

6.4.
Inadequate conceptions of freedom

Our discussion so far has focused on the importance Machiavelli assigns to desires for *libertà*. It is not yet clear, however, precisely what he thinks those desires are for. In negative terms, people who desire *libertà* want to be rid of tyranny, servitude, or

---

[46] *D*, I.5.17–19/210–12.

[47] In Greek, the usual word for excessive or unlimited freedom is *exousia*; for exemplary uses that connect *exousia* to imprudent and harmful conduct, see Plato, *Euth.* 301e, *Gorg.* 494e, 525a. Compare similar uses of the word *exestai* in *Gorg.* 461a–d for unimpeded speech or choice. Both are related to the highly undesirable condition of lawlessness (*anomia*), which cannot sustain freedom (*eleutheria*) in any adequate sense of that word.

slavery. Machiavelli also suggests that they often want to get rid of princes or kings. In positive terms, they may identify freedom with independence from external control, self-government, and simply a "free way of life." For most commentators on Machiavelli's idea of freedom, it is enough to underline these elements, which can also be found in ancient and humanist conceptions of republican freedom. But if we ask what more precise conditions Machiavelli thinks are needed to satisfy any of these desires, it is harder to find answers in most of the scholarly literature, including that which sees Machiavelli as an important theorist of republics. It is even harder to find a probing discussion of how Machiavelli distinguished between more and less adequate conceptions of *libertà*. Indeed, much of the scholarly literature gives the impression that such distinctions are unimportant for Machiavelli.

To see what conceptions of *libertà* Machiavelli regards as reflectively adequate, we need to ask what conceptions he sees as inadequate. We have already encountered episodes in which the name of *libertà* was invoked to rally people behind a particular leader or cause, yet where Machiavelli suggests that those who make the appeal had a deeply flawed conception of *libertà*. The same pattern is repeated again and again in the *Histories*. First people desire freedom and demand the end of tyranny, thinking that this is enough. But then they fail to establish orders that secure a free way of life. In other cases when people are taken in by some persuasive leader's promise to satisfy their desires for freedom, this happens because they have naïve or confused notions of what freedom is and what actions support it. The main basis for Machiavelli's distinctions between more and less adequate conceptions is set out early in the *Discourses*. In the first few chapters, he uses the word "free" (*libera*) in two senses that do not deserve the name of *libertà*, although they have some relation to it. The notions of (1) becoming free and (2) having "free opportunity" (*libera occasione*) are both quite distinct from, and may easily be at odds with, living free (*vivere liberi*) or "in freedom."[48]

The basis for the distinction (1) between "becoming free" and living in freedom is whether or not freedom is a condition founded on *stable orders*. Becoming free is an event or process that does not necessarily lead to a stable condition of living freely. It may be a transient condition that does not lead to greater freedom, but rather to conflicts that lead people back to a greater yoke than they wore before. For Machiavelli the phrases "living free" or a "free way of life" refer to a stable, ordered condition. He reserves the word *libertà* for such conditions, never using it for "natural" conditions in which *virtuoso* ordering has not taken place. According to Machiavelli's reasoning, there cannot be a natural condition of freedom; becoming free from oppression may lead to *libertà*, but by itself it is not *libertà*. Men living outside human laws and orders are not yet living a properly human life, and Machiavelli's concept of *libertà* sets normative standards appropriate for human beings capable of *virtuoso* self-ordering. It is not a naturalistic concept that could equally describe a condition of wild animals "left free in a field." Machiavelli does acknowledge intermediate stages when the conditions adequate to the name of *libertà* are in the process of construction, but not yet firm. In Rome, for example, he says that Romulus and other early kings "made many and good laws conforming also to a free way of life." But these were still incomplete and therefore vulnerable to corrosion. So "when that city was left free [*rimase libera*]" from the rule of kings, it was not properly speaking a free city, providing conditions for a free way of life. For "many things that were necessary to order in favor of freedom were lacking, not having been ordered by those kings."[49] The word *libertà* is used only for the stabler conditions established after the kingship was abolished and replaced by republican orders.

The basis for the second distinction (2) between having "free opportunity" and "living free" or in freedom is whether or not an agent's actions and choices are *limited*.[50] Machiavelli never uses *libertà* or its cognates for actions that respect no limits except those imposed by brute force. Individuals and peoples can only be said to live in freedom when they have freely imposed constraints on their own actions, optimally through "laws and orders" authored by themselves. Machiavelli stresses throughout the *Discourses* that "men never work any good unless through necessity," especially *necessità* applied by their own laws. On the other hand, "where choice [*elezione*] abounds and one can make use of license, at once everything is full of confusion and disorder." Unlimited "free opportunity" leads to disorder, allowing those who do not observe limits to impose their *malignità* without respect for others. The formal basis for the distinction between *libertà* and *licenza* is clear here. *Licenza* involves unlimited private choice. *Libertà* is an ordered condition where a number of people live in freedom because all of their actions are constrained under laws. In Machiavelli's vocabulary, having "free opportunity" in the sense of recognizing few or no constraints on one's actions deserves the name of *licenza*, not *libertà*.[51] The phrase "excessive liberty," like "excessive *virtù*," is an oxymoron because *libertà* in any adequate sense is by definition a non-excessive, limited, and regulated condition.

Stable order (1) and limits (2), then, are the two main formal characteristics distinguishing normatively adequate desires for *libertà* from desires to become free or have "free opportunity." When people express the second type of desire without tying it to the first, they do not normally refer to either order or limits as a necessary part of what they want. Instead they think of being or becoming free as a matter of removing constraints, or acting in an unconstrained manner. Obviously, Machiavelli recognizes the removal of *some* constraints as a necessary step toward recovering freedom lost or founding free orders anew. But as argued in chapter 4,

---

[49] *D*, I.16.44/240; I.2.14/206.

[50] *D*, I.3.15/207.

[51] Machiavelli's consistent use of words is striking by comparison with other Roman and Roman-inspired republican writers, who frequently use the phrases "excessive liberty" and "excess of liberty" as a synonym for license; see Cicero, *Republic* 99–101, Livy, *LH*, I.107. Also compare Plato (*Rep.* 562b–d), whose Socrates speaks of insatiable and excessive desires for freedom as the main cause that destroys the order of *politeia* and brings tyranny. The freedom/license distinction derives from the Greek contrast between true *eleutheria* (freedom) or *autonomia*, and *anarchia*, *exousia* (license) or *paranomia*, *anomia* (lawlessness), which many mistakenly call freedom. See Plato, *Rep.* 557b–c, 562d–564a, 569c, 572d–e and similar passages in *Laws*; and TPW, III.82–84, VII.69/485, VIII.63–64, 67.

he also regards the imposing of other constraints authorized or authored by agents themselves as a necessary condition for *libertà*.

Once these distinctions are spelled out, it becomes easier to see why Machiavelli regards some conventional republican appeals to *libertà* as dangerously vague "generalities" that need to be rethought in a more rigorously reasoned way.[52] In the *Histories* and the *Discourses* he gives many examples of how legitimate desires for freedom may be expressed in ways that reflect confused, self-serving, or incomplete notions of what freedom requires. Some of the most serious confusions and abuses of the good name of freedom are discussed in the next section. Here I consider Machiavelli's appraisal of four conceptions of freedom frequently invoked in republican discourse: freedom as command, as non-subjection, as non-domination, and as non-dependence. None of these conceptions is entirely wrong on Machiavelli's criteria; all have a place in his account of freedom, as they do the wider republican tradition. But unless they are tied explicitly to criteria of stable order and self-imposed constraints, they remain deficient. By itself, none supplies a sufficient account of what freedom is or why it is valuable.

6.4.1. Freedom as command

According to a first conception, freedom is understood primarily as a right of individual or collective agents to seek positions of *command*. As we have seen, Machiavelli says that those who desire freedom in order to command men or peoples are a minority in any city. Nevertheless, he does not dismiss their conception of freedom as a right to seek command as nothing more than a mask for excessive ambition. Although in some cases that is all it is, in others the desire to be free in this sense stems from motives that deserve respect. Some want to be free to command because they have strong natural drives toward leadership. Others seek this kind of freedom because they see that if they do not put themselves forward for positions of command, others who are less competent or trustworthy will seek to command them. Whatever the motives, Machiavelli insists that good *ordine* should accommodate desires to be free to command. Insofar as governments that thwart such desires are not ordered "in favor of freedom," addressing them is a necessary condition for *libertà*. But it is by no means a sufficient condition. Desires to be free to seek command must be regulated by more fundamental constraints on those desires since, if left unchecked by strict laws, they invariably lead to excessive self-assertion. *Licenza*, not *libertà*, results when agents see freedom simply as a condition that removes restraints on their desires to command, but does not demand that they accept limits on their own "free opportunity" in acting.

6.4.2. Freedom as non-subjection

A second conception of *libertà* mentioned in Machiavelli's works views freedom primarily as a condition of *non-subjection*. Subjection, servitude, and slavery are

---

[52] See *Discursus*, discussed in chap. 1, sec. 1.7.

direct ways of exerting vastly unequal power, whereby the subjecting agent exerts extreme, asymmetrical constraints on the subject. Shedding subjection is clearly necessary for any condition that deserves the name *libertà*. But again, it is far from sufficient. As Machiavelli points out, people often say that they desire freedom when they mean that they want simply to be relieved of the extreme asymmetrical constraints inflicted by servitude, slavery, tyranny, or the status of being subjects of another. Yet they have no clear notion of what—if any—orders should replace those that currently subject them. Machiavelli's distinctions imply that two steps are needed for people living in subjection to achieve any satisfactory kind of *libertà*. First they need to shed the extreme constraints that subject them; then they need to build new orders for themselves that place reasonable, reciprocal constraints on everyone living under those orders, instead of the extreme, arbitrary, and asymmetrical constraints imposed by tyrannies. In examples described in the *Florentine Histories*, the first part was often easy enough once the fractious people was moved by common hatred of a tyrant to overcome its divisions. The hard part was the second step: getting different sections of the liberated people to agree on the new, self-imposed constraints needed to constitute secure *libertà*. It usually transpires that many of the people roused to action by the name of *libertà* lack any clear notion of the compromises and new constraints that the second, "building" step might require. The least prudent perhaps do not even conceive that conditions of stable *libertà* must be built by hard work, thinking that to regain the *libertà* they had lost, it was enough to throw off a particular yoke. This, Machiavelli explains, is why "cities, and especially those that are not well ordered that are administered under the name of republic, frequently change their governments and their states not between liberty and servitude, as many believe, but between servitude and license."[53]

Although escaping subjection is always good, then, the act of shedding tyranny may bring only fleeting benefits if it is not anchored in an account of what a stable condition of freedom would require, and how it might be constructed. Otherwise action aimed at satisfying desires to become free from subjection might fail dismally to establish freedom, and soon send the briefly liberated back to conditions of tyranny. Responsible uses of the word *libertà* should, Machiavelli implies, highlight the building more than the shedding aspects of freedom. It is easier to rally people to shed subjection with dramatic cries of *libertà* than to build free orders, and much easier to arouse them against an oppressor than to persuade them to subject themselves willingly to new constraints.

6.4.3. Freedom as non-domination

A third conception of *libertà* commonly associated with republican thinking sees freedom primarily as a condition of *non-domination*. I understand domination as more diffuse and less direct than subjection. Like subjection, it involves asymmetrical constraints imposed unilaterally by one party. Subjection normally exerts constraints by directly applying or threatening the use of force or other extreme

[53] *FH*, IV.1.146/473–74; III.27.142–43/468–69.

sanctions, such as the withdrawal of material benefits deemed crucial for the weaker agent's well-being. By contrast, when an agent charges another with dominating him, he often means that the dominant party exerts unauthorized constraints of an indirect kind, often without the overt use or threat of physical sanctions. One agent may dominate another in a limited way, with a view to achieving specific aims; or more continuously, with a view to controlling others' actions and choices on many issues and on a long term-basis.[54] Once again, some of Machiavelli's most vivid examples of how *dominare* or *dominio* undermine freedom come from the *Florentine Histories*. In the context of civil life, he describes how conflicts between Blacks and Whites, Guelfs and Ghibellines, or pro- and anti-Medici sects frustrated occasional efforts to build stable orders based on reciprocal constraints. Since none of the main *sètti* would authorize the same constraints on their own actions that they wanted to impose on rivals, each one sought to dominate the other at every turn, and insisted that public *libertà* depended on their own dominion. On Machiavelli's account, whereas in Rome parties favored by the "ignobles" had sought only "not to be dominated," in Florence the universal refusal to share power drove even such parties to seek "ultimate victory" over rivals, convinced that those who do not dominate others must end up being dominated.[55] He describes analogous struggles among Italian cities seeking to dominate the others for the sake of glory, security, or both.

Machiavelli suggests that such conduct must be appraised from two sides at once. On the one hand, agents who seek to dominate others clearly threaten conditions of public *libertà*, as well as the freedom of those they dominate. To this extent, public conditions of *libertà* are inconsistent with entrenched asymmetries of power that allow some agents to dominate others on a continuous basis. Moreover, agents are justified in regarding attempts to exert unauthorized constraints on their choices in specific instances as unjust incursions on their freedom. On the other hand, Machiavelli is extremely wary of republican rhetoric that treats the absence of domination as a sufficient or primary condition for *libertà*, though he does see it as a necessary condition. If conceived in negative terms of opposition to or the absence of domination, this still leaves open the question of what further, positive ordering is needed to secure conditions in which desires to dominate are kept within well-regulated bounds. Once again, unless people who conceive freedom as non-domination tie this conception to a clear notion of regulative orders, there is a risk that desires not to be dominated will take the form of merely negative resistance to *any* stable orders. The risk arises from a tendency, frequently noted by Machiavelli, for those whose main desire is "not to be dominated" to conflate *any* relations of authority and obedience with illegitimate *dominio*. People who have thrown off domination sometimes think that this suffices to give them freedom, and are loath to set up new relations of command and obedience that they fear might generate new forms of domination. They view all inequalities in authority as suspect, even those that are duly authorized by the will of citizens and that are

---

[54] For a valuable discussion see Pettit 2001, 138–49.
[55] *FH*, II.14.67/378–79.

subject to scrutiny under the laws.[56] In Machiavelli's view, however, laws that create unequal authorities—relations of command and obedience—are preconditions for any order that deserves the name. Well-ordered, publicly authorized inequalities are also preconditions for political *libertà*. Non-domination cannot mean dispensing with them in a radically egalitarian democracy. Many individuals have thrown off particular forms of domination; precious few have known how to build new cities ordered for freedom. One of the bedrocks of such knowledge is to realize that agents are most free not when they start out with few constraints, but when despite constant pressures they choose well how to order themselves to meet them. To move from a condition of non-domination to a condition of stable *libertà*, positive self-ordering is at least as important as the shedding of pressures or agents that dominated one before.

Another condition needed to anchor conceptions of freedom as non-domination concerns *how* domination is shed and how orders aimed at prohibiting domination are established. I argue later in this chapter that Machiavelli treats respect for free agency as a basic criterion of good ordering, thus ruling out various means for pursuing the end of non-domination.

6.4.4. Freedom as non-dependence

A fourth conception touched on in Machiavelli's writings considers *libertà* as a condition of *non-dependence*. Early passages in the *Discourses* refer to "free" and "freedom" as conditions of non-dependence, as in Book I, chapter 1, where Machiavelli writes that Rome "had a free beginning, without depending on anyone."[57] Dependence is distinct from both subjection and domination insofar as the asymmetrical constraints that operate in dependent relationships are not always imposed intentionally by one agent on another. Whereas domination involves some deliberate acts aimed at exerting unequal influence on the dominated, one party may be dependent on another even if the latter has done nothing to encourage that dependence. The relation may arise simply from the dependent party's comparative weakness in certain essential resources, which compels it to look to others for support. The resources most openly discussed in Machiavelli's writings are military. When he argues that princes, republics, "builders," and cities should seek to depend on themselves and avoid depending on others, he uses the phrases "one's own arms" and "others' arms" as metaphors for these conditions. In all his works, depending on one's own arms is treated as a necessary condition for *libertà* in individuals or in cities. Individuals or cities that depend on the arms of others, by contrast, cannot be regarded as stably free even if they are partly "ordered for freedom."[58]

---

[56] The Florentine people's obsession with non-domination led to very short terms of office, constant turnover in personnel at all levels of government and administration, and other destabilizing policies. Machiavelli suggests that polities without clearly ordered, stable ranks of authority never stay free for long.

[57] D, I.1.9/202.

[58] Examples of partly but unstably free orders include those made by Romulus and the other Roman kings, and those of the Veientes after they created a king in the midst of republican orders.

While non-dependence is a necessary part of Machiavelli's conception of *libertà*, however, it is both insufficient and stands in need of clarification. In all his writings Machiavelli implies the need to distinguish clearly between adequate and inadequate senses of non-dependence or independence. One inadequate sense equates independence with the absence of serious constraints. As Machiavelli stresses from the first chapter of the *Discourses, virtuoso* individuals and cities always depend to some degree on constraining conditions that they have not chosen. The notion of complete independence from constraints, including some imposed by the intentional or non-deliberate actions of others, is illusory, and desires to achieve independence in this sense are unreasonable. True, the *Discourses* describe free cities as "those that had a beginning far from all external servitude and were at once governed by their own will."[59] But Machiavelli also says that builders depend on constraining "necessities," both natural and man-made, to establish and maintain their cities in freedom. If agents must find pre-existing constraints in place that "necessitate" they exercise free will, then on Machiavelli's reasoning, free builders and other agents are in an important sense heavily *dependent* on natural and human necessities whose absence would render them less free. At the core of his notion of non-dependence is the following paradox: in order to be independent vis-à-vis *some* agents or environmental constraints, you first have to recognize—and authorize—your inescapable dependence others, and then build constructively on these constraints.

This suggests another inadequate sense of non-dependence or independence, one that equates these conditions with self-sufficiency. As chapter 11 suggests, the main argument of the *Prince* is structured around an implicit distinction between independence wrongly conceived as self-sufficiency, and independence adequately conceived as dependence on an expanded and enriched understanding of "one's own arms" (*armi proprie*). To "depend on one's own arms" does not mean that a prince can survive all alone, dictating his own terms to others unilaterally. A prince who depends only on his own arms knows two things: first, how to identify the people and resources he *must* depend on for any defenses he wants to build; and second, how to establish good orders for those people and resources so that they reliably serve as *his* arms and not someone else's. Princes who act on this knowledge may become independent of *foreign* arms only because and insofar as they realize that they have no choice but to depend on their *own* people. This realization should induce them to strengthen reciprocal obligations between themselves and the populace, not to break free of duties on their side. Any prince who thinks he can become independent of foreign powers *and* the goodwill of his own people is badly deluded. It is unrealistic to conceive independence or non-dependence in absolute, unilateral terms. The only reasonable forms of independence are those based on a prudent decision to authorize some people rather than others as conditions for one's own actions, acknowledging that one is necessarily dependent on them. Once that dependence is admitted, prudent agents can proceed to establish mutual obligations that correct any freedom-threatening asymmetry in a relationship, so

---

[59] *D*, I.2.10/202.

that agents who depend on one another tend to see themselves as interdependent rather than dependent. According to Machiavelli, individuals and cities, princes and peoples must always depend on others in some respects, but they can order their relations of mutual dependence in ways that tend to enhance or undermine their freedom of action.[60]

Dangerous misjudgments often occur because desires for freedom as non-dependence are not qualified in these ways. Clearly there are always some individuals and cities that are more powerful than others, or that have resources that others think they need for their own prosperity or defense. If the most free were those who seemed to depend least on any constraints they had not imposed themselves and the least free were those forced to work under physical or ethical necessity to others, it would make sense to conclude that power and *libertà* go hand in hand. Since on this view power always expands freedom, it would follow that power should not be limited, since limits might undermine freedom. But while Machiavelli certainly thinks that power and freedom are mutually supportive, it is not at all clear that he thinks that military or economic power are primary constituents of *libertà*. The relations between power and freedom are close, but capacities for political or personal *libertà* do not depend primarily on de facto resources or power. Rather, the lesson of many examples in all the works—perhaps the core Machiavellian argument—is that personal and political power ultimately depends on something that agents can choose, however strong or weak they are at a given time: the choice to consider oneself as a free agent even under severe constraints, and to act accordingly.

6.5.
The rhetoric of *libertà* in republics

Before considering how Machiavelli seeks to improve on these conceptions, let us look at some examples of what happens when people apply normatively deficient conceptions of *libertà* to specific conflicts. Even if their conceptions are partly right, the failure to reason more carefully about what is needed to complete them can lead to serious misjudgments committed in the name of freedom. The *Florentine Histories* are full of cautionary examples of how freedom may be misconceived even in republics. Sometimes the word is cynically abused by men who want to become prince or tyrant in a republic. Sometimes it is used with good intentions by men who sincerely want to uphold republican orders, but who fail to grasp the conditions needed for stable *libertà*.

Almost everyone in Florence, Machiavelli observes, claimed to be a champion of freedom. Since the language of republican *libertà* was the dominant idiom of Florentine politics, anyone who sought public authority was obliged to use it. There was, however, usually a vast gulf between *onesto* words and *disonesto* deeds.

---

[60] Compare TPW, IV.108, IV.126, VI.18, and VI.78 on the limits of workable *autokratos* and *autarkos* (self-rule, self-sufficiency), noting that both stand in tension with good orders and tend toward *anomia*.

"Only the name of freedom" was fulsomely praised, on behalf of deeds undeserving of the name. On the one hand it was "extolled by the ministers of license," who were mostly "men of the people." On the other it was brandished "by the ministers of servitude, who are the nobles."[61] All the main parts of the city, he suggests, were chronically prone to confuse freedom with license. Instead of realizing that stable freedom for individuals, groups, or cities depends on setting some limits on the exercise of everyone's will, Florentines stubbornly resisted attempts to regulate their own freedom by means of laws. The whole city, Machiavelli writes, was "accustomed to do and to speak about everything and with every license and could not bear to have its hands tied and its mouth sealed."[62] None of the city's governments ever amounted to what the *Discursus* calls a "true republic": all were dominated by poorly regulated humors that drove them toward either tyranny or license, both conditions in which "there neither is nor can be any stability, because the one state [tyranny] displeases good men, the other [license] displeases the wise; the one can do evil easily, the other can do good only with difficulty; in the one, insolent men have too much authority, in the other, fools." Machiavelli's damning judgment on his beloved city's history is that the Florentines "are unable to bear slavery," yet "do not know how to maintain freedom."[63]

Now and then, common desires for freedom appear to override partisan divisions in the *Florentine Histories*, but never for long. Too often those desires are mixed with private ambitions that undermine republican *libertà*, however earnestly it is desired. In one episode Machiavelli describes a Genoese character trying to restore his fatherland's freedom together with "fame and security for himself." He runs into the piazza shouting out "the name of liberty"; and "it was a wonderful thing to see with what haste" the Genoese people "ran to this name." The protagonist's aspirations are somewhat discredited by the fact that he himself shared responsibility for the previous loss of his fatherland's freedom. In Florence too, the narrative implies, such men could always arouse the multitudes to attack their rivals, "shouting" the good words "'people, arms, liberty' and 'death to the tyrants.'" Both the leaders of such risings and the Florentine people were less ready to put down their arms after shedding tyranny, and to reflect on what measures were needed to build up stably free orders. In particular, the Florentine people showed excessive desires not to be commanded. Refusing to recognize their opponents' status as free agents, they "fought to be alone in the government." This desire, Machiavelli remarks, was not just a recipe for disorder but "injurious and unjust."[64]

This uncompromising attitude, summed up in the idea that every party wanted "ultimate victory," made the city vulnerable to seduction by corrupt, self-serving uses of the word *libertà*. Already in the earliest days of the fledgling republic, Machiavelli identifies weaknesses in its foundations that would later pave the way

---

[61] *FH*, IV.1.146/473–74.

[62] While he judges it good to "reason about everything" or to give any opinion "with reasons," he describes the failure to punish those who make slanderous "accusations" as one of the main threats to republican freedoms (*FH*, II.36.95/410–11; *D*, I.18.49; I.7–8/217–22).

[63] *FH*, IV.1.146/473–74; II.36.95/410–11.

[64] *FH*, V.6–7.192–93/527–28; III.105–6/423–24.

for the Medicis to become de facto "princes" by popular acclaim. Recurring violence between people and nobles created ideal conditions for would-be princes to seek power by using means that did not obviously violate established laws and orders. The language of freedom was frequently (mis)used to mobilize people around "private" aims that were bound to destroy the very republic and *libertà* speakers claimed to defend. One of Machiavelli's earliest examples of such corrupt rhetoric occurs when the Duke of Athens courts popular support for his private ambitions by invoking the language of republican freedom, employing a simple rhetorical sleight-of-hand. First he asserts that freedom depends on civil "unity": "only disunited cities were enslaved and united ones free." It follows that if the people give him the authority to enforce unity, he will be able to give them the freedom they have lost. If "by his ordering" Florence "should rid itself of sects, ambition, and enmities, he would be giving it liberty," not, as his republican critics claimed, "taking it away." On Machiavelli's arguments, the idea that unity is a precondition for freedom carries an obvious appeal in conditions of violent civil conflict. Yet the premise that unity is a condition for freedom is dangerously misleading, for reasons already set out. If unity is understood in a strong sense, implying the need to eliminate conflicting humors, it is both impracticable and destructive of *libertà*. The only kind of union that might be compatible with freedom would be based on strong self-imposed laws and orders that regulate different parts of a city, so that each agrees to share authority with the others. Any prudent solution to Florence's conflicts would have to start with laws "ordered by which these humors of the nobles and the men of the people are quieted or restrained so that they cannot do evil." If and only if it has such *fondamenti*, "then that city can be called free and that state be judged stable and firm."[65]

While understanding how fear or exhaustion may confound popular judgments, Machiavelli is not uncritical of those who failed to see through the duke's self-serving rhetoric. The immediate cause of the failure, he suggests, may have been the people's understandable desire to find a solution to civil strife. But a deeper cause lay in a less excusable desire that created the strife in the first place: namely, the Florentine people's "unreasonable desire" not to share authority with the nobles. This generated interminable conflicts that often forced them to depend on "others' arms" for their own defense. Seeing this happen over and over, ambitious men like the duke—and later the Medicis—were encouraged to play the role of people's defender. They could, Machiavelli writes with barely concealed bitterness, see "how liberal the Florentines had been with their liberty, how they gave it now to the king, now to the legates, now to other men of lesser quality." Any ambitious man could think that "if he led" the people "into some necessity," raising the specter of some internal or external threat, "it could easily happen that they would make him prince." If Florence or any other city hopes to maintain freedom, then, it is not enough to place checks on would-be princes and tyrants. Free orders will lack stable foundations if the people who live under them do not accept reasonable limits on their *own* authority. If all the warring groups in Florence had

---

[65] *FH*, II.35.93/410–11; IV.1.146/473.

accepted limits on their private desires, agreed to share authority, dealt with their enmities by "disputing" instead of by "fighting," and ended their disputes "with a law" instead of "with exile and death," they would not have had the civil wars that drove them repeatedly into the arms of usurpers.[66] They would have realized that to deserve the high value people assign to the word *libertà*, freedom must be based on laws that limit private wills, so that none is allowed a licentious free rein. If citizens of republics frequently recalled that *libertà* is not *licenza*, that it depends on constraints imposed by laws and is destroyed by disrespect for laws, they would be much slower to give away their freedom to false defenders.

When dealing with the Medicis' rise to princely powers, Machiavelli examines some of the ingenious new ways in which the language of *libertà* was used to justify self-interested, crowd-pleasing policies. A noteworthy example occurs in Book VI, in the context of external relations. It shows that corrupt conceptions of *libertà* may be used not only to deny rivals inside a city their share of authority; they are also used to deny other cities and peoples the right to authorize or reject external interventions. Forced to take sides in the contest between Florence and Venice for dominance in northern Italy, the city of Milan opted for an alliance with the Venetians. Among "the chief articles" of their treaty, Machiavelli reports, was a Venetian promise "to do their utmost for the defense" of Milanese freedom. Threats to that freedom came from inside and outside Milan. Inside, Count Francesco Sforza was trying become prince in the city, thereby weakening its internal freedoms. He did so with external support from the Medici party in Florence, whose leaders hoped to install an authoritarian ruler in Milan who would keep the city on their side against the Venetians. Against this background of power-political rivalries, Machiavelli has Cosimo de' Medici strike a transparently self-serving pose as a defender of other peoples' freedom. If the main reason why the Milanese signed up with the Venetians was to protect their *libertà*, Cosimo argues, then they made the wrong choice of protector. Pretending to share Milanese concerns for their own freedom, he insists that Sforza is more likely to keep Milan free. In this way Cosimo justifies Florentine support for the count's ambitions without openly referring to Florence's own desires for *dominio*.[67]

The ambitions that lurk behind Cosimo's apparent concern for Milan's freedom are revealed, however, in two ways. First, although he presents his preferred policies as a means of defending Milan's freedom, their effect is clearly to deprive the Milanese of both internal freedom and external independence. It may be true that Cosimo's proposals show the best means of preserving a temporary civil "peace" in Milan. But this is not the same as preserving freedom or lasting order. Second, Cosimo's liberating intentions are called into question by his haughtily dismissive judgment on the Milanese people's capacity for *libertà*. It was, Cosimo declares, "hardly a wise opinion to believe that the Milanese could keep themselves free" without external help. He insists that "the qualities of their citizenry, their mode of living, and the ancient sects in that city" were all "contrary to every form of civil

[66] *FH*, III.1.105/423–24; II.29.83/397–98.
[67] *FH*, VI.22.254/602–3.

government."[68] Since someone has to dominate them, it had better be the party that can do so most directly. Cosimo uses the language of freedom in much the same way as the nobles in Florence or Senate in Rome when, by branding the many as a turbulent multitude, they denigrate the plebs' capacities to live in ordered freedom. This argument paves the way for the few to present themselves as indispensable guards of freedom, when their deeds show that they are really interested in *dominio* rather than *libertà*.[69] Here it is not a part of one's own city but an entire foreign city that is judged incapable of "keeping itself free." Inside Florence, nobles and people used the name of freedom to demand a free hand for themselves; they sought, that is, license to dominate other parts of the city. Outside, the same people who misconstrued *libertà* as *licenza* sought to give Florence a licentious free hand in controlling regional affairs. The basic rhetorical stratagem is the same, and the use of the good word *libertà* is corrupted in both contexts.

Machiavelli's account implies that by failing to set limits to Florentine ambitions for regional dominance, Cosimo helped set in motion a series of actions that would undermine Florence's own internal and external *libertà*. His own critical views are expressed in the warnings issued by Cosimo's opponent Neri di Gino Capponi. Neri points out that if Florence supports Sforza's ambitions to become prince in Milan, in time "the Milanese, out of indignation against the count, might give themselves entirely to the Venetians—which would be the ruin of everyone." Machiavelli has Neri propose a solution based on treaty law rather than violence: a division of Lombardy into two separate powers that agree never to unite or dominate each other. Both rivals for control in Milan should agree to set limits on their own ambitions. In this way both Venice and Florence would help to preserve Milanese freedom instead of undermining it through their competition. By obstructing both Florentine and Venetian designs for dominion over the region, this plan would oblige both powers to look harder for common forms of defense based on mutual agreement.[70] In having Neri outline this prudent alternative to an escalating power struggle between Florence and Venice, Machiavelli implicitly questions Cosimo's argument that the Milanese people's internal qualities render them permanently incapable of sustaining freedom. Had all three cities accepted Neri's proposal to regulate intercity relations by multilateral agreement, one of the chief causes of instability in Milan—foreign intervention—would be removed. Instead of seeing the movements of neighboring cities as threats to their own freedom, each city might have come to see the freedom of others as a complement to its own freedom, and stopped pursuing policies that would eventually drive them to seek support from "others' arms" outside Italy.[71] Through Neri Machiavelli indicates that there was no genuine necessity for any Italian city to dominate another in order for any of them to secure freedom. Other solutions were available that would not have involved depriving Milan of its freedom, and that might have forced Venice and

---

[68] *FH*, VI.23.255–57/603–4.
[69] *FH*, IV.9.154/482–83.
[70] *FH*, VI.23.255/603–4.
[71] As Machiavelli says of Florence's subject cities in *FH*, II.38.99–100/416–17.

Florence to cooperate in defending freedom throughout the region. Machiavelli implies that by backing the use of unilateral means to gain dominion instead of Neri's cooperative plan for wider Italian *libertà*, Cosimo's rhetoric set back chances of creating any stable regional orders in Italy. His party's insistence on asserting unilateral solutions to regional disorders made it harder for Italian cities to form stable alliances against foreign interlopers.

Given the tendency of most Florentines to mistake license for *libertà*, it is unsurprising that Neri's multilateral proposal for defending the common freedom of neighboring cities has little appeal. Whether out of ambition or ignorance of any meaning of "freedom" other than self-assertive license, most citizens rally behind Cosimo's arguments. The basic flaw in these arguments can be expressed in terms of the Greek word *hubris*.[72] Cosimo's ambition makes him take a dim view of other peoples' desires not to be dominated. This depreciation of others leads to dangerous defects in his understanding of politics. Behind his version of the unilateralist fallacy is the notion that some peoples, cities, or sections of the people are incapable of "keeping themselves free" and therefore need a strong master. This furnishes a pretext for some parties, families, social groups, or cities to demand unauthorized dominion over others. In the *Florentine Histories,* the upshot of such demands is invariably to increase "indignation" among the depreciated people. Their struggles to regain freedom are intensified, while their methods become more violent. Even peoples who have long lived without freedom resent being treated as if they are incapable of governing themselves, and resist attempts to conquer them. By depreciating the Milanese people's desires and capacity for freedom, Cosimo's arguments betray his poor grasp of an *ordinario e naturale* "inconvenience" that makes it very difficult to dominate men for long. In external affairs more obviously than at home, Cosimo fails to take his father Giovanni's prudent advice: those who want "others' share" of authority or freedom always "lose their own, and before losing it live in continual unease."[73]

6.6.
Free will and free agency

This episode brings out another important aspect of Machiavelli's concept of freedom. I have been arguing that for Machiavelli any adequate sense of *libertà* must be tied to some notion of stable *orders*, and to the related idea of accepting *limits* on one's own actions. But Machiavelli is far from indifferent to the way in which limiting orders are founded. He implies that they can only be established securely if this is done in ways that respect agents' freedom in a sense different from the ones discussed so far. To see this, note that the cause of Milanese indignation

---

[72] The main victim of *hubris* is not Cosimo personally but Florence itself, and indirectly Italy—although Machiavelli has the dying Cosimo regret that he may have been deceived into giving Sforza too much power over Florence. The Medicis and other *dominio*-seeking princes are presented as instruments of the Florentine people's own self-destructive actions.

[73] *FH*, I.16, 161/491–92.

anticipated by Neri Cappone was not just their desire to preserve internal freedoms and avoid princely rule. It also had to do with the *methods* used by Sforza to gain a foothold in Milan. By emphasizing the formal agreement between the Milanese people and the Venetians, Machiavelli highlights the contrast between this public, lawful mode of conduct and the private, extralegal means used by Sforza, with Florence's blessing. The Venetians were of course also motivated by narrow self-interest and ambition. Machiavelli's implied criticisms of Sforza and the Medicis do not entail sympathy with their opponents in this crisis. But in this case at least, the Venetians acted openly, and made a formal commitment to defend Milan's internal freedoms. Sforza took power by pulling strings behind the scenes. He made no similar public commitment, based on reciprocal obligations, to keep Milan a free republic. On the contrary, he was set up with Florentine backing as a duke in Milan, making him a one-man ruler or prince. Venice agreed to protect Milanese freedoms by means of a bilateral treaty agreed by two free parties. Sforza-Florence's "protection" was imposed unilaterally, against the will of the Milanese people.

We have seen that Machiavelli regards indignation as the natural and ordinary response of people treated in this way. Even if a policy or government imposed by others has certain merits, they may quite reasonably see the very act of unauthorized imposition as a depreciation of their innate freedom. Expressed in terms of limits, one might say that people resent agents who impose authority on them unilaterally, since these agents fail to recognize other people's desires for freedom as a necessary limit on their own freedom or ambitions. The main object of "desires for freedom" is not a specific "way of life" or political order. It is something more fundamental: namely, the desire to be recognized as having a free will, and therefore possessing the capacity to authorize or reject constraints imposed by other free agents. As earlier chapters argued, for Machiavelli the presumption that people have free will does not depend on their being unconstrained or undetermined by *any* pressures greater than themselves. Free will is not a power to do whatever one chooses or to remake one's environment without constraint. As Machiavelli describes it in the *Prince* and elsewhere, it is simply a capacity that must be presupposed in any being whom we wish to treat as a responsible agent, susceptible to judgments of praise or blame. At minimum, someone considered as having free agency in this sense must be considered capable of accepting or rejecting authority; authorizing it as a self-imposed necessity or rejecting it as unacceptable. When someone is recognized as a free agent, he is seen as having the innate capacity to authorize laws, orders, or other people to govern him. This desire can be seen as more fundamental than the desire to live in a particular way or under a free forms of government, since people who want to be treated as free authorizers presumably want to authorize any form of government they live under, whether free or unfree.

I propose that this sense of desiring freedom—the desire to be treated as a co-authorizer of the laws and orders one lives under, or a free agent—is the bedrock of Machiavelli's reasoning about freedom. In all his main works, he treats respect for free agency as the main precondition for establishing stable orders, whether optimally free ones or not.[74] Moreover, as argued further in chapter 7, his account of the laws and orders that satisfy desires to "live in freedom" is grounded in and conditioned by this (primary) sense of freedom as demanding respect for limits set by others' free will. The rest of this section goes behind Machiavelli's analyses of rhetoric and politics to clarify the basic idea of free agency that underpins his conception of free orders. (1) First, I sketch my reading of key passages where Machiavelli sets out his basic reasons for presupposing that human beings have free will. (2) Then I ask what specific capacities as agents he thinks can be presupposed of human beings by virtue of their free will, including *virtú* itself. (3) Finally, I touch briefly on a question to be pursued further in the next chapter: namely, should other people's free will be respected only when one judges that it is used well, or should it be treated as a serious ethical constraint irrespective of the manner of its exercise? Since Machiavelli does not pose these questions directly, my answers involve reconstructing his likely positions from remarks that have an indirect bearing on the question at hand.

6.6.1. Arguments

Machiavelli's philosophical case for presupposing free will is set out most clearly in the *Prince*. Here he uses the phrase "free will," *libero arbitrio*, to describe the capacity for self-responsible ordering that human beings must presuppose in themselves even in the face of overwhelming constraints. Machiavelli admits that he himself has been tempted to embrace the "opinion" that "worldly things are so governed by fortune and by God, that men cannot correct them with their prudence," and "indeed that they have no remedy at all." His descriptions of *fortuna* stack the cards heavily against free will. Fortune, he writes, is like "one of those violent rivers which, when they become enraged, flood the plains, ruin the trees and the buildings, lift earth from this part, drop in another," so that "each person flees before them, everyone yields to their impetus without being able to hinder them in any regard." Nonetheless, he concludes that "our free will" should not be "eliminated," since "it is not as if men, when times are quiet, could not provide for them with dikes and dams" so that when floodwaters rise later, "either they go by a canal or their impetus is neither so wanton nor so damaging."[75]

Viewed from one angle, these passages might seem simply rhetorical, revealing little of philosophical interest. Among Machiavelli's chief aims in the *Prince* is to exhort Italians to resist foreign incursions, and his remarks on free will appear to have a mainly hortatory function. They are addressed to Machiavelli's compatriots in the extended sense, that is, to Italians not just Florentines; and they summon them to self-liberating action despite the daunting obstacles posed by

---

[74] Compare TPW, III.46–47, IV.19, IV.107–8, V.17, VI.76 on the importance of willing as a foundation of order. In ancient Greek, both *eleutheria* and *autonomia* refer to conditions of non-subjection or non-slavery; but Thucydides, Xenophon, and other writers suggest that these cannot be secured by means of force or deception.

[75] P, XXV.98/187–88.

fortuna. Clearly the passage does function at this hortatory level. The description of fortune as a "violent river" obviously underscores the great difficulties faced in exercising free will, challenging *virtuoso* men to oppose fortune anyway. But behind the rhetoric, the arguments also embody a well-considered, philosophical conception of free will that forms the bedrock of Machiavelli's ethical and political reasonings in all his major works. The specific political context and audience are important for understanding the philosophical arguments. But our understanding of the *Prince* is greatly impoverished if its arguments are reduced to rhetoric intended only for that context.

Why is it reasonable to assume that people have free will even under the kinds of overwhelming constraints described here? In the key passage in the *Prince* Machiavelli defends his presupposition in a distinctive way. To summarize arguments outlined earlier, he is not primarily interested here in how the proposition that human beings have free will can demonstrated with evidence. Instead he considers why we human beings might want to attribute it to ourselves. His reasoning implies that as individuals we want to account for our own actions to ourselves. In our relations with other agents, we need to render such accounts. It might be said that rendering accounts of actions to others is one of the "ordinary and reasonable" necessities of human life. By opting to judge that fortune leaves us a measure of free will notwithstanding contrary evidence, Machiavelli implies that his claims about free will are not factual claims but arguments about what is practically necessary for any adequately human existence.[76] It is up to each person to hold on to a self-conception as an agent with free will, or to let fatalistic broodings "eliminate" its conscious exercise. For Machiavelli this is a choice based on reasons, not an irrational leap of faith. To be sure, there are good empirical reasons to support the opinion that free will is an illusion. But if we allow our free will to be "eliminated" by such opinions, we not only have to accept the miserable consequences of being fortune's slaves; we also cease to live in ways proper to "men." These ways necessitate people to give accounts of their actions to others; judgments of responsibility are a basic condition for stable coexistence in any complex political unit or city. Free will must not be eliminated, in short, because human responsibility would be eliminated with it.

In the *Prince* Machiavelli's arguments for free will appear at the end of the book, where he finally sets out the philosophical foundations of his apparently instrumental-political arguments. If one goes back to the beginning after reading the last chapters carefully, it becomes easier to see how Machiavelli builds up his arguments about human self-responsibility from the start, culminating in the defense of free will. The *Discourses* start where the *Prince* leaves off. As I have already argued, the opening chapter set outs the main elements of Machiavelli's core

---

[76] Observers may have empirical evidence that casts doubt on some or all human beings' capacities to perform specific acts, or to act in an unconstrained manner. But Machiavelli first considers "free" as an attribute of *wills*, before considering how or how far free willing may determine *actions*. This allows him to hold out prospects of exerting free will to virtuous effect even in very adverse constraining conditions.

ethical concepts. Although it does not use the phrase "free will," the idea is implicit in the first chapter's rigorous analysis of the relations between *necessità* and *virtú*. There are two differences in the way that the two works approach questions of free will and free agency. First, the end of the *Prince* considers these questions in abstraction from particular historical or social environments. Here Machiavelli simply asks whether and on what grounds human beings may be considered as having free will, in relation to fortune, natural forces, or God.[77] The discussion in the *Prince* considers human beings generically, not as particular persons involved in interactions with others or identified with specific social groups, polities, historical epochs. By contrast, the *Discourses* begins by considering questions of free agency in relation to particular historical environments, using particular examples of cities such as Rome, Venice, or Florence to represent general types of "beginnings" that impose different kinds of constraint or necessity on agents. Second, the discussion in the *Prince* focuses on *whether* and *why* human beings can be considered to have free will. The *Discourses* begin by assuming that these fundamental questions have already been answered. When Machiavelli discusses the various options available to "builders" of cities under diverse conditions, he now assumes that they can reasonably be regarded as having some margin of free will. The *Prince* takes fatalistic determinism seriously before giving reasons to reject it. The *Discourses* start by "presupposing" free will as a condition for any human "building," even when under harsh *necessità*. The end of the *Prince* asks how beings who labor at every turn under *fortuna* or necessity can be expected to take the responsibilities appropriate for free agents. The *Discourses* repeatedly point out the dire practical implications of their failure to do so. The two works approach the case for free will from different angles, then, but their underlying premises are the same.

6.6.2. Capacities

The philosophical line of reasoning that runs through the first chapter of the *Discourses* raises two questions about the capacities we ascribe to agents when we assume that they have free will. First, what does free will allow human beings to do in relation to other causalities that they could not otherwise do? Second, what capacities should *not* be ascribed to all agents who are presumed to have free will? As argued in chapter 4, Machiavelli's most general answer to the first question can be expressed in terms of capacities to *authorize* and capacities to *author* necessities. Even builders who labor under the most onerous constraints may exercise free will in a variety of ways. They may choose to accept or not to accept pre-existing constraints as legitimate conditions for their actions (authorizing). Or they may impose new constraints on themselves and their environment, so that pre-existing constraints do not overwhelm them (authoring). The opening paragraphs of Book I, chapter 1 make it clear that Machiavelli does not see capacities for exercising free will—that is, free agency—as wholly dependent on agents' external environments. The first uses of the words *libera* and *libertà* refer

[77] *P*, XXIV–XXV/185–89; XXVI/191–92.

to a human capacity manifested in a pre-political, though not a natural, condition. This suggests that free agency should not be conceived as an ideally *unconstrained* capacity. On the contrary, Machiavelli insists that what he calls free building always takes place under severe natural and man-made constraints. Acts of building can be called free in the brief interval when people have been cast adrift from their ancestral homelands and are forced to authorize new constraints as pre-existing conditions for their building, or to author new laws and orders from scratch.[78] On this account, pre-existing *necessità* is conceived not as an obstacle to the exercise of free agency, but as a positive inducement for agents to "order" their own laws, thereby exerting their innate capacities for self-legislative freedom. This freedom is revealed not simply through the *shedding* of old rulers, customs, and corruption that weighed agents down before, but through constructive acts of building new orders and imposing new laws in the face of external constraints.

These basic capacities conferred by free will give agents considerable causal powers to influence their fields of action. Because they have these powers, they can be held responsible for a wide range of actions. One implication of Machiavelli's analysis is that people cannot reasonably deny that they lack any capacities for free agency, and should therefore be exempt from responsibility, because they were heavily constrained. Builders are not freer, or more likely to produce good orders, if they have carte blanche to order new cities however they choose. Being unconstrained by old modes and disorders makes it easier to build new cities. But lack of constraint, or actual capability, is not what identifies builders as more or less adequately *free*. In fact, facility and freedom are inversely related according to Machiavelli's arguments. Free agency always is manifested in relation to constraining forces or necessities, whether natural, supernatural, or imposed by other men. It is put to more *virtuoso* use, and more likely to produce stable orders, where free agents recognize the need to order new, human, self-imposed laws.

Another implication is that people cannot reasonably claim that they should not be regarded as free and responsible agents whenever they act in conditions that lack the orders needed to sustain *libertà*. The examples of free builders in the *Discourses* make it clear that free agency does not depend on the prior existence of any laws and orders at all. If builders could only consider themselves as free and responsible *agents* after they laid down *orders* of their own, especially if these had to be optimally free orders, then some other agency would have to be held responsible for the laws and orders that allow them to be free. On Machiavelli's arguments, this is an unreasonable position, since it presumes that responsible human actions can only occur by the grace of God, fortune, or others' *virtú*.

It is important to distinguish clearly, then, between the demanding conditions needed to satisfy Machiavelli's normative concept of *libertà* on the one hand, and the weaker conditions that make it reasonable to postulate *free agency* on the other. *Libertà* or a "free way of life" is the product of human acts. As the next chapter shows, Machiavelli sees it as a complex construction based on prudent

---

[78] Note that this moment cannot be said to represent a "natural" condition, since the causes that drove people away are as much the result of human political disorders as of natural "accidents."

deliberations and the rule of law. The capacities for free agency furnished by our *libero arbitrio* depend on few external conditions. While acts of (unauthorized) coercion and force can be criticized for *failing to respect* freedom, Machiavelli denies that that they successfully *deprive* individuals of innate freedom. People can be denied or deprived of free orders or a free way of life, but not of free agency. Machiavelli implies that anyone who possesses the basic cognitive capacities and maturity of judgment to reason prudently can authorize and author laws and orders. Neither the possession nor the exercise of these basic capacities depends on an agent's external environment, whether this is seen as primarily restrictive or enabling.

These positions are confirmed by a philosophically sensitive reading of the *Prince*. The passage comparing fortune to a violent flood suggests that the margin for human self-responsibility is often very narrow indeed. Nevertheless, Machiavelli argues that free will gives human beings capacities to exert their own causality, that is, to act as free agents, even when constraints of some kind affect every aspect of their actions. On this account, people do not deserve to be considered as free agents only when they are largely or significantly unconstrained, or where pre-existing orders ensure that their actions contribute in a positive way to *libertà*. If princes or builders could only act freely and take responsibility for their actions within established free orders, there would be no place for praise or blame, or indeed judgments about the prudence or imprudence of actions, in most of human life. While Machiavelli clearly sees a "free way of life" under free orders as the optimal condition for innately free persons, it is their capacity for free agency that makes this condition valuable and grounds their claims for respect.

This position connects capacities for free agency with capacities for self-ordering *virtù*. I suggested in previous chapters that *free will is the basic precondition for virtue and order*. In chapters 24–26 of the *Prince*, free will and *virtù* are nearly synonymous. Both concepts single out distinctive human causal powers, and both are defined in contrast to the powers of necessity and fortune. Machiavelli implies that both taken together are fundamental requirements for a properly human existence: what makes human beings capable of civil life unavailable to other animals. Freedom, however, is the precondition for *virtù*, not the other way around. In the passage about free will and fortune and the first chapters of the *Discourses* Machiavelli defines *virtù* in terms of innate self-legislative freedom. He never defines free will in terms of a prior concept of *virtù* because his concept of *virtù* already includes innate freedom in its basic meaning. The logic behind this seems to be that free will must be presupposed if the concept of *virtù* in its wider sense of a capacity for assuming ethical responsibility—optimally by imposing one's own laws—is to be intelligible at all.

This brings us to the second question: what capacities should not be ascribed to all agents who are presumed to have free will? On Machiavelli's arguments, *the exercise of free agency does not necessarily lead to virtù and order*. Free will and free agency may be asserted as "free opportunity," or manifested passively as being "free in a field." On the one hand, capacities to exercise free will are connected quite specifically to *virtù*: fortune "demonstrates her power where virtue has not

been put in order to resist her."[79] Recall that Machiavelli's *virtú* is not simply virtuous resistance or extraordinary power in fighting back. Free will exercised in
conjunction with *virtú* is always linked to the activity of ordering. It is an "ordinary" power. This rules out readings that see the capacities conferred by free will as
capacities to break away from or transcend all constraints in some extraordinary
way. On the other hand, free will is not identical to *virtú*, although it makes *virtú*
possible. *Libero arbitrio* is the more basic capacity that must be presupposed if hu
man beings are to be considered as capable of *virtuoso* ordering. And to suppose
that human beings have free will is not necessarily to suppose that they exercise it
in optimally *virtuoso* ways to impose good laws and orders. Free will itself should
be recognized as a condition of responsible agency. But its *works* may be virtuous,
or not. A distinction should be made between recognizing people as free agents
insofar as they are considered to have free will, and judging what they do with
their free will. Capacities for free will are capacities to act either well or badly, in
ways that deserve praise or blame. They are not capacities that predispose agents to
do good or to order virtuous works. Free agents may or may not set due limits on
their actions, and may or may not choose to live in free political orders.

6.6.3. Exercise and conditions for respect

There is a deep ethical ambivalence in Machiavelli's paradoxical insistence that
free agency involves choice under severe constraint. His arguments about free
agency under constraint point to two ways of considering the capacity that may
conflict. One the one hand, *free agency alone is a reason to respect anyone presumed
to have it.* The will to act as free, to assert oneself in the world with a sense of one's
capacity to affect it against whatever odds, gives rise to self-respect; and the same
sense of "glory" and reasons for respect apply to *other* agents recognized as free
in this way. Thus reasons for respecting free agency as such may come into play
independently of judgments about what particular agents do with their free will.
On the other hand, Machiavelli's arguments also suggest that *free agents may use
their capacities weakly or badly,* failing to produce stable orders or producing grave
disorders.[80] Does he thereby imply that the value of free agency depends on how it
is used? Should people be recognized and respected as fully free agents only when
they are judged to be using their free will for virtue and order? Or does he suggest that there are reasons to recognize people as free agents and give them ethical
recognition as such, prior to judging their particular actions?

Although Machiavelli does not directly pose these questions, the tension in
the *Discourses'* opening account provokes readers to ask them. Various strands of
his ensuing discussion imply that while people who consider themselves as free
agents may use their capacities for *libertà* and *virtú* well or badly, orderers should
still respect the free agency of anyone affected by their building. Indeed, they

---

[79] *P*, XXV.98/186–87.
[80] A similar view is presented in mythical form at the end of Plato, *Rep.*, esp. 617d–621b.

should treat such respect as a strict priority when deciding how to "build."[81] The good orders of the early Roman republic, presented as an adequate embodiment of political freedom, are the paradigm case. On Machiavelli's account, what made these orders stably virtuous was precisely that they were built on the presumption that men have diverse humors that make them use their freedom in different ways: a few to seek command or to dominate, most to live secure or avoid being dominated.[82] The Romans' prudent solution to this "natural and ordinary" source of conflict was not to deny or suppress the exercise of free will in men of either humor, but to accept the capacities for free agency of all citizens high or low, ambitious or not, as a basic limiting condition on their orders. Instead of treating these conditions as obstacles to any stable order, orderers treated the "tumults" created by different people's different uses of their free will as the foundation of stably free orders. "I say," Machiavelli writes,

> that those who damn the tumults between the nobles and the plebs blame those things that were the first cause of keeping Rome free, and that they consider the noises and the cries that would arise in such tumults more than the good effects that they engendered. They do not consider that in every republic are two diverse humors, that of the people and that of the great, and that all the laws that are made in favor of freedom arise from their disunion. . . . Nor can one in any mode, with reason, call a republic disordered where there are so many examples of virtue; for good examples arise from good education, good education from good laws, and good laws from those tumults that many inconsiderately damn. For whoever examines their end well will find that they have engendered not any exile or violence unfavorable to the common good but laws and orders in benefit of public freedom.[83]

The argument here builds directly on the idea, outlined in the *Discourses'* first chapters, that human self-legislative freedom—as distinct from the illusory freedom of merely being let loose "in a field" without constraints—is only exercised in relation to various constraining necessities. The most important necessities are posed by other people's drives and capacities for freedom, which are the chief stimulus to imposing one's own laws and orders—that is, human self-legislative necessities—to establish conditions for civil life.

Machiavelli's discussion of how the Romans dealt with conflicting *umori* illustrates his general argument that people's capacities for free agency may pose problems for order if badly regulated, or they may help to create and maintain it. The result depends not only on how particular individuals use their free will, although this too is important. It also depends on what orders one adopts to regulate them. From the start of the *Discourses*, good order is defined in relation to respect for

---

[81] Examples illustrating this position are discussed in the next chapter.
[82] *D*, I.16.46/242; I.5.18/211.
[83] *D*, I.4.16–17/208–10. Note the important difference between *disunione* and *tumulti*, which are conditions for freedom, and *disordini* or *discordie*, which undermine it.

citizens' free agency; respect for free agency, not some teleological notion of the common good, is the chief criterion for order. This means that good orders should give priority to procedures and restraints that recognize those who live under them as free agents, and respect them as such. Judgments about their particular uses of freedom are secondary.[84] Although Machiavelli does not explicitly announce these priorities, both his general arguments and examples strongly imply a basic sense of free *agency* as an innate, pre-political capacity, distinct from and ethically prior to freedom as a self-imposed political *condition*. Since innate freedom is what enables people to establish political freedom, it must be considered as freedom in the more fundamental sense. Innate freedom is *causally* prior because it explains why political freedom is possible and desirable for human beings, and *ethically* prior because innate capacities for free agency underpin and regulate Machiavelli's distinctive conception of political freedom. The next chapter further examines the relation between free agency and *libertà*.

---

[84] This is the basis for an egalitarian and anti-paternalist conception of freedom, arguably one of Machiavelli's most important legacies for later political philosophy.

CHAPTER 7

Free Orders

This chapter seeks to clarify the relationship between specific forms of political freedom that Machiavelli discusses and his more general, ethical ideas of free will and free agency. The main capacities that Machiavelli ascribes to free agents were discussed in the last two chapters. Insofar as human beings have free will even under the most severe necessity, they are nonetheless capable of authorizing or withholding their authority from whatever orders are imposed on them. Recognition of this basic human power of giving or withholding authority is, I will argue, among the most basic conditions for Machiavelli's political *libertà*. If agents try to impose free political orders without seeking the willing authorization of those who live under those orders, the quality of freedom in those orders will be undermined from the outset. When the priority of free agency over political freedom in Machiavelli's arguments is recognized, this calls into question the views that he cares only about political freedom; that he gives collective freedom priority over individual freedoms; and that he gives the independence of polities vis-à-vis others priority over the internal freedoms guaranteed by republican orders. Moreover, the fundamental role of free agency in Machiavelli's ethical and political thought sets his conception of *libertà* apart from much conventional humanist and Roman thinking. Despite superficial affinities between his language of *libertà* and that of other republicans, his own ethical arguments are fundamentally incompatible with many of the conventional republican doctrines that are often ascribed to him.[1] Interpretations that simply assimilate his arguments about freedom to these traditions fail to do justice to the philosophical depth of his ethical arguments, and underestimate the originality of his contribution both to republican thought and to modern ethical thinking about freedom.

---

[1] Especially with republican ideals based chiefly on the ethics of virtues or the common good, where the definition of that good is not subject to specific procedural or principled constraints; and with doctrines that give moral and political priority to independence from external control over internal freedoms. Even some scholars who recognize the importance Machiavelli accords to individual freedoms impute ideas to him that are foreign to his reasoning. Viroli (1998, 148–65), for example, closely identifies Machiavelli's concept of *libertà* with patriotism, treating the latter as a "passion" rather than a position based primarily on reasoned judgement. Since he also describes liberty as a passion, the role of reasoned principles in Machiavelli's idea of the republic—and for that matter, the role of prudential reasoning—is obscured.

7.1.
Priorities I: Respect for free agency as a condition for stable orders

While Machiavelli's arguments might inspire hope in the very weak and give them grounds for self-respect, why should others respect them simply *qua* free agents even if they lack effective power to exercise their freedom? Machiavelli usually answers this question by appealing to the reflective prudence of powerful agents. In episodes where he describes confrontations between a very weak and a very strong party, the implications he draws almost always include warnings to the strong not to think that victories can be clear or lasting unless they are pursued with appropriately limited means.[2] Many of the most memorable examples in the *Florentine Histories* and *Discourses* show that excessively violent, dishonest, or lawless methods bring future trouble to victors, often on a large scale. Prudent agents who examine carefully the sources of their own power and freedom must, Machiavelli suggests, see how much both depend on respecting the freedom of other individuals, parties, humors, and peoples.

I now want to suggest that although prudential reasons are most *conspicuous* among Machiavelli's arguments for respecting others' free agency, they are not the most *fundamental* reasons he offers. He gives prominence to arguments from self-interested prudence because he doubts that ethical arguments are likely to move powerful agents in corrupt times. Like Thucydides' Diodotus, Machiavelli assumes a dispassionately instrumental voice when discussing examples of strong parties seeking to take advantage of weaker ones. He often writes as if his only concern is to advise the strong on how to become stronger. His apparent indifference to ethical restraints is belied, however, by remarks he makes in the context of these discussions.[3] The same is true of his arguments about respecting others' desires for freedom. His most conspicuous arguments say that those desires should be respected because people tend to fight obstinately against anyone who flouts them, rendering many initial victories unstable. But Machiavelli sometimes hints at a more fundamental reason for respecting those desires: that innate capacities for free agency confer a dignity on those who assert it that deserves respect. In one of Machiavelli's most moving examples, "worthy of much-praised antiquity," a nobleman trapped in his burning fortress addresses his enemies with the defiant words: "Take for yourselves the goods that fortune has given me and that you can take from me; but those things I have of my spirit, wherein lie my glory and my honor, I will neither give you nor will you take from me." Hearing these words, the enemy were seized with regret at the imminent loss of a man who asserted his freedom so confidently at the point of death. They rushed to save his children and "brought ropes and ladders to him that he might save himself; but these," Machiavelli reports, "he did not accept, for indeed he preferred to die in the flames than to be saved by the hands of the adversaries of his

---

[2] *P*, XXI.90/181.
[3] See, for example, the Diodotus-like arguments he gives to Niccolò da Uzzano, discussed in chap. 9, sec. 9.3.

fatherland." The enemy's reaction made "one aware of how much the virtue of men is admitted even by the enemy." The latter "restored what things they could to save his children and sent them with utmost care to their relatives; the republic was not less kind to them, for as long as they lived they were supported at public expense."[4]

The virtue that commanded such spontaneous respect here includes the nobleman's love of fatherland. But his demand to be considered as a free agent under severe constraints is what arouses respect, and a sense of obligation to his posterity, even among enemies.[5] The example alludes to ethical reasons for respecting others' desires for freedom that hold independently of powerful agents' own security. People who assert their capacity for free action under constraint are, it suggests, inherently worthy of respect, even if their actions under constraint do not threaten the constrainers. Indeed, if an agent asserts his free will in the face of overwhelming asymmetries of power and demands respect for it, he merits respect all the more than if his material forces were better balanced with those of his opponent. Nor does Machiavelli imply that people are simply reckless who risk their lives and posterity by standing up against overwhelming odds, placing their desire for respect as free agents above physical survival. On the contrary, while agents in an extremely weak position cannot be sure of changing their enemies' conduct by asserting their freedom in this way, the example shows that they sometimes can.

But since more powerful agents seldom alter their conduct out of spontaneous ethical respect for the free agency of others, as the nobleman's enemies did in this example, Machiavelli identifies numerous instrumental and prudential reasons why they should. His main, recurrent argument is that innately free agents have the power to give or to withhold something of the greatest importance to those who seek to "order" or command them: namely, authorization for their future orders and commands. The capacity to authorize or to withhold authorization expresses people's innate freedom, and can be exercised even under severe repression. Over and over in the *Histories* and *Discourses*, Machiavelli has prudent individuals point out that free orders cannot be securely established in ways that fail to respect even very weak subjects' desires to have a say about how they are ordered, and by whom. Among numerous other examples, Giovanni de' Medici warns his sons that "in regard to the state, if you wish to live secure, accept from it as much as is *given* to you by laws and by men. This," he adds, "will bring you neither shame nor danger, since it is what a man takes himself" from unwilling subjects, "not what is given" to him, that inspires hatred and future disorders. Another prudent character confirms the same position with regard to relations among cities, regretting that his countrymen recurrently flout or forget it to their detriment. If, he says, the Florentines had "received" a nearby city into its dominions "by accord," they would have gained "advantage and security from it"; but since they had "to hold it by force," the constrained city would surely bring "weakness and trouble"

---

[4] *FH*, IV.11–12.156–57/484–86.

[5] This implication is underlined with a contrasting example of a leading citizen in another city who gave in to the enemy without defense, and was mocked, then starved by the enemy (*FH*, IV.11–12.156–57/484–86).

to Florence in bad times "and in peaceful times, loss and expense."[6] The *Discourses* expresses the same simple, but frequently neglected, precepts about the need for new or old orderers to seek "willing" authorization from the people who are expected to live under their orders. This is the import of such statements as, "not fortresses but the will [*volontà*] of men maintains princes in their states."[7]

The message in all these passages is that stable *autorità* depends above all on seeking free authorization from one's subjects, no matter how weak or disordered they may appear at present. It is *prudent* to seek "voluntary" authority because even when people lack the material powers needed to enjoy a fully "free way of life," they can still make stable victory impossible for those who offend them by denigrating their desires to be treated as free agents. Moreover, it is *advantageous* to respect these desires, because people who freely authorize orders or dominion have the power to underwrite stable victories. By authorizing a victor to propose terms for their future relationship, they give victors much more power to hold what they acquire than they have if losers refuse to accept defeat. By authorizing, and perhaps co-authoring, the terms of a settlement within or between cities, losers willingly "give" the victors one of the most important resources needed for cities that seek power: their assurance of good faith based on promises. Armed with such willed authorization, erstwhile enemies and subjects may in time become friends who gladly help to defend the victor's freedom, as Machiavelli says happened with Florence's subject towns when their free agency was respected.[8]

These positions are illustrated by Machiavelli's recounting of an episode from Livy's histories: the tense confrontation between the conquering Romans and a defeated neighboring people, the Privernati. The episode shows how people in an extremely weak de facto and de jure position may nonetheless assert their desires to be treated as free agents, thereby commanding respect from the stronger party. In Machiavelli's version, after a failed rebellion against Roman dominion the Privernati sent "many citizens" to ask pardon from the Roman Senate. Their recent disloyalty placed the Privernati in an exceedingly weak position vis-à-vis the Romans. They were disarmed, suspect, and at the mercy of Roman power. In these circumstances they might well have considered themselves as vanquished, and resigned their fate entirely to Roman judgment. But when their delegates went before the Roman Senate and a senator asked one of them what punishment he thought the Privernati deserved, the response was an unapologetic: "That which they deserve who consider themselves worthy of freedom."[9] Asked to explain his answer, the delegate showed what it means to consider oneself constrained by extreme necessity, yet not subservient to it. First he appealed to the Romans' self-interested prudence. If the Romans wanted a "faithful and perpetual" peace, he reasoned, they must respect their subjects' love of freedom. If they did not, they could expect fresh rebellions in the future, however weak the Privernati appeared

---

[6] *FH*, IV.16.161/491; VII.30.308–9/668–69; compare II.34.92–93/406–8.
[7] *D*, II.24.187/394; compare I.5, 38, 53; II.24, 32; III.6–7, 11, 30, 46.
[8] *FH*, II.38.99–100/416–17.
[9] *D*, II.23.183/389.

at present. Then the outspoken delegate stated the Privernati's basic demands. The Romans should negotiate with them as men who consider themselves worthy of being treated as free agents, and who ought therefore to have a say in consenting to or rejecting whatever authority might be set over them. The vast asymmetry between their present power and Rome's did not stop them from asserting their free agency. Moreover, although less reflective Romans might see the Privernati assertions as toothless, the prudent recognized that this was not the case, since their own security depended on the willing obedience of their subjects. When the Roman consul asked the outspoken delegate, "If we remit your punishment, what sort of peace can we hope to have with you?" the Privernate answered, "If you give a good one, both faithful and perpetual; if a bad one, not long-lasting."[10]

The Romans' response to this challenge is as striking as the Privernate's confident display of self-respect. Instead of treating the delegate's words as audacious, "the wiser part of the Senate" applauded the response, declaring, "The voice of a free man had been heard, nor could it be believed that any people or indeed any man should remain in a condition that was painful longer than was necessary." By declaring their awareness of their own innate freedom to others, people who lack material power here assert a wholly persuasive claim to be respected as free agents.[11] Machiavelli points to two related reasons for this positive reaction. First, the wiser senators perceived that people who *regard themselves* as free in harsh conditions of *objective* servitude thereby manifest the self-respect appropriate to agents who consider themselves free, and thus deserve the respect of others. For this reason the Senate decided to give Privernati privileges of citizenship, declaring, "Only those who think of nothing except freedom are worthy to become Romans." Second, the senators praised the Privernate delegate for his truthfulness, which demonstrated his confident assurance that he and his compatriots deserved to be treated as free agents even in abject defeat. Their honesty reinforces the ethical reasons for respecting their free agency, and reassures the Romans that they can trust the Privernati to uphold any peace that they willingly authorize. The Privernati might have feigned humility and begged pardon to the Romans' faces, only to rebel against them later. Instead they were courageous enough to state openly their intention to foment further rebellions if their desire to be treated as free men were not respected. Any other reply would have been "deceptive and cowardly," not because the defeated men in fact had subversive intentions, but because a pretense of passive resignation would have belied their character as free men.

For their part, the Roman senators are commended for avoiding a form of self-deception all too common among the powerful: that which fails to see that other people's desires for freedom place very serious constraints on their own authority. As the last chapter suggested, one of Machiavelli's main arguments is that people deceive themselves when they do not recognize how widespread the desire for

---

[10] *D*, II.23.183/389; *LH*, VIII.21.

[11] Machiavelli's point is not that there is no ground for respecting people as agents until they have publicly asserted their own awareness of themselves as innately free. Others should realize this without having to be reminded.

freedom is, even among people who do not presently have independence or free institutions. "Those who believe otherwise of men"—that is, who underestimate the motivational power of others' love of liberty—"especially those used to being *or seeming to themselves to be free*, are deceived, and under this deception take up policies that are not good for themselves and not such as to satisfy them. From this," he concludes, "arise frequent rebellions and the ruin of states."[12]

The Privernati example shows, then, that people who demand that their capacities for free agency be treated as a ground for respect, irrespective of their empirical powers, can hope to alter their opponents' conduct if the latter are prudent. From the side of the more powerful, it suggests both ethical and prudential reasons to respect the free agency even of much weaker parties, and to invite them to authorize "orders" that give the powerful authority over them. Even people who face a crushing defeat can choose to authorize the results of a war, or to resist the terms imposed on them. If they do authorize the result, this act gives them room to negotiate for terms of settlement and postwar orders that give them considerable powers of self-legislation. This also helps the victors "hold" what they "acquire." If losers do not authorize the victors' settlement, stable orders are unlikely to take root. The same simple, procedural precepts recur throughout Machiavelli's writings. Willing authorization, whereby people are asked to "give" authority, is a precondition for stably legitimate or free orders; authority "taken" from others by deception or force is never a stable basis for freedom. It is true that Machiavelli usually advances these arguments in an instrumental form. Nevertheless, they presuppose a more basic judgment about the ethical necessity to respect free agency, since the ethically reasonable desire to be treated as free agents explains *why* people fight so obstinately against those who flout this desire. If prudent reflection shows the instrumental necessity to respect people as free agents, it also points toward an ethical necessity to do so.

7.2.
Priorities II: Willing authorization as the foundation of free orders

Given the strength of "ordinary" desires for freedom, one of the main problems for the conception of political order I am attributing to Machiavelli is to find ways of setting mutually acceptable limits on the desires of each individual, party, or city. If Machiavelli treats respect for free agency as the indispensable foundation for free orders, how does he propose to set limits on every agent's freedom that all consider as legitimate?

In Machiavelli's vocabulary, the word whose meaning is closest to "legitimacy" is *autorità*. *Autorità* may be taken or given, by force or by laws. People

---

[12] *D*, II.23.184/389–90; emphasis added. Compare Nicias' remarks on the dangers of attacking cities that consider themselves free, TPW, VI.20–23. Also see the Melians' claim that it would be "base and cowardly for us who are still free [*eleutherois*] not to encounter anything at all rather than accept servitude [*douleusai*]," TPW, V.100; and the warning that those enemies are most terrible (*deinoi*) who, having been subjects (*hupēkooi*), attack and overcome those who ruled them before (TPW, V.91).

give other people, laws, or orders *autorità* over them by "willing" this grant. Although Machiavelli does not explicitly lay out this quasi-contractual procedure, it is strongly suggested by examples and comments in each of his main works. His general answer to the question of how to set limits on freedom that are acceptable to everyone is, therefore, to do so through transparent procedures allowing for free, public authorization of orderers and laws that establish those limits. As the Privernati episode in the *Discourses* and numerous civil and regional wars described in the *Histories* illustrate, *authority* should be given freely in ways regulated by transparent public procedures, even if *power* was acquired by force or war. Not only republics, but even powerful princes and dominant cities, too, should pay scrupulous attention to how they "found" their power. If they lack *autorità* given without force or fraud, they soon find that they have built on dust. These positions are reiterated so frequently in Machiavelli's writings that it seems reasonable to identify a general *principle* of authorization as the bedrock of his account of political legitimacy. The principle is grounded in his defense of free will as a necessary condition for responsibility. Procedures for giving or withdrawing *autorità* are the most basic political expression of respect for the free agency of people who live under a given set of *leggi e ordini*. People who authorize orderers, laws, or leaders in a regulated way—as distinct from the unregulated, chaotic ways shown in episodes where the mob "shouts" for a strongman savior—freely give a commitment to support the political arrangements they authorize. They take responsibility for the laws, and share responsibility for defending their city and its duly appointed leaders.

Machiavelli's main criteria for legitimate authorization are therefore procedural, based on acts of voluntary consent. This proceduralist position supports a strongly anti-paternalist view of what both freedom and political legitimacy require. It should be distinguished from two other accounts of what make orders free or legitimate that may justify paternalism. A first account says that peoples' free agency ought to be granted full political respect only when agents are able to express their will under free institutions, or in independent polities. On this view, the ethical quality of free agency remains somehow deficient when it is asserted under less than optimally free orders. If an *ordinatore* seeks to impose laws and orders on people who currently live in an oppressed or incompletely free condition, he need not consider himself constrained by his subjects' innate capacities to meet their demands to authorize his actions. Only the free willing of people who already have a "free way of life" under free orders constitutes a "necessary" constraint on orderers. Machiavelli's arguments clearly undercut these positions. While treating free orders and independence as appropriate expressions of innate human freedom, Machiavelli does not see either as a necessary condition for respecting individuals, parties, or peoples as free agents. As the previous chapter argued, Machiavelli denies that people who lack free political orders therefore lack capacities to change their fate by exercising their powers of self-ordering. Moreover, he rejects the paternalistic view that people who currently lack political or military freedom should be seen as dependent on the more free for their advancement.[13] The *Discourses* argue that it is extremely unwise to underestimate the obstacles posed even to the most powerful by others' desires for freedom, especially that of people "used to being *or seeming to themselves to be free* [*o a essere o a parere loro essere liberi*]."[14] On this reading, people who are "used to being or seeming to themselves to be free" are not primarily or exclusively those who do or seem to themselves to live a free "way of life" under free orders. They may also be people who live under the yoke of tyranny or foreign *dominio*, such as Thucydides' Corcyrans and Livy's Privernati. Such people may not regard their conditions of life as free, yet nevertheless "be or seem to themselves to be" *liberi*, free agents who demand respect for their capacities to accept or reject *autorità*. If they do not think of themselves as free agents but as wholly subject to natural instincts, divine purposes, or fortune, then others may find it easy to overcome and control them without *respetto*. But if they do assert their self-conception as free agents even under severe constraints, this is enough to give pause to those who seek to conquer them.

A second account of freedom and legitimacy is often linked to the first, and may also support paternalistic policies. It holds that respect for free agency is conditional on judgments about the ways in which particular agents use their free will. According to this view, people should be regarded as fully free agents, and granted powers to authorize their laws and orders, only insofar as they use these powers for *ends* that are deemed reasonable by whoever grants them. The most compelling version of this argument says that weaker parties who want others to respect them as free agents must, at the very least, adopt free orders as their end. Agents who choose to live under kings instead of republics, or who prefer to live a little longer with homegrown tyrants rather than risk living under the tyranny or license inflicted by foreign conquerors, thereby cease to deserve respect *qua* free agents. As the last chapter argued, however, Machiavelli's precepts implicitly reject the view that the morally necessitating force of constraints imposed by other peoples' innate freedom depends on the specific ends they pursue. As the Privernati example implies, orders that conform to the requirements of a "free way of life" cannot be regarded as fully free or legitimate if they are not authorized by those who live under them. The manner of their initial founding matters more than the ends. The Privernati are only "pacified" by the Romans' demonstrated respect for their free agency, not by the offer of free political orders per se. They do not say: we will be faithful to Rome and her laws on condition that you share with us your free way of life. They say: we will be faithful if you give us a peace based on respect for us as free men who have the innate power to choose the path of rebellion again at some future time, even if our material power at present

[13] In this respect Machiavelli's conception of freedom can be seen as more supportive of weaker agents than, for example, Locke's (1988 [1698], V.34.291) or Mill's (1991 [1861]), 453–56) conceptions, which give priority to the claims of the "rational and industrious" or to those deemed to have advanced further in their level of civilization, measured in terms of free government.
[14] *D*, II.23.184/390; emphasis added.

appears to be destroyed.[15] Machiavelli's examples suggest that legitimate *autorità* depends on acts of consent, not on the quality of *ordini* irrespective of how they are established.

Note that on Machiavelli's account, neither the Romans nor the audaciously freedom-loving Privernate delegate acted as they did for prudential reasons alone. The delegate took a big gamble with his people's security when he stood up to his victors and effectively demanded that the Privernati be treated as free men, although they appeared wholly dependent on the Romans' will. Machiavelli's account of the Roman response links prudence to principle. Reflective reasoning suggests very strong instrumental and prudential motives for powerful agents to take weaker agents' desires for freedom as a constraint on their actions. The positive instrumental reasons are that through acts of authorization, authorizers come to see themselves as co-responsible for upholding civil laws and orders. In this way acts of free authorizing give *leggi e ordini* strength that they otherwise lack.[16] The negative, prudential reason is that men who want to be treated as free agents never remain subjects for long. Whereas *autorità* freely given is one of the greatest sources of power in polities, people who are not asked to authorize the laws and orders they live under are unlikely to feel responsible for them. They are unreliable supporters for those in command, and unlikely to cooperate in maintaining common security. If agents reflect deeply enough, they should recognize that principled respect for free agency is a sufficient reason for self-restraint, whether or not they acknowledge additional prudential or instrumental reasons. The general principle of authorization saves powerful agents the trouble of trying to decide in each particular case whether or not they should consult the wishes of people affected by their actions. The principle simply says that they should always do so, regardless of the relative power of agents and subjects. So long as they let this principle guide them, the Romans would not have to wait for further rebellions to recall that innate capacities for freedom give the Privernati, and other subject peoples, a good reason to rebel against servitude.

7.3.
Conditions I: Universal security

Let us now consider a familiar challenge to the view that Machiavelli treats desires for freedom as a basic consideration for prudent political "ordering." This concerns

---

[15] Machiavelli (*D*, II.26.191–92/398–99) stresses the importance of respect expressed through words and procedures, writing that "one of the great prudences men use is to abstain from menacing or injuring anyone with words. For neither the one nor the other takes forces away from the enemy, but the one makes him more cautious and the other makes him have greater hatred against you and think with greater industry of how to hurt you." Quoting Livy later, he notes (*D*, III.22.267/478) that a prudent man "was no less mindful of the freedom of another than of his own dignity."

[16] As noted in chap. 6, Machiavelli recognizes that not all people do think of themselves as free. Nevertheless, they usually want others to treat them as if they are. This shows that the presupposition of free will and free agency does not stand or fall entirely on agents' self-conceptions. It may be imputed to them even when they doubt that they have free will.

how to situate desires for freedom within Machiavelli's broader account of human nature and motivational psychology. Surely, the skeptical argument goes, desires for freedom can be explained in terms of more fundamental human drives or desires. When Machiavelli first asks why people assert such strong desires for freedom, he answers: "a small part of them desires *to be free* so as to command [*desira di essere libera per comandare*], but all the others, who are infinite, desire *freedom* so as to live secure [*desiderano la libertà per vivere sicuri*]."[17] This is easily assimilated to the notion that freedom is valued by the "many" only because and insofar as it contributes to their own self-preservation. Might it be that Machiavelli is cutting moralistic views about freedom down to size here, reducing disruptive desires for freedom to natural drives that are, in the last analysis, identical with ambition and desires for self-preservation? Indeed, the desires might be explained in terms of evolutionary struggle for survival, where the stronger few seek freedom to dominate and the weaker majority value freedom as a condition that increases their chances of survival. If so they are just brute natural facts, with no inherent connection to *virtú* or political order.

Because many people think about their reasons for wanting freedom in this instrumental way, Machiavelli often uses instrumental arguments when trying to show why others' desires for freedom should be taken seriously. But he also identifies a different set of reasons why people desire freedom. People are assumed to have capacities to exercise free will, that is, free agency, as well as natural drives and dispositions. People who consider themselves as free agents, or who want others to treat them as free agents, may desire freedom for non-instrumental reasons having to do with ethical respect. Let us look more closely at what Machiavelli thinks is required for "freedom so as to live secure," paying close attention to the ethical as well as instrumental aspects of his reasonings.

Three initial observations undermine readings that reduce popular desires for freedom to "private," purely self-interested desires for security. First, Machiavelli insists that the security needed to guard freedom must be *universal* security. Popular desires for *libertà* are only "satisfied by making orders and laws in which *universal security* is included together with one's own power [*facendo ordini e leggi, dove insieme con la potenza sua si comprenda la sicurtà universale*]."[18] Princes and other powerful agents have the greatest potential to threaten freedom, and therefore stand in greatest need of checks. But *sicurtà universale* also requires security for the powerful against arbitrary attacks on their legitimate freedom. In order to build and maintain orders that provide the genuinely universal security needed to support *libertà*, both the many and the few must come to consider *sicurtà* and *libertà* from perspective wider than that of their own private interests. If people at first value freedom because and insofar as it provides for their personal security, prudent reflection on what measures would satisfy this natural desire for self-preservation shows that the only reliable foundations of one's own security are universal laws that equally protect that of everyone else in the polity.

[17] *D*, I.16.46/240–42; I.5.17–19/210–12; emphasis added.
[18] *D*, I.16.46/242.

Second, in the same chapter Machiavelli alludes to the ethical value of *libertà* when he suggests that a "free way of life" is the indispensable foundation of the most basic conditions needed for a self-respecting, human existence. Such an existence is one where each "is able to enjoy one's things freely [*liberamente*], without suspicion, not fearing [*non temere*] for the honor of wives and that of children."[19] Here Machiavelli defines security in relation to freedom rather than vice versa. His primary sense of the term is not brute physical survival or security with respect to property; security is defined essentially as security *in* human freedom, not in survival or particular property rights. He later connects this sense of security for individuals to the good orders, and therefore safety, of whole cities and provinces. Under free orders one sees larger, well-ordered peoples because

> marriages are freer [*più liberi*] and more desirable to men since each *willingly* [*volentieri*] procreates those children he believes he can nourish. He does not fear that his patrimony will be taken away, and he knows not only that they are born free and not slaves, but that they can, through their virtue, become princes. Riches are seen to multiply there in larger number, both those that come from agriculture and those that come from the arts. For each *willingly* multiplies that thing and seeks to acquire those goods he believes he can enjoy once acquired.[20]

Third, *libertà* is not valued only insofar as it protects people against harms; it is also valued for the substantive powers and possibilities it furnishes. As Machiavelli notes in a later chapter, the man who lives under free orders not only "does not fear that his patrimony will be taken away." As regards his offspring, he also "knows [*conosce*] not only that they are born free and not slaves [*nascono liberi e non schiavi*], but that they can, through their virtue, become princes [*che possono mediante la virtù loro diventare principi*]."[21] The opportunity for all in a free city to "become princes" gives citizens a crucial motive to work for the public good. People who know that they are "born free and not slaves" may have in that freedom a motive to resist enslavement, but not a motive to work for the public as well as their private good. By contrast, people who know that they and their children "can, through their virtue, become princes" are more likely to cultivate their own virtue for the public good.

Machiavelli therefore implies that the value people attach to freedom is connected to much more than physical self-preservation. It also stems from their desire to be treated as agents capable of assuming responsibility for their own conditions of life. Free agency is more fundamental to most people's conceptions of themselves as responsible persons than desires for command or security. People want security, but not on any terms; they feel secure only when they have been consulted and have co-authorized the laws and orders that are supposed to underwrite their security. If at first the "causes" of people's valuing freedom seem merely instrumental and

---

[19] *D*, I.16.45/240–41.
[20] *D*, II.2.132/334–35; emphasis added.
[21] Ibid. See chap. 3, sec. 3.5., 128, sec. 7.5., 272–73 below, and chap. 8, sec. 8.5., 318.

derived from organic-natural urges for self-preservation, in specifying the conditions that would satisfy those urges Machiavelli expands the concept of security beyond the narrowly self-regarding sense implied by a naturalistic anthropology. Natural desires for security can only be satisfied by "making orders and laws" that meet very demanding criteria. These must be worked out and established by human reasoning, since they cannot be discovered in human nature (N1) alone. This implies a distinction between the natural "causes" that make people desire freedom and the reflective *reasons* that make freedom *objectively* valuable.

The distinction is important because when people are "caused" to desire freedom by their natural, personal concerns for security but do not grasp the objective reasons why freedom is valuable, they may fail to take the measures needed to maintain it in good health. From a standpoint of naturalistic anthropology (N1), it may be true that most people form desires for freedom in the sense of freedom-under-laws because and insofar as this condition confers personal security. But when people realize that these basic forms of security depend on laws and orders that guarantee them universally, their desire for freedom acquires a reasoned ethical basis that supplements rather than supplants its initial, natural cause. The reasons for valuing freedom give people a motive to support a free way of life even when they are presently unmoved by strong natural fears for their security. As Machiavelli points out, most people take the benefits "drawn from a free way of life" for granted, unaware that free laws and orders—not unregulated human nature or good fortune—are wholly responsible for them. Thus he observes that the "common utility that is drawn from a free way of life is not recognized by anyone while it is possessed."[22] If Machiavelli's discussions of freedom have one main purpose, it is to bring readers—both those whose main concern is security and those who wish to command—to step back from these natural causes and consider more general reasons why freedom is *both* valued subjectively *and* objectively valuable. Armed with a more reasoned understanding of its value, they will be better equipped to design and defend laws and orders that can protect a free way of life.

If universal security is a basic condition for stably free orders, does this mean that conditions establishing universal security must be in place before free *ordini e leggi* can be established? Should orderers make security their first priority, and turn to the work of ordering for *libertà* only after basic *sicurtà* is in evidence? Proceeding in that order would open the door to the various inadequate conceptions of freedom discussed in the last chapter. Ambitious men who seek to dominate others often appeal to popular desires for security, especially in periods wracked by disorder, as a pretext for asserting their own power under the *colore* of defending civic freedom. Against these priorities, Machiavelli's discussions suggest the clear priority of respect for freedom and the rule of law over physical conditions of security. Indeed, his concept of *sicurtà* entails respect for freedom and the rule of law, which regulate the methods used to pursue *la sicurtà universale*. The regulative priority of freedom as rule of law is implied in Machiavelli's insistence that the

---

[22] *D*, I.1 6.45/240–41.

kinds of security that support *libertà* and the *vivere libera* must be universal, since universal security can only be the product of laws and orders authorized by those who live under them. Policies that seek to promote security in ways unregulated or weakly regulated by laws only provide security for some, at the expense of others. These merely partial forms of security undermine the foundations of political *libertà*, which in turn undermines internal stability and external security.

7.4.
Conditions II: Transparency and publicity

A second set of conditions needed to maintain free orders is laws designed to ensure that public offices, honors, and penalties are distributed on the basis of transparent, publicly known procedures. A recurrent theme of the *Discourses*, *Florentine Histories*, and the *Prince* is that nothing corrodes universal security, and hence political freedom, more than partisan or private modes of applying laws regarding public honors and the punishment of crimes. The distinction between private, non-transparent and public, transparent procedures is drawn clearly in Book III of the *Discourses*. Machiavelli notes that any individual may acquire "reputation" for his merits as a counselor to political leaders "by counselling well, by working better in the public benefit." The active demonstration of these merits should, he argues, be the basis for the selection of counselors in free polities. Individual merit as judged by fellow citizens, not heredity or personal friendship, ought to be the sole qualification for public offices and honors. "One should," Machiavelli writes, "open to citizens the way to this honor and to put up rewards both for counsel and for works so that they have to be honored and satisfied with them." To those gentlemen who fear that meritocracy would unleash the "restless spirit of the plebs" against their lives and property, Machiavelli replies: "If these reputations, gained by these [public] ways, are *clear and simple*, they will never be dangerous; but when they are gained by private ways" often favored by those who stake their claims on birth or power rather than commitment to public service, "they are very dangerous and altogether hurtful."[23]

Machiavelli sets out several conditions that should regulate the distribution of offices, honors, and punishments in order to ensure transparency and therefore *libertà*. A first condition is *impartiality*, or judgments of merit based on reasons that are independent of personal or party relationships. Freedom cannot be maintained unless laws are authorized and applied with a view to maintaining the freedom of all parties, with each accepting limits consistent with the freedom of others. Machiavelli stresses the importance of this condition especially in relation to the distribution of public honors. "A free way of life," he observes, "proffers honors and rewards through certain honest and determinate causes, and outside these it neither rewards nor honors anyone." Honest and determinate causes are those one can state publicly with reference to the public good; mere personal preferences or partisan interests are not such causes. Upholding "honest and determinate" principles of distribu-

---

[23] *D*, III.28.278/488–89; emphasis added.

tion further guards freedom because people who achieve public honors through their own merit, not through patronage of the rich and powerful, are less likely to be indebted to such men or to support them without good publicly stated reasons. As Machiavelli puts it, "when one has those honors and those useful things that it appears to him he merits, he does not confess that he has an obligation to those who reward him."[24] A second condition for public transparency is *generality*: laws regarding such distributions regulate commanders, citizens and peoples, strong and weak in the same way. Public freedom depends on placing all the citizens under the same laws, "together with" the power of princes and commanders. Those who authorize laws have a special responsibility to apply them in a transparent way, since nothing "sets a more wicked example in a republic than to make a law and not observe it, and so much the more as it is not observed by him who made it."[25] A third condition is strict *impersonality*. Applications of the law should be impersonal in the sense that they should judge not the characters or personal history of men, but only their deeds. This is particularly true of laws that order punishments for public transgressions. Officials who apply the laws in a strictly impersonal manner will not be more lenient to a transgressor just because he has performed good services to his city in the past. "No well-ordered republic," Machiavelli insists,

> ever cancels the demerits with the merits of its citizens; but, having ordered rewards for a good work and punishment for a bad one, and having rewarded one for having worked well, if that same one later works badly, it punishes him without any regard for his good works. When these orders are well observed, a city lives free for a long time; otherwise it will always come to ruin soon. For if a citizen has done some outstanding work for the city, and on top of the reputation that this thing brings him, he has an audacity and confidence that he can do some work that is not good without fearing punishment, in a short time he will become so insolent that any civility will be dissolved.[26]

All three conditions require *strictness* or "harshness" in applying the laws aimed at maintaining public freedom. "It is a very true rule," Machiavelli writes, "that when one commands harsh things one must make them observed with harshness" or people will begin to take advantage of the evident laxness. Although his main example here concerns military commands, Machiavelli broadens the discussion to include the most general, public "commands" in a polity: those given through the laws. If someone charged with the task of upholding the laws is too lenient in enforcing them or exempts some people from due punishment on personal or partisan grounds, he may succeed in gaining friends and a reputation for "humanity," as did the Roman general Valerius Corvinus. But "in a citizen who lives under the laws of a republic," that is, in a free polity, publicly "determinate" punishments should be applied in a strictly impersonal manner, following the example

[24] *D*, I.40.88/286–87; I.16.45/240–41.
[25] *D*, I.16.46/242; I.45.93–94/291–92.
[26] *D*, I.24.59/255–56.

of another general, Manlius Torquatus. This mode is "more praiseworthy and less dangerous" because it

> is wholly in favor of the public and does not in any part have regard to private ambition. For by such a mode, showing oneself always harsh to everyone and loving only the common good, one cannot acquire partisans; for whoever does this does not acquire particular friends for himself, which we call, as was said above, partisans. So a similar mode of proceeding cannot be more useful or more desirable in a republic, since the public utility is not lacking in it and there cannot be any suspicion of private power. But the contrary is in Valerius' mode of proceeding, for if indeed the same effects are produced as to the public, nonetheless, because of the particular goodwill that he acquires with the soldiers, many doubts resurge as to the bad effects on freedom of a long command.[27]

Punitive laws should be "harsh" in the sense of strict, rigorous, and impartial, but not "cruel" in the sense of causing harm disproportionate to a crime. Moreover, as strictness is different from cruelty, so self-regulation is not the same as repression. Lawmakers should not aim to stifle natural human urges, only to limit them so that they do not clash with the non-excessive movements of others.[28]

These conditions for maintaining public transparency, Machiavelli suggests, require the following "orders," which form the basis of both political *libertà* and the *vivere libero*:

1. *Public courts* staffed and based on procedures that can be trusted to apply known standards of evidence and make judgments based on evidence presented, not on private or sectional interests. Thus "an orderer of a republic should order that every citizen in it can accuse without any fear or without any respect."[29]

2. *Popular assemblies* (*concioni*) where the populace can examine the merits of different leaders and policies, and thereby get prudent counsel so that they do not have to make political choices in ignorance.[30] According to Machiavelli, elected assemblies serve the populace in much the same way as several counselors serve princes. When they comprise a variety of views and interests and are unafraid to express them, assemblies—like a prince's advisors—can help people to avoid serious errors of judgment by weighing matters from diverse points of view, considering the weaknesses as well as the

---

[27] *D*, III.22.265–67/476–78.

[28] Compare the chapter in the *Prince* entitled "Of Cruelty and Mercy." Here Machiavelli (*P*, XVII.65–68/162–63) at first seems to endorse a ruthless political realism that sees "cruelty" and an ability to inspire "fear" as qualities needed in good commanders. But on closer reading, it becomes clear that his main point is not to recommend "inhuman cruelty" but to criticize the use of "excessive mercy" or leniency with soldiers or subjects.

[29] *D*, I.8.26–28/220–22. Compare Plato, *Rep.* 464d–465e on the need for public channels where citizens can vent their anger through accusations and lawsuits.

[30] *D*, I.4.17/210; III.34.287–90/500–503.

advantages of a policy, and questioning judgments that are based on flawed information or self-deception.

3. *Free and open procedures for examining the fitness of candidates for high public office* and for holding accountable those who have this rank. Every citizen whatever his rank should have the right to make public any knowledge of a candidates' defects, subject to laws against calumny upheld by public courts.[31] Thus "good orderers" have laid down that in creating "the supreme ranks of the city, where it would be dangerous to put inadequate men, and when it is seen that the popular vogue is directed toward creating someone who might be inadequate, it is permitted to every citizen and is attributed to his glory to make public in councils the defect of that one, so that the people, not lacking knowledge of him, can judge better." Public discussion uninhibited by fear of reprisals and conducted within the limits of laws against slander helps to ensure that "in the election of magistrates peoples judge according to the truest marks that they can have of men; and when they can be counseled like princes, they err less than princes."[32]

4. *Modes for seeking reputation through holding public office should be public and open, not private.* Citizens of all ranks should be rewarded for good political counsel and works and offered the chance to advance in the ranks of public service. Honors and rewards are proffered only "through certain honest and determinate causes."[33]

7.5.
Conditions III: Equal opportunity

A third fundamental condition needed to maintain free orders are laws designed to check the emergence of significant inequalities, where these are not themselves "ordered" by public laws. The general risks to freedom posed by inadequately "ordered" inequalities are underlined in the *Discourses*. "Many times," Machiavelli notes in Book I, "a citizen is allowed to gather more strength than is reasonable, or one begins to corrupt a law that is the nerve and the life of a free way of life."[34] The question then is: how much and what kind of unequal "strength" possessed by individuals or sections in a city does Machiavelli think are compatible with the *vivere libero*? How should readers judge what are "reasonable" or unreasonable degrees of relative "strength" or weakness among fellow citizens, parties, or cities?

It is important to stress that Machiavelli sees well-ordered inequalities, not strict egalitarian orders, as the basic conditions needed for stable *libertà*. Clearly, the purpose of some laws is to establish unequal shares of various public goods such as authority, rewards, or revenues. Laws regulating the distribution of public

---

[31] *D*, 1.8.26–28/220–22.
[32] *D*, III.34.289–90/502–3.
[33] *D*, III.28.276–77/488–89; III.31.281–84/494–97. See also *D*, III.16.254–56/465–67; *FH*, III.1.105/423–24.
[34] *D*, I.33.71/269.

offices, for example, give people who gain office a larger measure of authority to command or to make laws than citizens who do not hold office. In Machiavelli's language, the latter are "ordered" by law to accept the superior authority in relevant matters of whoever enters public ranks through transparent procedures. Those duly authorized have greater public *autorità*, whereas those who hold no office are legally obligated to "obedience." In all his main works Machiavelli stresses the need for a clear division of political labor between the few who exercise authority and the many who obey. This is his prime example of a form of inequality needed to uphold political freedom. The ill-defined division of labor between public authorities and citizens obliged to obey them was, in his view, one of the main causes of Florence's debilitating *licenza*. When all the citizens in a republic demand equal authority to command, judge, and order new laws all at once, the result is all-out partisan rivalry that tends to corrupt the very notion of public *autorità*.

Machiavelli's positions are very far, then, from a leveling egalitarianism. He is as critical of such leveling as of extremely hierarchical social orders and forms of government that give excessive power to the one or the few. Yet he does not suggest that the forms of inequality needed to maintain *libertà* can be discovered simply by striking a balance between extremes. Free orders do not depend on moderating or mixing egalitarian and authoritarian forms of government. Unless such mixed forms are regulated by principles that are defined independently of their constituent elements, the mixing more often produces unstable hybrids of popular government and aristocracy or kingship than a well-balanced constitution.[35] On Machiavelli's arguments, there can be only one fully adequate basis for determining forms and degrees of public inequality: a justification based on reasons that are not perceived by citizens as private or arbitrary, but which persuasively demonstrate that specific kinds of inequality are necessary for public freedom.[36] This is in part a merely formal constraint on ways of determining inequalities. It still allows for different kinds of reason to justify different forms of inequality; Machiavelli does not suggest that only one set of reasons is self-evidently correct in advance of any closer examination. But his specific conception of public freedom provides a touchstone for judging some kinds of reason for inequality as more adequate than others. As I have argued, Machiavelli conceives of public freedom as a condition where individual wills are reciprocally limited by laws that they authorize themselves. He rejects conceptions of *libertà* as a condition where individual wills are minimally constrained, or one where they are brought into tumult-free harmony or unity. His criteria for deciding what count as good justifications for inequality are informed by his substantive conception of political *libertà*, as well as by the formal requirement that the justifying reasons should relate to general, public considerations rather than to private, partial interests. Let us now look more

---

[35] See chap. 1, sec. 1.7.

[36] Note that at this secondary level of argument Machiavelli's arguments have a teleological and consequentialist form: they say that inequalities must be justified with reference to some good, in this case sustainable *libertà*. I have argued, however, that the basic good itself is justified in non-consequentialist terms in Machiavelli's discussions of free will.

closely at the criteria he suggests under three main headings: political equality, social inequalities, material and economic preconditions for equal opportunity and universal security.

7.5.1. Political equality

Machiavelli's meritocratic principles imply that competition for public offices and honors should be regulated by a general requirement of what in present-day language might be called "equal opportunity." We will see later that Machiavelli is cautious in his specific proposals for political reform in Florence, where opportunities to seek high offices and honors were usually limited according to guild membership and associated gradations of status. For both pragmatic and principled reasons, he does not demand the abolition of all restrictions on who may seek certain ranks and honors. He does, however, consistently demand reasoned justifications for any restrictions that are ordered. One criterion is teleological and consequentialist: namely, whether particular restrictions on equal opportunity tend to support or to undermine a condition of public *libertà*. Another, more basic criterion is non-consequentialist and deontological. This is whether a set of restrictions on equal opportunity is consistent with the "ordinary and reasonable" desire of any person to be treated as a free agent and who, *qua* citizen, is considered as co-responsible for upholding laws and orders. The second criterion is the basis for Machiavelli's meritocratic principles, including the idea that all citizens should be permitted to put themselves forward for public "rewards and honors" whatever their wealth, social background, or party preferences, even at the highest levels: all can become princes "by their virtue." It is more fundamental than the first criterion because it embodies the basic conception of individual freedom that gives rise to Machiavelli's specific, derivative conception of public *libertà* as a condition of reciprocally limited individual freedom. As with other principled arguments, Machiavelli often sets out these reasons for a strongly meritocratic principle of equal political opportunity between the lines. They are less conspicuous in his writings than overt, prudential arguments that point toward the same conclusions.

The chief instrumental reason to prefer meritocratic forms of political equality is that "orders" requiring a prince's successors to be chosen from among the best men in a city, wherever they may be found, serve the "common utility" of princes and peoples. A key to early Roman successes was that "the way to any rank whatever and to any honor whatever was not prevented for you because of poverty," and "one went to find virtue in whatever house it inhabited."[37] Readers who do not share Machiavelli's ethical preference for the *vivere libero* cannot easily ignore his prudential argument: since stable orders depend importantly on *virtú* in leaders and *virtú* seldom corresponds with birth, the hereditary principle is harmful for any political order, whether free or not. In Rome, for example, "it was necessary that in its first beginnings an orderer of a civil way of life emerge." Romulus provided the rudiments of civil orders, though these remained incomplete. But

---

[37] *D*, III.25.271/483–84; see I.2.11–13/204–7 on how hereditary monarchies degenerate.

after he died it was "then necessary that the other kings take up again the virtue of Romulus; otherwise that city would have become effeminate and the prey of its neighbors." The monarchy established by Romulus did indeed degenerate after succession was made hereditary, since the virtue of princes chosen "by their virtue" was unmatched by that of sons and grandsons who gained the kingship by birth. Machiavelli concludes that so long as Rome "lived under the kings, it bore the dangers of being ruined under a king either weak or malevolent."[38]

The next, short chapter of the *Discourses* explains the utility of political orders that adopt a principle of equal opportunity for any citizen to stand for highest office in free elections:

> After Rome had expelled the kings, it lacked those dangers that, as was said above, it must endure if either a weak or a bad king should succeed. For the highest command was brought to the consuls, who came to that command not by inheritance or by deception or by violent ambition but by free votes [*per suffragi liberi*], and were always most excellent men. Since Rome enjoyed their virtue and their fortune in one time and another, it could come to its ultimate greatness in as many years as it was under the kings.

The chapter ends with another instrumental argument, this time designed to move readers who think it is good to expand or "acquire" in the manner of Alexander the Great. "It is seen," Machiavelli writes, "that two virtuous princes in succession," as were Alexander and his father Philip of Macedon, "are sufficient to acquire the world." But whereas virtue ended with the son and was followed by disorders, free republics can do "much more, as through the mode of electing it has not only two in succession but infinite most virtuous princes [*infiniti principi virtuosissimi*] who are successors to one another. This virtuous succession," Machiavelli concludes, "will always exist in every well-ordered republic."[39] These arguments have an overtly instrumental and consequentialist form: they say that meritocratic principles of equal opportunity are most likely to promote the utility of princes, peoples, and cities, and that these good consequences supply a reason to uphold such principles. But the more basic reasons for preferring meritocratic principles of equal opportunity have to do with ethical respect for free agency. Free agency is a condition for exercising *virtú*, and *virtú* is needed to uphold any stable *ordini*. These ethical reflections explain why equal opportunity promotes order and security for princes and peoples. They would hold even if in particular cases, or from particular perspectives, these consequences did not seem to flow from laws guaranteeing equal opportunity to seek political office.

7.5.2. Social inequalities

In the passage just cited Machiavelli proposes that equal opportunity should become the principle for selecting "princes," understood there in an unconventional,

[38] *D*, I.19.52–53/249–50.
[39] *D*, I.20.54/250–51.

republican sense as public officers in positions of supreme command. This raises questions about whether and how far public laws should aim to improve the chances of less well-born and well-connected men to "become princes" by their own virtue.[40] Does Machiavelli think that political freedom based on political equality in this meritocratic sense can only be sustained where there is a high degree of social and economic equality? Are there degrees of social or economic inequality that are compatible with equal political opportunities needed for a "free way of life," and others that clearly destroy freedom?

Some passages in the *Discourses* imply that a free, civil, or political way of life depends on laws that check the formation of excessive social inequalities, since these work against meritocratic principles of political equality, as well as against universal security and transparency. For example, Machiavelli notes drily that

> those republics in which a political and uncorrupt way of life is maintained do not endure that any citizen of theirs either be or live in the usage of a gentleman; indeed, they maintain among themselves an even equality, and to the lords and gentlemen who are in that province they are very hostile. If by chance some fall into their hands, they kill them as the beginnings of corruption and the cause of every scandal.

Lords and nobles claim superior rank or public entitlements on the basis of birth; gentlemen (*gentiluomini*) on the basis of wealth. Despite the gleefully provocative reference to killing at the end of the passage—Machiavelli adds that "he who wishes to make a republic where there are very many gentlemen cannot do it unless he first eliminates all of them"—it would be wrong to conclude that he wants to recommend a reign of terror against anyone unlucky enough to be born a lord or a gentleman. If any killing of nobles is authorized by his principles of universal security and equality, it is at worst a metaphorical elimination of their distinctive status; it should be effected by ordinary legal means, not by extraordinary and violent modes.[41] Machiavelli's metaphorical and ethical meaning is not that people who currently hold the status of gentlemen should be physically eliminated, only that the laws should eliminate any reference to those private ranks as a basis for public rank. While unequal ranks and honors should remain as an essential requirement for free orders, inequalities should be ordered and distributed according to general reasons stated by law and authorized by the public.

As we have seen, Machiavelli argues that serious threats to public *libertà* come from both the excessive ambition of the few and the unreasonable rejection of authority by the many. But "very great tumults" and hence the greatest threats to free orders are "most often caused by him who possesses," not by those who have little to lose. The "nobles" and more generally the "great" (*grandi*), a term Machiavelli uses for any higher-ranking or wealthy men, are more inclined than the "ignobles" to make excessive demands, and more able to create "great tumults" through their

---

[40] See the introduction to chap. 11.
[41] *D*, I.55.111–12/311–12.

wealth and influence.[42] Thus the onus is on the more powerful to accept laws and orders that check the formation of excessive inequalities, thereby helping to sustain public *libertà*. Machiavelli notes that nobles and gentlemen often show a shortfall of *industria* in defending the common good. "To clarify this name of gentlemen such as it may be," Machiavelli remarks, "I say that those are called gentlemen who live idly in abundance from the returns of their possessions without having any care either for the cultivation or for other necessary trouble in living." Their idleness in all these respects makes so-called gentlemen and nobles "pernicious in every republic and in every province," including several kingdoms and towns in contemporary Italy. Worse still, their internal power makes these provinces more vulnerable to external attack as well as to internal corruption. In provinces full of noblemen "no republic or political way of life has ever emerged, for such kinds of men are altogether hostile to every civilization." This is why "he who wishes to make a republic where there are very many gentlemen cannot do it unless he first eliminates all of them."[43]

These arguments suggest that Machiavelli's primary sense of equality as *political* equality under laws depends on a basic condition with regard to *social* inequalities: namely, that civil and political entitlements should be completely decoupled from hereditary status and private wealth. Machiavelli argues that well-regulated meritocracy makes wealth less desirable by removing one of the main incentives people have to seek ever-greater riches. Where individuals may seek any rank and honor whatever knowing that this would not be "prevented . . . because of poverty," this "mode of life" based on equal opportunity "made riches less desirable" than where riches are a condition for public rank.[44]

7.5.3. Material and economic preconditions

Does Machiavelli think it possible or desirable to specify certain modes of economic and social organization that are ideally suited to sustain political freedom? Or if he offers no explicit prescriptions, does he at least identify a threshold of acceptable inequalities in status and wealth beyond which freedom is threatened? Machiavelli does not address these issues in ways that allow us to reconstruct a developed account of his political economy.[45] Yet he does say enough about the material preconditions needed to sustain a *vivere libero* to rule out both strongly laissez-faire and proto-communist readings of his positions.

The *Florentine Histories* vividly illustrate the corrupting effects of great material and social inequalities on *libertà*. The work considers these effects from two angles, top-down and bottom-up. When the wealth of some individuals or families is so great that they are able to provide expensive favors to other citizens, including those who hold public office, some may be tempted to use their private economic

[42] *D*, I.5, 19/212.
[43] Ibid. Venice is his main example.
[44] *D*, III.25.271/483–84; also I.6.35; I.17.67; I.55.134–36.
[45] Though see Nelson's (2004) valuable discussion comparing Machiavelli's political economy to Greek writers.

power to control political and juridical processes behind the scenes. Public transparency is the first casualty of such conduct. Instead of doing things "in the sun" like the Romans in their best days, matters of great public import are decided "in the shade [*sotto l'ombra*]" in the manner of "false and corrupt" examples from antiquity.[46] Meritocratic principles of political equality are then eroded, as offices and honors are procured through loans, favors, and the partisan loyalties they help to purchase. These "shady" practices transform security in a city into a privatized and partisan good, accessible to the few who can afford it but increasingly elusive for the many who cannot. When the conditions of universal security are destroyed, so is the rule of law, the foundation of political *libertà* and the free way of life. Machiavelli's analysis of the Medici party's rise to power puts these corrupting processes under close scrutiny. The analysis does not conclude that great disparities of wealth in a city make these forms of corruption inevitable. It does suggest that, given natural human ambitions and self-indulgence, they are extremely likely to develop once such disparities emerge.

Machiavelli sees individual men who come to great wealth by their own *onesto* labors as analogous to kings elected for their own merits. From every *onesto* patriarch whose *industria* makes his family a potential power-broker in a city, there may issue one or two scions whose merits and honesty are comparable to his, and numerous other heirs who fall short of the original. And even the more worthy scions are unlikely to acquire their forebears' qualities of *virtuoso* responsibility and self-restraint. Since they came to their position by another man's fortune, they seldom develop the high quality of *virtú* that comes only when individuals are constrained to work under harsh necessity.[47] When after a few generations such men come to dominate political and legal processes—even if they do so mainly with methods that do not openly violate public laws—they are less well equipped to defend their city's freedom against others who seek to undermine it. If the wealthy few are not themselves corrupt, those who inherit their wealth may still lack the reflective prudence needed to defend free orders against corruption. *Necessità* has not obliged them to confront others' freedom as a serious constraint on their own wills, since fortune leads them to imagine that they can steer others' wills to their own ends by means of inducements.

Machiavelli's analysis of the bottom-up effects of extreme material inequality on *libertà* occurs early in the *Histories*, with his dramatic account in Book III of the Ciompi (woolworkers) revolt of 1378.[48] Here he describes the flip side of the inequalities that enable the very wealthy to increase their control over political processes. As political power came to be correlated to wealth, less wealthy citizens were deprived of civil powers that they had previously held. On Machiavelli's account, poorer artisans were gradually squeezed out of public ranks by the larger guilds that represented the wealthier sections of society. The "lesser guilds" were demoted to dependent status, depriving members of any independent voice for their concerns.

[46] *AW*, I.17.10/534.
[47] *D*, I.2.11–13/202–7.
[48] The uprising lasted for months.

Previously, their official status as a group publicly authorized to express collective interests gave them a stake in helping to preserve civil order alongside the wealthy. Once they lost this status and the political power it conferred, however, they ceased to consider themselves as co-responsible for upholding laws and orders that no longer enabled them to "live secure." The "lesser people [*popolo minuto*]" conceived a searing hatred for "the rich citizens and princes of the guilds," since "it did not appear to them that they had been satisfied for their labor as they believed they justly deserved [*che giustamente credevano meritare*]."[49] So long as these reasonable grievances were not addressed, the effects of extreme inequality harmed everyone in the city. Made desperate by poverty, political impotence, and the arrogance of the greater guilds, the poorest artisans and laborers turned violently on the wealthy, attacking their property and their families. The episode illustrates the point that when inequalities in wealth are allowed to undermine political equality, any sort of order is destroyed, not only free orders. By destroying universal security, such inequalities seem at first to create insecurity only for the poor and weak. But the poor and weak are still human, however hard the powerful might try to dehumanize them; and it is a "natural and ordinary" inconvenience that human beings fight back when they consider themselves injured. When they do fight back, it becomes clear that their insecurity jeopardizes the security of the wealthy—demonstrating that order as well as freedom depends on general *sicurtà*.

According to Machiavelli's analysis, the main cause of the Ciompi revolt was not economic inequalities per se, but the fact that these were allowed to undermine the established political rights of the lesser guildsmen. Had wealthier citizens stood firmly on the side of established rights protecting the lesser workers instead of agreeing to erode them to their own advantage, material inequalities might not have generated social and political disorders. Again, Machiavelli does not say that inequality inevitably leads to disorder, only that family feeling and ambition constitute *naturale e ordinario* temptations for the wealthy to use their wealth in ways that deprive others, de facto or de jure, of equal chances to seek public ranks and honors. When this happens on a large scale, and the less wealthy find that they lack resources for effective representation of just grievances, disorders become both likely and reasonable. Although Machiavelli does not say so directly, his arguments strongly suggest that the preservation of political *libertà* is incompatible with unrestrained laissez-faire economic practices. When he declares in the *Discourses* that "One could show in a long speech how much better fruits poverty produced than riches, and how the one has honored cities, provinces, sects, and the other has ruined them," the hyperbole has a more reasoned judgment at its core: that "the most useful thing that may be ordered in a free way of life is that the citizens be kept poor," or at least discouraged from gaining exorbitant *private* wealth.[50]

Machiavelli leaves it up to citizens in particular cities to judge whether the kinds of inequalities they face have begun to undermine public freedom. He does not say

[49] *FH*, III.12.121/442–43.
[50] *D*, III.25.271–72/483–84.

what the appropriate limits to inequality are, only *that* there are limits that must be identified and guarded by any city in relation to its own orders, forms of property, and wealth. Prudent orderers should legislate to avoid excessive inequalities, counteracting the political effects of those that remain with other "laws and orders." Machiavelli's general and formal criteria for judging these questions follow from arguments discussed earlier. *Libertà* depends on the public regulation of private wealth according to two general criteria. The expansion of private wealth should be limited, first, by laws aimed at ensuring that public freedom—understood as the reciprocally limited freedom of individual citizens—is not undermined. The criterion for setting limits here is consequentialist: whether public freedom is preserved or undercut. The second criterion is non-consequentialist. It is grounded in judgments about what any human being, fellow citizen or not, may reasonably demand from others by virtue of his capacities for free agency. These criteria do not supply specific practical rules for deciding how to set limits on private wealth. They do urge citizens to weigh very carefully the consequences and wrongs that may ensue if they fail to set *some* lawfully authorized limits to material inequalities.

At the same time, Machiavelli underlines the dangers to freedom and order that stem from ill-considered forms of regulation. Early in the *Discourses* he notes that while inequality leads to corruption and "a slight aptitude for a free way of life [*poca attitudine alla vita libera nasce da una inequalità*]," the notion that men can be made equal in possessions or abilities is a dangerous pipe-dream. The most extraordinary means would be needed to realize it, and even then it would remain elusive.[51] The *Histories* contains several examples of disastrously counterproductive attempts to eliminate economic inequalities by means of "extraordinary"—in Machiavelli's lexicon, a synonym for extralegal, unauthorized, or excessive—forms of taxation leveled against the rich.[52] Since the wealthy saw these forced redistributions of their private wealth as punitive and unjust, they reacted by stirring up disorders that destabilized the republic. Machiavelli shows almost as much sympathy for these concerns as he does for the plight of the disenfranchised lesser guildsmen. If material inequalities may lead to political injustice, remedies that can reasonably be judged unduly coercive by the better-off seldom result in stable or free orders.[53] Here is a case where redistributive measures do not meet the criterion of respect for free agency, because they are imposed unilaterally by one section of society on another, instead of being authorized through procedures regarded as authoritative by rich and poorer citizens. This violates the maxim that what we call justice "must be believed by others as by us."[54] The failure to seek the authorization of the rich for higher taxes showed that the policy was motivated not by a concern to preserve common freedoms, but by the partisan desire to reduce the economic freedom of the rich beyond what was necessary to sustain public *libertà*. The rich, Machiavelli implies, might have been more inclined to accept higher levels of taxation if they had been treated as equals

[51] *D*, I.17.48–49/245.
[52] See chap. 10.
[53] See chap. 8, sec. 8.5.
[54] *FH*, IV.27.174–15/506–8.

in the legislative process. Instead of force, prudential and principled reasons might have persuaded the wealthy that some limits on their private economic freedoms were needed to maintain public freedom. Freedom is most secure where the opulent few recognize for themselves that their own security depends on social conditions that can sustain equality of opportunity for the many. If they are reflectively prudent, they will freely authorize policies that redistribute private wealth for public purposes. Where they fail to do this, they must bear some responsibility for whatever punitive measures the majority may take against them. The majority, however, must also realize that extremely punitive measures will be seen as unjust, and provoke new cycles of unrest.

While the economic orders that satisfy Machiavelli's conditions uphold procedural constraints, optimally free orders also have a certain substantive form. Under free orders, the rule of law regulates interactions *among* individuals with a view to preventing the free movements of any individual, party, or social group from overstepping due limits and dominating others. It does this, however, in ways that leave individuals a good deal of private room to choose for themselves how to order their own productive and reproductive lives. Public laws and authorities that overregulate these choices, Machiavelli implies, threaten *libertà* as much as governments that fail adequately to regulate citizens' free motions. The economic order most likely to sustain free orders, then, is one founded on laws that protect the private rights of individuals to acquire property and pass it on to their children.[55] This is the bedrock of Machiavelli's political economy. But at the same time, the principle of respect for free agency that underpins these private rights requires that they be limited by law to protect conditions for public freedom. Procedures for deliberating and setting those limits should be clearly defined by law according to conditions of impartiality, generality, and impersonality to minimize suspicions that they are punitive or partisan.

Machiavelli does not say in general terms how much public regulation is needed to satisfy these general, principled criteria, or describe an ideal model of political economy that all polities should adopt. Broadly speaking, his principles imply that moderate forms of public regulation are preferable to extreme forms of public control or redistribution. Individual citizens' desires to choose for themselves what and how to produce and reproduce, and how to pass on their goods to offspring, are fundamental. This moderate position is confirmed by his extremely critical accounts in the *Florentine Histories* of the effects of punitive redistributive measures frequently imposed by the people on the nobles and *grandi*.[56] Yet he also implies that some publicly authorized redistribution may be required by the criterion of preventing great inequalities, in order to prevent permanent monopolies that allow the some parties or families to dominate others by non-transparent means. Redistributive measures should not be imposed extraordinarily, when disparities of wealth have already become so great that those asked to give more to the public see this transfer as revenge for their success, stemming from envy. Prudently or-

---

[55] *D*, I.16.45/241–42.
[56] See *FH*, IV.8.153/48; IV.14–15.159–60/447–49.

dered polities always have ordinary means in place to check excessive inequalities, so that the wealthiest citizens never have good reason to see taxation as unjust, and the less well-off have no reasonable cause for resentment.

7.6.
Foundations of political freedom: Procedural constraints and the rule of law

Machiavelli's conception of free political orders is implicitly critical of other familiar concepts, especially those that understand *libertà* as the absence of constraints on one's own will, movements, or choices.[57] These conceptions view freedom primarily as a self-assertive capacity, stressing individuals' power to do or to choose without interference or obstruction. Machiavelli, by contrast, views innate freedom primarily as a capacity for self-ordering and self-restraint. He uses the word *libertà* not to describe conditions where individuals face few constraints or have a wide range of choices, but for conditions where innately free people authorize orders and laws to *regulate* their own choices and actions in relation to those of other free agents.

In informal, personal relationships, people author and order their own restraints on a continuous basis. They refrain from demanding excessive free rein for reasons of reflective prudence (otherwise others might feel it necessary to do the same, leading to conflict) or ethics (respect for other people's capacities for free agency, and valuing these as well as one's own). In political and juridical contexts, choosing to accept limits on one's own freedom normally does not involve continuous assessment of every relationship. Rather, people accept that their freedom is limited in numerous ways by laws. On Machiavelli's conception of political freedom, citizens regard themselves not only as coerced by the laws, though laws are always backed by coercive force. Citizens who regard themselves as "living in freedom" also consider themselves as responsible for upholding laws they have authorized.

Why should public authorization be necessary if a lawgiver "orders" laws that satisfy all the conditions set out above with respect to security, publicity, and equality under the rule of law? The answer is that Machiavelli does not define any of these conditions for free orders *only* in terms of specific institutions or outcomes. All have an important perceptual element, especially trust (*confidenza, fede*).[58] Security depends partly on trust that more powerful neighbors and rulers will not seize one's patrimony, or limit one's personal choices at will. Publicity depends on expectations that rich and well-connected candidates for public office will not be able easily to conceal their true qualities from those who elect them. Political equality depends on trust that economic and social inequalities need not deter citizens of any background from standing for office and developing the virtue needed to become princes. In short, all depend on mechanisms

---

[57] Compare similar distinctions in Plato, *Rep.* 359c, 557b–d, 562b–569c.

[58] Trust (*pistis*) is an essential basis for stable civil and intercity orders in Herodotus, Thucydides, and Xenophon. Also see Iamblichus 1997, chap. 20.

designed to ensure transparency and accountability needed to maintain public trust. Throughout the *Discourses* and *Histories* Machiavelli argues that such mechanisms can only be maintained if the authority of laws is based on *procedures* of public authorization, not on judgments about whether the laws successfully realize all the elements of political freedom.[59] Chapter 4 outlined the idea that laws and orders imposed by human beings' own *virtú* have a quality of necessity—that is, a very strong kind of causality—that enables *virtuoso* agents to avoid complete determination by external necessities, whether natural, supernatural, or human. A philosophically sensitive reading of the first chapter of the *Discourses* suggests that Machiavelli identifies this kind of self-imposed *necessità*, necessity imposed by one's own *leggi e ordini*, as the optimal expression of *virtú* and foundation of stable human orders. For Machiavelli, laws understood as *self-imposed* constraints are the single most important means of establishing political *libertà*. That (1) the constraints needed for any civil or political life are established by means of laws, and (2) that the laws in question are authorized by means of procedures that respect the free agency of citizens, are the most fundamental conditions for free orders. The rule of law undergirds and regulates the three conditions for free orders just discussed: universal security, public transparency, and equal opportunity. *Leggi* are the chief means of confirming and giving authority to any human *ordini*. Strong laws provide the quality of *necessità*, in the senses of physical compulsion and ethical *obligo*, without which there can be no *virtú* and no *libertà*.[60] Citizens are under necessity to obey the laws of a free city because through procedures of free authorization they assume full responsibility for upholding them, and accept the penalties for transgressing the laws as self-imposed and reasonable.[61]

Machiavelli alludes very pointedly to the fundamental importance of the rule of law for his political theory in chapter 3, before going on to examine other less reliable modes of maintaining civil order and *autorità*. Men, he says, "never work any good unless through necessity," since license and disorder run amok where there are no compelling limits on their actions. "Therefore," Machiavelli continues, connecting the requisite form of *necessità* to the ethical and practical necessity imposed by laws, "it is said that hunger and poverty make men industrious, and the laws make them good [*le leggi gli fanno buoni*]." He then reiterates classical arguments for giving priority to the rule of laws over individual "wise" men or habits and customs. "Where a thing works well on its own without the law, the law is not necessary"; but "when some good custom [*consuetudine*] is lacking, at once

---

[59] Thus the authority of laws in the early Roman republic was greatly strengthened by the fact that "people had seen that the laws had been made for its benefit, such as the one appealing to the plebs" in which the benefit in question is the procedural requirement of seeking authorization from the plebs (*D*, I.32.70/267–68). Also recall Livy's procedural maxim, "that rule is certainly the firmest that is obeyed gladly" (*D*, II.23.182/388).

[60] On Machiavelli's "covert" writing about political obligation in the *Prince*, see chap. 11, sec. 11.6.

[61] Among ancient texts, these arguments are most fully developed in Plato, *Laws* 690c et passim.

the law is necessary."[62] Machiavelli's point is not that when possible, prudent orderers of cities should seek to rely on customs and habits to regulate civil conduct, and avoid using laws, since these always appear as coercive constraints on agents who reasonably prefer to be left "free in a field."[63] As we will see in chapters 10 and 11, he tries to show throughout the *Discourses* that it is never prudent to rely *primarily* on good habits, customs, or virtues in citizens or leaders. These qualities vary widely between individuals, and may change overnight even in those who appeared altogether good before. Even if a rare individual could be found who was consistently good in his customs, after his death there is no guarantee that others will emerge who are good enough to carry civil virtue on their shoulders. It follows that the rule of law should be given strict priority over customs and particular virtues of character. Good customs and particular virtues such as reflective prudence or steadiness of conduct, whether in individual leaders or the body of citizens, contribute greatly to a polity's well-being.[64] But if no laws are in place to make men good in their outward actions when their natural or customary dispositions are not good, civil order cannot last long.

At the end of Book I, having considered assorted difficulties of adopting modes of authority that are not anchored in strict legal restraints, Machiavelli reiterates his opening arguments to offer a robust defense of the rule of law as the foundation of political *libertà*. Laws freely defended by the people, he argues in chapter 58, are the best means human beings have of maintaining civil orders that are stable and free. Echoing his philosophical argument in chapter 1 that *virtú* is only elicited under necessity, Machiavelli now points out that freedom depends on rigorous restraints, whereas unshackled (*sciolta*) multitudes and princes invariably threaten *libertà*. The shackles needed for freedom are laws, which acquire authority through procedures whereby people freely authorize constraints on their actions.[65] A mass of individuals unshackled by laws for which they assume responsibility is a mere "multitude," prone to *licenza* and tyranny. The same individuals shackled by laws to which they freely give authority constitute a "people" well-armed to defend orders they regard as their own against internal and external threats. It is not, Machiavelli argues, the nature of multitudes that should be faulted for disorders, but the absence of non-natural, self-regulating laws that demand *rispetto* for civil orders.[66] Whereas "all err equally when all can err without respect," a free people governed by its own self-authorized laws will be disinclined to cause disorders. For "a people

[63] Phrases often translated as "customs and laws," *ethē kai nomima/nomoi*, are often used by Thucydides, Plato, and other Greek writers, who do not distinguish sharply between laws and customs but treat them as mutually supportive.

[64] And when found in a few remarkable individuals in corrupt times, these virtues may even save the city from great self-inflicted harms, as the examples of Camillus and Fabius Maximus show; see chaps. 8, 12.

[65] Compare Rousseau 1964 (1762), II.6.377–80.

[66] Compare the shifts from *dēmos* (people under laws) to *plēthos* (multitude) or *ochlos* (mob) in Thucydides' Athens, especially after that city's decision to attack Sicily; TPW, VI.60–64.

that commands and is well ordered" by its own laws "will be stable, prudent, and grateful no otherwise than a prince, or better than a prince, even one esteemed wise. The variation in their proceeding," Machiavelli concludes, "arises not from a diverse *nature*—because it is in one mode in all, and if there is advantage of good, it is in the people—but from having more or less respect for the laws [*rispetto alle leggi*] within which both live."[67]

The close relations between *libertà* and the rule of law are a familiar theme of classical and humanist republican thought. Here I draw on earlier discussions to summarize what I take to be Machiavelli's distinctive positions on three related questions that republican authors answer in diverse ways. (1) Which should take priority when assessing the quality of laws, formal procedures or end-states? (2) Which should be the primary concern of the laws, to protect individual rights or to protect or promote the common good? (3) How and how far can good laws avoid the problems of poor judgment that constantly undermine free orders, with respect to both the choice of public officials and the conditions needed to maintain *libertà*?

7.6.1. Formal procedures and end states

I have already tried to make the case that, contrary to first appearances, Machiavelli's arguments consistently imply that procedures of public authorization should take priority over the pursuit of specific end-states, including the pursuit of fully-fledged political *libertà*. As previous sections suggested, when agents try to establish conditions of *libertà* without due respect for the wills of those who are expected to live under them, prospects for success are slim indeed. This suggests two main conditions that should regulate actions aimed at "ordering for freedom":

1. *Authorization.* The rule of law depends as much on the judgments of people subject to the laws as on particular institutions. If large numbers of people judge that the laws given to them are unjust in substance, or that the laws lack authority because they have not given authority to them, the laws cannot be said to rule.

2. *Reasons as a source of authority.* Respect for the laws depends on good reasons, not on terror or unregulated force.[68] People will have good reasons to respect laws where laws have the authority of reasons valid for all, not for a few or for some sections of a population. The identification of publicly acceptable reasons depends on procedures that allow a free exchange of views, followed by transparent processes of authorization that are regarded by all participants as just.

These conditions can be seen as Machiavelli's optimal criteria for political freedom, not his minimum. But while he acknowledges that it is possible to have some elements of political freedom while omitting others, orders last much longer

---

[67] *D*, I.58.116–17/317–19.
[68] See chaps. 5, 10.

and thrive more when the optimal criteria are met.[69] As we will see in chapter 10, Machiavelli acknowledges that there are conditions in which particular civil freedoms must be curtailed in order to secure or restore general conditions of *libertà*. But when setting limits, those who undertake to order the laws for any particular set of people should be guided by the following considerations.

First, there are no rules for setting reciprocal limits on free agents' freedom, only principles that should guide deliberations about how to do so. The orderers who set limits should always seek the free authorization of the people who live under their orders, avoiding methods of imposition that may reasonably be seen as unjust. This formal and procedural condition is all that orderers have to guide them. Machiavelli does not suggest any more specific rules for setting boundaries between different agents' proper spheres of freedom. He occasionally speaks of limits set by common utility, injury to others, and so forth. But unlike later utilitarians, he does not suggest that any such criteria are able to serve as universally valid rules to determine where one agent's freedom reaches its limits and another's begins. In this respect the social and political implications of his egalitarian conception of free agency are more open-ended than utilitarian arguments, or arguments such Locke's that set pre-political or natural limits on equality. Readers who want political philosophers to include a precise set of rules for deciding how individual freedoms should be limited might find this open-ended approach unsatisfactory. Others might see open-endedness as a strength, indicating Machiavelli's awareness of the epistemic and practical difficulties of fixing universal rules that set specific boundaries on individual freedom. Since human knowledge of any natural or supernatural criteria for such boundaries is unreliable, legislators and philosophers who claim to have it should not be trusted. Even if their intentions are good, their choice and definition of freedom-limiting principles may be more affected than they realize by self-interest or the standpoint of their own party, city, or people. Without natural laws or universal rules that determine how freedom should reciprocally limited, human legislators are on their own; they must work out criteria for themselves by reasoning with other human legislators. If they cannot reach reasoned agreement about the criteria for limiting everyone's freedom, no appeal to higher reason, natural law, or common utility can spare them conflicts.

This suggests, second, that wherever established orders already exist for seeking authorization—for example, public assemblies or public courts—these should be treated as the authoritative source of judgments about what limits may legitimately be placed on anyone's freedom. If assemblies or courts have been affected by corruption in the past or delivered bad judgments for other reasons, that is not a sufficient reason for an orderer to usurp their functions by extraordinary means. He should rather strive to renovate such malfunctioning *ordini* by bringing them back

---

[69] Thus kingdoms and principalities may introduce elements of political freedom, as in early Rome, where "Romulus and all the other kings made many and good laws conforming also to a free way of life." But "because their end was to found a kingdom and not a republic, when that city was left free, many things that were necessary to order in favor of freedom were lacking, not having been ordered by those kings" (*D*, I.2.14/335).

to their original purpose: to provide forums for the public to deliberate, authorize, or reject the laws proposed by those designated as "orderers."

Third, procedural principles take strict priority over the realization of particular ends. The procedural principle of respect for public authorization rests on a more basic ethical principle: namely, that the right of free agents to authorize laws they are expected to obey takes precedence over particular conceptions of the common good. As I have been arguing, Machiavelli's own conception of the common or public good is grounded in a prior, deontological account of the respect due to free agents. Though laws should aim at the common good, the content of that aim has to be decided by self-legislating agents themselves. Respect for their freely given authority is a condition for any conception of the good to become authoritative in public life. When Machiavelli appeals to the notion of the public good, then, he does not consider it an intrinsic ethical value that may sometimes take precedence over the rights of agents to authorize their laws and orders. He conceives the public good as a good because and insofar as it is based on procedures that respect individuals' free agency, procedures confirmed by the rule of law. Other, more substantive notions of the common good or utility may be brought to bear on public deliberations; many are reflected in the opinions Machiavelli himself canvasses in his works. But the more general, procedural principle of authorization regulates *how* these are brought to bear in public reasonings, preventing any private or partisan conception of the public good from claiming authority in advance of acts whereby the general public authorizes it.

Fourth, when setting legal limits on everyone's freedom with a view to maintaining public *libertà*, orderers should not make the error of treating some individuals', parties', or peoples' freedom as less worthy of respect than that of others. The innate freedom imputed to free agents does not come in measurably larger or smaller portions between different people. Everyone who is considered a free agent must be considered to have the same capacities to author and authorize laws.[70] Thus the idea of equality, understood as a broad regulative notion rather than a specific set of distributive outcomes, should regulate deliberations about how to set reciprocal limits on everyone's freedom. Machiavelli's arguments preclude the idea that public freedom is the aggregate of individual or sectional freedoms, where the criterion for judging freedom is the overall sum, not the equal distribution of limits on everyone's free motions in accordance with procedures that all see as reasonable. Prudent orderers should avoid treating the freedom of some as exchangeable against the freedom of others, realizing that free *ordini* cannot be founded on laws

[70] Unequal empirical capacities must be decided by some agreed criterion that all can reasonably see as fair. The most obvious candidate for a non-arbitrary, uncontroversial criterion is age, since all human beings age in the same way. Machiavelli makes age his chief criterion for entry into the highest political ranks in his *Discursus*. Although he follows Florentine tradition in treating guild membership as a criterion for membership in other civil ranks, he says nothing to rule out civil rights for people who live in the countryside. Since Machiavelli—unlike Plato and, implicitly, Xenophon—says nothing about sex as a criterion for civil rights, it seems safe to assume that his private views followed Roman and Florentine tradition in this respect too. However, I find nothing in his principled positions, examples, or correspondence that precludes moral and political equality between men and women.

that give too much "free rein" or *licenza* to one sct of people—say, the "ignobles" or the wealthy—while placing excessively punitive limits on the freedom of the *nobili,* or doing nothing to improve opportunities for the poor.

7.6.2. Individuals and the common good under the rule of law

This way of conceiving political freedom as grounded in the rule of law differs in an important way from the conceptions of public *libertà* sometimes ascribed to Machiavelli. A common view is that Machiavelli thinks of freedom in the republic mainly in collectivist or communitarian terms, whereby the ethical claims of individual citizens come second to the claims of the city or *patria* as a whole. In the scholarly literature one often encounters the view that Machiavelli's concept of *libertà* ultimately places communal values such as the common good or the safety of the fatherland above personal freedoms.[71] These non-individualist ethical foundations are sometimes seen as characteristically "republican," and contrasted to the strongly individualist premises of "liberal" political theories. Although thoughtful readers recognize that Machiavelli's reasonings in favor of republics have an important individualist dimension, they still argue that his most important ethical commitments are rooted in claims about the intrinsic value of the city as such, not in claims about the value of individual free agency.

My reading questions this non-individualist view of Machiavelli's basic commitments. I have been arguing that for Machiavelli, any adequate conception of the public good or of common safety must be grounded in the rule of law; and that his conception of the rule of law is derived, in turn, from his conception of individual free agency as an innate capacity that deserves respect. According to this view, the primary purpose of the laws is to protect individual freedoms. Conceptions of the public good that do not treat this protection as a priority do not deserve the good names of "public" or of *libertà*. If a given conception of the good has not been identified as the *authoritative* conception, that is, the one given legitimate authority through transparent public procedures, there is no good reason why citizens should consider it to be their own public good. They may, on the contrary, have reason to see it as only a particular person's or party's idea of the common good, imposed on the rest without public deliberation or acts of authorization. Such conceptions will lack firm *autorità* or legitimacy, which, in Machiavelli's view, can only come from the free acts of a particular set of human beings.

These premises preclude the kind of collectivist republican arguments that have sometimes been ascribed to Machiavelli. To clarify, it is correct to see Machiavelli's conception of political *libertà* as one that requires extensive limits on every individual citizen's freedoms. But the basic reason for setting such limits is not to protect or promote the common good, but the ethical necessity to protect the equal freedom of each individual citizen. Indeed, any common good that is genuinely common or public must satisfy this requirement. In these respects, Machiavelli's conceptions of political freedom and the rule of law are firmly grounded in the

[71] See chap. 9, sec. 9.7.

prior value of individual free agency. The basic relations that constitute a free way of life or political freedom are relations among individuals. In any city whatever, different individuals have diverse humors, customs, ambitions, opinions, and powers. No reasonable conception of the public or common good can ever eliminate these differences or bring citizens to ultimate unity. On Machiavelli's anthropological premises as well as his ethical ones, the only reasonable way to identify an authoritative common good is freely reasoned debates among the individuals who are expected to support it.

On my reading, then, the *ethical* premises of Machiavelli's conception of political freedom are strongly individualistic. But his argument that individual free agency is necessarily constrained by other agents leads to a distinctive form of *political* individualism. Machiavelli's position is that although free agency is a basic ethical premise, this does not mean that it should not be subject to severe constraints. On the contrary, precisely because everyone is presumed to have equal *capacities* to exercise free will, everyone's *powers* to do so must be limited or no stable orders will ever be achieved. Machiavelli's individualism is perhaps best described as a regulated individualism. It is clearly distinct from varieties of laissez-faire individualism that treat individual freedom as an intrinsically valuable power as well as an innate capacity, and deny that individual powers must be curtailed in order to ensure that everyone's capacities for freedom are respected. While ascribing fundamental ethical status to *capacities* for free agency, Machiavelli recognizes that these capacities give free agents the *power* to work for good and for bad, for order or disorder. He therefore refrains from granting intrinsic value to the powers of individual free agency, insisting that specific uses of those powers must be judged on one basic, formal criterion: do agents impose limits on their own free will out of respect for the presumably equal free agency of others? Whereas laissez-faire individualism is based on an ethical picture of agents as ideally unconstrained, for Machiavelli this is both an unrealistic and an unappealing picture. If taken as the basis for political reasoning, it tends to lead orderers to license, not to *libertà*. A more realistic and ethically attractive picture accepts that since agents are under ordinary necessity to interact with other free agents, they must constantly adjust their actions and choices to those of others. To maintain free public orders under such inescapable constraints requires a fairly high degree of regulation, and constant vigilance against corruption.

7.6.3. Problems of willing: Free authorization and bad judgment

According to Machiavelli, one of the most serious problems in maintaining free orders is that people often freely authorize policies that undermine public *libertà*. The *Histories* present numerous examples where the Florentine people willingly give authority to leaders or parties that proceed to destroy the freedoms they promised to protect. To some extent, Machiavelli implies, such misjudgments may be attributed to the shrewd manipulations of the leading men who seek popular approval. As we have seen, his account of the Medicis' extraordinary rise to power shows how skilled politicians may preserve impeccable appearances of legality while undercutting freedom and the rule of law by means of informal, quasi-legal practices. Ultimately, however, citizens themselves must be held responsible for how they respond to such seductions. More adequate kinds of reasoning are undoubtedly needed to alert citizens to the risks of acting on poor information, financial or other inducements, or other forms of manipulation. But these risks cannot be eliminated by setting up a theoretical criterion such as an a priori notion of a rational will. The best that humans can do is to improve on, and guard against corruption in, procedures designed to appraise candidates for public office and policies proposed by incumbents. The chief correctives for the ineliminable problems of mendacity and manipulation in free orders are, once again, procedural. In concrete terms, they can be found in well-ordered public assemblies and courts placed under rigorous public scrutiny. These orders allow citizens to scrutinize the methods used by leading men in the city, and to deliberate their merits openly and without fear.

7.7.
Persuasions: Why should people choose free orders?

Throughout this chapter I have discussed two distinct sets of reasons that Machiavelli gives for preferring free political orders to unfree forms of government. Prudential arguments for political freedom appeal to particular agents' interest in securing various goods that they value, especially goods deemed necessary for self-preservation. Machiavelli's prudential arguments address two main audiences whose interests often appear to conflict: princes and powerful minorities who seek to command or dominate, and the great majority in any city who want above all to "live secure." The other set of reasons is principled, or ethical. What I have been calling Machiavelli's ethical arguments are based on reasons that he judges as compelling irrespective of any particular agent's standpoint, interests, or values.[72] Arguments that point to the innate freedom of human beings, and make this freedom a ground for preferring free orders, exemplify Machiavelli's principled reasonings.

This raises the question of whether Machiavelli treats prudential self-interest as a sufficient ground of arguments in favor of political freedom, or whether he implies that people should also recognize more fundamental, principled reasons for preferring free orders. When one's aim is to dissuade agents from overstepping the limits set by others' free agency, it might seem enough to point out that this would harm their own interests, since people who believe that their just claims to freedom are violated tend to make life hard for the violators. Moreover, many of

[72] I distinguish between "prudential and ethical" rather than "prudential and moral" because the words "moral" and "morality" are often—in my view wrongly—associated with "abstract" reflections or set in sharp opposition to prudential considerations, and I want to make it easier to recognize the close connections between prudence and ethics/morality in Machiavelli's thought. I further reject the view that he draws a sharp distinction between "ethics" (or morality) as applicable only to private life, and "politics" as a realm where only maxims of prudence apply; see, for example, Wolin 1960, 195–238. As I have been arguing, Machiavelli sets extremely demanding ethical (or moral) standards of conduct for all aspects of "public" life.

Machiavelli's examples imply that stronger agents are often persuaded to act with greater self-restraint by reasons of prudence alone, without acknowledging the general ethical significance of free agency. The overt form of his own reasonings is prudential and consequentialist, not principled or deontological. So even if my argument that he develops a less overt line of principled reasonings is plausible, the question remains whether it is *needed* to make Machiavelli's arguments for self-restraint as a condition for free orders. If appeals to self-interested prudence point to the same practical conclusions as appeals to respect for free agency, and if the strong are more easily dissuaded from overassertive actions by prudential reasonings, what can possibly be gained by making ethical respect an important reason for action?

I suggest two answers. One is that logically, prudential arguments presuppose the principled ones. The presupposition of innate freedom explains why it is always and everywhere prudent to order polities for *libertà*. Free orders make whole cities more prosperous and its citizens more contented; and these benefits help to secure them against internal or external threats. But the basic reason why freedom has these good effects lies in the intrinsic value of free agency, which tends to cause good effects when it is respected and well-ordered, and bad ones when it is denigrated or disordered. Although Machiavelli does not spell out this position, he strongly implies that the reason people are more likely to fight harder, produce more wealth, and obey the laws in free orders is that they are innately free, and thus more likely to flourish and contribute to public flourishing when their free agency is respected. Conversely, the reason why people always and everywhere are unreliable fighters, poor workers, and prone to act as blind multitudes in unfree polities is that their innate capacities for freedom are frustrated there. When Machiavelli says that "all towns and provinces that live freely in every part make very great profits," the profits in question are not only material. They include the great advantage for *individuals* that they are free under laws to exercise their own wills on matters of great private and public importance. Political freedom increases public profits *because* each individual is allowed to choose how many children to procreate, and to judge for himself how to feed them. It tends to support stable orders, and thus increase a city's power, *because* men who know that they and their children can "by their virtue become princes"—commanders and co-legislators in their city—are inclined to accept and defend the authority of the laws and whoever leads according to them. And if they judge that the men in authority at a given time are not doing their job well, they can put themselves forward as *capi* and *magistrati* to try to do it better.[73]

A second, practical answer is that even prudent judgments can be placed on firmer, reflectively reasoned ground if people grasp the basic ethical reasons for self-restraint. Ethical reasons are practically necessary if orderers wish to save themselves—and those for whom they order—time and trouble. No matter how carefully people calculate the other likely consequences of their actions, if they fail adequately to weigh in the certain (imminent and future) costs of failing to

---

[73] *D*, II.2.129/330–31.

respect the free agency of others, they have omitted the most important factor that influences the outcomes of any action that affects other people. As many of Machiavelli's examples show, it is natural for men in command to imagine that their private ambitions or partisan notions of the public good are in tune with other people's interests. Such wishful thinking often leads even commanders who claim to love freedom to behave in licentious or tyrannical ways, undermining the conditions for *libertà*. This is less likely to happen when commanders and orderers take the principle of respect for free authorization as their guide. Instead of waiting for experience to show that unauthorized measures are less prudent than those backed by free "willing," prudent agents should start by making sure that their orders conform to principles of equal innate freedom. If they reflect carefully enough, they should come to regard other people's freedom as a basic *ethical* constraint on their own free agency.

CHAPTER 8

Justice and Injustice

Machiavelli often uses the word "justice" (*giustizia, iustizia*) in his political and historical writings and correspondence. He seldom uses it, however, in the same ways as many Christian political theorists and humanists. This leaves the impression that Machiavelli is uninterested in developing a more adequate account of justice as part of his political theory. The impression is reinforced by the overtly prudential form of his reasonings. He does, of course, frequently discuss topics that classical and humanist authors place under the heading of justice. The distribution of public goods and offices, appropriate punishments for bad conduct or rewards for good, and the value of keeping promises and pacts are among the most prominent themes in all Machiavelli's best-known writings. But his arguments seem to treat self-interested prudence, not justice, as the touchstone for evaluating distributions, punishments, and rewards, and for deciding when obligations are binding. These appearances explain why so many perceptive and sympathetic readers conclude that Machiavelli wanted to separate judgments grounded in reflective prudence from ethical considerations, especially considerations of justice, and to limit—if not obviate—the role of justice in political deliberations.[1]

This chapter tries to show that, appearances notwithstanding, reasoning about justice is at the very center of Machiavelli's ethics and political thought. Indeed, questions of justice and injustice arguably form *the* main, implicit subject-matter of all Machiavelli's main political works. Although he uses the word "justice" more sparingly than more conventional republican writers, between the lines Machiavelli is always writing about justice and injustice. Even when he does not speak directly of *giustizia* or *iniustizia*, he often uses paraphrases or related words that signal a concern for justice, especially *leggi, respetto, obligo*, or *termini* (limits). Machiavelli employs these indirect modes of writing to discuss some of the most fundamental questions of political justice: how to define the limits of free action for individuals and sectional groups, how to regulate conflicts that ordinarily arise among free agents, and how to order various civil and judicial procedures under laws that everyone sees as fair. Moreover, Machiavelli does not set out standards

---

[1] Eric Nelson (2004, 85), for example, accepts the usual view: "as has been noted repeatedly, Machiavelli is not at all interested in 'justice,'" and "in this respect Machiavelli's account lacks the moral apparatus that would make real dialogue with the Roman or Greek traditions possible." Also see Cassirer 1946, 148–49; Strauss 1958, 281; more recently Skinner 1988, 433–34 and 2002, 146–17; Ball 1984, 521–28; Philp 2007, 37–54.

for political justice that are separate from, and potentially competitive with, ethical principles. As previous chapters argued, while his standards of political prudence are expressed more directly than his ethical judgments, fundamental ethical principles are implied by his reasonings about what reflective prudence requires. He frequently invokes justice even in the *Prince*, though that work assumes that many readers are unlikely to be moved by appeals to justice unless these are concealed within arguments from self-interest.

8.1.
Justice as the basis of order and *libertà*

A central argument of the *Prince* is that brute force is seldom enough to underwrite political power. This is the thrust of the statement in chapter 21 that "Victories are never so clear that the winner does not have to have some respect, especially for justice [*le vittorie non sono mai sí stiette che el vincitore non abbia ad avere qualche respetto, e massime alla iustizia*]." Here Machiavelli is arguing that princes become strongest when they are true friends to their allies in victory and defeat, refusing to be swayed from their commitments by "present dangers" or fleeting advantages. By showing themselves steadfast, they acquire a source of strength that is the necessary complement to military power: the firm, reciprocal commitments of those they have supported through good and bad fortune. Consistent reliability toward friends inside and outside one's own city is one of the pillars of genuine *potenza*, as distinct from merely apparent power. Machiavelli acknowledges that a cynical realist might see this maxim as a recipe for self-destruction. A prince who offers unwavering support might find that his ally becomes strong through victory, then turns his new strength against him; or if his ally loses, that he brings losses to his friends. Machiavelli's response to both concerns is that the benefits of long-term mutual trust are likely to counteract these disadvantages. If "the one to whom you adhere loses" yet you remain his friend, he will be under an obligation to return the favor if needed: "he helps you while he can, and you become the companion [*compagno*] of a fortune that can revive." If your ally wins, "though he is powerful and you remain at his discretion," nonetheless "he has an obligation [*obligo*] to you and has a contract of love [*contratto lo amore*] for you." One source of this *obligo* is the human decency that can always be found alongside human *malignità*. Contrary to the cynics, "men are never so indecent [*disonesti*] as to crush you with so great an example of ingratitude." And if powerful allies are not restrained by decency, they should be restrained—as the passage already cited suggests—by reflecting on why it is expedient to respect justice.[2]

As ever in the *Prince*, Machiavelli expresses these views by arguing from self-interest: it is in a prince's own best interests to form transparent, uncoerced contractual ties (*contratto*) of *obligo* with allies, and to meet obligations irrespective of changing fortune. Yet the prudential form of the arguments does not mean that

---

[2] *P*, XXI.90/181. A rare scholar who argues that the ethical message of this passage on justice should be taken literally, not as mockery, is de Alvarez (1999).

they have no independent ethical content. It is *both* prudent *and* just to fulfill one's obligations irrespective of changing fortune or self-interest. For persuasive purposes the argument can be made through an appeal to self-interest. But reasons of justice provide a firmer, more reliable guide to action than considerations of prudence alone. The initial premise of the *Prince* is that most readers live, as Machiavelli puts it in the *Florentine Histories*, "in such a way that just and unjust do not have to be of much account [*in modo che del giusto e dello ingiusto non si aveva a tenere molto conto*]." If one's aim is to persuade such people to act justly, the best strategy is to "leave out" explicit references to justice and injustice and "think only of utility [*utilità*]" for themselves or their city.³ Nevertheless, the prudential form of argument is ultimately subservient to its ethical substance.

The idea that justice is an indispensable foundation of political and military power is a recurrent, central theme in Machiavelli's writings. It appears in texts written before and after the *Prince*. Among the earliest extant sources of Machiavelli's views on justice is a series of proposals for reforming Florence's military defenses written in 1505–6. A letter from Cardinal Francesco Soderini thanks Machiavelli for outlining his "new military idea," adding: "You write wisely that this idea [*questo principio*] requires justice [*bisogna la iustizia*] above all, both in the city and in the countryside."⁴ Although Machiavelli's letter to Soderini is lost, some of its contents may be inferred from remarks made in his writings from the same year on the reorganization of Florentine arms. His *Provisione della ordinanza* begins by noting that all republics that have maintained and enlarged (*accresiute*) themselves over time have had two things, justice and arms (*la iustizia et l'arme*), as their principal foundation (*principal fondamento*).⁵ The same idea appears in another short piece written around the same time:

> Whoever speaks of empire [*imperio*], kingdom, principality, or republic and whoever speaks of men who command, starting from the highest rank and descending to the captain of a brigantine, speaks of justice and arms. You have little justice, and no arms at all [*Voi della iustizia ne avete non molta, et dell' armi non punto*]. And the only way to recover the one and the other is to order arms through public deliberation, and to maintain them with good orders [*ordinarsi all'armi per deliberatione pubblica, et con buono ordine et mantenerlo*].⁶

While it is true that the emphasis on justice in this military context connotes discipline as well as the notion of justice in an ethical sense,⁷ Machiavelli's concept of justice here is not reducible to military standards of well-ordered command. The *Cagione dell'ordinanza* ties it to *libertà* as well as to security and stable order.⁸ The

³ See *FH*, IV.19.165/496, and chap. 2 on Thucydides TPW, III.42–49as a source of this persuasive strategy.
⁴ Soderini to Machiavelli, 4 March 1506, *MF*, 120/119.
⁵ Machiavelli, *Provisione, Opere* I·31.
⁶ Machiavelli, *Cagione, Opere* I:26–17.
⁷ As noted by the editors of *MF*, 463.
⁸ *Cagione*, 27, 29.

Provisione does propose measures that at first glance may seem to treat justice as a mere means to military ends. Machiavelli underlines the need to uphold "severe justice" (*severa giustizia*) against the heads of private factions who prevent individuals from fulfilling their duties, and against anyone who shirks his military duties without legitimate reason (*absente sanza legitima cagione*).[9] But the main argument of the *Provizione* is that well-ordered military defenses cannot be maintained unless general political and legal justice is upheld. If the men of different ranks and occupations in a city are asked to serve in its defense, more than punitive force and military discipline are needed to motivate them to serve loyally; they also need persuasive "reasons to obey" public demands for their service. Cities whose governments are seen to uphold general justice are more likely to secure the trust and loyalty of citizens than cities where "the many" perceive that their interests are subordinate to those of the few. The citizens called on to serve as their city's *armi* are less likely to avoid service if they are confident that no exceptions to general conscription are made in exchange for political or monetary favors.[10]

Machiavelli's later works reaffirm these early ideas about why justice is needed to maintain political and military power. The argument that justice is a "foundation" of good military defenses reemerges in the last two chapters of the *Art of War*. Here Machiavelli has the chief speaker Fabrizio Colonna use the word *giustizia* in three distinct senses, all of which are needed for adequate civil arms. One sense identifies justice with respect for due limits, self-restraint, and moderation. "That army cannot flee hunger," Fabrizio declares, "which does not observe justice and which licentiously consumes whatever it wishes." *Giustizia* in this sense is said to make armies ordered and sober (*ordinati e sobrii*), whereas without justice they are licentious and drunk. A second sense of justice is punitive: it refers to the public judgment of anyone who transgresses established legal limits, and to the issuing of authoritative punishments. According to Fabrizio, an effective way to ensure that individuals who transgress the bounds of good orders are duly punished is to make the people at large responsible for judging transgressors. Whether within military ranks or in wider civilian orders, "to want one individual not to be favored in his errors by the people, a great remedy is to make the people have to judge [*giudicare*] him." This "mode of punishing [*modo di punire*]" helps to defuse disorders and "makes justice be observed [*da fare osservare la giustizia*]." A third sense of justice is distributive, referring broadly to judgments of what is due to different agents. At the start of the discussion about modes of punitive justice Fabrizio speaks more generally of distributing rewards and punishments to whoever "merited either praise or blame, either through their good or through their evil doings." A few pages later he mentions another kind of distributive justice, this time concerned with judgments about the ownership and use of goods or the stewardship of other human beings. Caesar Augustus Germanicus earned a name for justice (*nome di giusto*) by taking care to pay local tribesmen for the wood he used to build fortifications in France. This reputation, Fabrizio says, made it easy

---

[9] *Provisione*, 41–42.
[10] Ibid. See also *Frammento di discorso sulla milizia a cavallo, Opere* I:43.

for Caesar to gain support for further conquests in that province. Scipio Africanus gained his name for justice by returning a beautiful young hostage in Spain to her father and her betrothed. This act showed respect for the girl's honor and that of her family and, at the same time, gave back to each what was rightly theirs.[11] In discussing each of these three senses, Fabrizio emphasizes the value of justice as a means of improving military capacities. But the basic principles of justice he identifies have a much broader scope than this, and are ethically prior to military ends. They should, Fabrizio implies, serve as *fondamenti* for any human orders, civil as well as military.

In the *Florentine Histories* Machiavelli says less about justice than about various forms of injustice. Nevertheless, the main elements of his earlier accounts can still be found in the *Histories*. As we have seen, a leitmotif of the work is that the worst injustices are often perpetrated "under color" of decent words, so that their true character is discovered too late to prevent the disorders that flow from injustice. A deeply unsettling example occurs in Book II with the Duke of Athens' rise to tyranny in Florence. Having promised to restore Florentine liberties and to rid the city of factions, the duke soon revealed his unjust intentions through actions that belied his *onesto* rhetoric. Showing no "regard to civil life" and no "shame," "the severity and humanity that he had feigned" in order to win support "were converted into arrogance and cruelty." He "increased the old taxes and created new ones," took all authority away from the Signori, and delivered unjust sentences (*giudicii ingiusti*). His actions were arbitrary: at first he lifted restraints on the "great" to ensure that they help promote his designs, but later regarded them with suspicion. He distributed "splendid titles," money, and other favors not according to merit but with a view to buying off those who might otherwise oppose his tyranny, or to play off different sections of the population.[12] Later books in the *Histories* focus on injustice as a cause of disorders between cities. Among the most common sources of injustice is the ambitious desire to acquire control over the territory and *libertà* of others.[13] This includes the unjust desire to possess "the whole" (*il tutto*) of a province, or authority in a province, instead of resting content with "a part" (*la parte*).[14]

Let us now turn from particular cases to consider what they tell us about Machiavelli's general concept of justice. In its widest meaning, he uses the word as a general name for principles, rules, standards, and institutions that regulate the claims of different agents and bring them into some kind of order. *Giustizia* or *iustizia* is the quality that produces order among different parts of a city or agents interacting beyond the borders of cities, including cities and empires themselves. The main order-producing element of justice is expressed in Machiavelli's related concepts of *respetto* and *termini*, translated as "limits" or "bounds."[15] In any *ordine* that is

---

[11] *AW*, VI.128–39/654–65.

[12] *FH*, II.36.94–95/410–11.

[13] As the Florentines do over Lucca, though never for long without fresh resistance; see *FH*, V.14.203/539–40.

[14] *FH*, VI.20.251/410–11.

[15] Instead of as "end" in the sense of conclusion. The sense of *termini* as limits or bounds is much more usual in Machiavelli; see, for example, *D*, I.7/218; II.27/402; III.35.292/506, *inter alia*.

founded on justice, the claims of all parties are limited by criteria that do not derive from the particular interests of any one. Instead the limits are justified by principles that can be judged reasonable by all parties. This point is expressed clearly by Niccolò da Uzzano, Machiavelli's chief spokesman for prudent policies in the *Florentine Histories*. Whatever order may be established in the city and called just by its architects, appearances of order and the name of justice are never enough to underpin stable authority. This is especially true when those who make the order claim to have all "just cause" on their side while giving no credit to the claims of their opponents, for "this justice must be understood and believed by others as by us [*questa giustizia conviene che sia intesa e creduta da altri come da noi*]."[16]

Here Uzzano spells out another element of Machiavelli's general conception of justice: the idea of impartiality. The idea is expressed in a different way at the end of the *Prince* chapter 21, which examines several different notions of justice "between the lines." On the one hand, Machiavelli says that a prudent prince should always fulfill his commitments to those with whom he takes clear "sides" in conflicts, however his or their fortune may change. These remarks seem to refer mainly to allies in other cities. On the other hand, the chapter concludes by stressing the need for princes to avoid taking permanent sides in conflicts within their *own* city's population. A prudent prince should rather show an evenhanded solicitude for the interests of different "communities" (*università*) within his own city, shunning partisan tactics of divide-and-rule. Since "every city is divided into guilds or clans," Machiavelli's prince should "take account [*tenere conto*] of those communities, meet with them sometimes," and thereby "make himself an example of humanity and munificence" as a leader who retains the "majesty of his dignity [*la maestà della dignità sua*]" needed to arbitrate conflicts among his subjects. Princes who identify too strongly with particular clans, guilds, or parties arouse resentment among those of which they take less account or with whom they meet less often. The argument can be expressed either in the language of utility or in the ethical language of humanity and *dignità*. Either way, it implies an account of justice as requiring the impartial treatment of different elements in a city and the evenhanded consideration of their diverse claims. Justice in this sense is a fundamental component of a prince's *potenza*, since it ensures that he will be highly "esteemed" (*stimare*) by all sections of his city.[17]

This raises a question: how is it possible to make impartial judgments about whether or not a prince, a policy, or a law is impartial, and therefore just? Machiavelli does not underestimate the difficulties involved in making such judgments, or in persuading others to endorse them. At this stage, two distinctive features of Machiavelli's epistemology of justice may usefully be outlined; more will be said later about each.

First, judgments about impartiality have an extremely important perceptual dimension. Claims that just orders have been instituted or that justice has been done in any given case "must be understood and believed by others as by us." While

---

[16] *FH*, IV.27.174–75/506–7.
[17] *P*, XXI.91/182.

formal criteria are important for ensuring that orders meet standards of impartiality, they are not always sufficient. If, for example, the formalities of justice have been instituted through processes that many see as unjust or partial to special interests, then the resulting institutions themselves may be rendered suspect, however impeccable their formal qualities of impartiality. The ultimate judges of whether particular standards or institutions that go under the name of justice are adequate to that name are the people who are expected to uphold them. If standards and institutions are placed by others over people who do not "understand or believe" their claims to embody justice, their doubt is a sufficient test of these institutions' inadequacy. However, this reasoning does not entail the subjectivist and relativist view that *whatever* is "understood or believed" to be just by a particular set of people at a particular time is rightly viewed as just. Machiavelli's perceptual test applies to the practical exposition and implementation of standards of justice, not to those standards *qua* ethical standards. When large numbers of people do not understand or believe the claims of justice made on behalf of the institutions they live under, their skepticism may relate to three different things: the content of formal standards of justice, the procedures used to apply them, or the manner in which standards and procedures were established in the first place. Most of the problems Machiavelli discusses arise not because people disagree about the general standards needed to uphold justice, but because they do not believe that the procedures set up to implement justice or the means used to establish the procedures are impartial. When different parties insist on sharply differing or incommensurable standards of justice, Machiavelli implies that such conflicts are often rooted in something other than moral disagreement alone. Mistrust, or a narrow conception of self-interest, may also motivate refusal to submit one's own claims to reasoned adjudication on the basis of independent standards.

The other distinctive feature of Machiavelli's epistemology of justice confirms a non-relativist reading of the argument that people need to "understand and believe" in the justice of orders they live under. This is the claim that correct judgments about the justice and injustice of actions always come to light in due course, though in corrupt conditions this may take a long time. One of the most serious forms of injustice for Machiavelli is the breaking of faith or obligations, whether these are formal or tacit. He frequently has prudent characters express the view that ignorance and imprudence cannot serve as *post facto* excuses for injustice. In the *Histories* a spokesman for the Milanese people, who were enraged by the treachery of Count Francesco Sforza, declares to the count that nothing can

> excuse your perfidy or purge the infamy that our just quarrels [*giuste querele*] will bring upon you throughout the whole world. Nor will it keep the just pricking of your conscience [*il giusto stimolo della tua coscienza*] from tormenting you when the arms that were prepared by us to injure and frighten others will come to wound and injure us, because you yourself will judge yourself worthy of the punishment parricides have deserved. And even if ambition blinds you, the whole world as witness to your wickedness will open your eyes; God will open them for you, if perjuries, if violated faith [*la violata*

fede] and betrayals displease Him. . . . So do not promise yourself sure victory, for that will be kept from you by the just wrath of God [*giusta ira di Dio*] . . . have firm faith that the kingdom you have begun with deceit and infamy will come to an end for you or your sons with disgrace and harm.

The surrounding narrative acknowledges that deception and bad faith were the immediate cause of many of Sforza's victories. But the *Prince's* maxim that such victories are seldom lasting is borne out over time. On Machiavelli's account, Sforza soon found himself politically isolated and was forced to "request aid urgently from the Florentines, both publicly from the state and privately from friends," especially Cosimo de' Medici. The wider, corrupting effect of his deceptions was to deepen mistrust among Italian cities, whose republican orders were rapidly being eroded by "princely" entrepreneurs such as Sforza and Cosimo, paving the way for rival cities to invite French and imperial forces into Italy.[18]

Broadly speaking, then, we can say that the word "justice" for Machiavelli refers to standards, procedures, and judgments that are derived from reasoning about the conditions for ordered existence among free agents. Setting *limits* on any one party's claims is one hallmark of justice. The attempt to view claims *impartially* is another. Machiavelli discusses three main forms of justice in his works. One involves claims made with respect to *promises* or "keeping faith," where violations of faith are considered as a prima facie injustice. A second involves claims made with respect to *distributions* of goods, praise or blame, or rights to stewardship over human beings. The third involves claims relating to the *punishment* of violations of promises or rules and principles regulating distributions. As we will see, Machiavelli uses the word "justice" for informal standards and practices as well as formal rules and institutions. Informal standards such as respect for personal honor, duties of gratitude, and obligations to keep promises are very much part of Machiavelli's concept of justice. *Giustizia-iustizia* includes, but is not exhausted by, formal laws and juridical institutions. Indeed, Machiavelli often treats the standards embodied in informal practices of justice as a valuable touchstone for evaluating particular laws and legal systems.[19]

What is the relation between Machiavelli's concept of justice and two other key ethical concepts, order and freedom? Drawing on examples discussed earlier in this section, it seems clear that justice is a necessary element—indeed, a *fondamento*—of any *ordini* that deserve that name.[20] If *virtú* is the capacity that enables human beings to work out and institute standards of justice, *giustizia* is what confers the quality of order on some laws and institutions; for Machiavelli, laws and institutions that lack *giustizia* are always disordered. Order and justice are not two discrete values that sometimes come into conflict so that one must choose

---

[18] *FH*, VI.20/655–67; VI.22–23.254–55/600–603; VI.27.261/665;VI.32.267–68/672.

[19] See sec. 8.4. As noted in previous chapters, Thucydides and other ancient authors often speak of "customs and laws" as foundations of decent human life.

[20] Among recent scholars, this is recognized most explicitly by Fischer (2000), 197. He does not analyze the relationship in detail, however, and argues that Machiavelli has a "positivist" conception of justice as a convention that should be put aside when it is not useful to authorities.

which to put first. Since order depends on justice, justice must always come first, even when this seems to some observers to threaten what they take to be order. Institutions that fall short of standards of acknowledged justice, or that are perceived as unjust by those who live under them, lack legitimacy and therefore stability. They do not deserve to be called orders at all; at best, they may be described as apparent orders for as long as they do not collapse due to lack of legitimacy. This view casts doubt on the widespread opinion that lasting order can be imposed by unilateral force or violence, whether the imposing agent is an individual, a city, or an empire.

When considering the relation between justice and freedom, it is important to distinguish between free agency as a capacity of individuals and political freedom or *libertà*. On the one hand, Machiavelli seems to treat the value of justice as derivative from the value of individual free agency. The need for standards and institutions of justice arises because individuals are innately free; and their prepolitical freedom generates unavoidable conflicts over the proper limits of each agent's freedom. Different accounts of justice can be appraised by asking how well each does two things: first, accommodate the "ordinary and natural" phenomenon of innate freedom; and second, limit the potential for disorders that arise from conflicting claims. On the other hand, although free *agency* has moral weight independent of the standards and institutions of justice, Machiavelli treats justice as a necessary condition for any political freedom or *libertà* that deserves that name. He conceives *libertà* as a condition where conflicting claims are regulated by laws that are not tied to any particular private or partisan interests. The laws that maintain *libertà*, that is, are grounded in standards of justice. Justice is therefore the principal ethical foundation of political *libertà*.

If justice is as important to Machiavelli as the preceding discussion suggests, why does the concept seem to play a marginal role in his writings? We have already touched on the main reason: namely, that of all the *onesto* words used in public life, the concepts of *giustizia* and *giusto* are perhaps the most susceptible to misuse or abuse. Human *malignità* is only partly to blame for this. A more general explanation is that people often fail to reflect prudently on the causes of conflicts that impel them to seek justice. Appeals to justice are made when claims relating to promises, distributions, or punishments conflict. Several aspects of such conflictual settings tend to make the concept of justice appear ambiguous or multivalent. The language of justice is used both to assert the particular claims of each claimant, and to set up an impartial standpoint for arbitrating those claims. If those responsible for arbitration fail to persuade the parties that their standards and procedures are impartial, they will fail to ensure that their more general conception of justice takes precedence over the particular conceptions of the claimants. What remain are rival conceptions that go under the name of justice, none of which fulfill the conditions of reciprocal limits and impartiality needed for any adequate concept of justice. Machiavelli's discussions of justice and injustice treat these non-ideal, adversarial conditions as the inescapable starting-point for identifying more adequate notions of justice. Precisely because rival parties infuse the word with rival, self-serving interpretations, it is necessary to see what is wrong with these in order to get beyond them. In all his main works Machiavelli recognizes that the initial standpoint for anyone who seeks justice is always a particular, partial standpoint. Unsurprisingly, the first thing people do when demanding justice is to assert standards and demand procedures that reflect their own narrow interests. Only when they see the shortcomings of these partial accounts are they likely to acknowledge more general standards of justice, and to give them authority to correct their initial self-serving views.[21]

8.2.
Partisan accounts of justice

The *Florentine Histories* are full of grim examples of how the ideas of honor, keeping faith, and justice were debased in Florence. In Book III a group of prudent citizens, "moved by love of their fatherland," paints a depressing picture of their city's moral bankruptcy. Having "reasoned much about these disorders among themselves," they go before the Signori to offer their diagnosis of Florentine disorders. The patriots single out partisan ambitions and sectarian rivalries as chief causes. "The common corruption of all the Italian cities," they tell the Signori,

> has corrupted and still corrupts your city, for ever since this province extricated itself from under the forces of the empire, its cities have had no powerful check to restrain them [*un freno potente che le correggesse*] and have ordered their states and governments not to be free, but divided into sects [*sètte*]. . . . And because religion and fear of God have been eliminated in all, an oath and faith given [*il giuramente e la fede data*] last only as long as they are useful [*utile*]; so men make use of them not to observe them but to serve as a means of being able to deceive [*ingannare*] more easily. And the more easily and surely the deception succeeds, the more glory and praise is acquired from it; by this, harmful men are praised as industrious and good men are blamed as fools.[22]

The last two sentences recall passages in the *Prince* where Machiavelli has often been taken to be recommending the skillful use of deception to gain private political ends.[23] In the *Histories* this same practice—ostensibly vintage Machiavellianism—is treated as a civic virus responsible for spreading *corruzione* throughout Italy. What most readers have read as non-ironic advice to seek praise from successful deception in the *Prince* is here identified as the main internal cause of Italy's ruin, making the province vulnerable to foreign predators. The view that successful deception deserves praise encourages harmful men to prey on their fellow citizens under cover of public laws. Their example encourages licentious conduct among the young, who

---

[21] Compare Socrates' approach in Plato, *Rep.* I–II, which starts by canvassing various unreflective or corrupt opinions about what justice is, and only afterward identifies more adequate standards of justice.

[22] *FH*, III.5.109–10/429; translation slightly modified. Compare VII.1.276–77/628–29.

[23] See *P*, XVIII–XIX.68–82/165–75.

learn from experience that mendacity and excessive self-seeking bring "glory and praise," while observing that men who keep their promises and stay within due limits lose out to the others: the reputedly great men who see nothing wrong with acquiring by deceit. Before long the whole city, indeed the entire province of Italy, is used to living "in such a way that just and unjust do not have to be of much account" in public life.[24] If standards of justice are invoked they are relativized to private and sectarian whims, while "good laws, because they are spoiled by wicked use, are no remedy" for bad customs. These developments arouse "the appetite, not for true glory, but for the contemptible honors on which hatreds, enmities, differences, and sects depend; and from these," Machiavelli's patriots continue, "arise deaths, exiles, persecution of the good, exaltation of the wicked." And

> what is most pernicious is to see how the promoters and princes of parties give decent appearance to their intention and their end with a pious word [*con un piatoso vocabolo adonestono*]; for always, although they are all enemies of freedom, they oppress it under color of defending the state either of the best or of the people. For the prize they desire to gain by victory is not the glory of having liberated the city but the satisfaction of having overcome others and having usurped the principality of the city. Having been led to this point, there is nothing so unjust, so cruel, or mean that they do not dare to do it.[25]

In examining the use of these corrupting methods by different *sètti*, the *Histories* are remarkably evenhanded. The broadest sectarian opposition portrayed in the work is that between the "great" and the "many," or the *popolo*. On Machiavelli's accounts, both are equally prone to abuse the language of justice and injustice to suit their own purposes. Machiavelli's narrative does not take sides in the clash of partisan conceptions of justice. The *Histories* is structured in such a way that readers view conflicting claims now from one side, then from another. In many cases both sides have some serious ground for their claims. But they then assert their demands for justice in extreme and partial ways, making it difficult for their opponents to offer a reasonable compromise. Instead of reaching a settlement based on acceptance of limits to both sides' claims, conflicts are frequently inflamed by excessive demands made in the name of *giustizia*. Machiavelli takes pains to acknowledge the legitimate concerns of each party while, at the same time, showing the futility of trying to address them without impartial standards of justice.

The main forms of injustice committed by the great in the *Histories* are to demand more than their share of *autorità* in the city; to act as if they were above the law by virtue of their birth, wealth, or status; and to seek exemption from ordinary punishments for such infractions. One of the rhetorical devices used by the *grandi* to excuse these actions is to portray the many as a mere multitude incapable of civil reasoning or good order, who could only be kept under control if the few were given free rein to govern as they saw fit. Machiavelli sometimes seems to accept

[24] *FH*, IV.19.165/496.
[25] *FH*, III.5.110/429–30; compare chap. 2, sec. 2.5, on Thucydides.

the classical aristocratic topos of an unruly *moltitudine* that needs to be kept in line by the strong leadership of the few. A closer reading suggests that he invokes the topos in order to question its conventional uses, not to second the opinion that the many are by nature prone to disorderly conduct which makes it necessary for the few to employ extraordinary modes—that is, modes not regulated by ordinary public laws—to keep them in line. Machiavelli puts bogeyman rhetoric evoking "the arbitrary will" or "audacity" of the multitude in the mouths of imprudent, excessively ambitious speakers such as the hotheaded Rinaldo degli Albizzi. Rinaldo's arguments are patently self-serving and unjust. At one moment he wants to use the plebs as cannon fodder to check the insolence of princes. In the next he condemns them as "insolent" for seeking a share of authority in the city, declaring that they must be put down even "through deceit or force." The prudent maxim set out by Giovanni de' Medici a few chapters later might have served as a warning against this characteristic attitude of the traditional nobility: those who covet "others' share" (*la parte altri*) usually "lose their own, and before losing it live in continual unease."[26]

The hallmark injustices committed by the many are demands for excessive forms of restitution, especially through punitive taxes levied against the *grandi*; and demands for unreasonably vengeful collective punishments of the great, whose individual members are penalized for their status rather than for specific transgressions. Often in the *Histories* the popular *parte* takes restitution to mean not the restoration of order based on giving each its share, but revenge for past injustices committed by the great against the many. In Book IV Machiavelli describes how the popular party sought to place increasingly heavy burdens of taxation on the *grandi*. These measures were supposed to establish a more equitable basis for public spending, and hence to underpin stable orders after a period of civil conflict. Their actual result, however, was the opposite. The *grandi* saw the escalation of burdens placed on them as egregiously unfair, their complaints were interpreted as provocations, and the seeds of fresh civil conflicts were planted. The citizens responsible for the punitive taxes, Machiavelli reports, "inspired by seeing the powerful . . . depressed by the last defeat, loaded them down without giving them any consideration [*sanza . . . alcuno rispetto*]." At first, although "this tax hurt the great citizens very much," in order to "appear more honorable, they did not complain of their own tax but criticized it as generally unjust [*come ingiusta generalmente*] and advised that it should be lightened." But when the many came to know this, they blocked the proposals in the councils. Their subsequent actions against the *grandi* created even more serious disorders.[27] These events bear out a behavioral observation made earlier in the *Histories*: namely, that "it is not enough for men to get back their own [*ricuperare il loro*]," for "they want also to seize what belongs to others and get revenge [*vendicarsi*]."[28] Machiavelli's narrative suggests that popular desires to punish the arrogance of the *grandi* are natural, but seldom reasonable. Measures

---

[26] *FH*, IV.9.154/482–83; IV.16.161/491.
[27] *FH*, IV.8, 153/481; IV.14–15.159–60/447–49.
[28] *FH*, III.11.119/440.

that burden some people *sanza alcuno rispetto* are, he implies, "generally unjust" on the most general standards of justice; in this case the *grandi* had good grounds for complaining. Vengeance is not justice: it is partial, often respects no limits, and seldom restores stable orders that assign shares acceptable to all.

The perils of confusing revenge with justice are underscored in one of the most pathetic and violent pieces of writing in the *Histories*: a speech that Machiavelli gives to a nameless artisan during the Ciompi uprising. The speaker repudiates aristocratic doctrines of natural inequality based on birth. Instead he borrows the idea of natural right from his opponents and uses it to defend a radical egalitarianism. Urging the disgruntled plebs to revolt against "the avarice of your superiors and the injustice of your magistrates," the artisan declares:

> Do not let their antiquity of blood, with which they will reproach us, dismay you [*sbigottisca*]; for all men, having had the same beginning, are equally [*ugualmente*] ancient and have been made by nature in one mode. Strip all of us naked, you will see that we are all alike; dress us in their clothes and them in ours, and without a doubt we shall appear noble and they ignoble, for only poverty and riches make us unequal.[29]

Like all skillful rhetoric, the artisan's speech makes some reasonable points. The claim that present distinctions between nobles and ignobles lack any natural basis, and are often little more than appearances created by *couture* and grandiose names, concurs with the *Histories*' generally skeptical view of traditional social ranks. To this extent, the speaker's egalitarian arguments appear more reasonable than the natural-aristocratic theories he rejects. In several other respects, however, they are deeply defective when judged by Machiavelli's own positions.

For one thing, the assertion that "poverty and riches" are the only basis for inequalities in cities is clearly at odds with Machiavelli's meritocratic principles, as is the implication that the distribution of wealth is based on nothing but brute luck. The principles agree that political and economic inequalities should be decoupled from claims about the natural superiority and inferiority of persons. But principles of meritocratic equal opportunity do not say that absolute equality in wealth, rank, or authority is either natural or desirable. They say only that inequalities should be regulated by law and assigned to individuals according to transparent criteria based on merit. Machiavelli consistently holds that such inequalities, especially in the distribution of political authority, should be rigorously upheld against calls for radical leveling.[30] On his self-legislative principles, assertions about natural human equality cannot be an adequate basis for justice, which depends on deliberate human ordering.

Another fault in the reasoning behind the artisan's rhetoric is that on Machiavelli's arguments, social leveling cannot provide a stable solution to the problem of class arrogance and the civil disorders that stem from it. Machiavelli has little time for the view that social equality, any more than inequality, is underwritten by

[29] *FH*, III.13.122–23/444–45.
[30] See chap. 7, sec. 7.5.

human nature. He does not treat the formation of unequal ranks as a gross devi-
ation from man's natural orders. On the contrary, the tendency of some human
beings to set themselves above others and seek to dominate them is a "natural and
ordinary" inconvenience in any city. The conflicts generated by scrambles for rank
are endemic in all social orders; their sources are anthropological, not structural.
If you raze one specific system of informal social ranks, another will soon rise up
from the ashes.[31] You can eliminate the present category of *nobili*, but a new category of superiors will soon be formed by the most ambitious among those who
once insisted that all men are naturally equal. Indeed, these men are likely to lay
claim to the very name and other outward trappings of nobility once the old lot
have been deprived of it. The artisan's speech reflects this dangerous, though quite
natural, temptation for erstwhile ignobles to set themselves up as arrogant new
nobili. Machiavelli alludes to the fresh cycles of injustice that are in store for those
who seek redress in this way when he has the artisan declare: "Now is the time
not only to free ourselves" from the oppressions of their social superiors "but to
become so much their superiors that they will have more to lament and fear from
you than you from them."[32] Almost imperceptibly, the speaker has moved from an
initial, leveling egalitarianism, based on reasonable-sounding premises of natural
justice, to an unjust call for new and vengeful forms of inequality. Given the presence of suspicious and domineering humors in all human associations, the project
of leveling is self-defeating.

Finally, in the name of just retaliation for the destitute *ignobili*, the artisan's
rhetoric attacks the most basic pillars of civil or "human"—that is, ethical—orders.
He urges his hearers to brush away the pangs of conscience that restrain them
from committing acts of violence against the *nobili*. "It pains me much," he declares, "when I hear that out of conscience [*per conscienza*] many of you repent the
deeds that have been done and that you wish to abstain from new deeds," adding
provocatively:

> and certainly, if this is true, you are not the men I believed you to be, for
> neither conscience nor infamy should dismay [*sbigottire*] you, because those
> who win, in whatever mode they win, never receive shame from it. And we
> ought not to take conscience into account, for where there is, as with us, fear
> of hunger and prison, there cannot and should not be fear of hell ... men
> devour [*mangiono*] one another and ... those who can do less are always
> the worst off. Therefore, one should use force whenever the occasion for it
> is given to us; nor can a greater occasion be offered us by fortune than this
> one. .... As a result, either we shall be left princes of all the city, or we shall
> have so large a part of it that not only will our past errors be pardoned but
> we shall even have authority enabling us to threaten them with new injuries
> [*nuove ingiurie minacciare*].[33]

[31] This can be seen in *FH*, I, where from the ashes of the Roman Empire new names and claims to
dominance crop up.

[32] *FH*, III.13.123/445.

[33] *FH*, III.13.123/444.

The assertion that victors never "receive shame" no matter what means they use is myopic and self-defeating according to maxims set out elsewhere in the *Histories*, and indeed in the *Prince*—notably that victories never last when the victors show no *respetto* for justice.[34] The speaker presents not a coherent account of justice, but an eye-for-eye call for revenge. Whatever injuries the nobles have done to us, he implies, should now be done to them. In a provocative exaggeration, the orator asserts that "all those who come to great riches and great power have obtained them either by fraud or by force," adding that "to hide the ugliness of acquisition, they make it decent [*adonestono*] by applying the false title of earnings to things they have usurped by deceit or by violence." He now exhorts his impoverished hearers to undertake a similarly violent usurpation against the wealthy. "These persuasions [*persuasioni*]," Machiavelli remarks at the end of the speech, "strongly inflamed spirits that were already hot for evil on their own." Acting under the "standard of justice [*il gonfalone della giustizia*]" these men "burned the houses of many citizens" and hunted down others.[35] In short, the effects of the speech were disastrous for order, while its arguments rested on a corrupt understanding of justice.

On a casual reading it might appear that Machiavelli depicts the so-called *infima plebe*, the "lowest plebs," as incapable of *civiltà* when left to their own devices.[36] When the artisan's oration is read in its full context, however, the reasons for the plebs' "inflamed spirits" become evident. In the chapter preceding the oration Machiavelli offers a background account of the economic and political conditions that drove the *infima plebe* toward extremist reactions. He makes it clear that these men were not naturally prone to irrational rage or, for that matter, incompetent to assume civic responsibilities. In fact, they had previously played a larger role in political discussions relating to their trades, participating as well-represented members of Florence's guild system. According to Machiavelli, the *infima plebe* emerged as a marginal group in the city as a result of the unreasonably inflated power of the greater guilds. Under popular republican orders the number of guilds multiplied, leading those in the more honored of these associations to demand an even higher status and more effective power than others. Despite the republic's egalitarian rhetoric, new pecking orders began to form among the people at large, and then among the plebs. Some parts of the *popolo* and *plebe* were designated as greater (*maggiori*), some as lesser (*minori*). These distinctions flattered the ambitious humors of some popular men, but fueled resentments among those who were assigned an inferior status. Obsessed with their own honor and ambitious to dominate others, the so-called *maggiori* treated the *minori* with "arrogance." Tensions between greater and lesser ranks of the people were exacerbated by relations with the great, who played on popular vanities to enhance their own power. Machiavelli remarks that many *grandi* "favored the people of the greater guilds and persecuted those in the lesser guilds together with their defenders," adding that this favoritism gave rise to "many tumults"

---

[34] *P*, XXI; compare *FH*, II.34.92–94, 38.100; III.11.119; IV.8.153; IV.16.161; VII.30.309.
[35] *FH*, III.13–14.123–26/444–48.
[36] Compare BH, III.1.

against the *grandi*.[37] Many of the lesser plebs were gradually pushed outside the main guild system altogether, thereby acquiring the humiliating title of *infima plebe*. These people found themselves "subordinated" (*sottomissono*) under larger guilds, deprived of key channels for expressing their concerns. "In consequence," Machiavelli writes, "when they were either not satisfied for their labor or in some mode oppressed [*oppressati*] by their masters, they had no other place of refuge than the magistracy of the guild that governed them." It "did not appear to them," however, "that they got the justice they judged was suitable [*quella giustizia che giudicavano si convenisse*]" from these larger magistracies.[38]

This analysis is remarkable for its time, particularly in its sympathetic portrayal of the plebs' motives. Machiavelli clearly registers his own judgment that the *infima plebe* had reasonable cause for anger. His account provides the historical perspective needed to understand and confront the unjust urgings in the artisan's speech. The lesser plebs are not unscrupulous troublemakers. Their conduct is explained by specific deprivations: the elimination of their guilds deprived them of both civic rights and means of effective self-help. Unable to seek restitution through ordinary political means, they turned to extraordinary and violent modes. If the hatred the artisan vents against "the rich citizens and the guilds" is expressed in unreasonably violent ways, it does not lack reasonable causes, since "it did not appear to them that they had been satisfied for their labor as they believed they justly deserved [*che giustamente credevano meritare*]."[39] Machiavelli's analysis suggests that unjust policies, driven by poorly regulated popular ambitions and vanities, were responsible for creating conditions that drove the *infima plebe* to violent revolt. In the preface to the *Histories* we read that "many who have not had the opportunity to acquire fame through some praiseworthy deed have contrived to acquire it with despicable things."[40] Here not fame and status but security and the avoidance of starvation—the most basic conditions for a decent life—were at stake for the workers. The argument sells to the *infima plebe* not because it is their nature to be irrational or violent. It sells because, having been deprived of effective political power, they are driven to economic desperation.

Another remarkable feature of Machiavelli's account of the Ciompi uprising is that the speaker, lowly though his birth and station, is one of the most brilliant orators in the *Histories*. Machiavelli introduces him as "one of the most daring and experienced [*arditi e di maggiore esperienza*]" of the assembled lesser-and-lower

---

[37] *FH*, III.12.121/442–43. Note Machiavelli's (III.17.130/453) ironic remark later that "the better guildsmen" considered "what ignominy it was for those who had overcome the pride of the great to have to bear to stench of the plebs"—thereby setting themselves up as the new "great" entitled to the same arrogance that they had fought against.

[38] *FH*, III.12.121–22/442–44.

[39] Ibid. When the speaker says that "we" lesser plebs must have "two ends," (1) "to make it impossible for us to be punished" for offenses recently committed and (2) "to be able to live with more freedom and more satisfaction than we have in the past," he is half wrong and half right. The first end is wrong when judged by standards of order and justice Machiavelli sets out elsewhere: people must get the punishments they deserve for breaking laws, or no order is possible at all. The second, however, is a perfectly legitimate demand.

[40] *FH*, Pref.7/310.

plebs.[41] His speech contains some of the most skillfully modulated rhetoric found in the work. It moves smoothly between particulars and abstractions, makes effective emotional appeals under the color of reasoned argumentation, and shows an excellent grounding in sophisticated arguments equating justice with vengeance. The artisan achieves all this without the benefit of the scholastic education enjoyed by his social superiors. If a man who emerges from the mob of lesser plebs can perform this kind of rhetorical tour de force, he is surely capable of civil reasoning at a very demanding level. In a better-ordered polity, his persuasive talents and experience might have earned him high public office; he might, as Machiavelli puts it in the *Discourses*, have become an elective "prince" by his own virtue instead of urging his colleagues to become *principi* through violence.[42] In this respect, Machiavelli's ambivalent portrait of the artisan orator challenges aristocratic and popular-elitist prejudices about the political incompetence of the "lesser" *plebe*. At the same time, the incendiary speech offers no just or stable solutions. Even if one side has *just cause* for complaint, this cannot helpfully be met through unjust means. What is needed are standards and procedures of *justice* that appear reasonable to their opponents as well as themselves.

8.3.
Non-partisan persuasions toward justice

Throughout the *Histories* Machiavelli is careful to examine both sides of any conflict, whether inside or outside the city. He recognizes that conflicts often have important historical dimensions that may make them extremely hard to resolve. In many cases the wrongs alleged on both sides have multiplied over time, previous attempts to rectify them have failed, and both parties have concluded that previous efforts to compromise only gave their opponents an unjust advantage. Often they see no good reason to trust their opponents' new overtures, while past experience makes them reluctant to relax their defenses. While historically generated anxieties make it difficult to identify non-partisan standards of justice that both sides can endorse, Machiavelli denies that finding them is hopeless. But because he takes historically generated concerns very seriously as an impediment to justice, the prudent speakers in his narrative do not ask rival parties to forget their old grievances as they look for solutions.[43] Machiavelli does not see history as irrelevant to political problem-solving. He approaches political problems through history because he sees a clear historical understanding of present problems as a *sine qua non* for finding

---

[41] *FH*, III.13.122/443.

[42] *D*, I.58.132/335.

[43] Although he does suggest that historical grievances should be put aside once such principles are agreed and authorized. See, for example, Giovanni de' Medici's prudent remarks on an attempt to impose a retroactive tax on the great: he quieted "excited humors" by pointing out that "it was not good to go back over things past, but rather to provide for the future; and if the taxes had been unjust in the past, they should thank God that a mode had been found to make them just and should wish that this mode might serve to reunite, not divide, the city, as it would if past taxes were looked into and made to be equal with the present ones" (*FH*, IV.14.159–60/488–49).

well-considered solutions. And since different parties start from their own partial and partisan views of a conflict's history, anyone who hopes to persuade them to adopt a wider view must start by showing what is wrong with their narrower ones.

A good example of prudent mediation occurs early in the *Florentine Histories* when Machiavelli describes attempts by men who "placed themselves in the middle [*si missono di mezzo*]" to end the cycles of violence between nobles and the people. These self-appointed mediators invoke a range of arguments to lead warring parties toward common standards of justice: self-interested prudence, the common good of the city as a whole, and ordinary decency. A crucial element of their persuasions is to try to bring people on both sides to acknowledge their share of responsibility for a conflict.

Addressing the side of the nobles, the mediators start with a historical account of the present impasse that apportions to the nobles their share of responsibility. The speakers start by pointing out that the nobles' own "pride and their bad government" had given rise over time to the popular hatreds now vented against them. To be sure, the people often used unjust means to fight the nobles, and these should not be excused. But their indignation was in large part justified, for the nobility's long history of arrogance and misgovernment were clearly "the cause of the honors taken from them and the laws made against them" by the vengeful people. Taking account of the historical injustices that the nobility and their ancestors had perpetrated, the mediators advise them against trying to reassert their authority through brute force. For one thing, this would only reinforce the existing perception that the nobles were indifferent to justice. By "taking up arms now to regain by force what they had allowed to be taken from them on account of their own disunion and their evil ways," they would merely be seen as adding further injuries to an already long list of historical injustices.[44] It follows, further, that the nobles' attempt to regain authority through force would provoke redoubled, justified resistance; and—here the mediators appeal to common civic interests—this would be "nothing other than to wish to ruin their fatherland." Finally, they appeal to the noblemen's narrower self-interest: such methods would also "worsen their own condition." The nobles, they warn, "should remember that the people were far superior to them in number, riches, and hatred." The "nobility by which it appeared to them that they were superior to others" might be considered a ground for granting them authority if their actions proved that they were willing to use it for the common good, instead of for their own private and class interests. But until they demonstrated this, their *nobilità* "would not fight" all by itself and "would turn out to be, when it came to steel, an empty name [*uno nome vano*] that would not be enough to defend them against so many."[45] In few words and without using the word *giustizia*, then, Machiavelli's men-in-the-middle give persuasive reasons for the nobility to put down their arms and accept non-partisan constraints on their claims.

---

[44] Note the implicit appeal to the principle of public authorization: the nobles "allowed" the people to take away their authority because they failed to respect conditions for keeping it.

[45] *FH*, II.14.66–67/378–79.

Addressing the side of the people, the mediators start by invoking considerations of prudence. Their main prudential arguments have a general form rather
than appealing to specific popular interests. First "they recalled that it was not
prudent always to want the ultimate victory" instead of seeking compromises, and
further that "it was never a wise course to make men desperate, because he who
does not hope for good does not fear evil." Next, the men in the *mezzo* point to a
common interest with the nobles that the enraged people have failed to see. The
more radical members of the popular party sought not only to place checks on
the arrogant conduct of nobles, but to eliminate all distinctions of rank within
civil orders. This, in Machiavelli's view, would destroy any order whatever and
lead straight to tyranny. He has the mediators remind the people that the original
meaning of the word *nobilità* was "that which had honored the city in war." The
qualities of nobility in this sense ought, the speakers suggest, to have a place in any
good civil orders. It was in the common interests of citizens of all backgrounds and
humors to resist the seductive rhetoric of political leveling. The popular party was
right to challenge the nobles' demands for rank and authority based on bloodlines
instead of personal merit, but wrong to condemn *nobilità* in its more adequate
sense. Machiavelli's mediators conclude that it was therefore "neither a good nor a
just thing" for the people to "persecute" the nobles "with such hatred." Their long
history of seeking revenge for past oppressions had made the nobles ever more
reluctant to put down their weapons and accept political equality in the republic.
Rather than persecuting noblemen, the people should seek "to mitigate [*mitigare*]
them and by this benefit to have arms be put down," while toning down their own
demands for absolute "victory" over the old class enemy.[46]

These persuasions were not, Machiavelli says, convincing to all. But those among
the people who were "wiser and of calmer spirit" saw that moderating the punitive
laws against the nobles "would not mean much but that coming to battle might
mean very much." These prudent voices prevailed, and punitive laws against the nobles were "mitigated."[47] Although the *mezzo*-men do not speak explicitly of justice
and injustice, ideas about justice and injustice are implied by all their arguments,
especially the idea that injustice—conceived in general terms as extreme partiality
and lack of *respetto* for the other party—is never prudent. Both people and nobility
have erred in the past in seeking dominance or "ultimate victory" in the city. While
acknowledging that both had historical reasons for doing so, the mediators show
that the aims were unjust and destructive of any order. The ethics of self-restraint
developed throughout the *Histories* treat the acceptance of limits as the chief condition for both justice and order. As Giovanni de' Medici says in Book IV, "he who
is content with half a victory will always do better from it, since those who wish
to do more than win often lose."[48] Reflective prudence and justice reach the same
conclusions. Those men, parties, and peoples "who do not know how to put limits

[46] Ibid.
[47] Ibid.
[48] *FH*, IV.14.159–60/488–49. Again compare Diodotus' argument in TPW, III 47. Also see IV.19 and
IV.62.

[*termini*] to their hopes, and, by founding themselves on these without otherwise measuring themselves [*sanza misurarsi*] . . . are ruined" are unquestionably imprudent. On Machiavelli's implied standards, they also act unjustly.[49]

8.4.
Why it is dangerous to violate the law of nations

I have argued throughout this study that Machiavelli does not apply different ethical principles or standards inside cities and in foreign relations.[50] That this is true of his standards of justice can be seen in one of the few parts of the *Discourses* where he uses the language of justice and injustice. The text comes from Book II, chapter 28. The title alludes to the importance of punitive justice, albeit under the harsher-sounding language of avenging injuries: "How Dangerous It Is for a Republic or a Prince Not to Avenge an Injury [*vendicare una ingiuria*] Done against the Public or a Private Person."[51] By comparison with the *Histories,* the *Discourses* use the words *giustizia—giusto* and *ingiustizia—ingiusto* very sparingly. Here Machiavelli expresses ideas about justice and injustice by using paraphrases or near-synonyms: sometimes nouns such as *leggi* and *respetto,* but often verbs that seem to call for extremely harsh measures: to avenge (*vendicare*), to eliminate (*spento*), or to punish (*punire*).

This choice of words does not reflect a judgment that public or private justice can be reduced to primitive, pre-judicial notions used in the context of private vendettas. Machiavelli's tough-sounding paraphrases should, I suggest, be understood as part of a dialectical enquiry that takes common opinions about justice, often corrupt or incomplete, as the starting point for more reflective reasoning. To understand the reasons for his frequent use of harsh language to discuss justice in the *Discourses,* it is helpful to recall the distinction outlined in the *Art of War* between the "harsh" and "delicate" modes of action found in antiquity.[52] Fabrizio Colonna uses the distinction to encourage his young interlocutors to consider the shortcomings of both extremes. If delicate modes are corrupt and weak, then harsh ones are clearly better. But if "harsh" is taken to mean cruel and unreasoning, it too is a poor standard. The question posed at the start of the dialogue, then, is: how can one move from a partly reasonable but incompletely reflective opinion—here, that harsh modes are better than delicate ones—to a fully reasoned, reflective account of the specific kinds of harsh ancient modes that deserve imitation? If participants in the dialogue or the *Discourses'* various *discorsi* accept the tough-minded view that it is sometimes necessary to avenge injuries or inflict harsh punishments, what forms of vengeance or harshness would they see

---

[49] *D,* II.27.195/402.

[50] In this respect he is closer to ancient writers such as Thucydides, Xenophon, Plato, and Livy than to modern authors who do make this difference.

[51] The title of the previous chapter (chap. 27) also hints at the theme of justice by stressing the need for prudent self-limitation: "For Prudent Princes and Republics It Should Be Enough to Conquer [*vincere*], for Most Often When It Is Not Enough, One Loses."

[52] See chap. 5, sec. 5.7.

as compatible with standards of *civiltà* and *umanità*, which they recognize as the *fondamenti* of any stable orders?

When Machiavelli declares that it is necessary to avenge, to eliminate, or to act harshly, then, the very boldness of such statements signals to readers that they still need to be qualified. Vengeance and harshness must bounded, at the very least, by basic standards of humanity as they were understood among the best ancients, since unlimited harshness and revenge generate grave disorders. Prudent readers of Machiavelli's discussions of the need for vengeance will realize that when modes of *vendicare* are restrained by the standards needed to uphold human orders, they might as well be called "justice" as "vengeance." Indeed, the excessively harsh sense of *vendicare* is no longer adequate for these maturer reflections. Machiavelli keeps the old word but gives it a new, more reasonable meaning: an ethical meaning that renders *vendicare* synonymous with *giustizia*.

Despite the dissimulating language of vengeance in its title, the chapter dealing with the Fabii episode is among the *Discourses'* most openly didactic—one might even say moralistic—discussion pieces. Its main points are reiterated at the beginning of Book III, where they are presented as a set of straightforwardly ethical precepts about "justice."[53] Closely following Livy, Machiavelli recalls "our historian's" account of the wrongs committed by Rome's Fabii ambassadors to Gaul. To summarize the main outlines of the episode, during their wars with Gaul the Romans sent three members of the Fabii tribe as ambassadors to the enemy; the Fabii then violated well-established conventions—known in Rome as the *ius gentium* or "law of nations"—that forbade ambassadors to fight their hosts. This action was only the first of a series of offenses perpetrated by the Romans against the law of nations. Rejecting the Gauls' legitimate request that the Fabii be handed over to their judgment, the Roman Senate rewarded the offenders by making them tribunes with consular powers.[54] Unsurprisingly, when the Gauls

> saw those honored *who should have been punished*, they took all to have been done for their disparagement and ignominy. Inflamed with indignation and anger, they came to assault Rome and took it, except for the Capitol. This ruin arose for the Romans only through the inobservance of justice [*solo per la inosservanza della giustizia*]. For when their ambassadors sinned "against the law of nations" and *should have been punished*, they were honored [*peccato i loro ambasciatori <contra ius gentium>, e dovendo esserne gastigati, furono onorati*].[55]

As we saw in chapter 5, Livy reports that these events were interpreted by many Romans as divinely ordained punishments for their multiple offenses. Machiavelli treats this interpretation sympathetically, implying that it reflected a reasonable—if belated—judgment about the Romans' own guilt, and a recognition that the Gauls had just cause for their ferocious assault on the city. The "prophets" who claimed

---

[53] The word *giustizia* occurs six times in the *D*, twice in III.1, once in II.28.

[54] *D*, II.28.195–97/402–4; III.1.209/416–17.

[55] *D*, II.28.195–96/403; emphasis added.

to foresee the disastrous consequences of Rome's violations only pointed out what anyone could have predicted who grasped the reasons why respect for principles of justice is always prudent. For as the last sentence of the chapter says, one "should never esteem a man," or in this case a people at war, "so little that he believes that when he adds injury on top of injury, he who is injured will not think of avenging himself [*vendicarsi*] with every danger and particular harm for himself."[56]

In Livy's dramatic narrative the Romans endure unprecedented suffering at the hands of the injured party, whose depredations caused most of the population to abandon the city. The future of Rome itself hangs by a thread. If the remaining citizens also flee, the city will return to dust. If they can be persuaded to hold back, physically by defending their city and metaphorically by returning to the limits set by religion and the *ius gentium*, Rome might yet rise from the ashes.[57] Redemption depends on the *virtuoso* use of "one's own arms" under the most extreme necessity. But it also depends on the restoration of the sound moral orders that had been destroyed by the Romans' injurious conduct. Their "external beating" forced the Romans to "examine themselves" (*si riconoschino*) critically and thus to recall "all the orders of the city" that had been destroyed by their lack of respect.[58] For Machiavelli as for Livy, one man serves as the symbolic agent of Rome's physical and moral redemption in the wake of the Gauls' attacks. The return from exile of the controversial general Marcus Furius Camillus heralds the restoration of strict justice after a period when commanders were chosen and praised for their so-called liberality, a code word in Xenophon and Machiavelli for corrupt leniency toward partisans.[59] Machiavelli treats Camillus as a devoted public servant whose unpopularity in corrupt times was due to his "severity" in upholding rigorous standards of justice. The general was "held marvellous" because of "the solicitude, the prudence, the greatness of spirit, the good order that he observed in employing himself and in commanding the armies; what made him hated" was that he was "more severe [*severo*] in punishing" his soldiers "than liberal in rewarding them."[60] Confronting Rome's imminent destruction, Camillus persuades his countrymen to hold back from flight and to defend their fatherland in its "necessity." Then he calls on them to restore the ethical orders they had violated at such high cost to themselves, orders based on self-restraint and respect for other peoples' claims under the *ius gentium*.

Machiavelli's retelling preserves Livy's suggestion that Rome's redemption depended as much on the restoration of ethical order as on a renewed show of military *virtú*. "As soon as Rome was retaken," he writes in Book III, the Romans "renewed [*rinnovarono*] all the orders of their ancient religion" that had been corrupted in the period prior to the sacking of Rome. A basic condition for this renewal was to make amends for injuries perpetrated in the past. The Roman people

---

[56] *D*, II.28–29.197/404–5.

[57] On the idea of "pulling back" (*ritirasse indietro*) see *D*, III.22.256/477.

[58] *D*, III.1.210/417.

[59] See chap. 2, sec. 2.2, and chap. 3, sec. 3.4.

[60] *D*, III.23.269/480. Machiavelli's (and Livy's) countermodel is Scipio Africanus; see chaps. 3, 12.

had to realize, Machiavelli writes, "that it was necessary not only to maintain religion and justice [*necessario mantenere la religione e la giustizia*]," but also to esteem "good citizens" such as Camillus who had been unfairly castigated in corrupt times, and to punish "the Fabii who had engaged in combat 'against the law of nations.'" These measures of just "renewal" were, Machiavelli says, *necessario* to rebuild civil order. The concurrence of prudential and ethical necessity is underlined again when Machiavelli writes that "it was necessary that Rome be taken by the French, if one wished that it be reborn and, by being reborn, regain new life and new virtue," and thus to "regain the observance of religion and justice, which were beginning to be tainted in it."[61]

In reviving and sharpening Livy's arguments about why it is "necessary" to respect the "law of nations," Machiavelli implies that there are compelling reasons to respect standards of justice even when these are not formally embodied in civil laws. The reasons can be expressed in terms of reflective prudence. Among the wiser of Machiavelli's "ancients," conventions regulating conduct in relations between "peoples" in war and peace were considered as sacred; hence the need to restore *religione* as well as *giustizia* as a basis for ordered relations between Rome and foreign peoples. Reflective prudence suggested the ethical necessity for "religious" respect for the *ius gentium*. The ancients understood that without them no stable human orders could be sustained. Orders depend on trust. If trust is violated without warning or reason, this destroys orders and inflames the "indignation" of those who have been wronged.[62] "It is therefore to be considered," writes Machiavelli,

> how much every republic and every prince should take account [*tenere conto*] of doing similar injuries, not only against a collectivity [*una universalità*] but even against an individual [*uno particulare*]. For if a man is greatly offended either by the public or by a private person and is not avenged according to his satisfaction, if he lives in a republic he seeks to avenge himself, even if with its ruin; and if he lives under a prince and has any generosity in himself he is never quiet until he avenges himself against him, even if he sees evil [*male*] in himself for that.

The suggestion here is not that the victims of a great offense are justified in using evil means for revenge. Machiavelli says simply that it is *reasonable* they will be angry and seek redress, and *probable* though not reasonable that they will regard themselves as relieved of any obligation to exercise self-restraint in avenging it. As a maxim of reflective prudence, then, republics, princes, and individuals should take careful account of these probable consequences and avoid violating commitments.[63] Machiavelli stresses that crimes of omission are as imprudent as those of commission, affirming ancient standards of justice that held authorities—whether individuals or collectivities—responsible for failing to punish transgressions committed under their watch. Having started with the case of an injustice

---

[61] *D*, III.1.209–10/417.

[62] See *D*, II.32.203–6/412–14, III.33.285–87/498–500.

[63] Compare TPW, I.84, III.45–49, V.97–98, VII.18.

between collectivities, the Romans and Gauls, Book II, chapter 28 ends with the case of individuals: the Macedonian king Philip's failure to punish a courtier who "by deception and by force" had his way with a young man under Philip's protection. Machiavelli notes that the victim, Pausanius, "turned all his indignation not against the one who had done him the injury but against Philip, who had not avenged him."[64] While Machiavelli does not recommend Pausanias' chosen form of revenge as an example of just retribution, he does imply that the youth was right to hold his negligent superior accountable for the crime.

Once again, the prudential form of these reasonings should not obscure their ethical content. When Machiavelli insists that prudent men should always expect fierce resistance when they violate "limits" set by conventions or laws, he implies that indignation and resistance are more than natural human reactions. They are often reasonable responses to actions that show agents' scant "esteem" for the claims of others. To act in ways that might be expected to provoke reasonable indignation is imprudent because it is dangerous for the perpetrator. But the reasons why it is dangerous can also be expressed in terms of justice and injustice. Injustices are rightly seen by victims as slights to their dignity. Those who show disregard for tacit or formal standards of justice seem to place themselves above other human beings who find it necessary to respect the "law of nations." The conventions of reciprocal self-restraint that made up much of the *ius gentium* in Roman times were established to promote a modicum of trust in conditions where deception and violence would otherwise have free rein, particularly conditions of war. To violate such conventions unilaterally was not just an order-destroying act of arrogance; it was seen as an insult to the other party's human dignity, and therefore as an injustice. These ethical reasons for respecting standards of justice hold independently of judgments about prudence. Moreover, they help to explain *why* it is always prudent to avoid committing the injuries prohibited by tacit conventions of justice even when they lack the force of civil laws.

For Machiavelli these ethical reasons clearly trump narrower considerations of utility, including what some assertive patriots called the "ultimate necessity" to defend the fatherland.[65] In Livy's much longer account, some of the Romans who defended the Fabii acted out of patriotic motives. Imprudent though their actions were, their intentions were not all bad. They were motivated by a sincere desire to defend their fatherland and possibly shorten an already drawn-out war; fear and exhaustion made them act unjustly, not ambition alone. Machiavelli might have given some credit to such motives of common utility or the "defense of fatherland," but refrains from doing so.[66] He simply accepts the Romans' own belated, severe judgment on themselves: that their actions were intrinsically wrong, and deserved the punishments inflicted by the gods and the Gauls. As we will see in chapter 9,

---

[64] *D*, II.28.196–97/403–4.

[65] See chaps. 4, 9.

[66] Even if these had been among agents' motives, their action was still shortsighted and irresponsible; for "peoples are often deceived" who, "greedy for present peace, close their eyes to whatever other snare might be laid under the big promises" (*D*, III.12.248/458).

he consistently maintains that when a people is faced with policies that are "very useful but very dishonest" honesty is always the better choice, since there can be no genuine, lasting utility in policies that violate agreements. Thus a people acts prudently and justly when it refuses to "break faith" even for the sake of a policy "that would be of great utility to their fatherland."[67]

8.5.
Forms of justice: Promises, punishments, and distributions

The discussion so far has touched on the three main forms of justice discussed in Machiavelli's works: promissory justice, punitive justice, and distributive justice. This section outlines his distinctive positions on each, especially as he presents them in the *Discourses*.

8.5.1. Promises and oaths

I have argued that for Machiavelli, trust in others' willingness to impose limits on their own actions is a condition for any ordered and sustained relations. The idea that it is prudent and just to act in good faith, keep promises, and respect conventions follows from this understanding of the conditions for order. When the Fabii and Roman Senate violated the *ius gentium*, they took away any reason for others, the Gauls or anyone else, to trust their good faith. By adding insult to injury, they appeared to set themselves above the most basic standards of human justice, which require human beings to respect each others' dignity and capacities for free agency even in the most uncivil conditions of war. This implied assertion of superhuman status by any agent constitutes a just cause for others to pull them back to the "limits" that they should have "held and observed" from the start.[68] We have already mentioned three more specific features of Machiavelli's arguments that are worth underlining.

First, as the Fabii episode suggests, for Machiavelli injustice does not consist only in violating formal codes of positive or civil law.[69] The injustices in this instance involved the breaking of customary commitments accepted by a large number of peoples who frequently interacted with one another, including explicit and tacit conventions regulating the conduct of war and diplomatic missions. The formal status of an agreement may have some bearing on questions of justice and injustice, insofar as formal agreement signifies an act of willed authorization on the part of both parties. But in discussing relations between cities and peoples Machiavelli clearly implies that it is unjust to violate even commitments that do not have the

---

[67] *D*, I.59.120–21/320–22.
[68] *D*, III.35.292/505–6.
[69] I have been arguing that for Machiavelli, basic ethical principles and prudence require (optimally) that any human orders should be expressed in the form of law, understood as a general, impartial, impersonal, and compulsory standard. But where the political conditions needed to impose that form are absent, standards of justice can stand in and set ethical limits on acceptable action that are confirmed by reflective prudence.

status of civil law, for the reasons outlined earlier. He does say that men deserve special condemnation who do not respect the limits of justice to which they hold others. The worst offenders are often found in the context of civil life, where they explicitly authorize a law, then exempt themselves or their friends from respecting it. "I do not believe," Machiavelli declares, "there is a thing that sets a more wicked example in a republic than to make a law and not observe it, and so much the more as it is not observed by him who made it."[70] Yet this kind of double standard may just as well apply in relations among peoples, where more powerful cities such as Rome played a leading role in defining and upholding conventions of the *ius gentium* yet frequently acted in ways that eroded the authority of those conventions.

A second noteworthy feature of his arguments is that Machiavelli recognizes no difference, from a standpoint of prudence or one of principle, between violating faith with friends and violating faith with enemies. As we saw in chapter 2, he accepts the convention—endorsed under the *ius gentium*—that fraud and deception are admissible in any of the conditions of war that are not regulated by tacit and formal conventions. But necessary limits are imposed by standards of justice in war as in peace, between enemies or allies. The conventions of *ius in bello* permitted the use of deception in battlefield tactics and communications, notably the writing of misleading codes that might be intercepted by the enemy.[71] They prohibited fraud and the betrayal of trust in other fields of activity relating to the conduct of wars, such as the declaration and holding of truces and the conduct of diplomatic missions between enemies. Contrary to a widespread prejudice, Machiavelli's views on these matters are old-fashioned, not daringly subversive. Observing that fraud in war is often praised, Machiavelli writes:

> I do not understand [*non intenda*] that fraud [*fraude*] to be glorious which makes you break faith given and pacts made [*la fede data ed i patti fatti*]; for although this may at some time acquire state and kingdom [*stato e regno*] for you . . . it will never acquire glory for you.[72]

It would be misleading to say that these views were conventional for their time, since Machiavelli judged contemporary conventions to be utterly corrupt. His view of how sound conventions were generally used is highly critical; and because of this, he gives them new life by placing them on more thoroughly reasoned foundations, in place of the fine-sounding clichés that had come to be identified with them. Instead of suggesting merely that it is good and just to keep faith with enemies, Machiavelli's examples show why it is also prudent and necessary to do so.[73]

---

[70] *D*, I.45.93–95/291–93.

[71] See *AW*, VII.154–56/678–80 on codes and chap. 2, sec. 2.4.

[72] *D*, III.40.299/514.

[73] Grave disadvantages accrue to leaders who acquire a reputation for being "a breaker of faith" as was Hannibal (*D*, III.21.263–64). Compare the *FH* where Machiavelli (VIII.33.355–57/725–76) offers a rare, uplifting example of Florentines, "since they were in league," putting "their faith ahead of convenience and danger to themselves" to support allies. The result was advantageous for them, since their just action showed the pope and other predatory foreign powers "with how much promptness and zeal the Florentines keep their friendships." If the Florentines behaved more consistently in this way,

A third distinctive feature of Machiavelli's arguments about promissory justice can be seen in the single exception he allows to the general requirement of keeping promises. This is expressed in the title of a chapter in the *Discourses*, Book III: "That Promises Made through Force Ought Not to Be Observed [*Che le promesse fatte per forza non si debbono osservare*]." Here Machiavelli argues that "it is not shameful not to observe the promises that you have been made to promise by force; and when the force" that compelled you to make a promise is later "lacking, forced promises that regard the public will always be broken and it will be without shame for whoever breaks them."[74] The reason for this exception is procedural: it has to do with the injustice of the procedures used to extract an avowed commitment. By contrast, Machiavelli admits no exceptions based on non-procedural considerations admitted on other accounts of promissory justice, such as feelings of enmity or compassion, special relations with one's co-compacters, or the balance of power between parties.[75] Nor, as we have seen, does he allow exceptions for the sake of utility, even that of "great utility to the fatherland." He cites an example of a judicious decision by the Athenian people to reject an attempt by a leading citizen to secretly break faith with the city's allies. The people's representative did not doubt that in the short term, the betrayal of faith "would be of great utility to the fatherland [*fare alla loro patria grande utilità*]." But the people judged this policy to be "very useful but very dishonest [*utilissimo ma disonestissimo*]" and therefore rejected it. The prudent presumably reasoned that those who are dishonest toward one party will be suspected of bad faith by others, and those who are under general suspicion find it harder to get support for their actions. Dishonesty is therefore not only unjust; it is not useful on a reflective conception of *utilità*.[76]

8.5.2. Punishments

For Machiavelli punishments are among the most primitive forms of justice.[77] Throughout the *Discourses*, the concept of punishment is closely linked to the concepts of justice and law. *Punire* almost always means to impose a just penalty for a violation of accepted conventions or civil laws, and is distinct from revenge taken for merely private reasons or by means that exceed the bounds of justice. Thus Machiavelli distinguishes between ordinary *punishments* and extraordinary *commands*, writing that anyone who does not overestimate his own "strength of

---

Machiavelli implies, they might find themselves less often "alone in their wars" without "anyone to aid them in the spirit with which they help others."

[74] *D*, III.42.301–2/516.

[75] Machiavelli frequently implies that promises and obligations should hold firm over even strong passions and feelings. For example, see *FH*, V.13.200–201; V.31.223; VI.21.253.

[76] *D*, I.59.120/321. From PL, *Themistocles*. On the idea that justice is always advantageous (*sumpherōn*) for the just, affording the most valuable kind of self-protection, see Plato, *Gorg.* 522d and 527b; TPW, V.105–7. For a recent collection of essays that examine the relations between morality and self-interest, see Bloomfield 2008. Bloomfield's introduction and contribution in chap. 12 draw heavily on ancient Greek ethics.

[77] See next section on *D*, I.2.

spirit" should "guard himself from extraordinary commands [*l'imperi istraordi-nari*] and . . . use his humanity in ordinary ones [*e degli ordinari può usare la sua umanità*]; because ordinary punishments [*le punizione ordinarie*] are imputed not to the prince but to the laws and . . . orders."[78] The careful wording suggests that as a general rule, for Machiavelli a *punizione* only deserves that name when it is ordered under *ordinario* standards and publicly known procedures of justice. Extraordinary commands or imperatives, on the other hand, arise from private wills and are not regulated by standards of justice or law. These deserve some other name than *punizione*.

As to how punitive standards and procedures are applied, Machiavelli sees this as a matter of the utmost importance for preserving orders within and among cities. If punitive justice is not upheld in a strictly impartial way, corruption will follow fast. Punishments must be applied in a non-partisan manner so that they are equally "harsh to everyone" who infringes them, and so that judges are not swayed by any "particular goodwill" toward friends or enmities.[79] Moreover, a man's past good works cannot absolve him of punishments for new infractions. Punishments relate only to particular actions, not to an agent's character or previous actions. For "no well-ordered republic ever cancels the demerits with the merits of its citizens; but, having ordered rewards for a good work and punishments for a bad one," if a man rewarded at one time "later works badly," he must be punished "without any regard for his good works." As usual, Machiavelli defends this severe precept in terms of reflective prudence. If, he observes, "a citizen has done some outstanding work [*qualche egregia*] for the city, and on top of the reputation that this thing brings him," there arises a risk that he will gain "an audacity and confidence that he can do some work that is not good without fearing punishment [*senza temere pena*]." If men who do good at one moment think they can get away with doing harm later on, citing their previous good works to deflect criticism, soon they "will become so insolent that any civility will be dissolved."[80]

Punishments, then, should meet harsh—that is, strict—standards of transparency, impartiality, and impersonality both in their formal or conventional definition and their modes of application.[81] These forms of harshness are not cruel, arbitrary, or extraordinary but humane, reasonable, and ordinary. Machiavelli treats them as the most effective ways of dealing with offenses committed within and between cities, in war or in peace. Since the goal of justice is not unilateral revenge but the restoration of limits needed for good order, even infractions caused by "malice" should be punished "humanely," not maliciously.[82] Machiavelli underlines this point by noting that the Romans punished military commanders "with fines of money," that is humanely, although the same acts would have been punished in "another republic . . . with the capital penalty." The Romans had less punitive

---

[78] *D*, III.22.266/477.

[79] *D*, III.22.267/479.

[80] *D*, I.24.59/256.

[81] Also see *D*, I.28.62, 45.93–94, 59.120; II.28.196; III.2–5.214–17, 8.237–38, 22–23.268–69, 32–33.285, 42.301.

[82] Recall Diodotus' arguments against the mass death penalty in TPW, III.44–48.

laws "not because their sins did not merit greater punishment but because . . . the Romans in this case wished to maintain their ancient customs [*antichi costumi loro*]." So long as their orders were robust they wanted to keep their punishments humane, relying on reason rather than brute force to uphold the laws' authority. Humane punishments helped to preserve a "free and ready spirit" among their soldiers and people, ensuring that the latter complied with the laws because they understood the reasons for them. Penalties that are too harsh rely too much on fear, and too little on reason and free will, to produce obedience. They "terrify" (*sbigottire*) people into obedience and, by adding "new difficulties and dangers to a thing in itself difficult and dangerous," make it harder for anyone to "ever work virtuously."[83] Since virtuous *opere* depend on leaving people as free as possible within the limits needed to protect common freedoms, punishments that inhibit freedom with terror are both unjust and bad for good orders. Machiavelli states this clearly: "it is harmful to a republic or to a prince," he writes, "to hold the spirits of subjects in suspense and fearful [*sospesi e paurosi*] with continual penalties and offenses."[84] So that harsh laws do not seem unjust, alongside punitive orders any well-ordered city should have a system of just rewards for good works.[85]

8.5.3. Distributions

A third form of justice discussed in Machiavelli's writings concerns the distribution of a range of goods: especially rewards and honors, shares of public authority, and shares of material goods. The most general principle that regulates all these distributions is meritocratic. Unless exceptions are justified by publicly known and accepted reasons, judgments about individual merit are the principal basis for apportioning any of these goods to some people rather than others. When in early chapters of the *Discourses* Machiavelli identifies what he regards as the most important *virtuoso* Roman orders, meritocratic principles are among their chief foundations. Later chapters apply these principles beyond the selection of personnel for public offices.[86] Meritocratic commitments inform Machiavelli's critical view of hereditary inequalities as a basis for social or political power. Anyone and their offspring should, as he says, be able "by their virtue" to become princes in a well-ordered city—that is, in a republic where the word "prince" means a high office held by different men in turn.[87] At the same time, Machiavelli's principles lead him to insist on the equal rights of individuals from the traditional nobility to be judged by their virtue, not by their estate. Meritocratic principles underpin his defense of a strong judicial order based on procedures designed to ensure that cases against any defendant, however rich or poor or well connected, are judged impartially. Ideally, long-lasting polities will establish such orders early on in their

[83] *D*, I.31.69/266.
[84] *D*, I.45.94/292–93.
[85] *D*, I.24.59/255–56.
[86] On merit see also *D*, I.60.121, III.16.255, 19.260, 22.265–67, 25.271–72, 28.277.
[87] *D*, I.58/318–19, I.60/322–23.

life, and maintain them by establishing systems for public scrutiny and the election of personnel designed to check corruption.

Machiavelli's conception of distributive justice therefore has strongly individualist foundations. In the *Discourses* and elsewhere, demonstrated individual merit is the primary basis for the most important procedures that allocate public honors, offices, and authority. As we saw in chapter 7, however, Machiavelli does sometimes suggest that meritocratic orders are easily corrupted by extreme social and economic inequalities. These often emerge through private transactions rather than as a direct result of public policy. Machiavelli's analysis of the causes of the Ciompi revolt points to the dangers of allowing poorly regulated shifts in economic power to dictate changes in public orders. He implies that in a less corrupt republic, citizens would have refused to accept new distinctions in economic rank among the guilds as a basis for depriving the lower ranks of effective political power. The surest way to preserve political meritocracy, Machiavelli suggests in the *Discourses*, would be to keep the citizens "poor." Good order in early Rome was preserved above all by "seeing that the way to any rank whatever and to any honor whatever was not prevented for you because of poverty, and that one went to find virtue in whatever house it inhabited. That mode of life," he adds, "made riches less desirable."[88] But since respect for free agency is the ground of Machiavelli's meritocratic principles and respect for free agency precludes forced equalization, a less brutally "harsh" way of preserving meritocracy is needed. Although Machiavelli does not spell out what this might be, his principles support moderate forms of public regulation and redistribution of wealth.

Once again, Machiavelli makes these arguments by appealing to the prudent self-interest of those who currently have a greater share of ranks and honors, authority, or material goods. On the negative side, he points to the disorders that arise in cities where some people find it extremely hard to compete for these goods on a level playing field. Those who perceive that they are marginalized or disempowered eventually grow "indignant" and, like the *infima plebe* in the Ciompi revolt, may turn to violent means of redress. Early in the *Discourses* Machiavelli offers a more general analysis of the sources and effects of exclusionary modes in cities. These arise, he says, when early in a city's life the population grows "to such a number" that if they wish to live together they need "to make laws." When it appears to those who constituted the government and legislative councils that there are "as many as would be sufficient for a political way of life," they close "to all others who might come newly to inhabit there the way enabling them to join in the government." Once there are many inhabitants who are left "outside the government," the bare fact that they are excluded is deemed "to give reputation" to those who govern. The insiders then come to be called gentlemen (*gentiluomini*) and the outsiders the populace (*popolani*). This mode, Machiavelli remarks, is given "by chance more than by the prudence of him" who gives them laws.[89] Machiavelli's account underscores the arbitrary, self-serving purposes of political exclusions that

[88] *D*, III.25.271/483–84.
[89] *D*, I.6.2–9/213–17.

are based on ambitious desires for status rather than the necessity for orders of command and obedience. He goes on to stress the dangerous effects of such unreasonable exclusions, noting that they make men "indignant in two modes: one, to see themselves lacking their rank; the other, to see unworthy men of less substance than they made partners and superiors to themselves."[90]

On a more positive note, Machiavelli emphasizes the advantages of inclusive meritocratic orders for civil order and *virtú*. He asks readers to "consider the generosity of spirit of those citizens whom, when put in charge of an army, the greatness of spirit of those citizens lifted above every prince. They did not," he goes on, "esteem kings, or republics; nothing terrified or frightened them." Many *grandi* might be wary of allowing such men of the people to assume high ranks. But Machiavelli's next words are reassuring. "When they later returned to private status," he points out, they again "became frugal, humble, careful of their small competencies, obedient to the magistrates, reverent to their superiors, so that it appears impossible that one and the same spirit underwent such change."[91] An argument developed throughout Book I of the *Discourses* is that exclusionary public modes waste valuable resources of *virtuoso* ordering that may be found in the wider population. The hard political work needed to maintain virtue and order cannot be done by a few remarkable men or a dominant social class. A *virtuoso* city is one whose laws induce all able-bodied citizens to contribute to the common good. Conversely, a polity may be said to suffer from degenerative political idleness when many are prevented from making a full contribution to its political life and defense. Popular desires to have a say in government and legislation and a role in military defense were, Machiavelli argues, among the main causes of Rome's greatness. Therefore "if you wish to make a people numerous and armed so as to be able to make a great empire," he argues, "you must give the population at large opportunities and political powers." These might make it impossible to "manage it" in a more exclusionary mode, but inclusive meritocratic orders would make any city stronger.[92]

8.6.
Ignorance of justice: Who is responsible for upholding just orders?

Like other elements of his ethics, Machiavelli's standards and procedures of justice derive from the two strands of his philosophical anthropology: prudent reflections on the conflict-engendering desires and humors found in "any city whatever" (N1), and ethical reflections on the conditions for coexistence among innately free agents (N2). This distinction raises a question about how people come to recognize fundamental standards of justice. Does Machiavelli imply that they can be known a priori through ethical reflections grounded in the concept of free agency? Or can human beings acquire knowledge of justice only through experience of

---

[90] *D*, III.16.255/465.
[91] *D*, III.25.272/484.
[92] *D*, I.6.21–22/215.

civil and uncivil life, which brings home the need for some regulative standards while showing them the defects of others?

Machiavelli frequently implies that various forms of justice and the principles underlying them are in some sense already known to the people who violate them. In the case of the injurious Fabii, for example, he does not suggest that the unjust parties were unaware that they were committing a grave wrong. Perhaps some Roman defenders of the Fabii transgression believed that they were acting for the common good by placing the apparent "utility" for their fatherland above good faith and the "law of nations." But if anyone did try to portray the wrong as a right, Machiavelli gives no credit to their claims. On his retelling of the episode, there are only two possible views of why the transgressors acted as they did. Either they knew what justice required and knowingly chose to act unjustly, thinking that advantages could gained from wrongdoing. Or they did not know what justice required and acted in sheer ignorance. Machiavelli suggests that ignorance is a poor excuse in this instance. Even if some Romans could say honestly that they *did* not know that they or their ambassadors acted unjustly, it would be irresponsible of them to claim that they *could* not have known this until the "heavens" began to reproach them. As Machiavelli emphasizes in Book II, chapter 29 and again at the beginning of Book III, at the time of the Fabii disaster the Romans had already lived for some time under orders that embodied reasonable standards of justice. Sound standards and procedures needed to uphold just civil orders were set out in the good laws of Romulus, and later improved by the founders of the republic. Standards and conventions regulating relations between peoples were well-established in the "law of nations," which the Romans themselves had done much to articulate.

If some Romans did not know that it was unjust to violate that law, then, they could not plead ignorance as the cause of their injustice, since the problem was not that the only accounts of justice available to them were primitive or naïve. Their violations were not due to excusable ignorance, but to a culpable failure to defend well-established standards of justice. No one could plausibly argue that the Fabii and the Roman Senate erred because the standards of justice relevant to their case were obscure or incompletely developed. Nor could they argue that the Romans needed the scorching experience of getting it wrong before they could be set on the right path to full *cognizione* of justice. On Machiavelli's account, the early Roman republic was already on the right path. It already had simple, sound notions of justice enshrined in civil laws and the law of nations. Although the sorry episode of the Fabii became an occasion to restore justice and good orders, Machiavelli does not suggest that the Romans needed to go through this "ruinous" experience in order to *acquire* knowledge of justice. He suggests only that such experiences sometimes bring people and cities back to knowledge that they or their fathers already possessed, but through their own fault forgot.[93] In the Romans' case

---

[93] In this respect again, I see Machiavelli's position as closer to Socrates' and Plato's than, for example, to Hume's. On the view I attribute to Machiavelli, there can be no progress in the content of ethical knowledge, including knowledge of justice, although there may be improvements in (*a*) education about justice and (*b*) practical applications in institutions and laws. He does not depict justice as a

ignorance of justice was a symptom of deep-seated corruption, not an extenuating circumstance.

Nothing in Machiavelli's account implies that every individual or generation must wait to experience the effects of other people's "indignation and anger" before they can recognize that certain actions are unjust. Indeed, people would spare themselves a good deal of trouble if instead of waiting to experience resistance, they simply presupposed that other people are innately free; exercised self-restraint whenever their actions encroached on others' claims; and freely acknowledged the need for impartial standards and procedures to arbitrate conflicting claims. If human beings were not eminently corruptible beings, a priori reasoning about the necessary conditions for order among free agents would suffice to give people knowledge of justice. Since human orders and human judgments are corruptible, harsh experiences are sometimes the only means of bringing them back to their previous sound principles. But the bottom line of Machiavelli's moral epistemology is, as I suggested in chapter 3, essentially non-empirical. Although he treats particular re-educative experiences as necessary for the restoration of justice, the content of the original standards of justice remains the same before and after the phase when they were corrupted. No progress occurs in people's knowledge of what justice is between the pre-corrupt phase and the later renewal. The basic standards are constant; if anything, Machiavelli consistently implies that their strongest, purest form is found in the most ancient *ordini* and *opere*. Novel features are added by individual restorers, but not substantive changes that can be said to represent progress in moral knowledge. The basic elements of that knowledge, including knowledge of justice, are clear enough to uncorrupt reasoners. They are expressed in different ways by different peoples at different times. They are compatible with a wide range of particular orders and laws. Yet Machiavelli's transhistorical arguments seek to demonstrate the remarkable universality, continuity, and simplicity of the most basic standards of right and wrong.

So while recognizing that most people *do* in fact gain their knowledge of justice through particular experiences, Machiavelli also implies that they *can* apprehend independent grounds for standards of justice as well as reasons discovered through experience. Moreover, they *should* try to do so as a matter of reflective prudence, since this can help them to avoid dangerous mistakes such as those committed during the Fabii *débâcle*. If individuals grasp basic standards of justice and the reasons that ground those standards, they will easily understand why it is always imprudent to violate them. Particular new experiences always test people's commitments to justice, revealing the need to stem corrupt dispositions in some quarters. Trying experiences of civil or external conflict force citizens to "examine themselves" and bring back to light the ethical standards that form the foundations of their city. Prudent citizens may put such experiences to good use, treating great dangers as occasions to purge corruption. But redemption is not inevitable.

---

set of rules gradually "discovered" or constructed through collective learning processes over successive generations. As argued in chap. 3, Machiavelli's arguments imply skepticism about the idea that steady, cumulative progress in moral knowledge can gained from experience.

It depends on the *virtuoso* choices of citizens who have not forgotten what justice is, and who are able to remind others why it is prudent to restore it. Regrettably, as Machiavelli's examples show, there are all too many people who wait for punishing experiences to push them back to the limits, instead of imposing limits on themselves by their own reasoning. The Romans were fortunate enough to have a Camillus to pull them back to a redemptive outcome. Other peoples, including the Florentines, did not have this good fortune after they perpetrated injustices. It is, Machiavelli suggests, extremely unwise to depend on either harsh experiences or the prudence of a few good men to make you respect the limits set by justice. Every citizen and reader of Machiavelli's works should come to recognize the need to impose those limits on themselves, whether or not they have directly experienced a physical necessity to do so. Moreover, while basic standards of justice are simple and easy to grasp, people's ability to grasp them may very easily be corrupted. Machiavelli suggests that ethical judgments may become corrupted even under the best laws and orders through the unjust actions of individuals. Referring to the Fabii incident and its upshot, he notes that "if what I say happened at Rome (where there was so much virtue, so much religion, and so much order)," then "it is no marvel that it should happen much more often in a city or a province that lacks" these qualities.[94] This serves as further warning against ethical complacency, and underlines the need to recall the principled grounds for justice as well as reasons learned from experience.

As Machiavelli describes it, then, the Romans' chief failure was a moral failure of collective self-examination, not an error stemming from ignorance. Had they reflected sooner on what their ancestors and even more ancient peoples already knew, they would easily have recognized that it was unjust to reward the Fabii who violated the law of nations, and avoided all the ensuing trouble. Had they re-examined the reasons for the standards upheld in the *ius gentium* and in their own "ancient" orders, they would easily have seen the imprudence in subordinating these standards to utility or private advantage. There would have been no need to wait for the onslaught of disastrous consequences to recognize that such conduct was reckless and unjust. The Romans must be held responsible, Machiavelli implies, for failing to uphold and continuously "renovate" the principles laid down by their "fathers." The failures of collective self-examination led them to take their orders for granted. They forgot the general standards and principles that served as *fondamenti* of their orders, and soon confounded justice with self-serving arguments from utility, natural superiority or natural equality, or other criteria that could never be "understood or believed" just by all concerned. When people allow these corrupt reasonings to obscure well-known standards of justice, they are bound to make disastrous errors of judgment. And when this happens, Machiavelli argues, responsibility is shared by those who offered the corrupt reasonings to the public and the citizens who failed to recognize that they were corrupt. Pleas of ignorance cannot exonerate either party. Both could have known better had

[94] *D*, II.29.197/404–6.

they simply reflected on the reasons for upholding standards of self-limitation and impartiality when addressing any conflict.

The Fabii case shows how easily people may lose sight of clear standards of justice that they or their ancestors already grasped through reasoning, ancient customs, or laws. Machiavelli treats the relationship between experience and ethical knowledge here as double-edged. Experience may stimulate the renewal of that knowledge. But it may also obscure it. Independent, self-critical reasoning about experience is what makes the difference. If people reflect prudently on their experiences, they may recover and refresh their knowledge of justice. If they fail to examine themselves in the light of various *accidenti*, they may be tempted to interpret their own experiences in a narrow or self-serving way, and soon forget that standards of justice must seem just to others as well as to themselves.[95]

[95] *D*, III.1.209–10/416–20.

CHAPTER 9

Ends and Means

The last chapter's account of Machiavelli's thinking on justice calls into question an-other widespread preconception about his ethics. The basic structure of that ethics is thought to consist in a strong form of consequentialism, sometimes described by the phrase "the ends justify the means." This kind of consequentialism differs from ethical and political theories that include judgments about results *among* other important considerations to be weighed when evaluating actions, but do not treat consequences as the sole or primary basis for judgment. The consequential-ism usually ascribed to Machiavelli holds that the goodness or badness, rightness or wrongness of actions should be judged solely or primarily by the results they produce, so that other considerations are subordinated to this criterion.

Scholars who see Machiavelli's reasoning as consequentialist disagree about *which* ends he thinks justify actions. One candidate is the "ends" of "state," where the state is identified with a particular prince or king. Another is the ends of state understood as the integrity of a historic territory and security of its entire popula-tion. Still another possibility is that Machiavelli's justifying ends are those appro-priate to the security and virtue of republics. On this view, the desire to preserve a free way of life justifies particular policies, not just the needs of physical self-defense.[1] These diverse accounts are connected to very different interpretations of Machiavelli's ethics. Some accounts hold that his account of justificatory ends is strongly ethical, in that the main end results to be secured by action are de-scribed by a doctrine of the good or the good life. Others hold that it is basically strategic, in that the main results are to maintain power or survival for their own sake, independently of any conception of the good. Nevertheless, most scholars agree that the *structure* of Machiavelli's reasoning is teleological and consequen-tialist. It starts, they think, by identifying basic ends or results that human beings must pursue, as a matter of nature or sound reasoning or both. It then goes on to judge actions by asking how far they tend to promote or impede the desired

---

[1] The first view is based only on a superficial reading of the *Prince*. Serious scholars who take Machiavelli's other works into account usually defend some version of the second two positions. Two of the most influential arguments for the reason-of-state view are offered by Meinecke (1998 [1925]) and Berlin (1981 [1958]). Recent arguments for the third, defense-of-republican freedoms view include Skinner 1981 and 2002 and Viroli 1998. More recently, Hörnqvist (2004) has proposed that Machiavelli gives priority to the ends of "reason of state" in external relations but priority to the defense of civil freedoms inside republics.

ethical ends and strategic results.² Machiavelli's alleged consequentialism is often contrasted with deontological ethics, which holds that some acts are morally
obligatory, and others wrong, regardless of their consequences.³ According to a
widespread view, Machiavelli's chief legacy for ethics was to abandon principles
grounded in theology or natural law, replacing them with a tough-minded consequentialism that refuses to apologize for subordinating procedural constraints
to more important ends.

This chapter argues that these various consequentialist readings should be re-
examined, taking account of Machiavelli's dialectical methods of writing.⁴ As in
earlier chapters, I suggest that the main passages that are usually taken as evidence
of Machiavellian's consequentialism have been read without due attention to textual context, and without reference to ancient writings that use similar dialectical strategies to encourage critical reflection on corrupt opinions. When a text
declares that the ends justify the means, or that actions should be judged by their
results, it cannot be assumed that these words express Machiavelli's own reflective judgments. More often they are presented as widespread views that stand in
need of critical examination. Relocated in their textual contexts and taken as the
starting point rather than the terminus of critical *discorsi*, Machiavelli's apparently
consequentialist assertions often turn out to be imprudent opinions expressed by
political leaders or men in the piazza. He offers subtle reasonings about sweep-
ingly consequentialist statements that undermine their overt claims. My reading
does not deny that Machiavelli treats judgments about ethical ends and strategic
results as extremely important for evaluating actions. I argue only that he does not
treat ends or results as the *primary* basis for assessing the quality of actions.

9.1.
Responsibility for bad outcomes: The dangers of giving counsel

The claim that actions are or should be judged by their results, effects, or ends
frequently appears in the *Florentine Histories*.⁵ It is almost always presented in a
negative light. Throughout the book Machiavelli presents various forms of the
argument as a source of disastrously irresponsible judgments made by the Florentines, especially in their foreign relations. For example, he observes that when
Lorenzo de' Medici's foreign policies lost wars and cities, he was loudly criticized
by the Florentine people. But when policies conducted on exactly the same precepts went well, "in Florence, a city eager to speak, which judges things by results
and not by advice [*dai successi e non dai consigli giudica*], the reasoning turned
around; and it celebrated Lorenzo to the sky." However, these favorable judgments
also proved unreasonable. For although some policies seemed to have good results

---

² Note that the main question here is not whether particular actions are compatible *in principle* with
the main ends. It is whether in a particular set of circumstances, actions or non-primary ends tend *in
practice* to produce consequences compatible with the desired ends.
³ See Meinecke 1998 (1925), 36–44; Cassirer 1946, 143.
⁴ For an unusually skeptical view of consequentialist readings of Machiavelli, see Kocis 1998, 114–27.
⁵ Machiavelli uses different words in different contexts; I identify them as they arise in the following.

(*successi*) at first, "the end [*il fine*] was unexpected and the cause of much evil [*inaspettato e cagione di assai male*]."[6]

Machiavelli says here that the Florentines *do* judge things "by results and not by advice," not that they *should*. In this instance and many others discussed in the present chapter, such judgments are clearly imprudent.[7] In the *Discourses* Machiavelli describes the widespread tendency to judge actions by "the end" (*il fine*) as a kind of blindness that must always be taken into account by those who counsel any course of political action. "All men," we read in Book III, chapter 35, "are blind in this, in judging good and bad counsel by the end [*giudicare . . . dal fine*]."[8] This does not mean that the outcomes of policies should be of no account at all when judging them after the fact. Machiavelli clearly holds that when anyone makes himself "head of a grave and important decision," it is reasonable for people to expect him to take great care in assessing the likely effects of actions he advises. If a counselor claimed to have made a prudent assessment of consequences before an action was taken, and these claims later turn out to have been unfounded, people have reason to hold him partly responsible for failures of policy. On the other hand, not even the most prudent of counselors can predict outcomes with complete accuracy. Machiavelli draws a clear distinction between actions that appear useful (*paiono utili*) to a counselor of good faith before they are undertaken, and the outcome of the action as it appears *post facto*. He himself had been in the uncomfortable position of recommending policies that seemed good to him and to others until they were put unsuccessfully into practice.[9] Since no one who counsels an action can completely control its outcomes, many who advise princes or republics are afraid to say what course of action they deem useful, aware that "since men judge things by the end [*giudicando . . . dal fine*], all the ill that results [*risulta*] from it is attributed to the author of the counsel; and if good results from it, he is commended for it, but the reward by far does not counterbalance the harm."[10]

It is unreasonable to judge courses of action *only* by their outcomes, Machiavelli suggests here, because it is always necessary to choose between different courses of

---

[6] *FH*, VIII.22.343–44/710. Book VIII describes how Lorenzo's government struggled to keep up appearances of Florentine greatness while being forced to call on foreign support, having destroyed chances of a common Italian front through its aggressive expansionism and deceptive dealings.

[7] Compare Livy, who frequently has prudent characters remark that it is unwise or unjust to judge policies by their results. For example, see *LH*, XXII.38, where the result [*eventus*] is described by Fabius Maximus as "that schoolmaster of fools [*stultorum . . . magister*]." In XXVII.44 Livy writes in his own voice that an action "would be praised or blamed according to the outcome, than which nothing is more unjust [*apparebat, quo nihil iniquius est, ex eventu famam habiturum*]."

[8] *D*, III.35.290–91/504–5. Compare the *Prince* (*P*, XVIII.71/166–67): because men in general "judge more by their eyes" than by other senses, "in the actions of all men, and especially of princes, where there is no court to appeal to, one looks to the end [*si guarda al fine*]. So let the prince win and maintain his state; the means [*mezzi*] will always be judged honorable, and will be praised by everyone. For the vulgar are taken in by the appearance and the outcome [*evento*] of a thing, and in the world there is no one but the vulgar."

[9] The unhappy experience with his citizen militia. Despite the militia's failure, he consistently maintained that the basic ideas behind it were sound, and continued to examine conditions for their success.

[10] *D*, III.35.290–91/504–5.

action before all the outcomes are known.[11] How then should anxious counselors deal with men's "blind" insistence on judging actions only by their results? "I do not," Machiavelli concludes, "see any way for it" but to "take things moderately [*moderatamente*]" when giving advice, avoiding passionate rhetoric that seeks to move people to act against their better judgment. If other people follow advice that you gave "without passion with modesty [*sanza passione con modestia*]" and clear reasons, they cannot reasonably blame you if they fail, since their own judgment concurred with yours.[12] Examples of this kind of prudent persuasion appear in the preceding chapters, both involving Fabius Maximus, Roman general and dictator during the Punic Wars. In Book III, chapter 33 Machiavelli commends Fabius for his methods of inspiring confidence among his soldiers.[13] Like all good captains, Fabius knew that he could not promise his soldiers victory, since the fortunes of war are never entirely predictable. The best he could do was to give his soldiers "many reasons [*molte ragioni*] through which they could hope for victory" in battle, and to assure them that he could tell them other "good things" that would inspire confidence "if it were not dangerous to make them manifest." Fabius strikes the right balance here. He avoids the "dangerous" route of overstating grounds for confidence about outcomes, which cannot be completely known; yet he gives many reasons for confidence that the soldiers themselves can understand and affirm. Whatever the results of battle, soldiers motivated by these persuasions would see victory as their own, not just the captain's; and defeat if it came as their shared responsibility, since they fought with the same confidence as the captain.

The next chapter discusses the need in republics for orders that help people to avoid disastrous errors of judgment about the quality of their chosen leaders. Machiavelli notes that leading men are often esteemed "greater than they are in truth" until some action they take in office exposes their faults. Here again, his point is that people can never be absolutely sure that the men they elect will live up to their hopes once they hold office. The best they can do is to uphold institutional checks on self-deception, especially public councils where every citizen may "make public the defect of that one, so that the people, not lacking knowledge of him, can judge better." Fabius Maximus, Machiavelli notes, used such councils to good effect to persuade the Roman people that a candidate for the consulship was unqualified.[14] Machiavelli makes it clear that Fabius' persuasions satisfy the criteria he sets out in the following chapter, where he speaks of people's blindness "in judging good and bad counsel by the end." Fabius invokes good reasons for choosing or rejecting magistrates, not personal passions; and he presents his reasons through public orders without using backhanded forms of influence. When he prepares his soldiers for battle, too, his exhortations have the essential qualities of reasonableness and transparency, which encourage the men to see their actions

---

[11] This implies that the choice of one policy over another must be guided by considerations other than expected outcomes. These might include one's prior commitments and undertakings, respect for established laws and orders, or the desire to preserve a name for virtue.

[12] *D*, III.35.290–91/505.

[13] *D*, III.33.286–87/498–500.

[14] *D*, III.34.289–90/500–503.

as their own responsibility, not as controlled by blind fate. If people view their actions in this way, Machiavelli implies, they are more likely to take responsibility for the outcome, whether they judge it good or bad.

The broader implication of both examples is that those who "counsel" cities should worry less about what they cannot entirely control—both the outcomes of policies and public criticisms if they go badly—and take more care about the methods they use when persuading others to follow their advice. Policy advisers should do more to present a reasoned case for their proposed course of action, and submit it to public scrutiny so that "the people, not lacking knowledge" relevant to the decision, "can judge better." By observing these procedural constraints on the way that they present advice, they ensure that others identify with it as their own and share responsibility for whatever outcomes transpire. This, Machiavelli suggests in chapters 33–35 of Book III, is the most realistic response to the fact that most people are blind in judging actions by outcomes. To think that one can completely control outcomes is unrealistic. So is the belief that one can control popular judgments indefinitely by playing on passions. This tactic may work for a while, but if the results of a policy are not what people hoped, they will turn against you all the more angrily if you raised their hopes without good reasons. The best that counselors can do is to observe procedural constraints on the way that they offer counsel, especially when "grave and important" policies are at stake. One should "give one's opinion without passion and defend it without passion" so that "if the city or the prince follows it, it follows voluntarily [segua voluntario], and it does not appear to enter upon it drawn by your importunity. When you do this," Machiavelli concludes, "it is not reasonable [non è ragionevole] that a prince and a people wish you ill for your counsel, since it was not followed against the wish of many." For "one bears danger where many have contradicted, who then at the unhappy end [infelice fine] concur to bring you ruin."[15]

If Machiavelli's reasoning conformed to standard "Machiavellian" pattern, he might be expected to give very different advice to counselors concerned about being blamed for failures of policy. Having noted the inconvenient fact that "all men are blind . . . in judging good and bad counsel by the end," he might have told advisers to adopt various ruses to make bad outcomes appear unrelated to their initial advice, thus putting blame on someone else. This, indeed, is among the "Machiavellian" tactics often imputed to the Prince. But even there Machiavelli ends up stressing the need for transparency and frank reasoning in taking counsel. The Discourses tells counselors to shed their inhibitions and make carefully reasoned arguments, submitting them to public examination so that those who accept their arguments can be held co-responsible for outcomes. The Prince tells princes to welcome truthfulness and transparency in their counselors, and urges them to take responsibility for whatever policies they adopt instead of blaming whoever advised them. "A prince," we read in chapter 23, "should always take counsel" from others. "But he should be a very broad questioner [largo domandatore]" and "a patient listener to the truth; indeed, he should become upset when he learns that

---

[15] D, III.35.291/505.

anyone has any hesitation to speak it to him." At first he should ask advisers "about everything and listen to their opinions," but then take full responsibility for whatever policy he decides to adopt: "he should decide by himself, in his own mode." A condition for responsible judgment, however, is complete freedom of speech among his counselors. With each of them the prince "should behave in such a mode that everyone knows [*conosca*] that the more freely he speaks, the more he will be accepted [*quanto piú liberamente si parlerà, piú gli fia accetto*]."[16]

The bottom line of Machiavelli's advice about counseling princes is therefore the same as his advice about counseling peoples. Counselors cannot be held solely responsible for the "end" or outcome of a policy. Ultimate responsibility lies with whoever authorized the policy they proposed: the prince in a principality, the people and their magistrates in a republic.[17] In any well-ordered republic or *principato*, procedures for giving and receiving counsel should include strong checks on self-deception, misinformation, and other sources of bad judgment. Princes and peoples are responsible for ensuring that these procedural checks function well. They can also be held responsible if they malfunction. It is up to princes and peoples to encourage freedom of speech or discourage it, to listen carefully to different opinions, and to scrutinize counselors' arguments in public assemblies. If counselors appear not to be telling the truth, it is up to princes and peoples to urge them to do so, or to question their opinions if these seem to be poorly founded. If advisers seem to appeal too much to passions, instead of reasoning "with modesty," they should be called into question by citizens in republics or by princes in principalities. Machiavelli consistently holds citizens and princes co-responsible if they allow themselves to be swept along by such arguments, then later blame those who sold them.

The question of who should held responsible for unhappy outcomes of policies pursued in and by republics is a recurrent focus of the *Florentine Histories*. Many episodes in the work illustrate the pitfalls of judging actions solely or mainly by end results, as later sections will show. The narrative often highlights the irresponsibility of political leaders who judged policies only by expected or *post facto* results. But where citizens failed to be "broad questioners" of their leaders, and supported policies without good reasons, they too are assigned their share of responsibility. The risks of such irresponsible conduct are especially great in foreign policy. In Machiavelli's Florence in almost all the periods he covers, sectarian divisions ensured that almost any matter of internal policy would be subject to intense disagreement, if not a cause for new outbreaks of violence. When Florence went to war against other cities, however, cross-party hatreds were sometimes put aside in the name of a greater *necessità* or the "common good" of the fatherland. Machiavelli's analysis suggests that while some of these wars could reasonably be judged as necessary, in others the rhetoric of necessity was little more than a fig leaf for self-serving ambitions. As always in the *Histories*, he urges readers to examine closely the reasonings and deeds beneath the rhetoric of necessary ends invoked to justify particular wars.

---

[16] *P*, XXIII.94–95/183–85.
[17] Compare Plato, *Gorg.* 518c–519c.

As the next two sections show, Machiavelli consistently argues that it is a dangerous error to judge the necessity or utility of wars solely by their consequences. The dangers are most vividly illustrated in Book IV, where he presents debates about two very different types of war fought in the name of the Florentine people. One war was fought against a new entrepreneurial prince, Filippo Visconti, who had expanded aggressively in Lombardy and begun to threaten Florence's leadership in Tuscany. The other war was fought against Lucca, one of the most rebellious Tuscan cities under Florentine *dominio*.[18] Lucca and the freedom-loving Lucchese people make regular appearances throughout the *Histories*, exemplifying the difficulties Florence faced in trying to establish greater control over the region. Machiavelli presents the war against Visconti as an example of a war that was necessary but badly conducted from the outset, and therefore judged after the fact to have been unnecessary. In direct contrast, he presents the war against Lucca as one that prudent citizens judged both unnecessary and harmful for Florentine interests. Nevertheless, this war was extremely popular at the beginning, and so received substantial funding. In each case, only a minority of citizens judged prudently. Most people complained about the necessary war with Visconti, then rallied eagerly to support the unnecessary war with Lucca. Machiavelli's narrative asks how popular judgments came to be so confused in a republic like Florence, and how the tendency to judge policies by their outcomes contributed to the dangers that ensued.

9.2.
Judging wars by *post facto* outcomes

Machiavelli points to two reasons why the war against Filippo Visconti might well have been judged as a legitimate response to two kinds of necessity. One was legal: Filippo had violated formal treaties with Florence and other cities. The other was military and geopolitical: he had already seized cities in Florence's generally acknowledged sphere of influence, thereby demonstrating clear belligerent intentions.[19] Machiavelli does not suggest that these two reasons constituted entirely sufficient grounds for war; they did, however, amount to a strong prima facie presumption in favor of it. Nevertheless, after the war had been fought and lost, it was widely condemned as unnecessary. People cited two bad effects as *post facto* reasons to deny the necessity for war: that heavy taxes were imposed to pursue it, and that Florence lost. Since taxes "weighed more on the lesser citizens than the greater," and there was no victory to celebrate, the Florentines "filled the city with complaints, and everyone condemned the ambition and greed of the powerful, accusing them of wishing to start an unnecessary war [*una guerra non necessaria*] so as to indulge

---

[18] See Brown 2000a on the use of the terms *imperio* and *dominio* in Florentine legislation and politics.

[19] *FH*, IV.4–5.148–50/476–78. In this case there is both a natural necessity for self-preservation against an overt threat, and an ethico-juridical necessity or *obligo* imposed by the "need" to uphold treaties against violators.

their appetites and to oppress the people so as to dominate [*per dominare*] them."[20] Forgetting the reasons why they had judged the war necessary before, with defeat "the whole of Florence grieved, but especially the great citizens who had advised the war." The people for their part "stung them with abusive words, complaining of the taxes they had borne" and "of a war begun without cause."[21]

On Machiavelli's account, *post facto* hostility to the war was rooted in a very common error: the tendency to judge policies only by their effects, especially on one's own immediate situation, instead of by reasons assessed on their own merits before implementing a policy. When the effects of wars appear good to them, people are easily persuaded of their necessity; when effects appear bad, they turn around and call them unnecessary. In the case of war with Visconti, these irresponsible attitudes led the Florentines to overlook other causes that explained their city's defeat and the economic difficulties it brought. Instead of insisting that defeat showed that war was unnecessary, Machiavelli implies, they should have examined more self-critically the way in which the war was declared and conducted.

The main problem was not, as *post facto* critics charged, that there was no reasonable cause or necessity for war with Visconti, whose breaches of faith and threats to Florentine interests constituted a strong case for war. The crucial question was whether the city's allies and neighbors thought it justifiable to prosecute war at the moment when Florence did so. The Florentines could, Machiavelli implies, have made a good case for war to other Italian cities had the Florentine war party been more patient. Instead the magistrates opted to act precipitately and unilaterally, showing scant regard for other interested parties' views. He puts the arguments for a circumspect approach in the mouth of Giovanni de' Medici, usually depicted as spokesman for policies that pursue Florentine and party interests through procedures that others also see as legitimate. Giovanni "publicly discouraged" the decision to go to war at that moment "by showing that, however sure they might be of the evil mind of the duke [Visconti], it was better to wait for him to attack you than to go against him with forces." He points out that at present other Italians viewed the duke's claims as no less "justified" (*giustificata*) than Florence's. Toward them it would be much easier to make the case for a defensive war than for an offensive one, since a first attack by Visconti would be seen by many as a threat to their own interests, "and they would defend their own things with a different spirit and with different forces than they would those of others." On the other hand, a preemptive attack from Florence would be perceived as a general threat no less than one from Visconti, and would arouse suspicions of Florentine ambitions in other Italian cities. Cities that might support Florence if Visconti attacked first would almost certainly withhold support if Florence was first to use arms. Given current tensions around Italy, and especially other Italians' historically well-founded suspicions of Florentine ambitions for *dominio*, the most prudent course for Florence was self-restraint.[22]

[20] *FH*, IV.4.148–49/476–77.
[21] *FH*, IV.7.151/479–80.
[22] *FH*, IV.5.150/478.

Machiavelli lets readers consider for themselves whether Giovanni's caution was more prudent than the voices that prevailed. These men urged that "it was not good to wait for the enemy at home but to go and find him; that fortune is more friendly to the one who attacks than to the one who defends; and that war is carried on in others' homes with less loss, even though at greater cost, than in one's own." This opinion easily prevailed against arguments favoring a defensive war fought with allies.[23] Instead of making a strong legal and defensive case for war and waiting for Visconti to attack first, the Florentines rushed into a war that strengthened their enemy and made Florence look like the main threat to regional stability. At this heady stage, the same people who would later complain that the war had been unnecessary expected an easy victory, with or without support from other cities. Significantly, however, arguments about the strategic or legal necessity for war do not figure in the war party's case. Machiavelli depicts their main *ante bellum* concern as a desire for what they naïvely expect to be a fairly easy victory over Visconti. If *post facto* critics complained that the war had been unnecessary yet supported it at the time without demanding reasons for its necessity, they themselves must be held responsible for the oversight. When he goes on to discuss the conduct of the war, Machiavelli suggests that poor military "orders" were partly to blame for Florence's defeat. The Florentines' main error in this respect was to put their army in the charge of a mercenary captain who made an irresponsible judgment in a key battle.[24] But the main reason for Florence's defeat is implicit in Giovanni's arguments against making a unilateral declaration of offensive war. Giovanni sees that success or failure in war depends importantly on judgments about a war's legitimacy, not just inside the main parties to a conflict but also to their neighbors. For Florence to be assured of strategic support—and to ensure that Visconti would not gain new supporters—it mattered greatly whether other Italian cities were persuaded of the war's necessity.

The more general lesson here is that even when just causes for war can be found in treaty violations and threats to security interests, the means chosen to prosecute a war matter greatly for its success. In this instance, the Florentines' hasty unilateralism is presented as one key error; their eagerness to launch an offensive war without regard for their neighbors' suspicions is another. The use of unilateral and offensive means always raises doubts about the justice of a war, Giovanni suggests, because those who fight good causes with means that seem excessive or self-serving make it hard for others to trust them. And those who are obliged to fight without firm allies are vulnerable, since those who do not rally to your side might go over to support your opponent. The limited legitimacy of the Florentines' offensive war was therefore a foreseeable cause of its failure. The example further suggests that people are prone to judge actions too much by their results when they lack habits of reasoning about actions from a wider, multilateral or non-partisan standpoint. Without this wider perspective, they assess every policy only from the standpoint of their own immediate and apparent

[23] Ibid.
[24] *FH*, IV.6.150–51/479–80.

interests. Machiavelli treats this as the usual way in which most people, not least most Florentines, judge complex policies. All Machiavelli's main writings encourage readers to view complex situations from more than one side, so that they become better at taking stock of the foreseeable—and often reasonable—responses of other agents to their own actions.

Recounting the bitter complaints of citizens who had supported the war at first but now deplore it, Machiavelli has the young Rinaldo degli Albizzi, in his first appearance in the *Histories*, try to calm the "excited humors in the multitude" with these "good words":

> it was not prudent to judge things by their effects [*effetti*], because many times things well advised do not have a good outcome [*fine*] and things ill advised a good one; and if wicked advice is praised for a good outcome, one does nothing but inspire men to err, which results in great harm to republics because bad advice is not always successful [*felice*]. So likewise it was an error to censure a wise course that might have an unhappy outcome [*fine non lieto*], because it would take away from citizens the spirit to advise the city and to say what they mean.[25]

Does Rinaldo's argument that it is imprudent to "judge things by their effects" represent Machiavelli's own view? If one closely follows the reasoning about this war and other conflicts in the *Histories*, including the war with Lucca discussed shortly, it seems reasonable to answer this answer in the affirmative. In this instance the youthful Rinaldo, whose judgment has not yet been corrupted by partisan embroilments, expresses views broadly similar to those later expressed by prudent characters such as Niccolò da Uzzano.[26] By portraying Rinaldo's judgments as sounder before he becomes leader of a "party," Machiavelli underlines the point that since experience can corrupt as well as instruct, the simpler ethical judgments made by less experienced observers are sometimes closer to the mark than the subtler pretexts and exceptions offered by seasoned politicians. On the other hand, Machiavelli leaves room to doubt whether Rinaldo's *onesto* words are not used in this context for questionable purposes. His argument about the inadequacy of judging by effects is basically sound. But he invokes it here not to encourage citizens to reflect more carefully on their judgments, but to silence critical voices and to excuse a badly conceived war. His "good words" seek to put a lid on public self-examination, not to encourage it. While it is true that "it is imprudent to judge things by their effects" alone, it is false and irresponsible to argue, as Rinaldo seems to, that since good advice often has bad effects, bad effects should be excused as brute bad luck.[27] Machiavelli has Rinaldo declare that "God had willed" Florentine defeat. But his narrative identifies purely human and avoidable causes.

---

[25] *FH*, IV.7.152/480.

[26] See next section.

[27] Moreover, Rinaldo's ambitions are already highlighted here, hinting that his words may be aimed at gaining a reputation for prudence rather than showing a sure grasp of what is prudent.

9.3.
Judging wars by anticipated outcomes

A new war, this time with the neighboring city of Lucca, follows several chapters after the account of Florence's war with Filippo Visconti. Machiavelli presents the second war as strategically, legally, and ethically unnecessary. "No cause [*cagione*] for a new war," he states bluntly, "would have been seen if the ambition of men had not set one in motion again." Though they had fought the first war badly, the Florentines had at least had reason to consider a war with Visconti as necessary "to defend their own city's freedom" against a pact-breaking aggressor. Now the same men who criticized that war *post facto* wanted a new one, on far weaker grounds. This time, Machiavelli writes, they desired a war that aimed "to seize [*occupare*] the freedom of others" with no other defensive or legal cause. Like many of Florence's confrontations with neighbors in the *Florentine Histories*, the war with Lucca showed how "much more ready is the multitude to seize what belongs to others than to watch out [*guardare*] for its own." On Machiavelli's account, the catalyst for war was a mercenary captain who had often fought for Florence. Finding himself out of work in times of peace, he connived with Rinaldo degli Albizzi "to attack the Lucchese under cover of some fictitious quarrel." The captain would then have a job, and Rinaldo a popular cause through which he could easily gain a reputation for political leadership.[28] Machiavelli evaluates the case for and against war with Lucca by juxtaposing Rinaldo's pro-war arguments, made before a council of 498 leading citizens, with the arguments of his chief opponent, Niccolò da Uzzano.

Rinaldo's pro-war case rests on optimistic but unfounded claims about its anticipated results. First on his list of expected good effects was the "utility [*l'utile*] to be gained from the acquisition" of Lucca for Florence's "dominions." His next arguments are opportunistic. It was now a good time to seize Lucca, he declares, since the pope was too involved in other matters to impede Florentine designs. The third argument was simply "the ease of taking [*espugnarla*] Lucca," which, he asserted, "had lost that natural vigor and ancient zeal to defend its own freedom." Having lived under several tyrants, Lucca was a mere "slave to one of its citizens" and had neither the freedom to defend nor the will to recover it. Rinaldo's fourth and final argument is the only one to touch on the questions of a war's necessity. He describes the injuries done by Lucca's lord against the Florentine republic and "his ill will toward it," concluding on these rather thin grounds "that no other campaign ever undertaken by the Florentine people was easier, more useful, or more just."[29]

[28] *FH*, IV.18.163/493–94. This epitomizes the dangers of relying on mercenary soldiers described in all Machiavelli's works: depending on war for their livelihood, they are discontented in peacetime and often created new causes for unnecessary wars. Rinaldo, aspiring "to reach the highest rank of the city with his own virtues," is one of the *Histories'* most ambivalent characters. On Machiavelli's account he is true lover of his country whose policies are nonetheless flawed by personal ambition, extreme partisanship, and a dangerous tendency to "jump the gun" in tense situations.

[29] *FH*, IV.19.164–65/495.

Since neither legal nor defensive necessity was the key issue in the case for war, its merits must be assessed by scrutinizing two of its central claims. First, was it reasonable to expect the profit gained by the *end* of acquiring Lucca to outweigh the disadvantages of acquiring it by *means* of an aggressive war? Second, was it reasonable to expect the acquisition to be easy because of papal negligence and the Lucchese people's current, unfree political condition? When it is his turn to address the council, Niccolò da Uzzano gives a resoundingly negative answer to both questions. Florence, he declares, "had never undertaken an enterprise more unjust [*una impresa più ingiusto*], more dangerous, or one from which greater losses must arise."[30] He starts by giving principled reasons for this judgment that have nothing to do with anticipated results. From these primary, non-consequentialist foundations, he goes on to build up a secondary, more reflective consequentialist argument against the proposed war.

A first principled argument invokes the obligations of friendship. Lucca, Uzzano points out, had always been friendly to Florence, and had often been a refuge for Guelfs exiled from their fatherland. His second argument questions the justice of the war itself. Surely, he reflects, there is no just cause to declare war unilaterally on a city whose people had never offended the Florentines in any way, and who had not asked Florence to rid them of their current tyrant. These opening arguments underscore the ethical and legal constraints that *ought*, in Uzzano's view, to guide reasoning about whether to go to war. So long as people still take such constraints seriously, he argues, it is necessary to take account of the views of the Lucchese people about a Florentine attack. Rinaldo dismisses their views as unimportant: since the Lucchese lack internal freedom anyway, he asserts, they are unlikely to see an external assault as a serious injury.[31] Uzzano disagrees. It is of the utmost importance, he says, to recall the difference between Lucca's relations with Florence when Lucca lived under tyrants and its conduct when the city was free. Since the citizens had never offended Florence when they lived in freedom, when it did offend, one should blame not the city but its tyrant. Uzzano treats this as a matter of justice, while pointing out that actions perceived as unjust always offend people at the receiving end. If it were possible to "make war on the tyrant without making it on the citizens," he considers, "that would displease him [Uzzano] less; but as this could not be, then he could not agree [*consentire*] that a friendly citizenry should be despoiled of its goods."[32]

Having set out the principled case against war, Uzzano then turns around and adopts a more pragmatic, hard-hitting tone. In a clear echo of Thucydides' Diodotus, he observes ruefully that his initial arguments are unlikely to sway many compatriots, "since one lives today in such a way that just and unjust do not have to be of much account." A different kind of argument is needed to make a case against the war that might persuade men who care little about friendship

---

[30] *FH*, IV.19.165/496.

[31] This foreshadows Cosimo de' Medici's derogatory views on the Milanese people's love of freedom, discussed in chap. 6, sec. 6.5.

[32] *FH*, IV.19.65/496.

and respect for others. Uzzano proceeds to lay out a second set of arguments, designed to appeal to corrupt listeners. Unlike the first set, these arguments are consequentialist: they assume that the goodness or rightness of a policy may be judged solely by its results. But while these premises are very different from the principled premises of Uzzano's first arguments, he draws identical practical conclusions from them. Declaring that he will now put duties aside and consider only "utility to the city," Uzzano starts by reconstructing a more sophisticated version of Rinaldo's crude consequentialist arguments. There is, he notes, a widely held presumption that wars are justified by public utility. He then suggests that utility is always served by gaining benefits for the city and avoiding losses. On this criterion, he then argues, it was unreasonable to expect the proposed war with Lucca to result in more gains than losses. Uzzano questions Rinaldo's claims that it would be easy to acquire Lucca through war as a viable part of Florence's dominions, and that the profits gained through war would outweigh its costs. Machiavelli has Uzzano argue that

> only those things could be called useful [*utili*] that could not easily bring loss: so he did not know how anyone could call that enterprise useful in which the losses were certain and the profits doubtful. The certain losses were the expenses that it would incur, which would be seen to be so great that they ought to make fearful a city at rest, let alone one wearied by a long and grave war as theirs had been. The utility they would gain was the acquisition of Lucca, which he confessed to be great; but he had also to consider the uncertainties that were in it, which to him appeared so many that he judged the acquisition impossible.[33]

Uzzano echoes the maxim set out a few pages earlier by the dying Giovanni de' Medici: if you accept only as much as is given to you, "always you will have more than they who, wanting others' share, lose their own, and before losing it live in continual unease."[34] Whether you seek to acquire within your own city or in others, acquisitions taken forcibly without good cause will be challenged by others, and make you less secure than before. The more general risk is that ambitions to acquire neighboring cities led Florentines to deceive themselves about the ease of secure victory. Like Thucydides' overconfident Athenians, Machiavelli's compatriots seldom achieve good results when they start off expecting easy success.[35]

These arguments suggest that the pro-war camp had a dangerously one-sided account of what results were desirable; that is, of what constituted the public *utilità*. They conceive of victory in the narrowest terms as immediate military success, while scarcely thinking about the political conditions needed to secure their new acquisition. This myopic view, Uzzano argues, greatly undermined the Florentines' chances of achieving good results beyond initial victory. His more reflective account of public utility considers a wider range of political and security

---

[33] Ibid.
[34] *FH*, IV.16.161/491.
[35] Compare TPW, IV.27–28, and Alcibiades' arguments for Athens' invasion of Sicily in VI.17–18.

implications that might be expected to flow from war with Lucca. Uzzano weighs the apparent advantages of acquiring cities that have not consented to one's authority against the uncertainties that issue from such unauthorized acquisitions. One risk was that the war would give powerful rivals like Filippo Visconti fresh pretexts for war with Florence, whose resources would be badly strained. A much greater risk came from the Lucchese people's desire to be treated as a free "partner" to Florence in Tuscany, not as a subject in their unauthorized empire. Thus Uzzano saw that his fellow citizens'

> humors were excited and that his words were not being heard. Even so, he wished to predict this to them: that they would make a war for which they would spend very much, would run into very many dangers, and, instead of seizing Lucca, they would free [*libererebbono*] it from a tyrant; and out of a friendly city, subdued [*subiugata*] and weak, they would make a free city, hostile to them and in time an obstruction to the greatness of their republic [*una città libera, loro nimica . . . uno ostaculo alla grandezza della republica loro*].[36]

Rinaldo assumes that the effects of Florentine actions can be assessed in isolation from the responses of people at the receiving end. In contrast to this unilateralist view, Uzzano treats the responses of the Lucchese people as among the most important results to be weighed in the case for or against war. His appraisal of their likely responses is based on a principled recognition of the Lucchese people's desire to be treated as free agents who would reasonably want to authorize Florentine dominion, if they choose to authorize it at all.

After hearing arguments for and against the war, the council of 498 voted secretly; only 98 opposed the campaign, so Florence went to war. Despite Florence's strength and Lucca's weakness, the enterprise was unsuccessful. Even if they had they fought fairly, after the war the Florentines would have faced difficulties in making the acquisition appear legitimate in the eyes of the Lucchese people. But already during the war their indifference to other people's perceptions, and their complacency about prospects for "easy" victory, compounded the Florentines' problems. Machiavelli notes that if one judged the military campaign solely by the number of new territorial acquisitions made, it was initially successful. But the actions taken in the field by the two commissioners of war, one of whom was none other than Rinaldo degli Albizzi, were nonetheless unhappy (*infelici*). This was "not because they did not acquire many towns but because of the charges made against both of them in the management of the war." The charges related to the Florentines' "cruel and avaricious" treatment of enemy civilians. Machiavelli has a delegate from Lucca accuse the other Florentine commissioner, Astorre Gianni, of the most inhumane treatment, declaring that he "has no more of a man than the appearance, nor of a Florentine more than the name." The Lucchese insist that they do not wish to "defoul so decent and compassionate a republic

[36] *FH*, IV.19.165–66/496–97.

with the indecency and cruelty of one wicked citizen." Yet they point out that the Florentines' unjust conduct in this war set a precedent that would make other cities wary of accepting Florentine friendship. Machiavelli has the Lucchese beg the Florentines "to relieve the distress of your subjects [*subietti*] so that other men may not be frightened by our example of coming under your empire [*imperio*]." When the commissioners' misconduct came to be known in Florence, Machiavelli says, "not only the magistrates but the whole city" was displeased and Astorre was "condemned and admonished."[37] But the damage to Florence's reputation and enterprise was done. The use of excessively harsh methods, allegedly sanctioned by an important official, created lingering "unease" in the occupied cities. The inhabitants of places acquired through such methods had good reason to mistrust the Florentines thereafter.[38]

This embarrassing episode illustrates a point that will be discussed further in section 9.5: namely, that a poor choice of means may undermine one's chances of attaining desired ends. Florentine hopes of increasing the city's regional power through the acquisition of Lucca were dashed, moreover, as their embarrassment encouraged rivals to launch new offensives against Florence. The city's magistrates responded by calling in more mercenaries, never a solution that Machiavelli deems effectual.[39] Not long after the war with Florence the Lucchese authorized another foreign power, Siena, to help them overthrow their tyrant. This effort succeeded where Florentine arms had failed. Then things transpired as Uzzano had foreseen.[40] Lucca, now "free of its tyrant," prepared strong defenses against a new Florentine assault. Florence's troops were defeated. "This defeat," Machiavelli remarks, "saddened all our city, and because the enterprise had been undertaken by the generality of people [*dallo universale*], the people did not know whom to turn against." As for the Lucchese, after their victory they "not only regained their own towns" but took many others in the surrounding district. Machiavelli describes how at a later date, Florence was "pressed" (*strinse*) to make an accord with the Lucchese that guaranteed Lucca's freedom from Florentine dominion. Appalled, the Florentines "filled all Italy with letters full of complaints." Machiavelli mocks his compatriots' excessive desires for dominion, observing drily: "rarely does it happen that anyone is so displeased at having lost his own things [*le cose sue*] as were the Florentines for not having acquired those of others."[41]

---

[37] *FH*, IV.20–21.167–68/497–99. In fact he was acquitted.

[38] See *FH*, IV.23.169–70/501 on continuing local resistance.

[39] *FH*, IV.24.170/502–3.

[40] Machiavelli's account of these events implies that judgments about how and when to dispose of internal tyrant are best left to the people he rules, not to external powers. The smaller cities of Italy often found themselves in this dilemma: to put up for a time with internal tyrants whom citizens wished to depose, or to ask for external help from stronger powers whose intentions could seldom be trusted. Machiavelli acknowledges that the Lucchese might have been glad to get rid of their tyrant. But he also takes it for granted that they did not want the Florentines to do the job for them, at least not on their own unilateral and self-serving terms.

[41] *FH*, IV.25.171–72/503–4; V.14.202–3/540.

9.4.
Reflective consequentialism or deontology?

Looking back at the debate about the anticipated results of the war with Lucca, Machiavelli's narrative suggests that non-consequentialist reasons—the obligations of friendship and justice laid out in the first part of Uzzano's speech—were sufficient for choosing the right course. The secondary arguments about utility simply confirm the judgments that Uzzano had already made by reasoning about duties. If most Florentines had not ceased to take account of "just and unjust" in their deliberations, he would not have found it necessary to make lengthy consequentialist arguments. The two sets of arguments differ in having a deontological or teleological and consequentialist form, but their practical implications are the same. The episode illuminates Machiavelli's reasons for presenting his ethical positions in the form of consequentialist arguments. In the debates about war with Lucca he draws an unusually explicit distinction between principled reasons for action, and reasons of utility or prudence. He has the most consistently prudent character in the *Histories* explain why, having already given only reasons of justice, he will now abandon principled reasoning and defend his preferred course of action without reference to "just and unjust." The explanation is his audience's corrupted judgment, not the inherent weakness of non-consequentialist arguments about justice.

When Uzzano distinguishes between arguments about what is just and unjust and arguments about expected utility, then relies on the latter to persuade hearers, he outlines a persuasive strategy that had been used at least since Thucydides' Diodotus tried to dissuade fellow Athenians from destroying Mytilene. Machiavelli himself uses the strategy in many passages where he seems to maintain that ends justify the means. Like Diodotus and Uzzano, Machiavelli does think that just and unjust should be of some account when deciding a policy. Aware that many readers do not think so, however, his rhetoric gives priority to arguments for utility. These rhetorical priorities should not be confused with his ethical ones, which remain unchanged by the persuasive strategy. In effect, Machiavelli conceals arguments for justice within arguments that *seem* to consider nothing but expected utility. As I have argued before, his ethical reasonings have two parallel aims. One is philosophical: to identify adequately reasoned principles that should serve as grounds for practical judgments. The other aim is persuasive: to persuade readers who already have opinions—often incompletely reflective or corrupt—about what constitutes goodness or badness in actions to reexamine these views. Most of Machiavelli's overt, persuasive arguments have a consequentialist form; but the structure of his implicit, principled reasoning is, I submit, deontological. In the examples discussed previously, the bedrock of his reasonings are obligations of justice that should hold irrespective of anticipated or actual results. These obligations form the grounding level of Machiavelli's ethical arguments, although they are far less conspicuous than the secondary and supportive, consequentialist level.

The rest of this chapter reconsiders some of the passages usually cited as evidence of Machiavelli's "ends justify means" reasoning. Many well-known passages have been misread because readers take persuasive arguments as a sufficient expression of Machiavelli's ethical judgments. In reexamining them I will argue that his principled commitments are always more fundamental, though undoubtedly less explicit. Once Machiavelli's dialectical methods of writing have been appreciated, the principles emerge more clearly. The basic pattern of argument is always similar:

> First, Machiavelli starts with an assertion or opinion (O) that treats certain "ends"—utility, victory, "eliminating enemies," or freedom, for example—as justificatory. The initial assertion often seems to weaken or discard principled constraints on pursuing those ends.
>
> He then invites readers to examine (E) the statement in the light of various examples and reasons. A key question is whether readers have an adequate conception of the ends posited in the initial statement. If the justifying end is utility, victory, security, or freedom, have readers reflected enough on what they want to achieve under these good names? Are they in danger of mistaking a very limited and unstable victory for true victory, license for freedom, apparent or partial security for stably secure orders?
>
> At the end of a series of reasonings Machiavelli usually concludes (C) with reflections that confirm the initial statement, but only when its key terms are understood in a reflective way. The prereflective meaning of the statement almost always turns out to be a deeply flawed guide to action.[42] If readers see this by reflecting for themselves, they are more likely to be purged of their initial, defective views than if a speaker or writer preaches to them about principles.

The following series of reasonings from the *Histories*, for example, begins by seeming to assert a crude version of the opinion that ends justify means:

> (O) It has always been the end [*fine*] of those who start a war—and it is reasonable that it should be so—to enrich themselves and impoverish the enemy. For no other cause is victory sought, nor for anyone else are acquisitions desired than to make oneself powerful [*fare sé potente*] and the adversary weak.

But the next sentences stress the need for a more reflective account of what constitutes a worthwhile "victory" or "acquisition":

> (E) Hence, it follows that whenever your victory impoverishes you or acquisition weakens you, you must forego it or you will not arrive at the result [*termine*] for which wars are made. A prince or a republic that eliminates enemies and takes possession of booty or ransom is enriched by victories in wars. He who in conquest cannot eliminate enemies is impoverished by victories [*delle vittorie impoverisce*]. . . . Such a one is unprosperous in his losses and very unprosperous in his victories [*nelle vittorie infelicissimo*].

---

[42] See Vlastos 1991, 31–36 on "complex irony" as a method of Socratic dialectical writing.

The reasoning here invokes consequences, but its terminus is ethical. Victories and acquisitions that enrich the victor and make him stronger are the "reasonable" ends of war. But some victories and acquisitions enrich and strengthen victors; others weaken him. One criterion is whether victories and acquisitions eliminate enemies. Those that leave old enmities intact or create new ones impoverish the victor, thus defeating his own avowed ends. The next lines suggest that the more desirable results cannot be attained if the means used to pursue them are regarded as unjust:

> (C) Ancient and well-ordered republics were accustomed to fill their trea-
> suries with gold and silver from their victories, to distribute gifts among the
> people, to forgive the payment of tribute by their subjects, and to entertain
> them with solemn games and festivals. But victories in the times we are de-
> scribing first emptied the treasury, then impoverished the people, and still
> did not secure you from your enemies. All of this arose out of the disorder
> with which these wars were conducted.[43]

Of course, arguments that start by assessing consequences may give rise to extremely demanding principles of justice. Conversely, arguments grounded in deontological principles of justice may concur with judgments of reflective prudence. When analyzing the structure of Machiavelli's arguments, it is not always clear what the grounds or basic reasons are. It might seem more plausible to view him as a reflective consequentialist who defends strong ethical principles, rather than as a proponent of deontological ethics who recognized the persuasive value of reflective consequentialist reasoning. Indeed, the practical difference between the two positions may look so small that the choice of which to ascribe to Machiavelli seems arbitrary.

I have already suggested reasons for preferring the deontological reading. First, Machiavelli does distinguish obligations of justice from judgments about consequences, and suggests that the former hold regardless of the latter. Second, he implies that there are important practical differences between deliberating with reference to principled obligations and deliberating about consequences. In some of the examples discussed earlier, principles of justice provide a stable point of reference for practical reasoning. Had they been accorded a more important role from the outset, Machiavelli implies, the pitfalls of reasoning mainly about consequences might have been avoided. When important matters are at stake, principled respect for the duties of friendship and justice is a more reliable basis for judgment than forecasts of effects that take no account of "just and unjust." Moreover, if one judges actions by giving priority to principles of justice and duties to friendship over expected results, then one does not need to wait for results in order to judge

---

[43] *FH*, VI.1.230–31/573–73. Compare Thucydides' Melians, who warn the Athenians that their over-bearing methods of exercising rule will continue to turn many cities that are now neutral into mortal enemies. And what would this do, they ask, but reinforce the enemies Athens already has, while creating new enemies among others who see that it cannot be trusted? TPW, V.98. Also see Nicias' warnings against bold actions taken from a position of strength that end up destroying one's power; TPW, VI.9–14.

whether a course of action is good or bad, prudent or unwise. Prudent men like Uzzano could foresee bad consequences *because* they judged by sound principles. The next four sections discuss four more specific problems found even in sophisticated forms of consequentialist reasoning and highlighted in Machiavelli's works.

9.5.
Problem 1: Unjust means corrupt good ends

A first problem is that the means used to pursue ends always affect end results in fundamental ways. If the ends in question are strategic results such as the secure acquisition of new cities for one's dominion, the use of means that many people consider unjust makes it harder to achieve the desired ends. The same is true if unjust methods are used to pursue ends conceived in ethical terms, such as the secure enjoyment of public freedoms or the defense of one's fatherland. While Machiavelli sees the defense of a "free way of life" as among the most worthwhile ends that human beings can pursue, he does not argue that it can or should be defended by any available means. A highly discriminating choice of means is needed to ensure that good ends are not discredited or frustrated by the way that they are pursued. A free way of life can only be defended by means that respect principles of justice, which are grounded in respect for individuals as free agents. Principles that regulate acceptable means are thus prior to ends: they help to determine what count as acceptable ends, and identify acceptable means of pursuing them. Even if a preeminently worthy end such as a free way of life is given as the justification for an action, it is still subject to constraints imposed by obligations of justice or friendship. If those obligations are subordinated to this end, agents run a high risk of strategic error and ethical corruption.

The *Florentine Histories* offer many examples that illustrate this problem, such as the war with Filippo Visconti, in which the legitimacy of certain claims was confounded by the unjust methods used to prosecute them. A similar case occurs in Book IV in relation to internal partisan conflicts. In chapter 30 Rinaldo degli Albizzi seeks to persuade "the heads of his party" to stage a coup against a new Signori that included many *partigiani* of Cosimo de' Medici. Rinaldo argues that the end of averting "a certain and imminent danger" justifies the use of means that clearly went outside established laws and orders: to take up arms, "assemble the people in the piazza . . . deprive the new Signori of the magistracy, and create new ones suitable to the state." To this end Rinaldo demands that the old bags (*squittini*) from which the names of magistrates were drawn should be burned and the new ones "filled with new lists of friends."[44] Here again is a threatening situation that might well turn into genuine necessity justifying civil war. Machiavelli has already portrayed the Medici party and the exiled Cosimo as serious threats to the Florentine republic; Rinaldo's assessment of the danger they pose is not purely speculative. But as with the war with Visconti, the question was under what circumstances threatened parties should take up arms, so that the wisdom of

[44] *FH*, IV.30.181/514.

Rinaldo's preemptive call to arms must be judged by asking whether the "certain and imminent danger" he evoked had been demonstrated by the Signori's actions. If strong evidence were discovered that the new Signori itself was about to stage a coup to bring Cosimo back to power, this would constitute reasonable grounds for Rinaldo's party and other citizens to take up arms against the magistracy. But if this were done preemptively, not in response to an illegal action on the part of the government, self-appointed defenders of the republic would themselves be acting illegally and without a cause that appeared just to people outside their own party. The use of illegitimate means by the Medicis' opponents would make a Medici coup look more legitimate.

At the time, Machiavelli writes, the course of action proposed by Rinaldo "was judged safe and necessary by many, by others too violent and likely to carry too much blame with it." Machiavelli does not declare his own agreement with one point of view or the other. He does hint that narrowly partisan ambitions were among Rinaldo's own motives for wanting preemptive action, saying that the magistrates "suitable to the state" were those who Rinaldo and his party deemed suitable, that is, their own friends. Their allegedly public interest in avoiding certain danger depended on a partisan conception of the results that would justify the use of extralegal methods. Machiavelli's main reflections are attributed to a man who was "among those who were displeased" with Rinaldo's plan. Messer Palla Strozzi, he writes, "was a quiet man, gentle and humane [*gentile e umano*], more suited to the study of letters than to restraining a party [*frenare una parte*] and opposing civil discords."[45] Himself a prominent member of Rinaldo's anti-Medici party, Palla Strozzi does not challenge Rinaldo's claims that the pro-Medici Signori posed a serious danger to the republic. He simply argues that the danger could not be judged as certain until the magistrates' actions overstepped legal bounds, which so far they had not done. Without evidence of a more "certain and imminent" threat, the most prudent course of action was for citizens to watch their magistrates very closely, preparing themselves for action if designs for a Medici-led coup were revealed. In short, the prudent course is to act within established orders and laws, even if one's ends are to secure the city's safety and freedom.[46]

Machiavelli's account of ensuing events confirms both Rinaldo's fears of a Medici revival and Messer Palla's judgments about how to respond to the danger. As Rinaldo anticipated, the Signori soon began to sound out leading members of the Medici party about bringing Cosimo back from exile. Summoned to discuss this with the Signori, Rinaldo and his friends refused to consider negotiating, but instead rushed to take up arms. Palla Strozzi and other citizens had assembled many armed men in case the Signori overstepped the bounds of the law. But since no illegal action had so far been taken by the magistrates, these other defenders of the republic saw

---

[45] This might seem to cast doubt on the value of Palla Strozzi's practical judgments. In the context of this episode, however, his views are clearly to be preferred to Rinaldo's. Machiavelli casts Strozzi in the role of world-weary mediator, a man-in-the-middle in times when corruption had advanced too far to be contained by a few good men. Machiavelli may well have seen this as his own position at the time of writing, after years of being forced to serve his country more through letters than through action.

[46] *FH*, IV.30.181/514.

no cause as yet for an armed confrontation. Eventually Palla went out "on a horse with two men on foot, unarmed," thereby registering his opposition to the Signori and his willingness to at least hear their proposals, but without going so far as to threaten violence. This elicited a torrent of abuse from Rinaldo, who declared that his moderate stance showed "either lack of faith or lack of spirit." "To these words," Machiavelli writes, "Messer Palla did not answer a thing that might be understood [intesa] by the bystanders, but muttering he turned his horse around and went back to his home."[47] A few pages later we read that when the Medici party prevailed and restored Cosimo to power, Palla Strozzi was banished "along with many citizens of such quantity that few towns in Italy were left to which they had not been sent in exile and many outside of Italy were filled with them." Thus, Machiavelli comments sadly, "was Florence deprived by the same accident not only of good men but of men of riches and industry."[48]

Machiavelli suggests that Rinaldo's preemptive coup backfired because of its imprudent and questionably legitimate methods, which fatally discredited the good cause he sought to defend. By painting its opponents' revolt as a partisan refusal to share power, the Medici party could easily present itself as the party that sought to transcend and heal the divisions that had wracked the republic. These appearances increased the popularity of the Medicis, effectively destroyed their internal opposition, and undermined the freedom and virtue of Florence itself. All these were unintended but foreseeable consequences of the means used for basically good ends.[49] If one's ends are the security and freedom of one's city, the episode suggests, it is prudent to make respect for established laws and orders one's firm priority.

The importance of seeking legitimacy for the use of force inside or outside one's own city is brought home again and again in the *Histories*. In Book VII Machiavelli describes a confrontation between Florence and the nearby city of Volterra that raised similar questions about choosing means to good ends. The conflict arose after alum mines were found in the countryside near the smaller city. At first the Volterrans did not recognize their value, and invited Florentine citizens to invest in the mines. When their value was discovered, the Volterrans sought to reconvert the land to their own public use. They submitted this request to Florentine authorities, who, "either because they had been corrupted by a party or because they judged it well so," denied that the Volterrans were "seeking justice [volere le cose giuste]" in this matter. They ruled that the mines belonged to private individuals, including Florentine shareholders, and not to the Volterran people. Nonetheless, they agreed to pay an annual fee to the Volterran public as a token "that they recognized the people as superior." This offer failed to satisfy the Volterrans, and the property dispute became a catalyst for popular agitation against perceived

---

[47] *FH*, IV.31.181–82/515–16. Machiavelli remarks that Rinaldo "had seen the coolness [freddezza] of Messer Palla"—a symptom of his lack of spirit in Rinaldo's eyes, of prudent reasonableness in Machiavelli's.

[48] *FH*, IV.33.183/518.

[49] *FH*, IV.30.181/514.

Florentine arrogance.[50] Up to this point, the question of which side had the more just cause remains arguable. Machiavelli implies that many Florentines refused to budge because of corrupt partisan motives; but he also says that others judged it best to insist on keeping the mines in private hands. He does not directly criticize the Volterrans' *volte face*, and notes their respect for legal procedures—in particular their efforts to win Florentine authorization—when seeking to deprivatize the mines. At the same time, he observes that the Volterrans were unnecessarily slow to recognize the value of their mines and then wanted "to remedy late and without profit what they could have remedied easily" had they acted sooner. On balance, then, the Florentines had more than arguably just grounds for refusing to give up their stake in the mines without further bargaining. The Volterrans also had arguably just claims, but Machiavelli's narrative suggests that the burden of justification for changing the status of the mines lay with them.

Any justice in Florentine claims was damaged, however, by the means chosen to prosecute them. As the conflict intensified, the Florentines deliberated whether to defend their claims to the mines by force or to enter further negotiations with the Volterrans. Machiavelli writes that the Medici party saw the conflict as an excellent opportunity to acquire Volterra as part of Florence's "dominions." Machiavelli has Lorenzo de' Medici call for a campaign to "punish with arms the arrogance of the Volterrans." As Lorenzo presents it, the desired end of military action was not to oppose what he regarded as unjust Volterran claims, but to deter Volterra and other nearby cities from challenging Florence's dominant geopolitical position in the region by furnishing a "memorable example" of Florentine superiority. Machiavelli writes that the smaller city was easily defeated by Florentine troops, then sacked and destroyed with great violence. "For a whole day," he reports, "it was robbed and overrun; neither women nor holy places were spared." The news of Volterra's defeat and sacking, Machiavelli reports, "was received with very great joy by the Florentines" and significantly boosted Lorenzo's "reputation."[51] Thus Florence "acquired" another city for its dominions. But the key question for Machiavelli is always this: did the acquisition amount to a genuine, secure gain for Florence? If the immediate end was the acquisition of territory and the wider end served by territorial acquisition is a city's greatness, security, or power, then one must ask whether a particular acquisition effectively promotes these wider ends. On these reflective criteria, Machiavelli leaves little doubt that Lorenzo's actions were counterproductive. In military terms, the conquest of Volterra appeared easy and complete. But by resorting to force instead of negotiation to defend their claims, the Florentines made it difficult to distinguish whatever had been just in their initial claims from the unjust motivations that made them choose such excessive means. These means produced undesired results. The addition to Florentine dominions of yet another hostile city raised the costs of imperial *grandezza* higher than ever, creating a new source of disorders for foreign powers to exploit. As usual, Machiavelli says that the most prudent Florentine citizens foresaw this unhappy outcome and tried to

---

[50] *FH*, VII.29.307–8/667.
[51] Ibid.

warn compatriots against it. He describes an exchange at the end of the war in which a triumphant supporter of the campaign mockingly asks an opponent what he thought now that "Volterra has been acquired." The opponent replies:

> To me it appears lost, for if you had received it by accord [*d'accordo*], you would have had advantage and security [*utile e securtà*] from it; but since you have to hold it by force [*tenere per forza*], in adverse times it will bring you weakness and trouble and in peaceful times, loss and expense.[52]

The view that means help to constitute and may undermine good ends is, of course, compatible with a highly reflective version of the view that ends justify means. At the most obvious level, the arguments Machiavelli gives to Palla Strozzi and the opponent of war with Volterra are simply reflective consequentialist arguments: they say that a reflective assessment of consequences should make people realize the importance of following certain procedures and respecting others' views. At a less obvious level, however, the same arguments point to procedural principles of justice that hold independently of judgments about the prudence of specific actions. They imply that reflectively prudent action always concurs with these principles, which should be taken as a guide to action regardless of consequences. This is the terminus of many passages that seem at first glance to offer typically "Machiavellian" advice.

9.6.
Problem 2: Who can be trusted to foresee effects?

Machiavelli's accounts of debates about the legitimacy of force point to a second problem for consequentialist reasonings: who can be trusted to make accurate prognoses of an action's likely consequences? The problem of trust in merely human prudence is at the heart of Machiavelli's critical examinations of how policy-makers relate means to ends. As his examples show, the main difficulty in assessing the consequences of actions is not that their most important effects could not have been foreseen. On the contrary, he often tells us that prudent judges did foresee them very clearly. The difficulty is that in almost any city at any given time, there are precious few prudent judges who in times of need can be trusted to assess the likely effects of actions. Only a few can usually be found in moderately corrupt times. In very corrupt times like Machiavelli's own, either they cannot be found at all or, like the quiet, bookish Palla Strozzi and Machiavelli himself, they have been driven out of public life and deprived of all authority.[53] Where such *prudentissimo* reasoners are nowhere to be found and justice is held to be of little

---

[52] *FH*, VII.30.308–9/668–69.

[53] As, for example, with Camillus in Rome. Compare Hobbes 1989 (1629), 571, on Thucydides' similar position: though "qualified to have become a great demagogue, and of great authority with the people" the historian evidently "had no desire at all to meddle in the government; because in those days it was impossible for any man to give good and profitable counsel for the commonwealth, and not incur the displeasure of the people." Also compare Plato's position as expressed in his *Fifth Letter*, 322a–b.

account, judgments that treat consequences as the criterion of good action are easily corrupted.

A distinction between corrupt and uncorrupt judgments about consequences is implicit in the *Histories'* debates over preemptive uses of force. Men on different sides of a debate, such as Rinaldo and Palla Strozzi, often agree on the main ends at stake, yet still make very different judgments about the likely effects of using force toward those ends. Exceptionally prudent consequentialist reasoners such as Palla Strozzi or Uzzano recognize the dangers of preemptive action because they are prudent. But their prudence is grounded in prior, independent judgments about what is just and unjust. If their sole criterion were whether an action would have desirable results, prudent judges might still reach the same conclusions as if they were guided by sound principles. But unless judgments about consequences are anchored in firmer principles of justice, those judgments are easily unsettled by every ephemeral or apparent shift in the political balance. Worse, they are easily corrupted by ambition, envy, self-deception, or precipitate fears.[54] If a few prudent men in Machiavelli's *Histories* are able to judge prudently in corrupt times, this is not only because they have an especially reflective analysis of likely consequences; it is also because their judgments are guided by clear, unwavering standards of what is just and unjust.

Machiavelli's examples illustrate three more specific features of judgments about likely consequences that make them untrustworthy. One is *indeterminacy*.[55] The effects of most actions are many and complex. If they are large-scale actions involving many people and the use of force, they seldom issue in a single, clear-cut set of results that will be seen as an undisputed basis for judging success or failure, even after a good deal of time has passed. To judge an action by its effects, someone would have to be given authority to make a prior judgment about *which* among its multiple effects should be seen as decisive. Is victory the clear consequence when an opponent has acknowledged military defeat? Or does the question whether victory is the result of a war depend on judgments about the wider political, economic, and strategic implications?[56] Without clear guiding principles, it is hard to know whose views to trust on these questions. A second feature of judgments about results is that they tend to be *partial*. Results appear differently to different parties. They are generally judged as good by those who think they benefit from them, and as bad by those who experience results as harmful or humiliating. Such divergent judgments may become a new source of disorders if they are not adjudicated by standards that seem just to all. A third feature is the *instability* of judgments based primarily on results. Consequences look different from different points in time, as well as to different people. As Palla Strozzi says, "courses of action" often "appear good in the

---

[54] As happens with Rinaldo in the course of Book IV: he begins political life with sound views about not judging by effects, but is soon making corrupt and opportunistic judgments that go against his initial, sounder maxims.

[55] See TPW, IV.62, where the Spartan general Hermocrates argues that the indeterminacy and uncertainty of future results should always inspire caution.

[56] Wars have unforeseeable consequences and tend to spiral beyond initial aims: "Wars begin at the will of anyone, but they do not end at anyone's will [*vuole*]" (*FH*, III.7.113/433).

beginning but turn out to be difficult to deal with and harmful to finish." Moreover, complex actions such as wars have diverse and variable effects. Not even the most prudent reasoners can foresee all the fortunes of battle or their political fallout; though some actions seem at first to have good results, the end may still be "unexpected and the cause of much evil."[57] Casual observers might easily judge one day that on balance the effects of an action were bad, but the next day see new things that change their judgment. By varying their assessment of consequences from day to day, people avoid the responsibility of committing themselves to a stable set of judgments instead of examining their past errors and working out better grounds for future judgment.[58]

Early in the *Discourses* Machiavelli sets out the infamous maxim that "where the deed accuses, the effect excuses [*accusandolo il fatto, lo effetto lo scusi*]."[59] The context of this statement will be examined later. For now, I want simply to point out the clear disparity between the crude form of consequentialism it expresses and Machiavelli's extremely subtle analyses of the relations between actions and effects. While I have so far focused on less well-known examples from the *Florentine Histories*, the *Discourses* offer equally nuanced reflections on the difficulties of judging the *effetti* of actions. If Machiavelli agreed that the maxim *accusandolo il fatto, lo effetto lo scusi* should be taken as the bedrock of sound political judgment, he would presumably believe that most people who adopt it have good chances of avoiding the problems just set out. But one of the *Discourses'* recurring themes is that such chances are very slim indeed. Here as in the *Histories*, Machiavelli argues that reflectively prudent individuals are able to foresee the most important repercussions of actions. But these individuals are rare in any city; and in corrupt times they are seldom found in positions of public authority. Most of the men who do occupy those positions cannot be trusted to judge whether or not the effects of their actions excuse the latter. The *Histories* analyze the problem of trustworthy judgment in relation to partisan divisions, which make even well-meaning people on all sides suspicious of their opponents and inclined to preemptive attacks. The *Discourses* examine the same problem in more general anthropological terms, by considering the ubiquitous humors and self-seeking dispositions that make it hard to trust most people's consequentialist judgments. Machiavelli identifies excessive ambition as the most corrupting disposition. Ambition often prevents powerful men from taking stock of foreseeably harmful effects of their actions, even when others see them very clearly.[60] "So great is the ambition of man," Machiavelli observes, "that to obtain a present wish he does not think of the evil that in a brief time is to result from it." A few chapters later he notes that bad consequences arise when ambitious men wish

---

[57] *FH*, VIII.22.343–44/709–11.

[58] This, for example, is the corrupt implication of Rinaldo's speech early in Book IV. Since outcomes cannot be predicted, no one can be held responsible for actions that helped to produce them—neither the leaders who gave bad advice nor the citizens who failed to question them.

[59] *D*, I.9.29/223.

[60] See chap. 2 for examples of likely Greek sources.

rather to enjoy the present utility of being able to plunder their peoples, and to escape an imagined rather than a true danger, than to do things that might secure them and make their states perpetually happy. If this disorder brings forth some quiet, with time it is of necessity a cause of irremediable harms and ruin.[61]

Here Machiavelli describes two common forms of self-deception that impair the judgment of many ambitious men, even those who start out with good intentions. First, they pick out certain short-term or intermediate effects that seem to serve their "present utility" and treat these as sufficient to justify actions, although longer-range effects discredit this justification. Second, they invoke an "imagined danger" to excuse extraordinary, illegal, or violent actions, deceiving themselves that others will accept this as an adequate justification. But if the danger is not generally seen as involving urgent necessity, this non-urgency will always be pointed out by some people at the time of action, and recognized by others later. And those attacked in the name of an imagined or manufactured necessity can usually be expected to fight back hard, demonstrating that the initial assessment of consequences was self-serving and incorrect.

As we have seen, Machiavelli argues that well-ordered republics contain many procedural checks against self-deceiving judgments: public debate in assemblies, the right of any citizen to publicize evidence that casts doubts on leaders' probity, and strict standards of accountability for magistrates.[62] Nonetheless, Machiavelli does not treat peoples in republics as immune to self-deception about the relation between actions they wish to take and the effects of those actions. A major concern of both the *Histories* and the *Discourses* is that popular judgments in republics can become corrupted by excessive ambition. In the *Histories* this problem is shown in popular enthusiasm for Florence's unnecessary—and unnecessarily violent—wars to assert *imperio* over Lucca and Volterra. In the *Discourses* Machiavelli describes how, in much the same way, imperial ambitions corrupted ordinary citizens' judgment in republican Rome. The effects of this corruption were often most conspicuous in military settings, where men were armed and could easily take advantage of others who were weaker or caught off guard. When such actions went unpunished by military or civil authorities, as in Livy's account of the Fabii ambassadors, it became clear that corruption extended to civilian life. Machiavelli gives an even more damning example of corrupt judgments under an "ambitious republic," this time involving the betrayal of a city that had asked for Rome's protection. Roman legions were posted in Capua with a clear and limited mandate: to defend the Capuans from the Samnites. On Machiavelli's account these legions, "rotting in idleness," began to think about "taking up arms and making themselves lords of

---

[61] *D*, II.20.176/381–82; II.30.200/407–9.

[62] *D*, I.56–59/313–22. "Examples could be brought up," Machiavelli writes, "in which the least utility has made a prince break faith and a great utility has not made a republic break faith" (I.59.120–21/320–21). Machiavelli contends that procedural constraints make well-ordered republics less prone to self-deception than princes or oligarchic governments, not the fact that their ends—the common as distinct from the merely private "utility"—are of a different quality.

that country that they had defended with their virtue." Their ambitions were fueled by the Capuans' relative weakness. "Although the intention of the Romans was not to break the accord and the conventions they had made with the Capuans," Machiavelli writes, "nonetheless the ease with which those soldiers could crush them appeared so great" that they could not resist the thought of "taking from the Capuans their town and their state [*la terra e lo stato*]." Machiavelli observes drily that "A prince or an ambitious republic [*una republica ambiziosa*] cannot have greater opportunity for seizing a city or a province than to be asked to send his armies to its defense." Taken out of context, this sentence might be read as Machiavelli's own corrupt—or "realistic"—advice to take advantage of such opportunities. Read in context, it is quite clear that his advice is the opposite:

> he who is so ambitious that he calls in such aid, not only to defend himself but to offend against others, seeks to acquire that which he cannot hold [*cerca acquistare quello che non può tenere*] and which can be easily taken away from him. . . . But so great is the ambition of man that to obtain a present wish he does not think of the evil that in a brief time is to result from it.[63]

Here Machiavelli writes as if only the men who "call in" foreign aid to defend their city are responsible for offenses committed by those foreigners. But far from exonerating Romans or others who take advantage of weak cities they have pledged to defend, he goes on to argue that the "ambitious republic" of Rome soon fell prey to the self-deception that it could hold all the peoples it acquired by such unjust means. Because of their overwhelming superiority in military and political power, the Romans did not foresee the wider, dangerous effects of "acquiring" an empire with broken faith.

The wider point here is that when it comes to actions that are motivated by ambition, even virtuous republics and peoples are untrustworthy judges of the likely effects of such actions. All human beings, princes, and republics are prone to make self-serving judgments. Prudent consequentialist reasoning must take this tendency into account. Perhaps Machiavelli would have sympathized with later attempts by philosophers to improve on the kinds of consequentialism he evaluates: by identifying less corruptible ends, specifying "side-constraints," or working out a more realistic and nuanced psychology as a basis for forecasting long-term reactions. The import of his discussions, however, is that even a highly refined consequentialism is too vulnerable to ordinary forms of human error to serve as the *bedrock* of ethical judgments.

9.7.
Problem 3: Who can be trusted to identify good ends?

Machiavelli mentions various ends that may be thought to justify vicious or ruthless deeds: to secure a prince's rule, the common utility or safety of a polity, freedom in a republic. Yet having stated any particular end, he goes on to raise two

---

[63] *D*, II.20.176/383.

related questions about how it can serve as the touchstone for ethical justification: what is to count as a justifying end, and who can be trusted to identify it? On the question of *what* ends or effects are so worthwhile that they justify the use of any available means, Machiavelli sometimes notes a widespread opinion that the safety of the "fatherland" is an important enough end. But his further reasonings ask readers to consider what they understand by the fatherland or indeed safety when making such judgments. On brief reflection, it should be clear that the identity of the good to be safeguarded is not easily known. Indeed, it may be a matter of serious dispute. Should the "safety of the fatherland" be identified primarily with the security, power, and territorial acquisitions of a prince, a party, or an entire people? Are the wider external conditions for what is called safety in all these cases similar or different? As for the second question of *who* can be trusted to identify fundamental, justificatory ends correctly, the last section argued that Machiavelli has serious concerns about the stability and incorruptibility of human judgments, especially among the powerful few. If most people find it difficult to choose adequate means to ends, it seems likely that their choice of basic, justifying ends is also likely to be arbitrary, changeable, and self-serving unless they are guided by some non-teleological criteria. If Machiavelli doubts that unproblematic ethical ends can be identified by any trustworthy moral or political authority, then it is hard to see how the bedrock of his practical reasoning can be teleological and consequentialist. If he thinks that justificatory ends are both *intrinsically* hard to know and often misidentified *in practice*, the view that he treats certain ends as justifying means seems puzzling indeed.

To reconcile this view with Machiavelli's doubts about how justifying ends might be identified, readers would have to assume that he is committed to one of two positions on the knowledge of good ends. One is that although there are different opinions about what constitutes the ultimate good or utility that ought to serve as a touchstone for judging actions, some people—the few, the many, or virtuous individuals alone—know best what that good consists in, and should by virtue of this knowledge have the authority to define it. A recurrent theme of the *Discourses* is that the men who hold the titles of prince, noblemen, or *gentiluomini* can seldom be trusted to recognize or uphold the good. But while Machiavelli does think that "the many" are more trustworthy guarantors of safety and freedom,[64] he is not at all confident that either set of people can be trusted to identify the most important justificatory ends of policy. If princes and nobles are led astray by their unchecked passions, peoples are easily "deceived by a false image of the good" and, pursuing this image, go to ruin.[65] Indeed, the same characteristic of peoples that makes them good guards of public order makes them bad at judging ultimate goods or ends. Because they have diverse opinions, they tend to disagree

---

[64] Recall Machiavelli's use of the example of Themistocles, who advised the Athenian people to break faith with their Greek allies so that Athens could easily become "wholly arbiters" of Greece. When the people's appointed counselor advised them that this policy was "very useful but very dishonest," they "wholly refused it." *D*, I.59.120–21/321–22; I.58.118/318–19.

[65] *D*, I.53.106/305.

on what the good is and, once they have agreed, on whether to abandon it. But even prudent peoples find it difficult, if not impossible, to agree on what constitute good *fundamental* ends. They find it easier to agree on laws, orders, and standards that are not defined primarily in relation to particular ends, but are designed to regulate "ordinary and natural" disagreements over ends in ways that respect everyone's freedom.[66]

A second possibility is that where the common good, the safety of the fatherland, or other important ends are concerned, Machiavelli believes that it is relatively easy to distinguish flawed opinions from sound judgments. He might think that such matters stand in little need of debate, since their essential content is clear to all. At first glance, Machiavelli sometimes seems to use phrases such as "the common utility" or "safety of the fatherland" as if their meaning were unproblematic. But his further reasonings suggest that such stock phrases are deeply ambiguous. Consider, for example, a much-quoted passage which appears near the end of the *Discourses*:

> (O) Where one deliberates entirely on the safety of his fatherland [*dilibera al tutto della salute della patria*], there ought not to enter any consideration of either just or unjust [*alcuna considerazione né di giusto d'ingiusto*], merciful or cruel, praiseworthy or ignominious; indeed every other concern put aside [*poposto ogni altro rispetto*], one ought to follow entirely the policy that saves its life and maintains its liberty.

Read out of context, this looks like a straightforward instance of the argument that ends justify any means. Restored to its context, it becomes much harder to ascribe this argument to Machiavelli himself. Machiavelli places this passage (O) between two examples, one ancient and one modern, which stimulate further examinations (E) of the initial opinion. The first example comes from Livy's account of Rome's wars with its Italian neighbors. Machiavelli recounts that after the Samnites had besieged the Roman army and "set very ignominious conditions on the Romans,"

> (E1) Lucius Lentulus, the Roman legate, said that it did not appear to him that any policy whatever for saving the fatherland was to be avoided; for since the life of Rome consisted in the life of that army, it appeared to him it was to be saved in every mode [*salvarlo in ogni modo*], and that the fatherland is well defended in whatever mode one defends it, whether with ignominy or with glory. For if that army saved itself, Rome would have time to cancel the ignominy; if it did not save itself, even though it died gloriously, Rome and its freedom were lost.[67]

This invites readers to go back to Livy's text, where Lucius Lentullus gives a speech to despairing Roman troops. Those who expect to find Lentullus urging Romans to reject the "ignominious" terms of peace and fight to the death will be surprised. In fact, he recommends the opposite course of action as the best means of saving

---

[66] *D*, I.9.29/223–24.
[67] *D*, III.41.301/515.

the *patria* and Roman freedom. Lentullus starts by acknowledging that many of his soldiers "say that surrender is shameful and humiliating" and prefer to hurl the rump army back at the enemy. They should reflect, however, that such a passion-driven response to defeat would be unlikely to save their city and the people within its walls. On the contrary, "these are surely betrayed, not saved" if the Roman army were wiped out, "for who will protect them then?" The only way to defend the fatherland and cancel its ignominy was not to use reckless violence or refuse to enter treaties with the enemy. It was to accept defeat and "bow to necessity" by agreeing to the Samnites' terms of peace. Lentullus' speech ends by urging the consuls to go home and "buy back the City by giving up your arms" and submitting to the temporary humiliation of Samnite victory. If the end of saving the fatherland justifies the use of certain unsavory means, these cannot include the badly ordered use of arms, or refusal to accept humiliating defeat.[68] Those who adopt such reckless measures misidentify the defense of one's honor, rank, or ambitious desires with safety in a more adequate sense, that is, physical and political survival. As Lentullus points out, the price of defending one's fatherland against perceived ignominy may be physical and political destruction. The safety of anyone's fatherland is best guaranteed if soldiers and citizens know when to bow to the limits set by "necessity." For Livy as for Machiavelli, *necessità* signifies both the physical compulsion imposed by defeat and the legal and ethical obligations assumed by the signing of treaties. Lentullus' assertion that one should not avoid "any policy whatever" when seeking to rescue the fatherland conceals a more reflective argument that calls the overt, literal meaning into question. One should in fact avoid actions that reject all constraints of "necessity," whether physical, legal, or ethical. Those who regard themselves as superior to such constraints are unlikely to keep their fatherland or its freedom safe.

Having written that Lentullus' advice "deserves to be noted and observed by any citizen who finds himself counseling his fatherland," Machiavelli then offers the quoted opinion (O) as if it were his own advice. Now we read that no "consideration of either just or unjust, merciful or cruel, praiseworthy or ignominious" ought to bear on deliberations about the safety of one's fatherland. How can the foregoing interpretation of (E1) be reconciled with these bluntly consequentialist words? Machiavelli's next remarks raise further doubts about whether he subscribes to them himself. Referring to passage (O) as a whole, he now writes:

(E2) That [maxim] is imitated by the sayings and deeds [*imitata con i detti e con i fatti*] of the French so as to defend the majesty of their king and

[68] *LH*, IX.iv.219–22. Livy's narrative makes it clear that what was humiliating about the terms of Roman defeat by the Samnites was not the actual peace settlement, which was more than fair. The ignominy concerned only an embarrassing punishment for the Romans' refusal to accept defeat, whereby military leaders and consuls had to go "under the yoke": prostrating themselves unarmed to be jeered at by the enemy. "In other respects," as Livy has a Samnite leader note—Livy seems to agree—"the terms of peace would be fair for both vanquished and victors. If the Romans would evacuate Samnite territory and withdraw their colonies, then Romans and Samnites should live under their own laws henceforth on equal terms."

the power of their kingdom, for they hear no voice more impatiently than that which would say: such a policy is *ignominious for the king*. For they say that their king cannot suffer shame in any decision whatever of his, whether in good or in adverse fortune, because whether he loses or wins, all—they say—are the king's affairs.

Placed back in context between (E1) and (E2), passage (O) now looks like a clear example of a complex irony: a statement that is reasonable on one interpretation and unreasonable on another. As is usual in the *Discourses*, when an ancient use of a maxim is juxtaposed with a modern one, the ancient use is more reasonable than the modern, and less corrupt. Thus Machiavelli presents Lentullus' view "that the fatherland is well defended in whatever mode one defends it, *whether with ignominy or with glory*" as an example of a reasonable interpretation of passage (O). It has several features that are missing from the French monarchist interpretation. For one, it distinguishes clearly between the physical and political "safety" of a polity and questions of honor or "shame." For another, its primary concern is the safety of the city's people and their freedom, not that of its king and his "majesty." Finally, it does advise respect for limits of humanity and justice, whereas passage (E2) does not. Had the Roman army decided to fight to the death, this would involve the unjust "betrayal" of compatriots who relied on the army to defend it, and unnecessary cruelty by exposing defenseless citizens to the enemy. In the corrupt imitation of Lentullus' maxim, however, the only standard that defines the "safety of the fatherland" is the king's personal majesty.

Looking back from the corrupt view expressed in passage (E2), we may see that when Machiavelli speaks of ignoring considerations of "just and unjust" in the preceding passage (O), he is illustrating the process of corruption that often occurs when certain ancient "maxims" are adopted by modern imitators. Lentullus says nothing about suspending considerations of justice or humanity where the safety of fatherland is at stake. He says only that ignominy and glory matter less than the survival of a city and its freedom, which are best preserved by bowing to physical and political necessity. As Machiavelli puts it, present ignominy can always be "canceled" by subsequent deeds. The "necessary" conditions for political and physical security are less resilient than reputations and honor, and require more prudent defenses. Part of the complex irony in passage (O) is to repeat this reasonable ancient maxim while complicating—one might say muddying—it with corrupt elements. The claim that "just and unjust" are as immaterial to the ultimate safety of fatherlands as ignominy or glory is symptomatic of this corruption. Following on this development, passage (E2) represents a contemporary perversion of the reasonable Roman maxim expressed in (E1). At passage (O), though not (E1), just and unjust were as unimportant as praise and ignominy when defense of the fatherland was at stake. At (E2) the avoidance of shame and ignominy for the king has become the overriding concern—a complete reversal of the priorities defended in the sound Roman maxim. The differences between the three versions of the maxim are captured well by Machiavelli's distinctions between reasonably harsh, too-harsh, and delicate modes of imitating ancients. The Roman version

(E1) is reasonably harsh; the transitional, complicated version (O) goes too far; and the French monarchist version (E2) interprets ancient maxims in terms of the "private," self-indulgent concerns of men who undervalue laws or justice.

Though some might take issue with this interpretation, at least one thing seems clear: the presumption that Machiavelli is simply expressing his own judgments in passage (O) needs to be reexamined with closer attention to the context. When the passage is relocated between the ancient Roman and modern monarchist examples, it becomes harder to sustain the view that Machiavelli endorses the "harsh" version of the maxim. His main concern here and throughout the *Discourses* is not to set out handy maxims for readers to take on his authority. It is to encourage readers to reflect critically on the stock phrases used in political rhetoric, so that they will be armed against unreflective or corrupt persuasions that go under appealing "names." Some readers may want to seize on the simplest version of the maxim because it appeals to their sense of patriotic honor or ambition, and not take the trouble to work out the critical implications of Machiavelli's ancient and modern examples. But if passage (O) appears uncritically to embrace a set of ends that justify any means, passages (E1) and (E2) undermine the naïve acceptance of rhetoric invoking the safety of fatherlands, even when it is conjoined to the appealing rhetoric of *libertà*. The overall effect of these passages is to call for a critical approach to "ends justify means" reasoning, not to defend it. A contextualized reading suggests that Machiavelli did not believe that threats to the fatherland's safety constitute a reason to suspend ethical constraints on actions. Although he does not spell out an unambiguous conclusion (C), he leaves readers in little doubt that when political leaders invoke sweeping consequentialist arguments like those found in passage (O), citizens should do the opposite of what (O) seems to suggest. They should not exempt political leaders from explaining their policies in more carefully reasoned ways; and they should not refrain from demanding a reasoned account of the ends that are supposed to justify unjust or cruel means.

How then should we account for statements that express a similar "ends justify means" position in the *Florentine Histories*? For example, in Book V we read: "No good man will ever reprove anyone who seeks to defend his fatherland in whatever mode he defends it."[69] Read out of context, this seems to support the standard, rather crude consequentialist view of Machiavelli's ethics. When restored to context, once again it is clear that Machiavelli is presenting *onesto* words used for dubious political purposes. The context invites readers to reflect critically on how rhetoric invoking the safety of fatherlands may be abused. Here the words are part of a speech made by Rinaldo degli Albizzi, now in forced exile from Florence. Rinaldo is not addressing his own compatriots but a foreigner, the untrustworthy Duke of Milan. His aim is not to inspire Florentine citizens to defend their own freedom, but to persuade a foreign prince to attack Florence on Rinaldo's behalf. Machiavelli implies that Rinaldo's motives include sincere patriotism and the belief that the Medici-led government he seeks to overthrow is destroying his city's freedom. But his definition of the end "to defend the fatherland" is partisan and

---

[69] *FH*, V.8.193–94/529–31.

self-serving; and the arms he proposes to use are those of a foreign prince, who has already shown that he cannot be trusted to respect Florence's independence and internal freedoms. The majority of his countrymen were likely to see these methods as an unjust imposition, an affront to their freedom, and a threat to their fatherland rather than its salvation.

9.8.
Problem 4: Corrupting examples

The three problems discussed so far concern what might be called structural flaws in arguments that treat ends or outcomes as the ultimate justification for actions. A fourth and final problem has to do with the practical implications of accepting such arguments. As Machiavelli often notes, it is easy to find ancient and modern examples of men who committed deeds that are ordinarily seen as wicked or unjust, yet appeared to have great success. In a few cases, the effect of their deeds seems so good in itself that it more than cancels out the badness of the means used to achieve it. Throughout human history, men who wish to take a dangerous or audacious course of action have been able to point to examples of great men who used bad means to achieve good ends. By imitating these great men and their "extraordinary" deeds, new princes and ambitious republics seek to do the same.

The problem as Machiavelli sees it is that few if any of these imitators are as great, prudent, or virtuous as they imagine their role models were. Moreover, it is often doubtful whether the original models themselves were as successful as they are reputed to have been.[70] When ordinary people imitate men who committed bad deeds yet reputedly got good results, the chances that they will pull off the same astonishing feat are poor indeed. Even if it could be shown that bad deeds sometimes do lead to good results, this happens so rarely that it would seem imprudent to take the maxim "the ends justify the means" as a general rule. As for the rare examples of men who are reputed to have pulled it off, Machiavelli suggests that when the results of their deeds are examined closely, they often turn out to be less unambiguously good than imitators claim. As we saw in chapter 3, Machiavelli urges his readers to sharpen all their senses as they read both ancient authors and his own writings, putting aside preconceptions about this man's greatness or that man's follies and judge for themselves whether their deeds should—or indeed can—be imitated. Since his aim is to unsettle readers' preconceptions without attacking them, Machiavelli's discourses on such examples are often puzzling and elliptical. His remarks about Romulus early in the *Discourses* are a case in point. At first glance, some passages seem to support the usual consequentialist view of Machiavelli's ethics. In Book I he considers whether the legendary founder of Rome was justified in killing his brother Remus so that he could "order" Rome "alone." Here at last is the context for the infamous words *accusandolo il fatto, lo effetto lo scusi*:

---

[70] See chaps. 11, 12.

(O) a prudent orderer of a republic, who has the intent to wish to help not himself but the common good [*al bene comune*], not for his own succession but for the common fatherland [*comune patria*], should contrive to have authority alone; nor will a wise understanding [*ingegno savio*] ever reprove anyone for any extraordinary action that he uses to order a kingdom or constitute a republic. It is very suitable that when the deed accuses him, the effect excuses him; and when the effect is good, as was that of Romulus, it will always excuse the deed; for he who is violent to spoil [*violento per guastare*], not he who is violent to mend, should be reproved.

The ends postulated here might seem somewhat more precise, and therefore less open to abuse, than the sweeping phrase "defense of fatherland." If an agent has the *comune bene* as the avowed goal of his actions and appears to achieve it, perhaps Machiavelli believes that this obviates the need for critical scrutiny of his ends or means. The strong assertions made in passage (O) are qualified, however, in the following examinations. These set out conditions designed to check whether an orderer's "violent" acts might reasonably be expected to serve the common good. The first set of conditions is as follows:

(E1) [A prudent orderer] should indeed be so prudent and virtuous that he does not leave the authority he took as an inheritance to another; for since men are more prone to evil than to good, his successor could use ambitiously that which had been used virtuously by him.

This confirms the consequentialism of passage (O) but sets down a demanding set of conditions that restrict the range of acceptable means to ends. An orderer must himself use virtuously whatever authority he takes by force. He should then establish orders designed to check excessive ambition in his successors. The key point here is that although an orderer himself might have taken authority by force and without general authorization, the orders he establishes should not pass on this authority by inheritance, but seek unforced authorization for successors. The next sentence sets a further condition. If

(E2) one individual is capable of ordering, the thing itself is ordered to last long not if it remains on the shoulders of one individual but rather if it remains in the care of many [*alla cura di molti*] and its maintenance stays with many.[71]

If an orderer's "end" really is the common good, he will recognize that he should not seize sole power and continue to rule alone. Instead he will order the polity so that responsibility for maintaining order will accrue to the many.

At this first stage of his reasonings about passage (O), then, Machiavelli implies that the sweeping, permissive claim "when the deed accuses, the effect excuses" is not unconditionally true. It appears reasonable only if the actions following the violent deed—here, killing one's brother or "partner" (*compagno*) in order to

---

[71] *D*, I.9.29/223–24.

"rule alone"—meet the demanding conditions set out in (E1) and (E2). If Romulus' "extraordinary action" deserves to be excused—still an open question—this is not because it achieved the end of one-man rule. It might arguably be excusable if, having taken authority through violence, Romulus proceeded to order for the virtuous use of authority by his successors; ensured that succession was not hereditary; and transferred care of the city's orders to the many. In later chapters Machiavelli will raise further questions about whether or not Romulus fully satisfied these conditions.[72] For now his main concern is to show why the example of Romulus cannot be taken as a sufficient vindication of the maxim "when the deed accuses, the effect excuses." Before readers rush to interpret the Romulus legend in this way, they should reflect much more carefully on the specific conditions that make his example so attractive. Those conditions, Machiavelli will suggest, are not satisfied by most of Romulus' ancient or modern imitators.

So far, Machiavelli's reasonings do not question the central argument that the end of ordering for the common good justifies the use of extraordinary, even violent means. So long as orderers do their best to meet the conditions just set out, actions modeled on Romulus' fratricide might appear to deserve praise. But Machiavelli's next remarks raise the key question of trust. How far can one-man orderers who use violent means be trusted (E1) to use authority virtuously and not ambitiously, or (E2) hand it over to the care of the many? It is a thing well "known" through legendary reports that many founders of kingdoms and republics were able to achieve these remarkable feats.[73] Romulus, one may presume, succeeded in using bad means to good ends for two reasons. First, he is said to have possessed an almost superhuman prudence. Second, the people for whom he ordered were not yet corrupt. Very few *ordinatori* of ancient or modern times possess these advantages. Men who believe that they do possess them are far less trustworthy than those who show a healthy mistrust of their solitary judgments in matters of public import. Orderers who prudently examine themselves and their fellow men know how unwise it is to trust anyone to act alone, even if his avowed end is to serve the common good. These reflections imply that the conditions for Romulus' success were so rare that the actions he took to "order alone" are essentially inimitable. Anyone who tries to imitate Romulus' methods must face the probability that his good intentions will be defeated. The main stumbling-block might be corruption among the people for whom he seeks to order or his own ambitions, or fear, which almost always increases when men use violence to "take" power from others. While refusing to question the goodness of ancient founders whose actions are traditionally revered, Machiavelli gives this general guideline for judging other *ordinatori*:

> Because the reordering of a city for a political way of life [*il riordinare una città al vivere politico*] presupposes a good man, and becoming a prince of a republic by violence presupposes a bad man, one will find that it very rarely

---

[72] Machiavelli alludes to two different readings of the Romulus legend, one suiting the interests of kings and princes, the other more amenable to republicans; see chap. 11, sec. 11.2.

[73] D, I.9.30/224.

happens that someone good wishes to become prince by bad ways, even though his end [*fine*] be good, and that someone wicked, having become prince, wishes to work well, and that it will ever occur to his mind to use well the authority that he has acquired badly.[74]

Romulus and other ancient founders should be seen as exceptions to this rule, not as models to be imitated by aspiring servants of the common good. Far from endorsing the maxim "when the deed accuses, the effect excuses," Machiavelli argues that it is better as a general rule to avoid taking authority by violent means no matter how good one's ends. The discussion of Romulus is therefore subtler than it appears. It provokes readers to question would-be orderers who claim that what they take to be the common good can justify violent means; and suggests that particular conceptions of the common good should be subject to rigorous limiting conditions.[75]

9.9.
Corrupt judgments: Means and ends in the *Prince*

If Machiavelli's remarks on "judging by results" in the *Discourses* and *Histories* cannot be taken at face value, is the same true of his remarks in the *Prince*? I have already discussed some well-known passages that relate to justice and injustice. Here, let us look again at the well-known observation that princes should be prepared to use "vices" to defend the state. It begins with the statement that "since human conditions do not permit" any princes to observe all the various qualities that are "held good,"

> (O) it is necessary for him to be so prudent as to know how to avoid the infamy of those vices that would take his state from him and to be on guard against those that do not, if that is possible; but if one cannot, one can let them go on with less hesitation [*respetto*]. And . . . one should not care about incurring the fame of those vices without which it is difficult to save one's state [*stato*].[76]

The question then is, what can be considered as vices "without which it is difficult to save one's state"? Casual readings of the *Prince* usually take Machiavelli's list of conventional vices—cruelty, inhumanity, parsimony—and assume that Machiavelli thinks whatever conduct goes under these names is excusable if it helps princes to save their state.[77] Such readings fail to register the distinction between the names people use to evaluate actions and the true quality of the actions themselves. In cor-

---

[74] *D*, I.18.51/248.

[75] See chap. 11, sec. 11.2, on the "covert" proceduralist message of Machiavelli's discussions of Romulus.

[76] *P*, XV.62/160.

[77] The word *stato* refers to the general political order of a polity, including (but not primarily) its territoriality or status in relation to other polities. Here it refers to a prince's position of authority among his subject peoples.

rupt times, deeds that people describe with the names of specific virtues—liberality, humanity, mercy—often turn out to have vicious or corrupting qualities that hide under color of good words.[78] By the same token, conduct that in corrupt times is labeled vicious, parsimonious, or inhumane turns out on closer inspection to be genuinely *virtuoso*, and necessary for safeguarding good orders. Machiavelli's next sentence invites readers to reflect more carefully on statement (O) in the light of this distinction. It assumes that there are virtues and vices that can be objectively known, but that these are often misidentified and their "names" misused:

(E) for if one considers everything well, one will find something appears to be virtue, which if pursued would be one's ruin, and something else appears to be vice, which if pursued results in one's security and well-being.

This complicates statement (O), since it suggests that the modes of action often *thought* necessary for safeguarding the state may in fact lead to their ruin. If judgments about what constitute useful vices are often wrong, a secure basis for correct judgments must be found before a prince can know that he is adopting genuinely useful and not merely apparent vices. And until the distinction between apparent and genuine virtues and vices has been applied to the qualities Machiavelli discusses, it remains unclear what vices he thinks result in "security and well-being."

The next chapters of the *Prince* give examples illustrating the distinction outlined in passage (E). One example of a mode of action that appears to many as virtuous is the princely virtue of liberality. To gain a reputation for liberality, Machiavelli observes, many princes follow ways that lead to their own ruin and that of their countries. They do so because when in corrupt times men are applauded for their *liberalità,* this usually means that they use public funds to buy loyal supporters and create lavish appearances of *grandezza*. To corrupt cronies, such "liberal" men appear as virtuous. To disinterested observers, it is clear that their liberality ruins their state, since through such policies a prince squanders all his resources, "burdens the people extraordinarily," and imposes extortionate taxes. This makes him "hated by his subjects, and little esteemed by anyone as he becomes poor." Having "offended the many and rewarded the few with this liberality of his, he feels every least hardship and runs into risk at every slight danger." If these are the results of so-called liberality, Machiavelli proposes, princes should shun the conduct that currently goes under that name.[79] To safeguard their state instead of ruining it, they should do the opposite of what those praised as liberal do. People who benefit from a prince's liberality condemn the opposite of his behavior as "meanness" (*misero*) or "parsimony" (*parsimonia*). To the corrupt, a prince who exercises fiscal prudence, avoids wasting public money on self-promoting displays, and does not

---

[78] A few chapters later we read: "a prince who wants to maintain his state is often forced not to be good. For when that community [*università*] of which you judge you have need to maintain yourself is corrupt, whether they are the people or the soldiers or the great, you must follow their humor to satisfy them, and then good deeds are your enemy" (*P*, XIX.77/171). This is a description, not a prescription. Machiavelli does not advise princes to let this reality dictate their actions, only to treat it as an ordinary *inconveniente* that they should take into account.

[79] See chap. 2, sec. 2.2, for similar arguments in Xenophon's *Cyropaedia*.

try to buy supporters deserves to be called stingy. Nevertheless, Machiavelli writes, "in our times we have not seen great things done except by those who have been considered mean; the others have been eliminated." He draws this conclusion:

> (C) Thus since a prince cannot, without damage to himself, use the virtue of liberality so that it is recognized [*in modo che la sia conosciuta*], he should not mind getting a name for meanness [*nome del misero*]. For with time he will always be held more and more liberal when it is seen that with his parsimony his income is enough for him, that he can defend himself from whoever makes war upon him, and that he can undertake campaigns without burdening the people. . . . Therefore, so as not to have to rob his subjects, to be able to defend himself, not to become poor and contemptible, nor to be forced to become rapacious, a prince should esteem it little to incur a name for meanness.[80]

Here then is the first so-called vice that Machiavelli recommends as necessary to "save" the state: the vice of fiscal responsibility, which entails the avoidance of corruption. The next chapter discusses a similar inversion of the values ascribed to the "vice" of cruelty and the "virtue" of mercy. It starts by declaring that princes should "desire to be held merciful [*piatoso*] and not cruel [*crudele*]." But when considering ancient and modern examples, they should take care not to imitate some of the conduct that is widely praised as merciful. Much of that conduct is held merciful by people who dislike rigorous discipline and the strict justice it requires. They misuse the name of mercy (*pietà*) for actions that "allow disorders to continue, from which come killings or robberies" that "customarily hurt a whole community [*offendere una universalità*]." This in turn weakens the prince's position, confirming the argument that he "should not care about incurring the fame of those vices without which it is difficult to save one's state."[81]

The vice that corresponds to the virtue of mercy is cruelty, and conventional usage often mistakes virtuous mercy for corrupt—in this case "too delicate"—forms of conduct. Conventional usage might be equally wrong about what constitutes non-virtuous cruelty. In corrupt times people become self-indulgent; they wish to avoid public obligations, and regard it as cruel when they are duly punished for committing large or petty offenses. The "few" who have been bought off by princes are accustomed to get away with criminal behavior, thinking themselves above the rule of law. Such people denounce the cruelty of men or laws that use reasonable harshness to pull them back. Machiavelli says: let them. If what corrupt men call cruelty is the quality of actions that brings order to disorder, then princes should not shun a name for cruelty. If leaders are held cruel who uphold strict standards and punish offenses even when offenders are partisans, family, and friends, then cruelty in this sense is among the "vices" needed to safeguard the state.

The misfit between words and deeds is illustrated by the examples of two ancient generals, the Carthaginian prince Hannibal and his Roman rival in the Punic

[80] *P*, XVI.62–65/160–62.
[81] *P*, XVII.65–66/162–63.

Wars, Scipio Africanus. It is, Machiavelli declares, "above all necessary not to care about a name for cruelty" when one has to order and direct a very large army in combat. This is not always appreciated because the writers who discuss ancient military campaigns—virtually all Roman citizens or subjects of the Roman Empire—misjudged the qualities needed to maintain discipline. They applaud the "mercy" or "humanity" of Roman generals who failed to punish their soldiers' misconduct, while condemning enemy generals who upheld strict discipline. Machiavelli challenges these double standards. Among Hannibal's "admirable actions" was that "when he had a very large army, mixed with infinite kinds of men, and had led it to fight in alien lands, no dissension ever arose in it, neither among themselves" nor against Hannibal, "in bad as well as in good fortune." Roman writers assert, and Machiavelli seems to affirm, that Hannibal could not have achieved such good results by "anything other than his inhuman cruelty [*inumana crudeltà*]." But it is far from clear that Machiavelli agrees with this opinion. Whenever Machiavelli says that someone showed the ability to order for steady self-reliance in any "fortune," this is extremely high praise: it is among the defining qualities of *virtú*. This raises a suspicion that the qualities Roman writers call cruel and inhumane in their country's arch-enemy should properly be judged as virtuous. Machiavelli slyly intimates as much by pointing out that Hannibal's Roman detractors make contradictory judgments: they admire the Carthaginian's well-ordered army but "condemn the principal cause of it," his use of strict discipline—or as Romans corrupted by empire called it, his inhuman cruelty. By contrast, Hannibal's opponent Scipio gained a reputation for "mercy" among his fellow Romans. Machiavelli is unusually forthright in stating his own judgment of methods he imputes to Scipio: in relation to his own soldiers he showed excessive mercy (*troppa pietà*) in allowing his soldiers "more license than is fitting for military discipline." Scipio's armies might have defeated Hannibal's in the end. But here and in the *Discourses*, Machiavelli implies that his "excessive mercy" undermined the strict disciplinary standards that sustained the Roman republic. When in later generations men such as Julius Caesar imitated what they took to be Scipio's virtues, republican orders were finally destroyed.[82]

It is often said that Machiavelli's arguments in these chapters call for an inversion of "conventional" virtues and vices. This is true in one sense, but misleading in another. If "conventional" means "in corrupt times," then it is true that Machiavelli wants to invert corrupt conventional judgments. Since one symptom of corruption is to treat words and reputations as more important than deeds, Machiavelli's attempt to purge corruption does the opposite: it tells princes to care less about the names corrupt people call them so long as their actions work toward the safety and well-being of their *stato*. But if "conventional" refers to the "ordinary," non-corrupt senses of the words "vice" and "virtue," "cruelty" and "humanity," then Machiavelli does not advise princes to trade them in for a more "realistic" set of values resembling traditional vices. What he recommends in the chapters about the judicious use of "vices" is reasonable harshness regulated by

[82] *P*, XVII.67–68/164. See chap. 12, sec. 12.5.

standards of justice, as distinct from both license or leniency on the one hand and unrestrained cruelty on the other.[83]

The terminus of Machiavelli's reasonings about passage (O) trades in the initial ends-justify-means argument in favor of a strict proceduralism. His examples in chapters 16 and 17 show that what is needed to safeguard the state are respect for strict standards of fiscal responsibility; the refusal to squander public funds on sumptuous displays of one's *grandezza* or attempts to buy partisans; and rigorous discipline when dealing with offenses committed under one's watch. All these "vices" conform to Machiavelli's standards of justice, while the failure to observe them leads to corruption. By defending what he regards as virtues "under the name" of vices, Machiavelli reminds readers not to take ethical judgments—his own or anyone else's—at face value. He reminds them that judgments about vices and virtues are corruptible and stand in need of continuous, critical examination.

[83] *P*, XVII.66/163. He adds that a prince should not "make himself feared, and he should proceed in a temperate mode with prudence and humanity [*procedere in modo, temperato con prudenza e umanità*] so that too much confidence does not make him incautious and too much diffidence does not render him intolerable."

POLITICS

IV

CHAPTER 10

Ordinary and Extraordinary Authority

The last four chapters have tried to reconstruct the ethical principles of free agency and justice that inform Machiavelli's political judgments. This chapter examines one of the most important distinctions he uses to evaluate the necessity, and therefore the prudence and justice, of different policies: the distinction between "ordinary" and "extraordinary" ways of seeking and maintaining *autorità*. The import of Machiavelli's distinction between *ordinario* and *estraordinario* (or *straordinario, istraordinario*) modes of action is essential for recognizing his often oblique evaluations of various policies and institutions. If the ethical principles that underpin the distinction are overlooked, fundamental mistakes may be made about Machiavelli's own recommendations with respect to conspiracies, dictators, and religion.

10.1.
The antithesis between ordinary and extraordinary modes

Machiavelli's use of antithetical terms, especially *fortuna* and *virtú*, has been widely discussed in the scholarly literature.[1] Following ancient Greek and Roman practice, he employs this antithesis to present two alternative modes of action: one mode requiring fortune for success, the other *virtú*. Whatever his overt comments about the merits of each mode or the success of agents who used them, the antithesis tells attentive readers that one is deficient and the other adequate to the standards human beings should strive to meet.[2] Someone who relies on fortune, such as Alexander, may achieve a reputation for greatness. But if Machiavelli or one of his ancient writers implies that Alexander came to depend more on fortune than on his own *virtú,* they suggest that his modes of action were ultimately deficient, despite his reputation and undoubted achievements. The fortune/virtue antithesis was one of the most common tropes used by ancient authors for "double writing." By arguing that both fortune and virtue can be seen in Alexander's, Cyrus', or the whole city of Athens' deeds, but subtly stressing their excessive reliance on fortune, writers such as Plutarch, Xenophon, and Thucydides avoid direct criticism of their subjects, and

---

[1] For valuable discussions see Ball 1984; de Grazia 1989, 202–15.
[2] See chaps. 4–5.

may seem only to praise them.[3] Yet their allusions to the role of fortune in governing a subject's actions serve as a code suggesting that the man or the city was deficient in virtue, though this judgment is never spelled out. It is widely recognized that because the *fortuna/virtú* antithesis is used so consistently throughout Machiavelli's works, it functions almost like a code, whereby each word has distinctive connotations that are not part of colloquial usage. Readers who see that *fortuna* always connotes a deficiency in human self-responsibility, and that *virtú* is its antithesis, will find it easier to gauge Machiavelli's ethical judgments. They will be thrown off track if they lose sight of the antithesis, especially if they suppose that *virtuoso* agents depend on *fortuna* in order to work effectively. Translations that render Machiavelli's key words in different ways at different times can be highly misleading in this respect. When *virtú* is sometimes rendered as "virtue" but elsewhere as "ability" or "prowess," this obscures the recurrent contrast with *fortuna* as a deficient kind of causality. If *fortuna* is usually translated as "fortune" but occasionally as "luck," "chance," or "auspiciousness," the coded implication of its deficiency may be lost.

Another of Machiavelli's key antitheses, *ordinario/estraordinario,* has been a more serious casualty of colloquial-sounding translations. When Machiavelli describes actions or conditions for action as "ordinary," he is not just suggesting that that they are usual, accustomed, natural, or common. The word *ordinario* has extremely important normative connotations in Machiavelli's lexicon. He consistently uses it for modes and conditions of action that support stable human orders or *ordini*. "Ordinary" actions and conditions always have or confer the quality of order on relationships among individuals, parties, peoples, or cities. Whenever Machiavelli describes a mode of action as "extraordinary," the word connotes qualities opposed to those found in *ordinario* modes. If ordinary modes and conditions are compatible with stable orders, "extraordinary" ones stand outside and in tension with them. Actions taken "ordinarily" (*ordinariamente*) are regulated by good *ordini* and tend to uphold them. Actions taken "extraordinarily" are unregulated by ethical or civil orders, and tend to undermine them.[4] This antithetical usage implies that whereas *ordinario* actions can be considered as legitimate, the legitimacy of any modes that Machiavelli describes as *estraordinario* is doubtful. There are extraordinary *modi* but almost never extraordinary *ordini*; on Machiavelli's consistent usage, the phrase "extraordinary orders" is an oxymoron.[5] He does use the

---

[3] As noted in chap. 2, Thucydides employs the *tuchē/aretē* distinction throughout TPW, especially with respect to Athens. Plutarch uses it to structure subtly provocative essays titled "Fortune or the Virtue of Alexander" and "Fortune of the Romans," PM, IV.322–487. Among Roman writers, see Sallust's use of the *fortuna/virtus* antithesis in SBC, 1–12.

[4] Possible Roman sources are Livy, *LH*, V.37; Cicero, *Epistulae Famil.* VIII.8.1; *Ver. Orationes* I.39.102; *Let. Brutus* I.10.3, I.17.6 (2.88). A Greek term used in broadly similar ways to Machiavelli's "extraordinary" is *exaisios*, meaning transgressing right, lawless, excessive, or violent. Another related term is the verb *huperechein* (to stretch beyond measure, overstep limits) and other words with the prefix *huper-*. The word *taxis* (order) and cognates are used by many Greek authors in ways similar to Machiavelli's *ordine*, and related to a word referring to divine as well as natural and human order, *kosmos/kosmein*. See Plato's uses in *Rep.* 423a–c, 430e, 443d, 458b, 486b, 577e, 587a–c.

[5] In the *Histories* Machiavelli (*FH*, VII.13.291/646–47) once comes close to using the phrase: "if nothing extraordinary were ordered against" Piero de' Medici.

phrase "extraordinary laws," *leggi straordinarie*, once in the *Discourses*. Since *leggi* and *ordini* usually go hand in hand, the concept of extraordinary laws seems as alien to his vocabulary as that of extraordinary orders. We will later see, however, that the phrase *leggi straordinarie* occurs in the context of a heavily ironic, dialectical discussion of common "opinions" about the political uses of religion.[6]

Readings that overlook the normative basis of the ordinary/extraordinary distinction lack one of the main keys needed to understand the ethical dimensions of Machiavelli's political judgments. Since Machiavelli's normatively loaded usage of *ordinario/estraordinario* is foreign to colloquial usage in most modern European languages, many translations misleadingly highlight what are taken to be Machiavelli's meanings by using different translations for the same word. In English, *estraordinario* is rendered variously as "extraordinary," "exceptional," "remarkable," and "illegal," *ordinario* as "ordinary," "commonplace," "natural," "normal," and "legal."[7] Such varied translations obscure the evaluative import of Machiavelli's antithesis. For example, in chapter 2 of the *Prince* Machiavelli draws a clear contrast between the "ordinary industry" that maintains a prince in his state and the "extraordinary and excessive force" that may deprive him of it.[8] "Ordinary" industry brings anything but unremarkable results; on the contrary, it is a fundamental necessity for securing the state. But the antithesis is dissolved in a modern Italian translation, where *estraordinaria ed eccessiva forza* is given as "forza straordinaria e irresistibile" while *ordinaria industria* appears as "normali capacità."[9] The contrast between *normali* and *straordinaria* lacks the clear ethical import of Machiavelli's original antithesis. Indeed, it might even seem to invert the values that Machiavelli assigns to the words *ordinaria-industria* and *estraordinaria-forza* here, since *normali* has connotations of "commonplace" as contrasted with extraordinary—read as remarkable, impressive—*forza*. If Machiavelli's *estraordinario* is misread as the antithesis of commonplace, normal, or everyday and as a synonym for "exceptional" or remarkable, it is but a short step to the very serious error of identifying "extraordinary" with superior, supremely capable, or indeed *virtuoso* modes. Many standard English and German translations also encourage this kind of error, obscuring the strongly positive sense of Machiavelli's *ordinario* and the negative sense of *estraordinario*.[10] A casual reader might well conclude that

[6] See sec. 10.4., 389–90.

[7] English-language readers now have the benefit of translations by Mansfield (*Prince*) with Tarcov (*Discourses*) and Banfield (*Histories*) that avoid these misleading variations, found in virtually every other English translation. Similar variations occur in a standard German translation of the *Discourses*, with e/straordinario rendered as *außerordentlich* (extraordinary), *außergewöhnlich* (unaccustomed), or *ungesetzlich* (unlawful). Ordinario appears as *natürlich, gewöhnlich, in der Regel*, or *gesetzlich* (Zorn 1977). My French translations (Bec 1996) of the *Discourses* and the *Prince* are most consistent, almost always rendering ordinario as ordinaire and e/straordinario as extraordinaire.

[8] *P*, II.6–7/120.

[9] Melograni, trans. *Il Principe* (1994), 51.

[10] Translating the sentence just cited, one says that states can be maintained by a prince "of average capability," another by one who is "reasonably assiduous," thereby missing the normative contrast between good ordinary and less good extraordinary modes; see translations of the *Prince* by Milner (1995, 38) and Bull (1961, 34).

Machiavelli sees no special qualities of *virtú* in "ordinary industry," and suspect that princes who are able to exert "extraordinary and excessive force" have above average "capabilities"—perhaps including superior *virtú*.

On first reading any of Machiavelli's political works, one is struck by phrases that use the word "extraordinary," and realizes that the concept plays an important role in Machiavelli's political judgments. But unless the antithesis between *estraordinario* and *ordinario* is also noticed, the negative import of "extraordinary" is easily underestimated.[11] Ordinary methods of seeking authority are often so familiar as to seem uninteresting, while extraordinary ones leap out from the page and appear "great in themselves." Given Machiavelli's fondness for coded, enigmatic writing, it is not farfetched to surmise that he intended to create this somewhat misleading effect, using it to encourage readers to look beyond first appearances. Like Xenophon's *Cyropaedia*, Machiavelli's *Prince* and other writings expect readers to start by noticing what appears on the surface of the text, taking impressive words and appearances at face value. If they reread more carefully, however, they will spot subtle clues given in the use of words and accounts of deeds that disturb the initial, surface reading. I suggest that Machiavelli's extraordinary/ordinary distinction is among his main vehicles for this kind of double-writing. While attention-grabbing remarks about extraordinary modes seem to convey his most important views, a closer look reveals more reflective judgments expressed by the concept of *ordinario*. If ordinary modes are less exciting, their benefits are unjustly—indeed dangerously—underappreciated, since they are the *sine qua non* for any sustainable human orders.

The *Prince* often pairs the word *ordinario* with three other words: "natural" (*naturale*), "reasonable" (*ragionevole*), or "necessary" (*necessario*). Constraints that are described as "ordinary and natural" arise either from human dispositions that seem to be part of the basic makeup of the human animal, or from their innate capacities for freedom, or both. The desire to acquire is thus "natural and ordinary." Yet it is a "natural and ordinary *necessity*" that "one must always offend those over whom one becomes a new prince." Princes who fail to observe "any of the conditions observed by others who have taken provinces and wished to hold them," that is, the *ordinario* conditions set out earlier in the chapter, always lose what they acquire; "nor is this any miracle, but very ordinary and reasonable."[12] The necessity for anyone who wishes to maintain his *stato* to observe "ordinary" constraints is also stressed in the *Discourses,* where Machiavelli describes the mix of good and evil in human works as an "ordinary and natural inconvenience [*inconveniente*]" that all prudent commanders must take into account, and refers to the "natural and ordinary dangers [*pericoli*]" that tyrants bring on their subjects and themselves.[13] By contrast, the conditions that Machiavelli describes as *estraordinario* are never natural or reasonable, nor does he speak of "extraordinary necessities." Whereas ordinary modes use

---

[11] One of very few exceptions is the excellent study by Whitfield (1969, 141–62). Also see related observations in de Grazia 1989, 237–40, 259.

[12] *P*, III.8–16/120–26.

[13] *D*, III.37.294/508; III.6.234/442; *P*, XIX.73/168–69.

prudence and self-imposed orders to manage constraints, extraordinary modes are overassertive: instead of respecting natural or reasonable limits, they act outside or above them. These characteristics are underlined early in the *Prince,* where *estraordinari/a* occurs twice in the second chapter, paired with "excessive" (*estraordinaria ed eccessiva forza*) and "vices" (*estraordinari vizi*).[14]

Among the most conspicuous features of extraordinary modes is that they rely more on supernatural aid, fortune, or on "others' arms" than on agents' own *virtú*. Machiavelli often uses this sense of "extraordinary" ironically to characterize excuses made by agents who blame some *estraordinario* causality for their own avoidable failures. He notes that "the extraordinary and extreme [*estrema*] malignity of fortune" is sometimes invoked as an excuse for foreseeable defeat caused by the failure to observe "ordinary" constraints. More often, Machiavelli reports that people invoke miracles, the heavens, or God as accompaniments to actions unregulated by "ordinary" human orders. The chapters dealing with the rise of the Medici "princes" in the *Florentine Histories* report many "extraordinary" supernatural events, which parallel the extraordinary actions used by Cosimo and Lorenzo to take power. Near the end of the *Prince* Machiavelli waxes lyrical about the "extraordinary things without example" that may be seen to be "brought about by God as a result of princely actions: "the sea has opened; a cloud has escorted you along the way; the stone has poured forth water, here manna has rained, everything has concurred in your greatness." While such miracles cannot harm a prince's reputation, in the end he must rely on his own quite ordinary *industria* and *virtú* since "the remainder," the passage continues, "you must do yourself."[15]

This normative point is reiterated in a discussion of different modes used by private citizens to become princes. Machiavelli notes that Francesco Sforza "became duke of Milan from private individual by proper means [*per li debiti mezzi*] and with a great virtue of his own." As evidence of his *virtú* Machiavelli adds, "that which he had acquired with a thousand pains he maintained with little trouble." Sforza exemplifies the maxim that a prince of "ordinary industry," that is who works hard and virtuously, can easily maintain his *stato* even against great force. The counterexample is Cesare Borgia, who "acquired his state through the fortune of his father and lost it through the same," that is, through fortune and someone else's virtue. Though he did many things that "should be done by a prudent and virtuous man to put his roots in the states that the arms and fortune of others had given him," he failed because unlike Sforza he did not "lay his foundations at first" but relied on *l'arme e fortuna di altri*. Unless readers are careless or corrupt, they will reject the irresponsible opinion that if Cesare's "orders did not bring profit to him, it was not his fault." The context and vocabulary indicate the irony in Machiavelli's statement that Borgia's failures "arose from an extraordinary and extreme

[14] *P,* II.7/120.

[15] *P,* VII.27/134; *FH,* VII.5.281/635; *P,* XXVI.103/190. The *Discourses* note that after miraculous "accidents" such as thunderbolts and heavenly interventions are seen to occur, "extraordinary and new things supervene in provinces" (*D,* I.57.114/314–15). Compare Plato's (*Tim.* 25d) "excessively violent [*exaidōn*] earthquakes and floods" that accompany violent civil conflicts, and similar remarks in Thucydides and Livy.

malignity of fortune." Defeats that stem from the failure to observe ordinary constraints are not "any miracle, but very ordinary and reasonable."[16]

In addition to the contrast between *ordinario*—self-reliant and *e/straordinario*—irresponsible, Machiavelli associates the antithesis with three other contrasts. First, "ordinary" modes *stabilize* human conflicts by means of self-imposed orders; extraordinary modes are destabilizing and endanger order. When different humors lack "an outlet by which they may be vented [*sfogarsi*] ordinarily," Machiavelli writes, "they have recourse to extraordinary modes that bring a whole republic to ruin"; for "there is nothing that makes a republic so stable and steady [*stabile e ferma*] as to order it in such a mode so that those alternating humors that agitate it can be vented in a way ordered by the laws [*una via da sfogarsi ordinata dalle leggi*]." The prince who resorts to extraordinary measures "never secures himself; and the more cruelty he uses, the weaker his principality becomes."[17] Second, ordinary modes of venting, punishing, crushing, or eliminating are done *publicly* and regulated by clear public standards; extraordinary modes of doing these same actions rely on private methods such as manipulation by means of private economic power, or the use of private connections and forces. If "a citizen is crushed [*oppresso*] ordinarily," Machiavelli argues, "there follows little or no disorder in the republic" because the action "is done without private forces and without foreign forces, which are the ones that ruin a free way of life; but it is done with public forces and order, which have their particular limits [*i termini loro particulari*] and do not lead beyond to something that may ruin the republic."[18] Third, ordinary actions or conditions respect human or civil *limits,* while extraordinary ones ignore them. The first use of "extraordinary" in the *Discourses* pairs it with another word connoting a form of existence that has not been placed under constraints of *civiltà,* referring to modes that might be called "extraordinary and almost wild [*quasi efferati*]"; later a mode of defending someone against accusations is described as "violent and extraordinary."[19] The *Histories* graphically describes an "extraordinary example" made by Lorenzo de' Medici of an executed conspirator, involving the desecration of the young man's grave and dragging his naked body through the city by the noose used to hang him.[20]

Stability, publicity, and respect for limits are features that characterize justice and the rule of law in Machiavelli's ethics. *Ordinario* actions are regulated by public laws and therefore secure order in polities, whatever their form of government. Extraordinary modes are unregulated by laws and invariably produce disorder,

---

[16] *P*, VII.26–27/134; III.16/126.

[17] *D*, I.7.24–25/27–29; I.16.45/241–42; I.34.74/271.

[18] *D*, I.7.24/218; I.5.19/212; III.34.288/501.

[19] *D*, I.7.24–25/218. The same distinction is expressed more dramatically when in Book II Machiavelli contrasts princes who govern themselves by "human and ordinary orders [*ordini umani ed ordinari*]" with a "barbarian prince, a destroyer of countries and waster of all the civilizations of men [*dissipatore di tutte le civiltà*]" (*D*, II.2.133/335; I.59.121/321–22; I.4.16/209; III.34.287/501).

[20] *FH*, VIII.9.326–27/689–90. In another bitterly ironic juxtaposition, Machiavelli's description of this act follows a few lines after having seemed to praise "the fortune and the grace that had been acquired by this house through its prudence and liberality."

even if they sometimes appear to be a necessary evil. From the start of the *Discourses* Machiavelli identifies ordinary modes with those that deal with natural humors so that they may be "vented in a way ordered by the laws," emphasizing the close connection between ordinariness, laws, and self-legislative *virtú*. It is "useful and necessary that republics give an outlet *with their laws* to vent the anger that the collectivity conceives" against a leading citizen, "for when the ordinary modes are not there, one has recourse to extraordinary ones, and without doubt these produce much worse effects [*peggiori effetti*] than the former." Here ordinary modes are associated with actions regulated by public laws, and ordinary venting is legally regulated venting. Extraordinary venting is not regulated by laws. It therefore tends to boil over into sectarian conflicts, threatening order and undermining the public good. The identification of *ordinario* modes with the rule of law is sustained throughout the work. In Book III we read that a prudent prince "ought to guard himself from extraordinary commands and . . . use his humanity in ordinary ones," since "ordinary punishments are imputed not to a prince but to the laws and . . . orders." A mode of seizing a kingdom is "extraordinary and hateful" not only because it involved acts of extreme violence, but also because the perpetrator "had broken the laws of the kingdom and governed it tyrannically." And "princes may know," Machiavelli writes, "that they begin to lose their state at the hour they begin to break the laws and those modes and those customs that are ancient."[21]

10.2.
Are conspiracies ever justified?

If Machiavelli casts doubt on the *legitimacy* of "extraordinary" modes, it is not yet clear that he regards them as *unjustified* in all circumstances. Indeed, he sometimes seems to argue that they may be justified by extreme necessity or danger. Though risks of disorder loom large whenever citizens or leaders use extraordinary modes, he acknowledges that there are situations where these risks appear to be well worth taking. Romulus' fratricide to "order alone" and conspiracies to overthrow tyrants are among the extraordinary modes that Machiavelli is sometimes thought to endorse.[22] There can be little doubt that Machiavelli sees extraordinary methods as extremely dangerous and lacking, at least, in initial legitimacy. Nonetheless, it might seem reasonable for people oppressed by a tyrant to resort to extraordinary measures, since they are deprived of effective ordinary means of resistance.

Machiavelli himself refuses to give an unambiguous defense of such measures. Instead he weighs various examples and arguments for and against them, and his remarks are often teasingly ambiguous. One probable reason for this is that he could not openly advocate conspiracies (*congiure*) in his writings, especially after he himself had been arrested, tortured, and excluded from public service under suspicion of conspiring against the Medici restoration in 1512. Another explanation

---

[21] *D*, I.7.24/218; III:22.266/477; III:5.216–17/424–25.
[22] For example, Mansfield 1979, 318–43.

is that the main audience for Machiavelli's discussions of conspiracies consisted of young men who were tempted to become conspirators themselves.[23] One of the dedicatees of the *Discourses*, Zanobi Buondelmonti, and other young friends from Machiavelli's Orti Oricellari circle took part in a conspiracy against the Medicis in 1522. This resulted in exiles, deaths, and further punitive measures against critics of the regime. Some readers have speculated that Machiavelli wanted to egg his young friends on "between the lines," implicitly advocating the use of extraordinary and, if necessary, violent modes against princes who had taken power extraordinarily. On balance, however, Machiavelli's lengthy discussion of conspiracies in the *Discourses* casts doubt on this reading. The conclusion drawn at the end of every example is that "it is almost impossible to succeed," and that rare examples of successful conspiracies are celebrated by the writers "as a thing rare and almost without example." Those that appeared successful for a time were usually "conspiracies made against the fatherland" by a prince. When these men succeeded in taking away a city's freedom, they "no longer bore any dangers than the nature of the principality bears in itself," for "when one individual has become tyrant, he has the natural and ordinary dangers that tyranny brings him."[24] The principal danger is, of course, that a tyrant's subjects will conspire to overthrow him. Although this danger is *ordinario*, the modes needed to execute a conspiracy are always extraordinary. So we are back full circle: whether conspiracies are used to create a tyranny or to overthrow it, they carry a great many dangers that either lead to failure or make it nearly impossible to establish stable orders afterward.

A similar cautionary message is conveyed through the *Florentine Histories*, where Machiavelli describes an attempt by a group of well-intentioned young men in Milan to overthrow a tyrant. The conspirators met an unhappy end, though Machiavelli says that the memory of their undertaking stood as an inspiring example for future generations. The episode foreshadows Machiavelli's later discussion of the Pazzi conspiracy in Florence, and has parallels with his own experience. He ascribes responsibility for the conspiracy and its disastrous results to Cola Montano, "a lettered and ambitious man" who taught Latin to wealthy Milanese youths and inspired them to conspire against the "prince" of their city. Montano, Machiavelli implies, recklessly goaded these hotheaded, inexperienced young men to attempt their perilous enterprise.[25] In view of his very critical judgments about the role played by an older man in encouraging his young charges to risk their lives, it would be surprising if Machiavelli hoped to play the same role vis-à-vis his friends. The cautious approach he adopts in his own writings represents the more responsible way for an older friend to reason with would-be conspirators. On the one hand, he expresses guarded sympathy with their good intentions to get rid of tyrants and restore legitimate orders. On the other, he stresses the need to exercise

---

[23] Especially in the long chapters *D*, III.6 and *P*, XIX.

[24] *D*, III.6.229–34/426–44.

[25] *FH*, VII.33–34.312–16/674–77. Machiavelli portrays Montano's motives as deeply ambiguous. On the one hand he praised life in republics over life under princes. On the other, he was driven partly by his own ambitions; his main argument in favor of republics was that all "famous men" had been nourished by them. Compare *D*, III.6 on this episode.

circumspection when choosing the best means to these ends. Here and elsewhere, Machiavelli's comments show a deep avuncular concern about the risks his friends incurred through these actions, both for themselves and for other citizens. As in the *Discourses*, his bottom line is that most conspiracies fail. When they do, they provoke countermeasures that strengthen the regimes they sought to overthrow. The final book of the *Histories* begins by noting that

> the whole state had been so restricted to the Medici, who took so much authority, that it was required for those who were malcontent either to endure that mode of living with patience or, if indeed they wanted to eliminate it, attempt to do so by way of conspiracy and secretly. Such ways, because they succeed only with great difficulty, most often bring ruin to whoever moves them and greatness to the one against whom they are moved. Hence, almost always the prince of a city, attacked by such conspiracies ... rises to greater power and many times from being a good man, becomes bad. For conspiracies by their example give him cause to fear; and in fearing, to secure himself; and securing himself, to injure; hence arise hatreds later, and often his ruin.[26]

This passage touches on both sides of the question. The last sentence acknowledges that there may appear to be good reasons to conspire against illegitimate princes when no ordinary means of expelling them remain. By provoking a prince to become a tyrant, conspiracies may spell the beginning of the end of his illegitimate rule, since the tyrant's own excessive reactions make him more widely hated. And as the examples of conspiracies by republicans show, even those that fail can have salutary side-effects. They destabilize princes and tyrants whose rule lacks "ordinary" authority, warning them that they cannot last long if they deprive people of freedom. Conspiracies linger in the memory of other citizens as examples of courageous risk-taking by men who loved freedom, inspiring later generations to make similar attempts.[27] While stressing the risks for conspirators and the high price compatriots must pay for their failure, Machiavelli also applauds whoever stands up for his own and his country's freedom under adverse conditions. Initially bad results do not discredit good ends; and for Machiavelli, the end of defending freedom is intrinsically good.

On the other hand, he also stresses that an imprudent choice of means may undermine or corrupt even the best ends. Since the means used in conspiracies are inescapably "extraordinary," they can easily defeat good liberating and reordering ends. Machiavelli mentions two main ways in which this happens. First, as he points out in the passage just cited, if a conspiracy fails, the punitive measures are likely to inflict a far worse oppression on one's fatherland than existed before. Conspirators must be prepared to take responsibility for this outcome. They should be aware that if they fail, as they very likely will, their actions may be the catalyst

---

[26] *FH*, VIII.1.317/678–79. Compare *D*, I.46.95/293–94: "when men seek not to fear, they begin to make others fear; and the injury that they dispel from themselves they put upon another, as if it were necessary to offend or to be offended."

[27] *FH*, VII.34.315–16/675–77.

that turns a tolerably "good" prince into an outright tyrant. This happened after the tragic failure of the conspiracy against Lorenzo de' Medici and his relations. Until then a cautious, low-profile sort of prince on Machiavelli's account, Lorenzo became a bad man almost overnight, taking extraordinary and violent measures of revenge against the conspirators. Machiavelli's painful account of the Pazzi conspiracy and Lorenzo's recriminations certainly does not read as if it were aimed at encouraging contemporary imitators. It seems more likely to have been penned with a prophylactic intent: to dampen naïve enthusiasm for such adventures, and to warn readers about the dangers that conspiracies pose to their fatherland's freedom. Machiavelli intimates these reservations by attributing them to prudent and grave men who "detested" the plan, although they shared the conspirators' desires to get rid of Medici power and restore republican orders. His own commentary also offers a stern warning to spirited young men. "If ever any deed requires a great and firm spirit made resolute in both life and death through much experience," experience that the youthful conspirators lacked, "it is necessary to have it in this, where it has been seen very many times that men skilled in arms and soaked in blood have lacked spirit."[28]

Second, Machiavelli touches on two key relationships that may defeat conspirators' good ends: that between conspirators and their compatriots, and that between the people and the prince or tyrant. Even when their enemy is an unquestionably illegitimate ruler, conspirators risk alienating compatriots if their methods are deemed suspicious, excessive, or partisan. And since conspiratorial modes are by definition "extraordinary" even when their ends are to restore order, there is a very high risk that their actions will be perceived in this way—or that the men they conspire against can successfully color them in a suspicious light. The *Histories* are filled with examples of conspiracies by a handful of men who sincerely believed that they acted for the common good. Yet in every case, many of their compatriots saw them as self-interested partisans seeking to install their own *amici* and *partigiani* in power. Concerns about legitimacy are greater still when there is no general agreement among a city's population that its government is tyrannical. Regimes often come to power through questionably legitimate means, yet appear to many to have good effects, and gain popular assent despite extraordinary beginnings.[29] When a group of conspirators seeks to overthrow this kind of government, they not only run the usual risks of premature detection or betrayal; they also risk doing something in the name of the public good with which the wider public may disagree. As Machiavelli writes in the *Discourses*, "of all the dangers that can come after the execution" of a conspiracy "there is none more certain nor more to be feared than when the people is the friend of the prince that you have killed."[30] Before acting, then, conspirators must consider carefully whether most people would want this particular group of men—themselves—to make such a grave decision on their behalf. If serious doubts remain, aspiring

---

[28] *FH*, VIII.4–9.320–27/682–91.

[29] Machiavelli portrays Medici rule in this way; see chap. 1, sec. 1.1.

[30] *D*, III.6.232/441. Machiavelli cites Julius Caesar as the best-known ancient example.

destroyers of tyrants should hold themselves in check. Otherwise it is unclear why their compatriots should trust them to install a more legitimate order than the one they depose. Machiavelli suggests that if a handful of conspirators believe that their compatriots will unanimously applaud them and trust their intentions, no matter how extreme or secretive their methods, they almost certainly delude themselves.[31]

In the end Machiavelli leaves it to his readers to judge whether the risks of conspiratorial action are worth taking, and whether or not their ends are likely to be compromised by the use of extraordinary means. But the balance of his arguments and examples weighs on the side of circumspection. As a prime example of an extraordinary mode, conspiracies use private rather than public channels, and violent methods unregulated by laws. They are potentially destabilizing for entire populations, and their success hinges on a large element of luck, however prudent the conspirators may be. Some readers may judge that a conspiracy conducted by a few men in secret has better chances of success than an open revolt involving "the many." This, however, is precisely the kind of "private" judgment that renders conspirators suspect in the eyes of their compatriots. All these features call into question the legitimacy of conspiratorial modes, even if many people sympathize with their basic ends. Prospective conspirators would do well to consider alternative routes to eliminating what they regard as illegitimate governments.[32]

One alternative is the organized, popular uprising against illegitimate princes and tyrants. In the *Histories*, conspiracies conducted by a handful of men acting in secrecy invariably meet tragic ends. Open revolts involving large numbers of people do not. Machiavelli gives an encouraging example of such a revolt in Book II, where three separate conspiracies planned by the main social groups in Florence—the great, the people, and the artisans—come together in a single popular movement to overthrow the tyrannical Duke of Athens.[33] This example suggests that publicly known, "universal" revolts not only have better chances of success than conspiracies by a single group. They also have better chances of establishing legitimate authority afterward, since all the main parts of a city are involved in the subsequent "ordering." But how should such uprisings be analyzed in terms of Machiavelli's ordinary/extraordinary distinction? The open revolts he describes have two of the main features found in extraordinary modes. They are potentially destabilizing, and in the absence of civil orders that people recognize as legitimate, they take place outside the bounds of the law. Yet such revolts also have two qualities found in ordinary modes. Although they may begin as secret conspiracies, the secret is widely shared among different groups, and their actions soon become

---

[31] Plutarch's *Lives* contain many examples of this.

[32] See Spinoza 1958 (1677), V.7.312–13 for a similar interpretation. Machiavelli's purpose, he writes, "was probably to show the folly of attempting—as many do—to remove a tyrant when the causes which make a prince a tyrant cannot be removed, but become rooted more firmly as the prince is given more reason to be afraid." Spinoza's own political theory also stresses these hazards of conspiracies, but like Machiavelli only after first considering their attractions at some length; see Spinoza 2007 (1669–70), XVIII.7–9.

[33] *FH*, II.36.95/412; II.34.91/407.

public and seek public support across a broad spectrum. And because they rely on popular arms instead of a few risk-taking men, fortune has much less influence on their success. If a popular revolt is reasonably well-ordered before the fact, it may harness considerable resources of popular virtue to its cause instead of depending on fortune. In these respects, revolts made with the cooperation of different sections of society are preferable to conspiracies. As the contrast between this early popular revolt and minority-led conspiracies suggests, the former have better hopes of reaching a more successful and more legitimate end, with different parties sitting down together to negotiate new orders.[34]

Another of Machiavelli's alternatives for shedding tyranny was discussed earlier: whenever an opportunity presents itself, citizens who care about freedom should seek to "reason" with rulers with the aim of encouraging peaceful reform. If reasoning with princes and tyrants bears no fruit, the option remains of reasoning with fellow citizens—if necessary through indirect, coded, covert means—about how they can put pressure on rulers, especially by making them fear a universal revolt.[35] While Machiavelli does not rule out the possibility that extraordinary modes may sometimes be justified, then, he does set extremely demanding standards for such justifications. The main purpose of his discussions of extraordinary modes is not to defend them as a valuable last resort to be used under necessity, but to underscore the importance of ordering cities in ways that make extraordinary modes unnecessary. Leaders who boldly take up extraordinary means to tackle dangers when they arise are not especially prudent. Those who anticipate and check them before they become serious threats to order are.[36]

If extraordinary modes are so dangerous, why are people so ready to paint as life-threatening "necessity" tensions that could probably be managed through ordinary means? Machiavelli's examples suggest that ambition is the disposition that most often inspires men to take up extraordinary modes. Like "extraordinary," Machiavelli's *ambizione* is sometimes interpreted in a positive light, and seen as related to *virtù*.[37] It is true that Machiavelli describes ambition as a "natural and ordinary" disposition that may be used for good or evil. Regulated by strong *leggi e ordini*, ambition can support "ordinary" orders and help keep "extraordinary" modes in check.[38] On the other hand, Machiavelli treats ambition as the "natural and ordinary" disposition that is most resistant to regulative ordering: it is "so powerful [*tanto potente*] in human breasts that it never abandons them at whatever rank they rise to."[39] Machiavelli's judgments about ambition are not evenly balanced as between the boons and dangers it poses to civil order. He frequently pairs the word with other terms that connote disorder, describing a man's or a polity's ambitions as incorrect, suspicious, hurtful, partisan, as showing "an ugly

---

[34] *FH*, II.39.100/417–18.

[35] See chap. 1, sec. 1.7, and chap. 2, sec. 2.3.

[36] For example, see *D*, I.7.25/218; compare Thucydides' Diodotus (TPW, III.46) on not letting the idea of rebellion enter subjects' minds.

[37] See, for example, Mansfield 1998, 59–60, 69.

[38] *D*, II.2.132; III:28.276/488–89.

[39] *D*, I.37.78/276.

greed for rule," referring to "incorrect and ambitious behavior," and contrasting Romulus' virtuous use of authority "for the common good" with his successors' use of power "for their own ambition."[40] While ambition can be regulated, keeping it in check demands constant vigilance from citizens, and continuous self-examination on the part of those in command. It poses the greatest challenge to legislative prudence just because it can work for good as well as harm, and because it often works in deceptively "ordinary" ways. "Under various colors" (*sotto vari colori*) the ambitious undermine the laws' authority by using "private" means without ever appearing to use modes that violate public orders. They acquire supporters "in ways honest in appearance," offering favors to this or that private individual by "lending him money, marrying his daughters for him, defending him from the magistrates, and doing for him similar private favors that make men partisans to oneself." Thus acquiring partisans who can be counted on to turn a blind eye to their excesses, this gives "spirit to whoever is so favored to be able to corrupt the public and breach [*sforzare*] the laws." "Many times," Machiavelli observes, "works that appear merciful, which cannot reasonably be condemned, become cruel and are very dangerous for a republic if they are not corrected in good time."[41] Since the intention of ambitious men often "appears virtuous, it easily deceives everyone"; and so "persevering without hindrance" these men can "ascend from one ambition to another" until as a result "republics break down."[42]

In all his political writings Machiavelli portrays ambition mainly as a destructive humor and the chief source of corruption in cities. This view of ambition has much in common with the judgments of Machiavelli's favorite Greek writers, as well as with Roman authors such as Sallust and Livy.[43] As we saw in chapter 2, the Greek *philotimia* (ambition) is closely related to the vice of *pleonexia*, variously translated as "excessive desire" for than one's share or "taking advantage" of others.[44] Machiavelli too argues that poorly ordered ambition drives men to seek more for themselves than is reasonable, and thus to demand unjust advantage over others. Although ambition may simply involve desires to acquire, which is "natural and ordinary," it is also at the root of the desire to dominate others; and this is among the main causes of civil disorders in Machiavelli's political theory. Domination is not just command or authority, both functions that are necessary for political orders. *Dominio* is not a neutral relation of authority that may be exercised well or badly, as are *comandare* and *autorità*. *Autorità* and command are "given" to particular individuals or offices through acts of public willing. *Dominio* involves the "taking" of others' freedom or authority by an agent who has not been authorized to take so much. The next section considers how reasonable desires to clean up corruption by renovating political orders may themselves be corrupted by desires to dominate on the part of those who call for renovation.

[40] D, I.5.19/210–12; III.8.237/446–48; III.21.263–64/474–75; I.45.94; III.8.237/446–47; I.9.29/223–25.

[41] D, I.46.95/294; III:28.276–77/488–89.

[42] D, I.46.95–96/293–94; compare the references to Sallust, D, I.46/293–94, III.28/488–89.

[43] See chap. 2, secs. 2.2 and 2.5.

[44] See the excellent analysis of *pleonexia* and ambition in Bloomfield 2008, "Why It's Bad to Be Bad," 251–71.

10.3.
Extraordinary and ordinary ways to renovate corrupt cities

Machiavelli frequently invokes the ordinary/extraordinary distinction under the heading of "renovating" (*rinnovare*) corrupt political orders. "All worldly things," he writes in the *Discourses*, "have a limit [*termine*] to their life." But "generally those go the whole course . . . that do not disorder their body but keep it ordered [*tengonlo in modo ordinato*] so that either it does not alter or, if it alters, it is for its safety and not to its harm." He describes republics and religious sects (*sètte*) as "mixed bodies" (*corpi misti*), which live longer "when by means of their orders," or "through some accident outside the said order," they are so renewed. As previous *discorsi* showed, "ordinary" modes of renovating happen "by means of their orders" in cities; renewals that occur "through some accident outside the said order" are "extraordinary" renewals. If these remarks on the value of *rinnovazione* are read without bearing in mind Machiavelli's earlier discussions, they might seem to present ordinary and extraordinary modes of renovating as equally viable. When political bodies are corrupt or threatened with corruption, the precise modes used to renew them are, one might suppose, less important than that renewal occurs. For "it is a thing clearer than light," he continues,

> that these bodies do not last if they do not renew themselves. . . . It is thus necessary . . . that men who live together in any order whatever often examine themselves either through these extrinsic accidents or through intrinsic ones. As to the latter, it must arise either from a law that often looks over the account [*una legge, la quale spesso rivegga il conto*] for the men who are in that body or indeed from a good man [*uomo buono*] who arises among them, who with his examples and his virtuous works produces the same effects as the order.[45]

This raises the question of whether these two different ways of renovating corrupt polities "intrinsically"—by law or by a "good man"—both qualify as "ordinary" ways. When this passage in Book III is read against the backdrop of earlier arguments in the *Discourses*, it seems most unlikely that Machiavelli sees the two modes of renovation as equally trustworthy. The safer way to renovate, one might expect, must be the more straightforwardly ordinary way: through "a law that often looks over the account" for citizens and prevents corruption from growing in the first place. It is not yet clear, however, that Machiavelli regards all modes of renovation that rely on *uno uomo buono* as dangerous or extraordinary. If that man's works produce "the same effects" as a law, then perhaps each of the two modes is as good as the other. How does Machiavelli evaluate these alternatives? Does he see them as equally legitimate modes of renovation, each appropriate to different forms of corruption?

Answers to these questions hinge on how Machiavelli rates prospects of finding a good man whose works can be expected to have the same effects as a publicly

---

[45] *D*, III.1.209–10/416–17.

ordered law. He frequently notes that people in corrupt cities may long for a man of exceptional prudence to come forth and purge corruption "all at a stroke."[46] The longing is understandable, but is it realistic? Or is it a pipe dream to hope that one good man will arise from the rot to put corrupt cities in order? And even if a man who appeared good enough should emerge, could such hopes be fulfilled by ordinary means, or would they require the good man to step outside the constraints of human laws, with all the risks that this entails?

Machiavelli's previous arguments raise doubts about the "good man" solution. To find any one man who can do the same work of renovation as publicly ordered laws is, he judges, "almost impossible"; and attempts to make even a good man do the work of laws always results in dangerous, extraordinary measures. In Book I, chapter 18 he gives several reasons for this judgment. First, "it is a very easy thing for not one of these [men] to ever emerge in a city." Even among the ancients, examples of men who consistently did good when they were unconstrained by the laws are rare indeed. In present corrupt times, there are none to be seen at all. Second, even if one were to emerge, it is likely that he will "never be able to persuade anyone else of what he himself understands [*intendesse*]. For men used to living in one mode do not wish to vary it," so an individual renovator who seems wise to a few or to himself may well have trouble swaying others. Third, if a good man cannot persuade people to renovate their orders, he must either resort to extralegal force or give up. The need to resort to extraordinary modes is all the greater when people seek to change existing orders "at a stroke" when "everyone knows [*conosce*] that they are not good." To do this "it is not enough to use ordinary terms [*termini ordinari*], since the ordinary modes are bad; but it is necessary to go to the extraordinary, such as violence and arms," and first set one man up as "prince of that city, able to dispose [*disporre*] of it in one's own mode." This takes us back full circle to the near impossibility of finding a man good enough to be trusted to renovate civil orders. On the one hand, "the reordering of a city for a political way of life presupposes a good man." But on the other, desires to introduce new orders "at a stroke" can only be satisfied by a prince who is prepared to use extraordinary modes. And since "becoming prince of a republic by violence presupposes a bad man," one finds that "it very rarely happens that someone good wishes to become prince by bad ways, even though his end be good." As we saw in the last chapter, Machiavelli consistently holds that bad "ways" corrupt good ends. Any man good and prudent enough to be trusted with extraordinary authority to renovate a city would know this, and therefore be reluctant to use that authority. By the same token one rarely finds "that someone wicked, having become prince, wishes to work well, and that it will ever occur to his mind to use well the authority that he has acquired badly."[47]

Thus the second way of renewing corrupt polities is neither compatible with ordinary ways nor likely to have the same effects as a public law. By default, we are left with the ordinary mode of renovating that relies on laws ordered and maintained by responsible citizens. When Machiavelli returns to this theme in Book III

[46] See chap. 11, sec. 11.4 on ancient sources of this theme and that of one-man redeemers.
[47] *D*, I.18.51/247–48.

he notes that the worse things get, the more tempting it is to hope that a polity's troubles can be solved through "the simple virtue [*semplice virtú*] of one man, without depending on any law" but by the awe and shame that his virtue inspires in the people. Harking back to Rome, readers may find examples of men who "with their rare and virtuous examples produced . . . almost the same effect that laws and orders produced." The problem with this approach is that once these individuals were gone, all the old disorders returned. "For after Marcus Regulus no like example may be seen there, and although the two Catos emerged in Rome, there was so much distance from him to them and between them from one to the other," that "they remained so alone." Without laws to enforce renewal in the absence of good men, all their isolated examples of virtue had no lasting effect, and despite all "their good examples they were not able to do any good work."[48]

This suggests a more positive reason why renovation through laws is preferable to renovation by a good man. The laws impose general obligations on citizens to improve the quality of their own actions. Renovation through a law involves returning to the *principio*—a word connoting both beginnings and first principles—of human orders. Citizens who acknowledge the force of law can also examine the reasonable grounds for the law, and in doing so renew their commitment to the first principles of civil orders. Reasoning about the *principio* of a law leads to firm knowledge of why it is necessary for order, knowledge that tends to strengthen public commitments to uphold *leggi e ordini*.[49] By contrast, Machiavelli points out that unlike public laws, the examples set by individual renovators neither "make the citizens better" nor give them a stable set of principles that can guide their judgments. An outstandingly good man who is supposed to cure a city of corruption may inspire admiration and imitation. But his particular works do not supply general reasons for all citizens to act in ways that uphold the public good. And the demise of that particular man removes the main cause of people's respect for the law. Of course, laws can never cure human beings of the dispositions that produce corruption. Yet they can "make men good" in the sense that they correct the quality of their actions, regulating them in ways that support public order.[50] To the extent that people consider the laws regulating their actions as reasonable, they will regard them as *their own* laws, not alien constraints imposed on them, and thus exert their own virtue to renovate them. This advantage is lost when citizens depend on a good man to purge corruption. The notion that one outstanding person can be trusted to do this casts the rest of his compatriots in the role of dependants. Instead of renovating orders through their own virtue, they rely on fortune or the heavens to send them such a man; and if by some "accident" he should "arise" among them, they must again depend on fortune or God to make him work for good and not for harm. Since their own role in the renewal is passive, there is nothing to make citizens themselves less corrupt than they were before the

[48] *D*, III.1.211/418–19.
[49] *D*, I.18 and III.1 use the contrast between *cognizione-conoscere* (knowledge) and *intendere* (understanding) to highlight this difference; see chap. 3 and compare *P*, III.12/124.
[50] *D*, I.3.15/208.

great man came forth. This is bad for civil virtue and for the renovator's enterprise. Since his authority is based on beliefs about his own personal qualities, whatever authority he gives to renewed laws and orders depends on citizens' feelings about him, and on their sustained belief in his special capacities. In most cases, however, such feelings and beliefs prove fickle and transient.[51]

Machiavelli's reasonings about extraordinary and ordinary modes have two main persuasive aims. First, they seek to purge readers of illusions about relying on high-risk means to promote what they see as good or necessary ends. The attractions of extraordinary short-cuts to establishing order are strong but deceptive. In all his main writings, Machiavelli stresses the limits of reasonable trust. No individual or small group should be trusted to use extraordinary modes for the common good.[52] "In a republic," Machiavelli writes, "one would not wish anything ever to happen that has to be governed with extraordinary modes," even when the ends are good: for "although the extraordinary mode may do good then, nonetheless the example does ill," since "if one sets up a habit of breaking the orders for the sake of good, then later, under that coloring, they are broken for ill [*si mette una usanza di rompere gli ordini per bene, che poi, sotto quel colore, si rompono per male*]."[53] Second, Machiavelli's arguments urge citizens and leaders under any form of government to establish corruption-preventing orders long before corruption advances. In the final chapter of the *Discourses* he writes: "It is of necessity . . . that in a great city accidents arise *every day* that have need of a physician, and according to their importance, one must find a wiser physician [*il medico più savio*]."[54] Although he does not say so explicitly, his arguments throughout the *Discourses* suggest that the laws, not individual men, are the most reliable physicians. For example, we read in Book I that "a republic will never be perfect unless it has provided for everything with its laws and has established a remedy for every accident and given the mode to govern it."[55] Well-ordered republics should not *need* to resort to dangerous extraordinary modes when faced with intrinsic or extrinsic necessities, because their laws already provide ways of dealing with these that are public, transparent, and regulated.

When citizens take a gamble with extraordinary modes instead of working harder to renovate through ordinary laws, they often blame fortune instead of their own bad choices when trouble ensues. For Machiavelli this passive, irresponsible attitude is a symptom of corruption among citizens themselves. If it runs

---

[51] As it was, for example, with Savonarola: see sec. 10.4, 392–93.

[52] There are, Machiavelli writes, "very evident reasons" why "magistrates that are made and authorities that are given through extraordinary ways, not those that come through ordinary ways, hurt republics." If a citizen "wants to be able to offend and to seize extraordinary authority for himself, he must have many qualities that in a non-corrupt republic he can never have," if he wants to gain stable and legitimate authority. Above all, he must have great wealth capable of buying supporters, which he cannot do in a well-ordered polity. Even if he had them, "free votes do not concur" in electing such formidable men. *D*, I.34.74/417–19.

[53] *D*, I.34.75/271–73.

[54] *D*, III.49.308/524. Compare *P*, III.12/124.

[55] *D*, I.34.75/272–73.

so deep that they persist in choosing apparently good men over laws as the chief means of solving their problems, this often spells the beginning of the end for a republic. It is, however, *their* choice. When citizens underestimate the corrosive effects of ambition even on men who seem good, they may opt for modes of renovation that fail to regulate ambitious "humors," perhaps even lifting restraints on them. This, in Machiavelli's view, is a massive failure of political responsibility. Strict laws designed to check corruption should be part of the bedrock of any well-ordered city, including emergency powers for dealing with very great threats. Laws and orders designed to hold public officials to account are among Machiavelli's main examples of preventive laws designed to stem corruption. These include "the remedy of assemblies" where the deeds and reputations of public officials can be freely scrutinized; orders that allow diverse humors to "be vented in a way ordered by the laws"; and public courts of law where officials or other leading citizens can be accused and judged according to transparent procedures.[56] Another Roman order was designed to deal with emergencies arising from "intrinsic or extrinsic accidents" such as conspiracies or wars. The office of dictator (*l'autorità dittatoria*) gave emergency powers to an individual "to do everything without consultation, and to punish everyone without appeal." While these powers were exceptional and extensive, however, Machiavelli refrains from calling them "extraordinary." Two legal constraints were designed to prevent dictators from seizing extraordinary powers: the authority of dictators was "given to them by the people" and subject to public scrutiny, and the dictator's tenure in office was strictly limited. As a general rule, "if a free authority [*autorità libera*] is given for a long time—calling a long time a year or more—it will always be dangerous." But the dangers were kept at bay so long as a dictator "was appointed for a time, and not perpetually" and "his authority extended to being able to decide by himself regarding remedies for that urgent danger" that had brought him to his position.[57]

Machiavelli's reservations about the use of extraordinary methods to renovate are further signaled by his ambivalent use of the word "fear" in relation to these methods. Virtue is undoubtedly strengthened when the ambition-deterring fear (*timore, paura*) involves fear of punishment under transparent public laws. When Machiavelli uses the words *timore* or *paura* in relation to the laws, the words connote two things: awe and respect based on a reasoned appreciation of the laws' value, and a prudent concern to avoid the punishments that are incurred

[56] *D*, I.4.17/209–10; I.6–8.22–28/213–22.
[57] *D*, I.34.74/271–72; I:5.19/210–12; I.34–35.75–77/272–74. Building on his reading of Machiavelli, Spinoza also evaluates the common opinion that diseases of state are best cured through "the wisdom of an outstanding man [*viri eximae virtutis*] instead of through a prudent law [*prudentia legum*]." The one-man solution, Spinoza suggests after reflections similar to Machiavelli's, depends too much on fortune. Thus "he who seeks to avoid the troubles which afflict a state [*imperii*] should use remedies consistent with the nature of that state, and deducible from its fundamental laws" instead of imported from outside; "otherwise the cure will be worse than the disease." Unless "dictatorial power is permanent and stable—in which case it cannot be vested in one man without destroying the form of the state—its very existence, and hence the safety and preservation of the commonwealth, will be very much a matter of chance [*incerta*]." Spinoza 1958 (1677), X.1.428–31.

when laws are broken. Fear in this sense is reasonable and order-promoting. But there is a different kind of fear that has order-corroding effects, and which is aroused not by reasoning about the laws but by the assertion of unrestrained wills. In Florence, Machiavelli writes, those who governed "used to say . . . that it was necessary to regain the state every five years." But what "they called regaining the state" was inspiring "that terror [*terrore*] and that fear [*paura*] in men" in the hopes of deterring anyone from trying to seize the state from them.[58] Whenever Machiavelli associates fear with *terrore* or "being terrified" or "dismayed" (*spaventare—spavento, sbigottire*) he describes an emotion that tends to destabilize civil orders.[59] While the "fear" aroused by extraordinary "executions" may have the salutary effect of making men draw back to due limits, it can also damage political virtue. It is appropriate to fear the consequences of violating duly authorized laws, and appropriate to feel "fear of the laws" if the meaning of fear is close to respect.[60] In the case of civil laws, such fear is based on known rules and penalties; it is not fear of the whims of rulers or shifts in power. In the case of the "law of nations," fear of laws means appropriate respect for human standards of justice. "Terror" is incompatible with stable orders because of its arbitrariness in these respects.[61]

Machiavelli does not argue, then, that extraordinary modes are justified by extreme threats to civil order. All the good effects that are commonly cited to justify extraordinary measures—forcing the ambitious to stay within due limits, purging corruption, preventing tyranny—can be produced more reliably through ordinary modes. Even when administered by the best of ancient men, extraordinary executions only produced "almost" the same good effects as those produced by good laws and orders. People who treat extraordinary acts and extreme necessities as the main stuff of politics miss a truth apparently so banal that it often goes unnoticed: namely, that the continuous renovation of ordinary modes is what makes for greatness, stability, and freedom. In cities made by and for human beings, not gods or beasts, questions about how to perform extraordinary acts are far less important than questions about how to regulate ordinary humors, desires, and tumults.

---

[58] *D*, III.1.211/418.

[59] For example, *FH*, I.5.14–15/367–68. Compare Hobbes (1996 [1652], 42), who also distinguishes between different senses of "fear" as religious awe and "panique terror," but suggests that those who experience the latter often have some apprehension of its reasonable cause.

[60] See Plato, *Seventh Letter* 337a–b; Iamblichus 1996, chap. 20.

[61] Similarly related Greek words for fear are *phobos* and *deinos*, roughly corresponding to Machiavelli's neutral or salutary *paura* and *timore*; his uses of *sbigottire*, *spaventare*, and *terrore* are comparable to many Greek authors' uses of words commonly translated as "dismayed," "extreme fear," or "terror," such as *kataplēxis*, *explēxia* or *explēxis*, and *dediotes*. Thucydides' Book VI contains numerous examples of these words used in ways that are comparable to Machiavelli's, especially in the last three books of the *FH*. See TPW, VI.33–34, 36–40, 98; VII.44, 71; VIII.1, 96.

10.4.
Unreasonable uses of religion: Easy ways to acquire authority

Ordinary modes and laws are grounded in merely human authority. But as Machiavelli frequently notes, no human being can be trusted to make good judgments about policies and laws all the time. To make the best of their fallible human matter, orderers should make it a priority to "order" procedures that allow the many to deliberate laws and policies openly, since free discussion improves their chances of judging well.[62] But did Machiavelli also think that transparent public reasoning was the best way to gain authority when new orders were still being established? He was well aware that historically speaking, most human laws and orders had not been grounded primarily in public reasoning. Most of the ancient *ordinatori* he discusses sought to anchor the authority of their laws in some more commanding source. They often combined an account of the human necessity for their laws and orders with an appeal to divine authority. It has usually been assumed that Machiavelli accepts the wisdom of this approach to "ordering" and advises both republics and princes to imitate it.[63] On this reading, prudent orderers should use appeals to God or religion to found their own authority and that of their laws. If this is indeed Machiavelli's view, how can it be reconciled with his argument that ordinary modes and transparent human reasoning should be the *fondamenti* of authority in human cities? This section takes issue with the most usual interpretation of Machiavelli's remarks on civil religion by distinguishing more clearly between its reasonable and unreasonable uses. Sections 10.5. and 10.6. try to clarify Machiavelli's grounds for treating some political uses of religion as reasonable, and asks how far these uses fall within the bounds of ordinary modes.

Despite his arguments for a politics founded solely on human reasoning, Machiavelli seems to endorse appeals to superhuman authority when he considers how religious modes may help to support new political orders. In Book I, chapters 11–15 of the *Discourses*, he considers how the first Roman orderers used religion to help them acquire political authority. "Whoever considers well the Roman histories," he writes, "sees how much religion [*religione*] served to command armies, to animate the plebs, to keep men good, to bring shame to the wicked [*rei*]." These beneficial effects of religion were attributed to Romulus' successor, Numa Pompilius. Although Rome's "first orderer" Romulus gave the city its main "civil and military orders," Machiavelli notes that Numa often receives more praise for treating religion "as a thing altogether necessary if he wished to maintain a civilization [*una civiltà*]." According to this opinion, Numa wisely realized that religion is an invaluable aid that makes it easier for orderers to introduce new institutions. As Machiavelli puts it,

> where there is religion, arms can easily [*facilmente*] be introduced, and where there are arms and not religion, the latter can be introduced only with difficulty. One sees that for Romulus to order the Senate and to make other

---

[62] On free speech, see chap. 9, sec. 9.1, and chap. 11, sec. 11.6.

[63] For example, Cassirer 1946, 138; Berlin 1981 (1958), 45–50. For valuable reappraisals of the view that Machiavelli had an entirely instrumental view of religion, see de Grazia 1989 and Viroli, forthcoming.

civil and military orders, the authority of God was not necessary; but it was quite necessary [*bene necessario*] to Numa, who pretended [*simulò*] to be intimate with a nymph who counseled him on what he had to counsel the people. It all arose because he wished to put new and unaccustomed orders [*ordini nuovi ed inusitati*] in the city and doubted that his authority would suffice. And truly there was never any orderer of extraordinary laws [*leggi straordinarie*] for a people who did not have recourse to God, because otherwise they would not have been accepted. . . . For a prudent individual knows many goods that do not have in themselves evident reasons with which one can persuade others [*conosciuti da uno prudente, i quali non hanno in sé ragioni evidenti da poterli persuadere a altrui*]. Thus wise men [*uomini savi*] who wish to take away this difficulty have recourse to God.[64]

Taken at face value, this passage might seem to endorse the following claims:

(1) Recourse to some form of religion or "divine cult" (*culto divino*) is "quite necessary" to order stable, well-armed polities.
(2) The chief advantage of religion for political ordering is that it makes it easier to introduce institutions and practices needed to sustain good orders, such as arms.

A broader implication of each claim is that if an orderer seeks to establish arms where ordinary means of persuasion do not suffice, he is wise to present the divine sources of his authority in ways that cannot be directly subject to public scrutiny. Since "evident reasons" are not always enough to persuade others to back one's orders, appeals to sagacious nymphs or God's will provide indispensable support. Numa is counted among the "wise men" because he found a way to persuade the people to accept his authority that could not be falsified by such reasons.

Clearly Machiavelli rejects theocratic doctrines that ground political legitimacy primarily or solely in supernatural authority. Yet if he endorsed these two weaker claims and their implications, his commitment to the values of transparency, accountability, and demanding standards of public reasoning must be more tenuous than I have argued. If the usual reading is right, Machiavelli must have subordinated these values to more fundamental "goods" known to a handful of exceptional "orderers." But this reading overlooks important nuances in Machiavelli's remarks on the political uses of religion.[65] The long passage just cited is teeming with ambivalent phrases and normatively loaded words that beg questions about the usual, crudely instrumentalist view of Machiavelli's idea of a "civil religion." The instrumentalist view has, I suggest, all the hallmarks of an insufficiently reflective opinion held by those considered "wise" that stands in need of critical examination. Bearing

---

[64] *D*, I.11.34–35/230.

[65] And misses the ironies. See Neville and Rousseau, whose *Social Contract* quotes the passage untranslated in a footnote at II.7. Unfortunately, many readers also overlook the irony in Rousseau's remarks on religion, mistaking (I would argue) him too to be arguing for the political instrumentalization of religion; see, for example, Grant 1997. This reading loses sight of the critical undercurrent of both authors' arguments about how religion is often used for partisan and oppressive ends.

in mind the codelike idiosyncrasies of Machiavelli's language, let us look again at the two claims he seems to make in the passage.

The first claim (1) that "recourse to God" or a "divine cult" is "necessary" to order stable, well-defended polities is subtly examined throughout Book I, chapter 11. Machiavelli's reasonings do not aim to undermine the claim altogether, but prompt readers to distinguish more carefully between genuine necessity and merely self-serving or partisan notions of what is necessary. A first suggestion that readers should demand a more reasoned account of claim (1) occurs in the very first sentence of the chapter. We read here that "since the heavens judged [giudicando i cieli] that the orders of Romulus would not suffice for such an empire [imperio], they inspired in the breast of the Roman Senate the choosing of Numa Pompilius" as Romulus' successor so that Numa could order the things "omitted" (lasciate indietro) by the first orderer. Here claims about the "necessity" of religion are traced to two sources whose authority in fundamental matters of human ordering is questionable: the heavens and the Roman Senate. The judgment of the heavens is a questionable basis for determining the necessity for new orders, since people who possess merely ordinary cognitive capacities, such as Machiavelli himself, cannot know with certainty what the heavens judge. They cannot, then, reasonably give heavenly wishes authority as a basis for civil orders. Though judgments attributed to the heavens often accord with reasonable ethical judgments, they are not an acceptable *foundation* for human authorities. Machiavelli's reference to the judgment of the heavens is thus tinged with irony. His reference to the judgment "inspired" by the heavens in "the breast of the Roman Senate" is doubly questionable: first because no mortal can be sure what the heavens might really have to do with it, and second because, as Machiavelli showed in preceding chapters, the Senate during the Roman monarchy was often driven by private ambitions and unreasonable fears of popular desires for freedom.

By way of these subtle hints, Machiavelli poses the question: who can be trusted to judge whether religion is necessary for political ordering? His careful phrasing in the long passage cited above casts further doubt on the divine sources of Numa's religious "orders" and the genuine necessity of the Senate's decision to give them authority. Machiavelli intimates doubts through his slyly drawn contrast between Numa's modes of ordering and those of his predecessor Romulus. Recall that "for Romulus to order the Senate and to make other civil and military orders, the authority of God was not necessary." By contrast, divine authority "was quite necessary to Numa" since "he wished to put new and unaccustomed orders in the city and doubted that his authority would suffice." Here Machiavelli suggests that each *ordinatore* made his own judgment about the necessity to rely on God's authority; and the basis for his judgment was whether or not he trusted merely human sources to authorize his orders. Romulus did not need to appeal to divine authority because he was prudent enough to ground his orders firmly in reasons "evident" to others.[66] Numa did judge it necessary to have "recourse to

[66] Machiavelli does not see Romulus' example as entirely worthy of imitation, as argued in chaps. 9 and 11.

God" because he doubted the sufficiency of his own authority and the judgment of his subjects. Numa and the Roman Senate, Machiavelli implies, used religion in ways that reflected mistrust of their own ordinary capacities to gain popular support for their "new and unaccustomed," aristocratic and monarchical orders. For Machiavelli such mistrust indicates a serious deficit of *virtú*, and leads orderers to rely too much on the "arms" of others—in this case, those of the heavens and counsel-giving nymphs. Orderers who deem it necessary to have recourse to God are probably underexercising their own self-legislative *virtú*, which requires them to give reasons for their laws that relate to purely human considerations.

If orderers doubt that they can rely on the authority of such reasons to found new orders, one must ask why this is. One answer might be that the value of some goods cannot be expressed or evaluated through ordinary reasoning. But even if it were sometimes true that "a prudent individual knows many goods that do not have in themselves evident reasons with which one can persuade others," it does not follow that the most prudent solution to this problem is, as "wise men" think, to "have recourse to God." When Machiavelli speaks of "wise men" he often means men who are mistakenly considered wise according to unreflective or corrupt opinions.[67] Wise men "wish to take away" the ordinary and natural difficulties that attend all human reasonings, seeking short-cuts that save them the trouble of persuasion. Prudent men know the disadvantages of such short-cuts. They judge that "it is good to reason about everything," and recognize that in any case the difficulties of seeking reasoned authority cannot be "taken away" as the "wise" might wish.[68] Readers of the passage on Numa should therefore ask whether so-called wise men seek to avoid the difficulties of reasoned persuasion because it is hard, or because they want to place some matters beyond the reach of critical public questioning. "Wise" orderers may prefer to pretend that nymphs or the heavens advised them to create a order from on high, so that these matters are insulated from the frequent public examinations that are, according to Machiavelli, essential to maintain civil order. But Machiavelli implies that Romulus' methods of gaining authority for his orders were superior to those used by Numa because they relied on human resources—his own *virtú* and appeals to ordinary reasons—alone.

When Machiavelli declares that "truly there was never any orderer of extraordinary laws for a people who did not have recourse to God, because otherwise they would not have been accepted," the irony should by now be clear. He is not saying that orderers must "necessarily" appeal to God's authority because people do not readily accept *any* laws when these are grounded only on ordinary reasons. He is suggesting that when orderers seek to enact laws based on *extraordinary*— that is, questionably legitimate—authority, they "must" have recourse to God because "extraordinary laws" would never be accepted on the orderer's merely human authority. Since a clear antithesis between ordinary and extraordinary modes was drawn in the *Discourses'* preceding chapters, when the phrase "extraordinary laws" appears in chapter 11 it looks suspiciously like an oxymoron. The suspicion

---

[67] This ironic usage is common in Greek (especially Socratic) writing; see chaps. 1–2 on the Sophists.
[68] *D*, I.18.49/247–48.

is that anyone who seeks to institute "extraordinary laws" is concerned to establish private or partisan powers under color of legal forms. This explains why people are unlikely to accept "extraordinary laws," making it seem necessary for proponents of such laws to appeal to some authority other than "evident reasons."

This brings us to the second claim (2) that Machiavelli seems to endorse, namely that the chief advantage of religion for political ordering is that it makes it easier to introduce new orders. The words "easy," "easily," and "easiness" (*facile, facilmente, facilità*) appear many times in Book I, chapter 11. Since Numa

> found a very ferocious people and wished to reduce it to civil obedience [*ridurre nelle obedienze civili*] with the arts of peace, he turned to religion as a thing altogether necessary if he wished to maintain a civilization; and he constituted it so that for many centuries there was never so much fear of God [*timore del Dio*] as in that republic, which made *easier* whatever enterprise [*facilitò qualunque impresa*] the Senate or the great men of Rome might plan to make. . . . Marveling, thus, at his goodness and prudence, the Roman people yielded to his every decision. Indeed it is true that since those times were full of religion and the men with whom he had to labor were crude [*grossi*], they made much *easier* the carrying out of his plans, since he could *easily* impress any new form whatever on them. Without doubt, whoever wished to make a republic in the present times would find it *easier* among mountain men, where there is no civilization, than among those who are used to living in cities, where civilization is corrupt.[69]

Here we are told bluntly that appeals to religious or superhuman authority are useful short-cuts to political ends. Orderers who have successful "recourse to God" experience less pressure to set out persuasive public reasons for their laws and orders. But can these easier means of achieving ends produce the same stability and virtue in polities as the harder work of ordinary, public reasoning? Once again, attention to Machiavelli's choice of words alerts readers to three critical judgments behind initial appearances.[70]

First, Machiavelli hints strongly at the private or partisan purposes of Numa's instrumentalized "religion." Those who make use of religion here are "the Senate and the great men of Rome," who after Numa were able to use it "for *whatever* enterprise" they might conceive. This suggests that Numa's introduction of "new and unaccustomed" religious modes did not provide the foundations for a stronger sense of the common good between the *grandi* and the people at large. By appealing to supernatural authority, this kind of civil religion made it easier for the few to "reduce" the many to obedience, and thus to pursue "whatever enterprise" they might conceive.[71] Readers must wonder, however, whether such a religion can contribute much to political virtue. The passage suggests that the use of religion

---

[69] *D*, I.11.34–35/229–20; emphasis added.

[70] Compare *AW*, IV.98–99/625–26 on religion making it "easier" to exert authority.

[71] See Sullivan 1996, 102–17, for a similar reading of this passage. Compare the ironic language of *FH*, I on the Crusades, which Machiavelli insists on simply calling the "enterprise" (*impresa*).

to reduce people to "civil obedience" is a method appropriate only for crude or uncivilized people, or for people regarded as crude by those who use religion to gain popular obedience. In not trusting the sole authority of good laws and orders to support *civilità*, Numa and his followers showed their low esteem for the capacity of the many to understand the reasons for obeying the laws. In effect, they treated the Roman people as "nothing other than a brute animal" that could only be tamed by the "fear of God," when it should have been ordered ordinarily by "knowing how to reason about . . . public defense or public offense." This made it "easier" for the great to command obedience, but harder for the people ruled in this way to develop an "aptitude for free life" that arises from such "inequalities." In the context of Machiavelli's analysis of Rome's early days in Book I, then, Numa's use of religion represents a corruption of Romulus' more prudent "first orders"; and its corrupting effects made it hard to reorder for freedom when Rome's kings were replaced by republican orders.[72]

Second, even if it were reasonable to believe that orderers have no partisan purposes but are motivated solely by the public good, one might still ask whether the "easiness" of appeals to divine authority is advantageous for political orders based on that authority. As previous chapters have shown, whenever Machiavelli says that certain methods make it "easy" to achieve ends, the words *facile* or *facilmente* signal skepticism about the genuine wisdom of the claim. If the first ten chapters of the *Discourses* make one thing clear, it is that good political orders are never founded or maintained easily. Continual *industria* is needed from the start to prevent any sect or "the few" from introducing elements that make for future disorders, such as those introduced by Numa and the Roman Senate. Easiness is not a political value for Machiavelli; it is almost always a symptom of corrupting vice.[73] Maintaining orders requires unceasing labor aimed at bringing polities back to sound first principles. Orders made or maintained easily are thus unlikely to support civil *virtú*.

Third, orders founded on freely given, publicly reasoned authority are more appropriate for human cities than orders based on facile appeals to nymphs or God, and hence more likely to be well maintained. Even non-partisan legislators who depend on divine authority may commit one of two common errors. They may make laws that demand too much of mere mortals because their standards are superhuman. Conversely, their laws may be too lenient because they trust that God will intervene to correct "natural and ordinary" human failings. Machiavelli's ethics seeks to avoid both errors by making human beings wholly responsible for the content and authority of their own laws. Moreover, people who are asked to accept laws on divine authority may fail to examine the more mundane, everyday reasons for the limits set on their actions by the laws. For Machiavelli, the

[72] *D*, I.16.44/242–43; I.17.48–49/244–45. In I.19.53/249–50 Machiavelli says that Numa depended less on *virtú* and more on fortune than Romulus. Compare Neville (1681, III.2), who writes that the "true religion" needs no Numa "to plant and establish it," but only the power and spirit of God.

[73] Thus when in *D*, I.1 he notes that the Athenians and Venetians sought to make life "easier" for themselves by moving to a more clement site, the resulting "idleness" they were able to enjoy brought a transient "happiness," but insufficient virtue to maintain it.

principles that underpin any human orders must be grasped through reasoning about the ordinary necessities of human coexistence, especially those posed by innate human freedom. When citizens understand the ordinary and reasonable necessity for public limits on their freedom, they are more likely to defend these limits against those who seek to overstep them, rejecting various decent-sounding excuses for compromising the rule of law. When the necessity imposed by laws is conceived primarily as a divine necessity, however, the ordinary run of people—those who, like Machiavelli, do not claim to know God's intentions—will be less clear about their own civic responsibilities. In corrupt or insecure times, they may be more vulnerable to appeals by men who do claim to know God's will, and who invoke it to support extraordinary modes.

These reflections almost completely undermine the two claims that Machiavelli seems to make in his remarks about Numa Pompilius' civil religion. Against claim (1), he suggests many reasons to doubt that appeals to God are necessary to give authority to human laws and orders. Against claim (2), he implies that if appeals to divine authority do make it easier to achieve particular political ends, they may also short-circuit the hard work needed to build stable foundations for legitimate authority. I say that the undermining is *almost* complete because, as the next section argues, Machiavelli does allow that appeals to God's authority may *supplement* ordinary human reasons to underwrite civil laws and orders. But the implicit message of Book I, chapter 11 is that divine authority should not be treated as a *substitute* for the authority given through the laborious work of human reasoning. If it is treated as a substitute, short-cut, or rival to ordinary reasons, it will be an inadequate foundation for civil orders even if the orderers are free of private or partisan aims.

Machiavelli does not suggest that when political leaders get away with using religion in unreasonable ways, only they and not the people who accept their extraordinary actions are responsible for the resulting corruption. People who place divine authority above their own ordinary and human authorization for public orders are also responsible for shortfalls of virtue. Machiavelli acknowledges that the motives of ordinary citizens and political orderers are often different. When large numbers of citizens rush to embrace a leader's claims to have the authority of God on his side—especially when this happens in a republic—they are often driven by weariness of civil conflicts or war, or by fear of others' ambitions. Even in better circumstances, it takes hard work to gain public authority by ordinary means alone. In threatening or unstable conditions, it can be extremely tempting to believe that some wise individuals might know "many goods that do not have in themselves evident reasons with which one can persuade others." If such individuals could be found, they would save everyone else a great deal of work.

Machiavelli took a great interest in the methods used by charismatic men to present themselves in this light. In his own times religious leaders such as Girolamo Savonarola (1452–98) acquired a huge political following among people who considered themselves to be sophisticated citizens. Machiavelli ends the chapter dealing with Numa by noting that although the Florentine people were not uncivilized "mountain men" who could easily be swayed by superstitious appeals, their enthusiasm for Savonarola proves that

Although coarse men may be more easily persuaded to a new order or opinion, this does not make it impossible also to persuade to it civilized men who presume they are not coarse. To the people of Florence it does not appear that they are either ignorant or coarse; nonetheless, they were persuaded by Friar Girolamo Savonarola that he spoke with God.

The critical implications of the entire chapter become more apparent here, as Machiavelli explicitly compares his compatriots' credulity with that of the less civilized Roman people at Numa's reported conversations with a nymph. "I do not," Machiavelli continues, "wish to judge" whether Savonarola's claim "is true or not, because one should speak with reverence of such a man; but I do say," he concludes with gentle irony, "that an infinite number believed him without having seen anything extraordinary to make them believe him."[74] Had they also demanded "evident reasons" why they should give him such authority, the friar's followers might have been less dismayed by his failure to deliver the results he promised. If so many non-coarse citizens were prepared to embrace the authority of such a man, this shows that they had either ceased to value their free orders or forgotten why transparent public reasoning must be their foundation.

The *Histories* describe other citizens who knew how to invoke God for "extraordinary" political ends. Here Machiavelli links this rhetoric to political "deceit" and the "tyrannical" methods of the Medici party. He has a group of exiles complain that Piero Medici and his followers "were accustomed to living tyrannically" and had "by deceit taken up arms" and "by deceit" driven them out of their fatherland. "Nor," continue the exiles, "were they content with this, but they used God as a means to oppress many others who remained in the city." And "so that God be a participant in their treacheries, they had many citizens imprisoned and killed in the midst of public and sacred ceremonies and solemn prayers."[75] Machiavelli gives no reason to question the exiles' account of these methods. Citizens of republican Florence were exhausted by centuries of partisan division and bewildering, often virulent rhetoric dramatized in the *Histories*. Many must have welcomed appeals to God as a relief from all the usual partisan arguments heard in the piazza. In the longer term, however, citizens who rely too much on divine authority and mistrust their own powers of authorization undermine the foundations of free civil orders. Machiavelli's analyses of various unreasonable uses of religion in politics encourage ordinary citizens to take responsibility for scrutinizing public appeals to God, so that they will not "easily" be induced to give up their own share of civil authority.

---

[74] *D*, I.11.36/231. See Machiavelli's detailed dissection of Savonarola's preaching in his letter to Ricciardo Becci, 9 March 1498, *MF*, 8–10/5–8.

[75] *FH*, VII.19.298/654–55. Rhetoric invoking God in the *FH* becomes more frequent and fearsome in later books, as the free orders of the republic are corroded and citizens forget why it is important to found public authority on transparent human reasoning. Compare Thucydides' increasing use of words describing extreme fear, including fear of divine retribution for alleged blasphemies, after the Athenians take their poorly reasoned decision to attack Sicily.

10.5.

Reasonable uses of religion: Fear of God and fear of human justice

The last section suggested two main criteria for judging political appeals to divine authority as unreasonable: when such appeals are used for partisan ends, and when they are used to avoid the work of seeking authorization through transparent public reasoning. This section argues that Machiavelli does not object to political uses of religion when they *supplement* reasoned arguments for the authority of human laws instead of circumventing them. But ordinary human reasons must retain clear primacy among sources of the laws' authority. The standards implicit in Machiavelli's concept of *ordinario*, I suggest, serve as a touchstone for distinguishing between more and less reasonable uses of religion in politics. To see how Machiavelli develops the distinction, let us start by examining another puzzle set out in the same chapter of the *Discourses* that we have been discussing. Here he mentions another ostensible advantage for orderers who have "recourse to God": the capacity of religion to instill fear (*timore*) and, through this fear, to secure commitment to the public good and respect for authority. Where the fear of God is widespread, it is easier to introduce good arms; where citizens fear divine punishment if they break oaths, they are more likely to fulfill their duties to serve the common good.[76] On the one hand, Machiavelli's reflective arguments support these *ends*. On the other, his preference for "ordinary" modes might seem to question the use of religious fear as a legitimate *means* of achieving the ends. How can these two positions be reconciled?

The answer is related to the distinction drawn earlier between two senses of "fear." Machiavelli distinguishes between two kinds of political fear: a virtuous fear (*timore, paura*) of human laws and justice on the one hand, and a virtue-corroding fear or terror (*terrore*) of arbitrary or extraordinary decrees on the other. His discussions of religion make a similar distinction between two kinds of fear toward God. One is a respectful fear of just punishment, based on ordinary reasoning about the rightness or wrongness of actions. The other is an unreasoning fear of supernatural forces, aroused by people who claim to know God's intentions but cannot or will not give "evident reasons" for them.[77] Machiavelli provides a good example of the second kind of religious fear in Book I, chapter 13 of the *Discourses*. When the aristocratic and monarchical institutions founded by Romulus had been replaced by the orders of a republic, the newly empowered Roman people at first gave high-ranking positions of authority to men of their own plebeian ranks. This caused resentment among the "nobles"—descendants of members of Numa's Senate—who were unhappy about having to share authority with the plebs.

> After the Roman people had created tribunes with consular power and they were all plebeians except for one, when plague and famine occurred that

---

[76] D, I.11.34–35/229–30.

[77] The distinction is made in a number of Greek texts. On the idea that it is necessary to cultivate fear (*phobos*) of the laws in citizens, and that this fear is closely related to respectful modesty or shame (*aidō*), see Plato, *Laws* 699c and *Seventh Letter* 337a–b.

year and certain prodigies came, the nobles used the opportunity in the next creation of tribunes to say that the gods were angry because Rome had used the majesty of its empire badly, and that there was no remedy for placating the gods other than to return the election of tribunes to its place. From this it arose that the plebs, terrified by this religion [*sbigottita da questa religione*], created as tribunes all nobles.[78]

When Machiavelli uses the words *sbigottire* (to dismay, terrify), *spaventare* (to frighten), or *terrore* (terror), he invariably alludes to the virtue-corroding effects of the fear so described. Another example occurs in the next paragraph, again involving attempts by the Roman *nobili* to deprive tribunes of the plebs of their legitimate authority. When a particular tribune proposed a law, "among the first remedies that the nobility used against him was religion." One of their methods was to have the city's oracles, the Sybilline books, "respond that through civil sedition [*civile sedizione*], dangers of losing its freedom hung over the city that year." Although this ruse was "exposed by the tribunes," it "nonetheless put such terror in the breasts of the plebs" that their support for the tribune's laws "cooled off" (*raffreddò*). Another mode in which the nobles used religion was to use the occasion of a siege of the Capitol by "a multitude of exiles and slaves" to instill fears of a more dangerous, external invasion. Although the tribunes persisted in proposing their law, "saying that the onslaught was pretended and not true [*simulato e non vero*]," the plebs at large were badgered into agreeing not to discuss the law that favored their interests. In these ways, Machiavelli concludes, "religion made the Senate overcome the difficulties that would never have been overcome without it."[79] He clearly is not presenting the Senate's uses of "religious" intimidation as prudent or deserving of imitation. These Roman examples furnish cautionary lessons for those who want to guard the freedom of vulnerable republics, alerting citizens to remain vigilant against attempts by the few to "terrify" the many in order to dominate them.[80]

What then might constitute a reasonable use of religious fear to support civil orders? Machiavelli gives examples of such uses alongside the less reasonable ones in the chapters under discussion. In Book I, chapter 11 we read:

Whoever reviews [*discorrerà*] infinite actions, both of the Roman people and of many Romans by themselves, will see that the citizens feared to break an oath much more than the laws [*temevono più assai rompere il giuramento che le leggi*], like those who esteemed the power of God more than that of men.

[78] *D*, I.13.39/234–35.
[79] *D*, I.13.40–41/235–36; see Livy, *LH*, III.15–21. The law was the Terentillian law.
[80] In the first book of the *FH* Machiavelli (I.5.15/318–19) remarks that changes of religion were introduced by means of terror: "the struggle between the *custom* of the ancient faith and the *miracles* of the new"—custom corresponding to ordinary, miracles to extraordinary modes—generated "the gravest tumults and disorders" among men. Sectarian divisions within Christianity produced "so many persecutions" that "men bore the terror [*spavento*] of their spirit written in their eyes, because, aside from the infinite evils they endured, for a good part of them the possibility of seeking refuge in God, in whom all the miserable are wont to hope, was lacking." Compare *D*, II.5 on Christianity eliminating other sects.

Here Machiavelli hints at the priority of reasoned standards of justice over specific, positive laws. The former are reasonably *represented* as having the "power of God." But they are *grounded*, as Machiavelli goes on to note, in an individual's "own honor to obey the oath [*giuramente*] he had taken."[81] In this context, men who esteem "the power of God more than the power of men" do so on the basis of ordinary human reasonings. They identify the obligations created by self-imposed oaths with whatever is held most sacred among men; and they regard the authority of these obligations as more compelling than any particular human power, including positive laws. "Keeping faith" is regarded by non-corrupt peoples as a fundamental human duty, whether or not it is enforced by civil laws: it is held "sacred" in private relations among individuals, and embodied in the "law of nations" held to apply to acts not covered by civil laws. The religious commitment to duties of keeping faith to other human beings has sources independent of civil laws, and is considered binding even when laws do not enforce such duties. This is the kind of religious fear that helps to support civil orders.[82]

As we saw with the Fabii who "violated the law of nations" and other examples, Machiavelli's judgments about what counts as reasonable fear of God presuppose judgments about the reasonableness of ethical "orders."[83] Human beings have always identified basic ethical duties to keep promises with commands from God. But in the absence of secure knowledge about divine intentions, ordinary reasoning can find strong and evident reasons for recognizing the same duties. If a credulous opinion turns out to be based on such judgments, leaders such as Camillus who "favor and magnify" it cannot simply be seen as playing on superstitions. It is reasonable for people to fear punishment when they have violated a human law that they know is reasonable. If no human punishment is forthcoming, they often project their awareness of their own wrongdoing onto "miraculous" signs that the heavens are angry, seeing their own guilt in every natural or human disaster. Fear of God in this sense arises from a sense of human justice, which reasonable forms of religion identify with divine commands. When Machiavelli says that in the early republic the Roman people were "full of religion" (*ripieni di religione*) and associates this religiosity with respect for oaths, customs, and laws, he implies that these attitudes were consistent with ordinary reasoning about what is necessary to sustain human orders. They stand in stark contrast to the spurious necessity evoked by forms of religion that rely on unreasoning intimidation.[84]

Machiavelli illustrates these judgments with another episode from Roman history. The tribunes of the plebs, he reports, gave a public oath never to depart from the wishes of whoever should hold the office of consul. But when the consul present at the original oath was killed and replaced by another man hostile to the plebs'

---

[81] *D*, I.11.34/229. Note the implicit contrast between the reasonable religious attitudes of the Roman people and a few individuals, and the unreasonable uses of religion by the nobles and Senate in the same chapters and periods.

[82] Compare Thucydides and Livy on the need for good customs and religion; see chaps. 2, 5.

[83] See chaps. 5, 8.

[84] *D*, I.12.37/232–33. Here Machiavelli contrasts the Roman people's reverence toward public temples with unvirtuous uses of religion by "the princes of the Christian republic."

aims, the tribunes refused to follow him, insisting that their oath had been given to the dead consul alone. The plebs themselves, however, adhered to the impersonal terms of the oath, affirming that they had sworn a principled oath of allegiance to an office, not to a particular man. They considered themselves bound by a self-imposed, impersonal obligation despite the new consul's hostility to their ends. This example shows, Machiavelli remarks, that "for fear of religion [*per paura della religione*] the plebs wished rather to obey the [new] consul than to believe the tribunes." They then declared "in favor of the ancient religion [*in favore della antica religione*]" that they refused to consider themselves so corrupt as to think that each could "make oath and laws suitable by interpreting for himself [*nec interpretando sibi quisque jusjurandum et leges aptas faciebat*]."[85] The phrase "fear of religion" here is nearly synonymous with respect for principles of human justice, which set the standards for civil laws and orders. This, not the manipulative use of un-reasoned fear, is the kind of religious supplement to established civil orders that Machiavelli has in mind.

Moreover, "fear of religion" in the sense of "fear of God's wrath" supplements these basic, principled reasons for adhering to oaths. Although God's feelings cannot be known, the apprehension of his disapproval is reasonable in two respects. It is reasonable to fear the bad consequences that always follow acts of injustice; and it is reasonable to judge that such acts are wrong in principle. Machiavelli touches on this second kind of reason for "fearing religion" when he remarks that the tribunes set aside their initial opposition to the new consul not out of deference to the plebs or fear of the nobles, but "fearing because of this thing lest they lose all their dignity." The context suggests that the loss of dignity they feared involved the loss of others' *ethical* respect, not just a loss of status or face.[86] Men who violate laws and oaths based on self-legislated justice lose their *dignità* because by contravening their freely given faith, they show a lack of respect for the undertakings that alone make dignified human life possible. Whether one calls it fear of God or fear of justice, this reasonable kind of fear is *necessary* to sustain any civil orders over time: as the observance of religion in this sense causes greatness in republics, "so disdain for it is the cause of their ruin."[87] Laws must be backed by plausible threats that public force will be used against offenders. But they also inspire awe and respect by virtue of the common labors that produce them, and by the recognition that without laws or justice there could be no stable orders worthy of human standards.

When religious fear is separated from these ordinary reasonings, however, Machiavelli implies that its role in seeking *public* authority should be strictly limited. His examples question whether any stable orders can be maintained through the use of fear in the sense connoted by the words *terrore, spaventare,* and *sbigot-tire*. Such uses of religion subvert rather than support ordinary modes of seeking

[85] *D*, I.13.40/236; quoting Livy, *LH*, III.20.

[86] Ibid.

[87] "For where the fear of God fails," Machiavelli writes, "it must be either that the kingdom comes to ruin or that it is sustained by the fear of a prince, which supplies the defects of religion." And since even virtuous princes have short lives, "it must be that the kingdom will fail soon." *D*, I.11.35/230–31.

political authority. Ordinary and reasonable fear of the laws is grounded in two conditions: respect for the processes of public authorization, and the threat that force will be used to punish violations of the laws. In relation to threats to use force, we have seen that Machiavelli insists on the difference between two kinds: threats of force authorized by law and applied according to ordinary, publicly known and authorized standards; and threats not authorized by law or applied according to such standards. The ordinary kind of threat is supposed to elicit fear that deters people from breaking the laws and disturbing orders. The second, extraordinary kind makes men "terrified" or fills them with "fright" (*spavento*). These emotions cause them to throw up their normal defenses, rendering them passive and easier to control. But they also disable them from acting prudently or virtuously. Terrified people are people whose capacities for self-legislative reasoning are paralyzed. When people are forced to flee in abject terror from their beleaguered fatherland, they can do it no good. When on the contrary they are forced by those authorized to uphold the laws "to remain and fulfil their duties to defend the common ground," people are forced not to suspend their own powers of reasoning but to recall them and use them more effectively.[88]

Machiavelli's distinctions between reasonable and unreasonable uses of religion point to two very different meanings of the word *religione* itself. One (R1) identifies religion with oracles, miracles, prophecies, and supernatural conversations that cannot be confirmed by "evident reasons." The other (R2) identifies religion with ethical principles and obligations that are the necessary foundation of human orders, and which are grounded in reflective reasoning.[89] (R1) goes hand in hand with excessive dependence on fortune, and hence tends to promote irresponsible attitudes to politics. (R2) supports a politics of self-responsible *virtú*. "The life of the Gentile religion," Machiavelli writes,

> was founded on the responses of the oracles and on the sect of the diviners and augurs. All their other ceremonies, sacrifices, and rites depended on them; for they easily believed that that god [*iddio*] who could predict your future good or your future ill for you could also grant it to you. From these arose the temples, from these the sacrifices, from these the supplications and

---

[88] *D*, I.11.34/229. This raises a question about means and ends: is it reasonable for political orderers to issue "terrifying" warnings of divine retribution if their aim is to reinforce ordinary, publicly authorized threats of force? The main thrust of Machiavelli's arguments opposes such attempts to combine ordinary ends with extraordinary means. If methods of religious *terrore* are introduced in the name of good civil ends, the use of "extraordinary" means is likely to corrupt these ends. By causing citizens to relinquish their ordinary powers of public reasoning, political intimidation makes the maintenance of order depend on the contingent, transient virtues of individual leaders.

[89] Compare Spinoza's usage in his *Tractatus theologico-politicus* (2007 [1669–70], Pref.1–6 *et passim*); and Rousseau, who does much the same in the *Social Contract*, II.7.381–85 and III.8.460–69. The relation between these distinctions in Machiavelli's thought and Hobbes' (esp. 1996 [1651], 245–59) discussion of more and less reasonable forms of religion also deserves closer study. As noted earlier, Hobbes uses the uncolloquial language of "ordinary" and "extraordinary" throughout his discussions of religion in the *Leviathan*, raising questions about possible ancient sources and influence by Machiavelli in this respects. See esp. ibid. 198, 224, 257, 281, 295.

every other ceremony to venerate them. . . . As these later began to speak in
the mode of the powerful [*parlare a modo de' potenti*], and as that falsity was
exposed among peoples, men became incredulous and apt to disturb every
good order.[90]

The distinction between (R1) and (R2) explains the ambivalent use of the word
"religion" that follows this passage: "princes of a republic or a kingdom should
maintain the foundations of the *religion* they hold; and if this is done, it will be
an easy thing for them to maintain their republic *religious* and, in consequence,
good and united."[91] This statement is true if the words "religion" and "religious" are
understood in sense (R2), but not if they are taken in sense (R1).

One of Machiavelli's clearest ancient examples of the distinction occurs in the
chapter on Numa Pompilius. After Hannibal's devastating defeat of the Roman
army at Cannae many citizens, "terrified for their fatherland [*sbigottiti della patria*]," decided to abandon Italy and move to Sicily. In one of his more praiseworthy
actions on Machiavelli's often critical accounts, Scipio Africanus went to these citizens and "constrained them to swear [*costrinse a giurare*] they would not abandon
the fatherland." Here Machiavelli identifies the obligation to defend one's fatherland
with the precepts of a reasonable ancient religion. The moral force of the obligation
does not arise simply from the fact that it is owed to the *patria*; it is related to the
sanctity of oaths and obligations per se. Whether the oath is to defend one's fatherland, to obey whoever holds consular office, or not to attack a foreign people, its
obligatory force—and thus its "religious" sanctity—are the same.[92] In this instance,
it is also true that the citizens who thought of fleeing did not show the dignity
appropriate for *virtuoso* men. Instead they let extrinsic pressures reduce them to
undignified passivity, making them the playthings of fortune. By examining Scipio's
action under the heading "instilling fear of religion," Machiavelli suggests that the
reasonable use of fear under (R2) instills a sense of responsibility for one's own difficulties, discouraging people from fleeing even onerous civil responsibilities.

Machiavelli then offers a counterexample illustrating the disorders caused by
methods that use "fear of religion" in very different senses of the terms "religion"
and "fear." He summarizes Livy's account of a religious rite used in war by the
Samnites, one of Rome's recurrently hostile neighbors. Though exhausted by numerous defeats and finding that "they could no longer stand either by their own or
by external forces," the Samnites still refused to "abstain from war, so far they were
from tiring even of freedom they had unsuccessfully defended; and they would
rather be conquered than not attempt victory." Clearly Machiavelli thinks that
the Samnites had worthy ends. But the extraordinary "religious" means they used
to pursue them had disastrous effects. Relying on sacrifice, terror, and spectacle,

---

[90] In all his works, Machiavelli consistently uses *iddio*, "god," for what he regards as superstitious
Gentile deities and *Dio*, "God," for the one true deity.

[91] D, I.12.37/276–79.

[92] D, I.11.34/229–30. Although here Machiavelli seems to approve of Scipio's action, there is some
ambiguity in that he forces people to take the oath; and as we saw in chap. 8, Machiavelli does not think
it is unjust to break forced oaths.

Samnite rites used "fear of religion" in ways that undermined their soldiers' fighting spirit. Instead of appealing to their responsibilities as reasonable men, they decked out their armies in impressive attire to intimidate the enemy, and used terrifying methods to deter their own soldiers from fleeing. Whereas the Romans instilled in their soldiers a reasonable "fear conceived out of past defeats," Samnite rituals used "words of execration and verses full of fright [*versi pieni di spavento*]" to terrify their own men. If a soldier fled from fight or failed to kill a fellow soldier caught fleeing, it was declared that retribution would fall "upon the head of his family and his line." As Machiavelli's chapter title says, these rites used religion as "an extreme remedy" (*estremo remedio*) for the Samnites' extreme difficulties. The Samnites were defeated, Machiavelli writes, because of superior "Roman virtue." Both sides used fear and religion in their armies. But one side used them to inspire confidence, the other to terrify. One invoked reasonable fears and respect for human commitments to supplement ordinary reasoning about duties. The other made terrifying spectacles and threats substitute for freely assumed obligations. One treated the soldiers as dignified, responsible agents. The other treated them as untrustworthy cannon-fodder who would leap at the chance to flee unless they were terrified by the penalty. As a Roman general is reported to have said, the oath taken by the Samnites "represented their fear [*timore*] and not their strength [*fortezza*], for they had to have fear [*paura*] of citizens, gods, and enemies at the same time." The citizens they had to fear were the Romans, whose religious modes in war aimed at strengthening civil *virtú* in their troops. Machiavelli expresses respect for the Samnites' "obstinacy" in defending their freedom up to the end. Nevertheless, their defeat shows that "extreme" modes of using religion to instill unreasoning *terrore* destroy military as well as political virtue.[93]

10.6.
Folk religion and civil reasoning

A final puzzle must be addressed before we can conclude that Machiavelli consistently evaluates public uses of religion by standards of transparency, reasonableness, and justice. In the *Discourses* Book I, chapter 12 he sets out another common opinion that is usually taken as his own: namely, that princes should "favor and magnify" all things "that arise in favor of that religion" even if "they judge them false." Not only those deemed "wise men" but also the prudent make use of this mode. Indeed, Machiavelli says that the prudent should use it "so much the more as they are . . . better knowers of natural things [*più conoscitori delle cose naturali*]." The use of miracles by leaders who know that they are false is, he observes, a particularly effective way of getting faith (*fede*) from the rank and file.[94] Taken out of context, these remarks seem to give "the princes of republics or kingdoms" a broad license to use false beliefs to "magnify" whatever religion serves as the *fondamento* of their polity. If Machiavelli does endorse this kind of mendacity without quali-

---

[93] *D*, I.15.43–44/238–39.
[94] *D*, I.12.37/232.

fication, his commitment to transparency in public reasoning must be less firm than I have argued. Does he suggest that while it is unacceptable to use religion to terrify believers, it is acceptable to influence them through milder forms of manipulation, including the deliberate use of falsehoods?

If so, this view must first of all be reconciled with the examples and arguments that immediately follow. In apparent contradiction to the statement defending the use of false beliefs and miracles, we now read that the contemporary church and Christian princes have signally failed to secure their states by appealing to miracles and priestly dogmas. Their religion has instead been the main cause of political disunity, weakness, and wars. If "the princes of the Christian republic" had instead maintained religion as it was "ordered by its giver [*datore*]," Machiavelli asserts, Christian polities and peoples "would be more united, much happier than they are."[95] In view of these robustly critical remarks, the earlier statement that princes should magnify all things that reinforce religion even when they "judge them false" seems either enigmatic or ironic. I suggest that it is both. It is another case of a complex, riddling irony: a statement that should be judged false if its key terms are understood in one way, but true if they are taken in another. Having introduced the riddle in chapter 12, Machiavelli goes on to set out a solution in chapter 13. First he gives an example of a corrupt interpretation of the statement that princes should "favor and magnify" all things "that arise in favor of that religion" even if they judge them false. This is the case where the Roman nobles deliberately magnified disasters such as plagues, famines, and other prodigies into expressions of divine fury in order to terrify the plebs into submission. This use of false beliefs "easily" achieved the nobles' desired ends. But it was neither reflectively prudent nor virtuous. If the nobles gained a political advantage through the mendacious use of religion, this weakened the citizen body as a whole, inducing the Roman people to act as unfree, irresponsible agents instead of free citizens.

By contrast, Machiavelli's next example shows how leaders may use religious beliefs that they judge false in ways that are compatible with public *virtú*. When Lake Albanus "rose wonderfully" in a year when Roman soldiers yearned to return home after a long siege, their leaders "found" that a number of oracles predicted the capture of a key enemy city in the year that the lake overflowed. This happy coincidence of prophecy and natural event inspired the soldiers to "endure the vexations of the siege," since it gave them hope of capturing the town after a ten-year struggle. With the help of this inspiration, the town was indeed captured. In this way, Machiavelli notes, religion "used well" helped the Romans to succeed.[96] Note the differences between the more and less acceptable uses of religious falsehood in these two examples. Most obviously, Machiavelli sees the *end* achieved in the second case as reasonable because it concerned the common good, whereas in the first case public ends were sacrificed to the partisan ambitions of the nobility. But the criteria he uses to appraise the two cases also concern the choice of *means*. The first used extraordinary methods, putting "terror in the breasts of the

---

[95] *D*, I.12.37–38/232–33.
[96] *D*, I.13.39–40/234–36.

plebs" or other political opponents. No terror is involved in the second example. Religious prophecies are used there to inspire hope, not fear. They make people conscious of their capacities to act as free men even in the face of necessity rather than weakening confidence in their own powers, as the Samnite rituals did. Moreover, while the leaders who claimed to have discovered oracles predicting Roman victory knew the claims to be false, their success did not require all the soldiers to believe that they were true. Whether they judged them true or false, soldiers could still recognize good practical reasons for acting as if they were true. Finally, these reasons did not clash with their duties to defend their city, but reinforced them.

The same implicit distinctions help to clarify Machiavelli's appraisals of a further example. Chapter 14 considers another case of how religion, including nonrational practices such as auguries, may be used well or badly: the Roman armies' use of augurs known as "chicken men" (*pullarii*) to predict the outcomes of battles. If the chickens ate what was set before them, Roman soldiers "engaged in combat with a good augury"; if they did not eat, the soldiers abstained from battle. Machiavelli suggests that this religious rite could be used in "modes" that were consistent or inconsistent with "ordinary" reasoning. Prudent Romans simply interpreted the chicken's conduct in ways that tended to encourage solidarity, fidelity, and fighting spirit among their soldiers even when the results were inauspicious. If chickens did not eat but there was good reason to fight anyway, Machiavelli says that the following maxim prevailed: "when reason showed them [*ragione mostrava*] a thing they ought to do—notwithstanding that the auspices had been adverse—they did it in any mode."[97] Once again, the criteria of reasonableness here are not just teleological or instrumental. Machiavelli does not say that the use of superstitious auguries is always justified when the results seem likely to strengthen the troops. Such modes are justified only if they do not intimidate, mislead, or manipulate people, but encourage conduct already recommended by transparent reasons. The Roman *pullarii* ritual supplements reasons already given to soldiers for fighting bravely, and gives priority to those reasons when the results of the rite contradict them. The Romans' use of *pullarii* as augurs was reasonable, then, so long as it met two strict limiting conditions. The first relates to means: the rite itself was not used to strike terror in soldiers, thus weakening their capacities for *virtuoso* fighting. The second relates to ends: the chicken men were not used to blind, mislead, or coerce the rank and file of soldiers, but only to make their reasonable duties clearer to them through a public ritual. Both conditions clearly subordinate religious and superstitious practices to "evident reasons" for acting in certain ways.

In Book III Machiavelli again stresses the priority of "evident reasons" in evaluating various uses of religion. Here he declares that the main reason to use religion when ordering an army is to inspire confidence. "The things that make it confident are: that it be armed and ordered well," and "that [its members] know [*conoschinsi*] one another." The necessary confidence and order can only arise in soldiers who "have lived together" and serve under a captain whose prudence

---

[97] D, I.14.41/237.

they trust. And "they will always trust [*confideranno*] if they see him ordered, solicitous, and spirited and if he holds up the majesty of his rank well and with reputation." This majesty turns out to depend on the captain's transparently just conduct toward his soldiers. It will always be maintained, Machiavelli argues, "if he punishes them for errors and does not tire them in vain" and "observes promises" to his men. Most importantly, he should recall that although all good captains must remember that "holding the soldiers united and confident . . . is the first cause of every victory," nevertheless "virtue must accompany these things; otherwise they have no value [*accompagnata la virtú: altrimenti, le non vagliano*]." The virtue needed is not the captain's alone, but that of all his men.[98] The means—ordinary modes and reasoning—are again the touchstones for assessing an army's virtue here, not the end result of victory alone. The foundations of a good army's religion are principles of human justice, not superstitious beliefs. While the latter may help to motivate troops, they elicit *virtuoso* efforts only when they supplement good principles and practices already followed by prudent captains and soldiers.

The same chapter goes on to distinguish between responsible and irresponsible ways of inspiring soldiers to fight. A good captain "shows the easy way to winning, and conceals or makes light of things that at a distance could show up as dangers." At first glance, the notions that captains should show an "easy way to winning" and make light of potential dangers sound distinctly hostile to Machiavelli's standards of *virtú*. Surely winning should not be easy, and good captains should not play down distant dangers but face up to them? The solution to this puzzle lies in the difference between qualities of leadership in wartime and those needed in peace among citizens. Military orders need clearer ranks than civilian ones; and captains need to know more than their troops about their own army's overall strategy, the enemy's orders or disorders, and the physical terrain. With respect to what is most reasonable, military orders are not entirely analogous with civil ones. But even in the military, prudent captains do not knowingly blind or mislead their troops. They may, however, "dissimulate" insofar as they avoid dwelling too much on potential dangers before battle, so that their soldiers' confidence remains firm. Ordinary, evident reasons are still the main touchstone in Machiavelli's Roman example. "I do not wish," he writes,

> to omit a means used by Fabius [Maximus] to make his army confident when he had newly entered into Tuscany. . . . So speaking to the soldiers before the fight, and having said that he had many reasons through which they could hope for victory, he said that he could also tell them certain good things, in which they could see victory was certain, if it were not dangerous to make them manifest. As that mode was wisely used, so it deserves to be imitated.[99]

---

[98] *D*, III.33.285–86/498–500. Compare *AW*, VI.129/655 on religion backing up the "fear of laws and men."

[99] *D*, III.33.287/500. Compare Plutarch on Fabius' use of religion in PL, *Fabius Maximus*, 212–15.

This is not advice to captains to use falsehood to mobilize gullible troops. To claim evident reasons for certain victory *would* be deceptive and dangerously irresponsible, because no one can have such absolute certainty in advance. Since no captain knows what the outcome will be, it is better to focus on the "many reasons" to hope for victory, and to avoid both negative forebodings and auguries that claim certain victory. Fabius' argument is not based on unreasonable prophetic claims to know what will happen. It is based only on good reasons to hope for a good outcome, especially self-fulfilling reasons relating to the troops' own confidence. This view is consistent with Machiavelli's ethical principles because it does not presume that fortune or God's will can be affected by human appeals, but leaves the outcome to be decided by "natural things" such as human *virtú*.[100]

These arguments might seem to support the conclusion that so long as methods are "ordinary" in these respects, the use of religious beliefs "judged false" by leaders counts as an acceptable part of a civil religion. But this would still stand in tension with the view that only modes of seeking authority that can be assessed by evident public reasons are suitable for human ordering. One of Machiavelli's key distinctions between reasonable and unreasonable Roman uses of oracles, however, is that reasonable uses did not involve *political* authority at all. In the first, corrupt example in Book I, chapter 13, Roman nobles used oracles and prophecies as means to terrify the plebs toward the end of giving nobles the plebs' share of political offices. In the second, non-corrupt example, Roman military captains used oracles and prophecies as means to inspire soldiers toward the end of fighting with confidence in their own capacities. The means used in the second case do not directly involve ordinary, evident reasoning, but on closer scrutiny are founded on natural and reasonable confidence in human *virtú*. Just as important, the second use of religion cannot directly threaten ordinary modes of seeking authority because it is not used in the context of seeking civil authority. To make this more explicit, Machiavelli's discussions of religion suggest two different *ends* of using religion:

(E1) To elicit certain kinds of conduct or emotions, such as fear or confidence, in the context of specific contests such as war or attempts to pass a law; and

(E2) As a means of seeking authority for political orders, laws, or officials.

We have already identified his two distinct senses of "religion":

(R1) Beliefs in oracles, prophecies, or supernatural signs that cannot be evaluated by ordinary reasoning based on evidence or reflections on ethical necessities; and

(R2) Ethical principles that are the necessary foundation of human order, which are grounded in such reasoning.

---

[100] It also elucidates Machiavelli's argument that the prudent "enlarge upon" (*augumentano*) miracles and other superstitions "from whatever beginning they arise," and do so "much the more are they are . . . more knowing of natural things" (*D*, I.12.37/232).

In relation to these distinctions, the position I am ascribing to Machiavelli may be summarized as follows. Religion of type (R1) may sometimes serve legitimate purposes if it is used for (E1). But if forms of religion of type (R1) are used to seek political authority (E2) rather than as a supplementary and subordinate aid to policy, this undermines the foundations established by ordinary norms of public reasoning. The only form of religion that directly supports the foundations of civil order and is necessary for political authority is (R2). (R1) may sometimes support them indirectly in pursuit of specific aims (E1), but only (R2) is essential.

Similar criteria are reflected in Machiavelli's sympathetic views on traditional folk religion, as distinct from the doctrines and practices of the organized Christian Church. Some of these views are expressed in the poem "The Golden Ass":

> There is assuredly need for prayers; and altogether mad is he who forbids people their ceremonies and their devotions;
> because in fact it seems that from them can be reaped union and good order [*unione e buono ordine*]; and on them in turn rests good and happy fortune.
> But there should be no one with so small a brain that he will believe, if his house is falling, that God will save it without any other prop, because he will die beneath the ruin.[101]

Here Machiavelli denies that religious rites that are not founded on *ragioni evidenti* are irrational or irresponsible per se. The "mad" ones are those who want to prohibit these practices, not those who engage in them. He judges it unreasonable to forbid popular "ceremonies and devotions" partly because of the good effects they seem to have.[102] But the judgment is also consistent with his remarks elsewhere about the limits of human knowledge. Most people do not know "things supernatural"; they can neither prove nor disprove the existence of God, or be sure of what God wills. If mere human beings cannot know these things, it is not unreasonable for them to speculate that God or other supernatural forces may affect human actions. Indeed, it may be quite reasonable to speculate that reasoned principles of human justice *also* have divine origins and support. If these judgments are understood as speculative elements that have a proper place in traditional religions, not as claims that should be judged as true or false, no conflict need arise between popular devotions and basic, human standards of ethical and political reasoning. Popular prayers and confidence-raising oracles may not be able to control events, and it would be unreasonable to believe that they could. It is not unreasonable, however, to hedge bets with a prayer or appeal to an oracle when one knows that conditions are not entirely susceptible to one's control. Popular superstitions that provide backup support in adverse situations are not derided by those who are "more prudent and more knowing of natural things": they may even amplify them "from

---

[101] *L'Asino*, 118–27, *Opere* III, 67–68.

[102] Although on the arguments just outlined, this does not mean that *any* "religious" practice that cannot be appraised according to "evident reasons" is acceptable if its effect is to produce "union and good order" or other ends that deserve to be rationally endorsed.

whatever beginning they arise" to promote civil orders.[103] Forms of religion that present speculative judgments about God's will as sectarian dogmas are, in Machiavelli's view, much less reasonable than allegedly more "primitive" popular devotions. Dogmatic sects that demand complete credulity from followers invariably collide with the standards needed to uphold ordinary political orders. Ordinary orders need to be renovated by continuous, critical reasoning; dogmatic sects are threatened by independent thought. Traditional folk religion is more compatible with *ordinario* orders because it does not demand a commitment to dogmas alien to "ordinary and natural" reasoning.

The foundations of Machiavelli's true "religion" consist of this-worldly, self-imposed commitments underwritten by human standards of justice. This ethical religion is the only religion that is "altogether necessary" to maintain *civiltà*. It is reasonable to speculate that supernatural powers might approve of such principled religious commitments, and that divine retribution might result from their breach. But unlike the principles themselves, theological speculation about their divine sources is not strictly necessary to uphold religion and religious fear, since both are grounded in reflections on ordinary and natural human relations. This is very different from the ideal of civic religion usually ascribed to Machiavelli: one based on a revival of Roman patriotic convictions or "passions," and aimed at restoring the pre-Christian unity of religion and politics. The principles of Machiavelli's civil religion do not support particularistic patriotism, but are founded on reasoning about the necessary conditions for virtuous order in "any city whatever." Nor is their main concern to make it easier to govern, mobilize, or establish "union" among citizens. Contrary to a widespread view, Machiavelli does not subordinate the ethical dimensions of religion to political utility. Like the religious respect or *aidōs* defended in Thucydides' and Livy's histories, Xenophon's *Cyropaedia*, and Plato's *Laws*, Machiavelli's preferred kinds of *religione* encourage people to fulfill duties that are both ethical and political: duties of justice to other human beings, to honor promises, and to limit their own claims out of respect for other people's freedom.

---

[103] *D*, I.12.37/232.

CHAPTER 11

Legislators and Princes

Although he offers many reasons to reject one-man "orderers," Machiavelli sometimes seems to say that these reasons do not apply in two sets of exceptional conditions. One is at the first founding of a new city, where there are no laws yet and
no "people" duly constituted under laws. The other is in times of extreme corruption when civil orders must be renovated.[1] Where there are no laws or orders, the
authority of one *prudentissimo* man may help to found them swiftly and firmly.
Where previous orders have become disordered, it may be "necessary to turn"
a republic "more toward a kingly state than toward a popular state, so that the
men who cannot be corrected by the laws because of their insolence should be
checked . . . by an almost kingly power."[2] Even in the generally pro-republican *Discourses*, Machiavelli's remarks about the need for individual reorderers to purge
corrupt polities seem to justify the claims of new "entrepreneurial" princes in
Machiavelli's own times. These men, among them the Medici "princes" in Florence, often justified their actions with reference to ancient founders and reorderers
who used their kingly powers to impose good laws and orders for the public good.[3]
The *Prince* is often read as a manual for new princes who face the task of imposing
order in conditions so disordered, corrupt, or unsafe that they cannot trust others,

---

[1] This reading is accepted both by scholars who underscore Machiavelli's strong commitment to
republican principles, such as Viroli (1990, 171; 1998, 146–47); and by those such as Strauss (1958, 293)
who argue that he defended "tyranny pure and simple" as well as for the sake of founding republics.

[2] *D*, I.18.51/248.

[3] Machiavelli gives various meanings to the word "prince." One set of meanings is compatible with
republican orders: *principi* are those who hold the most highly ranked public offices in a republic.
Thus anyone can see his children become princes (*D*, I.58), since in republics there are potentially
"infinite most virtuous princes" (*D*, I.20); the dedicatees of the *Discourses* "deserve to be" princes in
this republican sense (*D*, I.Pref). On a more conventional set of meanings, a *principe* is a man who
holds preeminent authority for life, whether he inherited this position or "acquired" it by his own efforts. Machiavelli's usage implies a rough distinction between prince/principality and king/kingdom
(*re, regno*). Kings are usually one-man rulers whose powers are formally and effectively limited by some
other body, such as the Senate in Romulus' Rome or French kings so long as they were held accountable
to the *parlements*. By contrast, princes are not effectively under strict constraints, although formally
they may be. In Machiavelli's lexicon the word "prince" in this sense has some of the "extraordinary"
associations discussed earlier. Princes attain or hold power partly through extraordinary modes. The
distinction between princes and tyrants is thus inherently unstable; men who set themselves up as
princes partly through extraordinary means often turn into tyrants who recognize no formal or ethical
limits on their actions. See the similar readings of Mattingly (1958) and de Alvarez (1999, 10).

but must rely on their own *virtù*. In both the *Discourses* and the *Prince* numerous references to the great founders and orderers of ancient times—such as Lycurgus, Theseus, Romulus, and Moses—seem to exhort contemporaries to imitate their actions. When these actions were "extraordinary" or violent, it is widely assumed that Machiavelli exonerates them as necessary modes of purging corruption.

This chapter looks more closely at arguments in Machiavelli's works that seem to defend a role for one-man, extraordinary orderers in certain conditions. The first four sections locate Machiavelli's nuanced appraisals of ancient orderers in their literary and philosophical context by comparing his use of the topos of *virtuoso* legislator with that of Roman and Greek authors who inspired it. Against this background, the last two sections reconsider the *Prince*'s apparent support for one-man, *virtuoso* orderers.

11.1.
Spartan founders and refounders: Lycurgus, Agis, and Cleomenes

The second chapter of the *Discourses* sets out two different ways in which cities may acquire laws and orders. Some cities "had them by chance and at many different times, and according to accidents, as had Rome." Others "were given laws by one alone and at a stroke, either in the beginning or after not much time." This was the case for Sparta, which acquired its remarkably durable system of laws through the work of one man, the lawgiver Lycurgus. Machiavelli declares that this second mode of acquiring laws and orders is more likely to make polities "happy." A "republic can be called happy [*felice*]," he declares, "whose lot is to get one man so prudent that he gives it laws ordered so that it can live securely under them without needing to correct them." Having been shown the way to civil happiness by one outstanding *ordinatore*, Sparta went on to observe Lycurgus' laws for over eight hundred years "without corrupting them or without any dangerous tumult."[4]

In contrast, "that city has some degree of unhappiness that, not having fallen upon one prudent orderer, is forced of necessity to reorder itself." The most unhappy polities are "altogether off the right road" to order, "the true and perfect end" (*perfetto e vero fine*) of all polities. Clearly Rome was not such a city, since it did eventually "reorder itself" for the right road—for a time. Rome's first founders and builders (*edificatori*) neither got it right all at once, nor took the wrong path from the start. They exemplify those cities that, although "they do not have perfect order [*l'ordine perfetto*], have taken a beginning that is good and capable of becoming better." They may therefore "by the occurrence of accidents become perfect." These less than ideally happy cities, however, must face perils that do not threaten polities ordered all at once by one prudent man. Cities that lack such a one-man *ordinatore* will, Machiavelli declares, "never order themselves without danger" because they will be forced to make their own laws amid endless tumults, partisan and sectarian strife, and attempts by ambitious individuals to dominate the polity. All these natural and ordinary difficulties make the work of self-legislation extremely arduous,

---

[4] *D*, I.2.10/202.

for "enough men never agree to a new law that looks to a new order in a city unless they are shown by a necessity that they need to do it." And "since this necessity cannot come without danger, it is an easy thing for the republic to be ruined before it can be led to a perfection of order."[5] The path of continuous self-legislation, involving many fallible orderers instead of one supremely prudent lawgiver, is littered with risks. Even the fortunate Romans came close to ruin a number of times before they reached their height of greatness, notably in their early wars with the Samnites and Gauls, and later in their wars with Carthage. It is easy to see why the Spartan model of one-off, one-man legislating carries perennial appeal.

Machiavelli's comments on Spartan and Roman ways of acquiring laws echo a well-established topos of Greek and Roman writing. Ancient writers started by marveling at Lycurgus' achievement in founding such durable legislation. This work, they enthused, seemed to suggest that Lycurgan laws had divine inspiration. But the tradition of praising Lycurgus did not claim that his legislation was flawless. Nor did it conclude that his solitary *modus operandi* should be imitated. On the contrary, the topos was deliberately ambivalent. It presented Lycurgus as a case of an ancient figure whose deeds are widely and rightly praised, yet whose achievements seem to be inimitable. Historical and philosophical writers used the case to stimulate discriminating reflections on the pros and cons of various ways to establish civil laws. Their accounts of Lycurgus do not present a naïve, idealized model of a godlike lawgiver. Machiavelli's favorite authors depict the great Spartan's works as subtly and, in the long run, fatally flawed.[6] One set of flaws relates to Lycurgus' methods of legislating. Another relates to the content of his laws. An overview of the main criticisms casts valuable light on Machiavelli's references to Lycurgus.

The writers who served as his main sources on Sparta identify three main limitations in the Lycurgan model of lawmaking. First, they point out that outstanding individual orderers such as Lycurgus are not needed for cities to attain excellent internal orders or external greatness. Greek writers under the Roman Empire held up the example of Rome, which reached greater heights than Sparta although its laws and orders were not imputed to a single legislator. Polybius, for example, observes that the Romans arrived at the same good results as the Spartans through a process of trial and error. Their admirable constitution evolved after "many struggles and troubles" forced successive generations to choose "the best by the light of the experience gained in disaster."[7]

Second, though these methods are fraught with hardships and setbacks, they also have important advantages over those of individual, all-at-a-stroke lawgivers. Each new generation of Romans had to reexamine existing laws and orders, aware that they were mainly the work of ordinary human beings like themselves. Since they did not have the good fortune of having had one legislator who did the hard work for them, they had to rely on their own self-legislative *virtù* to stay on the

[5] *D*, I.2.12–13/203.
[6] Xenophon, "Lacedaemonians" in *Scripta Minora*, 136–89; PolH, VI.9.288–93, 48.378–83; PL, I.204–303, 382–401; Cicero, *Rep.* II.110–12, 158–59.
[7] PolH, VI.10.291–93.

right path. The Spartans considered themselves so fortunate in having perfect laws set out by Lycurgus that they seldom found it necessary, or indeed desirable, to reexamine their foundations. Because they relied heavily on the virtue of one man, later generations risked underexercising their capacities to reason about laws and orders. Extreme conservatism bred complacent pride in Sparta's long-lasting modes of government, even when they became corrupted. In the end, this attitude proved fatal for Spartan freedom. Had later generations been prepared to modify Lycurgus' constitution to meet new necessities, Spartan defenses against expansionist empires such as Rome's might have improved.[8]

Third, ancient writers ask whether Lycurgus' desire to establish unchanging laws for an incorruptible city was realistic. Xenophon observes that Lycurgan legislation honored Spartan kings "not as mere men, but as demigods [*ouk hōs anthrōpous, all' hōs hērōas*]." He invites readers to consider whether this deference was reasonable, and whether perhaps Lycurgus' laws set standards of civil virtue too high to be reached by ordinary mortals. This might help to explain why, despite the rigidity of Lycurgus' laws and the reverence in which they were still held in Sparta, they had become little more than an empty shell of legality in a deeply corrupted city. It would also explain why "in spite of their antiquity [*palaioi*], they are wholly strange to others even at this day. Indeed," Xenophon adds, "it is most astonishing that all men praise such institutions, but no state chooses to imitate them [*mimeisthai . . . oudemia polis ethelei*]."[9] Plutarch too says that Lycurgus hoped "ardently to make his laws immortal [*athanaton*]" and let them "go down unchanged to future ages." This was a worthy aim, but Plutarch's appraisals invite readers to question whether it was reasonable. Lycurgus' polity proved to be "beyond imitation" (*amimēton*), and though "his fame rightly transcended [*eikotōs huperēpe tē doxē*] that of all who ever founded polities among the Greeks," this could not prevent Sparta's eventual corruption.[10]

As for the content of Lycurgus' legislation, ancient authors point to two broad sets of defects. First, Lycurgus' laws are said to have paid insufficient attention to external relations. Polybius commends Lycurgus for having secured Laconian territory and leaving "to the Spartans themselves a lasting heritage of freedom [*eleutheria*]." But when it came to "the annexation of neighboring territories, supremacy [*hēgemonia*] in Greece, and, generally speaking, an ambitious policy," Lycurgus "made absolutely no provision for such contingencies." His one-sided focus on internal matters encouraged Spartans to remain inward-looking and inflexible when forced to deal with new external pressures.[11] Unused to accommodating other

---

[8] PolH, VI.48–49, 378–83. On this point Greek writers are ambivalent. While critical of Spartan inflexibility in external relations, they implicitly commend Lycurgus' laws for making internal order a priority instead of external conquests. Their judgments of Roman methods are ambivalent in the opposite way: good when Rome dealt flexibly with other cities and peoples in ways that made them firm allies, less good when Rome's methods turned overambitious and domineering.

[9] Xenophon, "Lacedaemonians," 184–89, 170–71. Machiavelli echoes this last passage in *D*, I.Pref.5–6 and again in relation to Roman modes of expansion in *D*, II.4.

[10] PL, *Lycurgus* 300–301, 292–93.

[11] PolH, VI.48, 378–80.

cities' needs, they tended to oscillate between isolationism and ill-judged attempts to dominate their neighbors. Polybius holds Lycurgus' omissions responsible for these defects. While his laws made the Spartans "most unambitious [*aphilotimotatous*] and sensible people as regards their private lives and the institutions of their city [*poleōs nomima*]," he left them "most ambitious, domineering, and aggressive [*philotimotatous kai philarchotatous kai pleonektikōtatous*] towards the rest of the Greeks." Lacking homegrown resources to meet all their military needs during the Peloponnesian War, the Spartans "were compelled to be beggars from the Persians" and had to realize "that under the legislation of Lycurgus it was impossible to aspire . . . to any position of influence" in Greece. In this respect Lycurgus' constitution was sorely defective, while "that of Rome is superior and better framed for the attainment of power."[12]

A second set of criticisms relates to the internal constitutional orders laid down by Lycurgus. Plutarch praises the Spartan's aspirations to create an incorruptible city, yet touches on several flaws in his legislation. His political orders were too "rigid and aristocratic [*austēra . . . kai aristokratikē*]" to develop civic virtues among ordinary people. While his laws regulating the education of citizens had many admirable features, they tended to sacrifice individual freedom to civic unity. "No man," Plutarch writes, "was allowed to live as he pleased, but in their city, as in a military encampment, they always had a prescribed regimen and employment in public service," and it was considered that individuals "belonged entirely to their country and not to themselves [*ouk autōn, alla tēs patridos einai dieteloun*]." A further shortcoming concerns what Lycurgus omitted to do with his otherwise excellent legislation. If his laws did not directly enjoin the Spartans' "savage and lawless [*ōmotaton . . . kai paranomōtaton*]" treatment of the Helots, their large serf class, they did not do anything to mitigate this mistreatment.[13]

Machiavelli's appraisal of Lycurgus' legacy builds on these nuanced ancient evaluations. It is both admiring and critical. Its main function in the *Discourses*, however, is not to encourage modern imitators but to caution readers against the pitfalls of undiscriminating imitation. In referring to Lycurgus' methods of legislation Machiavelli agrees, first of all, that to attain a "perfection of order" there is no *need* for a single, godlike lawgiver. After all, Rome "did not have a Lycurgus to order it in the beginning in a mode that would enable it to live free for a long time." Yet natural and ordinary necessities, especially the "disunion between the plebs and the Senate," forced the Romans to work hard to impose their own laws and

---

[12] PolH, VI.48–49, 378–89. Plutarch (PL, *Lycurgus* 298–99) gives a more positive assessment of Sparta's external relations before the Peloponnesian War, describing the Spartans as prudent "regulators and chasteners of peoples and magistrates [*andras harmostas kai sōphronistas tōn hekastchou dēmōn kai archontōn*]" who "implanted in the Greeks not only a willingness to obey, but a desire to be their followers and subjects." The deliberate idealization of Sparta's merits in foreign policy obliquely criticizes Rome's overassertive imperial policies.

[13] Plutarch (PL, *Lycurgus* 290–93) says that in this respect the Roman Numa was "far more Hellenic as a lawgiver [*Hellēnikōteron . . . nomothetēn*]" since he gave slaves "a taste of the dignity of freedom [*timēs eleutheras*]."

orders. Thus "what an orderer had not done, chance did."[14] On the second point too Machiavelli intimates his doubts about the desirability of one-man legislators who give a city its laws all "at a stroke." The Spartans might have been "happy" to have a Lycurgus at the beginning. But happiness in cities never lasts unless *industria* and *virtú* sustain it. The Spartans' happiness was based on the rare good fortune of having a *prudentissimo* lawgiver; and even for them, fortune proved fickle. The Romans were less happy in their beginnings, but their comparative disadvantage at the outset made them rely more on their own efforts than on fortune. Therefore they developed greater civil virtue, and surpassed the Spartans in the "perfection" of their political orders. Necessity constrained them to realize that orders can "by the occurrence of accidents become perfect" if citizens see accidents not as threats to their happiness, but as occasions for imposing better laws and orders by their own labors.

Machiavelli does not directly address the third criticism, that Lycurgus' desire to legislate immortal laws was unrealistic. In some respects, his arguments favor Lycurgan modes of legislating through reasoning and foresight over the Romans' often fumbling trial-and-error pragmatism. Against the one-sided view that the best path to good orders is to trust the lessons of experience, Machiavelli denies that experience can teach anything worthwhile if it is not evaluated through reflective reasoning, guided by independent standards of truth and ethical principles.[15] Readers should learn from Roman errors that they need such reasonings as well as experience to keep from veering off the right path. This much they can learn from Lycurgus: that it is possible to grasp and hold on to the most basic principles of good legislation even if recurrent "disasters" do not remind people of their value. The principles defended in Machiavelli's own works are presented as unchanging and universal, though they are compatible with diverse forms of polity and government. On the other hand, his account of these principles makes him doubt that their most adequate political instantiations can be discovered by one supremely wise man, let alone maintained by the wisdom of *uno solo*. General principles of human justice can be worked out by solitary observers of human dispositions and conflicts. But legitimate laws and orders must be established *among* men. The only means human beings have to establish them are either unilateral force, or discursive and persuasive reasoning. The latter always provides a more secure basis for authority, and must involve more than one guiding intelligence. However reasonable Lycurgus' laws may have been in other respects, the lawgiver's desire to fix his system for all time discouraged later generations from reexamining their orders with free and open minds. As we will see shortly, Machiavelli suggests that this rigid conservatism impeded several well-meaning attempts to "renovate" Lycurgus' legacy.

Machiavelli's comments on the content of Lycurgan laws also recall ancient criticisms, though he develops his own distinctive analysis of the relation between the external and internal defects. His argument can be summarized as follows.

[14] *D*, I.2.14/206-7.
[15] See chap. 3, sec. 3.5, and chap. 8, sec. 8.6.

Internally, Lycurgus' laws regulating citizenship left Sparta with an extremely small and narrow citizen body. Moreover, its oligarchic and monarchical institutions made it hard for civic virtue to flourish on a wide scale. Further, Lycurgus' concern to maintain civic unity blinded him to the advantages that well-ordered "tumults" may have for cities. These three internal defects crippled Sparta's ability to meet the growing demands placed on the city by external wars.

According to Machiavelli, Lycurgus' principal error was to order a constitution designed to maintain an extremely narrow citizen base, so that the "body" of the city could never grow to a greatness comparable to that of the Roman republic. The restrictions he placed on foreign commerce and immigration were supposed to prevent corruption. But if the end was good, the means were problematic:

> For since Lycurgus, founder of the Spartan republic, considered that nothing could dissolve his laws more easily than the mixture [*commistioni*] of new inhabitants, he did everything so that foreigners should not have to deal [*conversarvi*] there. Besides not admitting them into marriages, into citizenship [*alla civilità*], and into the other dealings [*altre conversazioni*] that make men come together, he ordered that leather money should be spent in his republic to take away from everyone the desire to come there, to bring merchandise there, or to bring some art there, so the city could never thicken [*ingrossare*] with inhabitants. And since all our actions imitate nature, it is neither possible nor natural for a thin trunk to support a thick branch. So a small republic cannot seize cities or kingdoms that are sounder or thicker than it.

The Spartan "stem"—its core citizen body—was so narrowly based that when it began to acquire "branches" thicker than itself, "it supports it with labor, and every small wind breaks it." Eventually "the trunk alone remained without branches. This could not happen in Rome," Machiavelli contends, "since its stem was so thick it could easily support any branch whatever."[16] The lesson he draws about Lycurgus' laws is that imitators of ancient legislation should prefer the Roman republic's policy in this regard. By encouraging immigration and admitting newcomers to citizenship, Rome continually "thickened the body" of its citizenry, making the city formidable vis-à-vis other powers.

The particular "mix" of kingship, aristocracy, and popular government in Lycurgus' constitution further contributed to its eventual decline. Not only foreigners but also most of the native population was excluded from Sparta's government. Machiavelli argues that both forms of exclusion undermined the city's power, although their original rationale had been to prolong the life of its ancient laws. If later generations failed to recognize the disadvantages that flowed from their reluctance to "accept foreigners in their republic," this was due in part to the built-in conservatism of a mixed constitution with a large monarchical element. Sparta, Machiavelli writes,

---

[16] *D*, II.3.134–35/336–37.

was governed by a king and by a narrow [*stretto*] Senate. It could maintain itself for so long a time because they could live united for a long time; there were few inhabitants in Sparta, for they blocked the way to those who might come to inhabit it, and the laws of Lycurgus were held in repute. (Since they were observed, they removed all causes of tumult.)

The exclusion of the majority from government caused few "tumults" partly because "there was an equal poverty" among different parts of the population, due to Lycurgus' strict laws that regulated the distribution of property. But the absence of tumults was also due to the fact that only a few citizens were eligible for any government offices. "The plebeians were less ambitious" than in governments with a stronger popular element "because the ranks of the city were spread among few citizens and were kept at a distance from the plebs." Moreover, the nobles and kings "had no greater remedy for upholding their dignity than to keep the plebs defended from every injury, which made the plebs not fear and not desire rule."[17] Machiavelli suggests that those who see this kind of paternalism as a strong point in Sparta's constitution should think again. Compared with Rome, its great disadvantage was that the Spartan population as a whole was less able to develop its capacities for civic virtue. Since the majority remained dependent on kings and nobles for their protection, they could not acquire the independence needed to give the city a strong "stem." Since ordinary people could not aspire to public offices, they did not develop a robust sense of responsibility for the public good or public defense; the main work in these areas was left to a small minority of men.

Finally, Machiavelli questions whether the apparently reasonable desire to keep the city united was pursued by reasonable means under Lycurgus' legislation. Lycurgus sought to ensure a long, corruption-free life for his laws by demanding a high degree of conformity in Spartan education and customs. As Plutarch and other ancient writers argued, individual freedoms were subordinated to patriotic ends defined by the laws. Spartan political life left little room for the ordinary tumults that Machiavelli sees as the lifeblood of a free way of life. His *tumulti* are not necessarily disorders; they are a condition for free and stable orders. They always occur in cities where men are able to vent their diverse humors, compete for public office, and publicly debate the merits of different candidates and policies. Machiavelli urges readers to imitate those who made laws for the early Roman republic in these respects. Accepting *tumulti* as "an inconvenience necessary" (*uno inconveniente necessario*) for civil life, they should seek to regulate them under firm but tolerant orders. The Spartans, he argues, failed to realize that cities grow more powerful when their laws tolerate and regulate tumults caused by diverse humors than when they are repressed in the name of unity. In Rome "the many" were employed in war and given rights to compete for high office, "which gave the plebs strength and increase [*forze ed augumento*] and infinite opportunities for tumult." If "the Roman state had come to be quieter" through attempts to impose more unity, "this inconvenience would have followed: that it would also have

---

[17] *D*, I.6.21/214.

been weaker because it cut off the way by which it could come to the greatness it achieved." In short, if like Sparta Rome had "wished to remove the causes of tumults," it would have "removed too the causes of expansion [*cagioni dello ampliare*]." Machiavelli concludes that had the Romans imitated Sparta by having "a prince for life and . . . a small Senate," then it could not at the same time "wish to make a great empire [*un grande imperio*]." For such an empire needed a strong enough trunk to support newly added branches; and no republic that wants this strength can reasonably "refuse to increase the number of its citizens" both by opening the ranks and rights of citizenship to the many at home and foreigners who enter.[18]

Machiavelli argues that these three shortcomings in Lycurgus' internal legislation paved the way for what proved to be Sparta's downfall: its inflexibility in addressing new challenges in foreign relations. The basic aims of Lycurgus' laws were defensive rather than expansive. They sought to preserve a high degree of unity within the polity, on the assumption that unity within a small, exclusive citizen body must be best for external defense. In Machiavelli's view, this assumption was wrong. Its defects came to light when Sparta was forced to deal with new external pressures, especially during its wars with Macedonia in the third century BC. In this period, several attempts were made to refound Lycurgus' laws. Machiavelli mentions Agis IV and Cleomenes III, two Spartan kings who tried to clean up corruption in the city. Agis "desired to return the Spartans to the limits [*termini*] within which the laws of Lycurgus had enclosed [*rinchiusi*] them." He judged that because the city had deviated from those laws, it had "lost very much of its ancient virtue, and, in consequence, its strength and empire." But when Agis tried to take emergency powers in order to save his country's laws, he was murdered by the Ephors "as a man who wanted to seize the tyranny." After reading Agis' records and writings, Cleomenes conceived the same belief that he could redeem his native city only if he were "alone in authority." His plan succeeded in the short term: Cleomenes "murdered the ephors in order to rule alone" and afterward "employed this authority . . . well." Nevertheless, his initial success proved short-lived. Cleomenes' action, Machiavelli suggests,

> was apt for making Sparta rise again [*a fare risuscitare*] and for giving Cleomenes the reputation that Lycurgus had, if it had not been for the power of the Macedonians and the weakness of the other Greek republics. For after such an order, when he was assaulted by the Macedonians, found himself alone and inferior in strength [*forze*], and had no one with whom to seek refuge, he was conquered; and his plan, however just and praiseworthy, remained imperfect.[19]

The argument here seems to be that the sole cause of Cleomenes' failure was geopolitical bad luck. As we have seen, however, Machiavelli has little time for this kind of fatalistic explanation. Whenever he declares that an action seems to have

---

[18] *D*, I.6.21–22/214–17.
[19] *D*, I.9.30/224–25.

failed because of external necessity, a closer look at his analysis usually shows that the agent's own errors were at least partly at fault. If Cleomenes' plan remained "imperfect," this suggests that his failure was not due only to bad luck in foreign affairs, but also to his own omissions or misjudgments. Machiavelli does not specify what these were. He does imply, however—following Polybius—that Cleomenes did too little to reorganize his country's defenses. Cleomenes found himself alone and inferior in forces because he made poor use of opportunities to build new alliances with other Greek republics in response to Macedonian expansionism. His ambition to hold sole command when making league with the Achaeans may, as Plutarch implies, have left him alone and "no one with whom to seek refuge."[20] Moreover, he was too conservative in refusing to grant citizenship and training in arms to newcomers and non-nobles.[21] Reluctant to reform laws that excluded much of Sparta's population from military training, Cleomenes remained "inferior in strength" and dependent on foreign mercenaries.[22] If Cleomenes "found himself" weak and isolated, then, this was not just because of the unfortunate superiority of Macedonian forces and weakness of Greek republics. The fatal imbalance was also due to his and his predecessors' failure to increase their own forces, through internal reforms and strong external alliances.

Machiavelli hints at a deeper problem with these attempts to refound the Lycurgan laws. Cleomenes' renovation strategy was "imperfect" because it was too deferential to tradition. He and Agis were right to uphold the rigorous standards that underpinned Lycurgus' laws. But they could have done more to update their content, innovating as they renovated. Admirers who see Lycurgus as an "expert" in a naturalistic science of legislation are likely to err even more in this respect. Some might think that by copying his works, they could repeat his good results. But this would be a misguided view of what is most valuable in Lycurgus' legacy. What most deserve imitating are Lycurgus' demanding standards of self-legislative *virtú*, not the specific practices he prescribed. If imitators judge that some of these standards were too demanding for mere mortals, they should not be so deferential that they refuse to modify them. Modifying does not mean abandoning the standards. Successive generations have rightly admired Lycurgus for recognizing that for all their bad humors and *malignità*, human beings can still regulate themselves with self-imposed laws and orders, thereby warding off corruption for a long time. The Spartans went too far for Machiavelli, as for most of his ancient writers; their

---

[20] Machiavelli hints at this obliquely through references to Aratus, Cleomenes' rival and leader of the Achaean League (*D*, II.32.205/412–13, III.5.217/424–25). What Aratus did that others did not was, among other things, "to obey laws rather than wish to command them." If readers turn to Plutarch's *Life* of Aratus, they will read that Aratus was a ferocious foe of tyranny who, by respecting the ancient laws and customs of peoples defeated in war, brought them into a powerful alliance of cities. By contrast, Cleomenes was defeated by his overambitious interest in dominion, which was greater than his desire for the common good of all Greeks. Eventually he was forced to seek refuge with non-Greek despots in Egypt, whose suspicions of Cleomenes led to his death; see PL, *Aratus* and *Cleomenes*.

[21] According to Plutarch (PL, *Agis* 22–25) Agis did want to admit some foreigners to citizenship; in this respect his reforms improved on Lycurgan laws.

[22] Polybius (PolH, VI.48–52, 378–87), whose criticisms of Lycurgan laws Machiavelli mostly seconds, adds that among the things Cleomenes "left undone" was to continue to use mercenaries.

discipline involved too much control by others, leaving too little room for individual choice and self-discipline. Nevertheless, imitators can moderate methods while upholding the basic aims: to found cities on rigorous laws and orders imposed by human *virtú*, instead of on the scarcely regulated play of natural instincts, ambitions, and fears.

If Machiavelli shares Lycurgus' desire to uphold demanding, reasoned standards of legislation, how does he reconcile these standards with the Roman mode of legislating by trial and error? For ancient writers, Lycurgus' methods represented the extreme philosophical mode of lawmaking, while the Romans represented other extreme of pragmatic empiricism. Machiavelli concurs with Polybius' implied judgment that the two modes should be treated as complementary.[23] Neither is adequate by itself, and imitators-of-ancients who admire one method while scorning the other will both go off the good "path." On the one hand, legislation that depends on the mind of one man alone is unsuitable for most cities. The strongest and most human cities are those like Rome where "new necessities in managing that city were always discovered," making it "necessary to create new orders" that work toward its "perfection."[24] On the other hand, Roman methods of legislation were far from faultless. Following ancient topoi, Machiavelli suggests that the chief weakness in those methods was excessive pragmatism, which sometimes prevented Romans from recognizing the difference between good and bad *principles* of order. Not valuing general principles enough, they made serious misjudgments that could have been avoided had they examined their orders—and themselves—more philosophically.

When Machiavelli's comments on the Spartan constitution are brought together, they cast doubt on the view he sets out at the beginning of the *Discourses*. On reflection, it may not be so good to have "one man so prudent that he gives it laws" in a way that people "can live securely under them without needing to correct them." Republics ordered in this way might "be called happy." But imitators of the ancients should not let the word "happy" lead them down a false legislative path. Human laws are not immortal, and citizens must always be ready to correct their defects with new legislation. Ultimately, excessive deference to one man's ancient laws harmed Spartan virtue and safety more than it helped. Had later generations of Spartans been less concerned with internal unity and the continuity of old practices—including some that were excessively "harsh"—they might have modified some of Lycurgus' laws for the better defense of their city.

---

[23] Polybius (PolH, VI.10.291–93) implies that if the Spartans relied too much on the reasoning of one man, the Romans relied too much on experience, chance, and accidents, and not enough on reasoning about general principles of good order. The Roman state, Polybius writes, "more than any other, has been formed and has grown naturally [*kata phusin*], and will undergo a natural decline and change to the contrary." Lycurgus "constructed his constitution untaught by adversity" through foresight and a "process of reasoning [*dia logou*]" alone. He did not need to go through the same process to grasp the basic principles of a mixed republic, since he "understood that all the above changes take place necessarily and naturally." If the Romans could learn not simply to go with the natural flow but to regulate it with reasoned laws, they might be able to slow down their present decline into tyranny.

[24] D, I.49.100/298–99.

11.2.
Roman founders and legislators: Romulus and Aeneas

Early in the *Discourses* Rome's first king Romulus is mentioned to exemplify the "general rule" that "it never or rarely happens that any republic or a kingdom is ordered well from the beginning or reformed altogether anew . . . unless it is ordered by one individual [*da uno*]." Further, "it is necessary that one alone give the mode and that any such ordering depend on his mind [*dalla cui mente*]."[25] In ancient and modern times, many aspiring one-man *ordinatori* took these maxims as their rationale for seizing extraordinary powers. In ancient Rome, Caesar and his admirers claimed that a single ruler with imperial powers was needed to set the corrupt republic in order. Similar claims were made by the new self-styled princes who seized power in Italian republics. Weary of civil disorders, many citizens in Machiavelli's Florence were ready to accept both the "general rule" and the individuals who put themselves forward as redeemers of their troubled city. The *Florentine Histories* describes how endless killings, exiles, and civil distress gave rise to popular longings for a new Romulus, a man willing to assert kingly powers to rebuild the foundations for a new and improved republic. We have already discussed how Machiavelli uses the Romulus legend to provoke critical reasoning about the value of one-man orderers.[26] This section focuses on his judgments about the content of the Roman founder's orders, although, as we will see, Machiavelli suggests that the quality of his works was strongly influenced by his "modes" of working.

For Machiavelli, the main historical question that readers should ask themselves is the following: how far did Romulus' "modes and orders" help to set Rome on a path to the free republic that it later became? If readers approach this question in a philosophical and ethical way, they should also ask how far the "general rules" that guided Romulus' ordering are compatible with reasoned standards of good order. As usual, Machiavelli's own answers to these questions are deliberately ambivalent. In historical terms, whoever established the orders attributed to Romulus can be credited with giving Rome many orders that were later "renovated" to form the republic. In ethical and philosophical terms, moreover, at least some of the principles that informed Romulus' orders were the same principles needed to found a "true" republic. Whether considered from a historical or an ethical standpoint, however, Romulus' orders remained incomplete. Before attempting to imitate his modes or his orders, readers should consider carefully what he got right and what remained undone in his works. They should then consider whether or not the omissions were rooted in errors of reasoning about the basic principles of good order.

If they pay close attention to the distinctions drawn in the first chapter of the *Discourses*, readers will notice some initial reasons to question Romulus' contribution to Rome's republican orders. Roman tradition acknowledged two different founders: the "native" Romulus and Aeneas, the Trojan prince cast adrift from his homeland after it was destroyed in war. Machiavelli does not overtly express

---

[25] *D*, I.9.29/223.
[26] See chap. 9, sec. 9.8.

a preference for one founding legend over the other. He simply says: "if whoever examines the building of Rome takes [*prenderà*] Aeneas for its first progenitor [*primo progenitore*], it will be of those cities built by foreigners, while if he takes Romulus it will be of those built by men native to the place." He adds that either way, one can see that Rome "had a free beginning, without depending on anyone [*principio libero, sanza dependere da alcuno*]." But Machiavelli's appraisals are not evenly balanced as between the merits of native and foreign "builders." Paradoxically, native builders are less free than foreigners. They face fewer necessities that force them to exert their free will in imposing new "laws and orders," whereas foreign builders are free precisely because they are constrained to leave their ancestral country and seek a "new seat." The same causes that make foreign builders more free oblige them to exert more *virtú* than native ones. Machiavelli's examples of free, *virtuoso* foreign builders are Moses and Aeneas. Romulus, however, was a native to the country where Rome was built. If these distinctions are applied in a precise way, Aeneas should clearly be regarded as the more fully free and *virtuoso* builder than Romulus.[27] A tentative normative conclusion seems to follow: those who want to represent Rome's beginning as free and optimally virtuous should choose Aeneas rather than Romulus as their symbol. Aeneas is the more suitable model for those imitators of ancients who want to order for a free way of life.

This conclusion is reinforced by Machiavelli's observation that the builders he calls natives have different motives for building cities than those who are driven out of their ancestral lands. On his allegorical account, men who build new cities in or near their place of birth are driven by concerns for a more secure or easier life. "Moved either by themselves or by someone among them of greater authority"—an oblique reference to the role often played in such building by kings or "great men"—they flee their current dangerous situation to "inhabit a place elected by them, more advantageous to live in and easier to defend."[28] Builders who are constrained to leave their homelands are free, by contrast, because they are under a much greater necessity to build new cities. Unable to "flee" from hardships, they are constrained to face them head-on, working hard to establish laws that regulate pressing necessities.

In relation to these distinctions, Romulus' status as founder of Roman freedoms looks ever more ambivalent. On the one hand, Machiavelli credits him with displaying more self-legislative virtue than the Venetians or either of the traditional founders of Athens, Theseus and Solon. If Rome's beginnings under Romulus were free although he was a native, this was due to the numerous "necessities the laws made" by him and his successors "imposed, so that . . . the greatness of its empire could not corrupt it for many centuries."[29] On the other hand, when Romulus founded Rome his end was not to establish an optimally free way of life. Presumably like the Athenians and Venetians, his priority was to order scattered settlements into

---

[27] *D*, I.1.7–9/200–202.
[28] Athens and Venice are Machiavelli's main examples of cities founded in this mode; he suggests that the foundations of these cities left much to be desired.
[29] *D*, I.1.9/202.

one city for greater security and "ease." The modes most suitable for pursuing such ends are kingdoms and the rule of the few, not republics. And while Romulus himself came to his authority by his own virtue, not by birth, the orders he established remained imperfect because they were directed to inadequately virtuous ends. As Machiavelli puts it at the end of his next chapter, "Romulus and all the other kings made many and good laws conforming also to a free way of life." But "because their end was to found a kingdom and not a republic . . . many things that were necessary to order in favor of freedom were lacking, not having been ordered by those kings."[30]

Machiavelli shows little interest in discussing Romulus or Aeneas as historical figures. His main questions are evaluative: which of the actions imputed to Rome's founders deserve most praise, and which should be imitated? How should their actions be taken as allegorical representations of what is most admirable—or most insidious—in Rome's political foundations? Since the legends of Romulus and Aeneas depict quite different motives and methods of founding, the choice of whom to "take" as Rome's *primo progenitore* may reflect different judgments about the proper ends of cities, and about what "modes and orders" of founding deserve to be imitated by modern orderers. Machiavelli's remarks at the beginning of the *Discourses* imply that if one's priority is to order for freedom and virtue, one should perhaps study the founding deeds of Aeneas as well as those of Romulus. Machiavelli himself says much less about the legendary Trojan founder. What he does say, however, is consistent with his arguments about how legitimate authority may be established among individuals and peoples who consider themselves free.

Aeneas is mentioned only one other time in the *Discourses*, in a chapter that discusses how he dealt with populations already settled in the area where Rome was built.[31] Here Machiavelli distinguishes between two modes of "free" building done by builders who have been forced out of their ancestral homes. One is the mode used by Moses and his followers when, since they "had not been able to defend their own country [*paese*]," they "were able to seize [*occupare*] that of others." This "very frightful" (*formidolosissimi*) method of free building, Machiavelli says, is usual when the people forced out of their homelands are many. But when the refugees are "not many," they are constrained to use means other than violence to establish a new seat for themselves. This second, non-violent mode was used well by Aeneas. Having relatively few followers, Machiavelli observes, foreign founders "cannot use violence but must seize some place with art [*con arte*], and having seized it maintain themselves there by way of friends and confederates [*per via d'amici e di confederati*]." Machiavelli implies that this method has been used more frequently than the violent mode. It is, moreover, a far more stable basis for civil orders. "Aeneas, Dido, the Massilians, and the like" all followed this second *via d'amici e di confederati*, and all "were able to maintain themselves through the consent [*per consentimento*] of the neighbors where they settled."[32]

[30] *D*, I.2.14/206.
[31] Compare Livy, *LH*, I.i.8–15.
[32] *D*, II.8.145/348.

Though these remarks on Aeneas are tantalizingly brief, they indicate an important normative and practical advantage in "taking" him as Rome's *primo progenitore*. Whereas the aspects of the Romulus legend mentioned by Machiavelli deal only with his internal orders, his account of Aeneas addresses a more basic question about the foundations of any city: the question of how it orders relations with other peoples on its territory, and with neighboring peoples. Rome's recurrent failure to secure the goodwill of its Italian neighbors is one of Livy's central themes. Machiavelli too presents this failure as one of the chief causes of Rome's eventual corruption. He draws frequent, cautionary parallels between Rome's mismanagement of relations with its Italian neighbors and Florence's similar errors. Aeneas' consensual modes of gaining legitimacy when founding a new country suggest a better way—the *via d'amici e di confederati*—in which Rome and Florence might have founded their security vis-à-vis other peoples.[33] Machiavelli does not directly contrast Aeneas' modes to Romulus', or accuse Romulus of negligence in the way that he ordered the city's external security in Italy. However, when one reads the last chapters of the *Prince*, the sanguinary evocations of intra-Italian violence in the "Tercets on Ambition," or the entire *Florentine Histories*, it becomes clear that fratricide among fellow Italians was among Machiavelli's main concerns. Romulus' founding act of fratricide so that he could "order alone" may have served as a model for princes seeking to impose extraordinary modes inside cities. But it could also be a metaphor for Rome's early and late attempts to dominate Italy through methods that antagonized its nearest neighbors. Florence and other cities whose leading men (or peoples) aspired to become "princes" of neighboring cities risked making the same fratricidal mistakes.

If Machiavelli is silent on Romulus' legacy in relation to Rome's external foundations, he says a good deal about his legacy for its internal orders. As with his analysis of Lycurgus' constitution, Machiavelli's appraisal of Romulus' building is mixed. His main implicit criticism is that the constitution ordered by Romulus and "the other kings" was an unstable mix of monarchical and republican, or at least proto-republican, principles. In the end this form of government could not reach a "perfection of order" without a great deal of further work. Many others did this work after Romulus. Some of it was done by later kings, such as Numa Pompilius. But as we saw in the last chapter, Machiavelli subtly criticizes some of the dubious "orders" made by Romulus' successors, implying that these institutions tended to prevent the Roman people from exercising civil *virtú*. The most important new orders were made not by Roman kings but by later generations, after kingship was abolished and a republic established in Rome. This, Machiavelli stresses, was not the work of any one godlike man, but was publicly commemorated as the work of the entire Roman people. If one must give credit to any one

---

[33] The main literary source for Aeneas' founding legend was the *Aeneid* of Virgil, a native of Etruria—Machiavelli's Tuscany. Virgil was celebrated by Florentine humanists as an esteemed forerunner, and his version of Rome's founding as one that gave Etruria-Tuscany special claims to preeminence in Italian political as well as cultural history, ancient and modern. See Garin 1994, 38–59 on Aeneas in Florentine humanism.

individual for founding Roman freedom on stable internal *fondamenti*, this should not be Romulus or Aeneas but the man who put an end to kingship in Rome. Thus "although the actions of the kings were great and notable," Machiavelli writes, "I shall omit them; nor shall I speak of them otherwise except for anything they may have worked pertaining to their private advantage; and I shall begin with Brutus, father of Roman liberty."[34]

While giving Romulus credit for imposing many good orders, then, Machiavelli gives him only partial credit for the orders that brought Rome to unparalleled greatness by liberating and regulating the virtue of its people. Machiavelli states quite bluntly that Rome would never have grown to greatness if it had remained a kingdom. "I judge," he writes, "that it was necessary either that the kings be extinguished [*estinguessono*] in Rome or that Rome would in a very short time become weak and of no value [*debole e di nessuno valore*]." Though excellent in many respects, Romulus' orders soon fell prey to the same corruption that befalls all kingdoms, and this corruption would have destroyed Roman virtue had its people already been corrupted. Because they were not, "they lost the head when the trunk was sound" and thus "could easily be brought to live free and ordered."[35] This was mainly their own work, not that of any solitary *edificatore*.

Does this mean that Romulus made a serious error in ordering Rome as a kingdom, and if so, did he operate with the wrong principles of ordering from the outset? The answer, Machiavelli suggests, depends on one's interpretation of the Romulus legend. Machiavelli's own account questions the ethical and political import of some interpretations, especially those that favor extraordinary modes of one-man ordering. But instead of repudiating Romulus as a standard-bearer of free, *virtuoso* republican orders, Machiavelli shows how his actions can be interpreted in ways that support the founding principles of such orders. One argument relates to Romulus' methods of founding, which did not make Romans "happy" by ordering everything "at a stroke," but left plenty of work for others to do. Whether Romulus left his orders imperfect on purpose or by accident, that he did so was not a bad thing. By experiencing both advantages and disadvantages of government under kings, the Roman people learned valuable lessons about how to order a judiciously "mixed" republic. Accordingly, they expelled the kings and repudiated the "name" of kings but retained the "kingly power [*la potestà regia*]" by ordering "two consuls there who stood in the place of kings in that republic."[36] Without the experience of rule by kings, the Roman people might never have arrived at this sound republican solution. They might have simply swung from kingship to oligarchy to licentious rule by the many, never hitting upon the reasonable "limit" that could arrest the endless cycles. Experience of kingship reinforced the Romans' dislike for it later, making them work hard for over four centuries to avoid falling back toward monarchy. This implies that republican virtue may be

---

[34] *D*, III.1.212/420. The reference is to Lucius Junius Brutus, one of Rome's two first consuls and ancestor of the conspirator against Caesar.

[35] *D*, I.17.47/243.

[36] *D*, I.2.14/206-7.

easier to sustain when memories of past, defective monarchy or tyranny are still vivid. Citizens who live under constitutions set up by one man at a stroke, such as Lycurgus', lack this advantage.

Machiavelli finds a second freedom-supporting feature of the Romulus legend in the content of his laws and orders. After killing his brother Remus, Romulus' prudent choice of orders ensured that his mixed kingly republic lasted longer than most such unstable mixes do. Later on, they made for a smooth transition to a more perfect republic. His key *prudentissimo* act was to place his own authority under the strict rule of law. Machiavelli commends him for immediately establishing a Senate and giving it authority to oversee his ordering. This move, his first act as *solo* legislator after killing off Remus, immediately set limits on his own actions and instantiated the principle of power-sharing as the foundation of the republic. This principle then served as a norm for Romans to evaluate Romulus' successors, demanding that they not take more than the share of power ordered by the *fondatore* for Roman kings. Further, he left the choice of his successor to this body, thereby asserting the principle that a king may not bequeath his authority to his own progeny or to any other successor chosen by himself.[37] These principles of power-sharing and elective kingship, Machiavelli suggests, are worth imitating by modern orderers, even if Romulus' extraordinary methods are not.

Once these merits in Romulus' orders are recognized, republicans as well as aspiring princes can appreciate the positive aspects of his ambivalent legacy. They will then be better able to judge what is worth imitating in his works, and what forms of imitation should be avoided. Machiavelli's appraisals offer a selective, republican interpretation of the Romulus legend as an alternative to princely interpretations that focus on his "extraordinary" determination to "order alone." If those who want to imitate Rome's native founder do so with a view to ordering stable republics, they should interpret his legends in a principled and not a literal way, and take his example as an allegory of the proper limits that a virtuous orderer must set on himself. Anyone who "considers well the authority that Romulus reserved for himself," Machiavelli notes, "will see that none other was reserved except that of commanding the armies when war was decided on and that of convoking the Senate." His self-restraint in these ordering acts illustrates the procedural principles that would become the chief foundations for Roman *libertà*. This is virtually a mirror image of interpretations that treat the Romulus legend as an ideological justification for extraordinary one-man ordering. Those who favor this reading stress the need for a self-assertive individual who is willing to step outside the bounds of public order, following the dictates of his mind alone. In contrast to this, Machiavelli's generous interpretation singles out Romulus' acts of self-restraint as most deserving of praise and imitation.

Through a series of finely discriminating reasonings, then, Machiavelli reinterprets the Romulus legend as an allegory defending the idea of a principled, procedural republic. Among its core elements are the principles of power-sharing under the strict rule of law, and the retention of a "kingly power" at the first rank of

---

[37] *D*, I.9, 29–30/224–25.

government while dispensing with the name and hereditary trappings of kingship.[38] Without openly rejecting more princely interpretations, Machiavelli's republican reading implicitly questions those who take Romulus as a model of extraordinary one-man founding to be imitated by modern princes. This is the other, cautionary side of his discussions of Romulus. In their eagerness to embrace—or perhaps to become—one-man orderers, many contemporaries held up Romulus as an ideal of one-man ruler unrestrained by traditional moral scruples. These men, Machiavelli suggests, commit serious errors of judgment—as do readers who ascribe this view to Machiavelli himself. They forget that Rome became great only after it expelled its kings, restored the principle of kingly authority by dividing it between two officials, and vested the "guard of freedom" in the people. Most importantly, they forget that there is a reason why ancient writers seldom depict Romulus as an ordinary mortal: to warn ordinary mortals against trying to do exactly as he did.[39] If modern would-be princes and their followers take Romulus' achievements as godlike and nonetheless try to imitate them in a literal way, this only shows how grossly they overestimate human powers. No one man, however prudent, has the powers needed to do all the ordering for others as well as himself, and none should be entrusted with such powers. Whenever a city's virtue or greatness depends on one man's extraordinary abilities and does not come "through the virtue of the collectivity that sustains good orders," that city may briefly find happiness, but not stability.[40] Prudent orderers should imitate Romulus' self-limiting methods while avoiding his excessive ones; and adopt as ends his commitment to the public good, not his desire to "order alone."

11.3.
God's executors and modes of free building: Moses

Another ancient *ordinatore* whose deeds are examined in the *Prince* and *Discourses* is Moses. Passages in both works seem to hold up the lawgiver of the Israelites as a model for imitation. The *Prince* describes him as a great liberator who took an abject, scattered "multitude" and made it into a "people" under its own laws. Noting that Moses' outstanding leadership enabled the Hebrews to throw off Egyptian servitude and establish their own homeland in conditions of extreme necessity, Machiavelli appeals to his own countrymen to produce an Italian able to do the same.[41] He observes in the *Discourses* as "a thing known" (*cosa nota*) that Moses

---

[38] Compare Cicero, *Rep.* II.124–33.

[39] Romulus' divinity is much discussed by Roman authors: for example, see *LH*, I.56–58; Cicero, *Rep.* II.112–13;II.124–29. Machiavelli follows convention in not openly questioning his divinity, using the topos to cast a critical light on contemporaries who want to imitate Romulus' actions.

[40] *D*, I.17.47–48/243–45. The same message is the terminus of the discussion of one-man restorers in III.1.211. When Machiavelli says that if a corrupt city "ever manages to rise again," this happens "through the exceptional ability of a single man . . . and not through the exceptional ability of the people as a whole who support good institutions," the sentence continues to depict not a successful conclusion but the recurrent downward cycle described in *D*, I.2.

[41] *P*, XXVI.101–5/189–92.

had been praised since antiquity, along with Lycurgus and Solon, for working to "form laws for the purpose of the common good [*formare leggi a proposito del bene comune*]" that were nonetheless credited to his sole authority.[42] Moses appears together with Aeneas in the first chapter of the *Discourses* as an example of a "free" builder: a foreigner constrained by famine, war, or other necessities to seek a new seat for his people. Moses' specific modes of building are later discussed in more detail. In Book II, chapter 8 he exemplifies free builders who, being forced to establish a new home for large numbers of refugees, find themselves under an "ultimate necessity" (*una ultima necessità*) to use extreme violence. Machiavelli notes that Moses and his followers were constrained to inhabit foreign countries, eventually seizing them for themselves and changing their names. Thus Moses "called that part of Syria seized by him Judea." Similar renaming, Machiavelli points out, occurred when various peoples moved in large numbers to seize the corrupted Roman Empire.[43]

Although Machiavelli's remarks about Moses are consistently admiring and respectful, this does not mean that he agreed with all those who sought to imitate his example. His remarks pose questions about whether Moses' actions are imitable, and if some are, what kind of imitation this must be. In one obvious sense, the *Prince* does treat Moses as a model for the man or men who Machiavelli wants to unite divided Italians and lead them out of their "servitude" to foreign powers. These liberating *ends* are indeed worth imitating. But does Machiavelli also suggest that the *means* used by Moses are suited to the task of redeeming Italians, or any other downtrodden people?

When considering whether Moses' methods can or should be imitated, readers may start by comparing them with the other modes of city-building described in the first chapter of the *Discourses*. In this context, Moses' mode of building sounds promising enough. As a foreign builder, Moses had to show more *virtú* than peoples such as the Athenians and Venetians who fled their original habitation in order to make life "easier" for themselves. His modes were freer than those of Romulus, who was a native of the place where he built. Later in Book II, too, Machiavelli underscores Moses' iron determination to overcome his people's servitude by forging them into a well-armed, independent *popolo*. These features undoubtedly deserve to be imitated in some way, not least as a corrective to the conduct of Italian princes in Machiavelli's era who, as he saw it, had sold their own peoples into foreign *servitú*. On the other hand, Machiavelli compares Moses' achievements with those of another founder whose actions are at least as worthy of imitation: his fellow "free" founder Aeneas. In Book I, chapter 1, Moses is presented as a builder for peoples who "inhabit the cities they find in the countries they acquire." No more is said here about his methods of inhabiting and acquiring other cities. We learn only that Moses used his powers of "free" building to occupy an existing city built by others, not to create a new one. Aeneas, by contrast, used his powers of free building to "build anew." Only "in this case," Machiavelli

---

[42] *D*, I.9.30/224.
[43] *D*, II.8.144/347–48.

remarks—apparently referring to the second, "new" mode of building—does one "recognize [*conosce*] the virtue of the builder" in all its aspects.[44]

The subtle contrast between free foreign builders who seize existing cities and those who build anew is drawn more starkly in Book II. Here Moses exemplifies orderers of peoples who are "many" and constrained by extreme necessity to abandon their homes. Wars fought by such vast numbers of refugees are extremely "cruel and frightful" (*crudelissima e paventosissima*), since it often appears to them that they have no choice but to use ruthless means for their own survival. Aeneas exemplifies leaders of migrants who are "not many." Even if they wanted to, such smaller bands have little chance of seizing others' cities and making them their own. Since they "cannot use so much violence" they are constrained to "seize some place with art." But the greater constraints on their own physical power elicit greater *virtú* in the laws and orders they make in their new seat. Instead of imposing themselves with violence on foreign cities, foreign builders such as Aeneas and Dido were constrained to build anew among pre-existing inhabitants of the lands that took them in. They maintain themselves in a new country "by way of friends and confederates" through "the consent of neighbors where they settled."[45]

Compared with these modes of free foreign building, Moses' methods look more dangerous, and ethically more ambivalent. Before trying to imitate Moses, aspiring redeemers of debased peoples should perhaps consider whether or not the modes used by Aeneas are an option for them. Clearly Moses deserves high praise for ordering his people to resist slavery. But resistance does not always lead to stable freedom or independence. A great deal depends on how one founds new orders aimed at securing a people's *libertà*. When new orders are founded on a violent conquest of others' cities, these controversial foundations can undermine the newly liberated people's free orders. It may be that more complete self-legislative *virtú* is shown by builders who are constrained to build new cities of their own, and who because of their small numbers must use persuasion to gain the goodwill of previous inhabitants.

Of course, Machiavelli acknowledges that Aeneas' mode of building may not seem a realistic option for every free foreign builder. If the refugees are very numerous, their leaders might judge that they have no choice but to emulate Moses and use more violent methods. Finding no vacant lands where they can build anew for so many, they must occupy places that are already inhabited by others. Nonetheless, Machiavelli's comments suggest the need for extreme circumspection about following the Mosaic model in these respects. The main reason is suggested in the *Prince* when Machiavelli remarks coolly: "one should not reason about Moses, as he was a mere executor of things that had been ordered for him by God [*uno mero esecutore delle cose che gli erano ordinate da Dio*]." Out of respect for this tradition, Machiavelli refrains from judging what Moses himself did. But he implies that if

---

[44] *D*, I.1.8/200. What "this case" refers to is ambiguous, and could include both types of free building. But further remarks confirm the suspicion that this is one of Machiavelli's deliberate ambiguities: a judgment that seems to relate to two or more subjects, but on reflection turns out to apply only to one.

[45] *D*, II.8.143–45/346–48.

Moses was a "mere executor" of God's will—meaning that God and not Moses was the real *ordinatore* of the Hebrew people—then this in itself is a good reason for ordinary human orderers to avoid imitating his methods. The chapter goes on to suggest that while latter-day imitators of Moses such as Savonarola claim to be "executors" of God's orders, these claims are untrustworthy.[46] It is therefore imprudent to follow men who claim to employ Moses' methods of free building. Unlike Moses himself, no one can be sure that his imitators really have God's authority to seize the cities of others with violent means. If they lack divine authority and do not seek *ordinario* human authorization from the inhabitants of their new seat in the manner of Aeneas, they will almost certainly fail to build securely.

How then should ordinary people respond when they encounter a man who, claiming to act as God's executor, calls on them to support such extreme and violent modes of action? Machiavelli's reasonings suggest that people who regard their leaders as fallible mortals should consider two questions very carefully. First, are violent methods really the *only* effective response to whatever extreme necessity confronts them? If Moses was just following God's orders, he obviously had no choice in his methods. Free will did not guide him; divine orders did. Ordinary human agents, on the other hand, always have a margin of choice even in the face of "ultimate necessity." Indeed, they have no choice but to choose their methods and take responsibility for their choices, not impute their results to some higher agency. Machiavelli subtly prods readers to ask: could the constraints described by some as irresistible necessity, and cited to justify violent reactions, have been addressed through less extraordinary methods? It may be very difficult for numerous migrants to get the people in a new place to consent to their presence, let alone to their authority. But if their numbers are many, this raises the question whether they faced an irresistible necessity to leave their previous home at all. Machiavelli considers this question in relation to the Maurusians, "a people of Syria in antiquity" who fled before the onslaught of Moses' troops:

> Since they heard the Hebrew peoples were coming and judged that they could not resist them, they thought it was better to save themselves and leave their own country than to lose themselves also in trying to save it. They removed with their families and went from there into Africa, where they placed their seat [*sedia*], expelling [*cacciando*] the inhabitants they found in those places. Thus those who had not been able to defend their own country were able to seize that of others.

Like the people from whom they fled, the Maurusians proceeded to seize others' lands and build by means of conquest and violence. But the passage quietly raises the question of why they were unable to defend their own country. Machiavelli does not say that in this case failure was due to a deficit of virtue, any more than it was for Moses' Hebrews. He does imply that anyone who thinks of imitating the Maurusians should consider this possibility in their own case. After all, even the most "frightful" inundations of peoples can be contained if they "encounter good

---

[46] *P*, VI.22/131.

arms [*buone armi*]." The Maurusians evidently did not have such arms or judge it possible to build them. They may have been right, but not all their imitators are in identical straits.[47] Before fleeing in large numbers to do to others what was done to you, beleaguered peoples should consider other means of self-defense. They should ask whether more virtuous leaders and orders might induce large peoples to stay and fight, as the Romans did when faced by comparably ferocious onslaughts by the Gauls.[48]

When evaluating the choices of peoples driven by necessity to invade others' lands, Machiavelli is more directly critical of the Gauls' modes than those of the Maurusians and Hebrews. Like the Hebrews under Moses, Machiavelli says that the Gauls judged that they were compelled by an "ultimate necessity" to seek to "eliminate everyone, since they wish to live on what others were living on." It appeared to their leaders that many of their people had to seek new land, and if necessary to "expel or kill the ancient inhabitants of it." But Machiavelli goes on to intimate that this necessity was caused partly by deficient domestic orders. Had the Gauls been better organized to feed and govern their growing population, there might have been no need to move *en masse* into others' lands. Machiavelli makes this critical point obliquely, by setting example of the ancient Gauls alongside those of Germany and Hungary in his own times. In the past, he notes, these countries were sources of massive migrations and "barbarian" violence. If these fearsome inundations had now ceased, this was because those peoples had since "improved their country so that they can live there comfortably" and were thus not "necessitated to change their place." From being a source of violent population exchanges, had become a "bastion" of order holding back invaders.[49]

A second question for followers of the more ruthless kind of free builder concerns the consequences of using these modes. Are violent methods such as seizing other peoples' cities likely to achieve their intended results: to give unfree people more control over their destiny by establishing them securely in a new "seat"? If a large people does have to deal with hostile new neighbors yet lacks a *redentore* who is guided by God, it may have to consider methods other than those used by Moses. Without assurance about their leaders' divinely given powers, its members face the responsibility to choose their methods with care. The basic choice is, as Machiavelli puts it here, to deal with pre-existing inhabitants of a new seat by way of force and fortresses, or "by way of friends and confederates." Moses, he observes in Book III, was able to take the way of unrestrained force. "Whoever reads the Bible judiciously will see," Machiavelli writes, "that since he wished his laws and his orders to go forward, Moses was forced to kill infinite men who, moved by

[47] *D*, II.8.144–45/348.

[48] Thus after the Romans were nearly frightened away from their city by the "ultimate necessity" of Gaulish onslaughts, the Roman people were reordered under Camillus' leadership, thus overcoming the apparent "necessity" to resettle on someone else's land. In the end there proved no need for the Romans to have "extraordinary" recourse to the conquest of others' land, since they were "in the ordinary course armed and warlike" (*D*, III.30.280–81/491–93).

[49] *D*, II.8.143–45/346–49; compare Machiavelli's more positive account of Germanic "orders" of emigrating in *FH*, I.1, discussed in chap. 4, sec. 4.2.

nothing but envy, were opposed to his plans."[50] Once again, Machiavelli refrains from judging Moses' ruthless methods because they were ordered by God. But unless people in later times are sure that their leaders are God's true executors, they must not exempt their methods from judgment, but should weigh matters very carefully before imitating Moses' modes. As Machiavelli notes in another context, it is necessary for a new prince who occupies a foreign city to destroy it and expel or kill its previous inhabitants "when his foundations are weak and he may not turn to civil way of life by way either of kingdom or of republic." These methods may enable him to assert power over a new territory. But they make it hard, if not impossible, to establish secure authority or any "human" way of life:

> to build new cities, to take down those built, to exchange the inhabitants from one place to another; and, in sum, not to leave anything untouched [intatta] in that province, so that there is no rank, no order, no state, no wealth there that he who holds it does not know [riconosca] it as from you; and to take as one's model [mira] Philip of Macedon, father of Alexander, who from a small king became prince of Greece with all these modes. He who writes of him says that he transferred men from province to province as herdsmen transfer their herds. These modes are very cruel, and enemies to every way of life, not only Christian but human [crudelissimi e nomici d'ogni vivere, non solamente cristiano, ma umano]; and any man whatever should flee from them and wish to live in private rather than as king with so much ruin to men. Nonetheless, he who does not wish to take this first way of good must enter into this evil if he wishes to maintain himself.

The "first way of the good [prima via del bene]" was described in the preceding chapter, which argues that those who want to introduce new forms of rule in an old state (stato) should allow the people to retain many of their "ancient modes" even while seeking to turn them toward "a new and free way of life." Read in its full context, Machiavelli's point in the next chapter is clearly not that men who occupy new countries should rush to imitate the modes of Moses and the inhumane, tyrannical ones of Philip. If they regard themselves as having some margin of free will, rather than being thoroughly determined by external necessity, they should wish to take the first mode of respect toward the people for whom they rebuild. And if they do not wish this because they are ambitious for "absolute power, which is called tyranny by the authors," they must be prepared to take full responsibility for their actions.[51] They must realize that if they imitate Moses' or Philip's methods, they cannot do so halfway. At the end of chapter 26 Machiavelli touches one of the Discourses' recurring arguments: that from a standpoint of reflective prudence—which concurs with judgments based on sound principles—when new foundations are built, there are no reliable middle ways between that of seeking willing consentimento and imposing new modes through violence. If you choose the second, you will destroy the trust needed to pursue the first, and

---

[50] D, III.30.280/492.
[51] D, I.25–26.60–62/256–58.

create a situation where only the total destruction of your enemies can save you. Either you must choose respectful persuasion as your guiding mode, or seek "ultimate victory" over your enemies, perhaps even their total destruction. If you opt for the latter mode, be prepared to face the consequences. Once you resolve to use extraordinary violence to establish a new *stato*, be prepared then to perform and take responsibility for the most inhumane—not "only" un-Christian—acts. As Machiavelli has a group of magistrates say when trying to dissuade the Duke of Athens from becoming a tyrant, his choice is clear. Either "you have to hold this city with the greatest violence [*con massima violenzia*]" since all the halfway measures—fortresses, guards, friends outside—"are not enough"; or "you have to be content with the authority that we," the citizens of Florence, "have given you [*data*]. And we urge you to this," the magistrates continue, "reminding you that that dominion is alone lasting which is voluntary."[52]

A common "realist" reading of Machiavelli's arguments against taking "middle ways" says that he advises readers to bite the bullet and adopt un-Christian, and if necessary inhumane, methods when doing so seems the only way to assert one's *dominio*. As I have argued elsewhere, however, he poses these stark either-or alternatives in the same way as Livy's and Thucydides' most prudent orators: to warn hearers about the prohibitive costs of violent action, usually to their own security as well as their reputation for humaneness. Machiavelli's bottom line is that if there is the slightest doubt about your own divine calling or that of men you follow, beware of endorsing extraordinary means while presuming that God commands them. Violence always provokes hatred among human beings, even if some judge that it was directed by God. And while "those lords can make their lordship safe who have few enemies . . . amidst universal hatred one never finds any security" since "he who fears every man cannot secure himself against anyone."[53] The main thrust of Machiavelli's reasonings about Moses, then, is not to encourage imitation in a literal or straightforward sense. It is rather to warn readers against imitating all his modes even when they pursue ends, such as liberating a downtrodden people, that resemble his. Ordinary mortals need to find other, more *ordinario* means to achieve similar ends, since only men whose every move is directed by God can always get away with using extraordinary means. All the others may go a certain distance with such means and think that they too can get away with it. But once they choose the path of violence, they usually find themselves under an "ultimate necessity" that is at least partly of their own making: a necessity to do things that are incompatible with "any way of life," let alone any way of *civiltà*. People who choose this path corrupt their own moral judgments and, what is worse, defeat their own hopes of living a secure civil or "human" life.

When Machiavelli refers to contemporary imitators of Moses, he most often has one man in mind: Friar Girolamo Savonarola, who sometimes claimed to have Moses-like powers of prophecy. The parallels Machiavelli draws between the two men relate not to modes of founding but to their ability to persuade others that they

[52] *FH*, II.34.92–93/408.
[53] Ibid.

knew God's will and acted on divine instructions. In the context of the *Prince*, the comparison serves as a warning to men presumptuous enough to claim that they are God's chosen agents. Here Machiavelli includes Moses among the innovative "princes" who gained authority by way of *virtú*. One of the distinctive qualities of *virtuoso* innovators (*innovatori*) is that they "stand by themselves." The unvirtuous sort are those "who depend on others." The latter, Machiavelli says, must "come to ill and never accomplish anything" because they must "beg" (*preghino*, lit. "pray") to achieve their ends; the former are more successful because they "depend on their own and are able to use force [*dependono da loro proprii e possono forzare*]." If Moses is counted among the "armed prophets" (*profeti armati*) of ancient times, this was because the Bible tells us that he was a man of outstanding *virtú* in his own right, although he acted strictly on directives from God.

Machiavelli counts Savonarola among the "unarmed prophets" (*profeti disarmati*) who "come to ill and never accomplish anything." He does not simply mean that Savonarola lacked military troops to defend himself. The word "arms" is used in a richly metaphorical way throughout the *Prince*. In its broadest sense, *armi* is Machiavelli's word for whatever conditions are necessary to "hold" secure authority. Among the arms Savonarola lacked were those ordinary persuasions needed to give stable authority to ordinary mortals. Such reasons acquire "force" when they are given the form of human laws and orders. Throughout the *Prince* Machiavelli plays on two meanings of *forza*. The word may refer to physical compulsion, or to the juridical and ethical authority exerted by publicly authorized laws. Force in the second sense is not opposed to law or persuasive reasoning, but depends on them.[54] The *Prince*'s contrast between armed and unarmed prophets refers to this juridical aspect as well as to the more obvious military one. Moses, Cyrus, Theseus, and Romulus were "armed" not just because they commanded armies, but because they relied to some degree on ordinary human persuasions to establish durable laws and orders.[55] Moses may have been a mere instrument of God when he led his people out of Egypt; but in order to impose new orders in a new land, he had to work as one human being obliged to persuade others to follow his lead. If the Bible tells us that God was the true author of Moses' works, the works themselves show the authority of a *virtuoso* man. Savonarola, by contrast, "was ruined in his new orders as soon as the multitude began not to believe in them." Having relied for his authority on unreasoning belief in his prophetic powers, as soon as one or two of his prophecies failed, he lost all credibility and "had no mode for holding firm [*tenere fermi*] those who had believed nor for making unbelievers believe."[56] The kind of belief people had in Savonarola's prophecies was infirm, unfounded, and therefore an unstable basis for any well-ordered program of reforms. The implicit message for citizens is

---

[54] In Greek the word for necessity, *anangkē*, has a similar ambivalence: it is sometimes associated with force (*bia*), sometimes with what must be done as a matter of moral duty (*deonta*, related to *deos*, fear in the sense of awe or reverence.)

[55] Cyrus is something of an odd man out in this series; but in Xenophon's account, he still used the forms of old laws and good Persian traditions to make his corrupt deeds appear good. See chap. 2, sec. 2.2.

[56] *P*, VI.24–25/132–33. Savonarola suddenly lost popularity after making predictions that failed.

to be wary of men who present themselves as saviors of their people. They should be equally wary if the man is a friar, a nobleman, or an ordinary citizen. Italy might stand in urgent need of a *redentore*, but not just any self-styled redeemer will do. If any one man emerges who believes he can do all the necessary work alone and with little difficulty, he is almost certainly not up to the task.[57]

11.4.
Ordinary mortals and the ancient ideal of the one-man legislator

Let us return briefly to some of Machiavelli's dramatic-sounding general statements about one-man "orderers." As we have seen, early in the *Discourses* he states that "it never or rarely happens that any republic or a kingdom is ordered well from the beginning or reformed altogether anew . . . unless it is organized by one individual."[58] This seems to imply that Machiavelli's reasons for rejecting unrestrained one-man rule do not apply at the "beginning" when new cities are being founded, or in times of extreme corruption when they must be "reformed altogether anew." Perhaps Machiavelli sees these situations as involving uniquely limitless individual freedom where *virtuoso* men can act "alone," unimpeded by ordinary orders? If a rare, *virtuoso* man emerges who knows "goods" unknown to the ordinary run of people, perhaps he is justified in using unilateral violence, deception, or any other extraordinary means to make others obey him?

Preconceptions of this kind have dominated discussions of Machiavelli's work for so long that it is hard for dissenting interpretations to get a serious hearing. By examining Machiavelli's finely discriminating treatments of ancient founders, however, I hope to enlarge the question mark over the presumption that he urges *virtuoso* individuals to throw off ethical and juridical constraints. Machiavelli recognizes that in corrupt times many people do take it as a "general rule" that rebellion against constraints is necessary for their salvation. Individuals who show a willingness to ignore constraints are seen in such times as "wiser" than the average run of men, who blindly accept the hollow conventions that constitute whatever is called morality or religion. More than anyone else in his times and arguably

[57] Compare the discussion of Moses' "stratagems" for persuading people to follow their laws and preserve their states in Spinoza 2007 (1669–70), XVII.6–16. "A person's judgement," he writes, "admittedly may be subjected to another's in many different and sometimes almost unbelievable ways. . . . Yet however much skilful methods may accomplish in this respect, these have never succeeded in altogether suppressing men's awareness that they have a good deal of sense of their own and that their minds differ no less than their palates. Moses . . . subjected his people's judgement to himself, not by trickery but rather by his divine virtue, as he was believed to be a man of God and to speak and do all things by divine inspiration. But even he could not prevent malicious rumors and innuendoes. Much less can other rulers." Moreover, "while the prophets themselves were endowed with divine virtue, they were still private individuals, and . . . therefore the warnings, rebukes, and denunciations which they took the liberty to deliver to men merely antagonized them and failed to set them on the right path." For these reasons a city needs its own laws and a citizen body of armed and equal individuals to restrain "the leaders of a merely human state [*humani imperii*]" but also those of theocracies. Ibid., XX.2, XIX.18, XVII.18–19.
[58] *D*, I.9.29–30/449–50.

in ours, Machiavelli offered a penetrating analysis of these convictions. But his analysis is not prescription. He does not advise readers to act as these men act, or to judge actions by corrupt standards of prudence or virtue or freedom. Machiavelli tries to diagnose the causes that lead so many to judge in this way; to get readers to reflect on both these causes and their consequences; and to persuade them to modify their defective beliefs, without sermons or aggressive harangues.[59] The self-assertive amoralism described in the *Prince* can be called "Machiavellian" in the sense that no one since ancient times had given such a complete description of the disease. It is not Machiavellian if that word refers to judgments *defended* by Machiavelli.

To clarify the connection between his remarks on ancient "orderers" and the persuasions Machiavelli offers to modern princes, let us briefly consider similar arguments made by ancient writers. The idea of the almost godlike lawgiver was a recurring topos of ancient writing, used to stimulate reflections on whether and how mere mortals should try to imitate quasi-divine legislative achievements. The topos was a favorite among writers who were concerned about the rise of assertive, charismatic leaders seeking to assume princely powers in a republic. It enjoyed a revival when Julius Caesar persuaded the Roman Senate to give him the powers of dictator for life, promising the people that he would use these extraordinary powers to restore good republican orders. At the time, critics evoked the ancient Greek motif of the ideal legislator to warn fellow citizens about the dangers of encouraging one-man rule. In his dialogue the *Republic*, Cicero has the main interlocutor set out the traditional Roman view of one-man founders, which also implies skepticism about one-man reformers:

> Cato used to say that our constitution was superior to those of other States on account of the fact that almost every one of these other commonwealths had been established by one man, the author of their laws and institutions; for example, Minos in Crete, Lycurgus in Sparta. . . . On the other hand our own commonwealth [*res publica*] was based upon the genius, not of one man, but of many; it was founded, not in one generation, but in a long period of several centuries and many ages of men. For, said [Cato], there never has lived a man possessed of so great genius that nothing could escape him, nor could the combined powers of all the men living at one time possibly make all necessary provisions for the future without the aid of actual experience and the test of time.

Cicero invokes the ideal of one-man orderers precisely in order to reject its normative value for Rome. He argues that if the superiority of Rome's constitution was due to its development by many men, not one, it was easily ruined by the actions of one alone. The dialogue warns readers not to let traditional praise for Romulus serve as an excuse for such men.[60] Machiavelli agrees with Cato's and Cicero's view that neither founding, maintaining, nor reordering is best done by one alone, but

[59] Compare Glaucon and Adeimantus' devil's advocate arguments in Plato, *Rep.* II.
[60] Cicero, *Rep.* II.110–13, 156–59.

requires the ongoing work of many. Even if a single man using "extreme force" could bring a corrupt city back to some semblance of goodness, "as soon as such a one is dead" the city will revert to its former bad habits. This, Machiavelli notes, happened in Thebes, "which could hold the forms [*forma*] of a republic and its empire through the virtue of Epaminondas while he lived, but returned to its first disorders when he was dead." The cause of this pattern is clear: "there cannot be one man of such long life as to have enough time to inure to good a city that has been inured to bad for a long time." Until extraordinary individuals become immortal, the ambition to reform corrupt people single-handedly and "at a stroke" is doomed to fail.[61]

In their use of indirect methods of reasoning, Machiavelli's arguments frequently resemble the original Greek models used by Roman republican writers such as Cicero, Sallust, Livy, and Tacitus more than the Latin writings. Simply to restate Cato's words would have sounded hopelessly naïve in his own corrupt times, when many people seemed to favor a Caesarist interpretation of ancient legislators. Accustomed to hearing the good name of republic abused for all manner of partisan and private ends, readers' eyes would surely glaze over if they read yet another idealistic defense of republics. Machiavelli's approach to the problem of one-man orderers has much in common with Plato's subtly dialectical treatment in his dialogues *Statesman* and *Laws*. Near the end of the *Statesman*, the dialogue's participants agree that government by a wise individual or a few would be their "first choice." But further discussion shows that this ideal is unsuitable for cities where human beings, not gods, are responsible for government. If statesmanship depended on the wisdom of one man or minority, citizens would often be subject to the arbitrary whims of men who claim to have superior expertise. Even the best human experts err: they imagine that their knowledge of good and bad is more secure than it is, and misjudge the best means for achieving what they deem to be good. While such men should rely on persuasion (*peithō*) to move other less knowing people to do what they judge to be correct, this does not always happen. When men who regard themselves as expert statesmen cannot persuade their fellow citizens but believe that they know what is good for them, they claim that their superior wisdom justifies the use of force even if this is "contrary to what has been written down [*para ta gegrammena*]" in established laws. Asking "what will be the name to give to the use of force [*bias*] in this case?" the dialogue's main character says it may be called an "unhealthy mistake" (*hamartēma*) contrary to the proper expertise of statesmanship (*hē politikos*). A true statesman, this implies, should know that judgments about the means used to direct others to good ends are a fundamental part of the true knowledge (*epistēmē*) of statesmanship.

By a process of elimination, the interlocutors find that they are left with a "second-best" strategy. They agree that the idea of statesmanship calls for a kind of authority that places restraints on abuse by experts, yet still allows genuine exper-

---

[61] *D*, I.17.47–48/467–68. Compare Livy (*LH*, II.1): "My task from now on will be to trace the history in peace and of a free nation, governed by annually elected officers of state and subject not to the caprice of individual men, but to the overriding authority of law."

tise to rule. What is needed is to produce a "good imitation of that true constitution of one man ruling with expertise [*meta technēs archontos politeian eis dunamin mimēsesthai*]." And the principal requirement for such an imitation is that as far as possible, all constitutions—assuming they have their own laws (*autois tōn nomōn*) "must never do anything contrary to what is written or to ancestral customs [*para ta gegrammena kai patria ethē*]." By treating laws and ancestral customs as the foundation of political knowledge, instead of depending on one or a few to provide the expertise of statesmanship, this "second best" choice avoids the pitfalls of arbitrary rule. The precept "there must be nothing wiser than the laws" emerges as the central pillar of the knowledge "of the statesman" and "of statesmanship." Thus "when some ruler [*archōn*] acts neither according to laws nor according to customs, but pretends to act like the person with expert knowledge [*epistēmōn*], saying that after all one must do what is contrary to what is written down if it is best," such a person must be called a tyrant. What he demonstrates is not true statesmanship but only a bad imitation (*mimēsis*) of it, guided not by knowledge but by "some desire or other combined with ignorance."[62]

The problem of one-man orderers is posed again in Plato's *Laws*. As they prepare to embark together on the enterprise of legislating for a new city, the Athenian Stranger asks his friends to consider how a city can establish "as quickly and efficiently as possible a political order [*hōs dunaton esti taxista kai arista schēsein politeian*] that will enable it to live a life of supreme happiness [*eudaimonestata*]."[63] They agree that there is clearly "no quicker or easier [*thātton kai rhāon*] way" to legislate than to follow the leadership (*hēgemonia*) of one or a few supremely wise men. But what "is difficult, and a very rare occurrence in the history of the world," is a situation in which a godlike love (*erōs theios*) for prudent restraint and justice (*sōphronōn . . . kai dikaiōn*) guides those who wield great power. The Stranger evokes the theme of an ancient golden age of godlike men, saying that "In Trojan times, they say, such a paragon did exist, but he is certainly unheard of today."[64] If by some wonderful accident one could find a single man who combined "supreme power" (*megistēs dunamis*) with "wise judgment and self-restraint" (*phronein . . . kai sōphronein*) this would give birth to the best political order and laws (*politeias tēs aristēs kai nomōn*). The Stranger then laughs at his own "somewhat oracular fiction [*muthos*]," recognizing that such happy conjunctions do not occur among mortals.[65] Ancient myths describe a golden age where legislators were "not men, but beings of a superior and more divine order [*genous theioterou kai ameinonos*]," who found it "easy enough" to look after human interests. But "where the ruler of a state is not a god but a mortal [*mē theos alla tis archē thnētos*], people have no respite from toil and misfortune."[66] The merely human legislator's art resembles that

---

[62] Plato, *Statesman* 296a–301c.

[63] Plato, *Laws* 710b–e.

[64] Compare HH, I.207, II.3, II.45.

[65] Ibid., 711c–712a. The entire Book IV of the *Laws* playfully examines the longing for easy legislative solutions, implying that it is understandable but misplaced; esp. 712, 715.

[66] Ibid., 709a–b, 713c–e. Compare Hobbes' (1998 [1642], 117–18) version of the Greek myth of Prometheus.

of doctors who must know their material with all its imperfections. Like doctors, legislators cannot remold their human subjects or control future accidents. They must work within limits, and know their own limitations.

The terminus of these reasonings is not that mere mortals should avoid emulating godlike rulers and legislators, but that they should imitate the ethical precepts represented in the myths instead of actual deeds. Myths of a golden age of superhuman beings urge men to obey "whatever little spark of immortality lies in us" by dignifying the "edicts of reason with the name of law [tēn toû noû dianomēn eponomazontas nomon]." Plato's Laws sets the rule of law over even supremely wise men, since "where the law is subject to some other authority and has none of its own [an archomenos hē akuros nomos], the collapse of the state, in my view, is not far off." In a sharp retreat from the initial call for a quick and efficient dictator to establish a "supremely happy" city, the Stranger now says that any man who nurtures

> the arrogant [hubreōs] belief that so far from needing someone to control and lead him [oute archontos oute tinos hēgemonos deomenos], he can play the leader to others—there's a man whom God has deserted. And in his desolation he collects others like himself, and in his soaring frenzy he causes universal chaos. Many people think he cuts a fine figure, but before very long he pays to Justice [dikē] no trifling penalty and brings himself, his home and state to rack and ruin.[67]

Similar warnings against the hubris of one-man rulers occur in all Machiavelli's writings. In his poem "On Fortune" he writes:

> If then your eyes light on what is beyond, in one panel Caesar and
>   Alexander you see among those who were happy [felici] while alive,
> From their example we well realise how much he pleases Fortune and how
>   acceptable he is who pushes her, who shoves her, who jostles her.
> Yet nevertheless the coveted harbor one of the two failed to reach, and the
>   other, covered with wounds, in his enemy's shadow was slain.
> After this appear countless men who, that they might fall to earth with a
>   heavier crash, with this goddess have climbed to excessive heights.[68]

Like Plato and other ancient writers, Machiavelli sees the longing for quick-fix solutions to deeply rooted problems as ordinary and human. So is the desire to avoid the labors of self-legislation by finding one man to order things all "at a stroke," guaranteeing supreme happiness.[69] These desires are so perennial that people recur

---

[67] Plato, Laws 714a, 715d, 716a–b.

[68] "On Fortune" (Opere III.37), in Machiavelli: The Chief Works and Others, trans. and ed. Allan Gilbert, vol. 2, pp. 745–49.

[69] Compare the dialectical (and enigmatic) appraisal of one-man rule in Rousseau 1964 (1762), III.6.407–12. He concludes: "But if according to Plato, a King by nature is such a rare person, how many times will nature and chance combine to crown him; and if a royal education necessarily corrupts those who receive it, what is to be hoped for from a series of men brought up to rule?" See Plato, Laws 875a–876d. Rousseau further echoes Machiavelli's complex ironic uses of e/straordinario with regard

to them time and again when they are exhausted by conflict, afraid, or weighed down with self-doubt, even after they have seen the ruinous effects of one-man solutions. It is "almost impossible" to find men who can pull off one-man redemptive acts, but very, very easy to find ambitious men willing to try. This explains why Machiavelli returns so often to the theme of one-man orderers.[70] It is of the utmost importance to him, as it was to his ancient writers, that people should reason for themselves about why one-man solutions are unstable. It is not enough that they should see particular examples as pernicious but make exceptions for other one-man rulers, saying that these conditions or that individual will not fall prey to weakness or *hubris*. The Florentines spurned many tyrants and princes, yet they embraced the Medicis and Savonarola. People must grasp the reasons why *no* human individual who is released from strict legal constraints should be trusted to order well. Otherwise they will remain susceptible to appeals by *some* individuals who claim to be different from the rest.

11.5.
Persuasion in the *Prince*: On maintaining one's own arms

Machiavelli's views on the comparative merits of princely and republican governments in the *Discourses* are stated plainly in the final chapters of Book I. We read there that even the best princes are less trustworthy, less powerful, and have worse judgment than well-ordered peoples. Most importantly, peoples have more respect for laws than princes. While both princes and peoples in long-lasting republics "have had need of being regulated by the laws [*bisogno d'essere regolato dalle leggi*]," if one compares a prince who is obligated (*obligato*) to the laws with a people "fettered" (*incatenato*) by them, "more virtue will always be seen in the people than in the prince." For these reasons, "cities in which peoples are princes [*città dove i popoli sono principi*]" are most stable and make greater increases (*augumenti*) in a short time.[71] In the *Florentine Histories* too, Machiavelli's regard for the political expertise of most princes is ambivalent at best. Even princes whom he appears to

---

to the "extraordinary" (*extraordinaire*) legislator whose "superior activity . . . has nothing to do with human dominion. For if one who commands men should not command laws, one who commands laws should also not command men. Otherwise his laws, ministers of his passions, would often only perpetuate his injustices, and he could never avoid having private views alter the sanctity of his work." Rousseau, 1964 (1762), II.7.381–82.

[70] This helps to explain Spinoza's reading: if Machiavelli "describes at great length" the means used by "a prince whose sole motive is lust for despotic power," Spinoza writes, surely he did this for "some good purpose, as we must believe of so wise a man." The most likely purposes were to warn peoples against the risks of trying to topple tyrants by force or conspiracy, since this tends to make tyrants even more cunning and despotic; to warn a free people against "entrusting its welfare entirely to one man"; and to warn aspiring one-man rulers of the dangers of tyranny. Too many rulers have "evidently believed their subjects would willingly allow themselves to be ruled by them and readily submit only if their subjects and everyone else regarded them not as equals but as gods." But "it is only where men become wholly barbarous that they allow themselves to be so openly deceived and become slaves useless to themselves rather than subjects." Spinoza 1958 (1677), V.7, XVII.6.

[71] *D*, I.58.118/318–19; also I.57–60.

praise for their personal qualities leave behind a mixed legacy of reputed glory and de facto corruption. When they die, the results of their shadier deeds come to light in their city's loss of internal freedoms, the corrosion of the rule of law, and vulnerability to foreign intrusions.[72]

This brings us back to the old question: if Machiavelli's views of princely government are this critical, why did he write an entire book dedicated to a Medici prince that, moreover, seems to give helpful advice to aspiring one-man rulers on how to increase their power? The easiest way to explain the apparent discrepancy between the line on princes taken in the *Prince* and the more critical line taken in later works is that Machiavelli changed his mind. Chapters 1 and 2 proposed a different explanation: that the main differences between the works are formal, not substantive. The *Prince* and other works put forward the same arguments and principles, but develop them through different genres of writing addressed primarily to different kinds of reader. The main addressees of the *Discourses* are readers well disposed to republics but who, because of their youth or lack of philosophical background, have not critically examined the principled or prudential reasons for their preference. The work's main aim is to reexamine the philosophical foundations of republican principles through the medium of history, thereby placing these principles on a more adequately reasoned basis. The *Florentine Histories* is addressed to citizens of all political persuasions. It analyzes the disorders that come from overassertive partisanship of any kind, including that which turns the preference for popular republics into an intolerant "sect" pitted against citizens who have other preferences. The *Histories'* aims can be described as purgative: its descriptions of the disorders that stem from sectarian intolerance in republics seem designed to purge readers of such extreme dispositions. At the same time, its accounts of wiser persuasions that should have been heeded more consistently suggest non-partisan principles of moderate government that any republic, or indeed prudent prince, should observe.

The same principles are defended in the *Prince*. As Rousseau suggests, at one level the work can be read as a "satire" of corrupt political and ethical judgments. When Machiavelli uses words that usually have positive connotations to describe corrupt deeds, such as "liberality" for bribery and "humanity" for the failure to punish partisans, he imitates similar parodies by ancient authors who showed how ethical language becomes corrupted in corrupt times. But at a less overt level, the work has serious purgative and persuasive aims. It addresses readers who are already princes, who want to become princes, or who find it reasonable that some men should be given one-man princely powers over republics. It assumes that these readers are either extremely ambitious themselves, or so disillusioned by the weak republican orders in their city that they are willing to entrust civil reordering to ambitious individuals. Machiavelli never directly criticizes this pro-princely perspective in the *Prince*. Instead he uses a range of classical literary and philosophical techniques to question it in indirect ways. In the manner of Xenophon's

[72] See chap. 1, sec. 1.1, on the Medici "princes," and chap. 2, sec. 2.2, on Cyrus. Compare the *Castruccio*.

Hiero, a dialogue between a tyrant and a man of letters, Machiavelli tries to engage princes and their supporters in reflections that lead them to see for themselves why princely governments are flawed. The *Prince* is best approached, I suggest, by identifying the methods of double-writing that give it the outward appearance of a treatise defending the amoral pursuit of princely ends. When Machiavelli's modes of writing are set alongside similar literary and philosophical techniques used by ancient authors, it becomes clear that many of the *Prince*'s most notorious statements should not be taken at face value.

One technique is ironic dissimulation, whereby the writer's declared intentions or judgments are contradicted by the substance of his discussion. For example, in the second chapter Machiavelli announces that his book will deal only with principalities, since he discusses republics elsewhere.[73] While appearing to tell princes how to secure a *principato* for themselves, however, those who pay close attention to the book's most reflective advice will discover that a truly secure principality must include many "orders" found in well-ordered republics. Machiavelli's rhetorical standpoint in the *Prince* is comparable to that stated by the prudent elder statesman Niccolò da Uzzano in the *Histories*. When opposing a policy supported by his less judicious compatriots, Uzzano says that he could denounce it as unjust, *disonesto*, or sacrificing public order to private interests; but since he presumes that most readers will be unmoved by such considerations, he will leave out justice and speak only of utility.[74] Despite this disavowal, Uzzano goes on to examine considerations of justice and injustice without explicitly speaking of *giustizia*. The *Prince* treats republics in a similar, oblique way. Since its author assumes that princes who pick up his book are uninterested in forming or maintaining republican orders, he will speak to them only about principalities. The overt perspective is the princely readers' own self-interest, narrowly conceived. Yet close attention to the work's reasonings and examples reveals a very different message beneath these appearances.

Another technique is the ambivalent use of concepts, so that the meaning of famous "Machiavellian" maxims differs according to the meaning readers ascribe to key words. The *Prince* can be seen as setting the pattern for the use of dialectical ambivalence in the later works. One subspecies of dialectical ambivalence is "complex irony," a Socratic technique of double-writing whereby a statement is true if key words are understood in one way, false if understood in another. On narrower, more conventional or literal meanings, one gets corrupt "Machiavellian" maxims. On richer, more reflective meanings, the same statement stands in tension with or subverts the overt message.[75] Another form of dialectical ambivalence occurs when key words in a statement turn out on close reading to be richly layered metaphors. For example, many Socratic writers who inspired Machiavelli used the word "hunting" in the context of arguments that take on new, deeper dimensions when the

---

[73] As many other scholars have noted.

[74] See chap. 9, sec. 9.3.

[75] As de Alvarez (1999, 78) puts it, in the *Prince* Machiavelli "conceals a far more moderate teaching beneath the shocking surface."

word is understood metaphorically: not just meaning "to chase wild animals" but also as a metaphor for philosophical dialogue in practical matters, and for "hunting down" wild human animals, that is, tyrants and others who set themselves above human laws.[76]

The core persuasive argument of the *Prince* is developed through the ambivalent use of a central metaphorical phrase: "one's own arms," *armi proprie*. The phrase occurs in the opening paragraph of the first chapter, when Machiavelli declares that a prince may acquire new dominions "either with the arms of others or with one's own, either by fortune or by virtue [*o con le armi d'altri o con le proprie, o per fortuna o per virtú*]."[77] Readers learn from the outset that any prince who wants to "hold" whatever he acquires should prefer to rely on his *armi proprie* and avoid depending on *le armi d'altri*. As the sentence just cited says, princes who rely on their own arms thereby manifest virtue; those who rely on the arms of others depend on fickle fortune. The question considered throughout the book is therefore: how can a prince come to rely only on his "own arms," making him independent, secure, and praiseworthy? In the later chapter entitled "Why the Italian Princes Have Lost Their States" Machiavelli explains why self-reliance is the primary condition for fulfilling these other princely desires:

> For one should never fall in the belief you can find someone to pick you up. Whether it does not happen or happens, it is not security for you, because that defense was base [*vile*] and did not depend on you. And those defenses alone are good, are certain, and are lasting, that depend on you yourself and on your virtue.[78]

A key to recognizing the *Prince*'s "covert" message is to notice the different meanings expressed by the phrase "one's own arms," and especially the word *armi*. What kind of "arms" do princes need to consolidate power, and what makes arms securely "their own"? The most obvious answers suggest the need for particular forms of military organization. This is indeed one of the most important aspects of Machiavelli's proposals in the *Prince* and elsewhere. He starts by writing in a conventional tone, using the word "arms" as if the word connotes simply the means of military defense. As the argument progresses, however, Machiavelli identifies several further conditions that are needed to secure a prince's "own arms." These conditions are economic and social, political, and juridical. Each set of conditions helps to constitute the prince's *armi proprie* in an extended sense, more adequate to the phrase than any of them taken alone. The persuasive argument of the *Prince* can be reconstructed as a series of steps that take readers—or at least those uncorrupt enough to follow—toward an ever more reflective understanding of what a prudent prince must do if he wants to have reliable arms of "his own."

If there is one relatively uncontroversial aspect of Machiavelli's thought, it is his preference for civilian militias over mercenary armies. This is clearly one of

---

[76] See chap. 3, sec. 3.4.

[77] *P*, I.6/119.

[78] *P*, XXIV.97/186.

the policies he wants to recommend as part of any prudent prince's "own arms." Machiavelli was a keen student of military organization and strategy, and his book *The Art of War* deals with these issues in great detail. In the *Prince*, however, he does not argue that new technologies, wealth, or organization within the military are the *foundation* of successful defenses. A more fundamental condition is how well the population of a country is ordered for its own defense. Most polities in Machiavelli's era failed to utilize their "own arms" in this sense because they relied too much on the military arms of "others": that is, on mercenary soldiers and foreign allies. In Machiavelli's view, polities that maintained restrictive citizenship laws and refused to arm or train its own populations for war deprived themselves of their most important source of strength. By contrast, when the Roman republic faced enemies it fought back by mobilizing its own people. Moreover, it continually augmented its fighting powers by granting citizenship to some immigrants and peoples defeated in war. Machiavelli concludes that by imitating these policies a wise prince can always avoid mercenary arms and "turn to his own." Such a prince "has preferred to lose with his own than to win with others, since he judges it no true victory that is acquired with alien arms [*con le arme aliene*]." He advises princes to establish militias comprised of ordinary citizens who are armed and trained in peacetime as well as in war. When one's own subjects are armed, "those arms become yours [*quelle arme diventano tua*]; those whom you suspected become faithful, and those who were faithful remain so; and from subjects they are made into your partisans [*di sudditi si fanno tua partigiani*]."[79]

Here then is a first, essential set of reforms that princes should undertake if they want to rely on "their own arms" to attain reputation and *gloria*. But if a prince is "wise" enough to see the necessity for these military reforms, he should also have the wisdom to understand that they cannot take effect without further reforms to the princely *stato* itself. In order to organize and train his own people to serve as "his own" military arms, a prince needs to secure the people's friendship and *favore*. These, Machiavelli argues in the *Prince* as elsewhere, are a more important "foundation" for princely power than military technologies or wealth. "Let no one," he declares, "resist my opinion on this with that trite proverb, that whoever founds on the people founds on mud."[80] It is a matter of the greatest importance that a prince should "have the people friendly; otherwise he has no remedy in adversity." Popular *favore* is especially necessary in modern times. "Since princes cannot fail to be hated by someone," Machiavelli writes, "they are at first forced not to be hated by the people generally [*dalle università*]; and when they cannot continue this, they have to contrive with all their industry to avoid the hatred of those communities which are most powerful [*quelle università che sono più potenti*]." In times of the Roman emperors, he observes, the most powerful "communities" were the soldiers; "and so those emperors who because they were new had need of extraordinary support [*favori estraordinarii*] stuck to the soldiers rather than the people." But in his own times and those to come, the "most powerful" *università* was the popular. If

---

[79] *P*, XIII–XIV.55/155; XX.83/176–77.
[80] *P*, IX.41/144–45.

in Rome emperors had to satisfy the soldiers "because the soldiers could do more than the people," it has since then become "necessary for all princes except the Turk and the Sultan to satisfy the people rather than the soldiers, because the people can do more than the soldiers."[81] If a prince hands out weapons to hostile or suspect subjects, they may turn their arms and military training against him.

These reflections suggest that the more adequate military *armi* furnished by peoples only become a prince's "own" arms if certain *political* preconditions are met. Machiavelli is teasingly vague about the specific modes and orders needed to convert popular *favore* into princely power. "The prince," he writes, "can gain the people to himself in many modes, for which one cannot give certain rules [*certe regula*] because the modes vary according to circumstances, and so they will be left out [*si lasceranno indreto*]."[82] There is more than a touch of irony in this "omission." Many recent princes, notably the Medicis, had of course discovered the value of popular friendship and knew well how to manipulate it for their partisan ends. There are no "certain rules" for such modes of gaining popular *favore*, not just because the modes are diverse, but also because many of them are extraordinary and corrupt. Those who use them often operate "in the shade," refusing to submit to ordinary laws and standards of civil conduct. Machiavelli describes some of these corrupt modes of gaining favor in chapters 15–19, which consider the appearances and actions that make princes praised or blamed. As we have already seen, his discussions of liberality and parsimony, cruelty and mercy, and keeping faith (chapters 16–18) draw a key distinction between modes that gain favor easily, quickly, and give princes a "name" for competence on the one hand, and those on the other that gain *favore* less quickly and require more *industria*, but hold it more securely than the first. Princes who are prudent as well as wise should see that the easier, extraordinary modes are more corrupt and less effective than the second, more *virtuoso* ones.

Despite his assertion that he will "leave out" discussing non-corrupt, ordinary modes by which princes may gain popular *favore*, Machiavelli does deal extensively with these modes in the *Prince*. He often does so obliquely, under *colore* of chapter headings and openly announced themes that seem to address the prince's narrow self-interest alone. But while appearing to discuss conventional topics—how to measure a prince's forces, on avoiding contempt and hatred, who princes should have as secretaries, and so on—Machiavelli quietly smuggles in arguments that undermine the overt, unprincipled appearances of his advice. When close attention is paid to his "covert" reasonings, a number of *ordinario* ways can be identified that help to secure a prince's "own arms" by increasing popular favor.

In chapter 10, for example, Machiavelli explains the impressive defenses found in "the cities of Germany [*le città della Magna*]" under the chapter heading "In What Mode the Forces of All Principalities Should Be Measured." These cities "are very free [*liberissime*]" and only "obey the emperor when they want to; they do not fear [*non temono*] either him or any other power around, because they are so

[81] *P*, XI.40–41/144; XIX.76, 81.
[82] *P*, IX.40–41/144.

well fortified that everyone thinks their capture [*espugnazione*] would be toilsome and difficult." The fortifications in question are not simply walls and artillery; they also include well-stocked public stores of food and drink. And just as important, the plebs are kept well fed "without loss to the public" because they are given work "in employments [*esercizii*] that are the nerve and life of that city." A first set of preconditions for secure defenses, then, is that the people who provide them have basic material security: a secure employment and livelihood, and therefore freedom from fear of hunger.[83] Further conditions are intimated through the different meanings that Machiavelli ascribes to the word *esercizii*. *Esercizii* include regular military exercises performed by all able-bodied male citizens, as in the next sentence: "They still hold military exercises [*esercizii militari*] in repute, and . . . have many institutions [*molti ordini*] to maintain them." But the *esercizii* in which the plebs are engaged are not only military. The orders that maintain the military in repute include various civil orders that enable the plebs to feed themselves without depending on public largesse or the charity of the wealthy, through employment—military or civilian—that is highly regarded as part of the "nerve and life" of the city. On this idealized account of German cities, princes and wealthy citizens do not treat the plebs as mere cannon fodder, but must respect them as free men on whom their own security depends.[84]

Machiavelli's covert message here is that a well-ordered public economy that ensures a decent living for all a city's people is among the necessary foundations of a prince's military power.[85] This is not just a matter of keeping one's martial herds well fed. Since the plebs are free men, they must be motivated to do whatever is needed to keep a city defended. The economic advantages of Machiavelli's quasi-fictive "German model" are inseparable from their motivational benefits. Plebs who are able to feed themselves through highly valued work are also more content with their princes, and more willing and able to perform their military duties. And princes in cities whose subjects are "very free," secure in their livelihood, respected, and self-respecting will be harder to attack than those who think that walled fortresses, not well-"armed" subjects, are their best defense.

So far, Machiavelli's argument says (1) that popular favor is the most important condition for a prince to secure his "own" military arms; and (2) that *favore* is best secured when a prince orders civil life so that the people can make a decent, independent living for themselves. By themselves, these arguments do not necessarily imply that the people should be granted civil *authority*. The *Prince* says nothing explicit about the value of public assemblies where the people can "vent" their humors. Nor does it spell out other republican positions stated in the *Discourses* and other works: that peoples are better guards of freedom than princes, for example, or that anyone among the people should be permitted to hold princely offices. The

[83] *P*, X.43–44/146–47. See chap. 8, sec. 8.2 on the bad effects that ensue when these conditions are lacking, exemplified by the Ciompi uprising.

[84] See also *AW*, VI.130–39/657–65 and "German Affairs [*Rapporto di Cose della Magna*]," *Opere* I:69–84, where Machiavelli "imitates" Tacitus.

[85] These passages recall his memoranda to the Soderini government, where he argued that the creation of a civilian militia depended above all on *giustizia*; see chap. 8, sec. 8.1.

Prince's advice seems to respect the parameters of traditional princely aims and responsibilities. In chapter 9 Machiavelli tells princes that they may think of their friendship with the people in instrumental terms as a means of making them "obligated [*obligano*] . . . to your fortune." This should be easy enough if they undertake to "protect" the people from overambitious *grandi*. The language of friendship, protection, and making peoples obligated conveys an old-fashioned, top-down image of princely relations with the people, suggesting that the prince may "gain the people to himself" while retaining clear control. By simply leaving subjects to live in their traditional way and affording them a degree of material security, a prince might gain his people's friendship for a time without increasing their role in government.[86]

But Machiavelli suggests that other, less traditional measures are needed to make the people one's "own" faithful defenders. If peoples are expected to assume this important role, princes will have to offer them more than old-fashioned protection handed down from princely heights. Readers who progress through the initial stages of reflection on what is needed to secure a prince's *armi proprie* should recognize a third step in the *Prince*'s reasonings, which says (3) that popular goodwill can only be secured if the people are given a share of political authority. Between lines skillfully crafted in the unthreatening, traditional language of *favore* and *protezione*, Machiavelli hints at the need for far-reaching changes in existing relations between rulers and ruled. As in the *Discourses*, his main point is that princes who seek sustained popular goodwill and assurance that the people willingly participate in civil militias must increase popular authority in the *stato*. This is a condition for making "one's own" people the foundations of "one's own" arms. Machiavelli makes this point by subtly modifying traditional "advice to princes" in ways that pave the way for more republican orders.

A first modification concerns the form of obligations between princes and subjects. Traditional princely thinking holds that princes protect, while subjects are duty-bound to show gratitude for that protection. Machiavelli's new advice for princes is to recognize that subjects are *their* best protectors. Having previously seemed to affirm the traditional notion that popular friendship depends on getting a prince's *protezione*, in chapter 10 Machiavelli says that both sides have to do the protecting, and both therefore have obligations to each other. In a *stato* where the people's arms are also the prince's *armi proprie*, the responsibilities of protection cannot just be those of princes toward subjects; subjects also have responsibilities to protect their prince. Their dependence is reciprocal. And if a prince wants to be sure of his own people's good faith in fulfilling their side of the bargain, their relationship should not be asymmetrical, with one side giving favors to the other while holding the reins of power. Only two-way obligations make people reliable partisans and partners. It follows that princes owe obligations of gratitude and respect to peoples just as peoples owe them to friendly princes. Subjects "come to unite with their prince so much the more, since it appears he has an obligation to them, their houses having been burned and their possessions ruined in his defense." The reason, one

---

[86] *P*, IX.40–41/144–45.

may infer, is that the most binding obligations are formed between equal and free agents, not between superiors and inferiors, masters and dependents. For "the nature of men is to be obligated [*obligarsi*] as much by the benefits [*benefizi*] they give as the benefits they receive." Presumably, one of the modes of gaining the people to a prince is to treat them as equals in obligation, and to show gratitude for the protection they afford him as he expects them to be grateful for his.[87]

A second subtle modification in traditional princely thinking concerns the importance of free speech and consultation. In chapter 23, under the deceptively conventional heading "In What Mode Flatterers Are to Be Avoided," Machiavelli poses an apparent dilemma. On the one hand, "there is no way to guard oneself from flattery unless men understand [*intendino*] that they do not offend you in telling you the truth." On the other hand, "when everyone can tell you the truth, they lack reverence for you." At first glance Machiavelli's advice seems to endorse restrictions on freedoms of speech. A prince must choose "wise men in his state" and give only to them "freedom to speak the truth to him [*dare libero adito a parlargli la verità*]." But subsequent passages mitigate the apparent harshness of this advice. While a prudent prince should choose his trusted advisers carefully, once they are chosen he should give them no cause to fear frank speaking. A prince's *armi proprie* are strengthened much more by getting the fullest possible truth from trusted advisers than by uncritical or timorous forms of "reverence." In conferring with his "wise men" the prince

> should ask them about everything and listen to their opinions; then he should decide by himself, in his own mode; and with the councils and with each member of them he should behave in such a mode that everyone knows that the more freely he speaks, the more he will be accepted. . . . A prince, therefore, should always take counsel, but when he wants, and not when others want it. . . . But he should be a very broad questioner [*largo domandatore*], and then, in regard to the things he asked about, a patient listener to the truth; indeed, he should become upset when he learns that anyone has any hesitation to speak it to him.

To illustrate how free consultation helps princes to gain public trust and public support, Machiavelli offers a counterexample of a contemporary emperor, Maximilian, who weakened his position by acting differently.[88] Maximilian "did not take counsel from anyone," for he was "a secretive man who does not communicate his plans to anyone, nor seek their views." Then when his plans were introduced and

---

[87] *P*, X.44/147. On the idea that well-armed friends are the best source of one's own arms, see TPW, I.82 and Plato, *Sixth Letter* 322d: more than military equipment or gold, there is "no greater source of power for all purposes than in the gaining of steadfast friends possessed of a sound character." In a passage recalling the *Prince*'s account of philosophical hunting, Plato identifies knowledge of how to gain such friends with the "fair science of ideas [*tōn eidōn sophia tē kalē*]," adding that philosophy properly understood provides a "safeguard against the wicked and unjust, and a kind of self-defensive power [*sophias tēs peri tous ponērous kai adikous phulaktikēs kai tinos amuntikēs dunameōs*]."

[88] Significantly, Machiavelli only presents an example of a ruler who erred in the second direction and not the first: he was too unwilling to take advice and hear the truth, not too tolerant of free speech.

others began to question them, "he, an agreeable [*facile*, lit. "easy"] person, is dissuaded from them." The result was that "the things he does on one day he destroys on another" and that "no one ever understands what he wants or plans to do" so that "one cannot found oneself [*fondarsi*] on his decisions."[89] Maximilian's conduct exemplifies the point that one-man rulers are prone to make arbitrary, unstable judgments unless they submit their views to advisory bodies on an "ordinary" basis. Prudent princes realize that depending on "one's own arms" does not require secretiveness or an aversion to taking counsel from others. Self-reliant princes are both independent-minded and open to others' freely expressed views. Princes who encourage freedom of speech and consultation in a well-ordered polity, ensuring that no adviser is afraid to speak the truth, greatly strengthen their *armi proprie*. Machiavelli's own Plutarchian candor in writing the *Prince* is a good example of indirect truth-telling that princes are wise to heed.

A third modification of traditional princely notions concerns the role of laws as foundations of a prince's rule. Up to chapter 12, whenever Machiavelli speaks of the foundations of princely power he explicitly identifies them with military power on the one hand, and popular *favore* on the other. Toward the middle of the *Prince* he mentions another kind of foundation:

> We have said above that it is necessary for a prince to have good foundations for himself; otherwise he must of necessity be ruined. The principal foundations [*principali fondamenti*] that all states have, new ones as well as old or mixed, are good laws and good arms. And because there cannot be good laws where there are not good arms, and where there are good arms there must be good laws, I shall leave out the reasoning on laws and shall speak of arms.

This is the third time that Machiavelli has said that he will "leave out" discussing some topic. First it was republics; then the various modes that princes use to gain popular support; and now "reasoning on laws," *ragionare delle legge*. Here in chapter 12 he "reasons about" all three, both obliquely and directly. Republics are mentioned more times in this chapter than in any other.[90] The use of arms by republics, moreover, is compared in gently provocative ways to that of princes. Similar forms of dissimulation can be detected behind Machiavelli's claim that he will leave out reasoning on laws. Although the word "laws" appears less frequently in the *Prince* than in the *Discourses*, Machiavelli alludes obliquely to the rule of law under other headings and paraphrases. In chapter 12, for example, he writes that "arms have to be employed either by a prince or by a republic." Princes, he says, should perform the office of captain themselves. But republics have to send their citizens to battle. If a republic sends as captain a citizen "who does not turn out to be a worthy [*valente*] man, it must change him; and if he is, it must check him with laws so that he does not step out of bounds [*tenerlo con le leggi che non passi el segno*]." While Machiavelli does not explicitly say that princes who act as

---

[89] *P*, XXIII.94–95/183–84.
[90] *P*, XII.48/150; five times (twice in VIII, twelve all together).

captain should be subject to similar constraints, his remarks and examples imply this. There are two problems with princes who are also captains, analogous to problems with one-man orderers. If they prove unworthy they cannot be easily changed; and if they step out of bounds, it is unclear what will stop them. Here we have an example of how good laws are necessary to forge and maintain good arms. Republics that deal with military or civil captains by providing ordinary ways of changing unworthy ones and keeping them within bounds can be considered to have good arms. Princes who are unconstrained by such orders or lack corrective mechanisms are poorly armed. Some fortunate individuals manage to retain popular favor and reputation although they do "step out" of lawful bounds. But without founding themselves on good laws, they are seldom able to pass their authority on to their chosen heirs. The arms they appeared to wield as their "own" turn out to be founded on their private fortune, not on "a state who lived on in industry" beyond their own ephemeral successes.[91]

This explains why "where there are good arms there must be good laws," and why there is no need to speak about laws when speaking about good arms. Reading between the lines, it turns out that good *armi* presuppose good *leggi* as one of their chief foundations. The statement "good arms are the foundation of good laws" remains true; but the reverse is also true, since on an adequate understanding of the terms *leggi* and *armi* each presupposes and helps to constitute the other. The arms needed for a prince's security now include much more than military *armi*; they also include the economic and political and legal preconditions already discussed. Good laws do depend on good arms in this enlarged sense. At the same time, the ordering of good economic and political conditions requires laws as their main foundations. Laws and arms turn out to be interdependent.[92]

11.6.
Princely knowledge and the "knowledge of peoples"

These modifications of traditional princely maxims suggest two broad options for princes with respect to the form of government they should adopt. One option is to establish princely government on the basis of popular consent. Although Machiavelli does not spell this out in so many words, it is strongly suggested by affinities between passages that do spell it out in the *Discourses* and more oblique references to popular willing in the *Prince*. Both works identify "fortresses" (*fortezze*) with the use of unauthorized compulsion to secure power. The *Discourses* treats "will," *volontà*, as the antithetical means of securing it; thus "not fortresses but the will of men maintains princes in their states." A prince or orderer of republics who founds his state on popular *volontà*, Machiavelli writes, displays his own "virtue and prudence." Fortresses are both a symptom and a contributing cause

---

[91] *P*, XII.49–50/150–51; 53/153.
[92] Compare Book III of Plato's *Laws* on the interdependence of "the rule of law that governs willing subjects, without being imposed by force" (690c), distributive justice, and good military defenses (697b–698a), discussed through the example of Cyrus.

of illegitimate rule: princes who think they need to build them usually doubt that they can secure authority through ordinary means.[93] The same point is made in the *Prince,* though without the open contrast between *fortezze* and *volontà.* "The prince who has more fear of the people than of foreigners [*forestieri*]," Machiavelli writes there, "ought to make fortresses, but the one who has more fear of foreigners" than of his own people "ought to omit them."[94] The possibility that a prince's fear of his own people might be alleviated by inviting them to authorize princely laws and orders is not directly discussed. But if *fortezze* are not a prince's chief foundation, something has to be; and the main alternative seems to be *volontà.* Princes who omit or "leave out" fortresses must build on the will of the people.

When Machiavelli's remarks on fortresses in the *Prince* are placed alongside his more pointed remarks in the *Discourses,* it seems reasonable to infer that his position is similar in the two works. Some form of voluntary acceptance is the necessary basis of any government's power, whether princely or some form of mixed republic. And the surest way to keep the people on side as committed defenders of the prince's *stato* is to give them public *ordini* through which they may "willingly" authorize—and if needed criticize—the *principato.*[95] This can presumably be done by placing the office of prince under laws that reduce any individual officeholder's powers, thus creating a constitutional monarchy. Romulus took this road by placing his own authority under strict constraints, overseen by a powerful Senate. This, in Machiavelli's view, is the key act of Romulus that deserves to be imitated by anyone who reforms a corrupt *stato.*[96]

A second option is more radical. The prince can eliminate himself, or at least his office, *qua* one-man monarch for life. He can establish new orders that retain some of the strong powers normally called the *potestà regia* (Greek *basilikēs*) at the top rank of government, but subject these powers to far-reaching constraints: limits on the tenure of any individual officeholder, strict oversight by other powerful bodies such as a Senate and popular assemblies, and perhaps the sharing of the *principato* among two or more individuals. A man who is currently recognized as monarch for life, whether he rules in a constitutional monarchy or as a new prince with extraordinary modes, may choose to reform corrupt orders by moving away from *principato* toward a republic. As we saw in chapters 1 and 2, this option was intimated in the discourses-with-tyrants genre of ancient Greek writing that Machiavelli frequently alludes to in the *Prince.* The *Discursus* tries to persuade an actual prince, Giovanni de' Medici, to convert his *principato* into a republic with a strong "top rank" composed of many qualified citizens instead of one. At an overt level the *Prince* sustains the fiction of being an advice book for princes who want to strengthen one-man, lifetime rule that they can pass on to their offspring—the monarchical sense of the "name" of *principe.* But the work's examples and reasonings

[93] *D,* II.24.186–87/391–96.

[94] *P,* XX.86–87/178.

[95] This view is reaffirmed in *D,* II.24, where Machiavelli stresses the need for popular friendship, benevolence (*benivolenza*), or will (*volontà*) as foundations for any political "order."

[96] This is the basis for Machiavelli's relatively positive comments on some of the older kingdoms of his own day, although he thought that some were regrettably moving in a more absolutist direction.

tend to underline the difficulties faced by princes in that sense, while hinting at the advantages to be gained by those who transform their principality in ways that call for a redefinition of the "name" of prince itself.

The ancient role model for this alternative is not Romulus but Junius Brutus, who expelled the last kings from Rome. In reordering the city as a republic, Brutus and his colleagues prudently retained a kingly office in the consulate. But they ordered that there should be two consuls at any time instead of one, set limits on the terms of consular tenure, and subordinated consular powers to senatorial and popular scrutiny. The resulting republic was one where not one but "infinite most virtuous princes" could be found to serve the public at any given time; where it was judged appropriate "that the plebs have hope of gaining the consulate"; and where consequently even humble men knew that their offspring "could, by their virtue, become princes."[97] These ways of moving from a monarchical sense of *principe* toward a more republican sense of the word are not openly discussed in the *Prince*. But close attention to the work's examples and arguments suggests that such a transition would be the most logical means of realizing any prudent prince's ends: to secure his "own arms" beyond his own lifetime, thereby achieving true glory instead of the mere reputation for it gained by Caesar, Alexander, and other such "extraordinary" individuals. Princes who do not take this final self-eliminating step leave an ambivalent legacy. If like Caesar and Alexander they set no limits on their own authority but constantly extend it, they leave a legacy of grave disorders that often last for centuries. If like Romulus they do limit their own monarchical powers, but not enough to prevent their abuse by less virtuous kings than themselves, their good orders soon become tainted with bad.

The reflective judgments conveyed—though not spelled out—in the *Prince* are therefore paradoxical. Self-limitation, indeed self-elimination, turns out to be the best means by which a prince can strengthen his own arms in his *stato* and province.[98] The *prudentissimo* prince is one who makes himself redundant *qua* prince in the usual, monarchical sense. The *armi proprie* of any prince who wants to establish stable rule in and beyond his own lifetime are constituted by the steady commitment of the people he governs. This commitment is best secured if the prince makes himself into an accountable official subject to public laws, and if the people are ordered under laws that they regard as their own. A prince who does not recognize this risks separating himself from the popular body of the polity, which would then cease to constitute "his own" united arms.[99] Princely rule defeats itself unless

[97] *D*, I.20.54/250–51; I.60.122/322–23; II.2.132/335. Also see chap. 2, sec. 2.3., 83–84.

[98] Compare Neville's (1681) reading of Machiavelli and his comparisons with Plato.

[99] This explains why many early philosophers read the *Prince* as a "book of republicans" defending "the rule of laws over the rule of men." Spinoza suggests that Machiavelli wrote *Prince* as a warning to aspiring one-man rulers: any such "who is not a vain fool who thinks that he can please everybody, must go in daily fear of plots; and thus is forced in self-defense to plot against his subjects rather than to further their interests." Although "experience seems to teach that it makes for peace and harmony if all power is vested in one man," reflection shows that "it is slavery, not peace, that is furthered by the transfer of all power to one man"; and further, "those who believe that one man *can* hold the supreme right of a commonwealth by himself are greatly mistaken." Both Machiavelli and Plato argued that

it transcends itself. As Machiavelli says in the *Florentine Histories*, "a city based on good laws and good orders has no necessity, as have others, for the virtue of a single man to maintain it"; all other cities lack good *ordini*.[100]

Although Machiavelli opens the *Prince* by asserting that he will not speak there of republics and indeed uses the word sparingly, the *idea* of a republic—that is, the normative standards he uses the concept to express in the *Discourses*—is never far from the surface in his "little work on principalities."[101] The complementarity of the two works can be seen by comparing their dedications. The *Discourses* starts by saluting men who are not princes but deserve to be. It goes on to show how polities should be ordered so that all those who deserve to be princes may share in the honors and labors of *principato*—within a well-ordered republic. The *Prince* is dedicated to an actual prince, the younger Lorenzo de' Medici. But it tells him from the outset that he and other princes need to supplement their lofty perspective with the understanding of ordinary men if they want to maintain power. It goes on to show how princes should make themselves stronger by taking greater account of their subjects' judgments. Thus Machiavelli says he hopes it will not "be reputed presumption if a man from a low and mean state dares to discuss and give rules [*discorrere e regolare*] for the governments of princes." He then proposes that if "to know well the nature of peoples one needs to be a prince [*a conoscere bene la natura de' populi, bisogna essere principe*]" so "to know well the nature of princes one needs to be of the people." The overt tone is deferential, as is the use of high-and-low imagery to describe the status of prince and people, with the author humbly placing himself in the latter category. But the main thrust of the words is to question their own apparent premise: namely, that men of "low and humble status" should hesitate to offer princes advice on how to rule.[102] By denying that princes can fully grasp their own "nature" and responsibilities without consulting men of humble status, Machiavelli puts princes and ordinary men on a par with respect to *conoscere* in matters of governing, and challenges princes to reconsider their ambitious desires to dominate peoples or cities.

"right is determined by power," yet "the power of one man is far too small to bear so great a burden." Further, "if everything depended on the inconstant will of one man, nothing would be stable" (Spinoza 1958 [1677], VI.4–7, VII.1).

[100] *FH*, IV.1.146/473–74.

[101] See chap. 1, sec. 1.7.

[102] *P*, Ded.4/118. Compare Machiavelli's topographical imagery of mountains and plains with Plato, *Laws* 681e–662d.

CHAPTER 12

Expansion and Empire

One of Machiavelli's best-known maxims is that well-ordered republics must be prepared to "expand" if they wish to preserve their security and their internal freedoms. He discusses various forms of expansion in the *Discourses*, appears to prefer Roman modes over other ancient models, and seems to recommend them to contemporaries for imitation. We have seen throughout this study, however, that Machiavelli's appraisals of Roman modes and orders are extremely ambivalent. His praise for some Roman orders and individuals—the order permitting and regulating "tumults," for example, or the conduct of Furius Camillus—is unqualified. But his calls to imitate other Roman modes—those of Romulus, Numa, and other kings, the Senate in any period, or ambitious individuals who show excessive liberality to their friends—are mixed with warnings against the dangers of uncritical emulation. His remarks on the methods used by Rome to expand in Italy, westward toward Gaul, and later toward Spain and Africa, are among the most ambivalent and puzzling in the *Discourses*. This chapter examines these scattered remarks, asking how far and in what respects Machiavelli presents Roman methods of *imperio* or *dominio* as models that other cities, particularly Florence, should emulate. I consider throughout whether Machiavelli's judgments about imperial expansion can be reconciled with the general ethical commitments I have imputed to him in this study.

12.1.
Why republics must expand: The defects of non-expansionist republics

Machiavelli first sets out the argument for expansionist republics in Book I of the *Discourses*, where he observes that "when a republic that has been ordered so as to be capable of maintaining itself does not expand, and necessity leads it to expand, this would come to take away its foundations and make it come to ruin sooner." This view is reaffirmed in Book II, where he explains its basic premise:

> it is impossible for a republic to succeed in staying quiet and enjoying its freedom and little borders [*pochi confini*]. For if it will not molest [*molesterà*] others, it will be molested, and from being molested will arise the wish and the necessity to acquire; and if it does not have an enemy outside, it will find one at home, as it appears necessarily happens to all great cities.[1]

---

[1] *D*, I.6.23/216; II.19.173/378. Compare Alcibiades' "If others are not subjected to us, we might be subjected to them." TPW, VI.18.

As we saw in chapter 11, Sparta exemplifies the difficulties faced by any republic that builds excessively strict limits on expansion into its constitution. If maintaining a small, tightly controlled citizen body contributed to the remarkable longevity of Lycurgus' constitution for a time, it was also the main cause of its downfall. Expansion (*ampliare*) can thus be called "the poison of such republics." Whoever orders them "must, in all the ways possible, prevent them from acquiring territory, for such acquisitions . . . constitute [their] complete ruin."

Machiavelli acknowledges the great attractions of the non-expansionist republican ideal. Before rejecting it, he offers a sympathetic account of the best reasons in its favor. "I would well believe," he writes, "that to make a republic that would last a long time, the mode would be to order it within like Sparta or like Venice," while founding its external defenses on two things: one being "to settle it in a strong place of such power that nobody would believe he could crush it at once," the other to ensure that "it would not be so great as to be formidable to its neighbors." Deriving strength from its site and deterrent capacities from its comparative military weakness, such a republic could, one might surmise, "enjoy its state at length." For, the reasoning goes, "war is made on a republic for two causes: one, to become master of it; the other, for fear lest it seize you." The case for non-expansionist republics might well highlight three more specific conditions that, if met, would take away these two causes of war:

> (1) *if it is difficult to capture it*, as I presuppose, since it is well ordered for defense, it will happen rarely, or never, that one can make a plan to acquire it. (2) *If it stays within its limits*, and it is seen by experience that there is no ambition in it, it will never occur that one will make war for fear of it; and so much the more would this be if there were in it a constitution and laws to prohibit it from expanding. Without any doubt I believe that *if* the thing could be held balanced [*tenera la cosa bilanciata*] in this mode, it would be the true political way of life and the true quiet of a city.[2]

Having made this very appealing case for non-expanding republics, Machiavelli then identifies flaws in its reasoning. They emerge on closer scrutiny of the initial arguments about deterrence through strength of site and the unthreatening character of non-offensive orders. The first argument (1) is too optimistic in assuming that threatening new pressures, whether people call them "necessity" or bad "fortune," can be kept at bay by an advantageous location. This assumption betrays a deficit of *virtú*, since it expects a fortunate site to confer defensive foundations that should be built by deliberate ordering and maintained through continuous hard work. People who believe that its site allows their city to dominate fortune or necessity deceive themselves, and this complacent self-deception makes them easy prey of changing fortune.[3]

---

[2] *D*, I.6.21–23/214–16; emphasis added.
[3] As in Machiavelli's exemplary cases of Venice and Athens, *D*, I.1.

There are two fallacies in the second argument (2) that a republic is best defended if it "not be so great as to be formidable to its neighbors." One is that the factors that make for comparative greatness cannot always be kept under tight control. Sparta did not at first choose to become a great power seeking ever more partner or subject cities in Greece. It was placed under necessity to expand because others—first the Persians, later the Athenians—expanded in threatening ways. The pressures that appear to undermine a republic's security are not always intentional threats or direct attacks. The constant expansion of peoples through a variety of means—trade or migration following an unplanned population growth, famine, or external assault, as well as deliberate colonization or conquest—is for Machiavelli one of the fundamental facts of human social existence. Well-ordered republics should always be prepared to address it in "ordinary" ways, not respond to any shift in population or power as if they were dire necessities requiring "extraordinary" responses.[4] A second fallacy, Machiavelli implies, is the assumption that comparatively less powerful cities are less vulnerable to attack because others are unthreatened by them. The error becomes clear if one considers the two main causes of war, fear and desires for dominion. Although relatively weak republics may be spared wars made because of fear, they pose a standing temptation to those who want to become masters of other cities and peoples, including those who desire dominion for fear of other strong polities.

The non-expansionist formula, *strong site + comparative self-imposed weakness = security*, therefore does not add up. It underestimates the need for self-ordering *virtù* to contribute to durable defenses; and it underestimates the drives of others to dominate even when they have no immediate reason to fear. "Since one cannot, as I believe, balance this thing, nor maintain this middle way [*questa via del mezzo*] exactly," Machiavelli concludes, "in ordering a republic there is need to think of the more honorable part and to order it so that if indeed necessity brings it to expand, it can conserve what it has seized."[5] As we have seen, what Machiavelli calls "middle ways" seek to combine two opposing principles in their modes of action, and generally fail to achieve their desired ends. The end of lasting deterrence and security cannot be produced by the non-expansionist formula; its combination of geopolitical *strength* with relative military *weakness* fails to take full stock of ordinary human motions, ambitions, and conflicts. On Machiavelli's arguments, the only "true" modes are those that need no balancing because they are founded on a single, unmixed principle. In this case, strength is the only principle that can undergird durable defenses. A republic's external defenses should therefore be built on strength unmixed with weakness; and that strength should be founded on its own *virtuoso* orders, not fortunate site, so that when fortune changes, citizens are not caught off guard by the realization that their strong location cannot defend them indefinitely.

[4] See chaps. 4, 10.
[5] *D*, I.6.23/216.

12.2.
Three modes: Equal partnership, subjection to one, and the Roman mode

The question for Machiavelli, then, is not whether but how republics should expand. The main word he uses for "to expand" in the *Discourses* is *ampliare*, occasionally *augumentare*. Both words are used in connection with a variety of
methods of expansion. One key distinction is expansion by way of subjects (*subietti, suddditi*) or partners and friends (*compagni, amici*). The distinction between
expanding by making subjects or partners appears in Thucydides and is echoed
by Plato, Xenophon, and other Greek and Roman writers.[6] It recurs throughout
the *Discourses* and *Florentine Histories*, overlapping with other distinctions that
explain its basis. The most important is that peoples or cities may come forcibly
(*forzati*) or willingly (*voluntari, voluntariamente*) into another's *imperio*.[7] Authority may be "taken" by force or willingly "given." Similarly, those who want to "make
a great empire" may do so by force or "by love," which induces people to join one's
enterprises willingly.[8] A more metaphorical distinction between acquiring what
belongs to others "by siege" (*per ossidione*) or "by means of accords" (*mediante
gli accordi*) also occurs in both works.[9] Machiavelli implies a related distinction
between cooperative and multilateral methods of seeking *ampliare, imperio* or *comandare* on the one hand, and unilateral modes on the other. On his usage, expansion and empire may be achieved by making partners or subjects; but partners
are commanded or governed cooperatively with their consent, while subjects are
commanded by *uno solo* dominant power.[10]

Note that when examined in relation to these distinctions, the modes of expanding by making partners and by making subjects turn out to be antithetical.
They represent two opposing principles that cannot be stably combined in a single,
"middle way" mode of action. Machiavelli repeatedly insists that one must choose
between taking one or the other—subjection or partnership, siege or accords, forcing or gaining goodwill—as one's guide. The desire to combine these opposing
principles invariably produces indignation among people at the receiving end of
such policies, and eventual ruin for the imprudently ambitious perpetrators who
want to have it both ways. This analysis, as we will see, has important implications
for interpreting Machiavelli's remarks about the Roman Empire.

Together with the antithesis between *compagni* and *subbietti/suddditi*, a further
distinction between *imperio* (empire) and *dominio* (dominion) is essential for understanding Machiavelli's views on various modes of expansion. *Imperio* and *dominio* are not antithetical, but Machiavelli gives the words very different kinds of
normative value. His *imperio* is the broader concept, and more open-ended with

[6] The Greek words are usually *summachoi* (allies, partners) or *hetairoi* (companions, comrades) and *archomenoi* (subjects). For example, see Xenophon's uses in XH, xi.54–57 and Thucydides TPW, *passim*, discussed in chap. 2. Also compare Plato, *Seventh Letter* 331e–332a.
[7] *D*, II.15.159/361–63; II.21.178/383; II.23-4.183–87/387–90; II.32.205/411–12.
[8] *FH*, II.9.61/371–72; II.34.93/406–8; IV.18–19.164–65/494–97; *D*, II.3.133–34/336–37.
[9] *D*, II.32.205–6/411–14; *FH*, VII.31.309/670–71.
[10] *D*, II.4.136/338, 138/340; III.19.200–201/471–72.

respect to the means that may be used to attain it. He sometimes uses *imperio* for "acquisitions" taken by force or siege, or for rule imposed without the consent of the ruled. But empire-*imperio* may also be freely given to one city by others, who even under *imperio* may be considered as friends and partners rather than subjects. Indeed, an empire may be governed "by way of a league" of cities in which none dominates the others. Thus Machiavelli uses *imperio* to describe the Tuscan league of twelve cities that shared power on equal terms and expanded by means of voluntary association. *Imperio* in this broad sense—also called "mode of ruling," *d'imperare*—may thus involve well-ordered collaborative government among equals, or *comandare* by one city whose leadership is freely authorized by the rest.[11] Machiavelli's *imperio* is not always a legitimate mode of expansion or rule; it may be practiced well or badly, through ordinary or extraordinary modes.[12] Unlike *dominio*, however, *imperio* understood in a normatively adequate sense may be compatible with Machiavelli's demanding standards of legitimacy.

Machiavelli's *dominio* is a very different matter. In the *Histories* it is usually connected with ambition, insolence, or "lust for domination."[13] *Dominio* implies the aim of dominating others. The quest for dominion within or among cities is a principal cause of "ordinary and reasonable" resentments, disorders, and wars. At first glance, some of Machiavelli's remarks seem to connect *dominio* to other undeniable goods, as when he says that "cities have never expanded either in dominion or in riches if they have not been in freedom." But the word generally has undertones of doubtful legitimacy, implying that free or rich cities that seek *dominio* over others should not expect securely to hold their freedom or wealth for long: thus empires based on domination are often ruined "by having acquired dominion they could not keep."[14] More freedom, Machiavelli argues, could be found among the "cities and empires that arose among the Roman ruins" than in the Roman Empire itself. Although these smaller entities had "less dominion" than the sprawling empire that once contained them, some cities acquired considerable "authority and power" after Rome's fall, since "one did not dominate the others."[15]

Book II, chapter 4 of the *Discourses* applies these distinctions systematically to ancient examples. Machiavelli begins by identifying three modes of expansion employed by ancient republics. The first mode was to form a formally equal "league of several republics together, in which none was before another in either authority or rank." In "acquiring other cities," the members of such leagues "made them partners" in common defense. The most important distinguishing feature of expansion

---

[11] Recall that for Machiavelli "command," as distinct from "dominion," means a position of publicly authorized, first-ranking authority that he considers necessary for any political "orders."

[12] *D*, II.21.177/383–84; III.19.200–201/471–72.

[13] *FH*, I.29.41/349; IV.3.147/475–76.

[14] *D*, II.2.129/331; II.4.136/338–39; II.21.177/383–84;. In the *Discourses* it is often used in a subtly critical way for Florence's dominions (II.27.194/401, III.18.259–60/469–70).

[15] *FH*, V.1.186/520. This normative usage provocatively inverts the sense of the words *imperio* and *dominio* on Florentine republican conventions. To speak of Florence's dominions was not considered offensive to its subjects-client cities, whereas to speak of its *imperio* or *imperium* set off alarm bells; see Brown 2000a.

by leagues is its concern to maintain formal equality among league members or *compagni*. Partner cities are treated as equals in two respects: in the method of acquiring them as league members, and in the methods of exercising authority within the league itself. Machiavelli says that this mode of expanding by leagues was found among the ancient Tuscans, as well as the Achaeans and Aetolians in Greece; the modern Swiss confederates also practiced a version of this mode.[16] The expansion that occurs here is multilateral as well as voluntary: each member city expands together with the others by joining its arms to the defensive capabilities of allied polities and peoples. In terms of the distinction just discussed, expansion by leagues involves the formation of *empire without dominion*.

The second mode aims "to get partners, but not so much that the rank of command, the seat of empire, and the title of the enterprises do not remain with you." This mode respects members' free agency in one respect but not in another. It acquires new *compagni* by letting them enter "willingly" into *imperio* with the commanding power. Its methods of exercising power within the empire, however, are based on the "dominion of one," not on the principle of equal consultative freedoms. In effect if not in name, this mode converts initially willing partners into subjects who are neither asked to authorize the empire's actions nor given their share of credit for its enterprises. A single dominant city sees itself, and is seen by its nominal *compagni*, as sole author of whatever policies the *imperio* undertakes. This mode was practiced, Machiavelli says, by the Romans and no other known people. Rome began by getting "many partners throughout all Italy who in many things lived with it under equal laws" while always reserving "for itself the seat of empire and the title of command." Under the banner of at least partial, formal equality, its Italian partners "subjugate[d] themselves by their own labors and blood without perceiving it." By the time Latins, Samnites, Privernati, and others "perceived the deception under which they had lived" in considering themselves as free and willing partners in Rome's *imperio*, it was too late to renegotiate the terms of empire without violent rebellion. Many Italian peoples tried to "avenge their injuries" through war, but were easily defeated by Rome, so that "from partners they too became subjects."[17] Unlike expansion by leagues, this mixed mode tries to combine elements of legitimate *imperio* with unilateral, non-consensual *dominio*. Machiavelli's judgments as to whether and how this combination can succeed will be discussed shortly.

The third mode of expanding is the polar opposite of the first. It is based on the undisputed dominance of one power in its methods of both acquiring and exercising power. In contrast to both the first and second modes, the third uses direct force to subjugate new peoples instead of waiting for them to authorize the commanding power's leadership. Like the second mode and in contrast to the first, it seeks to exercise power through the dominance of one, through unilateral instead of multilateral methods of seeking authority for imperial policies. This mode is exemplified by Sparta and Athens, whose aims in the Peloponnesian War were "to get not

[16] *D*, II.4.135–36/338–39.
[17] Ibid.

partners but direct subjects" and who refused to share authority.[18] Here we have a straightforward case where "empire" is simply synonymous with "dominion," and involves no legitimacy in either its methods of acquiring or holding subjects.

In different ways, the first two modes share a concern to expand in ways that *appear* legitimate to the cities and peoples "acquired" through them. Although the second involves a degree of deception, those who practice it presumably grasp a point stressed repeatedly throughout the *Discourses* and *Histories*: namely, that authority is more firmly established and maintained when people give it willingly.[19] The first mode of expanding by leagues treats partners' willing acceptance as a necessary condition for acquiring and maintaining power. The second treats it as necessary to acquire power, though not to maintain it. Only the third ignores these precepts in both respects. For this reason, Machiavelli rejects the third mode as "entirely useless." Acquisitions made in this way can never be held, for reasons analogous to those he gives a few pages earlier to explain why neither internal nor external tyranny is ever secure. Moreover, such acquisitions are not just impossible to maintain; they also destroy good internal orders and undermine the external security of republics that make them. Thus Athens and Sparta were "ruined" by "having acquired dominion they could not keep." Such acquisitions, he remarks later, are "for the harm, not the greatness, of a state."[20] The chapter entitled "What Peoples the Romans Had to Combat, and That They Obstinately Defended Their Freedom" foreshadows these objections to the third mode. Here Machiavelli sets out the maxim that "freedom that is taken away from you is avenged with greater vehemence than that which is wished [willed] to be taken away [*voluta tòrre*]" This is echoed two chapters later, where we read that "taking care of governing cities by violence, especially [but not only] those accustomed to living freely, is a difficult and laborious thing."[21] The same point is hammered home throughout Book II. Amid his detailed discussions of ancient policies, Machiavelli insists on the need for cities to seek the willing authority of their newly acquired subjects, or face certain ruin. Peace in one's dominions "is faithful," he writes, "where men are willingly pacified," and not otherwise. The passage continues: "Those who believe otherwise of men, especially of those used to being or seeming to themselves to be free, are deceived in this," and "under this deception take up policies that are not good for themselves and not such as to satisfy them." Attempts to seize power over peoples instead of seeking their voluntary consent to one's *imperio* are always "dangerous or useless," whereas "good government" depends on having subjects who "willingly consign themselves" to one's authority.[22]

It seems, then, that there is no way for cities that rule others in the third mode to gain legitimate authority unless they abandon their aim of solitary, unilateral dominion. A city can only maintain secure command if it is "armed and massive

[18] Ibid.

[19] D, II.15.159/363, II.21.178/384, II.23–24.183–90/389–97, II.32.205/413–14; FH, II.9.61/371, II.27.81/395, II.34.92–93/407–8, IV.16.161/491, IV.18–19.164–66/494–97, V.14.203/539, VII.30.309/669.

[20] D, II.4.136/338–39; II.18.172/373.

[21] D, II.2.131/334–35; II.4.136/338–39.

[22] D, II.23.183–84/389–90; II.32.205–6/413–14.

with arms." But since the requisite "arms" must include reliable partners who aid the city in its enterprises, and partners must be treated as free agents, it follows that secure dominion can never be the dominion of one alone. The same conclusion is reached in later chapters. Cities that seek clear dominion over others, we read, are often driven to build "fortresses" to hold rebellious provinces. But those who judge that they "could live securely while offending their citizens and subjects" always lose their authority since, as the *Prince* also argued, "not fortresses but the will of men maintains princes in their states."[23]

This raises an unsettling question about the second, Roman mode. Machiavelli repeatedly affirms that the chief aim of *imperio* is lasting strength and greatness, and the main source of stable *potenza* and *grandezza* is loyal partners willing to devote their own resources to defend the empire. But if the Roman mode converts initially free and willing partners into dominated, resentful subjects, surely this constitutes a fatal flaw in the mode itself? Despite appearances of legitimacy fostered by its consensual modes of *acquiring* new members, it seems likely that its domineering means of *exercising imperio* must undercut the mode's avowed ends by turning onetime partners into enemies within the empire. How, if at all, can the two opposing principles that constitute Machiavelli's Roman mode—voluntary partnership and involuntary subjection—be combined without leading those who employ this mode to ruin?

12.3.
The Roman "middle way": Making subjects or partners

Having eliminated the third method of expansion, Machiavelli goes on to evaluate the other two. In the chapter as a whole, the first mode of expanding "by leagues" receives much more detailed attention than the other two. This is partly because the third mode is swiftly ruled out, while the second will be discussed at length in later chapters. Machiavelli apparently expects readers to be interested in the first mode only insofar as the Romans had to contend with it, particularly with the Tuscan league in Italy. "Since the Romans made war with the Tuscans very often," Machiavelli writes, "I will expatiate in giving knowledge [*dare notizia*] of them particularly to show better the qualities of this first mode." The Tuscans, who lived roughly in the region of Machiavelli's native Tuscany, were a people whose *imperio* flourished within much narrower limits than that of Rome. Noting that there are few historical records of the ancient Tuscans (or Etruscans), Machiavelli says that he will nonetheless try to recover some "little memory" of their modes of expansion and methods of achieving greatness, so that readers may better evaluate Roman examples discussed in later chapters. "In Italy, before the Roman Empire," he begins, "the Tuscans were very powerful [*potentissimi*] by sea and by land. . . . It is also understood that their arms were obeyed from the Tiber as far as the foot of the mountains that encircle the thick part of Italy." The Tuscans

---

[23] *D*, II.4.136/338–39; II.24.184–89/391–97.

thus lived with that equality and proceeded in expanding in that first mode said above. There were twelve cities—among which were Chiusi, Veii, Arezzo, Fiesole, Volterra, and the like—that governed their empire by way of a league. They could not go beyond Italy with their acquisitions and even a great part of [Italy] remained intact for the causes that will be said below.[24]

This "power [*potenza*] in Italy" remained "secure for a great time, with the highest glory of empire and of arms and special praise for customs and religion [*con somma gloria d'imperio e d'arme, a massime laude di costumi e di religione*]."

Machiavelli asserts that this first mode is second best of the three, after the Roman mode. Nowhere in the present chapter or elsewhere in the *Discourses*, however, does he offer direct or unequivocal judgments about the weaknesses of the first mode, as he does with the third. A single premise seems to determine his ranking of the first mode as second best: namely, that since republics must be prepared to expand, it is better if no "fixed limit" (*termino fisso*) is set on their prospects for further expansion. The first mode of expanding "by partners" has such a limit, whereas the second, mixed mode has none. Machiavelli observes that republics that expand in the more limited mode of leagues may achieve security for a long time, and even "the highest glory of empire and of arms." But since they "cannot expand very much with it," many readers might well regard this as a serious disadvantage, and prefer some other mode. Unlike Rome, the Tuscan league "could not go beyond Italy with their acquisitions." Readers who see Rome's imperial expansion beyond Italy as among its main sources of power and *grandezza* are unlikely to admire the modest ambitions of the Tuscan mode. Machiavelli himself, however, says almost nothing about this or any other disadvantage of the mode of "expanding by partnership"; on the contrary, he devotes most of the chapter to a detailed discussion of its advantages. One considerable "good" is that since partner cities in such leagues are constrained to "consult and decide" (*consultare e diliberare*) with all the others together, they do not easily undertake wars. Another is that since "there are many communities to participate in dominion [*molti comunità a participare di quel dominio*]," members are less interested in dominating other peoples outside the league, since no one of them alone would be able to "enjoy entirely" the esteem that comes from dominion.[25]

The chapter concludes on a disturbingly ambivalent note. On the one hand, Machiavelli remarks that the ancient Tuscan mode of acquiring should not seem difficult for modern men to imitate, and stresses that it achieved "highest glory" and security. On the other, he acknowledges that this "power and glory" were so successfully "eliminated by the Romans" that few people now remember ancient Tuscan power. Despite his praise for the first mode of expanding by partners, then, Machiavelli appears to concur with the conventional wisdom that ranks the Roman mode of expansion above all others. This second mode allowed the Romans to combine two policies: showing overt respect for the free will of its partners

---

[24] *D*, II.4.135–38/337–41.
[25] *D*, II.4.137/340–41.

when first *acquiring* them for the empire, yet refusing to set any limits on its own supreme power when *exercising* it. Through these policies Rome "rose to such excessive power [*eccessiva potenza*]" that it appeared invincible. And "since it was alone in living thus, it was also alone in becoming so powerful." This "mode of proceeding," Machiavelli declares, "has been observed by the Romans alone; nor can a republic that wishes to expand take another mode, for experience has not shown us any more certain or more true."[26]

This, of course, was the opinion of many of Machiavelli's fellow humanists in Florence, and of many political men in Italy and beyond. Since all polities, whether princedoms or republics, must expand in some mode, it seemed reasonable to judge that the Roman model was the only one able to combine formidable strength with a measure of—at least apparent—legitimacy. While Machiavelli evaluates various modes of expansion from the standpoint of these "wise" opinions, however, it is not yet clear that he agrees with them. If he does want to defend the Roman mode of expansion, this desire appears deeply puzzling when it is set alongside many judgments he has already made before, not to mention others he will make later. One of the most puzzling is his apparent praise for Rome's mixed mode, although it has all the hallmarks of an unstable "middle way."[27] Machiavelli's middle ways involve attempts to combine fundamentally incompatible principles or courses of action; the results are chronically unstable, and eventually fall toward one side or the other—usually the one less desired. Machiavelli reserves his praise for Roman modes for cases where these scrupulously "fled from the middle way and turned to extremes."[28] Although Machiavelli does not expressly call the Roman mode of expanding a *via del mezzo*, it has the defining element of seeking to combine two inherently opposed principles: acquisition by "partnership" and rule by "making subjects." These principles are as mutually repugnant as the principles of a "true republic" and "true principality" set out in Machiavelli's *Discursus*.[29] Hard as some may try to combine them "in words" or appearances, the deeds they call for necessarily conflict because their fundamental principles are opposed. Equal participation and respect for free agency are opposed to unilaterally imposed dominion of one. Throughout human history, those who seek empire have tried to strike some balance between elements of one and the other; but in the end they have had to move toward one fundamental principle or the other. The Roman mode, surely, is no different from any other in this regard.

Other general arguments reinforce the suspicion that Machiavelli may be dissimulating admiration for the mixed Roman mode of expansion. Like Thucydides' Diodotus and Nicias, Machiavelli suggests a simple criterion for judging whether a mode of acquiring is good: whether an agent of empire can maintain an "acquisition" in such a way "that it enriches and does not impoverish the country and his fatherland." Those modes fail when "it arises that acquisitions are for the

[26] *D*, II.4.136–37/338–40.
[27] Criticized in *D*, I.6.23/216–17, I.26.62/258 and elsewhere.
[28] *D*, II.23.182/388.
[29] See chap. 1, sec. 1.7.

harm, not the greatness, of a state."[30] Machiavelli sometimes seems to suggest that Rome passed the test with flying colors: by "deviating from the universal mode of others," for example, they made "easy for themselves the way to arrive at a supreme greatness."[31] But easy ways are seldom secure, since they do not make best use of virtue. Many chapters in Book II suggest that the Romans frequently overstepped the "limit" that makes acquisitions beneficial: that set by other peoples' desires to be treated as "partners," not as subjects. If this happened so often even "when they proceeded with so much prudence and so much virtue," it is hard to avoid doubts about whether the Roman way is as ideal as common opinion suggests. Perhaps, after all, Roman modes of exercising *dominio* acquired through partnership are prone to the same weaknesses as those Machiavelli sees in the third mode. Even if an empire acquires partners through means that they thought legitimate at the time, there is no reason why they should continue willingly to support imperial enterprises if at some later point they are subjected to the unilateral will of one. If power is exercised over them in ways they consider unfair, the dominant party will find it difficult to maintain *imperio* irrespective of how partners were "made" to begin with.[32]

Moreover, Machiavelli's scattered comments on the experience and legacy of the Roman Empire tell a profoundly ambivalent story about the success of the mixed mode. On one side of the scales, he observes that for nearly 450 years the Romans managed to "balance the thing." They almost fell off balance several times, notably with the Fabii episode and subsequent vengeance taken by the Gauls.[33] Prudent men took the opportunity to pull civil and expansionist orders back to due limits, restraining the ambitions and arrogance that had induced Romans to treat both partners and enemies unjustly. What Machiavelli calls good Roman *orders* of expansion—as distinct from the normatively neutral *modes*—depended on respecting strict limits in all the city's acquisitions. Thus he notes that in its early days of expansion, the Romans set limits to consular ambitions, gave foreigners' land sparingly to colonists, used booty prudently, and fought wars by making good citizen-soldiers instead of relying on money or others' arms. Above all, they set limits on their own ambitions and actions because they recognized the need to treat locals as partners in their enterprises.[34] They left "no sign of empire" (*non lasciavano alcuno segno d'imperio*) but allowed conquered peoples to maintain their "state and dignity" (*mantenevano nello stato e dignità loro*). By these self-restrained means the early Romans discovered that prospective allies voluntarily "throw themselves into your laps," removing any necessity to coerce them into one's empire.[35]

---

[30] *D*, II.6.140/343, II.18.172/377; *FH*, IV.19.164–65/495–97.

[31] *D*, II.6.140/343.

[32] Machiavelli suggests that the Roman mode involved excessive or extreme ambition (*D*, II.6.140/343, II.20.176/381–82) excessive virtue (II.2.129/330), and excessive power (II.4.136/382). As noted in chap. 6, the word "excessive" for Machiavelli is always critical even when coupled with a good quality, connoting a lack of respect for limits.

[33] *D*, II.28–29.195–97/403–6, III.1.209–10/417–18.

[34] *D*, II.6–7.140–42/343–46; II.8.145/348–49; II.10.147–49/350–53.

[35] *D*, II.21.177–78/383.

So long as Romans observed these limits, their mode of expansion seemed fair to their partners and newly "acquired" peoples; it seemed, that is, to involve legitimate *imperio* without *dominio*. But in the second mode, unlike the first, there are no fixed limits that forcibly obligated Romans to adhere to these prudent methods. The absence of fixed limits rendered the mixed mode inherently unstable. Roman efforts to expand soon bore out Machiavelli's maxim that men err "who do not know how to put limits to their hopes, and by founding themselves on these without otherwise measuring themselves, are ruined."[36] Soon after they recovered from the war with the Gauls, Machiavelli writes, "acquiring was about to be pernicious for the Romans" even "in the times when they proceeded with so much prudence and so much virtue."[37]

Machiavelli describes the experience of empire from a very different standpoint than that of Roman triumphalism. Numerous remarks in Book II repudiate nostalgic idealizations of Roman power, characterizing the effects of Roman expansion in a highly critical way. From the standpoint of Rome's closest neighbors, first, these effects were disastrous. Although its erstwhile Italian partners "conspired against" Rome "to avenge their injuries, in a little time they were losers of the war and worsened their condition." Rome's Italian partners soon found that they had been "reduced" from the status of kingdoms to provinces, then from partners to subjects, and then as subjects, not only deprived of freedom but "crushed."[38] These "injuries" inflicted a loss of freedom and security on Italy as a whole. Machiavelli notes that the more the Romans reduced their Italian partners to indignant subjects, the less they could trust them to bear arms in Rome's defense. Together with the people of Rome, the other "partner towns" in Italy had once been the "heart and vital parts" of the imperial body; once they were reduced to abject "subjects," they could no longer be counted on to defend the province against outside invaders. Thus Rome deprived itself of its "own arms" and had to "buy off" foreigners to guard it from enemies close to home. These "inconveniences," Machiavelli writes, arose from "having disarmed your people," for whoever practices the Roman mode of subjection "treats those subjects inside his empire badly and those on the borders of his empire well, so as to have well-disposed men to keep the enemy distant." This "mode of proceeding of theirs," Machiavelli emphasizes, "is against every good order. For the heart and vital parts of a body have to be kept armed and not its extremities, since without the latter it lives, but if the former are hurt it dies."[39]

From the wider perspective of Europe and other former territories under the empire, great disorders followed the loss of Roman virtue, with very long-lasting effects.[40] Machiavelli declares that the Roman Empire "eliminated all republics and all civil ways of life," a condition that has endured up to the present. For although

---

[36] *D*, II.27.195/400–402.
[37] *D*, II.19.175/380.
[38] *D*, II.4.136/339–40.
[39] *D*, II.30.200–202/407–9.
[40] See *FH*, I *passim*.

the empire itself "was dissolved, the cities themselves have not been able to put themselves back together or reorder themselves for civil life"; and the "free way of life" enjoyed in the past has been replaced by a "servile way of life now."[41] Last but not least, Rome's own republican orders were fatally undermined when Rome began to use what were perceived as illegitimate methods of expansion. The dangers were first brought home during wars with their own Italian partner-subjects, who called on neighboring peoples such as the Gauls for support against Rome. As we will see later, Machiavelli treats the wars against Carthage as a turning point in the history of the Roman republic's internal corruption and eventual fall, from self-inflicted causes. By the time Caesar seized power and overturned Rome's republican orders, the city's modes of expansion had already created so much internal corruption, and so many enemies close to home, that there was little hope of saving the republic.

In view of this ambivalent experience, it is perhaps unsurprising that no one has imitated the "mixed" Roman mode—at least not successfully. What responsibility should be ascribed to Rome's partners for allowing themselves to be reduced to subject status? After all, Rome's Italian partners-turned-subjects sought and voluntarily accepted Roman protection, and other benefits of association with the empire. They knew that Rome was the strongest power, and were happy to pay tribute in exchange for advantages conferred by its military power, its laws, and the commercial opportunities found in a "massively" expanding city. When Machiavelli says these parties "subjugated themselves by their own labors and blood without perceiving it," he implies that it they themselves must be held co-responsible for any loss of freedom they endured, as well as for the legacy of subjection suffered by their descendants many centuries later. Had they evaluated Rome's policies by clear, unmixed principles instead of pragmatic calculations of immediate self-interest, they might have seen that by leaving Rome the seat and title of dominion, they encouraged it to pursue its ambitions ever further, until their own equality and security also came under threat.[42] But the fact that the partners erred did not make the Roman mode more legitimate, or more stable.

There are many reasons to doubt, then, that Machiavelli's apparent praise of the Roman mode in Book II, chapter 4 is non-ironic. Both his general reasonings and examples suggest that orders founded on partnership *cannot* consistently be combined with modes that insist on maintaining one party's undisputed dominance. There are no middle ways, and no way to "balance this thing" so that ambitious cities can have *both* partners instead of passive, unreliable subjects *and* complete,

---

[41] *D*, II.2.132/334–35.

[42] *D*, II.23.181/387–88; II.30.200–202/407–9. The Spartan general Hermocrates offers a similar analysis of the origins of Athens' empire in TPW, VI.76. As with Rome, Athens' allies at first willingly (*hekontōn*) made Athenians their leaders (*hēgemones*) in the war against Persia; but later, Athens found fair-sounding pretexts (*aitian euprepē*, nicely translated by Hobbes as "colorable criminations") to reduce them all to subjection. However, Hermocrates argues that it is pointless to waste time accusing Athens now; its subjects should rather reproach themselves for not seeing through pretenses and defending their own freedom. Also see TPW, IV.60–61, VI.85.

unilateral *dominio*.[43] Partnership under the dominion of one is no partnership, however it first came about and whatever name you give it. Machiavelli's conception of "true" power is collaborative: it is based on freely consenting agents contributing to common defenses. As soon as the individual or corporate agents involved are deprived of freedom, the power of the body they inhabit is deprived of its main animating force: self-ordering virtue exerted by the many. If this is missing in an *imperio*, all its wealth and military might start to look more like trappings of tyranny than elements of true glory proper to republics.

12.4.
Bad Roman modes, good Roman orders: The choice between extremes

The foregoing discussion touched on a seemingly casual distinction between Roman "modes" and "orders" of expansion. Early in Book I Machiavelli declares: "I believe that it is necessary to follow the Roman *order* and not that of the other republics—for I do not believe one can find a mode between the one and the other."[44] This looks puzzling in view of Machiavelli's account of the Roman "mode" in Book II, chapter 4: there it is described as the mode "between one and the other," whereas the reference in Book I suggests that the "Roman order" represents one of two extremes. The puzzle is solved if the "Roman order" described in Book I is distinct from the "Roman mode" of expansion discussed in Book II, chapter 4. The "order" of expanding discussed in Book I and again in Book II, chapters 1 and 3 is based *only* on the principle of acquiring "partners." In Book II, chapter 1 Machiavelli plays on the ambiguity in Roman practice by describing "the mode taken by the Roman people," that is, by the republic before it became corrupted, "in entering the provinces of others," as follows: "in new provinces they always tried to have some friend who should be a step or a gate to ascend there or enter there, or a means to hold it." In this way "they never lacked similar supports to make their enterprises easier."[45] Here the Roman method of making partners might be, but is not necessarily, part of a two-pronged mode aimed at securing unilateral dominion. "Orders" are always based on ordinary, legitimate authority; this is part of what makes them orders. Machiavelli describes certain ways of gaining partners as orders because they respect principles that alone can secure legitimate authority for expansion. The middle-way Roman strategy, by contrast, is always a "mode," never an order. I suggest that it represents a corruption of the sound, unmixed principles that underpin Machiavelli's account of the early republic's well-ordered methods of expansion.

These principles are summarized in Book II, chapter 19. "Those who have in their hands a civil way of life," Machiavelli argues, should expand chiefly by "increasing the inhabitants of one's city, getting partners and not subjects." While they should "send colonies to guard countries that have been acquired," they should exercise restraint

---

[43] Comparable contradictions in Athens' methods are exposed in Thucydides' dialogue between the beleaguered Melians and their Athenian assailants, especially TPW, V.91–93.

[44] *D*, I.6.23/216–17.

[45] *D*, II.1.128/330.

in how they treat the property and sensitivities of existing inhabitants.[46] Instead of using profits from war for the private advantage of one city, they should "make capital out of booty" by addressing the public good. They should "maintain military exercises with the highest seriousness," both literally and metaphorically, "subduing the enemy with raids and battles and not with sieges," a metaphor for avoiding the use of violent or unilateral methods.[47] This, Machiavelli states, "is the *true way* to make a republic great and to acquire empire." Now there are no two ways about it: "if this mode of expanding does not please" some, "one should think that acquisitions made by any other way are the ruin of republics, and should put a check on every ambition, regulate one's city inside with laws and customs, prohibit acquisition, and think only of defending oneself and of keeping one's defenses well ordered."[48]

These lines stand in deep tension with the statement in Book II, chapter 4 that the Roman combined mode of partnership-and-subjection was the only "true" mode. When Machiavelli says that Roman methods of expanding should be imitated, it is reasonable to assume that he refers to these "orders," not to the unstably mixed "modes." On his account, the Romans developed a wide range of good orders for expanding by "making partners" with other cities, peoples, and migrants. They developed flexible orders for expanding internally: generous immigration policies, and laws that ordered incoming peoples into clear jurisdictions to ensure that they had access to government and legal recourse.[49] They had a wide range of methods for "expanding by partners" outside the city: defensive alliances, treaties of cooperation or mutual non-aggression, economic exchanges, partial or full rights of Roman residence or citizenship. Even when new partners were acquired as a result of war or colonization, the orders of making defeated peoples into partners were good so long as they involved respect for their wishes and gave them what they regarded as significant benefits: that is, did not treat them as subjects. Through these orders of expansion Rome gained *imperio* in its most adequate sense: the power and glory that comes from having so many willing, committed partners inside and outside Italy. Rome also held command of common enterprises conducted by the *imperio*, and might have continued in this leading role without insisting on unilateral *dominio*. When Romans did demand dominion, Machiavelli observes, one finds that their victories in wars inside and outside Italy show "a very great virtue and prudence mixed with fortune" instead of firm victories based on virtue alone.[50] The more Rome transgressed previous good orders to demand unquestioned dominion, fickle fortune began to play a larger role in its enterprises.[51] Machiavelli makes it clear that when Romans chose prudently

---

[46] Also an important argument in *P*, I–III.

[47] Compare *D*, II.32.203–6/411–14.

[48] *D*, II.19.172–74/377–80.

[49] See, for example, *D*, III.49.308–9/524–25.

[50] *D*, II.1.125–27/327–30.

[51] The fine lines between the Roman mode of partnership and the demand for excessive power are illustrated in the order of chapters. *D*, II.3. recalls the good "Roman order" of expanding by partnership, again contrasting it favorably to non-expansionist and exclusive modes. *D*, II.4. then introduces the more dubious "Roman mode" of expansion.

between extremes, as in early days they often did, this decision made their policies good. When they tried to combine two extreme principles, as they did later, their successes began to be mixed with serious disorders.[52]

The reflective judgment that one cannot achieve *both* dominion over partner-subjects *and* the true power that comes from firm loyalty given by partners is borne out by a critical episode late in Book II. Following Livy, Machiavelli describes the debilitating wars fought in Italy after Rome's nominal partners, led by the Latins, realized that they had been reduced to subject status in the ever-expanding empire. Once again, the Roman general Camillus assumes the task of trying to salvage the fractured empire in Italy. Camillus' great prudence, according to Machiavelli, was to recognize the harsh necessity to choose between extreme principles and courses of action. Most Romans wanted to have their cake, so to speak, and eat it; they wanted to keep up appearances of legitimacy while acting as sole, unquestioned *dominus*. Camillus tells them that they must give up the self-deception that they can have both things at once. They must choose either the way of partnership or that of subjection, seeking authority by free will or by force.[53] Of these two extremes, Camillus says that only one is prudent; the other is bound to bring ruin. He does not say which has which effects, but offers a standard of prudence that hearers may apply for themselves. The standard is simply whatever is needed to sustain any "government" worthy of the name. "A government," he argues, "is nothing other than holding subjects in such a mode that they cannot or ought not offend you." This can be done in only two ways: "either by securing oneself against them altogether, taking away from them every way of hurting you"; or "by benefiting them in such a mode that it would not be reasonable for them to desire to change fortune."

Camillus' next remarks make it quite clear that only the second option has any chance of dealing with subjects so that they "cannot and ought not offend you." "The immortal gods," he declares to assembled Roman senators, have "put the decision in your hands whether Latium is to be or not to be." He stresses the gravity of their decision, whichever way it may go: they must bear full responsibility for whatever course they choose, and all its consequences, foreseen or not. "You can provide perpetual peace for yourselves" in relation to the Latins "either by raging or by forgiving." Regarding the first, more violent option, he asks: "Do you wish to make very cruel decisions against those who have surrendered or been conquered?" The question itself implies that this would be unjust. Moreover, it would require very extreme actions that were bound to undermine Roman virtue. "You may," he says, "destroy all of Latium";[54] but if senators choose this path of "elimination," they must be prepared to go very far indeed, knowing that half-measures will not suffice at this stage of the conflict. The other, more moderate alternative is "to increase [*augere*] the Roman republic on the example of your forefathers by accepting the conquered

---

[52] *D*, II.23.181–83/387–90.

[53] Analogous oppositions are either "eliminate" or "caress," use raging or forgiving; see *D*, II.23.184/390; *P*, III.10/122.

[54] In a clear echo of Thucydides' Diodotus on Mytilene (TPW, III.46–47), Livy (*LH*, viii.13) also has "and create vast deserts out of the places from where you have often drawn a splendid allied army to make use of in a major war."

into citizenship." This mode of "caressing" the defeated enemy has clear advantages. If the Senate takes this path prudently, it will "expand" the Roman Empire and achieve the highest praise. "Matter is at hand for growing by means of the greatest glory." Camillus' penultimate words leave little doubt about which option he judges to be prudent: "That rule [*imperium*] is certainly the firmest that is obeyed gladly [*Certe id firmissimum imperium est, quo obedientes gaudent*]."[55]

In recognizing the need to avoid a middle course and choose between "extreme measures," then, Camillus is really urging his compatriots to see that in deciding how to deal with the basic problem that caused the Latins to revolt—the question of their status as partners or subjects in empire—only one course makes any sense at all. Benefiting the Latins by admitting them to citizenship also benefits the Roman Empire, giving it great "increase" in loyal populations and "holding" them in a mode so that they cannot and "ought not" harm the Romans. Making subjects into partners is one of the most effective means of making stronger "bodies" of citizens ordered together under "ancient discipline" and capable of great military and political virtue.[56] Elsewhere, Machiavelli stresses the near impossibility of destroying peoples who seem to themselves to be free:

> Whoever becomes patron of a city accustomed to living free, and does not destroy it, should expect to be destroyed by it; for it always has as a refuge in rebellion the name of liberty and its own ancient orders which are never forgotten either through length of time or because of benefits received. Whatever one does or provides for, unless the inhabitants are broken up or dispersed, they will not forget that name and those orders, and will immediately recur to them upon any accident as did Pisa after having been kept in servitude a hundred years by the Florentines.[57]

If Machiavelli wants to use Camillus' speech to underscore the advantages of the order of making partners, how then should his next remarks be explained? He reports that the Senate decided to follow the "words of the consul." Accordingly, they applied one or the other extreme policy to different major towns in Latium. Some towns were benefited, others eliminated. The towns that were benefited received "exemptions and privileges" from the Romans, who gave them citizenship and secured them "on every side." The other towns were "demolished," colonized by Romans, and their citizens relocated to Rome, where they were dispersed "so that they could no longer hurt either through arms or through counsel." The point might seem to be that both extreme options are equally useful, and should be combined in this way, not that only one is prudent.[58] The senators did not, Machiavelli repeats at the end of this passage, "ever use the neutral way [*la via neutrali*]

---

[55] *D*, II.23.182/389.

[56] *D*, II.16.161/364–65.

[57] *P*, V.20–21/129–30. Again compare Thucydides' Diodotus, TPW, III.46.

[58] See Hörnqvist's (2004) recent interpretation along these lines. While Hörnqvist works harder than most scholars to make sense of apparent contradictions in the writings on empire, his neglect of Machiavelli's ancient sources—here Livy and Thucydides—leads him to take Machiavelli at face value.

in affairs of moment."[59] The solution is found in a tension between the clear thrust of Camillus' arguments, which leave little doubt that only one extreme option is viable, and the Senate's corrupt interpretation of the consul's words. If the Roman Senate interpreted Camillus' words as a call to combine two extreme modes, perhaps they were unable to understand or reluctant to follow his clear implicit judgment. Unable or unwilling to reverse previous Roman policy and treat the Latins as partners in empire, they reverted to the mixed-middle mode of trying to have it both ways by other means: make some into partners while crushing others.[60]

This was not at all what Livy's or Machiavelli's Camillus advised. The difference between Camillus' meaning and the Senate's interpretation is clear in Livy's original narrative, to which Machiavelli refers readers. Here senators praise Camillus' treatment of "the main point at issue," but resist his call to make a clear choice between extremes, preferring to treat the Latin "peoples" differently under "separate decrees." Livy's description of policies adopted toward different Latin towns stresses their extreme harshness, remarking on the "savage" character of penalties imposed on peoples who had rebelled many times or joined forces with the Gauls. The tension between Camillus' prudent words and the senators' actions is palpable in Livy's narrative. Camillus' advice was simple, clear, and stressed the need for a settlement based on consistent principles. The policies adopted by the Senate are extraordinarily complicated, based on no clear legal precepts, and often appear arbitrary. Camillus argues for a principled peace that meets many of the Latins' demands for full partnership in the Roman Empire, yet the Senate reverts to the same kinds of "second mode" policies that led to war in the first place. Camillus' speech and the Senate's policies do not represent the same Roman methods of expansion at all. Camillus insists on the necessity to choose between ordinary orders and extraordinary modes; the Senate tries to follow a middle way that, Livy and Machiavelli suggest, proves unstable over time.[61]

12.5.
Why Roman *imperio* became pernicious: The wars with Carthage

Expansion became particularly "pernicious" to Rome's internal orders during the long wars with Carthage in the second century BC. Machiavelli's analysis of the wars' legacy is unsystematic, and must be reconstructed from remarks scattered through different works. His main judgments, however, are consistent. Their clearest locus is the contrast between sound older "orders" of military and civilian conduct, personified by Fabius Maximus, and corrupt new "modes" initiated by Fabius' young rival, Scipio Africanus. As generals, both men successfully used sharply contrasting

---

[59] D, II.23.182/388–89.

[60] Machiavelli imitates Livy's-Camillus' arguments in a fragmentary text, "How to Deal with the People of the Valdichiana Who Have Rebelled." Hörnqvist identifies this as a straightforward policy proposal, reflecting Machiavelli's own hardheaded view that rebellious "subjects" should be eliminated. I agree with Allan Gilbert's (1989, I:161–62) more cautious judgment that the text has much more of a literary than a programmatic character. The clear parallels with Livy and Thucydides strengthen this view.

[61] LH, VIII.13–14. Compare the similar corrupt upshot of the Mytilinean revolt in TPW, III.50.

tactics to baffle their Carthaginian enemy, Hannibal. As political leaders too, differences in their methods of seeking to gain popular support for controversial actions form a key theme in Livy's histories.[62] Machiavelli draws on Livy's characterizations to some extent, but puts the contrasts into even sharper focus.

Like the Roman mode of expansion itself, Scipio has virtuous beginnings. When Machiavelli first mentions him in the *Discourses* it is to commend an early act that demonstrated his superior talents as a military commander.[63] But having helped to save his country's virtue, Scipio's later actions contributed to undermining it. In the military context, the main flaw Machiavelli attributes to Scipio is an unwillingness to discipline those under his command. The *Prince* mentions an episode that carries ominous echoes of the earlier Fabii incident in the wars with Gaul. After the Locrians in southern Italy "had been destroyed by a legate of Scipio's they were not avenged by him, nor was the insolence of that legate corrected." As with the Fabii, basic duties of justice were violated by men under Scipio's command; yet like the Roman Senate in the earlier case, Scipio added insult to already grievous injury by failing to punish those responsible. "All of which," Machiavelli comments wryly, "arose from his agreeable nature."[64] Machiavelli portrays Scipio's failure to punish the violations committed at Locri as a symbolic milestone marking a parallel shift in Roman military tactics toward ever more violent and "extraordinary" modes of fighting.[65]

Behind Scipio's imprudent leniency was the desire to win partisans to support his political ambitions. The result was that Scipio's armies did not "fear" him enough, so that his allies in Spain—and "part of his friends"—"rebelled against him" because of his "excessive mercy, which had allowed his soldiers more license than is fitting for military discipline." Having at first been too indulgent in his "humanity and mercy," Scipio then swung to the opposite extreme to avenge his injuries, and was "constrained to use part of the cruelty he had fled from." Machiavelli leaves it to readers to judge whether modes of action that lead men to fly between extremes of indulgence and cruelty are governed by genuine *virtú*, or by an excessive ambition that makes a man underassertive in one "fortune," overassertive when it shifts. Machiavelli reports that Hannibal, by contrast with Scipio, "was held impious and a breaker of faith and cruel." While ironically mimicking these prejudices of Roman chroniclers, however, Machiavelli questions their judgment, at least as far as Scipio's comparative merits are concerned. Hannibal's often violent, tradition-defying modes certainly do not represent the pinnacle of military *virtú* for Machiavelli. But he questions judgments that value Scipio's over- and underassertive methods

---

[62] Livy is extremely critical of Scipio's "insatiable" ambition and corrupt *modi operandi*, while praising Fabius for saving his fatherland; see *LH*, XXVIII.17–21, 40–45; XXIX.14–27, XXX.26, 32. Livy contrasts the older and younger men in ways that closely resemble similar contrasts between Thucydides' *dramatis personae*; see Walsh (1963), 35–45, 93–106 on Thucydides' influence on Livy and resemblances between Nicias and Fabius.

[63] *D*, I.11.34/229.

[64] *P*, XVII.68/164. The only thing that prevented this "damaging quality" from sullying Scipio's reputation was that he lived in a republic "under the government of the Senate," which opposed some of his most reckless impulses, allowing him to keep up the good appearances that "made for his glory."

[65] In *D*, II.32 he notes that Scipio turned to siege, an unwise mode.

more than Hannibal's sterner discipline, noting "a very great advantage" that arose from them "which is admired by all the writers": namely, "that although his army was composed of various kinds of men, no dissension ever arose in it, either among them or against him." If this excellent effect was produced by the "terror that arose from his person, which was held so great—mixed with the reputation that his virtue gave him," perhaps what Roman writers call "terror" of their mortal enemy is better characterized as respect due to a general who used strict discipline to order his army and partner provinces.[66]

In the context of Roman politics, Machiavelli's remarks focus on the corrosive effects of Scipio's conduct on the ethical quality and stability of republican orders. In Scipio, he observes, one sees how far ambition corrodes the rule of law—the only foundation of common freedoms—under "honest appearances." Machiavelli depicts Scipio as a past master of self-promoting spin, one of those who know how "to acquire fame so as to obtain honors in their republic," a skill more appropriate to one-man "princely" rulers who want to "maintain reputation for themselves" alone. Scipio's methods prove that nothing makes men "so much esteemed as to give rare examples of themselves with some rare act or saying conforming to the common good, which shows the lord either magnanimous, or liberal, or just," so that it becomes "like a proverb among his subjects."[67] Like the Medici princes in Machiavelli's Florence, Scipio corrupted the judgment of citizens in his own time and after by generating false appearances of virtue. When Machiavelli alleges that Scipio's model was Cyrus, he underscores his corruption several times over. Scipio's job was to defend a republic. But he made his role model a hereditary prince, and moreover a prince who—according to Xenophon's narrative—introduced indolence, disrespect for old laws and customs, and the beginnings of tyranny into what had previously been a well-ordered country. Moreover, one of the main skills displayed by Xenophon's Cyrus is that of keeping up appearances of political and military virtue while acting in ways that corrupt it. Machiavelli refers readers of the *Prince* to Xenophon's authority: "whoever reads in the life of Cyrus written by Xenophon will then recognize in the life of Scipio how much glory that imitation brought him," and see how "in chastity, affability, humanity, and liberality Scipio conformed to what had been written of Cyrus by Xenophon."[68]

Piecing together Machiavelli's scattered remarks, Scipio emerges as the first of a long line of Roman commanders, culminating in Julius Caesar, who exploited popular fears and ambitions for his own purposes.[69] Thus "when Scipio was made consul and desired the province of Africa, promising the entire ruin of Carthage," he met opposition from the Senate. But then, Machiavelli notes, "he threatened to propose it to the people, as one who knew very well how much such decisions please peoples."[70] The success of this populist move encouraged others to imitate his

[66] *D*, III.12.262–64/456–59.
[67] *D*, I.46.95/293–94; II.4.136–37/338–40; III.34.289/503; compare *LH*, XXIX.21.
[68] *P*.XIV.60/158. See chap. 2, sec. 2.2.
[69] This is implied in Livy's account. See *LH*, XXX.45 and his account of the corrupt "oligarchy" introduced by Scipio in later years, resulting in his exile from Rome. *LH*, XXXVIII.50–60.
[70] *D*, I.53.106–8/305–8.

apparent virtues and excessive ambitions, hastening the ruin of the Roman republic. Scipio's career illustrates how corruption spreads: starting at the top with ambitious leaders failing to enforce standards, their disrespect spreads to the military or
civilian rank-and-file, who are not called to account and may even be rewarded for
conduct based on low standards. After Scipio's conquest of Carthage—until then
the dominant power in the Mediterranean and a much greater city than Rome—
Romans became less industrious in defending their internal and external freedoms.
"After the Romans had subdued Africa and Asia and had reduced almost all Greece
to obedience," Machiavelli writes, "they became secure in their freedom, as it did
not appear to them that they had any more enemies who ought to give them fear."
This complacency

> made the Roman people no longer regard virtue but favor in bestowing the
> consulate, lifting to that rank those who knew better how to entertain men
> rather than those who knew better how to conquer enemies. Afterward,
> from those who had more favor, they descended to giving it to those who
> had more power; so, through the defect of such an order, the good remained
> altogether excluded.[71]

These developments prepared the way for tyranny on pretexts provided by foreign
wars. According to Machiavelli, the crucial move was the extension of magistracies beyond limited terms. Although this was "started by the Senate for public
utility," he writes, "that thing was what in time made Rome servile. For the farther
the Romans went abroad with arms, the more such extension appeared necessary
to them and the more they used it." The longer magistracies produced two great
"inconveniences": they gave fewer men practice in commands and thus "came to
restrict reputation to a few." Then when one citizen remained commander of any
army for a long time "he would win it over to himself and make it partisan to him,
for the army would in time forget the Senate and recognize that head." It was "because of this," Machiavelli argues, that "Caesar could seize the fatherland." But he
suggests that even if the Romans had not prolonged magistracies and commands
or "come so soon to so much power," they would have delayed their coming to
"servitude"—but not stopped it—by changing only their internal orders.[72] To reverse the decline they would also have to examine their external policies, asking
whether it was possible to sustain a mode of expansion that conceived of partnership with other peoples as, in effect, a fig leaf for the dominion of one.

The deficiencies in Scipio's modes are underscored by pointed contrasts with
Fabius Maximus, whose prudent judgment Machiavelli holds responsible for persuading the Senate to oppose the younger man's early ambitions to seize all of Africa
and "ruin" Carthage. In the *Prince*, as in Livy, we read that Fabius Maximus called
Scipio "the corrupter of the Roman military." The key phrase Machiavelli uses to
describe Fabius Maximus is that he was "unvarying" in his nature and customs.[73]

---

[71] *D*, I.18.50/246–47.
[72] *D*, III.24.270/482.
[73] *P*, III.9/121–22; Livy XXIX, 592.

As we have seen, the quality of "not varying" is not equivalent to stick-in-mud inflexibility, though this was how Fabius Maximus was portrayed by admirers of his opponent Scipio.[74] In the stability of his military judgments, Machiavelli contrasts him to Scipio and Hannibal, both of whom showed "excessive virtue" in their nontraditional modes of fighting and use of siege. Fabius represents the older Roman "order" of using force as a last resort, in contrast to Scipio's and Hannibal's impulses to take the offensive.[75] In the political context, the phrase "not varying" signifies two qualities that are necessary to maintain republican orders. One is impartiality: not varying one's standards to benefit partisans, friends, or family. The other is integrity: not varying in one's principles in order to gain popularity. When men who uphold these qualities are in command, they can be trusted never to act arbitrarily, but always according to publicly known, ordinary procedures. Machiavelli's Fabius never changes his "modes" according to personal relations, feeling, or fortune; and he imposes the same high standards of discipline and obedience to laws on himself that he expects others to show on his watch. In direct contrast to Scipio, Fabius' methods of seeking public authorization for his modes of conducting the war are impeccably transparent. Machiavelli underlines Fabius' avoidance of easy routes to popularity. He insists on speaking in assemblies, seeking to correct popular judgments with good arguments; and when he lacks evident reasons for a policy, he does not use force, favors, or deception to manipulate public opinion.[76]

Machiavelli also considers modes of expansion from the perspective of Rome's mortal enemy. When his relevant comments are gathered together, they appear quite evenly balanced between praise for the Carthaginians' old-fashioned respect for established orders of conducting war and criticism of recent corruptions. On the critical side, Machiavelli suggests that the Carthaginians were fatally complacent about their own security. Since they already held all of Africa, Sardinia and Sicily, and part of Spain, they felt safe in their own empire—an unreasonable complacency that Romans would later display, far more egregiously.[77] Because of their great strength and the distance between themselves and Rome, the Carthaginians did not perceive their errors until "the Romans, having subdued all the peoples between them and the Carthaginians, began to combat them over the empire of Sicily and of Spain."[78]

On the other side, what Machiavelli says about Carthaginian conduct in war stands as an implicit reproach to Rome's eventual transgression of limits established

[74] See chap. 5, sec. 5.2. Livy has Fabius prudently insist that policies and tactics should not be judged by "the result—that teacher of fools—but by that same process of reasoning that held good before, and will continue to do so [sed eadem ratio quae fuit futura, donec res eadem manebunt, immutabilis est]." Never mind, he says, if people "call your caution timidity" or your generalship "unwarlike"; it is better that a wise enemy should fear you than that foolish fellow citizens should praise you." He advises Romans to "be master of yourself and all that is yours, be armed and vigilant, prepared when opportunity presents itself" taking care that "reason and not fortune should be your guide [sed ut agentem te ratio ducat, non fortuna]." LH, XXII.xxxix–xl.

[75] D, III.10.242/451; III.21.262–64/473–80; compare II.12.152–53/355–57, II.17.163/367–68.

[76] D, I.53.105–7/305–8; III.9.239–4/446–48; III.34.289–90.

[77] D, III.16.255–56; FH, II.2.53–54/362–64.

[78] D, II.1.127–28/328–30; see PolH, XV.6–9.

by the *ius gentium* regulating *ius in bello*. He describes traditional Carthaginian methods of expansion before Hannibal as similar to sound Roman orders of expanding by making partners. Instead of assaulting the rising new power in Italy, Carthaginian leaders "acted rather in their favor, as is done with things that grow, linking up with them and seeking their friendship." This trusting attitude proved a dangerous mistake. On Machiavelli's account, the Carthaginians were naïvely—but not unreasonably—old-fashioned in expecting Rome to impose limits on its own ambitions, and in believing that Rome's past adherence to customary laws of war could be taken as an index of future conduct, despite evidence of Rome's appetite for dominion in Italy and beyond.[79] Throughout Book II of the *Discourses*, Machiavelli argues that the best orders for expanding republics are based on well-ordered, collaborative power used prudently, not overassertively. The Carthaginians had reason to expect the Romans to continue in these self-restrained orders because, as we saw earlier, "for more than four hundred and fifty years" they had usually done so: they had "paid attention to tiring out their neighbors with defeats and raids and to gaining reputation over them by means of accords." On Machiavelli's account, both Fabius and his Carthaginian opponents observed the limits set by the "law of nations," conducting their battles in ways that stopped short of physically destroying important enemy cities or seeking to win an uncompromising, "ultimate" victory. Fabius adhered to what Machiavelli treats as a view consistent with good, older Roman orders, that violent seizures turn acquisitions into a source of weakness. Against this background, Scipio's siege methods represent a decisive break with sounder Roman customs upheld by Fabius. Although Scipio claimed merely to be imitating the extraordinary tactics practiced by Hannibal, by destroying Carthage and other great cities he outdid his enemy in "extraordinary virtue": Hannibal could have sacked Rome many years earlier after his massacre of Roman troops at Cannae, but refrained from overstepping that crucial limit.

These views oppose a widespread opinion that once Hannibal led Carthaginian armies onto Italian soil, the Romans had no choice but to seek to eliminate them as a rival power. According to this opinion, Scipio's ruthlessness was necessary and praiseworthy, while Fabius' avoidance of direct combat only delayed inevitable all-out war to decide which single power would dominate the Mediterranean. If Machiavelli sometimes seems to second this opinion in the dialectic of his "discourses," the main thrust of his reasoning strongly dissents from it. His arguments imply that had both Roman and Carthaginian leaders been more prudent, a clear division of regional power might have been worked out between the two empires. This would have been the most reasonable solution according to Machiavelli's principles: each would lead its part, agreeing to share power and respecting clear limits. He does not deny that many ambitious men in Carthage were as guilty as their Roman counterparts of harboring excessive desires to dominate the entire region. Livy and Machiavelli ascribe more moderate, traditional views to Hanno, an "old and prudent Carthaginian" who stands to the younger Hannibal as Fabius Maximus stands to Scipio in Rome. Hanno, Machiavelli writes, "counseled that

[79] *D*, II.1.127–28/328–30.

victory should be used wisely to make peace with the Romans, since they, having won, could have it with honorable conditions." He thought that the Carthaginians should show the Romans that they "were able enough to combat them and, having had victory over them, one should not seek to lose it through the hope of a greater." Like Fabius in Rome, Hanno strikes the appropriately virtuous balance between force and restraint, respecting limits set by others' "ordinary and reasonable" ambitions. Sadly, this policy was not taken up, because less prudent men wanted more. But "it was known well by the Carthaginian Senate to have been wise later," Machiavelli remarks, "when the opportunity was lost."[80] Ambition and intransigence on both sides encouraged a dangerous escalation of the war.

Machiavelli implies, however, that ambition and disregard for limits went further on the Roman side. He describes Carthaginian leaders as more willing than Romans to return to earlier principles of bounded and ordered empire, by which they would agree to limit their own empire to north Africa and Spain if Rome would agree to stay in its neighborhood. Machiavelli implies that when at last the Romans prevailed, they had reason to trust the Carthaginians to seal such a settlement by means of "accords." This becomes clear in his tragic account of Hannibal's defeat. Despite earlier, more ambivalent judgments about Hannibal, Machiavelli presents him on the verge of his last battle as a model of *virtuoso* generalship. Pushed into a corner by Scipio's armies and

> knowing that this was the last stake of his fatherland, he did not wish to put it at risk before he had tried every other remedy. He was not ashamed to ask for peace since he judged that if his fatherland had any remedy it was in that and not in war. When that was denied him, he did not wish to fail to engage in combat, even if he should lose, since he judged that he was still able to win or, losing, to lose gloriously.

This pathetic epitaph quietly evokes Rome's growing *hubris*: "And if Hannibal, who was so virtuous and had his army intact, sought peace before fighting, when he saw that by losing it his fatherland would become servile, what should another do of less virtue and of less experience than he?" In other words, it is wrong to see Hannibal's belated request for peace as evidence of deficient *virtù*. If his virtue was "excessive" earlier in the conflict, Hannibal later showed appropriately disciplined virtue first in seeking to reach peace by accords and then, when the Romans rejected his overtures, in fighting to the end. Hannibal brought harsh necessity on himself and his country by audaciously invading Italy. Men always err, Machiavelli concludes, "who do not know how to put limits to their hopes, and, by founding themselves on these without otherwise measuring themselves, they are ruined."[81] But this judgment applies as much to Rome after the defeat of Carthage as to Hannibal. Encouraged by Scipio's personal ambitions as well as Hannibal's terrifying early successes, the Romans had come to treat the war with Carthage as a total war where immoderate ends—total, uncompromising victory and the physical "elimination" of the

[80] *D*, II.27.193/400–402; *LH*, XXI.iii–iv.
[81] *D*, II.27.195/402.

enemy—were now thought to justify any means. In the longer term, these aggressive modes of expansion tended to undermine Rome's security together with its republican orders. "The city of Rome," Machiavelli notes ruefully, "at one time had a defense." But "after it had conquered Carthage and Antiochus" and "no longer feared wars, it appeared to it that it could commit armies to whomever it wished, with regard not so much to virtue as to other qualities that gave them favor among the people." The Roman conquest of Carthage seemed to render Italy "safe from foreign wars"; but by lowering ethical and political standards, it created more license for civil wars, which not long after "began in Rome, first between Marius and Sulla, then between Caesar and Pompey, and later between the killers of Caesar and those who wanted to avenge his death."[82]

12.6.
Expansion by partnership: The forgotten Tuscan league

All these arguments, I submit, constitute overwhelming evidence that Machiavelli does not favor the mixed Roman "mode" of expansion. He rather dissimulates admiration for it in order to provoke readers to examine a very common opinion. His preferred methods of *ampliare* are the sound "orders" described throughout Book II of the *Discourses*—though his accounts of these need to be disentangled from accounts in each chapter of superficially similar but corrupt modes. Section 12.4. touched on some of his specific "orders," but how does he characterize them in more general terms?

Recall the apparently casual remark that the Romans long maintained acquisitions through "the order of proceeding and its own mode found by its first lawgiver."[83] As we saw in chapter 11, there are two possible founder-lawgivers for Rome, Romulus and Aeneas. Machiavelli says nothing about Romulus' modes of acquiring subjects or partners. His brief remarks on Aeneas, however, go straight to this issue. Aeneas and Dido maintained their authority in a newly acquired country "by way of friends and confederates" rather than force. Because they led relatively small numbers instead of mass migrations, they could not "use so much violence" but were constrained to "seize some place with art," notably the arts of befriending local peoples and creating new partnerships with them. In this way they "were able to maintain themselves through the consent of the neighbors where they settled.[84] Later Roman orders, as we have seen, remained good so long as they expanded by confederates in this way and did not seek to assert unilateral dominion. Aeneas' example shows that while people are often under genuine necessity to leave their homelands or expand in various ways, it is not always necessary to confront pre-existing peoples in a violent or domineering way. In fact, aggressive modes only make it harder to maintain power, and impossible to establish genuine *autorità*, since "not fortresses but the will of men maintains

---

[82] *D*, III.16.255–56/465–67; *FH*, II.2.53–54/362–64; compare *D*, I.18.49–51/245–48.

[83] *D*, II.1.126/327–28.

[84] *D*, II.8.145/348–49.

princes in their states."[85] Conflicts with peoples already settled in a place can be addressed by prudently self-legislated orders based on principles of willing authorization, or "partnership."

Machiavelli's brief remarks on Aeneas and Dido echo his detailed account of the first mode of expanding by leagues, represented especially by the ancient Tuscans. He does not openly declare that this is the one most worth imitating; he claims that it is only the next best after the Roman. But just as the impossibility of well-ordered one-man rule makes it necessary to settle for second-best government under the "almost regal" rule of laws, so the impossibility of "balancing" the Roman middle way makes it necessary to expand in the next-best mode. Readers who notice all the problems that Machiavelli identifies in the Roman mode might begin to see "expanding by leagues" as a more promising and realistic option. The skills needed to keep the middle Roman mode balanced might be found in gods, since even the efforts of *prudentissimo* men such as Camillus and Fabius could not keep it balanced for long. By contrast, the Tuscans maintained their mode of leagues "in the highest glory and arms" for a very long time, without any special favor from heaven or fortune.[86]

We have noted that the chief disadvantage of this mode seemed to be that, unlike the Roman, it "could not expand very far." However, Machiavelli "lets drop" several arguments that might be thought to outweigh this limitation. First, the disadvantages of the first mode are comparatively far less dangerous than those of the second. Both share the weaknesses of all human modes and orders: neither can provide absolute security, perpetual defense against outside attack, or guaranteed loyalty from its "parts." But compared with the built-in tendencies of the Roman mode to unchecked ambition, violence, and tyranny, the self-imposed limits found in the mode of leagues seem more likely to achieve the benefits of strong *imperio* without the risks of *dominio*.

Second, when Machiavelli mentions the Tuscan league in Book II, chapter 5, he has just made the point that what is "seen" or "known" from past experience so far does not necessarily exhaust what reasonably might be. It may be that, as he said in chapter 4, expansion by leagues is "seen by experience to have a fixed limit" of approximately twelve to fourteen "communities" (*università*). Until now, no examples can be found of leagues that went beyond that number without falling apart; this number proved sufficient for defense for a very long time in the Tuscan case. If in other times it should prove insufficient, however, past experience alone cannot rule out the possibility that viable leagues may be formed with more members.[87] Machiavelli does not specify particular types or size of community that may form leagues: presumably they may be cities and their surroundings, but perhaps also regions such as Tuscany, Lombardy, and the like. If so, an expanding league could in principle encompass the Italian peninsula. On

---

[85] *D*, II.24.187/392.

[86] See the perceptive remarks on the untenable character of the Roman mode and Machiavelli's preference for the Tuscan in de Alvarez 1999, 22–26, 66, 120–23.

[87] *D*, II.4–5.135–40/337–43. See Machiavelli's letter to Vettori on Aristotle and the limited value of confederations, which makes a similar point; chap. 1, sec. 1.5.

this expansionist logic, wider if looser kinds of defensive league could presumably be formed as well: for example, the Italians with the Swiss, who together could oppose the aggressive expansionism of Habsburg emperors, French kings, and the papacy. Machiavelli does not outline these specific alternatives, but they are not obviously precluded by his general principles or ordering leagues. If a league reaches its reasonable limits for bringing members into full partnership, it can still augment its power by making partners of a less formally binding sort. Machiavelli mentions two supplementary methods when discussing contemporary Swiss uses of the mode of leagues: financial interdependence, and military alliances with powers outside the league.[88]

Third, Machiavelli stresses one very great advantage of the "mode of proceeding by leagues": it "is known to have always been similar and to have had similar effects." On a casual reading, this might sound dismissive or bland. But by the consistent standards of judgment established in the *Discourses* and other works, the words carry very high praise indeed. Whenever Machiavelli says that men or orders never vary or are similar in their nature, mode, or customs, he suggests that they are reliable, transparent, and ordered by laws they give to themselves instead of shifting according to changes in fortune. The Roman mode, by contrast, was governed by a mixture of virtue and fortune. Its attempt to combine incompatible principles, to have one's cake and eat it, eventually forced Romans to rely more on fortune and foreign arms than on the potentially formidable ones close to home.

Fourth and finally, Machiavelli identifies a number of specific advantages that flow from what is usually seen as the first mode's main weakness, that is, the limits it sets on expansion. "Since you cannot expand very much" with the mode of leagues, he points out, "two goods follow: one, that you do not easily take a war on your back; the other, that you easily keep as much as you take." The first mode therefore passes the key test set out by Thucydides and seconded by Machiavelli: modes of acquiring are good when they allow you to secure what you take, bad when your acquisitions are fiercely contested and create new enemies. Machiavelli enumerates three causes that prevent leagues founded in the first mode from expanding indefinitely:

1. *A plurality of equal members* ordered under a requirement to engage in mutual consultation when deciding policy. "The cause of its inability to expand is its being a republic that is disunited and placed in various seats, which enables them to consult and decide only with difficulty."

2. *Low stakes of dominion*: "It also makes them not be desirous of dominating; for since there are many communities to participate in dominion, they do not esteem such acquisition as much as one republic alone that hopes to enjoy it entirely."

3. *The slowness of decisions made through councils of formally equal members*: "Besides this, they govern themselves through a council, and they must be

[88] *D*, II.19.173–74/378–80; *MF*, 245–59, 295–301.

slower in every decision than those who inhabit within one and the same wall."[89]

Machiavelli presents his first mode of leagues as an order that creates collaborative power by setting clear, self-imposed limits on members' capacities to dominate others, within or beyond the league itself. It has the strengths of an extended "body" without the weaknesses caused by the dominion of one.[90] His dissimulated praise for the mixed Roman mode illustrates the truth that "Men always praise ancient times—but not always reasonably."[91] This is especially true of judgments about the Roman Empire. If readers want to avoid the self-deceptions that undermined Roman virtue, they should examine the less-known, underrated modes of republican expansion practiced by other peoples. And if the empirical examples are too few or too sketchy to serve as complete guides, they can infer reasonable principles for ordering leagues from what is known about human nature. Although the Tuscans' religion, virtue, customs, and ancestral language were all "eliminated by Roman power," their main ordering principles can be inferred by conjecture where empirical evidence is lacking. "If the imitation of the Romans seems difficult," Machiavelli argues,

> that of the ancient Tuscans should not seem so, especially to the present Tuscans. For if they could not, for the causes said, make an empire like that of Rome, they could acquire the power in Italy that their mode of proceeding conceded them.[92]

12.7.
Should Florence imitate Rome?

It is sometimes thought that Machiavelli participated in a self-assertive discourse of empire that flourished in Florence under the Medicis.[93] On this view, Florentines should imitate the *ends* of Roman *imperio* by uniting Italian peoples—Florentines, Romans, Venetians, Milanese—under a common political framework, as the Romans brought the Samnites, Latins, and Tuscans under their republican empire. My understanding of Machiavelli's ethical and political principles is wholly compatible with this view of his imperial *ends*. He harks back to the principles that might "reasonably" have underpinned the Tuscan confederation, suggesting that

---

[89] *D*, II.4.137/339–40.

[90] Some of the core ideas here can be found in Greek writers, notably Thucydides. The norm holding that cities should enjoy *autonomia* was of course fully compatible with the notion that they should form strongly binding, formal and informal obligations with one another; *autonomia* depended on shared structures of mutually guaranteed freedoms, underwritten by laws or customs that were regarded as sacred. On the strength of demands for the recognition of equal rights of small and "great" cities to participate in leagues, enjoy equal treatment under shared judicial processes, and preserve traditional freedoms under their own laws, see TPW, V.47 and 77.

[91] *D*, II.Pref.123–25/324–27.

[92] *D*, II.4.138/335. See chap. 3, sec. 3.3, and Livy's observations about the former greatness of the Etruscans and their league of twelve cities; *LH*, I.2–3, V.33–34.

[93] A view most recently argued by Hörnqvist (2004).

contemporary Florentines should consider applying similar principles on a wider territorial scale. In this way Florence could play a leading role in persuading other cities to set aside their fratricidal hatreds and join a voluntary league of formally equal Italian cities, whose combined power could counter French, Habsburg, and papal intrusions. Machiavelli has no qualms about calling this kind of voluntary league an *imperio*, though it contrasts sharply with the involuntary and unequal forms of rule now associated with that name. He is clear that while partner cities must expand to form such empires of the willing, further expansion is not the aim of *imperio* in this adequate sense. Its proper and sufficient aim is collaborative self-defense, based on reciprocal ties of friendship and respect for each others' freedom. He says little about how leagues on the Tuscan-Aetolian pattern should deal with other cities, peoples, or empires, especially those that threaten them. But the *Discourses'* arguments about Rome, the *Histories'* about Florence, and the *Prince's* opening chapters highlight the ruinous consequences of overassertive unilateralism, demands for dominion, and the refusal to respect due limits, especially limits of justice.

The foregoing interpretation disagrees, however, with most previous views about the *means* that Machiavelli thinks are justified when seeking to form a new Italian *imperio*; and with the assumption that he wants Florence's leading role to involve *dominio* on the Roman model, instead of leadership or *autorità* freely given by other partners who "share" in it.[94] Other scholars have proposed that Machiavelli wants Florence to imitate Rome by pretending to treat allies as equals, yet retaining clear superiority in power, especially when making conquests further abroad.[95] The present interpretation suggests that this undiscriminating pro-Roman reading must be thoroughly revised. Machiavelli's appraisals of Roman methods of expansion are at least as critical as they are positive. He invokes common opinions about the value of Roman imperial models not only to second them, but also to provoke readers to examine what lies behind appearances of Roman glory. His appraisals of corrupt Roman "modes" reflect a concern that contemporary Florentines were imitating the wrong Roman models: those that lent an aura of *grandezza* to their enterprises, while intensifying enmities between Italian cities whose citizens preferred to fight to the death than be treated as subjects. As earlier chapters have shown, Machiavelli portrays the resistance of cities such as Lucca, Arezzo, Pisa, Siena, and Volterra as implacable by means of force or deception alone. In the *Discourses* he notes that the Roman republic's defenses were recurrently undermined by wars with indignant Italian "allies," who saw through the pretense that they were Rome's partners instead of its subjects. There and in the *Histories* he draws clear parallels, and identifies similar dangers, with Florentine efforts to expand

[94] The distinction I impute to Machiavelli between *imperio* and *dominio* corresponds broadly to Thucydides' *hēgemonia* (leadership) and *archē* (rule); see chap. 2, sec. 2.5.

[95] Although some recent scholars take Machiavelli to be recommending the Roman middle-way mode, others think he sees it as "absolutely" best but "pragmatically" too difficult for Florence, and recommends the Tuscan confederal mode by default though not in principle; for example, Viroli (2001, 188–89). Unusually, de Alvarez (1999) argues that Machiavelli prefers the Tuscan mode as the only sustainable one.

without respecting the desires of neighboring cities to retain their collective free agency within a wider Italian entity.

On Machiavelli's accounts, an important difference between Rome's and Florence's experience of expansion is that whereas the early Roman republic was constrained to work out multilateral orders for expanding "by partners"—especially if Aeneas is taken as first *ordinatore*—the fledgling Florentine republic got off to an imprudent start in this respect. Having begun life as an unfree imperial city founded and run by Romans, when a millennium later Florence at last acquired its own republican orders, its first modes of expansion still resembled those of the parent city in its less well-ordered days. Machiavelli says that Florence began to acquire its own empire soon after establishing free internal institutions. By the end of Book I "the Florentines were lords of the greater part of Tuscany," with only Lucca and Siena still living "under their own laws." Under the first republic the Florentines "forced the people of Pisa, Arezzo, and Siena to league with them," seized Volterra, and destroyed other fortified towns. The new republic, Machiavelli writes, "would have risen to any greatness if frequent and new divisions had not afflicted it."[96] The divisions in question came, as we have seen, from within and without; and Machiavelli always traces them to imprudent policy, not bad luck. One of the main themes in the *Histories* is the resistance of other peoples to Florentine subjection. No sooner do the Florentines assert their own freedom than they turn around and "assault" the freedoms of others, who resist with the same natural, ordinary, and reasonable vigor as their opponents. The early republic still combined principles of expanding "by partnership" with expansion "by subjects": Machiavelli states that in 1298, "All in Tuscany, part as subjects and part as friends, obeyed [Florence]."[97]

The distinction between obedience given by friends-partners or taken from unwilling subjects is much more prominent in the *Histories* than in other works.[98] One might even say that the defense of principles of voluntary authorization, in both internal and external relations, is the central theme of that work's political philosophy. The principles are set out early on behalf of the republic's internal liberties, when Machiavelli has prudent magistrates tell an aspiring tyrant: "You have to be content with the authority that we," the citizens of Florence, "have given you. And we urge you to this, reminding you that that dominion is alone lasting which is voluntary." Identical principles are soon extended to cities subject to Florence's *dominio*. By overthrowing their internal tyranny, Florentines "inspired all the towns subject to the Florentines to get back their own freedom." Thus "Arezzo, Castiglione, Pistoia, Volterra, Colle, and San Gimignano rebelled, so that with one stroke Florence was deprived of its tyranny and its dominion [*dominio*]," words that for Machiavelli—as for Thucydides, Plato, and Plutarch—are nearly, though not quite, synonymous.[99]

---

[96] *FH*, I.39.50/359–60; II.6.58/368–69.

[97] *FH*, II.15.68/379–80.

[98] For example, see *FH*, I.9, I.29, II.30, II.34, II.38, V.1, V.14, VI.1, VII.30, VIII.13.

[99] *FH*, II.34.91–93/406–8; II.39.99/417–18. Although the status of "subjects" under "dominion" remains preferable to that of "slaves" under "servitude," Machiavelli implies that the lines between subjection-*dominio* and servitude are fine, and easily crossed under pressure.

It has been suggested that Machiavelli saw the loss of external dominion, if not of internal tyranny, as a bad thing for Florence.[100] Does Machiavelli treat this episode as a dangerous and humiliating defeat, or as an opportunity for the Florentines to renegotiate the unstable terms of their *imperio*? Instead of drawing inferences from what "Machiavellian realism" is supposed to recommend, let us look more closely at Machiavelli's own words. "In recovering its freedom," he remarks in this context, Florence "taught its subjects how to recover theirs." Thus "just after the expulsion of the duke and the loss of their dominion," the new magistrates

> thought it preferable to placate their subjects with peace than to make enemies of them by war, and to show them that they were as glad of their subjects' freedom as of their own. Therefore, they sent spokesmen to Arezzo to renounce the empire they had over that city and to sign an accord with them, so that, since they could no longer have them as subjects, they might profit from them as friends of their city. With the other towns also they made agreements as best they could, provided that they keep the Florentines as friends, so that, being free, the other towns could help maintain the Florentines' own freedom. This course, prudently adopted, had a very prosperous result [*felicissimo fine*]: for Arezzo, after not many years, returned to the empire [*imperio*] of the Florentines, and the other towns were reduced to their former obedience within a few months. And thus many times are things obtained more quickly and with fewer dangers and less expense by avoiding them than by pursuing them with all force and obstinacy.[101]

Note the direct parallels between these comments and the *Discourses'* remark that if you placate people or peoples, they will "throw themselves into your lap."[102] When Machiavelli says that neighboring cities returned voluntarily to Florentine *imperio*, it would be odd indeed if he meant that they were conned by the Florentines into accepting the same terms of subjection they had just revolted against. Instead he suggests that having regained their powers of collective free agency, they willingly authorized Florence to exercise leadership in their common enterprises. A condition for this legitimate *imperio* was that Florence should continue to respect the freedom of partner cities to authorize its actions. When Florentines later behaved like poorly disciplined Romans and sought to reassert dominion over these cities, ever more violent, fratricidal wars were the result, destabilizing the Italian peninsula and ultimately destroying Florence's own republican orders.

---

[100] Hörnqvist (2004, 153) argues that along with other humanists such as Bruni, Machiavelli was spellbound by "the ancient Roman triumph" of empire as "transmitted through the works of Livy, Plutarch," and others. It is hard to see how any careful reading could possibly derive imperial triumphalism from Livy or Plutarch; see Baron 1988, 90–93, on subtler, more critical aspects even of Bruni's writings on empire. As I have argued throughout, Machiavelli invokes triumphalist maxims in order to examine their weaknesses, not to second them uncritically.

[101] *FH*, II.38.99–100/416–17.

[102] *D*, II.30–32; again compare Thucydides' Diodotus on Mytileneans, Livy's Camillus on the Latins.

As with other ambivalent concepts, misunderstandings arise from the assumption that Machiavelli's *imperio* must be synonymous with *dominio*. But Machiavelli's *imperio* may be exercised in very different ways: as the dominion of one clear superior, or as the collaborative power of formal equals. The second kind of *imperio* is stable and just; the first is unjust and unstable. In the *Histories* the core distinction is made early in Book V. After the Roman Empire crumbled, Machiavelli observes, "nothing was built upon the Roman ruins that might have redeemed Italy" from the slings and arrows of fortune. "Nonetheless," he writes,

> so much virtue emerged in some of the new cities and empires that arose among the Roman ruins that, *even if one did not dominate* [*non dominasse*] the others, *they were nonetheless harmonious and ordered together* [*insieme concordi e ordinati*] so that they freed Italy and defended it from the barbarians. Within *these empires* [*imperi*] the Florentines, if they had *less dominion*, were *not the less in authority or power*; indeed, because of their position in the middle of Italy, rich and ready for attack, they either successfully resisted a war begun against them or they gave victory to the one with whom they sided.[103]

Machiavelli alludes here to the two senses of what might be called "empire": the dominion of one power, and several cities and regions "ordered together" by their own orders and "accords" for the benefit of common defenses. The passage makes it clear that *imperio* based on dominion is not necessarily better at maintaining "authority or power"; indeed, Machiavelli offers many reasons for the converse evaluation. *Imperio* in a "truer" sense can be achieved only through voluntary partnerships among free peoples; expansion creates strong *imperio* only if the parts commit themselves freely, and continue to give their willing authorization to whatever powers take command of their joint actions. Thus when Arezzo voluntarily returns to the "empire" of the Florentines in Book II, it is to a new kind of empire based on willing and equal collaboration under Florentine leadership, not on unilateral dominion.[104]

This explains uses of *imperio* that seem contradictory if the word is taken as synonymous with *dominio*. In Machiavelli's usage, as we have seen, *imperio* may be compatible with constraints and standards of legitimacy set out in his general political theory: willing authorization, respect for equal freedom of others, limits on all members' powers under rule of law. *Dominio*, on the other hand, is always

[103] *FH*, V.1.185–86/120–21; emphasis added.
[104] As a result of several centuries of heavy-handed "imperialism," this collaborative, voluntaristic, and egalitarian sense of "empire" has become virtually defunct in contemporary usage. It is important to recall that Machiavelli and other early modern republicans identified a normatively adequate sense of *imperio* that stood in direct opposition to the qualities usually associated with "empire" today: unauthorized imposition of standards and demands, and unequal power wielded according to the will of one predominant party. For Machiavelli *imperio* in the first, non-corrupt sense may include "empire" of rule of law and magistrates authorized by those who "obey"; see *FH*, V.6.192/527–28. Compare uses of the phrase "empire of laws" and reason versus the "empire of men" or private desires, and related distinctions between just and unjust "empire" in Harrington 1901 (1656), 183, 189–90, 193, 223.

illegitimate according to these criteria. In the *Discourses* Machiavelli argues that the Pistoese came voluntarily under Florentine *imperio* and are less hostile to Florence than many other towns in its dominions, not because they "do not value their liberty just like the others and do not judge themselves equal to the others," but because the Florentines treated them as brothers, not enemies. In other words, the Pistoese freely participated in *imperio* so long as they were not subjected to *dominio*. This "has made the Pistoese run willingly under their rule [*imperio*], while the others have exerted and exert all their force so as not to come under it. And without doubt," Machiavelli continues, "if the Florentines by way of either laws or of aids had tamed their neighbors and not made them savage, they would without doubt at this hour be lords of Tuscany."[105] The maxim that any kind of *imperio*—internal or external—is most stable if sought on the basis of mutually authorized orders and partnership is confirmed by the unhappy *dénouement* of the self-liberation of the Florentines and their subjects. Having freed themselves and restored republican orders within and the freedom of subject cities without, Machiavelli writes,

> the city would have settled down if the great had been content to live with that modesty which is required by civil life; but they acted in a contrary way, for as private individuals they did not want companions [*compagni*], and in the magistracies they wanted to be lords. . . . This displeased the people, and they lamented that from one tyrant who had been eliminated a thousand had been born.[106]

Like Livy's Romans and Thucydides' Athenians, the Florentines' own failures of self-restraint would lead to internal unfreedom and the loss of external independence. They might have benefited from reflecting more prudently on ancient histories, instead of rushing to imitate the most deceptively grandiose of ancient modes.

---

[105] *D*, II.21.213/383–84.
[106] *FH*, II.39.100/417–18.

CONCLUSIONS

Machiavelli's writings are not how-to manuals, whether for aspiring princes or for citizens who want to rebuild crumbling republican "orders." Nor do they simply reassemble conventional republican maxims in a rhetorical way, with the aim of reigniting Florentine passions for the lost republic. The underlying purpose of his historical and political works is philosophical in the specific, very ancient sense discussed in chapters 1 and 2. Machiavelli's texts seek to challenge, exercise, and improve readers' capacities to make discriminating moral and political judgments. They do this by examining a variety of "opinions" found in ancient and humanist literature, in the speeches or private ruminations of political leaders, and among ordinary citizens in the piazza. Some of the opinions canvassed involve naïve wishful thinking about human nature. Others eschew responsibility by counting on "extraordinary" or divine intervention to sort out human beings' self-inflicted political disasters. Still others lay claims to unflinching realism that collapse on closer scrutiny. Perhaps the main "realist" lesson of Machiavelli's writings is that it is unrealistic to think that power or victory can be secured by mendacious, violent, or wholly self-regarding means. Skillful spin-artists may "color" such means so that they appear for a time to show a decent respect for laws and justice. People whose judgment is untrained or corrupt may fall into their trap at first. But attractive appearances and passionate false beliefs cannot sustain policies that flout basic principles of good order. I argued in chapter 8 that for Machiavelli, the most basic principles of good order are also principles of justice. And a proper understanding of justice takes account of the claims and perceptions of all parties, considered as equally free agents whose power of authorization deserves respect, even if some are much weaker than others. This, I submit, is the sometimes covert, sometimes quite overt core "teaching" of all Machiavelli's political writings. It is a "realist" teaching, but not in the usual sense. It says in effect that the true foundation of any agents' own security, victories, greatness, and glory is respect for justice, since this is the foundation of stable order in all human relationships: public or private, within or between cities, and notwithstanding great differences in power.

Nothing could be further from Machiavelli's purposes than to teach readers how to generate appearances of *grandezza* or virtue for the sake of private ambition or, indeed, for the ostensible good of whole cities. His writings teach discerning readers how to spot potentially ruinous defects behind good appearances, not how to create them themselves. Both his methods and motives resemble those of Greek writers who, in the wake of the fratricidal Peloponnesian Wars, tried to serve their shattered country as civil "physicians." Their unblinkered diagnoses of that conflict's causes centered on the corruption of moral language and moral judgment in Athens. According to Thucydides' oft-repeated account, confusion about the proper meanings of words helped propel the city toward lawlessness, blind worship of irresponsible demagogues, and unjust attempts to dominate other cities.[1] That Machiavelli should choose to emulate Greek as well as Roman models is unsurprising. The closest ancient analogue to the factious, overassertive, tragically self-destructive Florence portrayed in Machiavelli's *Histories* is the corrupt Athenian democracy described by Thucydides, Xenophon, and Plato. Other Florentines liked to compare their expansionist republic with Rome, and drew on triumphalist versions of Roman history to applaud comparable deeds of the Florentine people. Machiavelli invites readers to look beyond impressive appearances in both Roman and Florentine history. While his *Histories* and *Discourses* draw on critical Roman histories, they also "imitate" themes, passages, and language patterns found in Livy's and other Roman historians' own more ancient source, Thucydides. The need for citizens to cultivate more discriminating judgment is a central theme too in Xenophon's *Cyropaedia* and Plato's dialogues. As chapter 2 suggested, Machiavelli invokes the former work to intimate that he, like Xenophon, may only appear to be commending Cyrus-like manipulative techniques as part of the *virtuoso* repertoire of the "ideal prince." The covert purpose of both authors is purgative and prophylactic. They "let drop" subtle hints or signs that warn readers not to take good appearances at face value; and implicitly exhort them to develop foxlike skills in recognizing the snares that often lurk behind decent-sounding words or seemingly prudent policies.

This reading of Machiavelli is not entirely new or *sui generis*. Many of Machiavelli's early philosophical readers recognized his close affinities with ancient Greek writers. Unlike some contemporary scholars, they did not differentiate sharply between historical, political, and philosophical writing. They recognized elements of all three genres in Thucydides', Xenophon's, and Plato's works, and therefore in Machiavelli's. Moreover, the Greek-inspired, dialectical features of his writings help to explain how Harrington and Neville could so confidently claim that Machiavelli defends the "rule of laws" against the "rule of men." An essential part of this defense was to arm citizens against the appeal of decent words used to color less decent deeds, especially those of men who demanded extraordinary powers to act outside the ordinary constraints of public laws. In his dialogue "Plato Redivivus" Neville has a speaker declare that Machiavelli, more than any other recent author, understood that in times of civil crisis well-meaning citizens "lay hold oftentimes upon unsuitable remedies, and impute their malady to wrong and ridiculous causes." If they could learn to better judge causes and remedies, they would be less easily swayed by the rhetoric of imprudent or overambitious politicians.[2] This Greek, philosophical reading of Machiavelli also makes sense of Rousseau's otherwise baffling claim that the *Prince* "is the book of republicans," which had, in his view, "so far" been explicated only by "corrupt or superficial" readers. Like Gentili and Spinoza before him, Rousseau—a gifted, hypersensitive reader

---

[1] See TPW, III.82–84 and chap. 2, secs 2.2. and 2.5.
[2] Neville 1681, III.9, II.2.

and writer if ever there was one in the past three centuries—states that Machiavelli sought to teach "great lessons to peoples" while "pretending to teach lessons to kings."[3] Rousseau's own intimate familiarity with ancient examples of philosophical dissimulation surely helped him to recognize, and perceptively interpret, Machiavelli's texts. In short, early readers who were well versed in the same canon of ancient writers had no doubt that Machiavelli did not purport to teach extraordinary men how to become princes, or princes how better to manipulate their subjects, or republics how to deceive and dominate their neighbors. Nor did he present maxims of a ruthless realpolitik as the necessary foundation of security for "any city whatever," whether republic or principality. He sometimes seems to offer these lessons because he dissimulates, using the ancient techniques of double-writing discussed throughout this book.

The Machiavelli who emerges from this reading is a highly ethical thinker. Behind first appearances of amoral instrumentalism or even cynicism, he sets out strong reasons for people to adopt simple yet rigorous ethical standards that apply in external relations as well as in civil life. I have argued that Bacon, Neville, and Rousseau were right to suggest that Machiavelli's most shocking passages should be read ironically and dialectically. By appearing to advance views that are not the author's own, they provoke readers to examine common maxims or opinions that have an "aura" of greatness, prudence, or realism, yet tend to cause grave disorders when put into practice. One advantage of this reading is that it does not deny or play down the presence of either amoral or moral passages in Machiavelli's texts. There are undeniable tensions between disturbingly harsh and surprisingly moderate words, examples, and counsels in all his writings. No reading is likely to be persuasive that focuses on one of these inflections without trying to account for the other. It makes more sense to confront the tensions head-on, and consider how best to explain them. The most plausible explanation is, I suggest, that the amoral and moral elements are related dialectically in various ways discussed throughout this book. Moral standards and principles are the terminus of a reflective reading. But to get a fully reasoned account of their foundations, readers first have to take prima facie persuasive arguments for immorality very seriously indeed. For Machiavelli as for his ancients, the closest possible examination of immoral or poorly founded moral arguments is an indispensable part of ethical and political education. Francis Bacon explains the thinking behind this dialectical approach in characteristically graphic language. Machiavelli, he suggests, learned from Greek writers that anyone who hopes to avoid ruinous errors of moral judgment must "know exactly all the conditions of the serpent; his baseness, and going upon his belly, his volubility and lubricity, his envy and sting, and the rest." The word "serpent" here does not only signify outstandingly evil individuals, but "all forms and natures of evil." Some of these may appear harmless or even righteous to the people who embrace them. Indeed, people who perform evil actions are often sincerely convinced that they are doing good.[4]

[3] Rousseau 1964 (1762), III.6.409.
[4] Bacon 2001 (1605), 169.

This account is more probing and complete than interpretations that see "evil" teachings as the terminus of Machiavelli's *ragionare*, or those that play down his harsher statements in favor of a somewhat whitewashed, one-dimensional "conventional humanist" reading. A dialectical interpretation also has more intellectual coherence and historical plausibility than "value pluralist" readings, which try to explain the relation between his moral and amoral "teachings" by anachronistically projecting onto Machiavelli the ideas of nineteenth-century German historicism or postmodern relativism.[5] As for the easiest of all easy attempts to explain the coexistence of apparently incompatible elements in his writings, the claim that Machiavelli was an inconsistent or sloppy thinker and writer, readers must decide for themselves whether they feel qualified to make such a call.[6] This will depend on how hard they think they have tried to understand his texts, and on how much labor of interpretation they think any text deserves. Readers who insist that all reading must yield an unambiguous message without their active participation will be the first to shout "contradiction" at writers like Machiavelli, or for that matter at Plato, Spinoza, and Rousseau. As I argued in the first two chapters, apparent inconsistencies are a hallmark of ancient writings that sought to teach readers to look beyond initial appearances. The main techniques of reading this kind of writing were expounded clearly by Plutarch, and practiced by Machiavelli's favorite ancients.[7] If my proposal that Machiavelli used similar techniques does not convince everyone, I hope at least to have offered a more precise and historically plausible explanation of apparent contradictions in his texts.

The sense in which Machiavelli's ethics can be called "philosophical" is less familiar today than it was in his own times, or to early readers who had an intimate knowledge of ancient literature. Many of these readers recognized in Machiavelli's works all the defining elements of a particular, very ancient tradition of philosophical writing. They were undeterred by facts often cited today against a philosophical reading: that Machiavelli did not call himself a philosopher, for instance, or write in the formal manner of scholastic philosophers, or declare allegiance to a particular "school" (what he might have called a "sect") of philosophy. None of these considerations stopped Alberico Gentili from declaring in 1594 that among recent political writers, Machiavelli above all "assumes the role of philosopher" and excels in "that branch of philosophy which deals with morals and politics."[8] In the seventeenth and eighteenth centuries, many philosophers embraced Machiavelli as one of their own, apparently unconcerned that he did not describe himself as a *filosofo* or try to acquire philosophical credentials through scholastic circles. This reception seems less surprising when we recall that readers such as Gentili, Neville, and Rousseau were well aware of a non-scholastic tradition of philosophy to which Machiavelli signals his own affinities—often through subtle clues, such as his use of the hunting metaphor. This tradition was especially associated with the

[5] For example, Berlin 1981 (1958).
[6] For example, Anglo 1969.
[7] See chap. 2, sec. 2.1.
[8] Gentili 1924 (1594), III.ix.

name of Socrates, who, according to his students Xenophon and Plato, regarded philosophy as a non-specialist activity in which all responsible citizens should engage to some extent. The aim of true philosophers was not erudition for its own sake. It was to "hunt" for perennial but easily forgotten moral truths that should, once recovered, be brought back into cities to fortify virtue and remedy disorders. The appropriate method for this kind of philosophical hunting was the dialectical examination of common opinions, first appearances, or dogmas imbibed on the unexamined authority of others. Neither ancient Socratic writers nor Machiavelli's early readers acknowledged a sharp distinction between philosophy in this sense and historical writing that had similar aims. Read attentively, Xenophon's historical pieces are also moral and philosophical, while Plato's Socratic and non-Socratic dialogues frequently use quasi-mythical history as part of the search for stable moral standards.[9] Comparable combinations can be found in Bacon's histories and Rousseau's Platonic use of "conjectural" history in many of his writings.

As I suggested in chapter 1, Machiavelli's sympathies with a broadly Socratic tradition would also help to explain why he did not call himself a philosopher as well as a historian, dramatist, and political animal. Both Socrates and later participants in this tradition disavowed the name of philosopher as a conceit when applied to oneself. Although the word properly means "lover of wisdom," this meaning had often been corrupted by self-proclaimed "philosophers" who used the word to advertise their own ostensible wisdom. Instead of describing a desire and an activity whose end, wisdom, must always elude even the most conscientious hunters, an ambitious minority appropriated the name of philosophy as a term of self-elevation. This in turn induced the majority who did not consider themselves "wise" to scorn so-called philosophers as preening pretenders to superior wisdom, or useless drones who cut themselves off from the hard work of practical life.[10] Like Plato, Xenophon, and Socrates himself, Machiavelli disassociated himself from "philosophy" in these corrupt senses, including those that placed such a high premium on "contemplating" transcendent goods that practitioners lost interest in serving their earthbound, unphilosophic cities and fellow citizens. His philosophy is practical, in the same sense as Socrates' and Plato's. It engages in deeply reflective reasoning about the conditions for virtue and stable order in "any city whatever." And it encourages others—both ordinary citizens and extraordinary men of action—to reason in similar ways.

I expect to be charged by some readers with imposing a more systematic philosophical structure on Machiavelli's writings than they in fact contain. Indeed, one purpose of this book has been to stimulate more focused debate on this question than currently exists. In the existing literature one often encounters bald assertions that Machiavelli was not a philosopher. Almost as frequently, scholars use the phrase "Machiavelli's philosophy" without explaining what they mean.[11] If readers think I have overplayed my hand in this regard, I hope that my attempt to make a

---

[9] See chap. 3, sec. 3.1.

[10] See Plato, *Rep.* VI 492a–500c.

[11] See chap. 1, introduction.

case for a specific kind of philosophical reading will move others to give a fuller, more carefully reasoned account of their own philosophical or non-philosophical readings. I also hope that in considering this issue, readers will take seriously the comments by Machiavelli's early readers that helped to inspire the present enquiry. Gentili, Bacon, and Neville were better acquainted with Machiavelli's sources and references than most of his more recent readers. Though they did not leave detailed interpretations of Machiavelli's texts, their remarks and "imitations" of different aspects of his writing should stimulate further research in the history of philosophy. Much more work is needed on Machiavelli's relationship to Greek literature and ethics; this book only begins to scratch the surface of this important and fascinating question. I have tried to show why it cannot be avoided by recycling the usual dogmatic assertions, such as "Machiavelli did not read Greek"—which we do not know—or "Machiavelli preferred Roman political models," which does not mean he does not also look to Greek models in ethics, or draw from Greek writings negative lessons about the dangers of "unshackled" popular government and unlimited "expansion." Since Machiavelli does not openly cite or discuss Plato, and since this book is already long enough, I have reined in the temptation to investigate apparent affinities with his philosophy. I have, however, identified many Platonic passages that express ideas similar to those I find in Machiavelli's texts, often in similar language. At this stage I am unprepared to advance stronger claims about the relationship between Plato's ethics and Machiavelli's. But I see no good reason in Machiavelli's texts, or in the very sparse information we have about his education, favorite reading, or views on philosophers, to exclude the possibility that Machiavelli was as careful and appreciative a reader of Plato as he was of Xenophon, Thucydides, or Plutarch.

While this book has concentrated on tracking down Machiavelli's philosophical antecedents, it also paves the way for a thorough reappraisal of his relationship to later philosophers. The main legatees of the "Machiavellian" ethics identified here are Spinoza, Rousseau, and—through Rousseau's influence—Kant,[12] not later German idealists or Nietzsche or postmodern skeptics. When read as a philosophical defender of the rule of law whose *Prince* is covertly "the book of republicans," Machiavelli's main ethical positions appear far closer to Rousseau's than is usually recognized.[13] A less obvious but no less intriguing candidate for comparison is

---

[12] Some scholars have noted affinities between Machiavelli, Rousseau, and Kant in one respect: namely, their view that human beings cannot take their most basic moral bearings from tradition, God, or historical experience, but must apply their own powers of reasoning to construct human laws and orders. See Münkler 1995, 327; Schneewind 1998; and Hoeges 2000, 25. Such remarks are made only in passing, however; I know of no extended, systematic treatments of the relationship between these authors in any language. The very important impact of Rousseau's writings on Kant's ethics is of course well known; see Cassirer 1970 and 1981 (1918); Levine 1976; Velkley 1989.

[13] The present author too used to accept the standard view of Machiavelli as a political "realist" in the usual sense, and contrasted him with Rousseau as a fierce critic of modern Realpolitik; see Benner 2001. Having read both authors' works more carefully, I now regard their principled positions as similar, in external and civil relations. Both authors often use hardheaded prudential arguments to make a persuasive case for policies that rest, ultimately, on more basic moral principles. As with Machiavelli, the proposition that Rousseau imitated ancient dialectical modes of writing better explains the mix of

Thomas Hobbes. Though he does not explicitly acknowledge Machiavelli in any of his writings, a comparative investigation of the two authors' uses of ancient—and especially Greek—sources might shed valuable new light on both. As a young man Hobbes worked closely with Francis Bacon, one of Machiavelli's most open admirers and occasional imitators. Hobbes wrote several short "Discourses" in this period, including two that seem to imitate Machiavelli in parts, and arguably employ similar techniques of dissimulation.[14] Another of Hobbes' early works was a translation of Thucydides, and he acknowledged his admiration for Plato more openly than did Machiavelli.[15] Yet systematic studies of how he used these Greek sources are scarce. If I am right that Machiavelli often imitated ancient Greek methods of enigmatic and dialectical writing, and so cannot always be taken at face value, might this also be true at times of Hobbes? If so, it may be that some of the more extreme positions he asserts should be reinterpreted in the light of similarly structured, Greek-inspired arguments.

This interpretation and others

It may be helpful if I highlight this book's main points of agreement and disagreement with what can, I think, be loosely characterized as the two dominant "schools" of contemporary Machiavelli scholarship. One school acknowledges the preeminent influence of Leo Strauss' readings of Machiavelli and his studies in the broader history of ideas. Methodologically, these scholars stress the importance of textual interpretation over historical contexts. Substantively, their conclusions tend to see some form of realpolitik as having ultimate primacy for Machiavelli over independent ethical considerations, including those dictated by republican principles. On the methodological question of how to read Machiavelli's texts, my approach agrees that they can never simply be taken at face value, whether one

---

"realist" and "idealistic" elements in his thought than claims that he was sloppy, unstable, or tragically torn. In any case, Rousseau's frequent references to Machiavelli in the *Social Contract* invite a closer comparative study of their ideas.

[14] See Hobbes 1995 (1620). The editors offer extended comparisons with Machiavelli (Hobbes 1995 [1620], 124–48). But because they read him in a standard "realist" way, they overlook both his and Hobbes' subtle ironies and Tacitus-like dissimulation—bearing in mind that Tacitus acknowledged Greek inspiration for his methods of writing.

[15] Hobbes declares in the *Leviathan* (1996 [1652], 183) that in discussing "Civil Lawes" his "design" is "not to shew what is Law here, and there; but what is Law; as Plato, Aristotle, Cicero, and divers others have done, without taking upon them the profession of the study of the Law." He concludes his second book "Of Commonwealth" by hinting that he and Plato have similar dialectical purposes. Both writers' attempts to set out general principles of good government may, Hobbes admits, prove "useless," for Plato "is *also* of opinion that it is impossible for the disorders of State, and change of Governments by Civill Warre, ever to be taken away, till Soveraigns be Philosophers" (254; emphasis added). When Hobbes returns to the perennially thorny question of the proper relations between politics and philosophy near the end of Book III, he refers—in passing, or so it seems—to "Plato that was the best Philosopher of the Greeks" (461). Of course, these scattered remarks may not indicate more extensive affinities between the two authors' ethics and philosophical premises. But the question of whether they might deserves serious attention.

focuses on the most shocking passages of the *Prince* or on the moderate-sounding parts of the *Discourses* and *Histories*. I further agree that the first task of Machiavelli scholarship is to try to understand his writings as highly individual products. This is a demanding task, and one that is bound to involve deep disagreement among individual interpreters. Nevertheless, studies of the wider cultural, political, and historical contexts cannot substitute for careful reading of texts that are as puzzling as Machiavelli's.

Despite these important agreements, I sympathize with a concern sometimes expressed about readings that treat Machiavelli as an "esoteric" writer whose true meaning is never quite what it appears to be. Unless scholars offer a fairly detailed, transparent account of their own interpretative methods, their exegesis of a controversial text may appear purely personal or arbitrary, or almost as esoteric as the texts it expounds. However stimulating such readings are, some readers may doubt that they illuminate Machiavelli's own purported meaning. To alleviate reasonable doubts, interpreters do well to identify some clear points of reference that lend their readings an independent anchorage. The anchor may be a "context," or other writings invoked in Machiavelli's texts that provide clues for interpreting their message. I have tried to do this by proposing that ancient Greek examples of dissimulation are an especially important key. As I acknowledged in the introduction, this "solution" is not unproblematic. But it does have the considerable merits of historical plausibility, non-arbitrariness, and transparency. Any reader can consult the ancient sources discussed here, compare key passages or choices of words to Machiavelli's, and decide for him- or herself whether there are similarities that aid interpretation.

I have much deeper disagreements with some of Strauss' more substantive conclusions. Most obviously, this study questions the claim that Machiavelli "broke with" all major traditions of ancient ethics, as well as with Christian moral doctrines. Strauss locates the basis of Machiavelli's radical challenge to other ethical traditions in a fundamental break with the "Socratic tradition." Unlike most "civic humanist" studies and many of his own students, Strauss does recognize Machiavelli's profound and complex engagement with the Socratic tradition. He discusses—albeit briefly—Machiavelli's allusions to Platonic philosophical themes and similarities to Plato, as well as to Xenophon.[16] These insights notwithstanding, my own reading of Machiavelli's major works alongside "his" ancients suggests that Gentili, Bacon, and Neville were right on this issue, while Strauss missed the mark. In the process of missing it, he touched on many points of comparison between Machiavelli and Greek authors that should inspire further exploration. Indeed, some self-declared students of Strauss have already explored them, and noticed far stronger substantive affinities between Machiavelli and the Socratic tradition than Strauss himself admitted.[17] Such studies tend to confirm my argument that the "radical break" thesis is far from proven, at least as far as Socratic ethics is concerned. This book has tried to make the case for the contrary thesis:

---

[16] Strauss 1958, esp. 291–96.
[17] See de Alvarez 1999; Kleiman, n.d.

that Machiavelli sought to revive, not cut loose from, a broadly Socratic ethical tradition whose teachings he saw as congruent with those of Thucydides and his Roman emulators Sallust, Tacitus, and Livy. If he "broke" with anything, it was, on the one hand, with the ethical doctrines of an authoritarian, hypocritical, obscurantist church; and on the other, with the corrupt ethical standards drawn by some humanists from self-serving, triumphalist accounts of ancient—and especially Roman—models. On this reading, Machiavelli should be seen not as a "late" humanist who rejected the most fundamental, classical values of his predecessors. He is better characterized as a critical humanist who thought that many recent devotees of "antiquities" had lost sight of the most valuable teachings found in ancient writings.[18]

At the core of those teachings is a conception of human nature as an incorrigibly unstable mix of animal drives and capacities for self-discipline; of natural selfishness on the one hand, and on the other capacities to recognize reasons to limit one's own appetites out of regard for others. Plato's Socrates often speaks of the human soul's striving for a higher good, while Machiavelli does not. This might seem to affirm an anti-Socratic reading of Machiavelli who, according to Strauss, reacted against the unrealistically high standards set by Socratic and Christian ethics by lowering standards of conduct to a more bestial level. My reading denies that the highest standards Socrates sets for human beings are as lofty, or Machiavelli's as debased, as this opposition implies. While they proceed from different directions, both end up defending similar standards. Plato's (and Xenophon's) Socrates starts with people mired in the earthbound muck of prereflective, self-serving, or order-destroying "opinions" about justice or philosophy or statesmanship. As the dialogues proceed he asks them to set their sights higher, and to search for better standards in their own concepts and self-understandings. But they must learn not to ask, "What standards are suitable for godlike men, who might save me from troubles I can do nothing about?" They should ask instead, "What are the highest standards suitable for ordinary, corruptible, yet reasoning people like myself, who have no choice but to solve our own problems with our own imperfect resources?" Machiavelli addresses people who long for an "extraordinary" savior, whether human prince or holy man. He asks them to lower their sights in a very specific sense: to seek solutions to their troubles that lie within their own, "ordinary and natural" powers. People should lower any expectations that they might be saved by divine intervention, or by an extraordinary man who can eliminate their disorders "at a stroke." At the same time, they should realize that their only realistic hope of salvation lies in clarifying and defending high—though not unreasonably high—standards of conduct.

For both Socrates and Machiavelli, the proper aim of dialectical enquiry is to identify standards appropriate to the human animal. The first duty of human beings is thus to "know themselves" warts and all. Having acknowledged and understood their own radical limitations, they should then to strive nonetheless to

---

[18] Such as Leonardo Bruni and others who exalted the Medici "princes" in the name of defending the republic; see chap. 1.

live according to the highest possible standards of justice and respect. On philosophical reflection, the highest possible standards may turn out to be less elevated
than many people suppose. However high they go, human strivings toward the
divine are still only human. In order to serve higher civil or divine purposes, then,
humans must know their own limits, rein in superhuman ambitions as well as bestial drives, and accept that neither they nor the cities they serve will ever transcend
all the evils that stem from both. The best they can do is to contain evils by defending suitably "harsh" standards of conduct, even when corrupt conventions and
authorities threaten to debase them. Mature reflection suggests that human works
come as close to the divine as they possibly can when their makers understand
that all human works have a mixed, corruptible, fragile character remote from the
godlike nature of mythical heroes or "ideal cities."

This is the truth that begins to dawn on Socrates' young friends through the
dialectic of the *Republic*, where they start by constructing a counternatural—if not
almost superhuman—"ideal city," only to doubt later whether these foundations
are altogether suited to their city's merely human denizens. Instead of forming
cities on principles that run against the grain of human nature, a philosophical
politics should respect its variegated, flawed human material. As Socrates puts it,
city-builders should "mix and blend the various ways of life in the city" to produce "a human image [*to andreikelon*] based on what Homer too called 'the divine
form and image' [*theoeides . . . kai theoeikelon*] when it occurred among human
beings."[19] It is this Socrates who asks his interlocutors to place high ethical demands on themselves, but an appropriately human kind of demand, whom I see as
Machiavelli's philosophical ancestor. Machiavelli's recognition of the radical evil
in human nature and human "works" does not lead him to recommend evil policies as the only means to self-preservation. His response to this "realistic" insight
is the same as that of Thucydides, Xenophon, and Plato's Socrates: to insist on the
necessity to work all the harder at defining rigorous standards proper for human
animals, and to defend them even in conditions of personal danger.[20]

The other main school locates Machiavelli in the context of a broader tradition of "civic humanism." Methodologically, proponents give priority to the wider
intellectual and political contexts that they see as having influenced Machiavelli,

[19] Plato, *Rep.* 501b.

[20] Some readers might wonder how such sensitive interpreters as Strauss or Cassirer could have
failed to see all this. My best answer is that they interpreted Machiavelli—as none of us can help doing to some extent—in the light of their own very hard "times." As political philosophers who lived
through the first half of the twentieth century, they sought to understand how people raised in strict
moral traditions could embrace cool-headed justifications for "ends justify means" realpolitik and, in
the worst of times, commit cold-blooded acts of human evil. The thesis of a radically "realist" break
with all older moralities is thus a vivid testimony to the experiences of those who posit it. It tries to
identify determinate modern origins for what later generations experienced as a violent break with
older moral restraints. Both Strauss' and Cassirer's readings reflect an urge to find in Machiavelli a
rational, well-meaning spokesman for anti-moral attitudes that had run to irrational extremes in their
own times. Read at one level, I agree that Machiavelli's writings do help to *explain* how rational and
otherwise decent people could agree to throw off traditional restraints. But this does not mean that he
advises them to do so.

and in particular to the writings of Florentine and Italian near-contemporaries who are regarded as his chief interlocutors. Substantively, they argue that Machiavelli's main ethical commitments were consistent with long-standing humanist conventions, and of no great philosophical interest. They see his political views as broadly republican, though scholars disagree about what form of republic he favored. My reading disagrees with the methodological priorities of this "school." Studies that give primacy to contexts over texts run a serious risk of underrating the depth, subtlety, and independence of Machiavelli's thought. His writings palpably demand hard interpretative work. They pose puzzles that cannot be evaded without missing the point, and set up tensions that cannot easily be written off as unintended contradictions or changes of mind. Moreover, when scholars begin with a contextual template identified in advance of a close reading of texts, they may overlook *other* contexts or sources that provide equally important clues to the latter's meaning. I have argued, for example, that civic humanist scholarship has tended to exaggerate affinities between Machiavelli's main positions and those of other humanists such as Bruni. At the same time, and with a few exceptions, it has neglected close comparisons with the ancient authors whom Machiavelli himself treats as his main interlocutors. His Greek sources have suffered the worst neglect, but even his Roman sources—Livy in particular—get rather short shrift in most civic humanist studies.

Substantively, my reading agrees that Machiavelli did not break sharply from older humanist commitments. He too sought to reinvigorate certain ancient moral and political ideas, including classical republican ideals of political liberty, the rule of law, and skepticism about the virtues of monarchy or *principati*. Whereas civic humanist scholarship focuses overwhelmingly on Machiavelli's political theory, however, the present study has argued that his political ideas cannot be fully understood without a closer study of his philosophical ethics. Once this deeper layer of his thought has been exhumed and reconstructed, it also becomes apparent that Machiavelli was a far less "conventional" humanist than some scholars have proposed. He evokes similar themes and sources in a critical way, often challenging what he saw as irresponsible uses of ancient maxims, historical examples, and philosophical teachings by other humanists.

This interpretation yields a much richer and more precise account of Machiavelli's conceptions of freedom, republic, and the rule of law than contextualist accounts. The most distinctive feature of these conceptions is, I have argued, the priority of respect for free agency over political freedom, and indeed over any particular notion of the public good. For Machiavelli, the primary object of "ordinary and reasonable" desires for freedom is not a particular "free way of life," but something more fundamental: namely, the desire to be recognized as having a free will, and therefore as possessing the capacity to authorize or reject constraints imposed by other agents. Although he identifies specific free political orders as the optimal condition for innately free persons, it is their capacity for free agency that makes this condition valuable and grounds reasonable demands for respect. Recognition of a human power of giving or withholding authority is among the most basic conditions for Machiavelli's political *libertà*. If agents try to impose free political orders without the "willing" authorization of those who live under those orders, the quality of freedom in those orders will be undermined from the outset, and fail to deserve the good name of *libertà*.

When the priority of free agency over political freedom in Machiavelli's arguments is recognized, several views commonly ascribed to him in the civic humanist scholarship are called into question. Perhaps the most common view is that his conception of freedom is essentially political, not individual or moral. On this account, collective freedom takes priority for Machiavelli over individual freedoms, while the independence of polities vis-à-vis others takes priority over the internal freedoms guaranteed by republican orders. I argue that the fundamental role of free agency in Machiavelli's thought sets his conception of *libertà* apart from humanist and later republican thinkers who defend these positions. The principles I have ascribed to him—respect for individuals' innate freedom, transparent public reasoning, and obligatory self-restraint under laws—are incompatible with many variants of republican doctrine. His individualism stands at odds with strongly collectivist republican ideals. His commitment to transparent reasoning cannot easily be married to a republicanism that concedes a large role to "passions," useful deceptions, or the authority of a few presumably enlightened leaders. His strict rule-of-law commitments, finally, are irreconcilable with what he and "his" ancients saw as a suicidal policy adopted by many unstable republics: to allow the rule of "extraordinary men" to take precedence over the rule of laws in times of perceived danger.[21] Interpretations that simply assimilate his arguments about freedom to these positions fail to do justice to the philosophical rigor of his ethical standards. They also underestimate the originality of his contribution to republican thought and, more generally, to modern thinking about autonomy and the rule of law. This philosophical reading brings Machiavelli much closer to critical Enlightenment thinkers such as Rousseau and Kant than to republican traditions based on the revival of neo-Roman virtues, patriotic common good, or passionate rhetoric.

Perhaps the most controversial part of my interpretation is the argument, developed in chapter 9, that Machiavelli's ethics are at bottom deontological. Machiavelli is widely supposed to be the anti-deontological thinker *par excellence*, who boldly proclaimed that certain ends justify whatever means are needed to attain them. While disagreeing on many other issues, most scholars from the different schools concur on this point: Machiavelli, they insist, urged readers to relax or set aside principled restraints on action in the face of one higher "necessity" or another. According to "realist" readings, the self-preservation of princes or polities is Machiavelli's ultimate justifying end; according to humanist republican readings, it is the "public good" or freedom from foreign control. Scholars in both traditions argue that he drives a deep wedge between moral principles that hold irrespective of consequences, and a political sphere governed by hardheaded consequentialist reasoning.

Some readers will resist my conclusions because they are unusual, whether they examine the arguments carefully or not. But I hope that the textual evidence

---

[21] Recall Harrington's claim that Machiavelli upholds the strict "rule of laws" against the "rule of men"; see introduction.

presented here, not least the ample evidence from the *Florentine Histories*, will persuade others to give the case for a deontological reading a serious hearing. The case has two main components. One is a close rereading in their textual context of statements that *seem* to say "the ends justify the means." The other is a comparison of how such statements function in Machiavelli's and in ancient texts where similar provocative maxims occur. My deontological interpretation is most likely to persuade readers who recognize similarly structured arguments in ancient writings. Like Thucydides, Machiavelli puts forward such maxims—usually in the name of individuals whose judgment is somewhat suspect, or in the context of a dialectical discussion—in order to provoke more prudent reflections. The bedrock of his reasonings are obligations of justice that should hold irrespective of anticipated or actual results. These obligations form the "grounding" level of Machiavelli's ethical arguments, although they are far less conspicuous than the secondary and supportive, consequentialist level. Over and over, his reflections point to the ultimate convergence of self-interested prudence and principled restraints. Again like Thucydides, he starts from prudential reasoning about self-preservation, but ends up demonstrating that truly reflective prudence must entail respect for reasoned principles of justice and respect for others' freedom. It is undeniably easier to establish "extraordinary" modes of rule through methods that disregard such constraints. But such modes insult the human dignity of people forced to live under them, because they do not ask for their free authorization. This invariably makes them unstable, short-lived, and dangerous for whoever tries to impose them.

Machiavelli and the ethical foundations of political philosophy

Let me conclude by pointing out two features of the ethics I have imputed to Machiavelli that should, in my view, be of special interest to contemporary political philosophers. Both relate to the question of whether political theory needs principled or philosophical foundations, and if so, what they should look like.

First, the basic ethical principles identified by Machiavelli do not depend on controversial religious or teleological premises. A belief in God or specific divine purposes may help to motivate actions that conform to the principles, but is not needed to ground them. He implicitly but clearly rejects the idea that there are knowable ends of history or nature or reason that can serve as a touchstone for evaluating human actions. It is sometimes assumed that in dispensing with such premises, Machiavelli must have also rejected *any* objective grounds for ethical standards. His declaration of independence from older natural law doctrines and Christian metaphysics is supposed to have led him toward a radical new moral anarchism or skepticism. I have argued, however, that Machiavelli does not divorce ethical reasoning from all objective or metaphysical foundations. On the contrary, his principles retain clear, objective moorings that are only partly empirical. The empirical part is his account of the "ordinary and natural" appetites and drives found in human beings everywhere. The non-empirical part consists, first of all, in an undemonstrable yet necessary presupposition that all human beings are innately free; and given this presupposition, the search for adequate meanings of the concepts used in "any city whatever" to establish moral and civil order among beings considered as free. Although standards of adequacy are objective and invariable over time, they are eminently corruptible. This means that they must always be hunted down through dialectical discussion, and hunted again when obscured or forgotten. The meanings of virtue, justice, or freedom more often than not *appear* to depend on particular times, practices, or interests. But the empirical (N1) and moral (N2) parts of Machiavelli's anthropology furnish stable touchstones for evaluating the adequacy of different meanings. This approach to grounding basic principles has a distinct appeal. It avoids highly speculative metaphysical and teleological premises, yet retains a modest metaphysics in the argument that innate freedom must be presupposed of any beings who are recognizably human. It avoids relativism and skepticism about values, or about the proper meanings of words. At the same time, it acknowledges that relativism and skepticism are prima facie reasonable responses to the inescapable facts of moral confusion and corruption.

Second, Machiavelli's arguments about the primacy of free agency over political freedom bear directly on one of the most important problems of political judgment in our times. What is the proper meaning of the word "freedom," and what do people want when they demand respect as free persons? For Machiavelli, the language of freedom is corrupted when it is used to defend the pursuit of particular ends—including a "free way of life"—in ways that fail to respect others' freedom to authorize their own "orders." His writings confront a perennial human tendency examined much earlier by Thucydides: a tendency to view other people's freedom as a brute, somewhat regrettable fact that has no intrinsic ethical import. In Machiavelli's times and often in ours, the language of freedom is so routinely associated with unlimited self-assertion that it is not always easy to understand how civil *libertà* could possibly depend on universal restraints. Individuals, parties, and polities demand respect for their own "freedom" in this self-assertive sense, but see others' free agency as an irritating or threatening barrier to their own.

On Machiavelli's principles, by contrast, the innate freedom of other persons should be regarded as a basic *moral* fact or, in his language, an ordinary and reasonable "necessity." It is true that he usually advances these arguments in a prudential or instrumental form. Nevertheless, they presuppose a more basic judgment about the ethical necessity or *obligo* to respect free agency, since the ordinary and reasonable desire to be treated as free agents explains *why* people fight so obstinately against those who flout this desire. If prudent reflection shows the instrumental necessity to respect people as free agents, it also points toward an ethical necessity to do so. Prudent agents, Machiavelli suggests, should presuppose this freedom of others in all times and places, and regardless of their differences in power or status. Respect for other people's freedom should lead even the mightiest agents to limit their own actions: to rein in excessive ambitions (*philotimia*), desires for more than one's share of power or other goods (*pleonexia*), and ultimately self-defeating urges to overstep one's proper bounds (*hubris*). Machiavelli showed that these simple, very ancient principles remained unsurpassed as "medicine" for the political disorders in his times. He sought to recover an ancient ethics of self-restraint and self-responsibility, based on respect (*respetto, aidō*) for other free agents and the self-imposed laws that protect common freedoms. Both experience and reason suggest that we still need this ancient remedy as much as Athenians, Romans, and Florentines ever did.

BIBLIOGRAPHY

Primary Sources

Machiavelli

CITATIONS IN ORIGINAL
Opere. Vols. 1–3. Turin: Einaudi-Gallimard, 1997–2005.

MAIN CITATIONS IN ENGLISH
The Art of War. Trans. and ed. Christopher Lynch. Chicago: University of Chicago Press, 2003.
"A Discourse on Remodeling the Government of Florence." In *Machiavelli: The Chief Works and Others*, trans. and ed. Allan Gilbert, vol. 1, pp. 101–15. Durham, N.C.: Duke University Press, 1989.
Discourses on Livy. Trans. Harvey C. Mansfield and Nathan Tarcov. Chicago: University of Chicago Press, 1996.
Florentine Histories. Trans. Laura F. Banfield and Harvey C. Mansfield. Princeton: Princeton University Press, 1988.
The Life of Castruccio Castracani of Lucca. In *Machiavelli: The Chief Works and Others*, trans. and ed. Allan Gilbert, vol. 2, pp. 533–60. Durham, N.C.: Duke University Press, 1989.
Machiavelli and His Friends: Their Personal Correspondence. Trans. and ed. James B. Atkinson and David Sices. DeKalb: University of Northern Illinois Press, 1996.
"On the Method of Dealing with the Rebellious Peoples of the Valdechiana." In *Machiavelli: The Chief Works and Others*, trans. and ed. Allan Gilbert, vol. 1, pp. 161–62. Durham, N.C.: Duke University Press, 1989.
The Prince. Trans. Harvey C. Mansfield. 2nd ed. Chicago: University of Chicago Press, 1998.
"Tercets." In *Machiavelli: The Chief Works and Others*, trans. and ed. Allan Gilbert, vol. 2, pp. 735–49. Durham, N.C.: Duke University Press, 1989.

OTHER TRANSLATIONS CITED OR CONSULTED
Discorsi: Gedanken über Politik und Staatsführung. Trans. and ed. Rudolf Zorn. Stuttgart: Alfred Kröner Verlag, 1977.
The Discourses. Ed. Bernard Crick, trans. L. J. Walker. London: Penguin, 1998.
Discourses on Livy. Trans. Julia Conaway Bonadella and Peter Bonadella. Oxford: Oxford University Press, 1997.
Der Fürst. Trans. Friedrich von Oppeln-Bronikowski. Frankfurt am Main: Insel Verlag, 1990.
Machiavel Oeuvres. Trans. and ed. Christian Bec. Paris: Éditions Robert Laffont, 1996.
The Prince. Trans. George Bull. Harmondsworth: Penguin, 1961.
The Prince and Other Political Writings. Trans. and ed. Stephen J. Milner. London: J. M. Dent, 1995.
Il principe. Trans. Piero Melograni. Milan: R.C.S. Libri & Grandi Opere, 1994.

Other Primary Sources

Aristotle. 1894. *Ethica Nicomachaea*. Oxford: Oxford University Press.

———. 1990. *Politics*. Trans. H. Rackham. Cambridge: Loeb Classical Library, Harvard University Press.

———. 1991. *On Rhetoric*. Trans. George A. Kennedy. New York: Oxford University Press.

Bacon, Francis. 1985 [1597–1625]. *The Essays*. Ed. John Pitcher. Harmondsworth: Penguin.

———. 2001 [1605]. *The Advancement of Learning*. New York: Random House.

Bruni, Leonardo. 1987. "Isagogicon moralis philosophiae." In *The Humanism of Leonardo Bruni: Selected Texts*, ed. G. Griffiths, J. Hankins, and D. Thompson, pp. 267–82. Binghamton, N.Y.: Center for Medieval and Renaissance Studies.

———. 2001–7 [1419–42]. *History of the Florentine People*. Vols. 1–3. Ed. and trans. James Hankins. Cambridge: I Tatti Renaissance Library, Harvard University Press.

Cicero, Marcus Tullius. 2000. *On the Republic and On the Laws*. Trans. Clinton Walker Keyes. Cambridge: Loeb Classical Library, Harvard University Press.

———. 2001. *On the Ideal Orator*. Trans. James M. May and Jakob Wisse. New York: Oxford University Press.

———. 2005. *On Duties*. Trans. Walter Miller. Cambridge: Loeb Classical Library, Harvard University Press.

Fichte, Johann Gottlieb. 1971 [1807]. "Über Machiavelli." In *Fichtes Werke*, ed. Immanuel Hermann Fichte, vol. 11, pp. 400–453. Berlin: Walter de Gruyter.

Ficino, Marsilio. 2004. *Platonic Theology*. Vol. 4. Trans. Michael J. B. Allen, Latin text ed. James Hankins. Cambridge: I Tatti Renaissance Library, Harvard University Press.

Gentili, Alberico. 1924 [1594]. *De legationibus libri tres*. Vols. 1–2. Trans. Gordon Liang, ed. John Brown Scott. New York: Oxford University Press.

Guicciardini, Francesco. 1932. *Dialogo e discorsi del reggimento di firenze*. Ed. Roberto Palmarocchi. Bari: Giuseppe Laterza e Figli.

———. 1949. *Ricordi*. Trans. Ninian Hill Thomson. New York: S. F. Vanni.

———. 1969. *The History of Italy*. Trans. and ed. Sidney Alexander. Princeton: Princeton University Press.

———. 1994. *Dialogue on the Government of Florence*. Trans. and ed. Alison Brown. Cambridge: Cambridge University Press.

———. 2002. "Considerations of the *Discourses* of Niccolò Machiavelli." In *The Sweetness of Power: Machiavelli's "Discourses" and Guicciardini's "Considerations,"* trans. James B. Atkinson and David Sices. DeKalb: Northern Illinois University Press.

Harrington, James. 1901 [1656]. "Oceana." In *Ideal Commonwealths*, ed. Henry Morley. London: Colonial Press.

Hegel, G.W.F. 1999 [1800–1802]. "Die Verfassung Deutschlands." In *Werke: Frühe Schriften*, vol. 1, pp. 451–620. Frankfurt am Main: Suhrkamp.

Herder, Johann Gottfried. 1971 [1793–97]. *Briefe zu Beförderung der Humanität*. Vol. 1. Berlin: Aufbau Verlag.

Herodotus. 2001–4. *The Persian Wars*. Trans A. D. Godley. 4 vols. Cambridge: Loeb Classical Library, Harvard University Press.

Hippocrates. 2004. *Works*. Vol. 1. Trans. W.H.S. Jones. Cambridge: Loeb Classical Library, Harvard University Press.

Hobbes, Thomas. 1989 [1629]. "On the Life and History of Thucydides." In *The Peloponnesian War*, trans. Hobbes, ed. David Grene, pp. 569–86. Chicago: University of Chicago Press.

———. 1994 [1650]. *Human Nature and De Corpore Politico*. Ed. J.C.A. Gaskin. Oxford: Oxford University Press.

———. 1995 [1620]. *Three Discourses: A Critical Modern Edition of Newly Identified Work of the Young Hobbes*. Ed. Noel B. Reynolds and Arlene W. Saxonhouse. Chicago: University of Chicago Press.

———. 1996 [1652]. *Leviathan*. Ed. Richard Tuck. Cambridge: Cambridge University Press.

———. 1998 [1642]. *On the Citizen [De Cive]*. Ed. Richard Tuck and Michael Silverthorne. Cambridge: Cambridge University Press.

Iamblichus. 1996. *Iamblichi Protrepticus*. Ed. H. Pistelli. Stuttgart. B. G. Trubner.

Kant, Immanuel. 1996 [1783–84]. *Religion and Rational Theology*. Trans. and ed. Paul Guyer and Allen W. Wood. Cambridge: Cambridge University Press.

———. 1998. *Critique of Pure Reason*. Trans. and ed. Allen W. Wood and George di Giovanni. Cambridge: Cambridge University Press.

Livy, Titus. 2000–2002. *History of Rome [Ab Urbe Condita]*. Vols. 1–30. Cambridge: Loeb Classical Library, Harvard University Press.

Locke, John. 1988 [1698]. *Two Treaties of Government*. Ed. Peter Laslett. Cambridge: Cambridge University Press.

Macaulay, Thomas Babington. 1910. "Machiavelli." In *English Essays: Sidney to Macaulay*. Harvard Classics, vol. 27. New York: P. F. Collier.

Manetti, Gianozzo. 2003. "Life of Socrates." In *Biographical Writings*, ed. and trans. Stefano U. Baldassarri and Rolf Bagemihl. Cambridge: I Tatti Renaissance Library, Harvard University Press.

Mill, John Stuart. 1991 [1861]. "Of Representative Government." In *On Liberty and Other Essays*, ed. John Gray. Oxford: Oxford University Press.

Neville, Henry. 1681. *Plato Redivivus: or, a dialogue concerning government*. London: Printed for S. I. and Sold by R. Dew.

———. 1691. *Nicholas Machiavel's Letter to Zenobius Buondelmontius, in Vindication of his Writings*. London: s.n.

Plato. 1991. *Sämtliche Werke*. Vols. 1–10 (Greek and German). Based on trans. by Friedrich Schleiermacher. Frankfurt am Main: Insel Verlag.

———. 1997a. *Complete Works*. Ed. John M. Cooper. Indianapolis: Hackett.

———. 1997b. *Politico*. Trans. Paolo Accattino. Bari: Laterza & Figli.

———. 2005. *Le Leggi*. Trans. Franco Ferrari and Silvia Poli. Milan: Biblioteca universale Rizzoli.

Plutarch. 1998–2002. *Lives*. Vols. 1–11. Cambridge: Loeb Classical Library, Harvard University Press.

———. 2000–2005. *Moralia*. Vols. 1–13. Cambridge: Loeb Classical Library, Harvard University Press.

Polybius, 2001–3. *The Histories*. Trans. W. R. Paton. Vols. 1–3. Cambridge: Loeb Classical Library, Harvard University Press.

Rousseau, Jean-Jacques. 1964 [1750]. "Discours sur les sciences et les arts." In *Oeuvres complètes*, vol. 3, pp. 5–30. Paris: Gallimard.

———. 1964 [1762]. "Du contrat social." In *Oeuvres complètes*, vol. 3, pp. 348–470.

Sallust, Gaius Crispus. 2007. *Bellum Catiline*. Ed. and trans. J. T. Ramsay. Oxford: Oxford University Press.

Scala, Bartolomeo. 1997 [1483]. "De legibus et iudiciis dialogus." In *Humanistic and Political Writings*, ed. Alison Brown, pp. 338–64. Tempe, Ariz.: Medieval and Renaissance Texts and Studies.

———. 2008. *Essays and Dialogues*. Trans. Renée Neu Watkins, ed. Alison Brown. Cambridge: I Tatti Renaissance Library, Harvard University Press.

Spinoza, Benedict de. 1958 [1677]. "Tractatus Politicus." In *The Political Works*, ed. and trans. A. G. Wernham. Oxford: Clarendon Press.

Spinoza, Benedict de. 2007 [1669–70]. *Tractatus theologico-politicus*. Ed. Jonathan Israel, trans. Michael Silverstone and Jonathan Israel. Cambridge: Cambridge University Press.

Tacitus, Cornelius. 1979. *Works*. Vol. 1. Cambridge: Loeb Classical Library, Harvard University Press.

Thucydides. 1989. *The Peloponnesian War*. Trans. Thomas Hobbes. Chicago: University of Chicago Press.

———. 1991. *Historiae*. Ed. Henry Stuart Jones. Vols. 1–2. Oxford: Clarendon Press.

———. 1998. *The Peloponnesian War*. Trans. Walter Blanco, ed. Walter Blanco and Jennifer Tolbert Roberts. New York: W. W. Norton.

Xenophon. 2000. "Hiero" and "Lacedaemonians." In *Scripta Minora*, trans. E. C. Marchant, pp. 1–57, 136–89. Cambridge: Loeb Classical Library, Harvard University Press.

———. 2000–2001. *Cyropaedia*. Trans. Walter Miller. Books 1–8. Cambridge: Loeb Classical Library, Harvard University Press.

Secondary Sources

Allen, W. B. 1997. "Machiavelli and Modernity." In Machiavelli, *The Prince*, ed. and trans. Angelo Codevilla. New Haven: Yale University Press.

Anglo, Sydney. 1969. *Machiavelli: A Dissection*. London: Gollancz.

———. 2005. *Machiavelli: The First Century. Studies in Enthusiasm, Hostility, and Irrelevance*. Oxford: Oxford University Press.

Ball, Terence. 1984. "The Picaresque Prince: Reflections on Machiavelli and Moral Change." *Political Theory* 12, no. 4: 521–36.

Baron, Hans. 1955. *Humanistic and Political Literature in Florence and Venice at the Beginning of the Quattrocento*. Cambridge: Harvard University Press.

———. 1968. *From Petrarch to Leonardo Bruni: Studies in Humanist and Political Literature*. Chicago: Chicago University Press.

———. 1988. *In Search of Florentine Civic Humanism*. 2 vols. Princeton: Princeton University Press.

Bec, Christian. 1996. "Preface." In *Machiavel Oeuvres*. Paris: Éditions Robert Laffont.

Benner, Erica. 2001. "Is There a Core National Doctrine?" *Nations and Nationalism* 7, no 2: 155–74.

Berki, R. N. 1971. "Machiavellism: A Philosophical Defense." *Ethics* 81, no. 2: 107–27.

Berlin, Isaiah. 1981 [1958]. "The Originality of Machiavelli." In *Against the Current: Essays in the History of Ideas*. Oxford: Oxford University Press.

Billings, Grace Hadley. 1979. *The Art of Transition in Plato*. New York: Garland.

Bloomfield, Paul, ed. 2008. *Morality and Self-Interest*. Oxford: Oxford University Press.

Bock, Gisela. 1990. "Civil Discord in Machiavelli's *Istorie Fiorentine*." In *Machiavelli and Republicanism*, ed. Gisela Bock, Quentin Skinner, and Maurizio Viroli, pp. 181–202. Cambridge: Cambridge University Press.

Bock, Gisela, Quentin Skinner, and Maurizio Viroli, eds. 1990. *Machiavelli and Republicanism*. Cambridge: Cambridge University Press.

Bonadella, Peter E. 1973. *Machiavelli and the Art of Renaissance History*. Detroit: Wayne State University Press.

Botwinick, Aryeh. 1986. *Participation and Tacit Knowledge in Plato, Machiavelli, and Hobbes*. New York: Lanham University Press.

Bringmann, Klaus. 2007. *A History of the Roman Republic*. Trans. W. J. Smyth. Cambridge: Polity Press.

Brisson, Luc. 1999. *Plato the Mythmaker*. Trans and ed. Gerard Naddaf. Chicago: University of Chicago Press.

Brown, Alison. 2000a. "The Language of Empire." In *Florentine Tuscany: Structures and Practices of Power*, ed. William J. Connell and Andrea Zorzi, pp. 32–47. Cambridge: Cambridge University Press.

——. 2000b. "Demasking Renaissance Republicanism." In *Renaissance Civic Humanism*, ed. James Hankins, pp. 179–99. Cambridge: Cambridge University Press.

Burckhardt, Jacob. 1960 [1860]. *The Civilisation of the Renaissance in Italy*. London: Phaidon Press.

Cartledge, Paul, and Anthony Spawforth. 1992. *Hellenistic and Roman Sparta: A Tale of Two Cities*. London: Routledge.

Cassirer, Ernst. 1945. "Rousseau and Kant." In *Rousseau, Kant, Goethe: Two Essays*. Trans. James Gutmann et al., pp. 1–59. Princeton: Princeton University Press.

——. 1946. *The Myth of the State*. New Haven: Yale University Press.

——. 1970. *Rousseau, Kant, and Locke*. Princeton: Princeton University Press.

——. 1981 [1918]. *Kant's Life and Thought*. Trans. James Haden. New Haven: Yale University Press.

——. 2000 [1926]. *The Individual and the Cosmos in Renaissance Philosophy*. Trans. Mario Domandi. Mineola, N.Y.: Dover.

Cawkwell, George. 1997. *Thucydides and the Peloponnesian War*. London: Routledge.

Chabod, Federico. 1960. *Machiavelli and the Renaissance*. Trans. David Moore, intro. A. P. d'Entrèves. London: Bowes and Bowes.

Coby, J. Patrick. 1999. *Machiavelli's Romans: Liberty and Greatness in the "Discourses on Livy."* Lanham, Md.: Lexington Books.

Coleman, Janet, ed. 1996. *The Individual in Political Theory and Practice*. Oxford: Clarendon Press.

Comparato, Vittor Ivo. 1996. "A Case of Modern Individualism: Politics and the Uneasiness of Intellectuals in the Baroque Age." In *The Individual in Political Theory and Practice*, ed. Janet Coleman, pp. 149–70. Oxford: Clarendon Press.

Connell, William J., and Andrea Zorzi, eds. 2000. *Florentine Tuscany: Structures and Practices of Power*. Cambridge: Cambridge University Press.

Contamine, Philippe, ed. 2000. *War and Competition between States*. Oxford: Clarendon Press.

Copenhaver, Brian P. 1988. "Translation, Terminology, and Style in Philosophical Discourse." In *The Cambridge History of Renaissance Philosophy*, ed. Charles B. Schmitt and Quentin Skinner. pp. 75–109. Cambridge: Cambridge University Press.

Covini, Maria Nadia. 2000. "Political and Military Bonds in the Italian State System, Thirteenth to Sixteenth Centuries." In *War and Competition between States*, ed. Philippe Contamine, pp. 9–36. Oxford: Clarendon Press.

Craig, Leon Harold. 1994. *The War Lover: A Study of Plato's Republic*. Toronto: University of Toronto Press.

Crick, Bernard. 1970. "Introduction. So Many Machiavellis." In *Machiavelli: The Discourses*. Harmondsworth: Penguin.

de Alvarez, Leo Paul. 1999. *The Machiavellian Enterprise*. DeKalb: Northern Illinois University Press.

de Grazia, Sebastian. 1989. *Machiavelli in Hell*. Princeton: Princeton University Press.

de Romilly, Jacqueline. 1956. *Histoire et raison chez Thucydide*. Paris: Société d'Édition.

de Romilly, Jacqueline. 1997. *The Rise and Fall of States According to Greek Authors*. Ann Arbor: University of Michigan Press.

Desideri, P. 1995. "Plutarco e Machiavelli." In *Teoria e prassi politica nelle opere di Plutarco: Atti del V Convegno plutarcheo, Certosa di pontignano, 7–9 June 1993*, ed. I. Gallo and B. Scardigli, pp. 107–22. Naples.

Dietz, Mary. 1986. "Trapping the Prince: Machiavelli and the Politics of Deception. *American Political Science Review* 80, no. 3: 777–99.

Dillery, John. 1995. *Xenophon and the History of His Times*. London: Routledge.

Due, Bodil. 1989. *The "Cyropaedia": Xenophon's Aims and Methods*. Aarhus: Aarhus University Press.

Duff, Timothy E. 1999. *Plutarch's Lives: Exploring Virtue and Vice*. Oxford: Oxford University Press.

Field, Arthur. 1988. *The Origins of the Platonic Academy in Florence*. Princeton: Princeton University Press.

Fischer, Markus. 2000. *Well-Ordered License: On the Unity of Machiavelli's Thought*. Lanham, Md.: Lexington Books.

Fornara, Charles William. 1983. *The Nature of History in Ancient Greece and Rome*. Berkeley and Los Angeles: University of California Press.

Gallo, I., and B. Scardigli, eds. 1995. *Teoria e prassi politica nelle opere di Plutarco: Atti del V Convegno plutarcheo, Certosa di pontignano, 7–9 June 1993*. Naples.

Garin, Eugenio. 1965. *Italian Humanism: Philosophy and Civic Life in the Renaissance*. Trans. Peter Munz. Oxford: Oxford University Press.

———. 1972. *Portraits from the Quattrocento*. Trans. Victor Velen and Elizabeth Velen. New York: Harper and Row.

———. 1993. *Machiavelli fra politica e storia*. Turin: Einaudi.

———. 1994. *La cultura filosofica del rinascimento italiano*. Florence: Sansoni Editore.

Garver, Eugene. 1987. *Machiavelli and the History of Prudence*. Madison: University of Wisconsin Press.

Gera, Deborah Levine. 1993. *Xenophon's "Cyropaedia": Style, Genre, and Literary Technique*. Oxford: Clarendon Press.

Gilbert, Allan. 1938. *Machiavelli's "Prince" and Its Forerunners: The "Prince" as a Typical Book de Regimine Principum*. Durham, N.C.: Duke University Press.

———, ed. and trans. 1989. *Machiavelli: The Chief Works and Others*. 3 vols. Durham, N.C.: Duke University Press.

Gilbert, Felix. 1953. "The Structure and Composition of Machiavelli's Discorsi." *Journal of the History of Ideas* 14:136–56.

———. 1965. *Machiavelli and Guicciardini: Politics and History in Sixteenth-Century Florence*. Princeton: Princeton University Press.

———. 1972. "Machiavelli's Istorie fiorentine." In *Studies on Machiavelli*, ed. Myron P. Gilmore, pp. 73–100. Florence: G. C. Sanzoni.

———. 1977. *History, Choice, and Commitment*. Cambridge: Belknap Press of Harvard University Press.

Gilmore, Myron P. 1956. "Freedom and Determinism in Renaissance Historians." *Studies in the Renaissance* 3:49–60.

———, ed. 1972. *Studies on Machiavelli*. Florence: G. C. Sansoni.

Glish, Marcia. 1998. "Machiavelli's *Art of War* reconsidered." *Renaissance Quarterly* 51.

Grafton, Anthony. 1988. "The Availability of Ancient Works." In *The Cambridge History of Renaissance Philosophy*, ed. Charles B. Schmitt and Quentin Skinner, pp. 765–91. Cambridge: Cambridge University Press.

Grant, Ruth W. 1997. *Hypocrisy and Integrity: Machiavelli, Rousseau, and the Ethics of Politics*. Chicago: University of Chicago Press.

Gray, Vivienne. 1997. "Reading the Rise of Pisistratus: Herodotus I.56–68." *Histos* 1:1–27.

Guarini, Elena Fasano. 1990. "Machiavelli and the Crisis of the Italian Republics." In *Machiavelli and Republicanism*, ed. Gisela Bock, Quentin Skinner, and Maurizio Viroli, pp. 17–40. Cambridge: Cambridge University Press.

Hale, J. R. 1961. *Machiavelli and Renaissance Italy*. London: Macmillan.

———. 2001. *Florence and the Medici*. London: Phoenix Press.

Hankins, James. 2000. "Rhetoric, History, and Ideology: The Civic Panegyrics of Leonardo Bruni." In *Renaissance Civic Humanism,* ed. Hankins, pp. 143–78. Cambridge: Cambridge University Press.

Hexter, J. H. 1956. "Seyssel, Machiavelli and Polybius IV: The Mystery of the Missing Translation." *Studies in the Renaissance* 3:75–96.

Hoeges, Dirk. 2000. *Niccolò Machiavelli: Die Macht und der Schein*. Munich: C. H. Beck.

Hopkins, Phil. 2007. "'To Say What Is Most Necessary': Expositional and Philosophical Practice in Thucydides and Plato." In *Philosophy in Dialogue: Plato's Many Devices*, ed. Gary Alan Scott, pp. 15–40. Evanston, Ill.: Northwestern University Press.

Hornblower, Simon. 1987. *Thucydides*. London: Duckworth.

Hörnqvist, Mikael. 2004. *Machiavelli and Empire*. Cambridge: Cambridge University Press.

Huovinen, Lauri. 1951. *Das Bild vom Menschen im Politischen Denken Niccolò Machiavellis*. Helsinki: Druckerei-A.G. der Finnischen Literaturgesellschaft.

Kahn, Victoria. 1994. *Machiavellian Rhetoric: From Counter-Reformation to Milton*. Princeton: Princeton University Press.

Kelley, Donald R. 1988. "The Theory of History." In *The Cambridge History of Renaissance Philosophy*, ed. Charles B. Schmitt and Quentin Skinner, pp. 746–61. Cambridge: Cambridge University Press.

Keveaney, Arthur. 1987. *Rome and the Unification of Italy*. London: Routledge.

Kleiman, Mark A. R. N.d. "Machiavelli's Socratic Dialogue: The Prince as a Seduction into Virtue." Unpublished.

Kocis, Robert A. 1998. *Machiavelli Redeemed: Retrieving His Humanist Perspectives on Equality, Power, and Glory*. Bethlehem, Pa.: Lehigh University Press.

Kraye, Jill. 1988. "Moral Philosophy." In *The Cambridge History of Renaissance Philosophy*, ed. Charles B. Schmitt and Quentin Skinner, pp. 301–86. Cambridge: Cambridge University Press.

Langton, John. 1987. "Machiavelli's Paradox: Trapping or Teaching the Prince." *American Political Science Review* 81:1277–88.

Levine, Andrew. 1976. *The Politics of Autonomy: A Kantian Reading of Rousseau's "Social Contract."* Amherst: University of Massachusetts Press.

Lohr, Charles H. 1988. "Metaphysics." In *The Cambridge History of Renaissance Philosophy*, ed. Charles B. Schmitt and Quentin Skinner, pp. 535–637. Cambridge: Cambridge University Press.

Luccioni, Jean. 1953. *Xénophon et le socratisme*. Paris: Presses universitaires de France.

Lynch, Christopher. 2003. "Interpretive Essay." In *The Art of War*, by Machiavelli, trans. and ed. Christopher Lynch, 179–225. Chicago: University of Chicago Press, 2003.

Major, Rafael. 2007. "A New Argument for Morality: Machiavelli and the Ancients." *Political Science Quarterly* 60:171–79.

Mansfield, Harvey C. 1979. *Machiavelli's New Modes and Orders: A Study of the "Discourses on Livy."* Chicago: University of Chicago Press.

———. 1998. *Machiavelli's Virtue*. 2nd ed. Chicago: University of Chicago Press.

Mansfield, Harvey C. 2000. "Bruni and Machiavelli on Civic Humanism." In *Renaissance Civic Humanism*, ed. James Hankins, pp. 223–46. Cambridge: Cambridge University Press.

Mara, Gerald M. 1997. *Socrates' Discursive Democracy: Logos and Ergon in Platonic Political Philosophy*. State University of New York Press.

Martines, Lauro. 2002. *Power and Imagination: City-States in Renaissance Italy*. 2nd ed. London: Pimlico.

Mattingly, Garrett. 1958. "Machiavelli's *Prince*: Political Science or Political Satire?" *American Scholar* 27:482–91.

McIntosh, Donald. 1984. "The Modernity of Machiavelli." *Political Theory* 12, no. 2: 184–203.

Meinecke, Friedrich. 1998 [1925]. *The Doctrine of Raison d'État and Its Place in Modern History*. Ed. Werner Stark. New Brunswick, N.J.: Transaction Publishers.

Moes, Mark. 2007. "Medicine, Philosophy, and Socrates' Proposals to Glaucon about Γυμναστική in *Republic* 403c–412b." In *Philosophy in Dialogue: Plato's Many Devices*, ed. Gary Alan Scott. Evanston, Ill.: Northwestern University Press.

Morfino, Vittorio. 2002. *Il tempo e l'occasione: L'incontro Spinoza Machiavelli*. Milan: Edizioni Universitarie di Lettere Economia Diritto.

Münkler, Herfried. 1995. *Machiavelli: Die Begründung des politischen Denkens der Neuzeit aus der Krise der Republik Florenz*. Frankfurt am Main: Fischer Wissenschaft.

Nadon, Christopher. 2001. *Xenophon's Prince: Republic and Empire in the Cyropaedia*. Berkeley and Los Angeles: University of California Press.

Najemy, John M. 1990. "The Controversy Surrounding Machiavelli's Service to the Republic." In *Machiavelli and Republicanism*, ed. Gisela Bock, Quentin Skinner, and Maurizio Viroli, pp. 101–17. Cambridge: Cambridge University Press.

Nelson, Eric. 2004. *The Greek Tradition in Republican Thought*. Cambridge: Cambridge University Press.

Newell, W. R. 1987. "How Original Is Machiavelli? A Consideration of Skinner's Interpretation of Virtue and Fortune." *Political Theory* 15:612–34.

O'Meara, Dominic J. 2003. *Platonopolis: Platonic Political Philosophy in Late Antiquity*. Oxford: Clarendon Press.

Ostwald, Martin. 1982. *Autonomia: Its Genesis and Early History*. Atlanta: Scholars Press.

———. 1986. *From Popular Sovereignty to the Sovereignty of Law: Law, Society, and Politics in Fifth-Century Athens*. Berkeley and Los Angeles: University of California Press.

Pangle, Thomas. 1994. "Socrates in the Context of Xenophon's Political Writings." In *The Socratic Movement*, ed. Paul Vander Waert, pp. 127–50. Ithaca, N.Y.: Cornell University Press.

Parel, A. J. 1993. "The Question of Machiavelli's Modernity." In *The Rise of Modern Philosophy: The Tension between the New and Traditional Philosophies from Machiavelli to Leibniz*, ed. Tom Sorell, pp. 253–72. Oxford: Clarendon Press.

Pettit, Philip. 1997. *Republicanism: A Theory of Freedom and Government*. Oxford: Oxford University Press.

———. 2001. *A Theory of Freedom*. Cambridge: Polity Press.

Philp, Mark. 2007. *Political Conduct*. Cambridge: Harvard University Press.

Pocock, J.G.A. 1975. *The Machiavellian Moment: Florentine Political Thought and the Atlantic Republican Tradition*. Princeton: Princeton University Press.

———. 1985. "Machiavelli in the Liberal Cosmos." *Political Theory* 13:559–74.

Popkin, Richard H. 1988. "Theories of Knowledge." In *The Cambridge History of Renaissance Philosophy*, ed. Charles B. Schmitt and Quentin Skinner, pp. 668–84. Cambridge: Cambridge University Press.

Poppi, Antonino. 1988. "Fate, Fortune, Providence, and Human Freedom." In *The Cambridge History of Renaissance Philosophy*, ed. Charles B. Schmitt and Quentin Skinner, pp. 641–67. Cambridge: Cambridge University Press.

Pulver, Jeffrey. 1937. *Machiavelli: The Man, His Work, and His Times*. London: Herbert Joseph.

Rahe, Paul. 2000. "Situating Machiavelli." In *Renaissance Civic Republicanism*, ed. James Hankins, pp. 270–308. Cambridge: Cambridge University Press.

Rawson, Elizabeth. 1961. *The Spartan Tradition in European Thought*. Oxford: Oxford University Press.

Ridolfi, Roberto. 1963. *The Life of Niccolò Machiavelli*. Trans. Cecil Grayson. Chicago: University of Chicago Press.

Rood, Tim. 1998. *Thucydides: Narrative and Explanation*. Oxford: Oxford University Press.

Rubinstein, Nicolai. 1990. "Machiavelli and Florentine Republican Experience." In *Machiavelli and Republicanism*, ed. Gisela Bock, Quentin Skinner, and Maurizio Viroli, pp. 3–16. Cambridge: Cambridge University Press.

Sancisi-Weerdenburg, Heleen. 1990. "Cyrus in Italy: From Dante to Machiavelli." In *The Roots of the European Tradition*, ed. H. Sancisi-Weerdenburg and J. W. Drijvers. Achaemenid History, no. 5. Leiden: Nederlands instituut voor het nabije oosten.

Sasso, Gennaro. 1958. *Niccolò Machiavelli: Studio del suo pensiero politico*. Naples.

Schmitt, Charles B., and Quentin Skinner, eds. 1988. *The Cambridge History of Renaissance Philosophy*. Cambridge: Cambridge University Press.

Schneewind, J. B. 1998. *The Invention of Autonomy: A History of Modern Moral Philosophy*. Cambridge: Cambridge University Press.

Schofield, Malcolm. 1999. *Saving the City: Philosopher-Kings and Other Classical Paradigms*. London: Routledge.

Scott, Gary Alan, ed. 2007. *Philosophy in Dialogue: Plato's Many Devices*. Evanston, Ill.: Northwestern University Press.

Siegel, Jerrold E. 1968. *Rhetoric and Philosophy in Renaissance Humanism: The Union of Eloquence and Wisdom, Petrarch to Valla*. Princeton: Princeton University Press.

Skinner, Quentin. 1978. *The Foundations of Modern Political Thought*. Vol. 1, *The Renaissance*. Cambridge: Cambridge University Press.

———. 1981. *Machiavelli*. Oxford: Oxford University Press.

———. 1988. "Political Philosophy." In *The Cambridge History of Renaissance Philosophy*, ed. Charles B. Schmitt and Quentin Skinner, pp. 387–452. Cambridge: Cambridge University Press.

———. 1990. "Machiavelli's *Discorsi* and the Pre-humanist Origins of Republican Ideas." In *Machiavelli and Republicanism*, ed. Gisela Bock, Quentin Skinner, and Maurizio Viroli, pp. 121–41. Cambridge: Cambridge University Press.

———. 2002. *Visions of Politics*. Vol. 2, *Renaissance Virtues*. Cambridge: Cambridge University Press.

Strauss, Leo. 1950. *Natural Right and History*. Chicago: University of Chicago Press.

———. 1952. *Persecution and the Art of Writing*. Chicago: University of Chicago Press.

———. 1958. *Thoughts on Machiavelli*. Chicago: University of Chicago Press.

———. 1964. *The City and Man*. Chicago: University of Chicago Press.

———. 1987. "Plato" and "Machiavelli." In *History of Political Philosophy*, 3rd ed., ed. Leo Strauss and Joseph Cropsey, pp. 33–89, 296–317. Chicago: University of Chicago Press.

Sullivan, Vickie. 1992. "Machiavelli's Momentary 'Machiavellian Moment': A Reconsideration of Pocock's Treatment of the Discourses." *Political Theory* 20, no. 2: 309–18.

———. 1996. *Machiavelli's Three Romes*. DeKalb: Northern Illinois University Press.

Sullivan, Vickie. 2004. *Machiavelli, Hobbes, and the Formation of a Liberal Republicanism in England*. Cambridge: Cambridge University Press.

Tarcov, Nathan. 1982. "Quentin Skinner's Method and Machiavelli's *Prince*." *Ethics* 92: 692–709.

Tarcov, Nathan. 2007. "Freedom, Republics, and Peoples in Machiavelli's *Prince*." In *Freedom and the Human Person*, ed. Richard L. Velkley, pp. 122–42. Washington, D.C.: Catholic University of America Press.

Tatum, James. 1989. *Xenophon's Imperial Fiction: On "The Education of Cyrus."* Princeton: Princeton University Press.

Triantafillis, Constantino. 1875. *Niccolò Machiavelli e gli scrittori greci*. Venice: Tipografia del Giornale "Il tempo."

Vander Waert, Paul, ed. 1994. *The Socratic Movement*. Ithaca, N.Y.: Cornell University Press.

van Gelderen, Martin. 1996. "Liberty, Civic Rights, and Duties in Sixteenth-Century Europe and the Rise of the Dutch Republic." In *The Individual in Political Theory and Practice*, ed. Janet Coleman, pp. 99–122. Oxford: Clarendon Press.

Vasoli, Cesare. 1988. "The Renaissance Concept of Philosophy." In *The Cambridge History of Renaissance Philosophy*, ed. Charles B. Schmitt and Quentin Skinner, pp. 55–74. Cambridge: Cambridge University Press.

Vatter, Miguel E. 2000. *Between Form and Event: Machiavelli's Theory of Political Freedom*. Dordrecht: Kluwer Academic Publishers.

Velkley, Richard L. 1989. *Freedom and the End of Reason: On the Moral Foundation of Kant's Critical Philosophy*. Chicago: University of Chicago Press.

Viroli, Maurizio. 1990. "Machiavelli and the Republican Idea of Politics." In *Machiavelli and Republicanism*, ed. Gisela Bock, Quentin Skinner, and Maurizio Viroli, pp. 143–71. Cambridge: Cambridge University Press.

———. 1998. *Machiavelli*. Oxford: Oxford University Press.

———. 2001. *Niccolò's Smile: A Biography of Machiavelli*. Trans. Anthony Shugaar. London: I. B. Tauris.

———. Forthcoming. *Machiavelli's God*. Princeton: Princeton University Press.

Vissing, Lars. 1986. *Machiavel et la Politique de l'Apparence*. Paris: Presses Universitaires de France.

Vlastos, Gregory. 1991. *Socrates: Ironist and Moral Philosopher*. Cambridge: Cambridge University Press.

Walsh, P. G. 1963. *Livy: His Historical Aims and Methods*. Cambridge: Cambridge University Press.

Whitfield, J. H. 1969. *Discourses on Machiavelli*. Cambridge: W. Heffer and Sons.

Whitmarsh, Tim. 2001. *Greek Literature and the Roman Empire*. Oxford: Oxford University Press.

White, Nicholas. 2002. *Individual and Conflict in Greek Ethics*. Oxford: Clarendon Press.

Wolin, Sheldon. 1960. *Politics and Vision: Continuity and Innovation in Western Political Thought*. Boston: Little, Brown.

Wood, Allen W. 2002. "What Dead Philosophers Mean." In *Unsettling Obligations: Essays on Reason, Reality and the Ethics of Belief*. Stanford, Calif.: CSLI Publications.

Wormald, B.H.G. 1993. *Francis Bacon: History, Politics, and Science, 1561–1626*. Cambridge: Cambridge University Press.

Zorzi, Andrea. 2000. "The 'Material Constitution' of the Florentine Dominion." In *Florentine Tuscany: Structures and Practices of Power*, ed. William J. Connell and Andrea Zorzi, pp. 6–31. Cambridge: Cambridge University Press.

corruption (*continued*)
beset by, 380–85, 407–8, 432; in Rome, 58,
140, 165, 204, 216, 350, 391, 421–22, 463–64,
470–73; in Sparta, 410, 413–17
Corvinus, Valerius, 267–68
counsel: beneficial, 112; dangers of giving, 326–
30, 347n53; given to princes and republics,
112, 266–69, 445-46; harmful, 467; Machiavelli's, 29, 66n11; meritocracy and, 266;
superhuman, 79, 387–89; and utility/safety,
352n64, 354; in Thucydides, 89, 89n84, 91, 93.
See also reasoning
courts, public, 268–69, 283, 287, 384
covert teachings, 39, 110, 113, 199, 201, 280n60,
360n75, 378. *See also* codes and coded language; dissimulative writing
critical humanism, 11, 492
cruelty, 268, 268n28, 362–64, 469
Crusades, 143–44, 390n71
customs: in Greek thought, 86, 88–90, 281n63;
Machiavelli on, 280–81
Cyrus: Machiavelli on, 72–78, 72n29, 117,
118n57, 123–24, 431, 438n, 470, 485; Plato on,
76n46, 367, 447n92; Xenophon on, 69, 72–78,
78n57, 84–87, 117–18, 118n62, 119n63, 367,
431n55, 470

de Alvarez, Leo Paul, 121n72, 479n95
deception: acceptable vs. unacceptable, 84–87;
in acquiring empire, 456, 479, 486; and corruption, 19, 25n37, 26, 64, 80, 207, 244n72,
272, 297, 299, 313, 379, 472; in *Cyropaedia*,
85–87; in *The Discourses*, 87–88; as distinct
from irony, 65; and extraordinary methods,
432; and freedom, 246n74, 258–59, 457; as
human skill, 198; and the law of nations,
313, 315; necessity for, 137; self-, 61, 112, 116,
124, 154, 225, 258–59, 269, 328, 330, 337, 348,
350–51; sophistry and, 120, 207; susceptibility
to, 64, 66n11, 116, 313, 352, 437n72, 457; useful,
495. *See also* appearances; fraud
dedications, Machiavelli's, 19, 43, 122, 128, 450
delicacy, in political ordering, 204–6, 206n98,
309, 355, 362
deontological ethics, 284, 325, 340–43, 431n54,
495–96
dependence: on foreign powers, 18, 83, 229; on
fortune, 176, 398; freedom from, 237–39; of
princes on peoples, 444–45
Devil, 61
dialectical methods, 4, 39–41, 111, 120, 125–26,
132, 136, 137, 148, 204, 206n98, 309, 326, 341,
369, 434, 436n69, 439, 485n8, 489n13, 490,
490n15, 492, 496–97

dialogue: philosophical, 4, 10, 39–41, 52; with
tyrants, 79–84, 79n58
dictatorship, 176, 328, 384, 433
Diodotus, 93–96, 106n35, 216n10, 255, 308n48,
317n82, 336, 340, 378n36, 460, 466n54,
467n57, 481n102
Diogenes, 53
discipline: ancient, 205–6, 417, 467; in the
Cyropaedia, 73–74, 74n38, 76, 86, 118–20; of
human nature, 190–97, 199–200, 228, 492;
in hunting, 76, 118–20; and justice, 292–93,
362–64, 469–74, 481; in military orders, 46,
121, 148, 205–6, 292–93, 362–63, 469–74; and
necessity, 148, 151n47, 165; in Thucydides,
151n47, 165n73
The Discourses (Machiavelli): aim of, 438;
audience for, 438; on cities, 214–20; on
conspiracies, 374, 376; on deception, 87–88;
dedication of, 43; on freedom, 214–20, 232;
on free will, 247–49, 251; on hunting, 116–17,
123, 130; on imitation of ancients, 101, 107; on
justice, 309–10; knowledge in, 122n77, 125–26,
128n89; necessity in, 136–38, 142–43, 147–49;
on Peloponnesian War, 97; philosophy in,
49n112; on prophecy, 185; publication of,
16n5; on religion and politics, 386–404; on
selection and ordering of sites, 154, 157–62;
on virtue, 157–62
Discursus (Machiavelli), 6n, 54–62, 78–79, 234n,
240, 284n, 448, 460
disonesto (indecent) words/actions, 19, 21,
26–27, 64, 71, 101, 109, 138, 198, 239, 439. *See
also* appearances; *onesto* (decent) words/
actions; rhetoric
disorders, moral and political: between cities,
294; as distinct from tumults, 414; and dominion, 455; in Florence, 17–25, 28, 31–35, 55,
153n53, 170, 188, 224, 244, 277, 294, 299–303,
346, 418, 438; justice and laws as antidote to,
3, 5, 175, 184, 281–82, 293, 298–99, 310, 348;
and one-man rule, 434, 449, 492; philosophical remedies for, 2–3, 40, 51–52, 70n23, 132,
134, 488, 490n15, 498; and religion, 391,
395n80, 399–400; remedies for, 2–3, 29, 38,
40, 57–58, 217; Roman, 141, 216, 382, 466. *See
also* corruption.
dispositions. *See* humors
dissimulation, constructive, 64–69, 65n6, 77–78,
80, 87, 486. *See also* irony
dissimulative writing: of the ancients, 113,
367–68; antithesis as means of, 367–70; as
civil medicine, 70, 77; on deception, 84–88;
defined, 65; on ends justifying means, 357;
Greek, 63–66, 491; Hobbes and, 490, 490n14;

on Machiavelli's peace settlement with Pisa, 43–44
guilds, 275–76, 295, 304–5, 319

Hankins, James, 33n63
Hannibal, 54n134, 88, 178, 315n73, 362–63, 399, 469–70, 472–74
Hanno, 473–74
happiness, not necessarily related to stability or virtue: in Greek thought, 69, 69n16, 77, 77n49, 80–81, 83, 435–36; in Machiavelli's thought, 61, 77n49, 177, 193, 391n73, 405, 408–9, 412, 417, 422, 424, 436
Harrington, James, 11, 482n102, 485, 495n21; *Oceania*, 3
harshness: in building sites, 160–61; in Greek thought, 78, 206n99; in political ordering, 158, 204–6, 206n98, 267–68, 309–10, 317–19, 339, 355–56, 362–64, 417, 468, 493
heavens, ethical judgment and, 140, 163, 171, 180–84, 207, 321, 371, 382, 388–89, 396
Herder, Johann Gottfried von, 63
Hermocrates, 173n, 348n55, 463n42
Herodotus, 24n37, 35n71, 70, 77n50, 83n70, 130n96, 141n19, 161n65, 181n33, 189n58, 196n76, 223n27, 279n58, 435n64
Hiero I, 10–11, 77n49, 80–83, 82n66, 84n72, 218, 221, 438–39
Hiero II of Syracuse, 82, 82n66, 219
historians: motives of, in corrupt times, 112–15, 140–41; and philosophy, 51–52, 183; responsibilities of, 4, 30–37, 126–27
historical justice, 306–8
histories: contingencies of survival of, 113–15, 129; critical, 102n3, 485; interpretation and judgment of, 111–16, 124–32; self-celebratory vs. self-critical, 30–37, 112, 127
Hobbes, Thomas: on fear, 385; and Greek thought, 10n27, 35, 89n83, 347n53, 435n66, 463n42, 490n15; and Machiavelli, 10, 213, 490, 490n14; and philosophy, 10, 52, 124n82, 128, 130n99, 131n; on prophecies, 189n59
honors. *See* public office
Hörnqvist, Mikael, 325n1, 467n58, 468n60, 481n100
"How to Deal with the People of the Valdichiana Who Have Rebelled" (Machiavelli), 468n60
hubris (arrogance), 76, 81, 89, 95, 96, 103, 119n63, 120, 165, 177n16, 183, 192, 196n76, 244, 436, 437, 474, 498. *See also* self-assertion
humanism: civic, 1, 5, 37, 135, 493–95; critical, 11, 492; Italian, 39–42, 49n113, 494
humanity/humaneness. See *umanità* (humanity)

human nature: animal nature and, 62, 118–19, 190, 196–202, 208, 492–93; corruptibility of, 6, 62, 64, 191–93, 195, 203, 205, 322; ethical standards appropriate to, 173n7, 192n67, 250, 370, 492–93; and freedom, 208, 227, 231, 391; and inequality, 302–3; judgments and predictions based on, 187–89; Machiavelli's view of, 186–87, 190–93; moral and political ordering based on, 190–97, 202–5; two aspects of, 186–87, 192
humors: as anthropological concept, 36–37, 139, 185, 286, 303, 320, 349; and human standards, 196, 203; laws for accommodating, 203, 241, 306n43, 372–73, 384, 414, 443; as natural and ordinary, 38, 150–54, 183–84, 186, 205, 252, 385; need to regulate, 29n51, 30, 57–58, 126, 191–92, 384, 416; of orderers, 178; overambitious, 223; of the people, 183–86, 191–92, 240, 252, 286, 303–4; in Plato, 153n52; social conflict arising from, 30, 36–37, 152–53, 203, 240, 320. *See also* passions; venting, of humors
Hungary, 428
hunting, 116–24; as metaphor for education, 119–23, 130; as metaphor for philosophy, 118–21, 488; as metaphor for rulership, 118–19; as preparation for war, 116–18, 121–22; Socratic metaphor of, 75–76, 124, 439–40; virtue and, 119–20. See also *cognizione* (knowledge)

imitation: of ancient legislators/reformers, 359–60, 382, 388n, 408–11, 418, 420, 423–26, 429–30, 433–36, 448; ancient tradition of, 101–7; of foxes and lions, 197–200; the Greeks and, 102–3, 105–7, 113, 114n43; issues in, 101; lack of, 101, 107–8; literary, of misleading appearances, 65, 68, 78; Machiavelli on, 107–16, 123–24, 132–34; Plato on, 60n168, 103nn5–6, 434–46; political, 108–10; of/by reputedly great men and deeds, 72, 123–24, 357, 362–63, 386, 470–71; of Roman practices, 214n16, 230, 355, 395, 403, 414, 451, 463, 465, 478–83; the Romans and, 103–5; standards for guiding, 103–4, 108–16, 132–34, 204–6, 309–10; technical/artistic, 108–9; of the Tuscans, 459, 478; unreasonable, 108–10, 115–16, 177
impartiality, 61n152, 266–67, 278, 295–96, 298, 317, 324, 472
imperialism, Machiavelli's *imperio* and, 482n104. *See also* dominion (*dominio*); empire
impersonality, 267, 278, 317
impetuosity, 175–79
indignation, 22, 149, 222, 243–45, 307, 310, 312–13, 322, 454
individualism, 104, 213, 285–86, 319, 495

inequality: acceptable forms of, 270–72; economic and social, 272–77, 302–3; human nature and, 302–3; natural, 283, 302–3; political corruption stemming from, 274–79; in political order, 269–70

infima plebe (lowest plebs), 304–6, 319

instrumentalism, 76, 169, 207, 255–56, 259, 262–63, 271–72, 386–90, 402, 444, 486, 497

integrity: moral, 178, 204–5, 472; territorial, 325

intervention, in other cities, 217, 242–44

irony: Greek forms of, 65, 341n42; Machiavelli's use of, 24, 123, 143, 199n86, 355, 371, 388, 389, 393, 401, 439, 442; in Rousseau, 387n65. *See also* complex irony; dissimulative writing

Italy and Italian cities, 9, 23, 35, 195, 214, 217, 227, 229, 236, 242–44, 274, 297–300, 332–33, 339, 345, 421, 432, 451, 456–62, 465–66, 473–83

judgment: of citizens in republics, 40, 64–77, 383–84, 392; concerning imitation of ancients, 102–6, 108–16, independent, 6, 10, 48–49, 65–67, 71, 106, 364; corrupt, concerning deception, 86–87; corrupt, concerning ends and means, 360–64; corrupt, concerning ethical standards, 88–97, 107–9, 323, 383–84, 438; corrupt, in readers and writers, 70, 72; empirical methods insufficient for, 48, 130, 196, 206–7, 322; ethical, 124–32, 180–84, 187–88, 291, 334, 351, 388; free will and the problem of errors in, 286–87; hunting as training in, 117–24; instrumental, 7, 76, 169, 255, 402; Machiavelli and ethical, 7, 9, 15, 38, 341, 368; philosophical, 130; weaknesses in human, 37–38, 116, 125, 209, 384–85, 434–37. *See also* ethics; standards

Julius II, Pope, 177

justice, 290–324; appearances of, 484, 497; concept of, 293–97; concepts related to, 6, 290, 294, 309; corrupt/inadequate uses of, 53, 89, 92–93, 108–9, 127, 131–32, 299–306; distributive, 293, 297, 318–20; and empire, 479; equality and, 302–3, 308, 323; expediency of, 91–97, 200n88, 223–24, 336–64, 439; experience's role in understanding, 320–24; forms of, 297, 314–20; freedom in relation to, 277–78, 298; in Greek thought, 196n76; and historical conflicts, 306–8; knowledge of, 320–24, 321n; and law of nations, 186–88, 310–14, 385; limits as characteristic of, 294–95; Machiavelli and, 6–7, 84, 87–88, 96–97, 169, 290, 294–97, 496; the military and, 292–93; ordinary reasoning and, 209; partisan accounts of, 299–306; political order grounded in, 290–98, 372–73, 484; in Plato, 51, 66, 95n103, 96n107, 102–3,

200n87, 435–36, 447n92, 492–93; in Plutarch, 105–6; popular perception of, 295–96; in *The Prince*, 84, 447, 449; promissory, 297, 314–16; prudence and, 290–92, 308–9, 340–43; punitive, 293, 297, 316–18; relative standards of, 147; religion and human, 94, 400–406; religious fear in relation to, 394–98; respect for, after victory, 7, 84, 179, 215, 226, 291, 304; responsibility for upholding, 321–24; restoration of, 165; as restraint, 293; revenge vs., 302; senses of, 293, 497; in Thucydides, 88–96; of/in war, 331–40, 469; in Xenophon, 66, 76–78, 80, 83, 85–87, 117, 119–20

Kant, Immanuel, 77n53, 196n78, 489, 489n12, 495

kings and kingship: contrasted to free government, 194, 217, 232, 261, 271; corruption of, 449; elective, 275, 423; Greek idea of, 72, 74n38, 81n64, 83, 448; and kingly power, 407, 422–23, 448; Machiavelli's concept of, as distinct from princes and tyrants, 407n3; Medici houses as if made for, 22, 24, 24n37; philosophical, 43n96, 79n61; Roman, 219, 233, 237n58, 272, 283, 359n72, 391, 420–24, 449, 451; Spartan 107, 410, 413–17

knowledge: a priori, 287, 320, 322; empirical methods insufficient for, 129–31; foxes as model of, 198–99; of histories, 30, 125–27; hunting analogy for, 122–23; Machiavelli's concepts of, 122n77, 128n89, 382n49. *See also* *cognizione* (knowledge); empiricism and experience

Landino, Cristoforo, 41–42, 42n95

law of nations (*ius gentium*), 165, 182, 186–87, 215, 225, 309–15, 321–23, 385, 396, 473. *See also* justice

laws: animal nature and, 201, 206; arms and, 446–47; authority, means of giving legitimate, 256, 259–62; authorization of, from the people, 282–83, 448; central to Machiavelli's thought, 3–6, 61n152, 449n49, 485, 489, 494–95; characteristics of, 164; citizens' improvement through, 382; corruption of, 18–20, 23, 26, 28, 56, 222, 299–301, 307–8, 362, 369, 379, 470; customs and, 281, 281n63; establishment of, 162–63, 408–10, 412, 417; as ethical/political necessity, 6, 164–65, 193, 200, 255; fear of, 394–98, 403n98; foundations of, principled vs. teleological, 282–85; force and, 197, 200–201, 206, 208, 398, 431; freedom, basis of political, 25, 58, 62n153, 194–95, 233–34, 237, 240–46, 249, 252, 266–87; Hobbes on,

157–66 (*see also* response to); law and, 164; Machiavelli and, 136–39, 143–68; Medicis and, 138n9; natural and ordinary constraints and, 150–53, 156, 179, 186, 215, 370–71, 411; as a pretext, 142–47; response to, 153–56 (*see also* imposing and removing); responsibility and, 136–39, 145–46, 148–49, 161n63; rhetorical uses of, 136–47, 138n9, 150–52, 330; sources of, 150; *Timaeus* on, 102; ultimate, 142, 145, 146, 149, 313, 425, 427, 428, 430; virtue and, 135, 151, 157–61, 167; war and, 142–49. *See also* constraints; limits

Nelson, Eric, 5n18, 290

Neville, Henry, 2n6, 3n8, 4n12, 10, 42n94, 61n152, 69, 391n72, 485–87, 489, 491; "Plato Redivivus," 2–4, 3n10, 485

Nicias, 69n18, 96–97, 177n16, 259n12, 342n, 460, 469n62

nobles, 17–18, 36–37, 58, 219, 273–74, 278, 302–4, 307–8. See also *grandi* (the great)

Numa Pompilius, 161, 162, 386–93, 391n72, 399, 411n15, 421, 451

oaths: in Greek thought, 75, 86–89, 119; in Livy, 104; Machiavelli on, 19, 299, 314–16, 394–400, 399n92. *See also* justice; obligations; promises

obligations: and the autonomy of cities, 478n90; as ethical necessity, 6, 165, 193, 280, 290, 331n19, 497; in external relations, 245, 291–92, 336, 340, 354; as fundamental to Machiavelli's ethics, 340, 496–97; justice/prudence and, 290–92, 296–97, 312, 342–43; laws and, 6, 165, 191, 193, 382; and oaths/promises, 396–97, 316n75; of princes and subjects, 238, 280n60, 444–45; and religion, 398–400; in republics, 267, 362. *See also* justice; oaths; promises

one-man orderers: Aeneas, 418–22; ancient writers on, 82, 433–36 (*see also* Plato on); conditions for, 407–8, 432; contemporary princes as, 132, 245, 407n3, 437–38, 446–49; drawbacks of, 357–60, 381, 384n57; 433–34, 437, 446; Guicciardini on, 40–41; Lycurgus, 408–17; Machiavelli on, 27n45, 137, 407–8, 432n70, 436–38, 449n99, 470; Moses, 424–32; Plato on, 40–41, 62n153, 434–46, 436n71; renovation of corrupt cities by, 380–85; Romulus, 359, 418–24; Rousseau on, 436n71

onesto (decent) words/actions, 19–21, 26–28, 37, 64, 71, 101, 108–9, 127–28, 138, 198, 239, 275, 294, 298, 300, 304, 334, 349, 356. See also appearances; *disonesto* (indecent) words/actions; rhetoric

"On Fortune" (Machiavelli), 436

oracles, 404

order and ordering: concept of, 7, 46, 139–40; ethical, 88–89, 130; in Greek thought, 79n58, 88–89, 118n57, 162n67, 196n76, 368n4; human responsibility for, 6, 36, 62, 102, 112, 170–209; justice and, 95, 102, 132, 291–92; laws and, 6, 157–67; necessity for, 146–49, 154–67; philosophy and, 38–41, 46–48, 47n106; standards for, 104–5, 110, 112, 114–15, 125, 129, 131–34, 139–41, 142n22, 144, 146–49, 152–68, 367–73. *See also* ordinary methods; political order

orderers: Cyrus as, 78n57; Moses, 424–32; one-man, 40–41, 380–85, 407–8, 418, 424, 432–37; political, 6; questionable judgment of, 349–50, 352; renovation of corrupt cities by, 407; renovation of corrupt cities by individual, 380–85; Roman founders, 418–24; selection of, 328; Spartan founders, 408–17. *See also* founders; one-man orderers; princes

ordinary methods, 367–406; limits respected by, 372; political order based on, 368–69, 372–73; as public, 372; and renovation of corrupt cities, 380–85; and rule of law, 372–73; self-reliance and, 371–72; as stabilizing, 372. *See also* extraordinary methods; laws; publicity, of laws and actions; transparency

"ordinary," meaning of, 139–40; 368–73. *See also* "extraordinary"; natural and ordinary

Orti Oricellari circle, 39, 43, 43n97, 128, 374

Palla Strozzi, 52n126, 344–45, 344n45, 347–48

partisans and partisanship: as central theme in the Florentine Histories, 18–19, 438; challenged by "men in the middle," 52, 306–7; extraordinary methods and, 376, 378–79, 390; in Greek thought, 71, 74, 78, 88–89; in histories, 33, 101, 108, 112–13, 115, 126–27; justice and, 132, 295, 298–306, 311, 317, 472; liberality/cruelty and, 20, 21n33, 78, 124n81, 311, 362–64, 438, 469, 471; Machiavelli as non-partisan writer, 2, 34–37; and passions, 29–30; and practical judgment, 333, 349; as "private," non-public mode, 20–21, 37, 78, 204, 266–68, 278, 284, 289, 434, 442; religion and, 387n65, 388, 390, 394, 401; as threat to freedom, 240, 266; as threat to political order, 18–30, 33, 41, 55–56, 153, 204–6, 270, 277, 334–35, 343–47, 356; on turning subjects into partisans, 441, 444; use of rhetoric, 26–28, 138, 145–46. *See also* private ambitions and their effects; sects (*sètte*)

partnership: in building new cities, with natives, 160; in government, 358, 444; in Greek thought, 445n87, 454n6; as opposed to subjection, 146–48, 218n, 338, 453–64, 479–83. *See also* arms; empire

standards (*continued*)
  knowledge, 125–27; virtue and, 166. *See also* judgment
statesmanship: Machiavelli's examples of, 26, 97; philosophical, in ancient thought, 2, 50–51, 66n10, 106, 128n91, 165n73, 434–35, 492–95. *See also* Camillus, Marcus Furius; Capponi, Neri di Gino; Fabius Maximus; Palla Strozzi; Uzzano, Niccolò da
Strauss, Leo, 1n1, 5, 9n25, 15, 67n12, 135, 407n1, 490–92, 493n20
strictness. *See* harshness
subjects/subjection: contrasted with citizens, 81–84; contrasted with friends/partners, 147–48, 218, 223n27, 454, 480; empire through, 91–97, 147–48, 206, 222–26, 339, 342, 454, 456–64, 475, 479–81, 480n99; freedom from, 222, 234–35, 262, 483; in Greek thought, 72–73, 75, 77–78, 78n57, 81–82, 92–95, 119, 173n, 223n27, 259n12; methods of holding/losing, 6, 223n27, 255–60, 259n12, 318, 361–62, 370, 374, 378n36, 437n72, 441–50. *See also* dominion (*dominio*); empire; partnership; tyranny, freedom vs.
Sullivan, Vicki, 5n19, 390n71
supernatural explanations, 180–84. *See also* prophets and prophecy
Switzerland, 456, 477

Tacitus, Cornelius: as critical historian, 102n3; "Dialogue of Oratory," 104–5; dissimulation of, 113n40, 490n14; on imitation of ancients, 104–5; Machiavelli and, 4, 443n86, 492; persecution of, 66n9; political analysis of, 9; sources for, 434, 490n14
Tarcov, Nathan, 369n7
Tercets on Ambition (Machiavelli), 195
terror, 385, 394–95, 397–400
Thebes, 434
Themistocles, 352n64
Theodoric, 142
Theseus, 78n57, 408, 419, 431
Thucydides, 83n70, 96n103, 116n50, 196n76, 223n27, 371n15; on appearances, 22n26; on Athens, 22n26, 35n71, 58n143, 71, 88–97, 281n66, 337, 368n3, 464n43, 483; causal explanations in, 180, 184n47; on corrupt values and judgments, 88–96; as critical historian, 31, 35n71, 102n3, 127, 130, 216; and dissimulation, 63, 71, 88–96, 89n84, 136, 367; on enemies, 151n47, 225, 477; and fear, 385n61, 393n75; on fortune, 173; on freedom, 216n11, 219, 246n74, 497; Hobbes and, 10n27,

35n71, 89nn83–84, 347n53, 490; on impetuosity, 177n16; Latin translations of, 9; and law, 281n63; Machiavelli and, 4, 8–11, 96–97, 133, 170, 292n3, 309n50, 336, 340, 430, 467n58, 468n60, 485, 489, 492, 496; mentor of, 10n27, 89n83; and morality, 89n83, 104–5, 162n68, 492, 493, 496; philosophical content in work of, 51; Plato and, 89n83; political participation of, 347n53; and religion, 396n82, 406; as Roman source, 8n, 102n3, 469n62; on rulership, 151n47, 188n54, 225, 342n, 454, 477, 478n90, 479n94, 480; Socrates and, 89n83; on Sparta, 151n47, 165n73, 173n; themes of, 88–89, 189n58; on trust, 279n58; on virtue, 165n73; on words and deeds, 71–72, 485
Tignosi, Niccolò, 138n9
Torquatus, Manlius, 268
translation, of key Machiavellian terms, 368–69
transparency, 26–29, 266–69
trust, 279–80, 291, 296–97, 312, 314–16, 359
truth: as best possible account, 30, 126; conception of, 126, 126n85; as defensive mechanism, 127; political role of, 29–30; as standard of judgment, 125–27; verisimilitude vs., 29–30
tumults: caused by changes in religion, 395; the "great" as source of, 273, 304; as ordinary and natural, 152–54, 160, 167, 205, 251–52, 252n83, 413–15. *See also* humors
Tuscans and Tuscany, 17, 114, 121, 217, 331, 403, 421n, 455–56, 458–59, 475–78, 479n95, 480, 483. *See also* Etruria
tyranny, freedom vs., 221–25
tyrants: Cyrus, 77; dispositions of, 76–77, 339n40, 373–79; educational dialogues with, 78–84; hunting analogy for, 119; princes vs., 407n3; rhetoric of, 26; rise to power of, 24n37, 62n153; unhappy experiences of, 80–81

ultimate necessity, 142, 145, 146, 149, 313, 425, 427, 428, 430
ultimate victory, 146, 148, 179, 205, 225–26, 236, 240, 308, 430
umanità (humanity), 124n81, 186, 203–6, 204n92, 438
unilateralism, 18, 91, 92, 96, 139, 148, 153–54, 238, 244, 298, 333, 338
unity: and the common good, 286; external enemy as source of, 34; freedom and, 222, 241, 270; and individual liberties (in Sparta), 411, 413–17; Italian, 44
Urban II, Pope, 143
utility: apparent vs. genuine, 349–54, 471; common contrasted with private, 18, 24, 26,